Stanley E. Porter is Principal, Dean
and Professor of New Testament,
McMaster Divinity College, Canada.

Dennis Stamps is Director of the West
Midlands Ministerial Training Course,
Queen's College, Birmingham, UK.

D1564051

JOURNAL FOR THE STUDY OF THE NEW TESTAMENT
SUPPLEMENT SERIES
195

Executive Editor
Stanley E. Porter

Sheffield Academic Press
A Continuum imprint

Rhetorical Criticism and the Bible

edited by
Stanley E. Porter and Dennis L. Stamps

Journal for the Study of the New Testament
Supplement Series 195

Copyright © 2002 Sheffield Academic Press
A Continuum imprint

Published by Sheffield Academic Press Ltd
The Tower Building, 11 York Road, London SE1 7NX
370 Lexington Avenue, New York, NY 10017-6550

www.SheffieldAcademicPress.com
www.continuumbooks.com

British Library Cataloguing-in-Publication Data

A catalogue record for this book is available from the British Library

Typeset by Sheffield Academic Press
Printed on acid-free paper in Great Britain by Bookcraft Ltd, Midsomer Norton, Bath

ISBN 1-84127-093-8

CONTENTS

This volume contains the selected and edited proceedings of the fifth inter-national conference on rhetorical criticism organized by Thomas Olbricht and Stanley Porter, and partially sponsored by the University of Pepper-dine, Malibu. Over 30 participants from seven different nations (Canada, Denmark, Great Britain, Finland, South Africa, Sweden, United States of America) gathered to discuss the rhetorical analysis of Scripture. We met from Monday evening, 27 July, to Thursday afternoon, 30 July 1998.

It was a hot conference. Temperatures in Fiorenza/Florence, Italy, were in the 30s (Celsius) for most of the afternoons, and on occasion reached the low 40s. Air-conditioning was limited, though fortunately available in our meeting room. As has been the experience of four of the five conferences, we stayed in the facilities of the University of Pepperdine. The facilities were, once again, first class. We were within easy walking distance of the great centre of renaissance culture, literature and art. A highlight of our time together was the feast of Italian cooking provided by our hosts as we began and as we departed.

Once again, the papers reflect the manifold ways the term rhetoric is understood, used and applied. In some papers, readers may question what is distinctive about rhetorical criticism as it is invoked by other traditional forms of biblical criticism, but readers should look for the nuances of the figure, especially as they relate to argumentation and the perceived effect of a text. Other papers lay out a methodology that seems not only different, but wholly distinct, with some wandering far from what is commonly understood as rhetorical criticism. This conference was marked by growing interest in the tapestry or textures of socio-rhetorical criticism proposed by Vernon Robbins (at least ten of the papers address this). In that vein, our discussions often settled on exploring enthymemes as a unit of rhetorical argumentation and cultural disclosure.

These papers represent a diversion from previous conferences as there is less intertextual dialogue between previous conference papers. Perhaps that represents a confidence in work that stands alone, a coming of age in the field of rhetorical criticism. If readers wish to peruse the previous proceedings, the papers continue to be available from Sheffield Academic Press (though this will be the last conference for which the press publishes the proceedings). Papers from the first conference have been published as S.E. Porter and T.H. Olbricht (eds.), *Rhetoric and the New Testament: Essays from the 1992 Heidelberg Conference* (JSNTSup, 90; Sheffield: JSOT Press, 1993), the second as S.E. Porter and T.H. Olbricht (eds.), *Rhetoric, Scripture and Theology: Essays from the 1994 Pretoria Conference* (JSNTSup, 131; Sheffield: Sheffield Academic Press, 1996), the third as S.E. Porter and T.H. Olbricht (eds.), *The Rhetorical Analysis of Scripture: Essays from the 1995 London Conference* (JSNTSup, 146; Sheffield: Sheffield Academic Press, 1997), the fourth as S.E. Porter and D.L. Stamps (eds.), *The Rhetorical Interpretation of Scripture: Essays from the 1996 Malibu Conference* (JSNTSup, 180; Sheffield: Sheffield Academic Press, 1999).

Finally, we must once again express our thanks for the ongoing financial assistance and support of Pepperdine University. We continue to be grateful to the editorial staff of Sheffield Academic Press for publishing our proceedings, in particular to Stanley E. Porter, as editor of the JSNT Supplement Series, for his commitment, time and energy in bringing these proceedings to publication. But the conference is nothing without its participants, and thanks must go to those who met in Florence and to those who have attended these conferences regularly, enriching our mutual scholarship and hopefully contributing to the important work of biblical interpretation in the worldwide academy.

Stanley E. Porter
Dennis L. Stamps

ABBREVIATIONS

AB	Anchor Bible
ABD	David Noel Freedman (ed.), *The Anchor Bible Dictionary* (New York: Doubleday, 1992)
AGJU	Arbeiten zur Geschichte des antiken Judentums und des Urchristentums
AJT	*American Journal of Theology*
AnBib	Analecta biblica
ANRW	Hildegard Temporini and Wolfgang Haase (eds.), *Aufstieg und Niedergang der römischen Welt: Geschichte und Kultur Roms im Spiegel der neueren Forschung* (Berlin: W. de Gruyter, 1972–)
ATR	*Anglican Theological Review*
AUSS	*Andrews University Seminary Studies*
BAGD	Walter Bauer, William F. Arndt, F. William Gingrich and Frederick W. Danker, *A Greek–English Lexicon of the New Testament and Other Early Christian Literature* (Chicago: University of Chicago Press, 2nd edn, 1958)
BBB	Bonner biblische Beiträge
BDB	Francis Brown, S.R. Driver and Charles A. Briggs, *A Hebrew and English Lexicon of the Old Testament* (Oxford: Clarendon Press, 1907)
BDF	Friedrich Blass, A. Debrunner and Robert W. Funk, *A Greek Grammar of the New Testament and Other Early Christian Literature* (Cambridge: Cambridge University Press, 1961)
BETL	Bibliotheca ephemeridum theologicarum lovaniensium
BEvT	Beiträge zur evangelischen Theologie
Bib	*Biblica*
BibB	Biblische Beiträge
BibInt	*Biblical Interpretation: A Journal of Contemporary Approaches*
BibLeb	*Bibel und Leben*
BIS	Biblical Interpretation Series
BKAT	Biblischer Kommentar: Altes Testament
BLG	Biblical Languages: Greek
BNTC	Black's New Testament Commentaries
BTB	*Biblical Theology Bulletin*

BZ	*Biblische Zeitschrift*
ConBNT	Coniectanea biblica, New Testament
CBQ	*Catholic Biblical Quarterly*
ConBNT	Coniectanea biblica, New Testament
DSD	*Dead Sea Discoveries*
FFF	*Foundations and Facets Forum*
FN	*Filología neotestamentaria*
FRLANT	Forschungen zur Religion und Literatur des Alten und Neuen Testaments
GTA	Göttinger theologische Arbeiten
Greg	*Gregorianum*
HNTC	Harper's NT Commentaries
HTR	*Harvard Theological Review*
HUCA	*Hebrew Union College Annual*
ICC	International Critical Commentary
Int	*Interpretation*
JBL	*Journal of Biblical Literature*
JR	*Journal of Religion*
JSNT	*Journal for the Study of the New Testament*
JSNTSup	*Journal for the Study of the New Testament*, Supplement Series
JSOT	*Journal for the Study of the Old Testament*
JSPSup	*Journal for the Study of the Pseudepigrapha*, Supplement Series
KAT	Kommentar zum Alten Testament
LCL	Loeb Classical Library
LEC	Library of Early Christianity
LNSM	J.P. Louw and E.A. Nida (eds.), *Greek-English Lexicon Based on Semantic Domains* (New York: UBS, 1988)
LOT	Literature of the Old Testament
LSJ	H.G. Liddell, Robert Scott and H. Stuart Jones, *Greek–English Lexicon* (Oxford: Clarendon Press, 9th edn, 1968)
MeyerK	H.A.W. Meyer (ed.), *Kritisch-exegetischer Kommentar über das Neue Testament*
MTS	Marburg theologische Studien
NCB	New Century Bible
Neot	*Neotestamentica*
NICNT	New International Commentary on the New Testament
NIDNTT	Colin Brown (ed.), *The New International Dictionary of New Testament Theology* (3 vols.; Exeter: Paternoster Press, 1975)
NIGTC	The New International Greek Testament Commentary
NIV	New International Version
NovT	*Novum Testamentum*
NovTSup	*Novum Testamentum*, Supplements
NTS	*New Testament Studies*

NTTS	New Testament Tools and Studies
OCD	*Oxford Classical Dictionary*
OTE	*Old Testament Essays*
OTP	James Charlesworth (ed.), *Old Testament Pseudepigrapha*
RILP	Roehampton Institute London Papers
SBG	Studies in Biblical Greek
SBL	Society of Biblical Literature
SBLBNSA	SBL Biblical Studies in North America
SBLDS	SBL Dissertation Series
SBLSP	SBL Seminar Papers
SBT	Studies in Biblical Theology
SEÅ	*Svensk exegetisk årsbok*
SNTSMS	Society for New Testament Studies Monograph Series
SR	*Studies in Religion/Sciences religieuses*
TB	Theologische Bücherei
TDNT	Gerhard Kittel and Gerhard Friedrich (eds.), *Theological Dictionary of the New Testament* (trans. Geoffrey W. Bromiley; 10 vols.; Grand Rapids: Eerdmans, 1964–)
TEV	Today's English Version
TRE	*Theologische Realenzyklopädie*
TS	*Theological Studies*
TTod	*Theology Today*
TU	Texte und Untersuchungen
TynBul	*Tyndale Bulletin*
TSJTSA	Theological Studies of the Jewish Theological Seminary of America
TZ	*Theologische Zeitschrift*
USQR	*Union Seminary Quarterly Review*
VCSup	*Vigiliae Christianae* Supplements
WBC	Word Biblical Commentary
WUNT	Wissenschaftliche Untersuchungen zum Neuen Testament
ZDPV	*Zeitschrift des deutschen Palästina-Vereins*
ZNW	*Zeitschrift für die neutestamentliche Wissenschaft*
ZTK	*Zeitschrift für Theologie und Kirche*

LIST OF CONTRIBUTORS

L. Gregory Bloomquist, Saint Paul University, Ottawa, Ontario, Canada

Douglas A.Campbell, King's College, University of London, England

Johan H. Coetzee, Rand Afrikaans University, Johannesburg, South Africa

Paul Danove, Villanova University, Villanova, Pennsylvania, USA

Marc J. Debanné, McGill University, Montreal, Canada

Anders Eriksson, University of Lund, Sweden

Craig A. Evans, Trinity Western University, Langley, British Columbia, Canada

Arthur Gibson, University of Surrey Roehampton, London, England

Gerhard van den Heever, University of South Africa, Pretoria, South Africa

James D. Hester, University of Redlands, California, USA

Richard Lemmer, University of South Africa, Pretoria, South Africa

Thomas H. Olbricht, Pepperdine University, Malibu, California, USA

Stanley E. Porter, McMaster Divinity College, McMaster University, Hamilton, Ontario, Canada

Vernon K. Robbins, Emory University, Atlanta, Georgia, USA, and University of Stellenbosch, South Africa

Gerrie Snyman, University of South Africa, Pretoria, South Africa

Dennis L. Stamps, Queen's College, Birmingham, England

Lauri Thurén, University of Joensuu, Joensuu, Finland

Hendrik Viviers, Rand Afrikaans University, Johannesburg, South Africa

Duane F. Watson, Malone College, Canton, Ohio, USA

K.K. Yeo, Garrett-Evangelical Theological Seminary, Evanston, Illinois, USA

INTRODUCTION: RHETORICAL CRITICISM AND
THE FLORENCE CONFERENCE

Stanley E. Porter and Dennis L. Stamps

The purview of rhetorical criticism seems to be expanding. In the past, the focus has primarily been upon patterns and modes of argumentation and the use of rhetorical devices as the ways and means of persuasion. More recently, as evidenced from the Florence conference, rhetorical critics are becoming more interested in how textual discourse constructs new socio-logical understanding and identity, even new patterns of behaviour which follow from such understanding and identity. In this perspective, rhetoric is more than how a text communicates and whether that 'how' is effective, but what a text communicates. Rhetoric becomes the means of positing a new reality and persuading others to adopt it. Much of this has come about through the influence of Vernon Robbins and his writings, *Exploring the Texture of Texts* and *The Tapestry of Early Christian Discourse*.[1]

Perhaps a key to understanding this shift is the particular and peculiar interest Robbins and others have in how Christianity established its iden-tity as a religion in the Greco-Roman world and culture, which included, of course, Judaism—and beyond that, how early Christians expressed this identity and persuaded others to adopt and retain this new world-view. It is a fascinating project to uncover how these early followers of Jesus took the cultural and social ideas and conventions of their day and age and converted them into a continuous, but distinctive, new cultural and social pattern. Add to this the interest in how these ancient texts continue to speak in different contexts throughout history and even today, and one has identified a multifarious interpretative project.

The roots of the interest in the 'power' of language and texts are ancient. It is precisely this power which worried Plato, especially if it was in the

1.   V.K. Robbins, *Exploring the Texture of Texts: A Guide to Socio-Rhetorical Interpretation* (Valley Forge, PA: Trinity Press International, 1996); *The Tapestry of Early Christian Discourse: Rhetoric, Society and Ideology* (London: Routledge, 1996).

hands of an unvirtuous person. Aristotle and others were more focused on the artistry of this power and how to teach it to others. Perhaps this recent return to the power of texts in modern biblical rhetorical criticism is a return to the ancient roots of rhetoric. Time will only tell if Robbins has provided a proper means for interpreting and assessing the power of the New Testament texts in his comprehensive socio-rhetorical criticism and its five (or six) textures.

In what follows, a few brief introductory comments are given about each of the essays in this volume. The back drop to these comments is this shift to a rhetorics of how a text constructs a new sociology of being, a concern about the 'power of texts'. It is hoped that these comments will put these papers into perspective against the larger canvas of rhetorical criticism. It is also hoped that they will give the reader an opportunity to judge whether the content and thrust of a given essay merits further detailed consideration (a judgment purely based on the reader's own interests and not on whether the essay is in itself worthy).

The first part is devoted to the theory of rhetorical criticism. T.H. Olbricht opens with an exploration of the writings of Philo and Clement of Alexandria 'in order to determine the nature and the reasons for the power of their approaches to communication'. More particularly, he seeks to analyze the way Philo and Clement use allegory in the way they cite and utilize the Old Testament in their arguments. V.K. Robbins takes up the power of texts in the second essay as he defends himself against the criticism of E. Schüssler Fiorenza. Her attack prompts him to analyze opposition rhetoric (which seeks to dominate and not promote equal dialogue—the form of rhetoric Robbins finds in Schüssler Fiorenza's criticism of his work) and to suggest that she misunderstands the intent of his socio-rhetorical analysis and its desire to create free and open dicussion.

In a long and complex essay, L.G. Bloomquist looks at the agenda of socio-rhetorical analysis and the use of C.S. Peirce's abduction logic by Robbins. Bloomquist suggests that the use of Peirce reveals a desire to maintain a form of 'objective' historicity which is not congruent with the overall aims of socio-rhetorical analysis. His critique of Peirce is partially based on Wittgenstein and his concept of private language. Bloomquist seeks to illustrate his points by interspersing a commentary on Gal. 3.21. It is an intricate essay which is worth the effort in the way it exposes a potential weakness of socio-rhetorical analysis.

Even more intricate is A. Gibson's essay on the relations between rhetoric and philosophical logic. In essence, Gibson shows that rhetoric and logic are philosophical friends, but not the kind of bedfellows that rhetorical critics often imply by their use of the enthymeme. He argues that the enthymeme was never meant to provide a kind of mathematical precision in reconstructing the argument of a rhetor as is often done in biblical rhetorical criticism. (His formidable knowledge of logic and his critique of rhetorical critics' use of the enthymeme certainly caused much discussion at the conference.)

Typical of much of D.F.Watson's writings on rhetorical criticism, this essay is a methodical exploration of why we need socio-rhetorical commentary and how one goes about doing it. His agenda is based wholly on Robbins's theory of socio-rhetorical analysis and the five (or six) textures of the text. His thorough exploration of the questions in his title are prompted by his own efforts to write a socio-rhetorical commentary on Philippians. One will go away impressed with the systematic way Watson tackles the questions and his essay should be foundational for future socio-rhetorical commentators. However, it does pose the question as to whether commentaries will only be getting longer in all they try to accomplish.

In Part II, there are three rhetorical critical readings of the Old Testament. Gerrie Snyman begins by looking at the book of Esther. The essay is a wonderful contemporary discussion of how a text's interpreters identify with biblical characters and ideology. He begins by looking at how two ministerial students exegeted Esther 9, defining a liberation theology in the characters and actions of Esther and Mordecai, and hence identifying with the characters as examples of political action in modern South Africa. Snyman evaluates this identification, exposing the fundamentalism (in many guises) which motivates such identification. He wonders if this type of biblical interpretation is an appropriate reading and is an appropriate example of moving from the text to the contemporary situation. J.H. Coetzee turns to the Psalms. In a fascinating analysis of politeness strategies, he examines Psalms 3, 13, 41, and 42/43 looking at how these public, cultic prayers and their argumentative strategies both reveal a rhetoric of appeal to God and influence listeners to have a sociological perspective on Israel and its enemies. H. Vivers takes up the Song of Songs and examines its rhetoric about the body. He notes its liberating and powerful potential for focusing on an embodied life rather than the dualism of much biblical spirituality. But he also notes that the rhetoric of the body in the Song of Songs did not succeed in providing this full-body perspective for the community of faith.

In Part III, the Gospels are subjected to rhetorical critical readings. C.A. Evans looks at the nature of Jesus' rhetoric of criticism in the parables, criticism of both his friends and his enemies. These parables and their criticisms have a flavour of the Old Testament prophetic parables and are unlike those found in the Tannaitic rabbis. P. Danove concentrates on the Gospel of Mark and its presentations of the disciples. His analysis is a multi-textured analysis echoing Robbins, but concentrates on narrative rhetorics showing how the pattern of Mark's construction of discipleship is a powerful call to the readers to a form of ideal discipleship. G. van den Heever also borrows the socio-rhetorical analysis of Robbins to explore the ideological rhetoric of John's Gospel. He concentrates on a more his-torical approach to reveal parallels between the rhetoric of empire and the cult of the emperor and John's anti-emperor rhetoric, which transfers the emperor-cult language to Jesus. His point is that the ideology of such language/rhetoric is to establish a utopian vision, hence John's Gospel becomes a counter-political utopian vision which is meant to supplant the exalted utopian vision centred on the emperor. For van den Heever, John's Gospel is a powerful ideological tract.

Part IV has nine essays that explore the rhetoric of the Pauline letters. A. Eriksson looks at the way Paul's letters use arguments from the contrary to cast doubt upon positions other than his own, a standard classical rhetor-ical ploy. D. Campbell attempts to solve the difficulties surrounding the enigmatic text, Rom. 3.27–4.25, by demonstrating how it employs a set of textual correlations in which a fourfold argumentative agenda is proposed followed by a corresponding series of responses to the four issues raised. Campbell is convinced that there is a rhetorical pattern that supports this reading of the study, which Paul may be employing. S.E. Porter offers a novel insight into the theological predilections of the scribe by examining the textual variants of Romans. This unique study of textual varients challenges the traditional way we understand and read the eclectic Greek text and implies that we must be more conscious of the textual tradition and the way that these traditions entextualize the rhetoric of the scribe(s).

L. Thurén tackles one of the most difficult passages in the New Testa-ment, Romans 7 and Pauls use of εγο. In analyzing Kümmel's proposed solution to this problem, Thurén notes that Kümmel's approach indicated that more than theology was needed to solve the problem, and that Küm-mel recognized the role that rhetoric played in the apostle's usage.

D.L. Stamps continues his exploration of the distinctive features of Pauline theological rhetoric by examining the appeal to Christology in

1 Cor. 1.4–2.5. R. Leemer looks at the nature of metaphor as a means and a rhetorical device for opening up the metaphysical dimension of the text to its readers/audience, and demonstrates this by exploring the use of metaphors in the letter to the Ephesians. M.J. Debanné looks at the nature and understanding of enthymeme as a way to analyze Paul's argument. He then employs an enthymemic analysis of Philippians, looking for common patterns or a typology of Pauline 'logic'. J.D. Hester takes a totally different approach to 1 Thessalonians by subjecting the text to a fantasy theme analysis suggested by E.G. Bormann. In particular, Hester is interested in how 1 Thessalonians through fantasy themes creates a group culture or dynamic, a group identity. K.K. Yeo approaches 1 Thessalonians in a more traditional way, examining the election and calling language and the effects of this language upon the readers and their situation. He uses a form of socio-rhetorical analysis to show that the language of calling established a rhetoric of honour and a rhetoric of hope to confirm a community in crisis.

As one can see by the wide range of topics and approaches taken by the essays in this volume, rhetorical criticism is often understood in a very loose sense that allows it to probe many different dimensions of a biblical text and its effect. A recurrent theme in these essays is the way the rhetorics of the text construct a social ideology. Another recurring theme is the potential of socio-rhetorical analysis to evaluate the various aspects and impacts of a biblical text. As has been noted in previous volumes, rhetorical criticism is not a monolithic practice. This volume continues the expansion of rhetorical criticism into different and intrguing realms of biblical interpretation. The reader will have to decide if it is useful and important.

Part I

THE THEORY OF RHETORICAL CRITICISM

GREEK RHETORIC AND THE ALLEGORICAL RHETORIC
OF PHILO AND CLEMENT OF ALEXANDRIA

Thomas H. Olbricht

1. *Introduction*

The perception now prevails that biblical texts must be interpreted from a larger provenance than previously.[1] Biblical critics have taken up various approaches, one of which is rhetoric, both classical and modern.[2] Rhetoric, however, in the classical mold only focused upon certain types of discourse even though the term today encompasses a much larger array of contexts. Most rhetoricians in the classical period limited their observations to discourse in the law courts (forensic), the political assemblies (deliberative), and the ceremonial occasions (epideictic).

Aristotle declared that there were many other types of discourse which he did not subsume under the rubric of rhetoric. He thought that rhetoric might apply to communication efforts in all areas of knowledge, but in regard to specific matters such as physics and other sciences, topics and forms arise, he avowed, which are peculiar to these specialties:

> Specific topics on the other hand are derived from propositions which are peculiar to each species or genus of things; there are, for example, propositions about Physics which can furnish neither enthymemes nor syllogisms about Ethics, and there are propositions concerned with Ethics which will be useless for furnishing conclusions about Physics; and the same holds good in all cases. The first kind of topics will not make a man practically

---

1.   For these various new directions see L.G. Perdue, *The Collapse of History: Reconstructing Old Testament Theology* (Minneapolis: Fortress Press, 1994), pp. 229-98; C. Holladay, 'Contemporary Methods of Reading the Bible', in L.E. Keck *et al.* (eds.), *The New Interpreter's Bible* (Nashville: Abingdon Press, 1994), pp. 125-49.

2.   See the bibliography of D.F. Watson and A.J. Hauser, *Rhetorical Criticism of the Bible: A Comprehensive Bibliography and Notes on History and Method* (BIS, 4; Leiden: E.J. Brill, 1994); and S.E. Porter (ed.), *Handbook of Classical Rhetoric in the Hellenistic Period 330 B.C.–A.D. 400* (Leiden: E.J. Brill, 1997).

wise about any particular class of things, because they do not deal with the particular subject matter; but as to the specific topics, the happier a man is in his choice of propositions, the more he will unconsciously produce a science quite different from Dialectic and Rhetoric. For if once he hits upon first principles, it will no longer be Dialectic or Rhetoric, but that science whose principles he has arrived at.[3]

Various features of the documents of late Judaism and early Christianity, it seems to me, Aristotle would relegate to a different sort of discourse. The topics would be different. The forms and power of proofs would be different. Certain forms of conceptual features might also be different. Jewish and Christian topics focus upon the mighty acts of God, past, present and future. A major form of proof would be a statement cited from an ancient privileged text, that is, the Scripture, rather than the enthymeme as Aristotle declared: 'Now arguments that depend on examples are not less calculated to persuade, but those which depend upon enthymemes meet with greater approval'.[4] I have previously designated this the rhetoric of the church or synagogue.[5]

In the past I have commented on a few contours of that rhetoric. Synagogue and church rhetoric are obviously multifaceted and require much descriptive and analytical work so as to set forth how it functions. One area with which I have been concerned has to do with the rhetorical power and function of biblical texts in Jewish and Christian documents and treatises. These texts most often in the ancient world were perceived as privileged in a manner not experienced, and therefore not investigated, by the Greco-Roman rhetoricians. How then do these citations and allusions function rhetorically in synagogue or church rhetoric? The answer is, of course, that they function variously. It depends, in part, on the manner of their interpretation; which leads me into another fascination of mine, that is, how analogical or allegorical interpretation functions rhetorically. It is my judgment that analogical or allegorical rhetorical vehicles and interpretation are much more likely to occur in the synagogue or church than in any other context, unless in poetry or the theater.

3.   Aristotle, *Rhet.* 1.2.21.
4.   Aristotle, *Rhet.* 1.2.10.
5.   T.H. Olbricht, 'An Aristolelian Rhetorical Analysis of 1 Thessalonians', in D.L. Balch, E. Ferguson and W.A. Meeks (eds.), *Greeks, Romans, and Christians: Essays in Honor of Abraham J. Malherbe* (Minneapolis: Fortress Press, 1990), pp. 216-36 (225-27).

Therefore I concluded, perhaps 40 years ago in scrutinizing Horace Bushnell's 'Dissertation on Language' in his book, *God in Christ*,[6] that until I had a clearer vision in regard to analogical aspects of religious discourse, I could not make progress in setting forth the contours of Jewish and Christian rhetoric, which would include the function of biblical or privileged texts. The ancient rhetoricians, it seems clear to me, did not comment on these rhetorical functions inasmuch as they did not encounter them in those kinds of discourse as exercised in the writings of, for example, Philo or Clement of Alexandria. Few observations may be found in classical rhetoric in regard to metaphorical, analogical, allegorical, typological or mythic discourse. Yet these were major rhetorical features of many treatises of late Judaism and early Christianity.

In this essay, therefore, I am especially interested in exploring the writings of Philo and Clement of Alexandria in order to determine the nature and the reasons for the power of their approaches to communication. While we may find some help from others regarding the means by which analogical discourse obtains its power, by and large it will not be from the ancient rhetoricians. Ultimately I am interested in ascertaining how the approaches of Philo and Clement differ from those of New Testament materials and from Antiochian communicators who have conventionally been declared different from their Alexandrine counterparts.

While the Greeks and Romans in their rhetorics commented on similes and metaphors, that is, analogical figures of speech, they discussed only to a limited extent the larger metaphorical constructs in discourse. We therefore need to explore the contexts in which the rhetoricians took up these rhetorical figures and determine in what manner they thought rhetorical power was attained thereby.

While something may be learned of rhetoricians prior to Aristotle commenting on the employment of comparison, it is with Aristotle that clear guidelines have come down to us.[7] The two major terms employed by Aristotle in regard to comparison are παραβολή and εἰκών. In discussing the proofs in *The Rhetoric* (c. 335 BCE), Aristotle highlighted two kinds: examples and enthymemes.[8] The examples are likewise two: those that have happened, which we may designate historical, and those invented,

6. H. Bushnell, *God in Christ: Three Discourses* (Hartford: Brown & Parsons, 1849).

7. M.H. McCall, Jr, *Ancient Rhetorical Theories of Simile and Comparison* (Cambridge, MA: Harvard University Press, 1969), pp. 1-23.

8. Aristotle, *Rhet.* 2.20.1.

that is, comparisons (παραβολαί) or fables (λόγοι).[9] It is the latter which interests us here. Aristotle, though providing examples from Aesop, does not state wherein lies their power. He argued that even though fables are easier to come upon than historical comparisons, 'those derived from facts are more useful for deliberative oratory, because as a rule the future resembles the past'.[10] He further argued that enthymemes have more power than examples, though both should be employed so as to reinforce each other.

One of Aristotle's fables invites further reflection on its power:

> Aesop, when defending at Samos a demagogue who was being tried for his life, related the following anecdote. 'A fox, while crossing a river, was driven into a ravine. Being unable to get out, she was for a long time in sore distress, and a number of dog-fleas clung to her skin. A hedgehog, wandering about, saw her and, moved with compassion, asked her if he should remove the fleas. The fox refused and when the hedgehog asked the reason, she answered, "They are already full of me and draw little blood; but if you take them away, others will come that are hungry and will drain what remains to me." You in like manner, O Samians, will suffer no more harm from this man, for he is wealthy; but if you put him to death, others will come who are poor, who will steal and squander your public funds.'[11]

The fable in this case shifted the focus away from the demagogue, against whom much animosity prevailed, to the fox, a neutral entity. The plight of the fox stirs compassion, as well as admiration in respect to her sagacity in rejecting help in removing the fleas. The point is simply and vividly made without stirring the inflammatory passions that arise in respect to the demagogue. The power of the fable, therefore, lies in its ability to make a telling point, while at the same time waylaying rancor.[12]

Aristotle discussed εἰκών in Book 3 on style and arrangement in chs. 2, 4, 10, 11. The word εἰκών is translated 'simile', though Aristotle stated that it is difficult to distinguish simile from metaphor. As a stylistic device Aristotle declared the metaphor crucial: 'It is the metaphor above all that gives perspicuity (σαφής), pleasure, and a foreign air, and it cannot be

9.   Aristotle, *Rhet.* 2.20.3.
10.   Aristotle, *Rhet.* 2.20.8.
11.   Aristotle, *Rhet.* 2.20.6-7.
12.   I have read the section in C. Perelman and L. Olbrechts-Tyteca, *The New Rhetoric: A Treatise on Argumentation* (South Bend: University of Notre Dame Press, 1969), pp. 371-410, on analogy, metaphor and simile. The comments are helpful, and set out schematically the argumentative and stylistic power, but do not really take up rhetorical power, that is, why rhetorically analogical materials enhance the argument.

learnt from any else; but we must make use of metaphors and epithets that are appropriate.'[13] In this case Aristotle has declared what it is that gives the analogical stylistic device power, that is, it brings clarity and liveliness. By doing so it increases the ease of learning:

> Easy learning is naturally pleasant to all, and words mean something, so that all words which make us learn something are most pleasant. Now we do not know the meaning of strange words, and proper terms we know already. It is metaphor, therefore, that above all produces this effect; for when Homer calls old age stubble, he teaches and informs us through the genus; for both have lost their bloom.[14]

Clearly then for Aristotle the purposes of allegory, fable, and metaphor, that is, all forms of analogical dimensions of discourse, are to clarify and supply greater liveliness, though to a lesser extent they can contribute to the substance of the argument and increased insight. He did not himself notice how they may clear the air of rancor and passion and thereby create a greater predisposition to hear out the argument. The purpose is not, as Aristotle envisions it, a penetration into a more fundamental level of reality, as is the case with Philo. The chief end is pragmatic, that is, to win the case in the law court, to persuade the citizens of the polis, and to praise and blame the forefathers of cities and civilizations.

I have continued this pursuit of reflection on the employment of the analogical in discourse in the following later Greco-Roman rhetoricians: Demetrius, *On Style* (c. second century BCE); the *Rhetorica ad Herennium* (c. 85 BCE); Cicero, *De inventione* (c. 89 BCE) and *De oratore* (55 BCE); Loginus, *On the Sublime* (c. first century CE); and Quintilian, *Institutio oratoria* (c. 92 CE). The details in regard to each will appear in another essay.[15] Here space only permits me to set out my conclusions.

From this perusal of the rhetoricians, I conclude that for them the power of analogical materials first of all lies in clarity, especially in regard to literal or historical comparison. Fictional or allegorical analogies supply vivacity, liveliness and emotion, and help dissipate overwrought antipathy.

13. Aristotle, *Rhet.* 3.2.8-9.

14. Aristotle, *Rhet.* 3.10.2-3. See also R. Moran, 'Artifice and Persuasion: The Work of Metaphor in the *Rhetoric*', in A.O. Rorty (ed.), *Essays on Aristotle's Rhetoric* (Berkeley: University of California Press, 1996), pp. 385-98.

15. See T.H. Olbricht, 'Analogy and Allegory in Classical Rhetoric', in J.T. Fitzgerald, T.H. Olbricht and L.M. White (eds.), *Early Christianity and Classical Studies: In Honor of Abraham J. Malherbe* (Harrisburg, PA: Trinity Press International, forthcoming).

They also contribute in an ancillary manner to the content and substance of the argument. These rhetorical devices function both to enhance style and to contribute toward proof by way of both λόγος and πάθος. As such, however, for these rhetoricians these figures of speech do not provoke profounder meanings which lie beneath the surface.

2. *Alexandria: Its Intellectual and Rhetorical Traditions*

Although Alexandria prior to Philo (c. 20 BCE–c. 50 CE) had sophists and rhetoricians, rhetoric in the Greco-Roman sense did not flourish there. The interests of the intellectuals of the city centered not so much in politics and legal affairs, but in metaphysical matters. As Johannes Quasten observed,

> The school of Alexandria is the oldest centre of sacred science in the history of Christianity. The environment in which it developed gave it its distinctive characteristics, predominant interest in the metaphysical investigation of the content of the faith, a leaning to the philosophy of Plato, and the allegorical interpretation of Sacred Scripture.[16]

The reason may be, as Robert Smith declared, the subjugation of Alexandria to Rome and therefore little opportunity for self-determination of basic policy:

> With the loss of Greek independence and the consequent subjugation of Egypt in the East, one would not expect to find in Alexandria the sort of oratory heard in Athens in the days of Demosthenes. Secular or sacred oratory…simply could not flourish in an oppressive atmosphere as it did in a freer society.[17]

It is for this reason that, though Smith believes that the teaching of rhetoric occurred in Alexandria, he found it difficult to locate information about specific teachers.[18] It is clear, however, that Alexandria had its share of sophists as Bruce Winter has shown in *Philo and Paul among the Sophists*.[19]

The person from whom we have the earliest, most extensive documents containing allegorization from the ancient world is Philo of Alexandria:

16. J. Quasten, *Patrology* (3 vols.; Allen, TX: Christian Classics, n.d.), II, p. 2.

17. R.W. Smith, *The Art of Rhetoric in Alexandria: Its Theory and Practice in the Ancient World* (The Hague: Martinus Nijhoff, 1974).

18. Smith, *Art of Rhetoric*, pp. 18, 147.

19. B.W. Winter, *Philo and Paul among the Sophists* (SNTSMS, 96; Cambridge: Cambridge University Press, 1997), pp. 19-112.

It is a surprising fact that though the practice of allegorizing an authoritative text had begun at least three hundred years before Philo's day and probably much earlier, his writings are the first extensive example of it that we possess, and the chief non-Jewish examples of allegorizing that have survived are either contemporary with Philo (Heracleitus) or later than his day (Plutarch and Porphyry). In spite of this state of affairs, nobody would today attempt to argue that Hellenistic allegory was an imitation of Alexandrian allegory, and we can in fact recover a few traces of the long tradition of Hellenistic allegory that had existed before Philo's day.[20]

The verb form of the word ἀλληγορία is first found in Philo and Josephus. The earliest instance or cognate apparently is in a fragment of the Stoic philosopher Cleanthes of the third century BCE. Heracleitus, who wrote *Quaestiones Homericae* in the first century, defined the term: 'That is called allegory which, as the name implies, says one thing but means something other than what it says.'[21] Heracleitus and Philo are the first authors to use the noun to mean 'figurative interpretation of an authoritative text'.[22] The earliest Jewish writer to employ allegory was apparently Aristobulus of Paneus sometime around 150 BCE.[23] He attempted to interpret the Torah by allegorizing it into philosophical or scientific truth. Fragments of his work may be found in Eusebius. Though it is known that Stoics and others interpreted Homer allegorically, yet their efforts are only extant in fragments. Hanson wrote of the assumption that Aristobulus was indebted to Hellenistic allegorizers for his modus operandi, even though documents from the latter are no longer available:

> The Scriptural interpretation of Aristobulus is obviously trembling on the verge of allegory even if it has not yet quite reached it. It is a surprising fact that his is the earliest text we possess which practices allegory, or near-allegory; no Hellenistic allegorizer's work has survived except in the smallest fragments of a period as early as this. Yet we must agree that Aristobulus is borrowing his allegory from Hellenistic models.[24]

Philo himself mentioned two precedents for allegorical interpretation, the first being the Essenes:

20. R.P.C. Hanson, *Allegory and Event* (London: SCM Press, 1959), p. 55.
21. Heracleitus, *Quaestiones Homericae* 22.32.
22. Hanson, *Allegory*, p. 39.
23. N. Walter, *Der Thoraausleger Aristobulos: Untersuchungen zu seinen Fragmenten and zu pseudepigraphischen Resten der jüdischhellenistischen Literatur* (TU, 86; Berlin: Akademie-Verlag, 1964).
24. Hanson, *Allegory*, p. 43.

> Then one, indeed, takes up the holy volume and reads it, and another of the men of the greatest experience comes forward and explains what is not very intelligible, for a great many precepts are delivered in enigmatical modes of expression, and allegorically, as the old fashion was; and thus the people are taught piety, and holiness, and justice, and economy, and the science of regulating the state, and the knowledge of such things as are naturally good, or bad, or indifferent, and to choose what is right and to avoid what is wrong, using a threefold variety of definitions, and rules, and criteria, namely, the love of god, and the love of virtue, and the love of mankind.[25]

The second group is the Therapeutae in whom Philo had a special interest. About them he wrote:

> And the interval between morning and evening is by them devoted wholly to meditation on and to practice of virtue, for they take up the sacred scriptures and philosophise concerning them, investigating the allegories of their national philosophy, since they look upon their literal expressions as symbols of some secret meaning of nature, intended to be conveyed in those figurative expressions.[26]

There is, however, a difference between Philo and the Palestinian rabbis and other Jewish scholars who preceded him. Hanson wrote:

> The psychological, moral or philosophical truths which he extracts from Scripture by the use of allegory are easily distinguishable from the sort of doctrine which the other two traditions derive by the use of allegory, and the two types of doctrine have little or nothing in common. The great difference between Philo and Jewish allegorizers of other traditions is, as has already been mentioned, that Philo exhibits no typology whatever… Philo is little interested in Messianic expectation and not at all in eschatology. He is not even much interested in historical events, for his attitude to history is ambiguous.[27]

3. *Philo*

The dates of both Philo's birth and death are uncertain, but he was born about 20 BCE and died around 50 CE. He was born into a Jewish family of affluence and received the standard, for someone of his status, Hellenistic education consisting of literature, rhetoric, mathematics, music, and logic. But at an unspecified stage in life he embraced fully his own Jewish

25. *The Works of Philo* (trans. C.D. Yonge; Peabody, MA: Hendrickson, 1995), 'Every Good Man is Free', (§§82-83) p. 690.

26. *Works of Philo*, 'On the Contemplative Life', (§28) p. 700; also (§78) p. 705.

27. Hanson, *Allegory*, p. 49.

culture and traditions as mediated through the Hellenistic backgrounds in which he grew up. John Dillon observed:

> It is unlikely that Philo had in his mind from his earliest years exactly what his philosophy of life was; it is much more probable that at a certain stage of his education he experienced a kind of conversion, a rediscovery of his own culture and traditions. This took a curious form. It was not a rejection of Greek culture and in particular of Greek philosophy, but rather an application of it to the Jews' sacred books, particularly the Pentateuch, the books of Moses.[28]

Philo knew very little Hebrew, but was immersed in Greek literature, and steeped in Plato, especially the *Timaeus* and the *Phaedrus*. Philo had a definite view of the succession of knowledge which Dillon designated Middle Platonism. Plato, according to Philo, was a follower of Pythagoras, and Pythagoras of Moses, and from the latter Greek thinkers borrowed their best ideas. Philo probably had little or no influence on Middle Platonism, but he influenced considerably Clement of Alexandria and Origen. Dillon concluded:

> My chief thesis (as against such an authority as H.A. Wolfson, for example) is that Philo was not so much constructing for himself an eclectic synthesis of all Greek philosophy, from Presocratics to Posidonius, as essentially adapting contemporary Alexandrian Platonism, which was itself heavily influenced by Stoicism and Pythagoreanism, to his own exegetical purposes. If this is the case, then, used with proper caution, he is plainly good evidence for the state of Platonism at Alexandria in the first decades of the Christian era.[29]

4. *Philo and Allegory*

Among the literary remains of Philo's writings are 35 documents with fragments from at least five more.[30] The majority of these documents are

---

28. J. Dillon, *The Middle Platonists 80 B.C. to A.D. 220* (Ithaca, NY: Cornell University Press, 1971), p. 141. Other studies include, C. Riedweg, *Mysterienterminologie bei Platon, Philon und Klemens von Alexandrien* (Berlin: W. de Gruyter, 1987); R. Mortley, *Connaissance Religieuse et Herméneutique chez Clément D'Alexandrie* (Leiden: E.J. Brill, 1973); T.M. Conley, *Philo's Rhetoric: Studies in Style, Composition and Exegesis* (Berkeley: Center for Hermeneutical Studies, 1987); M. Alexander, Jr, *Rhetorical Argumentation in Philo of Alexandria* (Atlanta: Scholars Press, 1999).

29. Dillon, *Middle Platonists*, p. 182.

30. For a list, see *The Works of Philo*, pp. xv-xvi.

commentaries on the Torah, mostly on Genesis and Exodus. Most of the allegorical interpretations Philo employs are found in these exegetical (commentary) writings. In the non-exegetical essays, for example, 'On the Eternity of the World' and 'On the Contemplative Life', any reference to the Old Testament is by way of allusion and what little allegorization may be found is based upon Hellenistic writings. As a general rule Philo's direct citations of the Septuagint text provide a point of departure and structural framework for his comments. He does not often engage in proof texting, so characteristic of Christian preaching and polemical writings, either in the exegetical discourses or the non-exegetical. Sometimes these quotations are taken to be literal, for example,

> (127) The lawgiver of our nation denounces the first curse as the lightest of evils, namely, poverty and indigence, and a want of all necessary things, and a participation in every kind of destitution; for, says he, 'The enemy shall lay waste the corn-fields before they are ripe, and when the corn is ripened they shall suddenly come and reap it'. [Deut. 28.33] Thus causing a twofold calamity, famine to their friends and abundance to their enemies; for the prosperity of one's enemies is more, or, at all events, not less painful than one's own misfortunes.[31]

But more frequently texts are put forth for their non-apparent meanings:

> For, says God, 'I will make the heaven of brass for you, and the earth iron'. [Deut. 28.23] Implying by this enigmatical expression that neither of them shall accomplish the tasks which naturally belong to them and for which they were created; for how could iron ever bear ears of corn, or how could brass produce rain, of which all animals stand in need, and especially that animal so liable to misfortune and in need of so many things, man?[32]

And,

> And yet, what need is there, either of long journeys over the land, or of long voyages, for the sake of investigating the seeking out virtue, the roots of which the Creator has laid not at any great distance, but so near, as the wise lawgiver of the Jews says, 'They are in thy mouth, and in thy heart, and in thy hands': [Deut. 30.14] intimating by these figurative expressions the words, and actions, and designs of men; all of which stand in need of careful cultivation.[33]

---

31. *The Works of Philo*, 'On Rewards and Punishment', p. 676.
32. *The Works of Philo*, 'On Rewards and Punishment', (§§131-32) pp. 676-77.
33. *The Works of Philo*, 'Every Good Man is Free', (§68) p. 688.

It is clear why Philo employed allegory to interpret the Septuagint Bible. His intent seems to have been chiefly apologetic. Peder Borgen wrote:

> He lived all his life in the double context of the Jewish community and the Alexandrian Greek community. Philosophy was Philo's life interest. The dialogues seem to be apologetic writings and thus to fall in line with the rest of his works.[34]

On the one hand Philo set out to create a viable means through which his own Jewish community could sustain its faith in a predominately Hellenistic context, and on the other to create respect for and perhaps win over the Alexandrian Hellenists to Jewish perspectives. Basic to his argument was that the learned Hellenists ultimately depended upon Moses for their insights. Moses set out the universal laws for the universe, and all persons will realize their highest existence through becoming familiar with these laws. Philo was confident that these laws were ultimately addressed to all humans:

> the law corresponds to the world and the world to the law, and that a man who is obedient to the law, being, by so doing, a citizen of the world, arranges his actions with reference to the intention of nature, in harmony with which the whole universal world is regulated.[35]

And in another treatise,

> We must say, therefore, that he is desirous here to teach that most excellent lesson to those who read the sacred scriptures, that each separate individual by himself when he is an observer of the law and obedient to God, is of equal estimation with a whole nation, be it ever so populous, or I might rather say, with all the nations upon earth. And if I were to think fit I might proceed further and say, with all the world; because in another passage of the scriptures God, praising a certain just man, says, 'I am thy God'.[36]

One puzzles, therefore, a bit in regard to Philo's rhetorical strategy. His non-exegetical discourses commence according to somewhat standard conventions, more after the manner of philosophical rather than political writings, though 'Flaccus' commences as with a political narratio. In these non-exegetical discourses it is not the text that provides the starting point. Examples are 'On the Eternity of the World' and 'Every Good Man is Free'. The latter commences as a standard treatise, 'My former treatise, O

34. P. Borgen, 'Philo of Alexandria', *ABD*, V, p. 335.
35. *The Works of Philo*, 'On the Creation', (§3) p. 3.
36. *The Works of Philo*, 'The Decalogue', (§§37-38) p. 521.

Theodotus, was intended to prove that every wicked man was a slave...'
But the exegetical texts commence either by citing a text or building to
such a citation. The approach in the exegetical documents therefore seems
ineffectual as a rhetorical introduction by modern, if not by ancient
rhetorical standards, if the purpose is apologetic. Even in the New
Testament, speakers do not address a Hellenistic audience by citing
biblical texts, for example, Barnabus and Paul's statement to the people of
Lystra (Acts 14.15-17), and Paul's sermon on the Areopagus (Acts 17.22-
31). Philo did not win a significant following among either the Jews or the
Hellenistic population, which may mean that he was not rhetorically
astute. However, his employment of the Septuagint text may result from
his conviction that these texts ultimately are reality for all persons, not just
the Jews. And it is true that 'philosophers' of the ancient world were
accustomed to citing ancient documents. But it is doubtful that any
perceived even the works of Homer in the privileged manner in which the
Jews reverenced the Torah as communication from the deity.

The Jews believed that the ancient scriptures merited exegesis precisely
because through these words God disclosed fundamental reality, as well as
laws, for both nature and humanity. For Philo, the more basic disclosures
resided in meanings that were not apparent on the surface:

> But the things which we have here been saying do not appear solely in the
> plain and explicit language of the text of the holy scriptures; but they
> appear, moreover, to exhibit a nature which is not so evident to the multi-
> tude, but which they who place the objects of the intellect above those
> perceptible by the outward senses, and who are able to appreciate them,
> recognise.[37]

These two horizons could be set out allegorically, the body representing
the ostensible meaning, and the soul the opaque. Both are crucial but the
latter the more fundamentally important:

> But it is right to think that this class of things resembles the body, and the
> other class the soul; therefore, just as we take care of the body because it is
> the abode of the soul, so also must we take care of the laws that are enacted
> in plain terms: for while they are regarded, those other things also will be
> more clearly understood, of which these laws are symbols, and in the same
> way escape blame and accusation for men in general.[38]

---

37. *The Works of Philo*, 'On Abraham', (§200) p. 428.
38. *The Works of Philo*, 'On the Migration of Abraham', (§93) p. 262.

5. *The Rhetorical Function of the Allegory in Philo*

The allegory in Philo functions neither with the ancient rhetoricians to clarify, and to add the dimensions of vivacity, liveliness and emotion, and waylay rancor, nor with theological/philosophical analogy to declare, however dimly, of heavenly (ontological) characteristics that may be recognized in the earthly (discrete), for example, that loyalty in the divine may be dimly glimpsed in the human, though divine loyalty as far exceeds the human as does the human that of the dog. Or in some cases, so philosophers and theologians have declared, the analogical may be pursued only via the negative.[39] It is likewise not clear that in Philo allegory functions according to Nielsen's theses concerning the function of metaphors however helpful these may be for understanding New Testament metaphors:

   a. Metaphorical language functions in a concrete context by means of reciprocal interaction between two different statements.
   b. One can derive from metaphorical language information in the form of new suggestions for understanding reality (informative function).
   c. The purpose of metaphorical language is to engage the audience in such a way that by entering into the interpretation they adopt it as their own understanding of reality (performative function).
   d. Metaphorical language can be reused in other contexts, which open up for the possibility of reinterpretation.[40]

Philo can and did employ metaphors of the sort that exhibited the characteristics proposed by the observations of the rhetoricians and Nielsen's functions. For example,

> And pilots again, sitting in the hindmost part of the ship, that is the stern are, as one may say, the most important of all the people in the ship, inasmuch as they have the safety of the ship and of all those who are in it, in their hands. And so the Creator has made man to be as it were a charioteer and pilot over all other animals, in order that he may hold the reins and direct the course of every thing upon earth, having the superintendence of

---

39. E.L. Mascall, 'The Doctrine of Analogy', in R.E. Santoni (ed.), *Religious Language and the Problem of Religious Knowledge* (Bloomington: Indiana University Press, 1968), pp. 156-81.

40. K. Nielsen, 'Old Testament Metaphors in the New Testament', in S. Pedersen (ed.), *New Directions in Biblical Theology: Papers of the Aarhus Conference, 16–19 September 1992* (Leiden: E.J. Brill, 1994), pp. 128, 129.

all animals and plants, as a sort of viceroy of the principal and mighty King.[41]

I will examine in detail a section in Philo's discourse 'On the Creation', in order to ascertain how allegorization functions. In commenting on Gen. 2.4, 5, Philo noted the return to the conditions before herbs and grass grew on the earth, even though ch. 1 reported their creation (§129). For Philo, the text thereby declared the priority of ideas over material existence. Philo had already set out the view that just as a king envisions a city in his mind before he puts a plan on paper, and then executes the plan (§§17-22), so God created everything in his mind before it discretely appeared. The vision is that of Plato, that beehood, or the idea or form of a bee, precedes the actual insect. Philo, however, under the weight of the Genesis vision, declared that the forms themselves were generated by God, unlike Plato, who held that the ideas were independent of deity:

> Does he not here manifestly set before us incorporeal ideas perceptible only by the intellect, which have been appointed to be as seals of the perfected works, perceptible by the outward senses. For before the earth was green, he says that this same thing, verdure, existed in the nature of things, and before the grass sprang up in the field, there was grass though it was not visible. And we must understand in the case of every thing else which is decided on by the external senses, there were elder forms and motions previously existing, according to which the things which were created were fashioned and measured out...for nature perfects none of those which are perceptible to the outward senses with an incorporeal model (§§129, 130).

Philo therefore employed what modern scholars believe is the beginning of a second document (Gen. 1–2.4a is Priestly [P], that is, the beginning of the Yahwist [J] account), as the grounds for declaring a quasi-Platonic vision of reality.

Next Philo took up Gen. 2.6, 'And a fountain went up from the earth and watered the whole face of the earth'. (The biblical statements as quoted here are from Philo's text.) The philosophers, Philo declared, envisioned all water the same, that is, as one of the four elements from which the physical universe is composed; but Moses, in contrast, distinguished the 'sweet and drinkable' water from that in the sea (§131). The sweet water of the earth, he further declared, holds the earth together, 'acting in the manner of glue'. Everything on earth, he believed, must have a moist essence. Philo likewise attributed this view to the natural philo-

---

41. *The Works of Philo*, 'On the Creation', (§88), p. 13.

sophers, held by among others Anaxagoras, though Philo did not mention any names. This moisture is obvious in the woman:

> for nature has bestowed upon every mother, as a most indispensable part of her conformation, breasts gushing forth like fountains, having in this manner provided abundant food for the child that is to be born (§133).

Philo, since he has brought up the mother, takes this occasion to disagree with Plato. The earth, he affirmed, is indeed a mother as early writers declared, naming her 'Demetra', that is, *ge* or *de* (earth) plus *meter* (mother). Philo is famous for etymologies of this sort. Plato believed, wrote Philo, that the earth imitates the woman, but rather, Philo declared, it is the woman who imitates the earth. So the earth has streams of rivers and fountains like breasts for the nourishing of the plants. In this, therefore, the woman emulates the earth.

It is clear therefore, in these two instances, that the privileged text, properly understood, discloses a reality beyond the immediately transparent sense. It is a meaning which both incorporates the insights of the philosophers, especially Plato, but at the same time modifies and corrects Platonic and other philosophical perspectives according to the Old Testament vision. This analogical interpretation, therefore, does not clarify or vivify a point of view. Rather it locates reality behind the discrete, and this covert reality is the more fundamental because it provides the foundation for the discrete. The text therefore sets forth a true account of creation, but it must be read, Philo asserted, in such a manner that fundamental reality is the center of attention.

Philo's allegorical rhetoric, therefore, works in this manner. The Septuagint text is the beginning point for discourse because in it fundamental insight is set out. But fundamental insight is not located in the discrete details of the text. It lies behind these overt expressions either by way of express declaration, or words as symbols, or words etymologically examined, or in some cases in numbers. The rhetoric of allegorization, for Philo, has its rules since even allegorization has its limits, but even in allegorization he respected affirmed biblical presuppositions over against those of the philosophers.

Frances M. Young more recently has examined metaphor, allegory and typology in the church fathers. She has offered a helpful, nuanced breakdown of types of allegory:

1. rhetorical allegory, where allegory is adopted as a figure of speech on a spectrum with irony and metaphor;
2. parabolic allegory, of a kind found in fables and riddles;

3. prophetic allegory, hidden and riddling revelation found in oracles, dreams symbolic visions, or narrative signs;
4. moral allegory, where the moral of a text is sought for paedeutic or paraenetic reasons, e.g., by particulars being universalized as examples;
5. natural or psychological allegory, where a mythological text is read as referring to forces interacting in the world according to accepted scientific norms;
6. philosophical allegory, where the transcendent world is revealed, in veiled fashion, through the material world, and/or a text employing earth language to convey heavenly meanings;
7. theological allegory, whereby Christ, or the creative and saving purposes of the Trinity, becomes the true meaning of life, the universe, the text and everything.[42]

Philo employed all of these types of allegory, but some more than others. He especially employed natural (though not so much from what he considered myths), philosophical and theological allegories. His theology, however, was not Christological, but focused on the God of Israel. None of these types, however, fully explicated the thrusts of Philo's fundamental allegorizing.

Just as the form or idea of plants were created in Genesis 2, and discrete plants in Genesis 3, so the form (idea) of a human was created in Genesis 1 and the empirical human in Genesis 2. Having quoted Gen. 2.7, he wrote:

For man as formed now is perceptible to the external senses, partaking of qualities consisting of body and soul, man or woman, by nature mortal. But man, made according to the image of God, was an idea, or a genus, or a seal, perceptible only by the intellect, incorporeal, neither male nor female, imperishable by nature (§134).

This discrete human was created both from material and from the divine since 'he breathed into' meant,

the divine spirit...sent to take up its habitation here on earth...[humans] may at all events be immortal according to that portion which is invisible... (§135).

Likewise the original human was more perfect than any who followed (§136), and thus for three reasons, first, because the materials from which he was created were unmixed, uncorrupted and pure. Second, God selected the most excellent clay from which to make him. Third, that God is good

42. F.M. Young, *Biblical Exegesis and the Formation of Christian Culture* (Cambridge: Cambridge University Press, 1997), p. 192.

and he made each part of the human body according to the numbers suited to it, so that it had 'admirable adaptation to the share in the universe of which it was to partake…' and gave it beauty as well (§138). God did not take the pattern for humans from any other animals, but created man from reason alone. Man was given the senses in order to perceive sounds, colors, flavors and odors (§139). Philo believed that since the first humans were perfect so also were their creations, and here he turns to the comparison of artists who imitate an original, the imitations always being inferior. Everything human has degenerated in succeeding generations (§142). In this Philo seems more Hellenistic (for example, Hesiod and the successively declining ages) than Hebraic since though periods of decline are found in the Hebrew Bible (for example, Judges) they are often followed by a new age of peace and prosperity so that no overall pattern of decline prevails.

The constitution by which the original humans lived was the universal constitution, 'the right reason of nature' (§143). This constitution for the earth, however, had to have been preceded by a like constitution for beings having rational divine natures (§144). In this case the constitution was not simply a plan in the mind of God, but he had already brought it to fruition in a 'divine' realm.

Not only are humans, when created, perfect, they also share all the dimensions of existence. They eat of the earth like mammals, they swim like fish, they even elevate themselves above the earth like birds; and furthermore, they share traces in themselves of the divine (§§145-147). That humans gave animals their names indicates that they were filled with wisdom, as was their God-creator. It is proper for a king to give names to his subjects. So God brought the animals to man to name, so that he might incite the powers with which he invested humans. Since man was yet pure he was able to devise names for them 'with great felicity and correctness of judgment…so that their natures were at once perceived and correctly described by him' (§150).

In his single state the man was at the height of perfection. When the woman was created, however, the male became attached to her as she to him. They in turn desired to generate a being like themselves. This relationship was the beginning of the decline of humans:

> And this desire caused likewise pleasure to their bodies, which is the beginning of iniquities and transgressions, and it is owing to this that men have exchanged their previously immortal and happy existence for one which is mortal and full of misfortune (§152).

Before woman was made God created a paradisal park. In the park all the trees bore suitable fruits and nuts and were disease free. Philo now expressed his views in regard to the trees of life and knowledge:

> And these statements appear to me to be dictated by a philosophy which is symbolical rather than strictly accurate. For no trees of life or of knowledge have ever at any previous time appeared upon the earth, nor is it likely that any will appear hereafter. But I rather conceive that Moses was speaking in an allegorical spirit, intending by his paradise to intimate the dominant character of the soul, which is full of innumerable opinions as this figurative paradise was of trees (§154).

The tree of life, Philo asserted, had to do with piety toward the gods, the means through which men become immortal, and the tree of the knowledge of good and evil, by which wisdom and moderation is obtained. When God discovered that the inclination of humans was wickedness, he drove them from the garden because immortal life is acquired by holiness or piety (§155). The serpent that appeared to the woman was a symbol of pleasure because he crawled on his belly, used lumps of clay for food, and bore poison in his teeth. It is the same with the human devoted to pleasure who likewise analogically bears these characteristics (§§157-159). The serpent is said to have a human voice because pleasure has innumerable defenders who speak on its behalf.

In the section examined here we have covered most of the ways in which Philo found 'hidden' meaning in the Scripture except for his exploration of numbers. In 'Allegorical Interpretation I' Philo explored 'secrets' of the number seven on account of the creation being six, plus the one on which God rested, totaling seven. 'Nature', he declared, 'delights in the number seven' (§8). There are seven planets, the constellation of the Bear is made up of seven stars, and the periodic changes of the moon are seven. He also argued that infants born in the seventh month are the most likely to live. Humans in turn maturate in steps of seven years. The importance of the number seven continues endlessly:

> Again, the irrational portion of the soul is divisible into seven portions; the five senses, and the organ of speech, and the power of generation. Again, the motions of the body are seven; the six organic motions, and the rotatory motion.
>
> Also the entrails are seven—the stomach, the heart, the spleen, the liver, the lungs, and the two kidneys.
>
> In like manner the limbs of the body amount to an equal number—the head, the neck, the chest, the two hands, the belly, the two feet. Also the most important part of the animal, the face, is divisible according to a

> sevenfold division—the two eyes, and the two ears, and as many nostrils,
> and in the seventh place, the mouth.
>   Again, the secretions are seven—tears, mucus from the nose, saliva, the
> generative fluid, the two excremental discharges, and the sweat that pro-
> ceeds from every part of the body (§§11-13).

Seven also applies in the arts, and grammar, music, the tones of the voice.
The number seven is the first compound of the perfect number six, by
adding one. He recognized his approach as being that of the Pythagoreans:

> On which account the Pythagoreans compare this number to the Goddess
> always a virgin who was born without a mother, because it was not gener-
> ated by any other, and will not generate any other (§15).

Clearly then, allegorization functioned most characteristically for Philo
as the manner by which to extricate from the text its concealed meanings.
He worked more than simply from the language of the text, drawing upon
allusions in its expressions. He almost always depended on something
explicit in the text to provide his point of departure. While what he set out
as hidden often reflected Middle Platonistic predilections, he departed
from these outlooks, when in his judgment they differed with the overall
presuppositions of the Old Testament.

6. *Clement of Alexandria (c. 150–c. 215 CE)*

Little is known of Clement's life. He was possibly educated, if not born, in
Athens. He studied Christianity and philosophy in several locations
including Palestine. He became a pupil of Pantaenus in Alexandria, and
then assumed the role of teacher himself about 190 CE. He left Alexandria
in 202–203 CE because of persecution, never to return. Much like Philo
from whom he borrowed extensively, especially in interpreting the Old
Testament, philosophically he reflected Middle Platonism.[43] Clement set
out to represent Christianity as the fruition of both the Old Testament
Scriptures and of Greek philosophy. His knowledge of ancient authors was

---

43.   A. van den Hoek, *Clement of Alexandria and his Use of Philo in the Stromateis* (VCSup, 3; Leiden: E.J. Brill, 1988). Other studies on Clement include T.F. Torrance, 'The Hermeneutics of Clement of Alexandria', in *idem, Divine Meaning: Studies in Patristic Hermeneutics* (Edinburgh: T. & T. Clark, 1995), pp. 130-78; S.R.C. Lilla, *Clement of Alexandria: A Study in Christian Platonism and Gnosticism* (Oxford: Oxford University Press, 1971); and E.F. Osborn, *The Philosophy of Clement of Alexandria* (Cambridge: Cambridge University Press, 1957).

prodigious, citing as many as 348.[44] In his major work *Stromateis* he spent much time criticizing the Gnostics, especially Valentinus and Basilides.

Much like Philo, Clement was convinced that Plato and Pythagoras were indebted to Moses, and for that reason the insights of the Old Testament Scriptures were the foundations of contemporary knowledge:

> (1) Aristobulus, in volume one of his *To Philometor*, wrote: 'Plato too was a follower of our system of law, and its precepts.' (2) There had been a translation by others before Demetrius, before the domination of Alexander or the Persians, recording the events concerning the exodus from Egypt of our fellow citizens the Jews, the realization of all that happened to them, the conquest of their own land, and the exposition of the whole system of law. (3) It is clear enough that the philosopher I mentioned, a man of wide learning, took a great deal from it, much as Pythagoras borrowed a great deal from us to form his own philosophic system. (4) The Pythagorean philosopher Numenius wrote directly: 'What is Plato but Moses speaking Greek?' This Moses was a theologian and prophet and, in the eyes of some, an interpreter of sacred laws. (5) The actual Scriptures—and they merit our full confidence—record his birth, actions, and life (150).

Clement believed that Scripture functioned in various ways though he did not with Philo emphasize the move from the more obvious to the more symbolic or esoteric:

> (1) The Apostle was certainly right in saying that he had come to know 'the mystery through revelation', as I wrote briefly earlier. In accordance with this, as you read you are able to realize my understanding in the mystery of Christ. (2) 'In accordance with this you are able', he said, knowing that some have only taken milk, no solid food yet, and perhaps not milk in its pure state. (3) There are four ways in which we can receive the meaning of the Law: it may present a type; it may show a symbol; it may lay down a precept of right conduct; it may pronounce a prophecy. (4) I am well aware that to make these distinctions and expound them is the work of fully mature men. The whole of Scripture is not, in the proverbial saying, 'a single Myconos'. If you wish to hunt down the whole process of God's teaching, you must approach Scripture with a more dialectical method to the best of your faculties (179).

Clement did not write exegetical philosophy/theology in the manner of Philo. Like Philo his intent is apologetic, but more explicitly so in continual overt declarations of his purpose. His treatises are sprinkled with quotes from both the Old and New Testaments, and from numerous

---

44. Clement of Alexandria, *Stromateis (Books One to Three)* (trans. J. Ferguson; Washington, DC: The Catholic University of America Press, 1991), p. 4.

Hellenistic authors. Clearly for him Scripture had a privileged status, but then quotations from Scripture often functioned in much the same manner as quotations from Plato or Pythagorus, that is, as a point of departure from which to expound a claim. He employed Scripture much more as proof texts than did Philo. But often quoted biblical texts were not so much proofs as the locations of allusions expressing sentiments Clement set out to develop.

In a section in the *Stromateis* titled, 'Philosophy, a Preparatory Science for Christianity', Clement argued that before the Lord's coming philosophy guided the Greeks to righteousness and was perhaps a direct gift of God and 'was what the Law was to the Hebrews, a tutor escorting them to Christ' (28). He alleged that 'There is only one way of truth, but different paths from different places join it, just like tributaries flowing into a perennial river'. In this section Clement claimed, not so much a higher meaning behind the text, but that the text expressed the same point he wished to make. He advanced two Scriptures, one from the Old Testament and one from the New. From the Old Testament he quoted Prov. 4.10, 11, 'Hear, my son, and accept my words, to have many paths of life. I am teaching you the ways of wisdom, so that its springs my never fail you'. It is doubtful that the text here attests to many routes to the truth, but rather the various aspects of uprightness. So at a minimum Clement is taking license with language so that it serves his purpose. From the New Testament he quoted words attributed to Jesus though he did not so identify them: 'Jerusalem, Jerusalem, how often have I wished to gather your children together to me like a bird with her fledglings!' (Mt. 23.37). Following the New Testament quotation, much after the manner of Philo, he employed etymology in regard to the meaning of Jerusalem, and then declared that the 'many fledglings' are different tutors. He regarded diversity of sources as not explicit in the text since he declared that his point was there prophetically:

> 'Jerusalem' means 'vision of peace'. He is showing us prophetically that those who have grasped the vision of peace have had a large variety of different tutors leading to their calling. (5) All right. He wished but could not. How often? Where? Twice: through the prophets and through his own coming. Therefore the phrase 'How often?' indicates the varieties of wisdom. It offers salvation in individual ways, qualitatively and quantitatively, universally, in time and in eternity 'since the spirit of the Lord has filled the world' [Wis. 1.7] (29).

Clement therefore drew more upon the language of Scripture than from the meaning of it as he himself seemed to recognize. The meaning he

wished to inculcate was not so much a philosophical insight so characteristic of Philo but a proleptic meaning for a later context, which he designated prophetic. In the rest of Section 29, Clement advanced a number of
Old Testament quotations to prove that one should 'make use of secular
education but not to settle there permanently'.

In Section 30, Clement argued that philosophy contributes to the
acquisition of wisdom. Wisdom is higher than philosophy and exercises
control over it. The Scripture, he declared, provided evidence for this
claim in the story of Abraham, Sarah, and Hagar. Sarah was long barren.
She gave her maidservant to Abraham, Hagar who was from Egypt:

> So Wisdom, who makes her home with the man of faith—Abraham was
> accounted faithful and righteous—was still barren and without child in that
> generation and had not yet conceived a child of virtue for Abraham. She
> sensibly thought it best that the man who had at the time a suitable oppor-
> tunity for progress should begin by going to bed with secular education
> [Egypt is an allegory of the secular world], and later come to her to father
> Isaac in accordance with divine Providence (30).

He also cited Philo as to Hagar being a resident in a foreign land. So it is
possible through Hellenistic education to reach Wisdom later, Sarah who
conceived later introducing Abraham to Wisdom. In this allegory Clement
is nearer Philo, but his point is more practical, that is, the manner in which
the Abraham story shows the progression of Wisdom, rather than having
to do, as in the case of Philo, with epistemology and ontology. Clement
pursued the allegory further:

> (3) Isaac represents the 'self-taught'; that is why he is identified as a type of
> Christ. He was the husband of one wife, Rebecca, who signifies 'patience'.
> (4) Jacob is recorded in association with several women, and is interpreted
> as 'man of discipline'. Measures of self-discipline involve a number of
> different dogmas. As the result, he has the alternative name 'Israel', 'the
> genuine visionary', with his wide experience and practice of discipline.
> (Something else becomes clear from these three forefathers; that the seal of
> true knowledge is sovereign, and it comprises nature, learning, and disci-
> plinary practice. You could have another image of what I have been saying
> in Tamar sitting at the crossroads and passing for a prostitute, so that Judah,
> eager to learn (the name means 'capable'), the man who never left anything
> unconsidered or uninvestigated, considered her and 'turned to her', while
> maintaining his confession of faith in God (31).

Additionally, Sarah condemned Hagar because she represented only
liberal (or Hellenistic) education, whereas the knowledge Abraham
possessed, that is, Wisdom, was more admirable. So philosophy is

concerned with questions regarding the truth and nature of the universe, but these are merely preliminary for those coming to Christ in whom is true wisdom (32).

Clement employed allegory, not so much to clarify or vivify a point of view, but in order to ground his arguments in the Scriptures. On occasion he declared a person or thing as a type, which Philo seldom does, for example, that Isaac is a type of Christ (31). Typology posits a world in which that which happens later brings to fruition an earlier declaration. Typology has a time line; it is horizontal. Philo, in contrast, believed that Scripture adumbrated fundamental reality to the one probing the mysteries and symbols of the text. His allegorization pointed upward (that is, beyond sense experience) and downward (that is, probing the foundational bed rock). The allegorization of Clement of Alexandria exhibited neither of these directions. His allegorization was essentially flat and immediate. Texts and persons in history adumbrated positions and persons about whom Clement set out to establish a viewpoint. These had mostly to do with practical affairs and in that sense were more in line with allegorization as discussed by the rhetoricians. But whereas the example of allegories offered by the rhetorician needed little elucidation to make them understandable, Clement normally had to explain why most of his allegories were suitable to his purpose. He employed Scriptures, in effect, more by way of allusion than proof. But he intended it to be proof because he explicated the texts in such a manner that he had, in his opinion, set out solid evidence for his conclusions from the Scriptures.

7. Conclusions

From this examination of the allegorical interpretation of Scripture in Philo and Clement of Alexandria I have arrived at a clearer vision of the manner in which these approaches to interpretation have rhetorical power. Their rhetorical effects are rich in textures that are constantly dependent upon the author and audience. There is still much work to be done. In the New Testament, for example, the employment of texts from the Old Testament most often insists that these declarations from of old have come to fruition in the last days of the age now passing away. It is typological interpretation. And typological interpretation must also be examined for how it functions rhetorically. Furthermore, some use of Old Testament texts in the New is employed in the manner of evidence as employed by rhetors in the law courts. Texts employed in this manner have another function still. What I have accomplished here, therefore, is an analysis of only one phase of the features of synagogue or church rhetoric in regard to the citation of biblical texts, that is, allegory as employed by Philo and Clement of Alexandria.

THE RHETORICAL FULL-TURN IN BIBLICAL INTERPRETATION: RECONFIGURING RHETORICAL-POLITICAL ANALYSIS

Vernon K. Robbins

> The issue is not *whether* we enact rhetorical practices from the literature we interpret; the issue is *what* rhetorical practices from that literature we enact.
>
> (Gnomic paraphrase of Moore 1992: 93)

In her address at the Rhetoric and Religion Conference held at the University of South Africa, Pretoria, 15–19 August 1994, Elisabeth Schüssler Fiorenza asserted that those who have reintroduced rhetoric into biblical interpretation during the last quarter of a century have 'become stuck in a rhetorical half-turn' (Schüssler Fiorenza 1996: 29). Her assertion is that in the context of the revival of rhetorical criticism 'biblical scholarship has not yet made the full epistemological turn to a rhetoric of inquiry insofar as it has barely recognized the contributions which feminist and liberationist scholarship have made to the New Rhetoric' (pp. 29-30). She provides both a rationale and a rationale for the rationale to explain the situation. The reason rhetorical biblical scholarship has not incorporated feminist and liberationist scholarship, she asserts, is that interpreters remain in 'captivity' to 'empiricist-positivist science'. This captivity takes the form of spending 'much of its energy in applying and reinscribing to Christian Testament texts ancient rhetorical methods, disciplinary technology, terminological stylistics and the scattered prescription of oratorical handbooks in antiquity' (p. 32). Then she explains the reason for this captivity. Rhetorical interpreters, she asserts, find themselves unable or unwilling to acknowledge 'their feminist and liberationist critical partners' because of 'the contested character of the field'. This means that 'The "fear" that it could be seen as "unscientific" prevents engagement with such critical political intellectual discourses' (p. 47).

1. *Oppositional Rhetoric as a Half-Turn in Schüssler Fiorenza's Analysis*

Schüssler Fiorenza equips the stage for her argument with two steps. First, she mentions Margaret Mitchell's *Paul and the Rhetoric of Reconciliation* and describes how '[f]ollowing in the footsteps of Hans Dieter Betz she defends the antiquarian approach and technological method still prevalent in biblical rhetorical studies with a spirited attack on the practitioners of the so-called New Rhetoric' (Schüssler Fiorenza 1996: 32). Second, instead of illustrating her thesis with work by either Betz or Mitchell, Schüssler Fiorenza presents a critical discussion of the socio-rhetorical analysis and interpretation I presented to organize a discussion at the 1992 session of the Society of Biblical Literature of the various versions of the story of the woman who anointed Jesus. She chooses this illustration because, as she says, 'his [Robbins's] is one of the few Christian Testament studies that attempt to take rhetorical and feminist theoretical insights seriously' (Schüssler Fiorenza 1996: 33). She begins with a critical discussion of my presentation of ideological criticism, since, in her view, my discussion implied that my own approach was free from any ideological orientation (Schüssler Fiorenza 1996: 33). I have always understood that my approach has an ideological grounding, but Bruce J. Malina had a similar opinion about my approach prior to 1996. It has been natural to presume, I suppose, that anyone who works with ancient rhetorical manuals and seeks a programmatic approach to interpretation must consider their work to be grounded in scientific objectivity rather than in ideological orientation. Moreover, placing ideological texture fourth in the sequence of analysis and interpretation led some people to think I held the opinion that my analysis of inner texture, intertexture, and social and cultural texture was free from an ideological orientation. I hope that the introductions and the chapters on ideological texture in my two books have clarified my position in this regard (Robbins 1996b: 1-6, 95-119; 1996c: 24-27, 192-236). The proper description of my position is not scientific or scientistic, but interactionist (Robbins 1998: 286-88; Lawson and McCauley 1990: 15-31). This means that, in the context of scientific explanation versus humanistic interpretation, my position is that both approaches yield important information about our understanding and interpretation of texts. It is important, in my view, to set scientific and humanist procedures of analysis and interpretation into energetic, interactive dialogue on an equal playing field in our work.

Later in her essay, Schüssler Fiorenza describes the task of rhetorical biblical scholarship in the following manner:

> How meaning is constructed depends not only on how one reads the social, cultural, and religious markers inscribed by the text but also on what kind of 'intertexts', preconstructed 'frames of meaning', common-sense understandings, and 'reading paradigms' one utilizes when interpreting linguistic markers and textualized symbols (Schüssler Fiorenza 1996: 40).

I agree fully with this description of our task. One of my purposes in the session at the SBL, therefore, was to assess the use of intertexts in the analysis and interpretation of the various versions of the woman who anointed Jesus. In the essay I criticized the limitation of the intertexts for the Markan version of the story to 1 Samuel 10, where Samuel anoints Saul as king. I called for a reading that places the story in a broader context of 'social values and dynamics in Mediterranean society' (Robbins 1992: 311). This procedure means that one observes the presence of Jesus at a meal in a house and asks about the function of oil in that kind of context in Mediterranean society.

Rather than opening a conversation about how one might negotiate a disagreement about the intertextual construction of a particular context for interpretation, Schüssler Fiorenza closed down a discussion of the issue with oppositional rhetoric that implied that her construction of a Jewish scriptural context is not a scholarly construct, but that my construction of a broader Mediterranean context is based on 'a twentieth-century theoretical fabrication that needs to be seen as "story" rather than as "social scientific" objective description of reality' (Schüssler Fiorenza 1996: 34).

The point I was making in that essay is that, as Bruce Malina has pointed out, we are 'low context readers' when we face a text like the story of the woman who anointed Jesus. We do not know the social and cultural context that provided the distinctive meaning effects of the various versions of the story. As a result, we 'construct' a context. If Schüssler Fiorenza had admitted that she also had constructed a context for interpretation, she could have opened a most interesting discussion about 'creating contexts' for interpretation of the variant versions of the woman who anointed Jesus. Instead, she closed the door with oppositional rhetoric that reached a conclusion in the following statement:

> Again, let me repeat. I am not interested here in arguing for the superiority of my own interpretation of this text in *In Memory of Her*. Rather I want to illustrate my contention that rhetorical criticism in biblical studies remains in captivity to an empiricist-positivist scientism which it shares not only

with literalist biblicism but also with its brother discipline, classics. Both biblical studies and classics were institutionalized as modern 'gentlemen' disciplines dedicated to the study of philology, text and history—pure and simple (Schüssler Fiorenza 1996: 35).

I want to acknowledge that Schüssler Fiorenza did not have my *Tapestry of Early Christian Discourse* to consult at the time, since it did not appear until 1996. This may have caused her to moderate a few of her comments, but I am not sure. Rather than choosing a strategy that put both of our constructions of the context on an equal playing field for discussion, she chose an oppositional strategy that closed the door to that discussion. In the essay she refers to her book *Discipleship of Equals* and calls for 'a political rhetoric of inquiry in biblical studies' grounded in 'the *ekklesia* as the public assembly of free and equal citizens in the power of the Spirit' (Schüssler Fiorenza 1996: 36). Instead of enacting a procedure of 'equality' that would have invited a full rhetorical turn in an assessment of the contexts of interpretation for analyzing and interpreting the various versions of the story, she used oppositional rhetoric containing inner attributes of domination and separation that she claims she would like to move beyond. Characterizing my work as objectivist, scientistic, empiricist, and malestream, versus her work as open, free, and based on equality, she took a political half-turn that set her work in opposition to mine in a manner that did not invite any further deliberation about the issues involved. Thus, there is a deep antipathy in Schüssler Fiorenza's essay between what she says and what she does. She says many excellent things about the manner in which rhetorical scholarship should proceed, but her discourse enacts a dominating, alienating, oppositional mode of rhetorical argumentation.

It has been of interest to me that Kathleen E. Corley, taking a feminist approach, has proceeded in a manner very similar to mine to establish a context of interpretation for the Markan account of the woman who anointed Jesus, and with highly similar results (Corley 1993). The issue in all of this is not, after all, a male-oriented, scientistic approach versus a feminist approach of equality in public assembly. The issue is what kind of full rhetorical turn we make as we construct a context of interpretation for a particular text. The scholarly issues at stake become lost when oppositional rhetoric takes the stage. Schüssler Fiorenza claims a goal of enabling 'biblical scholars to investigate the discursive arguments which perform particular kinds of actions in particular historical situations and at particular political sites' (Schüssler Fiorenza 1996: 36). I agree. The question, then, is the particular historical situation and political site that caused Schüssler Fiorenza in 1994 in South Africa to use oppositional rhetoric in her essay rather than rhetoric that would invite discussion and debate among equals.

2. *Oppositional Rhetoric in the New Testament*

Schüssler Fiorenza's adoption of oppositional rhetoric as a preferred mode of discourse in a context where she was pleading for a full-turn in rhetorical biblical scholarship presents an opportunity to reflect on the nature of oppositional rhetoric not only in our own personal discourse but also in New Testament discourse. Stephen D. Moore has made the point that as we interpret literature we reenact certain rhetorical practices present in that literature (Moore 1992: 93). Feminist scholars have helped us to understand how easy it is to reenact certain male rhetorical practices in the literature we interpret. In an address I delivered at the University of Stellenbosch at the Second African Symposium on Rhetoric, 11 July 1996, and subsequently published in *Scriptura*, I briefly described oppositional rhetoric in the New Testament as follows:

> Central to opposition discourse is the reasoning that people to whom God has given a tradition of salvation in the past currently enact a misunder-standing of God's saving action that must be attacked and replaced by an alternative system of belief and behavior… It presupposes an alignment of the speaker with God, against people who claim to understand God who really do not know the will and the ways of God (Robbins 1996a: 360).

Oppositional rhetoric is present in many places in the New Testament. One immediately thinks of Jesus' controversy with 'the Jews' in Jn 8.43-47, which reaches a point where Jesus asserts that the Jews are sons of the devil:

> [43] Why do you not understand what I say? It is because you cannot accept my word. [44] You are from your father the devil, and you choose to do your father's desires. He was a murderer from the beginning and does not stand in the truth, because there is no truth in him. When he lies, he speaks according to his own nature, for he is a liar and the father of lies. [45] But because I tell the truth, you do not believe me. [46] Which of you convicts me of sin? If I tell the truth, why do you not believe me? [47] Whoever is from God hears the words of God. The reason you do not hear them is that you are not from God.

This is not the time and place to present a socio-rhetorical analysis and interpretation of this oppositional discourse. Gail R. O'Day has many excellent observations about it in her New Interpreter's Bible commentary on it. Among them is the following:

> John 8 presents the reader of the Gospel of John with some of the Gospel's most difficult interpretive issues. The Jesus who emerges from these verses speaks with staggeringly sharp invective to his opponents and holds nothing back in his attack on his theological adversaries. It is very difficult to harmonize this picture of Jesus with the images of him that shape our theological imaginations: Jesus as the one who eats with outcasts and sinners, who cares for the lost sheep, who is the model of how we are to love…
>
> The virulent language of chap. 8 must be read against this backdrop of being cast out of the synagogue, of being excluded from the religious centers that once helped to define one's religious and communal identity. The language of this chapter is the language of the minority group spoken in protest to the majority culture. The Johannine Jewish Christians had no way to back up this language—that is, they had no power to take any actions comparable to their own exclusion from the synagogue. They were outnumbered by the Jewish community and had no political resources at their disposal. Their only 'power' rested in the force of their rhetoric, in their ability to denounce those who had excluded them (O'Day 1995: 647-48).

With her commentary O'Day speaks directly to one of the major pleas made by Schüssler Fiorenza, namely, 'to investigate the discursive arguments which perform particular kinds of actions in particular historical situations and at particular political sites' (Schüssler Fiorenza 1996: 36). Many New Testament scholars join with O'Day in a view that the Johannine community was a minority group speaking out in protest against a majority culture. She expresses concern about this kind of rhetoric and explains the difficulty of reconciling it with other discourse in the New Testament. In other words, she does not herself wittingly or unwittingly enact the oppositional rhetoric in the text. The discourse attributed to Jesus introduces strong polarities to separate Jesus fully from 'the Jews'. For various reasons which she explains in her commentary, she does not wish to enact this kind of rhetoric in her commentary.

Another passage of oppositional rhetoric is in Matthew 23. Luke Timothy Johnson wrote what is considered by many to be a classic article on the discourse in this chapter, entitled 'The New Testament's Anti-Jewish Slander and the Conventions of Ancient Polemic' (Johnson 1989). Distinguishing his approach from censorship, argument against the historical accuracy of the polemic, claims of mistaken attribution, and a critic's strong 'misreading' of the text to make the author an anti-Semite, Johnson

sketches the historical and social context which generated the language
and places the polemic within conventional rhetoric of slander in the
Hellenistic world (pp. 421-23). Johnson describes the first generation of
messianists as 'a persecuted sect' and suggests that '[t]he primordial
experience of suffering deeply influences all the New Testament rhetoric'
(p. 424). He explains that '[t]he messianic sect was diverse from the
beginning' (p. 425). As a result of these pressures of diversity within the
sect, 'New Testament polemic is mostly turned inward against fellow
members of the movement' (p. 426). Judaism itself was diverse at the
time, with the result that:

> When the New Testament writings were composed, neither Christianity nor
> Judaism had reached the point of uniformity and separation that would
> characterize them in later centuries. The messianists were part of a much
> larger debate within Judaism, a debate with many parties, concerning the
> right way to read Torah, the text that shaped the people (p. 428).

As Johnson explores and describes the historical circumstances that
produced the New Testament's anti-Jewish polemic, he suggests that such
a description is helpful, 'but the rhetoric itself still appears excessive and
filled with dangerous power' (pp. 428-29). Two more qualifications, he
suggests, can lead to a proper assessment: (1) one 'must understand the
social context within which such slander was at home'; and (2) one 'must
appreciate the conventions of the language itself'. He then proposes that
'the slander of the New Testament is typical of that found among rival
claimants to a philosophical tradition and is found as widely among Jews
as among other Hellenists'. Then he adds: 'I further suggest that the way
the New Testament talks about Jews is just about the way all opponents
talked about each other back then' (p. 429). Asserting that the proper way
to think about first-century Judaism is as a philosophy, he suggests that
philosophical groups and Judaism were both highly concerned about
morals, and the best way to pursue and reach their goals was through
fierce disputation. Analyzing the rhetoric of philosophical polemic, he
observes that typical actions, not specific actions, are the subject of the
disputes and that people were able to strike back, returning abuse with
attacks on those who called themselves philosophers. Listing the topics of
the philosophical debates, Johnson suggests that a person 'find(s) the same
language everywhere'. The 'charges became standardized and formed a
topos' (p. 432). New Testament literature, he suggests, represents a
secondary, 'literary' use of such polemic. The literary and rhetorical
function of Matthew's attack on scribes and Pharisees is 'to frame the

positive instructions of messianist disciples...in 23.8-11' (p. 433). He completes the article with a survey of this kind of polemic in Jewish literature and concludes with the proposal that, 'the New Testament's slander against fellow Jews is remarkably mild'. In addition, he suggests that 'Nothing relativizes plausibility structures like pluralism. Knowing that all parties to a debate spoke in a certain way forces us to relativize our party's version' (p. 441). Oppositional rhetoric, then, is a significant phenomenon in New Testament literature, and Johnson's proposal is that it was pervasive during the time of the beginnings of Christianity.

3. *Oppositional Rhetoric in Recent Writings of Luke Timothy Johnson*

Following Moore's proposal that interpreters regularly reenact rhetorical practices in the literature they interpret, one might suggest that Schüssler Fiorenza's adoption of oppositional rhetoric as a central mode of discourse in her essay has a strong precedent in New Testament literature itself. It is also instructive that Luke Timothy Johnson recently has enacted a similar oppositional mode of discourse both in a recent book (Johnson 1996) and in a lecture before the Catholic Biblical Society of America during 1997 (cf. Johnson 1998a).

Johnson's book *The Real Jesus* reenacts the oppositional approach he analyzed in his earlier essay. In his book he claims there was diversity in earliest Christianity, and there was vigorous disputation. He criticizes every scholarly endeavor to display that diversity and to display opposition, however, as engaged in an impossible task. The overall pattern of diversity and opposition in New Testament literature, he asserts, is widespread. This pattern, however, is only literary technique. Walter Bauer successfully showed that there was diversity and conflict in early Christianity, but there is no ability on the basis of New Testament literature, Johnson claims, to identify specific opponents or to locate specific diversity. Therefore, scholarly endeavors during the past quarter of a century to identify specific opponents and to locate specific diversity are misguided. In his words:

> There is no new evidence, and there are no controls. All that has happened is that, on the basis of subjective literary judgments, compositions have been disjoined, anointed as sources, and then appointed to their respective roles in a hypothetical community drama. It is a paper chase, pure and simple (Johnson 1996: 99).

The similarity between the style of this prose and Schüssler Fiorenza's prose in the essay discussed above is noticeable. Issues are described in wholesale terms, 'pure and simple'. The remarkable thing in the context of Johnson's argument is that there is new evidence: Qumran literature and archeology, extensive archeology in Judea and the Galilee, and new early Christian literature in the Nag Hammadi library. But Johnson disregards these phenomena as evidence for 'historical' reconstruction. He criticizes Dieter Georgi for bringing a discussion of opponents into the pages of the New Testament itself (pp. 97-98), and he criticizes Raymond Brown for his analysis of diversity with the Johannine tradition, saying that 'his entire reconstruction of Johannine "history" rests upon no more solid basis than a series of subjective judgments and suspect methodological presuppositions' (p. 100). His strategy is remarkably like the strategy he describes among philosophical groups during the first century. If Christianity is one more philosophical group, then the topics of its literature is morals, not history. Johnson adopts the position of one who disputes on the basis of 'typical' actions, just as he says philosophical and religious groups did during the first century—accusing people in cate-gorical terms rather than picking up specific pieces of evidence and entering into a discussion on an equal playing field. In this book the tone is not deliberative; it is epideictic, engaging in invective against groups of people who are 'misguided', a term he uses in the title of the book.

Both Johnson and Schüssler Fiorenza, then, engage in political rhetoric, and when they do they enact oppositional rhetoric that closes off issues rather than moves them into a context of free exchange among equal partners in dialogue. This kind of political discourse, then, is a rhetorical half-turn rather than a full-turn. Turning away from serious scholarly deliberation, it attacks typical rather than specific actions to establish a frame for instructing disciples rather than engaging seriously with col-leagues in scholarly investigation, exchange, and debate.

4. *Making the Rhetorical Full-Turn*

The question, then, is how to make a rhetorical full-turn that includes political debate and confrontation. Johnson presents an overview of the interpretive practices and goals he envisions in 'Imagining the World Scripture Imagines' (Johnson 1998b). Detailed assessment of his program will have to await another context. Here I will recall that underlying Johnson's approach to interpretation is a correlation of anthropological (human), social-historical (Jewish), literary, and religious (experiential) dimensions of early Christian texts (Johnson 1986: 5-18; 1998c). The anthropological and religious (experiential) dimensions have notable affinities with socio-rhetorical interpretation of the social, cultural, ideological, and sacred textures of early Christian texts. A significant difference emerges in Johnson's limitation of analysis to the 'complete and finished literary form' of early Christian writings (Johnson 1986: 6). One result of this focus is a limitation of analysis to the 'literary culture' of early Christianity, the products of the 'elite' religious and political leadership. Analysis and interpretation does not, in this approach, get to the interaction of oral and written traditions that give the early Christian discourses their distinctive social, cultural, ideological, and religious dynamics in the Mediterranean world (Robbins 1994, 1996a). To put it another way, limitation of analysis to the complete and finished literary form of early Christian writings bypasses the 'inner workings' of the 'networks of signification' within the texts and fragments of texts available to us (Robbins 1984: 5-6). 'Literary culture' is a limited sphere of culture within early Christianity. The largest sphere of early Christian culture for the first 150 or 200 years was oral. A major challenge, then, is to identify the interaction of oral and written discourses within extant literary writings (Robbins 1999). Analysis of the interaction among oral and written discourses in multiple early Christian environments as exhibited both by fragments of writings and by complete writings holds the potential to exhibit the inner workings of the discursive cultures that created distinctive modes of reasoning, feeling, believing, and acting among early Christians. Analysis only of the complete and finished literary form of early Christian writings, then, puts the interpreter in a position of a rhetorical half-turn in interpretation. An interpreter must explore the complex world of oral traditions, fragments of writings, and complete literary versions of writings to perform a rhetorical full-turn in biblical interpretation.

Concerning Schüssler Fiorenza's approach, there is a beautiful moment in her essay when she introduces the metaphor of the African American circle dance or the European folk dance to destabilize a binary frame of reference for figuring the practices of a critical feminist biblical interpretation. Within this description, I suggest, lies an image very close to the one that has guided my development of socio-rhetorical interpretation. Schüssler Fiorenza proposes:

> an image of interpretation as forward movement and spiraling repetition, stepping in place, turning over and changing of venue in which discrete methodological approaches become moving steps and artful configurations.

> Clumsy participants in this dance that figures the complex enterprise of
> biblical criticism may frequently step on each other's toes and interrupt
> each other's turns but they can still dance together as long as they acknow-
> ledge each other as equals conscious of dancing through a political mine-
> field (Schüssler Fiorenza 1996: 51).

This image of movement and spiraling repetition introduces a very different mode of procedure than one that places oppositional rhetoric at the
forefront, and I applaud it. It is an image that evokes well the goal of
socio-rhetorical analysis and interpretation. The forward movement and
spiraling repetition moves through and circles around analyses of inner
texture, intertexture, social and cultural texture, ideological texture, and
sacred texture. The stepping in place, turning over, and changing of venue
describes well the move from wisdom discourse to miracle discourse to
apocalyptic discourse, death–resurrection discourse, and pre-creation
discourse. Oppositional rhetoric has as its goal to dominate. Striking out
against real or imagined opponents, oppositional rhetoric discusses only
typical actions and makes generalized assertions and accusations. The
good thing is that not all New Testament discourse is oppositional
rhetoric. Widespread throughout New Testament literature are also patterns of conciliation within wisdom discourse, healing discourse, death–
resurrection discourse, and pre-creation discourse (Robbins 1996a). The
nature of New Testament literature is that it interweaves diversity and
opposition into a thick configuration of history, society, culture, and
ideology. If our rhetorical analyses reenact only one or two rhetorical
modes within this literature, then we are making only a quarter- or half-
turn within its rich discursive texture. To make our task complete, we must
engage in political rhetoric and we must do it not only by joining voices
and actions with women's voices and marginalized people in wide regions
of our global village. We must engage in dialogical interpretation that
includes disenfranchised voices, marginalized voices, recently liberated
voices, and powerfully-located voices. In order to make a rhetorical full-
turn as we do this, we must learn how to embed our oppositional strategies
in many forms and styles of rhetoric so that we enable free and open
discussion and controversy in an environment where we keep our colleagues on an equal playing field and keep the issues in an arena of
specificity rather than staging them as typical actions to be attacked.
Moving forward, spiraling, stepping in place, turning around, and changing venue, we explore with each other, debate with one another, and disagree with each other as equals, inviting other voices into the dialogue in a

manner that makes a rhetorical full-turn through scientific, humanist, malestream, feminist, ethnic, geographical, racial, economic, and social arenas of disputation, dialogue, and commentary.

BIBLIOGRAPHY

Corley, K.E.
1993 *Private Women, Public Meals: Social Conflict in the Synoptic Tradition* (Peabody, MA: Hendrickson).

Johnson, L.T.
1986 *The Writings of the New Testament: An Interpretation* (Philadelphia: Fortress Press).
1989 'The New Testament's Anti-Jewish Slander and the Conventions of Ancient Polemic', *JBL* 108: 419-41.
1996 *The Real Jesus: The Misguided Quest for the Historical Jesus and the Truth of the Traditional Gospels* (San Francisco: HarperSanFrancisco).
1998a 'So What's Catholic about It? The State of Catholic Biblical Scholarship', *Commonweal* 125.1: 12-16.
1998b 'Imagining the World Scripture Imagines', in L.G. Jones and J.J. Buckley (eds.), *Theology and Scriptural Imagination* (Oxford: Basil Blackwell): 3-18.
1998c *Religious Experience in Earliest Christianity: A Missing Dimension in New Testament Study* (Minneapolis: Fortress Press).

Lawson, E.T., and R.N. McCauley
1990 *Rethinking Religion: Connecting Cognition and Culture* (Cambridge: Cambridge University Press).

Moore, S.D.
1992 'Deconstructive Criticism: The Gospel of Mark', in J.C. Anderson and S.D. Moore (eds.), *Mark & Method: New Approaches in Biblical Studies* (Minneapolis: Fortress Press): 84-102.

O'Day, G.R.
1995 'The Gospel of John: Introduction, Commentary, and Reflections', in *The New Interpreter's Bible*, IX (Nashville: Abingdon Press): 491-865.

Robbins, V.K.
1984 *Jesus the Teacher: A Socio-Rhetorical Interpretation of Mark* (Philadelphia: Fortress Press).
1992 'Using a Socio-Rhetorical Poetics to Develop a Unified Method: The Women who Anointed Jesus as a Test Case', *SBLSP* 31: 302-19.
1994 'Oral, Rhetorical, and Literary Cultures: A Response', *Semeia* 65: 75-91.
1996a 'The Dialectical Nature of Early Christian Discourse', *Scriptura* 59: 353-62.
1996b *Exploring the Texture of Texts: A Guide to Socio-Rhetorical Interpretation* (Valley Forge, PA: Trinity Press International).
1996c *The Tapestry of Early Christian Discourse: Rhetoric, Society and Ideology* (London: Routledge).
1998 'Socio-Rhetorical Hermeneutics and Commentary', in J. Mrazek, S. Brodsky, and R. Dvorakova (eds.), *EPITOAYTO: Essays in Honour of Petr*

Pokorny on his Sixty-Fifth Birthday (Prague-Trebenice: Mlyn Publishers): 284-97.

1999   'Historical, Rhetorical, Literary, Linguistic, Cultural, and Artistic Intertextuality: A Response', *Semeia* 80: 291-303.

Schüssler Fiorenza, E.

1996   'Challenging the Rhetorical Half-Turn: Feminist and Rhetorical Biblical Criticism', in S.E. Porter and T.H. Olbricht (eds.), *Rhetoric, Scripture & Theology: Essays from the 1994 Pretoria Conference* (Sheffield: Sheffield Academic Press): 28-53.

A Possible Direction for Providing Programmatic Correlation of Textures in Socio-Rhetorical Analysis

L. Gregory Bloomquist

1. *Introduction: The Promise of a Programmatic Correlation of Textures in Socio-Rhetorical Analysis as an Interpretive Analytics*

Clifford Geertz wrote: 'Man is an animal suspended in webs of significance he himself has spun' (Geertz 1973: 5). Vernon Robbins's socio-rhetorical analysis (SR) has moved New Testament criticism from the limited examination of historical questions to an exploration of the fascinating web of reality spun by each of the New Testament writers and their worlds. Robbins has done so by posing in a fresh way the question of where we start when we want to talk about rhetoric. This has led us to consider multiple, non-exclusive arenas for rhetorical analysis.

Furthermore, Robbins has argued that we may consider these arenas in a programmatic way by using SR as an 'interpretive analytics'. As a wide-ranging interpretive analytics, SR promises a 'programmatic correlation of multiple textures of texts that invites resources from multiple disciplines of investigation into an integrated environment of analysis and inter-pretation' (Robbins 1996c). Robbins feels that this interpretive analytics is able to fulfill three promises: to correlate the textures programmatically, to provide systematic attention to texts and textures, and to identify the resources necessary to give a new account of first-century Christianity (1996c: 237). It is an ambitious goal, and it is one that has already stirred the imaginations of scholars in both first-century Christian studies, as well as in wider religious traditions and in rhetoric in general.

Nevertheless, it is a goal that has not gone unquestioned. For example, in his discussion of Robbins's work at the meeting of the Rhetoric and New Testament Section of the Society of Biblical Literature in San Francisco (November 1997), R. Alan Culpepper suggested that the promises made by Robbins remain to be fulfilled. Similarly, Gordon

Newby argued that there were problems with seeing how the correlation of textures could ever be fulfilled.

The purpose of this paper is to elucidate ways that may assist SR to move from text, to model, to category. If socio-rhetorical analysis is to be more than a bringing together of a variety of existing models for a kind of ongoing dialogue among them and to become in itself 'an interpretive analytics', what is required? We turn first to Robbins's own understanding of his present work, and then, after posing the question anew, to some reflections on this work.

2. *Two Stages in Robbins's Investigation*

a. *Phase 1: Exploration of Cultures through History*

Like the vast majority of twentieth-century New Testament scholars, Robbins began his work by examining New Testament texts historically, and then through literary genres. This diachronic discussion followed the lines set down by Rudolph Bultmann: the New Testament texts evidence the evolution of Christian thought as it moves out of the Jewish world of Palestine to the progressively more Greco-Roman world of the Jesus movement in Paul, the Gospels, and Johannine literature.

Even more particularly, it followed Koester and Robinson's search for trajectories, which 'expanded F.C. Baur's project by embedding early extra-canonical Christian discourses into his biographically conceived historiography' (Robbins 1996a: 354). The result, argues Robbins, had serious shortcomings, including not only its tendentiousness but also even more importantly in Robbins's eyes the willingness to presuppose the existence of orthodoxy at the beginning of Christian culture, and then to impose a developmental process on the data whereby orthodoxy in multiple forms programmatically and persistently wards off heresy until orthodoxy becomes a dominant culture toward the end of the second century (Robbins 1996b: 354).

A partial corrective was achieved by Burton Mack, who, according to Robbins, also sought 'trajectories' but who did so by first attempting to uncover 'local' voices embedded in the Gospels of the New Testament. Mack thus introduced the significant element of 'rhetorical culture' into the task. According to Robbins, Mack's *A Myth of Innocence* (1988) was

> the first to attempt a rhetorical historiography of early Christianity. Using source analyses performed by form critics, plus Bultmann's view of the Hellenistic cult of Christ, Mack distinguished five different early Christian

groups on the basis of: (a) miracle catenae; (b) collections of parables; (c) the Q gospel; (d) controversy chreiai; and (e) the Christ cult. Mack has taken this work further in *Who Wrote the New Testament?* (1995), describing early Christianity through five major discourses: (a) teachings from the Jesus movements; (b) fragments from the Christ cult; (c) Paul and his gospel; (d) Gospels of Jesus the Christ; and (e) visions of the cosmic Lord (Robbins 1996a: 355).

Mack's suggestions provided Robbins with the necessary impetus for and with the first configurations of what rhetorical cultures would look like. Nevertheless, Mack did not provide the programmatic correlation of textures that would allow for the determination of these cultures. Mack's insights lacked 'a programmatic approach to dialogical interaction among the different modes of discourse in earliest Christianity' (Robbins 1996a: 355).

b. *Phase 2: The Shift to an Interactive Exploration and Making Culture*
Challenged by his South African colleagues during a stay there, Robbins began to break with the essentially historical model. The result was a turn to an interactive consideration of texts, that is, a consideration shaped by an understanding of how humans 'make culture'. He became interested in the way 'discourses' created 'discursive cultures' and thus the way in which shifts in speaking allowed for an interaction between discourses and discursive cultures that eventually would produce a variety of 'literary cultures'. In pursuit of this goal, he turned not only to 'insights from Greco-Roman rhetoric, but also to Mikhail Bakhtin's writings, sociolinguistic theory, and cultural anthropology' (Robbins 1996a: 355).

The work of Bakhtin and Medvedev led Robbins to argue against the univocal traditions that Koester and Robinson had posited as the outcome of the trajectories of first-century Christianity. In Bakhtin, Robbins discovered the 'multivocal' nature of single texts, namely, the way in which all literature contains multiple voices that are in some way in dialogue with each other.

Cultural anthropological studies, including the important study by B. Shore, *Culture in Mind: Cognition, Culture, and the Problem of Meaning* (1996), led Robbins to adopt an essentially late Wittgensteinian approach that looked for the rules of the rhetorical game in texts and to see the multiple voices that were discerned as players in the game (Wittgenstein 1958a; Thiselton 1980), for example, that of the 'synoptic gospels' (Robbins 1989). It was a search that led Robbins to the all-important way that people play by rules, even—or especially so—in the midst of sacred ritual, and what happens when they change the rules (Robbins 1996b: 343). The result, he argues, was a further move toward the way discourse creates culture, since the 'followers of Jesus in various places at various times throughout the first two centuries renamed Jewish practices as Christian practices' and thus 'subtly or not so subtly changed the rules, and introduced new phrases and nuances to communicate their new under-standings of who they were and what they were doing' (Robbins 1996b: 343). The result was, according to Robbins, a proliferation of games (that is, rule-determined cultures) in first-century Christianity and in the New Testament. 'When we add literature outside the New Testament, we get even a fuller picture of the multiple games and versions of games in early Christianity. All of the games together comprise early Christian culture' (Robbins 1996b: 343).

Finally, sociolinguistics has contributed to Robbins's development of a programmatic approach. Robbins has begun to use the term 'rhetorolect' for 'a form of language variety or discourse identifiable on the basis of a distinctive configuration of themes, topics, reasonings, and argument-ations' (Robbins 1996a: 356). Accordingly, he argues that each of the various types of early Christian discourse (wisdom, miracle, apocalyptic, death-resurrection, and cosmic discourse) may be 'rhetorolects' since each is a rule-bound, and in some cases rule-breaking, discourse that

> certain early Christians may or may not have spoken and intermingled with other discourses. Speakers or writers may work primarily in the context of one rhetorolect, or they may energetically intermingle various rhetorolects in their discourse. Whatever rhetorolects emerge, either consciously or unconsciously on behalf of the speaker or writer, the choice introduces distinctive socio-rhetorical features to their discourse (Robbins 1996a: 356).

3. *Is a Programmatic Correlation of Textures Possible and, If So, How?*

The richness of Robbins's analysis is patent, as are the possibilities that his analysis affords rhetorical studies in general. And his drive toward a programmatic correlation of textures is important, not just for a fuller understanding of early Christian texts, but also for a variety of studies. Nevertheless, there are significant questions that arise from Robbins's present study, for example, has Robbins sufficiently broken with the historical tradition as it was bequeathed to him by an essentially positiv-istic approach to history in his correlation of textures? If one does not start with or privilege history, does one start with discourse or text? Can we really get inside the mind of another person or culture sufficiently to say that we have understood or interpreted that person or culture adequately?

I want to suggest the value of both the philosophical enterprise of Wittgenstein and those followers who have correctly understood him, and the stages of cognitional analysis in the work of Bernard Lonergan, for a methodological grounding of socio-rhetorical analysis. I will do so by reflecting on socio-rhetorical analysis in four stages: (1) cultural observation; (2) the formulation of possibilities; (3) the logic of these possibilities; and (4) the ultimate goal of socio-rhetorical analysis as an interpretive analytics.

a. *First Reflections: Cultural Observation*

It is possible to argue that at the basis of Robbins's approach there should be an essentially descriptive approach that, at its most basic, seeks simply to enter into the text via observation of its textures. There would be nothing really programmatic about this approach. It would simply be letting the 'facts' of the text 'wash over' one. It would follow the same approach that an anthropologist might take as s/he enters into village life, namely, with a view to 'taking birth' in the culture and finding out how the people of the village create and play their game by their own rules. No decision would be made beforehand as to what rules are to be found, where the results will fit, etc. It would be a stage of mere attention. Some of Robbins's comments appear to endorse this approach (Robbins 1996c: 26).

There is no doubt that this is a valuable stage for a correlation of textures, and Robbins's own work has shunned the peremptorily prescriptive nature of some analysis in favor of a wide-ranging ingathering of texts, methods, and discourses. Nevertheless, anthropologists themselves are now raising serious questions to this approach. While descriptive, anthropological approaches have moved anthropology along lines that Robbins has embraced for first-century Christian studies by helping to eschew 'the holistic persuasions of traditional anthropologists', by helping anthropologists to recognize 'that their representations are fundamentally the products of asymmetrical power relations', and by helping them to 'develop new forms of representation which could include the multiple voices of those being represented', it is also true that the same approaches have raised new questions about representational practices, the question of whose representations are in fact being presented, the form of the representations, and the politics and ethics of just such representations (James, Hockey and Dawson 1997: 1-4). Simply put, 'if we acknowledge the situated nature of other peoples' "realities" and social worlds, so we must finally reject any professional claim to being the purveyors of unmediated accounts or objective "truths"' (p. 5).

If this is the case, however, does it not enable us to see how different parts of an observed people's or an observed text's life—what socio-rhetorical analysis might call 'textures'—fit together? Does not the very notion of 'correlation' that socio-rhetorical analysis intends imply some notion of 'unmediated accounts' or 'objective truths'? Yet, if alterity is not allowed to dominate, is there any option but to speak of some universal or objective regime of truth?

These questions are serious enough, but they are merely the surface of fundamentally more difficult questions, such as the idiosyncratic nature of our knowing and communicating. Cultural anthropologists note that one of the first things that we encounter at a first stage of observation or encounter is that each of us knows and communicates largely on the basis of what we reflect on and learn from our immediate surroundings (Shore 1996: 3-5). But, if this is so, how can communication happen? Further, how can analysis of communication happen?

Here we come face to face with the problem that some Wittgensteinians highlight, and which is a more-or-less accurate reflection of Wittgenstein's own discussion of 'private language', which in his words was those 'sounds which no one else understands but which I "appear to under-stand"' (Wittgenstein 1958a: 94e [269]). As Wittgenstein noted, unless one is able to determine the function of a word, that is, its use, there is no way to communicate that word or to use it for communication, and this is true whether the user understands the word he is using or not. Never-theless, if it is possible to 'seem to be guided, seem to know what to do, yet neither conform in our actions to any existing rule nor act under its influence, immediate or remote', how can our words possibly be under-stood (Hallett 1977: 346)?

Now, it may seem odd to suggest this problem at the outset of a discussion of rhetorical analysis, given that rhetoric is geared to com-munication to others; nevertheless, it is a crucial problem in our approach to the rhetoric of others, especially in light of the contemporary rejection of the modernist universality of human psychological characteristics— what Shore calls the 'psychic unity muddle' (Shore 1996: 311)—and of the rejection of 'a common essential (and yet-to-be-realized) identity' that allows any human to understand another. Nevertheless, I raise it here because the answer to the problem stresses the essentially rhetorical (that is, other-directed-linguistic activity) nature of human activity. For communication evidences not a universal human identity but the universal human 'condition which is that of an absence of essential identity', such that 'human beings, who constitute themselves semiotically rather than instinctually, identify themselves with subject positions (placements in relation to the actions or emotions of others) presented to them by discourses in language and other signifying systems' (Bowman 1997: 46-47). In other words, communication—and meaning—occurs as discourse encounters discourse and discourse system, even if that discourse begins as essentially un-understood or private. What humans—not just anthropologists—are after is overcoming a 'lack of familiarity with the imaginative universe within which their acts are signs' (Geertz 1973: 13).

Thus, a first and highly preliminary stage in socio-rhetorical analysis seems to me to be a recognition and reflection of this reality that consists for the most part in the observation of encounters of language and language systems. This observation consists in just that: observation. Our experience of this encounter is necessary but also necessarily unsatisfying. Were it not both, we would rest content with a 'feast of meanings' which, while not a bad thing in itself, would ultimately disappoint by its very richness; however, by forcing us on through being essentially unsatisfying we are brought into a dialogue that would otherwise be preempted through an interpretive decision made too quickly.

An Example. If, for example, we wished to understand something about what Paul says in Gal. 3.21, we might begin with observation. We might note the use of terms, such as words commonly translated 'law', 'faith', 'works', 'promise', and so on. We would likely want to know something of the meaning of these words, that is, their use by this author.

This is not an insignificant step. One of the values of socio-rhetorical analysis here is to slow the interpretive process down by forcing one to 'walk around' in the text and see the elements from various angles (textures). One might start by noting how the author uses the word 'faith' or 'works' and how this function plays out in the text.

One of the things that the observer will discover is that these words seem to exist in some sort of relationship with each other, suggesting perhaps a relationship. What that relationship is, and thus what the use is, would seem to derive not only from the verse itself, but also from the chapter as a whole—at the least!—and likely from the letter as a whole. Thus, at the least, one would probably want to go back to Gal. 3.1 and begin to see how the language is used up to and including 3.21. It is only in this way that one will begin to hear over and over again repetitions of words.

One will also likely begin to ask questions: what is this 'law'? Does it exist only in the author's mind, or in the world of the audience? Does it still matter or is it a relic of the past? What possible relation does the mention of 'spirit' have to 'law'? Is this in the author's mind? Is he borrowing it from some other place?

At the outset, then, observation as an experience of an encounter seems a crucial starting point for socio-rhetorical analysis. It alerts us, as a ringing bell does, to something, though we may not know what. That comes later. At this point, there is no one angle that is right or primary; all that is important is that no angles be excluded from consideration.

b. *Reflections on Rules and the Linguistic Nature of the Rules in Socio-Rhetorical Analysis*

Socio-rhetorical analysis provides no direction as to the starting point or to the subsequent stages. One might begin with inner texture or any other texture. Nevertheless, a reflection on the programmatic correlation of textures surely demands some reflection not only on what is primary but also on the hierarchy or order to be followed. In section a I have suggested that what is primary is not a particular texture but rather the experience of encounter through observation of the language used. In this section, I would suggest that what is subsequent is again not a texture but rather a consideration of the trans-textural nature of the rules of the language that are being used.

Rules are central to the communication process, which is the encounter of discourses and discourse systems. Communication happens as specific rules for the function of words are picked up, even though they may not be understood. Eventually the person will begin to use words in ways that are common to ways in which others use them and will thus understand what someone means or 'the rule by which he proceeds' when he understands the other's 'use of words, which we observe; or the rule which he looks up when he uses signs; or the one which he gives us in reply if we ask him what his rule is' (Wittgenstein 1958a: 38e-39e [82]).

This means that when we talk about rules, we should not be looking for something that 'lies beneath use', which 'would have to have something like the generality and normative force that seem to characterize the functioning of rules' (Minar 1990: 3). Rather than 'digging beneath our practices', we need constantly to remind ourselves 'of where we already are'; the very demand even that we search 'behind our practices, for the source of their "objectivity" rests on a turning away from that which lies before us' (Minar 1990: 8) as we have it through observation.

Now, I would suggest that one of the elements of the genius of socio-rhetorical analysis is to point to various contexts or angles (what Robbins calls 'textures') of particular language games in order to see how language may be being used in each of those contexts or from each of those angles. Each of these textures or angles sets before us different angles on 'where we already are' and thus with different rules for the different textures. The function or meaning cannot be univocal but is thus radically multivocal since there are various contexts within which language games happen and from which meaning cannot be abstracted. 'Our meaning something by a word is prepared for by and inseparable from a background of practices and agreements' (Minar 1990: 3).

Nevertheless, it might be asked whether there is one texture that is primary and others that follow in some sort of necessary hierarchy? Can we privilege one of these textures to be correlated—for example, the social and cultural texture—and thus be led progressively through the remaining textures until the examination of the use of language has been exhausted? If so, could not social and cultural facts become the criteria for determining the use of the words?

While a tempting option, we should perhaps ask some questions about this approach. On what grounds would we adjudicate the textures thus; on the grounds that this context is somehow determinative of the way in which people use language? What then happens to the essentially idiosyncratic experience? Does it become irreducibly subsumed under some larger scheme?

In terms of rhetorical argumentation, I believe that there is no proper versus improper use of patterns, intertextural use, social and cultural uses and misuses, as well as ideologically and sacrally correct uses and misuses of words. There is, in other words, no use that demonstrates better any rules that are primary or misused. What this means is that one would simply be after the use of the words from whatever angle one could imagine for the imaginative use to which a writer could have put it.

For example, if we think of words that apparently have to do with healing in, say, Luke's Gospel, we could begin by assessing the use of these words in relation to the social and cultural texture of first-century eastern Mediterranean practice. While not reducing the meaning of the words to this one, we might suggest the primacy of this meaning. If, however, we start, as we have above, with observation first, and proceed to some discussion of how these words function from different angles, we might note something different, for example, that words for 'healing' appear to indicate something of what happens when Jesus encounters people who are in some physical need on his way from Galilee to Jerusalem. Our immediate leap to a socio-cultural meaning, or an etymo-logical (intertextural) meaning, might then void a particular and possible 'private' understanding of Jesus' actions as he moves from Galilee to Jerusalem, a meaning that may in fact be completely independent of the words' social and cultural meanings, as well as their historical meanings.

But, what then of the 'programmatic' correlation of textures? If we consider any angle as possible and any possibility as a valid starting point, are we not left in a complete muddle as to any 'program'? It seems likely that there will be some order involved, namely, the search for 'rules' as the way the language functions. This would suggest some resulting taxonomy and correlation of textures, though not necessarily in any 'transportable' way, that will enable us to determine the outlines of rhetorolects and their final topics. For while there is a certain givenness that may be carried across into our understanding of rhetorolects—resulting from geographic differences, historical circumstances, migrations, or other social differ-ences (interaction of upper and lower classes, education and the technical terminology necessary for social intercourse, etc.) (Ivic 1992: 570)—there is also change, which may be local (geographically or socially), and which is either adopted or rejected (Ivic 1992: 570). However, there is no rule that indicates how givenness or change will or should proceed, or even that it has to be one or the other, only that in other analogous settings these changes have or have not occurred.

Slang is a good example of a common discourse that, while not un-ruled, is certainly not strictly rule-bound and is thus unpredictable. For example, slang may arise from the upper or the lower classes, the domi-nant or the countercultural, the technically literate or the educationally impoverished. And, while it is likely true that 'slang emanates from conflicts in values, sometimes superficial, often fundamental' (Maurer 1992: 572), there is no rule that indicates against whom the conflict is waged, since it could be waged against the dominant culture that sees the origins of a gang—and then used normatively and non-conflictually within a gang—or it could be waged against dominant elements within a gang—and thus conflictually from within. Or again, while it is true that slang works through shock value, it is a shock value that is voluntary; thus, the shock value through 'the superimposition of images that are incongruous with images (or values) of others' (Maurer 1992: 572) could be addressed to those that are outside (so as to be shocking) or to insiders (so as to prove their insider-nature).

In sum, there do not appear to be any rules for the determination of rhetorolects that will provide us with the magical key to determining the developments of rhetorolectical trajectories, any more than—as Robbins saw—there are rules for historical trajectories that have proven able to identify anything more than the 'winners' of the various discursive debates in early Christianity. While 'winning' rhetorolects are limited, possible rhetorolects are innumerable precisely because there are innumerable rules by which the rhetorical presentation may be made in innumerable contexts.

My option here for the pragmatic assertion that rules determine only how specific problems and their solutions are identified and dealt with in actual situations of linguistic encounter is not merely an option for an understanding of language that accepts the significance of the later Wittgenstein's importance for our understanding, but also a rejection of 'discourse-bound' meaning of rationalist discussions. Pragmatic rules in contexts consider the vagueness or fuzziness that is 'an essential character-istic of language which enables optimal communication' in ways that the more law-based forms of discourse analysis cannot (Parret 1983: 57).

For example, if one were to say that 'winning' at chess can only be uttered when particular pieces are moved into position on the board rather than when one player—or even an observer standing by—slaps his knees at a particular point in the game, then one will not understand the 'use' to which the player who uses the word 'win' in that way has put the term. Furthermore, one would not only not be right in so misconstruing the meaning; one would thus also miss the whole point and joy of the game that would not be missed were one to allow for that fuzziness and vagueness.

An Example. In the example under Section a, I made necessarily pre-liminary—and thus unsatisfying—observations regarding Galatians 3. The next task in our encounter with Galatians 3 is not to decide which rules are normative for the possible meaning of Galatians 3, but rather to examine various possible rules for elements in play in Galatians 3, that is, the various ways meaning is at work in Galatians 3. To decide on the rules ahead of time is to make *our* rules necessarily *their* rules.

It is likely that we should start with some investigation into what the words mean—though there are other possibilities; nevertheless, in doing so, we must not limit our investigation to the merely philological, even the dictionary meaning. Yet, here is the first problem that needs to be surmounted: what do the words in Galatians 3 mean? As Wittgenstein showed, the meaning of words cannot be arrived at logically, but only through use. How can we decide on whether these words are used in a way that is related to other like words or whether they are used completely idiosyncratically?

Let us for the moment simply posit *some* common use, though not excluding the possibility of completely common use nor that of completely idiosyncratic use. Let us also for the moment simply posit some intuitive insights regarding what a common use of the words might reveal. Specifically, let us do so in light of the use to which the words are put after the discovery at the beginning of the chapter of what appears to be a crucial opposition that runs throughout the whole chapter between phrases commonly translated 'works of the law' and 'the hearing of faith' in the remainder of the chapter.

If we do so, we come up with something like the following: 'law' has something to do with 'a rule that governs one during one's life, apparently in the body', and 'faith' has something to do with 'the faithful or trustworthy fulfillment of a promise made'. If we then allow that these meanings may be picked up in some way that reflects these meanings throughout the chapter, we discover that the author (whom we will call Paul since he does so at the beginning of his letter—not that it makes much difference at this point) is posing to the readers of the epistle a question about whether they have the spirit (note: not 'are being justified', which seems to lie behind so many commentaries at this point and which I will go on to note below) through following the rule of life via their bodies or through the faithful fulfillment of the promise. Neither of these meanings for words commonly translated 'law' and 'faith' does violence to the accepted meanings of the words that we might discover through consulting a Greek or Hebrew dictionary, though each does expand considerably on the meanings given there by allowing the words to gain their meaning through their function in the context here rather than by an extra-contextual and predetermined meaning.

But what about Paul's expression that the Spirit comes through 'hearing' the faithful fulfillment of the promises? This word seems intelligible enough. It seems to have to do with sounds hitting the eardrum. But, even if we add that it has do with intelligible sounds hitting the eardrum in intelligible ways, what does this have to do with the meaning of the word in this context? Perhaps it has to do with a specific hearing, namely, that of Paul's preaching. But, why? How?

Again, we shall try an intuitive insight: given the above meaning of those apparently crucial words 'law' and 'faith', and the practice that is being alluded to in Gal. 3.15-18, what if 'hearing' here has to do with the hearing of a will read and confirmed at the death of a body? Could the author be speaking of a hearing that is the occasion of the faithful fulfillment of the promise when a will has been confirmed and ratified? If so, according to the author, this is the way that the audience has the Spirit, namely, as an inheritance that is given at the 'hearing' of a will read.

Now, given that we cannot ask the author or his audience about whether this meaning is correct, it is possible to see that programmatic correlation of textures is neither the absolute assurance of the function of use through the asking of the author whether this is what is intended nor is it the preemptive decision of which rules are primary and determinative. Rather, programmatic correlation is more a kind of dialogical assessment of meaning through multiple, tentative readings from various textures and in various combinations of order. Nor will we even have the luxury to say that this is the only way that 'hearing' might be interpreted nor that it would always be interpreted in this way either by this author or even in this same text, even though 'when words in our ordinary language have prima facie analogous grammars, we are inclined to try to interpret them analogously; i.e. we try to make the analogy hold throughout' (Wittgenstein 1965: 7)

Now, if 'hearing' in Galatians 3 does in fact function, at least from some angles or in some contexts, in the way we have suggested here, then other questions will follow, that may or may not be explicit in the text. For example, it may be that the question 'who died and thus had his/her will read?' is a crucial, though implicit, question in the text, though we might want to explore socially and culturally what is the context within which a will is read or ratified: is it death? is it a decision to hand on the inheritance (as in Lk. 15)? For the joy of exploration, let us assume that we wish to pursue this line of exploration. When we do so, might it not be that the answer to this implicit question surfaces in this chapter with the mention of Jesus the Messiah, whom we learn elsewhere in this letter is understood by the author as having died? And, if this be the case, our exploration of this rhetorical presentation and our initial insights into the rules of the picture reveal remarkable features: the Galatians are asked by Paul whether they are living a God-blessed life (*dikaios*) of spiritual riches and spiritual experiences through the Spirit that God gave them because of their following a rule of life that is valid only in life or a particular phase of life, or whether they are living that life because the inheritance of Jesus the Messiah, which he himself has from Abraham, has now been ratified to them and is thus now theirs in Jesus' faithful fulfillment of the promise of God, the same Jesus having died and his 'will' having been read to them as heirs.

This explanation not only does no violence to any part of the text but elucidates it. Nevertheless, it does not yet help us understand Gal. 3.21. Are there rules that we are missing for the interpretation of that verse?

c. *The Value of Peirce's Understanding of Abduction for Understanding the Rules of Rhetorical Argumentation*

The impetus to search for rules is powerful. For many, the discovery of the right rules will in fact open the way for future discoveries. It is felt that if only we can discover the operative rules, we shall be able to move forward with further discoveries.

Now, while observation impels us forward in a search for meaning, initial insights based on certain descriptive rules may satisfy. Certainly an insight gives one the feeling of having provided meaning. What is lacking, of course, is a sustained exploration of the rules.

Not surprisingly, this is a crucial feature of scientific exploration. There is a debate between those who believe that there is a logic of scientific discovery that is governed by rules and those who believe that the only logic there is is one that assesses what is already presented. The latter, of course, is similar to the kind of deductive logic that is understood to be operative in normal language games as described above: let us posit a possible scenario and then let us see how uses of words flow from that scenario in context. In this approach, as we have seen in some detail above, observations do not lead one to an hypothesis, for example, *that* a word means such and such because of such and such reasons; observations only allow one to test an hypothesis, for example, *whether* a word means such and such or does not.

The former is perhaps a less well-known logical approach that has come to the fore in light of attention to another form of pragmatics than that described in the previous section, namely, the pragmatism of C.S. Peirce and his notion of abductive logic (Peirce 1960–66). It is about how we get new ideas and is thus a logical, first stage of all enquiries (6.469). Peirce's abductive logic appears promising to those who believe that if we can find a logical starting point for our enquiry, either our own discoveries will ensue or we shall be able to see how others have so thought (Lanigan 1996).

Abduction, though discussed in a variety of ways and over a variety of diverse writings by Peirce, is essentially an ampliative (or synthetic) logical inference in which a conclusion is problematically or conjecturally asserted. Nevertheless, to understand it more fully, it is helpful to examine its meaning separately in Peirce's early writings and in his later writings.

1. *Abduction in Peirce's Early Writings.* The earliest use of abduction in Peirce's writings occurs in his April 1867 reflection on hypothesis, followed in May 1867 by a fuller reflection on abduction in light of Peirce's categories. Both of these works, though early, contain the essential seeds of what would become Peirce's view. (While there is no mention of abduction in this final part of the paper, Peirce's comments in a 1902 grant application suggest that what he means by the word 'hypothesis' is what he will later clarify as 'abduction'. In his 1902 grant application to the Carnegie Institution [Peirce 1986: 588], Peirce wrote that his paper of April 1867 'divides arguments into Deductions, Inductions, Abductions [my general name, which will be defended] and Mixed Arguments. I consider this to be the key of Logic.')

Induction, for Peirce, is when 'we generalize from a number of cases of which something is true and infer that the same thing is probably true of a whole class' (Fann 1970: 9-10). For Peirce, 'perfect' or 'formal' *induction* is when we have a valid demonstrative form of inference that follows when the second premise and conclusion of a deductive syllogism are known to be true and the first premise is true by *enumeration*. Thus, if 'any M is P, Σ^* S^* is M; therefore Σ^* S^* is P; where Σ^* S^* denotes *the sum of all the classes which come under* M', (my emphasis) then 'Σ^* S^* is P, Σ^* S^* is M; therefore M is P' (Peirce 1984a: 43). As we shall see, in later texts, Peirce will regard induction in terms of case (minor premise), result (conclusion), and rule (major premise), a terminological transition that we learn elsewhere had to do with his desire to be able to express 'propositions which are not reducible to subject-predicate form' in logical form (Fann 1970: 20). An example of induction might be: Jesus and Hanina ben Dosa and Akiba and ben Zakkai are charismatic Palestinians; Jesus *et al.* are healers; therefore all charismatic Palestinians are probably healers.

Abduction is not the same as induction. In his 1902 application (cited above), he notes that:

> abduction is not of the number of probable inferences...[Regarding the paper on Probable Inference in the Johns Hopkins 'Studies in Logic'] the only error that paper contains is the designation as Abduction of a mode of induction somewhat resembling abduction, which may properly be called abductive induction... Abductive induction is quite a different thing from abduction... I at first saw that there must be three kinds of arguments severally related to the three categories; and I correctly described them. Subsequently studying one of these kinds, I found that besides the typical form, there was another, distinguished from the typical form by being related to that category relation to which distinguishes abduction. I hastily identified it with abduction, not being clear-headed enough to see that, while related to the category, it is not related to it in the precise way in which one of the primary division of arguments ought to be, according to the theory of the categories.

Accordingly, Peirce describes abduction as a means of explaining, 'an inference from a body of data to an explaining hypothesis, or from effect to cause', while induction is a means of classification, 'an inference from a sample to a whole, or from particulars to a general law' (Fann 1970: 10). Abduction allows us to 'pass from the observation of certain facts to the supposition of a general principle to account for the facts'. Peirce's early discussions of abduction suggest that it is a 'demonstrative form of argument' that follows when the conclusion and first premise are known to be true and the second premise is true by *definition*. 'Thus, if "any M is Π* P*, Any S is M; therefore any S is Π* P*; where Π* P* denotes *the conjunction of all the characters of* M [my emphasis]", then "Any M is Π* P*, any S is Π* P*, therefore any S is M"' (Peirce 1984a: 43-44). In later texts, Peirce will regard abduction in terms of rule, result, therefore case; in other words, one will establish a general hypothesis, note a specific result, and conclude regarding the particulars of the specific result. For example, we might say that 'all charismatic Palestinians are, for example, prophetic, scripture-quoting, physical-illness-healing; Jesus is a prophetic, scripture-quoting, physical-illness-healing person; Jesus is probably a charismatic Palestinian'.

As is clear, this form of logic is far less convincing than, say, deductive logic, though its reach is wider. Second, this form of logic concerns essentially a series of observed characteristics, which is why the 'result' is not the conclusion but rather a premise. Abductive argumentation is not then simply an altered form of deductive logic, though its justification is deductive.

In an avowedly incomplete illustration of the state of his materials dating from September 1867 (Peirce 1984b), we move toward not only the word 'abduction' itself but also toward what it will eventually mean for Peirce. In this lexicographical entry Peirce says that abduction is the English form of the word ἀπαγωγή (*Prior Analytics* 2.25), which has been translated *deductio* by Boethius and *reductio* or *inductio* by others. Peirce then limits himself to his own translation of the term in Aristotle ('abduction') and to a translation of the *Prior Analytics* 2.25.69a20-37:

> when it is evident that the first term [that which occurs in the syllogism only as a predicate. See *Analytica Posteriora*, lib. i, ch. 21, p. 82.b.2.—Peirce's note] is predicable of the middle, but that the middle is predicable of the last [that which is only subject—Peirce's note] is inevident, but is as credible or more so than the conclusion, further if the media of the last and middle are few; for it is being altogether nearer knowledge (Peirce 1984b: 108).

The letters are those used by Aristotle, as is the example that follows: A = 'what can be taught' = major of a syllogism of the first figure; B = 'science' = the middle of a syllogism of the first figure; Γ = 'justice' = the minor of a syllogism of the first figure, thus B is A, Γ is B, Γ is A. Following Aristotle, Peirce writes:

> Now, that science can be taught [B is A] is plain, but that virtue is science [Γ is B] is inevident. If then ΓB [virtue is science] is as credible or more so than ΓA [virtue can be taught], there is an abduction. For by assuming the science of ΓA [virtue can be taught], we, not having it before, are nearer to knowledge. [That is, we come nearer to knowing that justice can be taught, on account of the credibility of justice being a science—Peirce's note] Or again, if the middles of ΓB [virtue is science] are few; for thus one is nearer knowledge… But when ΓB [virtue is science] is neither more credible than ΓA [virtue can be taught] nor are the middles few, I do not call it abduction. Nor when ΓB [virtue is science] is immediate, for that is knowledge (Peirce 1984b: 108).

Now, the value of this relatively slavish following of Aristotle is that it does show both Aristotle's and Peirce's interest in those weaker arguments, in which the minor and particular premise is inevident. The major premise is not in doubt; it is either self-evident or logically evident. The minor and thus particular premise, however, is in doubt and cannot be self-evidently or immediately logically supported. Given the doubts about it, the only way that it can be used in a valid argument is if it is *as* credible (Peirce) or probable (Aristotle) or *more so* than the conclusion and if the terms that are intermediate between B and Γ are few. It also suggests the heuristic direction that Peirce's work on logic will eventually follow.

What is striking about this form of argumentation is not its logical rigor, but rather its imaginative capacities. Can we, however, determine any logic that might pass as 'abductive' in New Testament writings themselves? I think that rhetorical presentation of the several woes of Matthew 23 has an abductive element in the way Peirce first described abduction:

- Those who are hypocrites, blind guides, etc. are for instance those who lead astray, those who swear deceitfully, and those who do not do what they tell others to do, etc.
- The scribes and Pharisees are those who lead astray, those who swear deceitfully, etc.
- The scribes and Pharisees are very likely hypocrites, blind guides, etc.

There are likely other examples, but, as this example illustrates, the argumentation is close to induction. Where it is different from what Peirce calls 'induction' and thus may be distinguished from it is that it involves a series of characteristics rather than a collection from which instances have been taken at random (e.g. Paul, Akiba, and Johannan ben Zakkai are random examples of Scripture teachers in first-century Palestine; Paul and Akiba and Johannan ben Zakkai are Pharisees; any scripture teacher in first-century Palestine is more than likely a Pharisee).

2. *Abduction in Peirce's Later Writings.* Peirce appears to have focused much of his later logic around the hypothesis. By 1901, he is calling 'the step of adopting a hypothesis as being suggested by the facts', abduction, and claiming that it is the first stage of scientific inquiry (Fann 1970: 30). In his 1901 paper 'The Logic of Drawing History from Ancient Documents' (7.162-255), a document that is pertinent to our exploration not only for its complete presentation of abduction but also due to the relevance of the context to our subject matter of textures and history, Peirce argues that the hypothesis to be adopted would be likely and render the facts likely (7.202). It would be required in cases 'in which a phenomenon presents itself which, without some special explanation, there would be reason to expect would *not* present itself; and the logical demand for an explanation is the greater, the stronger the reason for expecting it not to occur was' (7.194). Thus, though it is the 'most ineffective' of arguments (7.218)—and can even be considered mere 'guessing' (7.219)—it is useful.

In his lecture on 'Pragmatism and Abduction' (1903)—a lecture in which it becomes clear that 'pragmatism' as Peirce understood it not only involves abduction but also in fact rests upon it!—Peirce provides the formula for abduction, which 'although it is very little hampered by logical rules, nevertheless is logical inference, asserting its conclusion only problematically or conjecturally' (5.188):

> The surprising fact, C, is observed;
> But if A were true, C would be a matter of course;
> Hence, there is reason to suspect that A is true (5.189).

If we were to give this formula some New Testament related elements, we might argue for example that in the first century: 'A surprising fact is observed, namely, that wherever Jesus went healings happened; but if Jesus were a healer, healings happening wherever Jesus went would be a matter of course; hence, there is reason to suspect that Jesus is in fact a healer.'

The hypothesis so generated 'is merely preparatory' (7.218) and needs to be tested. This happens through deduction (7.203), which, already by 1898, had come to be for Peirce 'clearly regarded as the process of tracing out the necessary and probable consequences of an hypothesis' (Fann 1970: 30). Deduction will produce 'predictions as to what the results of experiment will be' (7.206). What it does is to trace out 'the ideal consequences of the hypothesis' by showing that 'certain admitted facts could not exist, even in an ideal world constructed for the purpose, either without the existence of the very fact concluded, or without the occurrence of this fact in the long run in that proportion of cases of the fulfillment of certain objective conditions in which it is concluded that it will occur' (7.207).

The testing that follows will allow for experiment after experiment to confirm the predictions deductively arrived at from the hypothesis; this is what Peirce calls 'induction' (7.206). It 'is not justified by any relations between the facts stated in the premises and the fact stated in the con-clusion; and it does not infer that the latter fact is either necessary or objectively probable' (7.207). Thus, in the later Peirce, abduction alone becomes synthetic, for it alone is able to add to knowledge; induction, which had been considered synthetic, now is seen only to confirm (Fann 1970: 34-35). 'Abduction seeks a theory. Induction seeks for facts. In abduction the consideration of the facts suggests the hypothesis. In induc-tion the study of the hypothesis suggests the experiments which bring to light the very facts to which the hypothesis had pointed' (7.218).

Because abduction is not just an insight but also a means of logical inference, there are rules that accompany it. The main rule is that one is after the 'best' hypothesis possible, in other words, the one most likely of receiving deductive description and inductive confirmation. As soon as the abductive hypothesis is found to be inadequate, it is jettisoned in search of another, better one. Thus, it must be able to explain the facts before us, be capable of scientific, experimental confirmation (and not just logical confirmation), and be economical (i.e. must not involve infinite amounts of time or money in its confirmation such that confirmation becomes unrealistic) (7.220).

3. *Abductive Arguments in the New Testament: Three Examples and Galatians 3.* In order to determine whether a search for abductive arguments in New Testament rhetorical argumentation is helpful, we may wish to determine first of all whether it can be seen to be operative in the New Testament, and possibly in rhetorical argumentation. We will look at three possibilities. We will consider settings in which an audience is invited to speculate on a surprising fact, and to consider whether the process that Peirce sets forth is presented there, namely, whether a hypothesis regarding the event is suggested, whether the author follows the stages of the determination of the necessary and probable consequences of the hypothesis, and whether the deductive examination is followed by experiment after experiment to confirm it.

a. *John 5.* The one set of texts that comes closest to this appears to be Jesus' own defense of his healing activity in John's Gospel, which not surprisingly has been viewed as an extended trial. Without going into a detailed examination of, for example, John 5, it would be possible to suggest that Jesus' argumentation there follows the following form:

> Jesus notes that the crowds are surprised by the healings he has done and the things that he has said (C);
> But if he is who he says he is (A), C would be a matter of course;
> Hence, there is reason to suspect that Jesus is who he says he is (A).

Furthermore, there is some deductive examination of consequences in 5.31-47. There is no clear inductive confirmation, though we may presume that subsequent miracles with repeated argumentation by Jesus as above were intended by the author as a means of showing how in fact the hypothesis is being confirmed.

b. *1 Corinthians 15.1-15.* Another possible example concerns the resurrection of Jesus as the surprising fact to be observed. Abductive logic might have led some early Christians to the hypothesis that, given the resurrection of Jesus from the dead, then there is a resurrection of the dead:

> The surprising fact C (the resurrection of Jesus) is observed;
> But if A (the resurrection of the dead) were true, C would be a matter of course;
> Hence, there is reason to suspect that A is true.

The explanation or communication of this hypothesis does look similar to 1 Cor. 15.12, with the deductive consequences spelled out in 15.13-15. Nevertheless an extended look into the argument there does not start with the resurrection of Jesus, but with the acknowledged fact of the resurrection of the dead, as is clear from 15.16, which then makes 15.12-15, including the resurrection of Jesus, appear more like a deductive explanation than like abductive hypothesis creation. (1 Cor. 15.12 would not then be the start of an abductive argumentation but an argument from the contrary.) Furthermore, there is inductive confirmation for the 'surprising fact' (Jesus' resurrection, 1 Cor. 15.5-8) but not for that which is sought to be supported (namely, the resurrection of the dead as such).

c. *Mark 2.1-12.* Finally, Mk 2.1-12:

> The surprising fact C (the forgiveness of the paralytic's sins by Jesus) is observed;
> But if A (someone other than God can forgive sins) were true, C would be a matter of course;
> Hence, there is reason to suspect that A is true.

While this would be the form that abductive argumentation would take from the elements of the story, is Mk 2.1-12 really about hypothesizing that someone other than God can forgive sins? This does not seem to be the conclusion from the story, for the focus by the end is on Jesus' introduction of a completely new feature into the story, namely, the Son of Man. While it is possible that the point is to introduce an hypothesis that is faulty (someone other than God can heal sins) in order to overturn it with the correct understanding (only the Son of Man, other than God, can heal sins), there is no indication of the consequences (other than that healing accompanies forgiveness), nor is their immediate confirmation through experimentation.

d. *Summary Look at the Three Examples.* While it is possible to look at the above three examples abductively, I would suggest that each of the above three examples works not abductively but deductively in their context. In other words, the apparent purpose behind the first argument is not to hypothesize that Jesus is who he says he is, nor is that of the second to hypothesize that there is a resurrection of the dead, nor is that of the third to hypothesize that there is a reason to suspect that someone other than God can forgive sins. Each of the above rhetorical arguments, though they can be expressed abductively and *would be* abductive if that were their purpose, are deductive and can only be expressed abductively because the corresponding deduction is valid. On this point, the early Peirce and the later Peirce agree (see Fann 1970: 52). Thus:

> If Jesus were whom he says he is (A and A is true), the fact that the crowds are surprised by the healings he has done and the things that he has said (C) would be a matter of course;
> Jesus is who he says he is (A and A is true);
> Therefore, it is no wonder that the crowds are surprised by the healings he has done and the things that he has said (C is true).

Again:

> If the resurrection of the dead (A) were true, the surprising fact of the resurrection of Jesus (C) would be a matter of course;
> There is a resurrection of the dead (A and A is true);
> Therefore, that Jesus is raised from the dead is true (A).

And finally:

> If someone other than God can forgive sins (A) were true, the surprising fact that Jesus can forgive the paralytic's sins (C) would be a matter of course;
> Someone other than God can forgive sins (A and A is true);
> Therefore, Jesus can forgive the paralytic's sins (C).

Accordingly, abductive logic provides us with no assured scientific logic that ensures our exploration. In the above cases, one still needs to determine the rhetorical intent of the argument before assuming the kind of logical argumentation that will apply. Unless the focus is on estab- lishing the probability of the case, it is likely that an argument that has deductive force has a deductive purpose, that is, to establish a Result. In each of the above three examples, that appears to be just what is in mind.

e. *Galatians 3.* Is the same true when we turn to Galatians 3? Recently, Vernon Robbins (in discussion on RHETORIC-L) has argued eloquently and forcefully in favor of an abductive argument in Gal. 3.21.

First of all, however, it would appear to me to be necessary to note just how crucial are the stages of observation and the consideration of the rules of a variety of textures. In the discussion of Gal. 3.21, there appears to have been a too-ready jump to determine the argumentative logic of individual units (if they are units).

Second, it is interesting that when we do turn to the argumentation, we note that elucidation happens deductively throughout Galatians 3. The author's exposition to his hearers may assume that they have not reached the same conclusion as he has, but then deductive argumentation assumes the same thing, as do induction and abduction. So, it is inadequate to argue, as Peirce did, that only abduction leads to discovery; the discovery that abduction leads to is of particulars (Peirce's 'case') but both deduction and induction lead to discoveries of results (in the case of deduction) and of rules (in the case of induction).

Third, based on our earlier abductions concerning Galatians 3, a sustained inquiry into the logic of Galatians 3 suggests that the argumentation follows this form:

> All who receive the spirit are heirs through the ratification of the faithful fulfillment of the promise in Jesus;
> You have received the spirit;
> Therefore, you are heirs through the ratification of the faithful fulfillment of the promise in Jesus.

Again:

> No one receives the spirit and thus becomes an heir through following a rule of life;
> You have not thus received the spirit;
> Therefore, you are not heirs through following a rule of life.

So, what role does the rule of life ('law') play? Paul's point appears to be not that it has no role, only that its role is not relevant to the inheritance or ratification of God's promises. Paul's question in Gal. 3.21 thus concerns what possible value the law can have, given this situation in which the faithful fulfillment of the promise has led to the will being ratified in the hearing of those who, whether they followed the rule or not, are given the opportunity to accept the inheritance.

Paul argues that the rule, unlike the inheritance, is temporally limited, for it is only valid until the ratification of the faithful fulfillment, which Paul goes on to describe in Galatians 4 as a coming of age. Thus the inheritance hearing what would take place not only at the physical death of a parent but also at the social death of the parent (i.e. where the child is no longer a child and thus the parent is no longer a parent) would suggest the following argument in 3.21:

> All who follow the rule of life do so in this life with a view to living this life as children of a parent.
> You followed this rule of life in your life.
> Therefore, you followed this rule with a view to living this life as children of a parent.

But,

> All who have had the will ratified are no longer children and thus do not need the rule of life that you had as children.
> You have had the will ratified.
> Therefore, you are no longer children and thus do not need the rule of life that you had as children.

There is no need to appeal to any abductive argument in all of this. The deductive logic here presented does, however, demand that we explore more fully the practice of wills and their ratification, for example, in a sacred and cultural context, as well as the beliefs concerning wills and their power.

Where abductive logic may be apparent in this text is in the implicit investigation and questioning that may have led Paul to some of the elements in the argumentation. For example, it may be that a 'surprising fact' was the inclusion of the Gentiles. Accordingly, it may be that abductive logic was active in Paul's thinking along the following lines:

> The surprising fact that the Gentiles have been given the Spirit (C) is observed;
> But if anyone who hears the faithful fulfillment of the promise as in the case of a will thus becomes an heir and recipient of the good blessings of God, including the Spirit (A), C would be a matter of course;
> Hence, there is reason to suspect that A is true.

While the approach that Paul took to these matters remains necessarily speculative and thus only somewhat helpful in the discussion of his actual, rhetorical argumentation in Galatians, what we can agree on as a valuable contribution of Peirce's attempts at logical explanation to our investigation has to do with his statement: 'Do not block the way of inquiry' (1.135). By this phrase he appears to have meant that he considered abduction a way around those attempts to pronounce a fact inexplicable.

4. *Tentative Conclusions regarding the Use of Peirce's Logic for the Analysis of Rhetorical Argumentation.* So, is there value in pursuing Peirce's 'abductive logic' as a possible logic at work in the rhetorical argumentation of the New Testament? I believe that a tentative conclusion is a modified no.

I do not think that what Peirce calls abductive logic, either of the early kind or of the later, is very widespread in the New Testament. While there are glimpses here and there of both the early abductive logic of hypothesis through characteristics (as in Mt. 23) and of the later abductive logic of 'surprising facts' (possibly in John's Gospel), there is no sustained abductive logic. Fann's examples of abductive style reasoning as found in the Sherlock Holmes stories of Sir Arthur Conan Doyle—stories in which it is not the result that is the focus but how to argue back from the result to something unknown (Fann 1970: 57-58)—suggest the kind of literature in which we are most likely to find it; it is doubtful that New Testament literature should be used as a mystery story. The so-called abductive features supposed to be found in the New Testament may be explained otherwise, primarily by reducing any supposed abductive inference to a corresponding deduction, since 'to explain a fact is to show that it is a necessary or a probable result from another fact, known or supposed' (Fann 1970: 52).

What Peirce calls deduction, as the tracing out of necessary and probable consequences of certain original hypotheses that were held, seems widely present in the New Testament argumentation and, in fact, appears to be the primary argumentative form. If the enthymeme is the main rhetorical device in the New Testament, as it was for Aristotle and for much Hellenistic rhetorical overview, then we might continue to suggest that the enthymeme is primarily deductive in nature. This is not a new conclusion, but rather a confirmation of the long-held view of enthymematic argumentation as a kind of deductive argumentation. The difference between my position and that of those who would view the enthymeme simply as a 'failed' or 'imperfect' deductive syllogism would be that, as I have suggested elsewhere and has just been noted, not all enthymematic argumentation is deductive, nor is that which is deductive in style strictly deductive. The 'unsatisfactory' way in which abduction was shown by Peirce to be necessarily valid means not only that 'this failure to provide an independent justification for abduction remains a difficult problem for contemporary philosophers who maintain that there is a logic of discovery' (Fann 1970: 54) but also remains a significant mark against the likelihood that following abductive logic will assist us in our own task of New Testament interpretation.

Finally, I think that the origins of abductive logic as an attempt to ground a scientific logic makes both it and Peirce's inductive logic (which is to be used for scientific confirmation) inadequate for use in the analysis of rhetorical argumentation. One of the most serious problems in using Peirce's logical theory for an understanding of rhetorical argumentation is, I would think, that for Peirce his theories are not descriptive but prescriptive: 'logic is not the science of how we *do* think; but, how we *ought* to think; nor how we ought to think in conformity with usage, but how we ought to think in order to think what is true' (2.52; cf. 2.7). Peirce's attempts to bring scientific rigor to imperfect hypothesization should make us wary of applying it to common language. Peirce's logical arguments, be it abduction, or deduction or induction, are not ways in which people normally function; they are intended to be the prescriptive ways people should function logically. This seems radically at variance with the very notions that are fundamental to socio-rhetorical analysis in terms of observation and finding the rules of the game that are operative in even the most idiosyncratic approach to experience. According to Wittgenstein, even if one identifies something wrong 'regularly', 'it does not matter in the least. And that alone shews that the hypothesis that I make a mistake is mere show' (Wittgenstein 1958a: 95e [270]).

In the end, we may not agree that abduction allows us to advance in the study of rhetorical argumentation. It may even be that we shall have to conclude that Peirce's attempts to make abductive logic the 'master' of all logic and science would have led in Peirce's mind to a time when 'pragmatism' would have succeeded and when it would be useless to admit any further hypotheses as hypotheses by defining which hypotheses alone are admissible (5.196); as such, abductive logic could be seen as blocking the very way of inquiry through the very attempt *not* to. The pragmatism of Peirce, which requires that abduction 'give us an expeditious riddance of all ideas essentially unclear' (5.206), is here at radical variance with the pragmatic acceptance of the fuzziness of language in normal communication and even that in rhetorical argumentation (see above). In spite of these caveats, however, we can agree that Peirce's reflections allow us to reflect for ourselves on how rigid the rules we wish to discover and apply to the language of others ought to be.

d. *The Goal of Interpretation*
Interpretation does not happen as a process of logical deduction. Coming to understand 'is a self-correcting process of learning that spirals into the meaning of the whole by using each new part to fill out and qualify and correct the understanding reached in reading the earlier parts' (Lonergan 1973: 159). What lies at the base of human activity are the 'cognitive foundations of meaning construction' (Shore 1996: 321).

Words alone cannot get at this. In his *Zettel*, Wittgenstein noted: 'How words are understood is not told by words alone' (Wittgenstein 1970: 144). Meaning lies beyond words, beyond even the psychological. Simple samples—even fuzzy ones—drawn from life or from the imagination (Hallett 1977: 47) may lead us further than clear, consistent ideas, expressed with perfect logical lucidity.

As in the later Wittgenstein's analysis, Bernard Lonergan, especially in his work *Insight* (Lonergan 1978), saw that what was lacking in much historical and positivistic analysis is quite simply a fuller appreciation of meaning: 'in the measure that one explores human experience, human insights, human reflections, and human polymorphic consciousness, one becomes capable, when provided with the appropriate data, of approximating to the content and context of the meaning of any given expression' (Lonergan 1978: 567). Like Shore, Lonergan seeks to meet the demands of the problem of understanding through a reflective approach to the problem of meaning, not through an appeal to psychic unity or universal language (Lonergan 1978: 567) but nevertheless through some sort of correlation of the different realms of meaning. Lonergan calls this unity a 'universal viewpoint', by which he means not a universal or totalizing view but rather the 'various ranges of possible alternatives of interpretations' (Lonergan 1978: 564).

In socio-rhetorical analysis this might entail the setting forth of various models by which or into which someone speaking might be seen to entertain ways of dealing with the world, some of which happens through words, some of which doesn't. In this way alone would we take seriously the fact that all our language use is metaphorical and has meaning only in particular contexts or textures that can be shown as models. It would neither be to say that these models are the only ways of dealing with the world nor that they are historically the way the world was dealt with; only, that these are the options or models as they suggest themselves in light of reflection from the various angles or textures. Models would thus be possible and would need to be adjudicated as to likelihood on the basis of criteria similar to those provided by Wittgenstein, for example, 'elegance of fit'.

Lonergan's understanding of expression, like Wittgenstein's under-standing of language in general, is both rich and contains a significant—and in Lonergan, explicit—rhetorical element. According to Lonergan, even mundane and common functional expressions depend upon three things: (1) 'a principal insight (A) to be communicated', (2) 'a grasp (B) of the anticipated audience's habitual intellectual development (C)', and (3) 'a grasp (D) of the deficiencies in insight (E) that have to be overcome if the insight (A) is to be communicated'. Each condition has direct bearing on the question of the rhetorical *inventio* and enthymeme: what is to be communicated and how what is communicated can be effective.

When Lonergan turns to interpretation of an expression, however, we begin to see something that is missing in the reflections we have carried on to this point, for up to now we have looked at observation and language rules as if they were somehow 'out there', much as the historical approach to the New Testament has looked at the New Testament texts as 'out there' and thus separated them from the people who read the texts. Lonergan's approach to interpretation of expressions—be they common or monu-mentalized—leads us to see that knowing the audience in any expression involves not only the historical moment but also a self-reflective moment, that is, a moment of self-judgment contained within the rhetorical approach itself. It is here, I believe, that Lonergan is able to provide a significant step forward to SR by helping refine our understanding of ideological texture.

A first stage of self-reflection occurs in a 'first-level interpretation', which he calls 'simple interpretation'. Here the interpreter seeks to re-state the expression, the 'principal insight (A') to be communicated' and which 'purports to coincide with the principal insight (A) of the original expression'. The difficulty in doing so is due to differences between the reasons for the communication (i.e., 'the practical insights (F) and (F')'), differences that depend upon further differences 'between the habitual insights (B) and (B'), (D) and (D'), and remotely upon differences between the habitual developments (C) and (C'), and the deficiencies (E) and (E')' (Lonergan 1978: 562). In other words, the interpreter, seeking to re-communicate the original expression, is faced with differences not only in terms of why he wishes to communicate, but also differences between the two audiences that are recipients of the communications and between the way the rhetor/interpreter understands how communication with the audience is to be bridged. We have already noted these problems, though in different terms, when discussing the problem of 'private language'. What is new here is the introduction of the element of self-reflection.

This element becomes more prominent and more crucial in 'second-level interpretation' or 'reflective interpretation'. This 'reflective interpretation' 'is guided by a practical insight (F") that depends upon insights (A"), (B"), and (D")', though it is so in both a positive and negative way. On the one hand, it is positive since now the habitual insight (B") 'is a grasp of the audience's habitual grasp (C") of its own intellectual development (C') and of the difference between that development and the habitual accumulations of the insights (C) in the initial audience'. On the other hand, it is negative since 'the insight (D") is a grasp of the audience's deficiencies (E") in grasping the differences between the habitual developments (C') and (C) and so in understanding the differences between the deficiencies (E') and (E) and between the practical insight (F') and (F)'. What is finally communicated in this 'reflective interpretation' is neither the original insight expressed (A), nor the insight communicated via a simple interpretation in apparent full agreement with the simple expression (A') but rather a self-reflective grasp of the identity of the principal insight (A) and the purported agreement with the insight (A'), so (A") (Lonergan 1978: 563).

This reflection, Lonergan argues, seeks not to gloss over historical, social, or cultural differences, but to accept and build upon these differences and, in so doing, to clarify the interpretation by reflecting not simply on the original expression or text, but by reflecting on the difference between the original expression and subsequent interpretations because of differences in the respective audiences. Such an interpretation might be as 'distant' as the discussion by a contemporary commentator of the history of interpretation of a New Testament text or as 'close' as the discussion by a New Testament figure of the use to which a chreia could be put. In either case, what is finally communicated in this 'reflective interpretation' is neither the original insight of an expression or text, nor the insight communicated via a simple, almost mimetic interpretation that is in apparent full agreement with the simple expression, nor even a biased interpretation that seeks to correct the original insight in light of later insights; what is communicated, according to Lonergan, is rather a self-reflective grasp of the identity or difference between the two. In Robbins's terms, we might say it is the difference between the world created by the text and the world of the interpreter (Robbins 1996c: 40).

This extraordinarily brief and dense glimpse at Lonergan's rich appreciation of the interpretive task suggests, as he himself noted, that in interpreting the expressions of others it is not only 'quite another matter to set about the investigation of such obscure objects, to reach something better than a mere guess about them, and to find an appropriate and effective manner of communicating the fruits of one's inquiry', but also that 'audiences are an ever shifting manifold' and that it would thus be 'a matter of considerable difficulty to work out a reflective interpretation that satisfied a single audience; but there is an enormous range of other audiences that will remain to be satisfied; and the single audience one does satisfy will not live forever' (Lonergan 1978: 563).

What Lonergan here underscores is the crucial role to be played by what Robbins has to this point called ideological texture. In Lonergan, this texture is seen not, however, as just another stage of historical analysis, whereby, for example, previous power brokers have understood texts—though that may be an element of it—but more importantly as a necessarily self-reflective stage of the interpretation of language. What Lonergan seeks to arrive at is some means whereby interpreters do not merely seek to bridge the gap between an expression (e.g. a New Testament text or passage) and themselves but also a means whereby they can understand the differences that separate them from that text by focusing on the differences between the language of the expression and their own.

It is an approach that at significant points is fully consistent with the initial stages as noted above, though I believe that Lonergan—like Peirce—is wrong to think that this approach will entail the development of a 'scientific' form of interpretation that will conceive of and determine 'the habitual development of all audiences' through techniques 'by which its expression escapes relativity to particular and incidental audiences' (Lonergan 1978: 564). Rather, it is a coming to listen to the other (in some cases the person speaking face to face with me, in some cases the past, in some cases another culture or society) not simply with a view to mimicking the other through equivalent utterances by me but rather with a view to understanding one's self in the light of our very understanding and lack thereof of the other. In other words, I will look not only at isolated utterances, and not only at the way those utterances or expressions fit within and thus function within a particular language game, but also how different that whole is from other functionings.

This is difficult since 'philosophers [and I would say 'interpreters' of expressions in general] come to their tasks with a certain conception of how things must be. This picture lies in the background, unexamined, and dictates the questions asked and specifies the form the answer will take' (Fogelin 1987: 109). Accordingly, the stage of judgment will reveal both that this is the case, what some of the preconceptions are, and finally what difference it all makes. It will not, as might be suggested by the post-modern nature of some recent 'ideological' analyses, simply allow that 'anything goes' or enshrine particular biases.

The result will be, according to Lonergan, not a shrinking of the horizons of the expression or text to be known and thus a mastery of it—the very thing that Robbins criticizes in the primarily historical, New Testament scholarship he encountered—nor will it be a retreat from rational reflection to a political bias, but rather a broadening of our own horizons as 'one comes to set aside one's own initial interests and concerns, to share those of the author, to reconstruct the context of his thought and speech' (Lonergan 1973: 163). In this way, we will begin to understand not merely the proliferating voices—though we will understand them more fully—but more importantly the difference between the voices and ourselves. This reflection will reveal as much about the voices as about us.

An Example. It was first of all an awareness of how unfamiliar Galatians 3 really was to me as I read, observed, and gained insights into the chapter that both excited and suggested to me a need for interpretation. Were I not to have experienced this unfamiliarity (a difference between the known and the unknown), I would not have engaged in the task of interpretation with such delight or perhaps not at all.

Second, the task revealed to me the way in which doctrinal and ideological concerns have given a particular ideological touch to subsequent interpretations of the passage. At various points in the history of the interpretation of Galatians 3, judgments have been made concerning what Galatians 3 is really about. Most often, the passage is couched in the 'big picture' of subsequent church disputes over law and grace, justification by faith and by law. The simple use of the word *dikaiosunē* in Galatians 3 thus becomes a focus and causes hearers/readers to disregard the rest of the context.

My approach thus far, however, would suggest that our observation of usage demands further questioning, not along prescriptive but along descriptive lines of particular contexts, in which the conjunction of apparently insignificant words or words whose meaning appeared obvious to me becomes crucial. 'To get clear about philosophical problems, it is useful to become conscious of the apparently unimportant details of the particular situation in which we are inclined to make a certain meta-physical assertion' (Wittgenstein 1958b: 66).

Third, the interpretation of Galatians 3 need not lead me to a repetition of what happened or even how the text envisions what happened. There is historical interpretation that will be driven by the difference between our understanding of what happened and our lack of understanding, but this is only one form of interpretation. As described above, however, it is inad-equate on its own but can be fleshed out by a realization of how many other angles (textures) there are from which to view the text. That these angles themselves reveal other textures suggests that this stage of judgment is not only the goal but also a transitional stage to further explor-ations of other textures. This would eventually lead to a programmatic elaboration of subsequent textures, not as necessary but as possible. For example, the focus on the will-ratification of Galatians 3 might lead us to query the way in which a person who understood himself as an undeserv-ing heir might begin to see the world. Or it might lead me to see how in other cultures will-ratification plays a role in sacred rites (even as it apparently does in the final oratorical display in the movie *Amistad*, which, following as it does on a reflective appropriation of the biblical story by the imprisoned slaves, becomes here highly suggestive).

4. *Conclusions*

At the beginning of Section 3, I mentioned that there were several questions that remain to be answered in Robbins's work. These included whether Robbins's identification of five or six rhetorolects in earliest Christianity is still too tied to Mack's historical intuitions, or even whether Robbins's identification of rhetorolects is too heavily dependent on the historical identification of these particular rhetorolects. Another question concerned the starting point of exploration, discourse or text, which again raises the question of history, namely, whether we start with the way language works or only how it works when it becomes monumentalized and sacralized in texts and thus obscures the formative influence of discourse. Another question concerned the so-called 'private language' problem, which is especially crucial in dealing with history and thus the impossibility of asking someone to clarify their language.

As is clear, then, the potential problems in the discussion of the programmatic correlation of textures all concern history. Nevertheless, the problem that I have addressed has sought to circumvent these individual problems not in order ultimately to avoid them but in order to deal with a more fundamental problem first, namely, the problem of history in New Testament interpretation, which touches on the third promise of SR according to Robbins. I have done so since I believe that the strength of SR is precisely in its potential for leading us out of the modernist focus on history. I believe that it will do so, however, only when an adequate approach to correlation of textures can be given. Toward that end, I believe that the reflections of both Wittgenstein and of Lonergan will prove important foci of attention.

There is of course a flow through time of persons and events, with individuals and cultures influencing each other; however, it is 'meaning' that is a 'constitutive element in the conscious flow that is the normally controlling side of human action' (Lonergan 1973: 178) and it is meaning that is the object of our study, not the flow itself, which is both unattainable and thus literally insignificant. (The essential nature of Lonergan's thrust is correct and it is one that SR can helpfully pick up on; nevertheless, the ultimate value of Lonergan's contribution at this point will only be realized when it is shorn of the drive toward a 'proper' knowing of history [Lonergan 1973: 195], a drive that he shares not only with other moderns like Peirce but with some insufficiently radical tendencies of SR.)

I believe that the interpretation toward which all reading drives is implicit in some of what Robbins says about ideological texture, though at present ideological texture appears to be a kind of sub-section of social and cultural texture (Robbins 1996c: 36; Eagleton 1983: 15). It is in this context of interpretation that Lonergan speaks of 'dialectic' and 'horizons' and even 'conversion', since as we aim at one horizon it is only upon reaching it that we see another stretch before us (Lonergan 1973: 235-36). According to Lonergan:

> intellectual conversion is a radical clarification and, consequently, the elimination of an exceedingly stubborn and misleading myth concerning reality, objectivity, and human knowledge. The myth is that knowing is like looking, that objectivity is seeing what is there to be seen and not seeing what is not there, and that the real is what is out there now to be looked at... Only the critical realist can acknowledge the facts of human knowing and pronounce the world mediated by meaning to be the real world; and he can do so only inasmuch as he shows that the process of experiencing [our observation], understanding [our initial insights into rules], and judging

[our further inquiry into rules in their contexts] is a process of self-transcendence (Lonergan 1973: 238-39).

As I have proceeded through this discussion I have used Lonergan's fourfold structuring of the process of cognition to set forth the outlines of these reflections. This structure, which can be simplistically reduced to experience, insight, inquiry and judgment, mirrors our stages of observation, initial hypotheses of rules governing the way language works, inquiry into the rules, and finally self-reflective and self-transcendent judgment as interpretation. I believe that these stages, while not synonymous with the textures of socio-rhetorical analysis, are stages that are operative within socio-rhetorical analysis and that it is the 'textures' of SR that are the contexts or angles through and in which one observes rules at work.

My work has thus sought to confirm not only the essential Wittgenstein-ian elements of SR and to discover value in the Lonerganian progression in interpretation—though in good Lonerganian style, my reading of Lonergan in light of SR has led me to seek also for a Wittgensteinian refinement of Lonergan's own thought!—but also to see how SR can provide a fuller picture of what Wittgenstein and Lonergan intuited.

In the end, I think that the results of my observations suggest some preliminary, methodological work that needs to be done with a view to allowing for an interpretive 'flow' through SR before we leap into the textures and suggest their implications. This is not intended to 'put the brakes' on SR but rather only to cause us consistently to attend to the dynamics at work as we observe through and in several textures. Whether these textures are viewed in a particular order and relation seems now less significant to me, for the picture of correlation of textures that I am left with is less one of linear ascent through starting with one privileged texture and moving on to the next and more one of juggling, whereby the balls in the air, while clearly and carefully ordered, cannot be said to be in relation to one another in only one, linear fashion or only occupying one space at one time. If we could somehow conceive of a juggler expanding his juggling with spirals, ever larger and wider, we would have a perfect image.

Finally, while it might be possible to think that both Wittgenstein and Lonergan are echoed in SR because of Robbins's extensive reading—which includes his reading of both the later Wittgenstein and Lonergan—I believe that it is more likely that they are there because of the way all three—Wittgenstein, Lonergan, and Robbins—have probed real life and have contributed to giving us a picture of real life in the rhetorical presentation of the New Testament, as opposed to the flatlands and boring midlands of so much scholarship.

BIBLIOGRAPHY

Bowman, G.
  1997   'Identifying Versus Identifying with "The Other": Reflections on the Siting
             of the Subject in Anthropological Discourse', in A. James, J. Hockey, and
             A. Dawson (eds.), *After Writing Culture: Epistemology and Praxis in Con-*
             temporary Anthropology (ASA Monographs, 34; New York: Routledge):
             34-50.
Eagleton, T.
  1983   *Literary Theory: An Introduction* (Minneapolis: University of Minnesota
             Press).
Fann, K.T.
  1970   *Peirce's Theory of Abduction* (The Hague: Martinus Nijhoff).
Fogelin, R.J.
  1987   *Wittgenstein* (New York: Routledge, 2nd edn).
Geertz, C.
  1973   *The Interpretation of Cultures: Selected Essays* (New York: Basic Books).
Hallett, G.
  1977   *A Companion to Wittgenstein's 'Philosophical Investigations'* (Ithaca, NY:
             Cornell University Press).
Ivic, P.
  1992   'Language: Language Variants: Dialects', in *Encyclopedia Britannica*,
             Macropedia: XXII, 569-71.
James, A., J. Hockey, and A. Dawson
  1997   'Introduction: The Road from Santa Fe', in A. James, J. Hockey, and
             A. Dawson (eds.), *After Writing Culture: Epistemology and Praxis in Con-*
             temporary Anthropology (ASA Monographs, 34; New York: Routledge):
             1-15.
Lanigan, R.L.
  1996   'From Enthymeme to Abduction: The Classical Law of Logic and the
             Postmodern Rule of Rhetoric', in L. Langsdorf and A.R. Smith (eds.),
             Recovering Pragmatism's Voice: The Classical Tradition, Rorty, and the
             Philosophy of Communication (SUNY Series in the Philosophy of the Social
             Sciences; Albany: State University of New York Press): 49-70.
Lonergan, B.J.F.
  1973   *Method in Theology* (New York: Herder & Herder, 2nd edn).
  1978   *Insight: A Study of Human Understanding* (New York: Harper & Row).
Maurer, D.W.
  1992   'Language: Language Variants: Slang', in *Encyclopedia Britannica*, Macro-
             pedia: XXII, 572-73.

Minar, E.H.
    1990   *Philosophical Investigations Paragraphs 185-202: Wittgenstein's Treatment of Following a Rule* (Harvard Dissertations in Philosophy; New York: Garland).

Parret, H.
    1983   *Semiotics and Pragmatics: An Evaluative Comparison of Conceptual Frameworks* (Pragmatics and Beyond; Amsterdam: J. Benjamins).

Peirce, C.S.
    1960–66   *Collected Papers* (Cambridge, MA: Belknap Press).
    1984a   'On the Natural Classification of Arguments (P 31: Presented 9 April 1897)', in E.C. Moore *et al.* (eds.), *Writings of Charles S. Peirce: A Chronological Edition: 1867–1871* (4 vols.; Bloomington: Indiana University Press): II, 23-48.
    1984b   'Specimen of a Dictionary of the Terms of Logic and Allied Sciences: A to ABS (MS 145: November 1867)', in E.C. Moore *et al.* (eds.), *Writings of Charles S. Peirce: A Chronological Edition: 1867–1871* (4 vols.; Bloomington: Indiana University Press): II, 105-21.
    1986   *Writings of Charles S. Peirce: A Chronological Edition*. IV. *1879–1884* (ed. C.J.W. Kloesel *et al.*; 4 vols.; Bloomington: Indiana University Press).

Robbins, V.K.
    1989   *Patterns of Persuasion in the Gospels* (Foundations and Facets: Literary Facets; Sonoma: Polebridge Press).
    1996a   'The Dialectical Nature of Early Christian Discourse', *Scriptura* 59: 353-62.
    1996b   'Making Christian Culture in the Epistle of James', *Scriptura* 59: 341-51.
    1996c   *The Tapestry of Early Christian Discourse: Rhetoric, Society and Ideology* (London: Routledge).

Shore, B.
    1996   *Culture in Mind: Cognition, Culture, and the Problem of Meaning* (Oxford: Oxford University Press).

Thiselton, A.C.
    1980   *The Two Horizons: New Testament Hermeneutics and Philosophical Description with Special Reference to Heidegger, Bultmann, Gadamer, and Wittgenstein* (Grand Rapids: Eerdmans).

Wittgenstein, L.
    1958a   *Philosophical Investigations* (trans. G.E.M. Anscombe; New York: Macmillan).
    1958b   *Preliminary Studies for the 'Philosophical Investigations' Generally Known as the Blue and Brown Books* (Oxford: Oxford University Press).
    1965   *Generally Known as the Blue and Brown Books: Preliminary Studies for the 'Philosophical Investigations'* (Harper Torchbooks/Academy Library; New York: Harper & Row).
    1970   *Zettel* (trans. G.E.M. Anscombe; ed. G.E.M. Anscombe and G.H. von Wright; Berkeley: University of California Press).

Relations between Rhetoric and Philosophical Logic

Arthur Gibson

1. *Introduction*

This study is concerned with relations between our contemporary research in philosophy of logic, the topic of original creativity in literary linguistics, how they impinge on Aristotle's connecting rhetoric with logic, and further work on attempted retrieval of his treatment of these matters. Such research strikes a contrast with some work on some recent trends in New Testament scholarship; the last part of the chapter will attend to the relation of the foregoing to this sphere of study.

History of rhetoric subsequent to Aristotle tends to be downloaded into discussion about his rhetoric as though such history is Aristotle's. No doubt we all struggle under imperfect presuppositions of influence; yet this state of affairs is not quite the same division of labour as assuming that the history of rhetoric subsequent to 322 BCE furnishes us with the access conditions to Aristotle's rhetoric.

This state of affairs indirectly pertains to the possibility of accurate criteria which are asymmetric concerning the relations of original creative language to its critical assessment. Such an issue itself has a magnetic family resemblance to another class of problems. This is that of an investigation into whether or not meta-language and object-language universes can be connected, together with the hope that the identity of their mapping relations is internal to this assessment; such a project is only in its earlier stages. These are almost untouched, unanswered, relevant, yet seemingly remote, recondite questions. Here are three examples, indirectly related to the present study. Is there a logical rhetoric of music, according to which semantics is enthymemic? What are the relations between precision in great original music composition (supposing in some suitable sense that music has a linguistic syntax and semiotic system for emotions and aesthetics) and precision in logical form? Could we one day infer that Mozart's *Figaro* is at least as precise as Russell's Paradox, and comparable? We are some distance from tackling these questions; rather, a modest one will engage us here with an eye to planning for a future route.

This study is a strand of a more widespread attempt to develop a new philosophy, which includes consideration of the above questions.[1] So it is expedient to indicate, albeit briefly, relevant general presuppositions and orientation. Although I am not a Wittgensteinian[2] (and apropos the second paragraph of this chapter reapplied to him, neither was Wittgenstein), it is apt to select a perspective struck by two of Wittgenstein's perspectives which are historical dipoles: philosophy as logic, and philosophy as grammar, though he himself, unlike some of his followers, never seemed entirely to have polarized this relation.

He used the notion of the bipolarity of a proposition.[3] I argue that grammar and logic can engage what could suitably be itemized as a conceptual monopole.[4] Within this focus, suitably extended, logic entails grammar, and this implication, suitably routed, entails a generalizable philosophy. The relations of logic to literary creativity are largely unmapped. One of its domains comprises the relations between 'following rules' with 'counter-intuitive originality'. Such a conjunction places deep questions against our grasp of what it is to be a rule, to the degree that we may not have a grasp of what it is to be the criterion for this notion of 'rule'.

The contention presupposed here is that great creative literature is in some perplexing senses logical; and that, recognition of this state of affairs is achievable by structuring the ways in which rhetoric in prose, prose-poetry, and poetry manifest and are dependent upon logic for some of their

---

1.   See A. Gibson 1987, 1997b, 2000a, 2000b.

2.   In view of the millions of words in the various manuscripts by Wittgenstein, which appear in the University of Bergen edited CD ROM edition (Oxford University Press, 1999), we need to reassess the view that there are only two Wittgenstein philosophies; perhaps 'continuum of philosophies' is nearer to the mark.

3.   Wittgenstein 1996: 8.

4.   I have lifted the term 'monopole' from physics to extend the notion of polarity, and construct it as a live metaphor: a counter-intuitive monopole. In astro-physics a *monopole*, predicted by Dirac (cf. Rees 1997: 194-98), is a unification and deconstruction of the dipole into a single identity, which is assumed to occur in cosmological situations. Thus some *terrestrial* physical states are accurately represented as propositions which are contraries, and under suitably exotic generalized states of affairs can be transformed into a singularity, a monopole. This characterization is pertinent as a metaphor for unifying certain disparate philosophical policies, assessed by logic (A. Gibson 2000a: Chapters 2–6).

persuasive power. This associates the concept of logic with what it is to be possibility.

Before proceeding to issues of rhetoric, let us reflect on elements for a logical foundation by which to develop a boundary (but not an electrified perimeter fence) between logic and rhetoric. If such relations hold true, the principle of bivalence applies. Consequently such a philosophy as canvassed above would be true or false. It would be an advantage to know the further criteria according to which a philosophy is true. The disputed question of whether or not philosophy should offer solutions, outside of its own technical realm, obtrudes here. I wish to develop an affirmative answer to this issue. Rhetoric is one bridge to facilitate that answer.

In Aristotle we have the founder of the sort of rhetorical theory from which, in varying ways and sometimes contrary, later rhetorical concepts derive. Many subsequent rhetoricians were either indebted to him or inferior in their insights; or dependent on the probity of his conceptions, even allowing for the obscurity, incompleteness or density of some of Aristotle's comments. Later accretions of rhetorical dogma, and competing views, have their places. Yet there is a need for some rhetoricians to be informed more than they sometimes are about current research in Aristotle's logical theory. The priority of the current analysis is not the important subject of historical development, however; it is that of a philosophical logician more interested in current research concerning what it is to be rhetoric and its relations to logic.

Aristotle not only adds a logical component to the rhetorical skill of persuasion; and we may note in passing that, for example, 'I fear you' is a logical proposition. As Schutrumpf[5] explains, Aristotle is also critical of writers who privilege the skill which plays on the emotions as if the latter were exclusive of logic. Aristotle maintains[6] that, in the relevant sense, such use of the skill is unrelated to the truth of the subject; Plato makes the same criticism in the *Phaedrus* (267c7). Schutrumpf's view is that Aristotle's position on the emotions in rhetoric is continuous with Plato's. Aristotle is concerned with both the logical basis of rhetoric and its contextualized natural history. Respecting the latter, the psychological character of decision-making in the light of the relativity of circumstance should be included and measured by logic in rhetoric.

5.   Schutrumpf 1994: 101-102.
6.   Aristotle, *Rhet.* 1.1.1354a.1-8.

2. *Argumentum ad hominem*

A response—i.e. a misunderstanding—of the foregoing might be, incorrectly, to argue the following: (α) Aristotle's *Rhetoric* using *argumentum ad hominem* gathers together the commonly held points of agreement evident upon reflection to rational animals; therefore, (β) Aristotle is not developing a deductive argument basis for rhetoric but proposing stylistics for assessing the presentation of (α). It should be obvious that (α) does not imply (β); nor has (β) internal properties of (α) that could imply (β). The present study will argue that (β) is false, though I presuppose that in some other sense Aristotle is concerned with style. One can simply remove or dissolve the problem composed in '(α) therefore (β)' by observing that Aristotle's use of evident truths common to rational people is a state of affairs to which he applies deduction of various types (not a metaphoric type of deduction). His relaxed use of deduction is still deduction, and not a strategy to acquiesce in what by agreement passes for reasoning at the hands of those who share such evident truths. Aristotle's employment of signs does not sacrifice objective logical standards in the interests of achieving whimsical persuasion relative only to a recipient's subjective values. Rather, a major part of his contribution is to challenge just that conflation of the evident with *ad hominem* patterns of audience expectation. Clearly there is a central place in the study of Aristotle's *Rhetoric* for Locke's[7] view of *argumentum ad hominem* according to which a person or people are faced with the consequences drawn from their own principles or concessions; this position does not require that 'consequences' have not to be consequences, however.

If one excludes or ignores the role of deductive logic within Aristotle's *Rhetoric*,[8] it is not possible to explain his early claim in the *Rhetoric* that 'enthymemes are the body of proof'. This quoted expression, puzzling though it can be, especially for those to whom rhetoric is 'persuasion', identifies 'proof' as a criterion of enthymemes. It hardly seems credible to reduce this to a subjective sense of persuasion.

One way which fails to recognize this state of affairs is where some studies of rhetoric, it seems unwittingly, employ metaphorical uses of terms such as 'syllogism', 'implication' (and its tautologies), 'necessity', 'entailment' and 'enthymeme', 'rule', 'law'. I argue that, even allowing

7.   Locke 1890 [1997].
8.   Aristotle, *Rhet.* 1.3.1354a.15-16.

for our own distance from Aristotle and the indeterminacy to which we are thus subject, we can recognize among some rhetoric researches that there are distinctions and views measurably quite alien to Aristotle's own theory and practice, and inconsistent with his logic. There is a situation in which a scholar selects a piece of narrative and incorrectly re-arranges it so that an enthymeme analysis is applicable to it. It is recast into something reminiscent of syllogism, and this sort of treatment is then ascribed to the narrative as though it were its internal character. The Appendix below presents a review of types of such activities and an outline theory of metaphor to characterize it.

3. *Aristotle's Dialectic, Syllogistic and Rhetoric*

Since the foregoing introduces the idea of metaphoric shift, it may be thought that, as with modern scholars, Aristotle treats rhetoric and logic relations in an evolutionary autobiographical way. He certainly should be interpreted as the developing philosopher he was, whose aim was to discover a universal framework for reason and knowledge, while he also attempted to represent and integrate their differences. This presupposition should underpin attempts to focus him, while regulating it with our knowledge and conceding our ignorance of influences on Aristotle. But this is very different from the sort of movement, often only implicit to the users, which is explicitly sketched in the Appendix. In some modern rhetoric studies, the emergence of imagination, and the implicit extension of terminological metaphor in dialectical interaction is a self-authent-icating process, whereas for Aristotle, in the relevant domains, it was assessed by deduction.

Aristotle probably had a qualified opposing reaction to the dominant function of Socratic dialogue, wary as he was of its potential, especially in the hands of philosophers less than Plato, to attract ponderous and incon-clusive examination of issues. Hintikka's[9] perspective on this sort of view, of the problem-solving character of Aristotle's thought, is certainly impor-tant: he presents Aristotle's syllogistic, in part, as a product of his struggle with dialectic, in which there is some overlap in the problem-solving roles between the two.

Aristotle was sharply aware of some distinctions between validity in a syllogism and argumentative strength in dialectic; he allowed controlled

9.   Hintikka 1996: 90-96.

interaction between the two domains without always perfectly conceiving this relation. But he was evidently aware of many differences, such as the importance of context and smaller number of premises in rhetoric. Hintikka's view is that Aristotle took it that, 'Logical inferences will then be those answers that are necessary *ad argumentum*',[10] and so including detection of fallacies. In this respect there can be a specific paraphrasing overlap between dialectic and deductive inference, distinct to inductive confirmation[11] since it is non-monotonic. One of the well-known gaps between Aristotle's dialectic and rhetoric is that the latter has an audience whilst the former has a responding participant. Aristotle is of course attentive to the conditions that act as bridges between logical inference and rhetoric. With the latter as well as the former assumptions and premises should be selected which are shared by either all of the audience or some of them.

If we are to focus on this bridge and its refinement or reconstruction, we should ask: what are the relations between rhetoric, logic and uses in an ancient Greek natural-language narrative? This multifarious question presupposes generalization which goes beyond our knowledge of its components; but it is possible to isolate some internal properties of its identities. These include elements of inference, form, necessity, relevance, content, and originality.

4. *Proof in Logic for Rhetoric*

Notoriously, the relations of form to content, which returns us to the Wittgenstein polarity, its relations to metaphysics and what he termed 'natural history',[12] together with the role of the relevance of content to implication[13] are among the concerns of this section.

As Smiley[14] judges the matter from the few extant traces of Chrysippus, we know that he deemed consequence necessary, but not formal; for Philo of Megara it was neither necessary nor formal. Aristotle avoided defining implication, and concentrated on necessity with topic-neutral expressions

10. Hintikka 1996: 89.

11. I have avoided terming this 'inductive inference', in conformity with, e.g., Sainsbury 1991: 9-11.

12. Cf. Garver 1996.

13. This topic can be more explicitly formulated by relatedness logic: cf. Epstein 1995: 92.

14. See Smiley 1998.

so as to generalize over more subjects than he could have, were he to have attended to the content of subjects. He conceived of formality by construction of what he presupposed are topic-neutral inference patterns, and invented the notion of validity along these lines. This state of affairs demarcated content from logical form. The general result was a competition whose game-rules were roughly that, if one selects form, then content is irrelevant and/or excluded and vice versa.

So what do we do? I argue[15] that deeply set in or under the foundations of what it is to be true communication is a complementary state of affairs: a functional fusion between content and logic. Formulation of such a conjunction should be stipulated by criteria of relevance. This notion of 'fusion' will have to be counter-intuitive just as, for example, the Newtonian and relativistic laws of physics collapse within the earliest phase of the universe.[16] In this scenario the criteria of recognition for identifying deviation are unknown. Surely, there is an inferential series between such superphysics and the normative physical universe resulting from it, however unclear their identity is to us. We can compare this connection with intertextual relations between apparently unconnected types.[17] Such an approach would have to incorporate the phenomenon of counter-intuition to isolate the unexpected from the incorrect. Godel's theorem is an instance of counter-intuition, namely where the negation or contrary of an expected inference is proved to the true. There are various classes of counter-intuition. In my view these logical results 'leak' facets of the deeper, still unexplored foundations of logic, three of whose empirical mirrors are astrophysical cosmology of the earliest universe, music and art. In this perspective, therefore, we are at an early stage of theory-construction in which the mysteries of knowledge yet future to us have been partially explored, and its subtlety obscured, by our partial ignorance in histories of logic and rhetoric. In scenarios and research projects like these it is confusing to allow pseudo-technical terms to go proxy for standard concepts of measurement. This is where, for example, rhetoric and logic come to be of special value. To be sure, there will be

---

15. See A. Gibson 1997b and 2000a: ch. 1.

16. Cf. A. Gibson 1987 and 1981/2001.

17. For example, comparing Beckett's *Waiting for Godot* and *Endgame* with Shakespeare's *Lear*. Consider the unexpected diachronically widely separated demon motif 'Huwawa' as a familiar spirit, plus the forest archetypes and adjacent figures in the earliest Sumerian versions of *Gilgamesh* which parallel elements in Baudelaire's poems 'Correspondence' and 'Obsession'.

dispute and counter-intuitive instability in interpretative disputes; yet these should be distinct to speculation which runs like a possessed metaphor out of control.

So, while there are problems in logic research, and it needs moral counseling with creativity, this state of affairs is fundamentally different from the production of arbitrary models.

5. *Counter-intuitive Solutions to Paradox*

At the side of this, a logician nevertheless should be embarrassed by failure to make more philosophically of what are usually taken to be established logical foundations. Should philosophers be creatively bolder than we tend to be, for example in application to issues outside of philosophy? Are we too easily imprisoned in the spirit of the age? Could we not recognize the possibility that Russell's Paradox[18] arose because of creative blindness in Russell, as with Frege? Was this partly due to typical analytical philosophy's attenuated and over narrow concepts of what it is to be a language, which artificially imposes a discontinuity between formal and creative (natural language) uses, correct though it is to contrast the two domains in various ways? If so, this would be a substantive case of having a concept not being necessarily a recognitional capacity. That is to say, such generalized truth is counter-intuitive. An odd background feature of this logicist historical situation is that Whitehead and Russell's *Principia Mathematica* explains almost all of its mathematics via 'natural English language', thus demonstrating the falsity of Russell's prejudice against recognizing some of the logical resources of natural language. So we have problems, yet here also a hint for a way forward: to conjoin logic with creative language.

The paradoxes of implication, which utilize formal validity and entail logical impossibility, are not a concept of implication based on content or relevance, since they require an impossible antecedent (or a true antecedent whose content is irrelevant to the entailed proposition) to imply a necessary consequence. It should be argued from this that (1) the paradoxes of implication are entailed by prior departure from logic itself; note that an ideal exposure of logic would contain paradoxes. If this point is not maintained, as it is not in some philosophy of logic, then some alternatives

---

18. Perhaps the basis for a solution is ontology: an ontology which converges into one universal set at the Universe's time t_0, and counter-intuitively reserves an infinite well-ordered domain outside of this closure.

are: (2) a schizoid relation between form and content in which content is irrelevant, or (3) an emphasis on relevance as the criterion of consequence, which excludes truth as a criterion of relevance and consequence. I argue that (1) to (3) have to be deployed to imply. (4) In principle a logic is to be had which matches validity to relevant content. The history of logic furnishes us with many hitherto unintegrated (and perhaps previously unsuitably formulated) steps toward (4), though some current interests can distract one from finding the route to later stages in the journey taken seriously by Aristotle.

A major programme of research for Aristotle's *Poetics* awaits the next stage subsequent to the previous paragraph's implementation, by which to facilitate the construction of a connection between logic and rhetoric. It is the investigation of what we can designate as the quite unexplored philosophical logic of creative language perhaps presupposed by, or partially submerged in, the *Poetics*. Most of the logic terminology in Aristotle's *Prior Analytics* and the *Rhetoric* recurs in the *Poetics*. These relations have not been subjected to extensive enquiry. Studies on the philosophy of emotion linking the *Poetics* and *Rhetoric* are important; yet there needs to be a new subject for research: the logic of the *Poetics*. Clearly historical analysis has its part to play, and involves urgent tasks within our cultural ethos. Internal to such research is the proposal that original creative literature, which may not comply with some formal canon of rhetoric, can be logical in ways that relate to counter-intuitive concepts of consequence, relevance, content and their relations to the enthymeme. Some medieval and modern attention to formal validity deems that a contradiction entails any proposition. This has discredited mere form as a criterion of any significant explanatory power for logic.

Contrariwise, it is now open to assess how a live metaphor of logical form should incorporate creative use of language as a candidate for logic. This unexpectedly reverses up to, but not over, the later Wittgenstein, though with a thesis distinct, though complementary, to his. We should not underestimate the concurrence of this approach with the early Wittgenstein's logic: in one of his notes he stated, 'The epistemological questions concerning the nature of judgment and belief cannot be solved without a correct apprehension of the form of the proposition'.[19] Since we do not have a perfect grasp of what it is to be a logical generalization, we do not know, in the relevant sense, what it is to be the sense of 'proposition' as a

19. Wittgenstein 1996: II, 67.

generalized property. I believe that 'proposition' here can be proved to stand for any communicative expression conveying a thought.

6. *The Relevance of Logical Propositions*

Part of the solution to this collection of problems rests on the significance of maintaining that content is irrelevant if and only if it does not belong to any concise subproof of such content. This concept of a subproof preserves[20] the features of proof for finite sequences in which abstract irrelevance and redundancy are distinct. Anderson and Belnap's[21] relevance logic is not right since it presupposes that only if a propositional variable is shared by 'A' and 'B' is 'A → B' valid, especially in view of the incompleteness of relevance proof and semantics for first order logic. Lewy[22] argued that there is a fundamental drawback to their work: their relation of logical implication forbids suppression of premises and principles. There is no true entailment respecting the law of the disjunctive syllogism. If this is applied to the metalanguage relations of logic to enthymemes, it blocks enthymeme omissions.

In this sense a concern with relevance does not necessarily have truth as an internal property, since (in the Anderson and Belnap thesis) a prior criterion does not permit enthymemes. So, if one slackens logic for relevance in the Anderson and Belnap mould, it backfires. Their approach prevents one from applying logical truth to a large class of discourse outside of the propositional calculus. The negation of their view therefore enables one to insist on truth as a precondition for developing a concept of consequence which treats necessity, formality and relevance. Consequently, a concern with truth is not a doctrinal requirement, but an internal property and precondition of a universalized explanation of inference in language. If the identity and role of such inference are clarified, then we will already have satisfied criteria for being a true concept of relevance conditions. Thus to isolate relevance as a competitor to Aristotle's own approach to inference splits what is properly fused together or associated in his concepts.

Outside of the (no doubt proper) pluralist ecumenical perspective assessing competing logics, history of logic has confidently furnished us with mangled accounts of some aspects of implication in ancient Greek

---

20. See Shoesmith and Smiley 1978: 181-86, 214.
21. Anderson and Belnap 1975, 1992.
22. Lewy 1976: 15-51.

logic, which we should demarcate from the more reliable history by the Kneales.[23] The pioneering researches by Lear,[24] Burnyeat,[25] Martin,[26] and Smiley[27] have provided new insights. Geach[28] showed in what way some untenable pseudo-Aristotelian doctrine is still conflated with Aristotle's own concepts. We should allow for the vast logic developments which are beyond the capacity of syllogism, and that to some degree Aristotle was aware of this gap. The Greek συλλογισμός is not of course always identical in sense or scope to the later Classical and subsequent use of the term 'syllogism'. Aristotle employed the term for other non-syllogistic deductions. These are sometimes ones which are too complex and/or cannot be represented by the syllogism. His attention to deductive inference—as a presupposition of some rhetorical properties—is at the heart of his and our concern to expose what it is to be the identity of logic. On the one hand, we should be concerned with historical accuracy, in which we attempt to retrieve the most accurate interpretation of what Aristotle wrote. On the other hand, a philosopher living now who wishes to understand what Aristotle wrote, partial though its survival is, will also wish to explore the logical scope of Aristotle's own desire to render explicit what it is to be logic, given that he in one lifetime could not possibly have completed what he initiated. A necessary internal property of this project is what it is to be possibility and its relation to logic. An historicist emphasis which neglects Aristotle as a working philosophical logician, and one which does not address and expand the abstract universe formulated by Aristotle's uncompleted research programme, will distort Aristotle's psychological autobiography and accordingly his creativity. Aristotle's conception of implication is self-evidently not explained solely in terms of his formal syllogistic theory. So, whatever scope one might deem syllogism to have, this scope is not itself the limit of Aristotle's view of logical inference, quite apart from his approach to dialectic. One does not have to be an enthusiast of Aristotle's conception of logical theory to agree that its deep range, implicit potential, and instinct are extraordinary. For example,

23. Kneale and Kneale 1984.
24. Lear 1980.
25. Burnyeat 1994.
26. 'William's Engine' was already attending to meta-language interests in entailment, necessity and relevance logic.
27. Smiley 1995.
28. Geach 1972.

Geach[29] has proved the truth of Aristotle's hunch, which he could not prove to be formally true, that no modalization of an invalid plain categorical syllogism is valid. Such syllogism is to be understood as existentially true (or false) of the universe of discourse. Insofar as this pertains to the present study, we should note, then, that the modal operator 'necessary' obtains for *de dicto* modal syllogisms.

Conversely, Geach[30] maintains that Aristotle's doctrine of the asymmetry of the subject (ὄνομα) and predicate (ῥῆμα) announced in Aristotle's *On Interpretation* was obscured by his later theory of terms (ὅροι) which his theory of syllogism implemented. Geach calls this theory of terms 'bogus' since it blurs fundamental elements in thought and its expression, which involve and change the truth-conditions of expressions. This concept of terms imposed a notion of symmetry over the proposition which discarded its internal functional structure; and of course this misleading doctrine of symmetry within the proposition's components was influential in the medieval world. Since the internal asymmetry of the proposition is indisputable,[31] though there are competing theses about its significance, Aristotle's choice, to formalize a theory of deduction in the syllogism using the theory of terms rather than the insights he uses outside of syllogism yet still in his deductive theory, should be kept in mind when noticing that he sometimes implements the asymmetry of propositional contents thesis in his *Rhetoric*. In other words, on occasions he utilizes a logic more complex and subtle than his syllogistic theory can absorb or formalize in the *Rhetoric*.

For those who puzzle as to why Aristotle should have proceeded to blur and discard his initial asymmetry of proposition thesis when engaging with the syllogism, there could be at least two, not necessarily exclusive, answers. First, if we follow Lear,[32] Aristotle's grasp of the underlying theory of the syllogism is analogous with our modernist logic's conceptions of a computable function and proof-theoretic techniques. In other

29. Geach 1989: 580.
30. Geach 1981, 1972; Geach (1991) argues that a similar confusion attended the development of Deontic logic, in which Von Wright's original conception in 'Deontic logic' did not have its natural development which would preserve the priority and difference of the subject, while binding the predicative elements and the deontic operator; later work in deontic logic took the role of obligation as a function over whole propositions.
31. Frege 1977.
32. Lear 1980: 11-33.

words, Aristotle was concerned with the valid conditions for a meta-theory of consequence, rather than a programme enabling one to formalize all statements which occur in natural languages. Second, having discovered many of the necessary conditions for what it is to be logic, perhaps it is too much to expect that, even Aristotle's, resourceful originality would have proceeded to invent the requisite predicate logic from which to derive quantification and its modal calculuses.

What stands theoretically and functionally between the theory of logical identity and rhetoric is the reasoning presupposed in rhetoricians' discussion of rhetoric. If this domain of discourse is not transparent, it will equivocate over the target subject. Such equivocation persists. Certainly, there are disagreements about the identity of rhetoric and questions within logic interpretation which may impact on rhetoric with uncertain significance, so as properly to attract dissenting opinion.

Yet there are neglected issues concerning potential ambiguity in syllogistic interpretation which, given suitable attention, can expose semantic indeterminacies in the syllogism that have family resemblances to equivocation in rhetoric. In certain respects this is a neglected area of research, which could reduce some actual and purported 'gaps' between the formal language of syllogism and use of natural languages in rhetoric. That is to say, the differences between syllogism and the use of deduction can be one of degree and not type. For example, Sorenson[33] argues that the Barbara syllogism 'All men are mortal; Socrates is a man; therefore Socrates is mortal' presents problems if we insist that, on all possible accurate representations of this syllogism, it has to be interpreted as valid: do we not overlook the 'innocent' equivocation between the major premise's use of 'man' as an unmarked generic property and the minor premise's shifted marked specific use of 'man'? If we were to switch these two uses around, as theoretically can be forced on us because the rules of validity do not mark the shift, then the syllogism would be invalid.[34] Sure, our intuitions about logical validity lead us to align the 'correct' interpretation with the valid use of the terms. The problematic point is, however, that if we are honest to the arbitrary 'fixing of the rules', we have here—internal to syllogistic theory—a semantic indeterminacy which preserves equivocation to ensure the intended inference, precisely where it is assumed to be excluded. So we need a logic of indeterminacy and vague predicates by which we identify these properties and how they pertain to determinate

33. Sorensen 1998: 322.
34. Boethius (1998: 43-45) seems to have been sensitive to similar problems.

rule uses and their scope; Haack[35] has already produced the basis for such an analysis, which could be deployed to such tasks.

This sort of problem is parallel with the informal mixture usually associated with some creative areas of rhetoric. Although the foregoing treats the issues as ones of equivocation, we could equally form a theory which would make explicit such phenomena and transcribe them as multiple levels of functions, more complex than Aristotle or many modern logicians allow.[36] Accordingly, we should regard with suspicion claims about semantic transparency and the absence of equivocation in syllogistic, or other, deduction. Consequently, Aristotle's own recognition, that logic lies at the heart of rhetoric, has an unexpected corollary: standard interpretation of the valid rules of syllogistic are actually incomplete and allow or require some manipulation in some semantics of equivocation to preserve or interpret for validity. So the link between rhetoric and syllogistic is two edged. This is not to be committed to the false consequence that unwitting intrinsically invalid equivocation, characterizable by fallacy, is coextensive with the above situation. Rather, the situation commits one to having to accept that there is correct inference, but we should articulate this comprehension in conjunction with the substantive proviso that even contingent implications and their semantics are more counter-intuitive and complex than many assume.

As mentioned above, Lear's[37] view is that Aristotle's motive in developing syllogistic theory was metalogical: Aristotle was not claiming that all logical consequences can be formalized as a proof in syllogism. He supposed that a direct deductive argument (for example, a triangle has interior angles equal to two right angles) can be recast as a series of syllogistic inferences; hypothetical syllogisms can be formalizable in syllogistic only if they properly contain a direct syllogism.

Once we have retrieved or constructed an explanation of the deductive status of the enthymeme, we can relate this to our modern formal logic. Epstein[38] argues that within the perspective of a formalized concept of relevance many classically valid arguments are enthymematic, that is, suppressed implicit premises exist. For example when material implication

---

35. Haack 1971.
36. For example, one could criticize Frege for his denouncing 'tone' as non-truth functional, and, for example, develop a natural logic along the lines of a tree structure to introduce tones as functions; see A. Gibson 1987: 11-14; 1981: 48, 157-64.
37. Lear 1980: 11.
38. Epstein 1995: 384-88.

produces consequences that act under a covering law for propositional contents with different and unrelated subject matter, there is a suppressed premise to do with a common function and presupposition of generalization over consequence relations. In Smiley's[39] sense, this is a theory of consequence relative to a basis of content and its internal properties, which follows the sort of view Bolzano[40] proposed.

7. *Enthymeme*

Burnyeat[41] appears to have proved that the origin of the idea of the enthymeme being an incomplete syllogism comes, not from Aristotle but from Cicero and his use of the third Stoic indemonstrable.[42] In *Prior Analytics* (2.27) the argument is that even if an enthymeme is completely furnished with what is absent, it still may be formally invalid. This contradicts the idea that an enthymeme is an incomplete syllogism whose validity is produced by adding missing premises. *Prior Analytics*[43] does indeed state that: 'a συλλογισμός is ἀτελής [incomplete] if it needs either one or more premises, which are indeed the necessary consequences of the terms set down, but have not been assumed in the propositions'. But it does not state, nor assume, and neither explain that this is an enthymeme.

Let us leave aside so-called (quasi) 'Aristotelian' logic, so as to ask: is the enthymeme in Aristotle an abbreviated syllogism? Burnyeat[44] argues that it is not. Ross asserted that the point Aristotle mentions—the omission of a premise in speech—'forms no part of his definition of the enthymeme'.[45] Typically, if the enthymeme is applied to such a syllogism, it has to be the case that the omitted premise—one of two orders[46]—is presupposed by the user in the mind (ἐν θυμῷ). Given that the application is

39. Smiley 1998.

40. Bolzano 1837.

41. Burnyeat 1994: 41-44.

42. Burnyeat traces this through Quintilian back to Archedemus and Antipater. Cf. Cicero, *Top.* 55 *init*, 56 *init*: 'Not both p and q; p; therefore not q.'

43. Aristotle, *Prior Analytics* 1.1.24b10.24-25.

44. Burnyeat 1994.

45. Ross 1965: 500.

46. As Burnyeat (1994: 4-5) notes, Aristotle did not develop an account of the omission of conclusion of a syllogism as an enthymeme. He mentions that Hamilton, *Lectures on Logic XX*, castigating the whole notion of the enthymeme, adduced that there could be a third order of enthymeme—the omission of a conclusion (cf. W. Hamilton, 'Lecture XX', in *Lectures on Metaphysics and Logic* [eds. H.L. Mansel and J. Veitch; Edinburgh: W. Blackwood, 4th edn, 1869]).

problematic of the notion of 'enthymeme' to a temporally remote dead language text, how one would achieve the knowledge of a missing premise is often problematic. Such knowledge would, of course, rest on the assumption, which in that case would be questionable, that there ever was such a premise. This terrain is fertile territory for equivocation which may disguise sterility.

Often premises are absent from the antecedents of consequents in syllogisms that are not enthymemes. This point is extendible to deductive inference outside of syllogistic: sometimes it is a matter of choices or subtlety as to which antecedent premises one may omit or has excluded. So it does not follow from someone arguing that a premise is omitted, that the logical remains are an enthymeme. Consequently, for those who have not implemented this distinction in their analysis of a narrative,[47] their assumption, that detection of a missing premise implies the presence of an enthymeme, is false. It equally could imply that nonsyllogistic deductive inference, which is not an enthymeme, is present or that the omission is not enthymemic nor deductive, or that it is a nonlogical elipsis.

A source for claiming that Aristotle advanced the 'incomplete syllogism' enthymeme is in the Aldine of *Prior Analytics* 2.27 (70a10):

ἐνθύμημα μὲν οὖν ἐστὶν συλλογισμὸς
ἀτελὴς ἐξ εἰκότων ἢ σημείων.[48]

Burnyeat observes that there is clear evidence for the conclusion that ἀτελής in the manuscript was deleted and restored by scribal inference, nor was it based on an earlier use of the term in *Prior Analytics*.[49] He points out that all other significant manuscripts omit ἀτελής, and there is a late arrival in 1597 of a gloss by Pacius, even though Pacius later volunteers the observation that other manuscripts which he checked did not have the term in them.

The statement ἐνθύμημα μὲν οὖν ἐστὶν συλλογισμὸς ἐξ εἰκότων ἢ σημείων recurs in the *Rhetoric* three times;[50] it occurs without ἀτελής.

---

47. For example in Mk 2–3, to be examined below.

48. 'An enthymeme is an incomplete syllogism from likelihoods or signs.' See Burnyeat (1994: 6-7) for textual data; he observes that this reading is from the Aldine of 1495, appears in the commentary by (which is usually but perhaps incorrectly ascribed to) Philoponus on the above passage, and both he and Alexander affirm that the enthymeme is a syllogism with one premise omitted, with their examples citing a major premise, whereas Ammonius permits suppression of the minor premise.

49. See Wallies 1909.

50. Aristotle, *Rhet.* 1.2.14.1357a.32-33; 1359a.7-10.

This use of the statement, which does not draw attention to the absence of a premise by noting the imperfect statement of what is present in that statement, can be understood in at least two ways. First, it adverts to no other premises than what it states. Second, the statement stipulates an inference which is not identical to a perfect deductive syllogism, yet which is still a proof (πίστις) and which accordingly should be studied without reference to specifying an absent premise. Burnyeat[51] comments that none of the uses of 'enthymeme' that precede Aristotle's pioneering technical definition(s), in Alcidamas and Isocrates, invite one to provide expressions that the speaker left out of his speech. So the second option above complies with the prehistory of 'enthymeme' and Aristotle's usage uninfected by a history of the future commentary after Aristotle. Burnyeat's argument here is that 'enthymeme' is a kind of συλλογισμός: a proof, not a συλ–λογισμός of a kind.

In short, 'enthymeme' is a deductive proof; it is not a defective proof, rendered imperfect by an absent premise. Nevertheless, of course, there are different strengths for the apodeixis and for syllogism. For example, one can infer another syllogism from a valid syllogism by strengthening the premises or weakening the conclusion.[52]

Aristotle's framework in the psychology of language for this proof is objectivist concerning the relation between speech and thought. The mental counterpart of the relevant enthymeme in speech is itself a piece of logic: the relevant aspects of thought are argued proof. This is rather like Frege's (1977) view that the status of a logical 'thought' is objective and parallel with its propositional expression. Burnyeat[53] notes that Philoponus derives the term ἐνθύμημα, not from ἐν θυμῷ but from ἐνθυμεῖσθαι: 'It is called enthymeme because it leaves one premise for the mind to *think*.' Both the sourcing of the function here and the mode of expression leave aside the certain origin of an actual presupposed judgment in the author's origination, and reposition the function in mental activity which need not be the author's, and presents it in such a way as to allow that it might not even have been considered by the author, but it could instead originate with a reader reflecting on the narrative. That these matters are only possibilities does not weaken the conclusion that if such a derivation were correct then it does not have to follow, as it would in a syllogism, that a premise has to be missing.

---

51. Burnyeat 1994: 11-12.
52. For proof of this, see Geach 1989: 573-74.
53. Burnyeat 1994: 13.

8. *How Short Is a Chain of Premises?*

In the *Prior Analytics* an ἀπόδειξις is a συλλογισός with antecedents and
a consequence demonstrated as a necessary implication of those premises,
of which a *reductio ad absurdum* can be an instance. Burnyeat[54] argues
that the qualification τις after συλλογισμός complies with Aristotle's
allowance that some such demonstrations function in a μαλακώτερον[55]
fashion, that is, in a more relaxed συλλογίζωνται in the *Rhetoric*.[56] Here,
even so, the definition of ἐνθύμημα is the same for συλλογισμός;
ἐνθύμημα is not presented as an abbreviated or deformed subspecies of
συλλογισμός. Someone might have expected that when the expression
'rhetorical syllogism' occurs in Aristotle's *Rhetoric* (1356b4-5),[57] it might
be defined as a species of συλλογισμός. Not so: it is defined as συλ–
λογισμός. We should again note that this term is often used with the sense
'deduction' and is not synonymous with 'syllogism'. Aristotle was not one
to confuse the basic difference between the criteria of definition with an
instance of an example thus defined, and even less with an extended or
attenuated type of example.

Minimizing the number of premises as a feature of enthymeme is
contrary, since, for this to apply to a normal syllogism, there would be just
one premise for some enthymemes; in contrast, two premises do not seem
to be too lengthy a set for the audience to follow.[58] Aristotle does not
make it a necessary condition for being an enthymeme that it has a
premise missing from a syllogism. Aristotle himself explains the conversion from maxim to enthymeme using the example from Euripedes'
Hecuba:[59] '"There is no man who is truly free" which is a maxim, but
with its continuation became an enthymeme, "For he is either slave of
wealth or chance".' Burnyeat points out that logically this sequence is
complex, possessing a disjunctive predicate which syllogistic cannot
represent, as with a number of other enthymemes in this section of the
Rhetoric, though the use of deduction is quite evident. This reveals, of
course, that Aristotle's συλλογισμός should not be restricted to, nor to

54. Burnyeat 1994: 14.
55. 'More relaxed'; cf. *Metaph.* 6.1; 1025b13, etc.
56. Aristotle, *Rhet.* 1396a.34-b.1.
57. As noted by Burnyeat (1994: 16-17); here Burnyeat has an important examination of the relations of 'example' and ἐπαγωγή in relation to definition.
58. Burnyeat 1994: 22.
59. Aristotle, *Rhet.* 1394b3-6; traced by Burnyeat to Euripedes, *Hecuba* 864-65.

have to include, 'syllogism', since it depicts deductive argument. So the determination of ἐνθύμημα is wider than syllogism, though not necessarily in the sense of being non-deductive. In particular, rather than being looser than syllogistic, enthymemic rhetoric is at least in some contexts more logically complex. From the perspective of logical technicality and depth, rhetoric can make more stringent requirements than syllogistic.

9. *For the Most Part*

An enythmeme is a demonstration from a large set of kinds in the *Prior Analytics*, which displays different levels of modalities. For all these variations the premises are sufficient to infer the conclusion.

If we have a narrow view of the powers of a strict deductivist, Aristotle's 'for the most' could exclude deduction and include probability, though this would not reflect clear understanding. We should, of course, distinguish between what we think Aristotle actually wrote, what it is possible to ascribe as the limit of its extended range of insight, and how these two are affected by our contemporary researches into what it is to be logic and rhetoric. There is an esoteric and yet functional set of relations between the inner conditions which constitute what it is to be a statement and its functional relation to the logical theory in the perspective of a statement's communicative use. But we do well to be wary here. Rules can indeed be presented as something underlying use in the sense of theoretical abstractions as properties external to the user's cognition. Yet since unrestricted abstractionism is wrong,[60] we need not attend to a schizoid division between use and grounds for use. Despite this, we need to allow that all theory is less than perfect; so we need to allow that there sometimes will be an overlap and gap between actual use and its theoretical representation. Since there is also a gap between a user's cognition of what she states and her grasp of what it actually states, we should not be reductionist by imposing the hypothesis that the sense of the statement is what is agreed solely by consensus, nor merely what is 'evident'. And we should ascribe this awareness to Aristotle as a qualification on our, sometimes too free, use of his deductively determined framing of the evident truths which he presupposed for rhetoric.

This situation also devolves on the psychodynamics of origination and to what degree inscription of meaning in linguistic form acts as a vehicle

---

60. For proof, see Geach 1971.

for types. Beyond the scope of current analysis there should be a dispute concerning a sort of complex general presupposition: if there are onto-logical universals, and these can be, or are, mapped by creative literature, can any such resulting generalized statements referring to, and/or true of, a piece of the universe be said to contain (use, presuppose, entail internal properties of) a truth condition which applies to circumstances other than its token instances?

10. *Plural Quantification of Probability?*

Although one should not argue that there is no probability in Aristotle's *Rhetoric*, yet its 'for the most part' quantification does not have to bear a probabilistic rendering, nor an inductive one, for 'most' is a quantifier, and can be expressed using standard logic or Boolean algebra.[61] In other words 'for the most part' has quantification within deductive inference,[62] while Aristotle isolates dialectical from rhetorical argument (συλλογισμοί). Obviously, Aristotle's view is that probability can attach to ἐνθύμημα, for 'ἐνθύμημα is a *deduction* starting from probabilities or signs'[63] and this can affect its validity. But it would be a genetic fallacy to confuse 'starting from probabilities' with the subsequent 'deduction'.

   What of Aristotle's claim that 'all our convictions come either through συλλογισμός or from ἐπαγωγή' ('induction')?[64] We should note that Aristotle proceeds by adding: 'Now induction, or rather the deduction which springs out of induction, consists in deducing a relation between one extreme and the middle by means of the other extreme'. He volunteers the use of the expression 'it is necessary that' to represent relevant relations. So Aristotle's aim is not to achieve 'probable knowledge', but by use of ἐπαγωγή ('induction') deriving deduction, to infer knowledge. This is akin to the use of 'true' in possible worlds: possibly true.[65] Aristotle is con-cerned to deduce knowledge adopting the evidence inductively achieved as a starting point, and not internalize the function of induction as a feature of deductive rhetoric's identity. So this is not, in this perspective, infor-mation induced by statistical probability. Accordingly, the typical result-ing inference-relation that is preserved in enthymemes in this situation is

61. Cf. Altham 1971 and Altham 1991.
62. Aristotle, *Prior Analytics* 1.30 and 2.12.
63. Aristotle, *Prior Analytics* 2.10-11, 27.
64. Aristotle, *Prior Analytics* 23.15-35.
65. Cf. Lewis 1976.

deductive. The result is not inductive, but deductive, with its range limited by appropriate plural, not probabilistic, quantification. Even an undecided truth-value is not required to be a probability, and one may even take statements involving probability and present them in deductive form, as Levi[66] demonstrates.

Where knowledge is qualified 'for the most part' and likelihood in such contexts, it is knowledge whose quality is not uncertain, but whose quantification may have limiting boundaries falling short of universalization. This resists the idea that degrees of repute in evidence should be read as degrees of probability in our modern senses.[67] When Aristotle wrote of pregnancy as an illustration of 'for the most part', it would have been bad taste to think that Aristotle was conceiving of a probabilistic partial degree of foetal existence, though he does write of invalid forms which are susceptible to refutation.

11. *Mark's Inference*

The position developed in the foregoing differs widely from the ways many theological rhetoricians analyze while attempting to discover rhetoric and enthymeme in the New Testament. Is it textually viable to apply a modern probability analysis merged with enthymeme[68] to Mark's Gospel, for example, ch. 3? Behind such a programme in biblical studies there is sometimes the assumption that somehow Peirce has shown that probability has superseded deduction as a technique for narrative analysis. No specialist research has proved that this is even a probability, let alone demonstrated it to be a requisite treatment of New Testament language. In such cases it appears that the assignment of probability is a psychological function of the scholar's expectation, and not a property of the ancient language which is the target of policy. Certainly, deductive mapping of language use, if correctly applied, itself supersedes probability, since the latter is presuppositional approximation, and not an internal identity of inference. The exception to this view, obviously, is where the object language is itself inductive. Contrariwise, this is not the case in a range of

66. See Levi 1967: ch. 6.

67. Hacking (1975: ch. 5) is an important study on 'signs' which exposes the development of modern uses of probability that can be applied to trace confusions about 'signs' and enthymemes in post-sixteenth-century scholarship.

68. I have argued in the foregoing that this probabilistic treatment of 'enthymeme' would in any case not be Aristotle's approach.

relevant uses (of course, this judgment should be focused within the present discussion of enthymeme theory).

Mark 3.24 uses the conditional inference, 'For if a kingdom is divided against itself, that kingdom cannot stand'.[69] Surely this conditional functions there as a token to coerce the reader into taking it to be a generalization? The implication relation in this statement is repeated in Mark 3 using 'household' and 'Satan' as a replacement for 'kingdom', thus entrenching other token uses to emphasize the inference as a generalization. A presupposition of the conditional inference is, of course, that Jesus has been selected by the scribes as the candidate subject for the conditional statement. This deployment of the inference relation presupposes an extensive use of generalization over typical opposed contexts.

The logic of questions is still in its formal infancy, so we should approach the logic of interrogative irony[70] cautiously. Mark 3.22 asks, 'How can Satan drive out Satan?' The function of the question is to posit it as an axiom, which is then used by conditional proof to convert it to a function reminiscent of a theorem. It presupposes logical functions concerning reference in relative identity, the law of non-contradiction, and predicate logic's negation. The succeeding statement, 'If a kingdom is divided against itself, that kingdom cannot stand', takes the question as a transformed axiom, and presupposes it to contain, as a premise for this inference, a generalizable rule of the consequence of contradiction, a rule which is taken to be transitive regarding subject. This implicitly presupposes a functioning scheme equivalent to or parallel with metalanguage, by which token replacement of a type operates as an underlying function in the object-language fused to the meta-language.

This logic is only a fragment of the literary senses in Mark 3; yet it proffers a mirroring[71] of the presuppositions of the collective consciousness obtaining for both synchronic and diachronic axes. For each the geography is important, since Jesus is presented as preaching in the old territory of Baal Zebub. He had just commanded a sick man to take up his bed and walk and healed the blind. In the same territory, at the time of Mark, the ancient Phoenician archives available to Josephus (which absorbed other Semitic influences on Greek, as well as Greek on

69. It seems clear that the use of this example has an intertextual relation to Isa. 19.2.

70. For a start on the literary theory of this where location is a function of ironic argument, see A. Gibson 1997a and 1997b.

71. Cf. Bowie 1993.

Semitic),[72] displayed the same liturgical myths as had the Ugaritic Keret myth cycles of Baal: 'he shall come down from the roofs...the sick man shall take up his bed...the blind shall be cured'.[73] In Mark 3 the scribes attempt to identify Jesus as a function of the medial product of such inter-textual history, so as to subvert his identity claims. So there is evident interplay of competing ontologies bound to different criteria of identity superimposed over 'Baalzeboul' and 'Satan'.[74] Mark 3's usage of logic, episodically outlined above, is a structure for the narrative's conceptual dynamics. Within this perspective, the reference of 'Satan' is an argument-place that simultaneously slips its anchor and criterion of identity as the transcendent power figure, and reattaches, with another criterion of identity, to the (false) god motif of Baalzeboul, only to be deconstructed by the narrative's presentation of Jesus' reasoning as he denudes Satan of Jesus' own interiority and Satan's external cultic geography. By these strict implications Mark presents the necessity that the criterion of identity for Satan is left for the original users—the scribes—to be the bearers of 'Satan'. 'Satan' is parallel with the logical dangling pronouns[75] and variables that can take a range of values. Although the scribes' application of demoniac descriptions to Jesus are presented as what is tantamount to intentionalistic falsehoods by the Markan narrator, the polemical redeployment secures a deconstructed ascription of 'Satan' to the collective state of those who are the source of the allegations.

The status of reference and the criteria of identity are at the forefront of the use of 'Satan' here. The roles of reference and identity have varying explications in philosophy of logic; yet a discrete core of features from a number of concepts have ready application to Mark's uses of 'Satan'. The

72. For general background, see Dalley and Reyes 1998.

73. Dalley and Reyes 1998 and J.C.L. Gibson 1978, citing Keret, I.ii.27-46. Notice how the sick man taking up his bed contrasts with the only Old Testament occurrence of Baalzebub, 2 Kgs 1, where it notes that Ahaziah, awaiting news of a cure from Baalzebub, is told by Elijah that he will not arise from his bed but dying, he shall die, implementing Gen. 3's curse; Mark's irony in the miracle reverses the curse.

74. As Salvesen (1998: 145-46) argues, the various Semitic, Persian and Greek rhetorical strands of dialogue poetry are one cluster among many traditions which attest to the centrality of disputes about Satan and moral teaching in the Levant before and during the New Testament period. This, in conjunction with the above analysis, indicates that Mk 3 tackles themes of archetypal concern for its first-century CE audiences, with its revolutionary use of deductive reasoning as a technqiue of confrontation and argument.

75. See Geach 1972.

tendency to the Phoenician spelling of 'Baalzeboul', which displaces the Hebrew ironizing spelling of 2 Kings 2, complements the popular aware-ness contemporary to Mark of the older Canaanite backcloth against which Jesus taught, with the geography of Mark 2–3.

Sketchily, I have mentioned this reference pattern as a complex function of the argument structure to make the point that the logic of Mark in these contexts is dense with subtle patterns and levels or multiple orders of use and mention. Analytical philosophy has given little attention to such uses, which partly stems from Frege's tardy remarks on complex tonal pun. Only a start[76] has been made to introduce the notion of 'tone' and asso-ciated phenomena to binary deductive logics, so as rightly to violate Frege's[77] restriction of 'tone' (*Beleuchtung* and *Färbung*) to non-logical domains. Syllogistic has no place in such an advanced literary and logical space. Of course this is not to presuppose that we can in principle provide a calculus of tone since, whatever the limits of logic, such a calculus has to engage with the little understood philosophy of the imagination, and 'tone' is a ragbag term, as Dummett notes in the foregoing citation. But, thinking of Aristotle's own approach to future contingents, by which we find a specific, single proposition engaging the field of investigation, rather than the task of attempting to solve the whole question of what a calculus for the future would look like, we can approach the occurrence of tone in a particular narrative to assess it for logical properties, employing a range of standard and deviant logics. A presupposition that I have, in addition to the present analysis, for suggesting this, is the idea that almost all logics have some causal and mapping relations to other human creativities and their creative expressions.[78]

Rightly understood, areas of Aristotle's rhetoric in the sphere of the enthymeme were presented to engage with some of these issues. It will take another study to suggest that Aristotle's *Poetics* also contribute to this perspective. So logical analysis should be sensitive to the thematic literary polemic; for war it is, against falsehood, in the narrator's hand. The fore-going example exemplifies the multi-layered functioning of the logic of polemical discourse. So we should be careful to avoid dividing the underlying functions of a narrative with its usage. Narrative is not a linear function, but more like a multidimensional universe. Certainly, we should

---

76. See A. Gibson 1987: Epigraph; 1997a; 1997b.

77. See Dummett 1981: ch. 2.

78. For a summary development of this programme in the literary framework, see A. Gibson 1997b.

avoid incorrect formulations fusing surface structure with underlying functions. One of these would be to conflate Aristotle's rhetoric with the foregoing example from Mark, since the latter does not employ partial quantification and Mark employs a single statement in the role as a token for a universally quantified type.

12. *Conclusion*

The significance of knowledge and the form of ignorance within an author's and critic's uses of reason are important in assessing the functional capability of their compositions to bear logical analysis. Obviously, to some indeterminate degree, this is a problem contingent on the expressibility of the intention of the ancient author in linguistic form, and a matter regulated by the presuppositions of the scholar's analysis. The logical identity of a proposition *and* its use as a piece of reasoning involve a complex set of issues which await fully successful analysis. Also, other uses which are present in a narrative should not be neglected by philosophers since they have a functional contribution in the context which will affect the sense. Thus, logical analysis is not merely the task of abstracting out of a discourse the bits that seem promising as objects for transformation into inferential or syllogistic form. Rather, in a certain sense, the ideal (which we cannot achieve) should be that logical analysis would leave meaning just as it is. To ignore this would be rather like finding the inference: '2 + 2 = 4 and possibly 3 extra', and assuming that the extra ingredient was a sort of bonus that did not affect the sum. This illustration is a naive form of complex muddles. In recondite areas of inference, it is rarely obvious such errors are being committed when they are. A true account of logic is a function of discovering the accurate relations for resolving when such slips are made.

Although philosophers and logicians diverge over the technical solutions and final form of the central problems, many applied strategies in rhetorical analysis have operated either in ignorance of the type of insights unquestionably achieved, or offer contributions which could massively benefit from quite basic research on the philosophy of logic. Sometimes these are a product of influences that intervene between ourselves and sources. One problem due for attention in the light of the present study, whilst beyond its scope, is the question of the relations between 'proof' (πίστις) and 'faith' (πίστις). Are they homonyms or polysemes in New Testament usage? Is there some deep structure concerning which a use of such 'faith' has?

Much of the New Testament world contests the cultures with which it battles. There is thus a danger of scholarly equivocation over such controversial writers by conflating the possible scope of social contacts within their world (but often not of theirs) as if they were conceptual influences. The routing of Greek rhetoric through Palestinian rabbinic Judaism would hardly be an attractive source to those writers whose reasoning disputes within a polemic to retrieve a vision of Old Testament fulfillment set against its perceived betrayal in such Judaism. There is need for a fresh approach to an aspect of this arena. The occurrence of pseudo-Aristotelian rhetoric and Platonic forms in the Sanhedrin's stylistics is evidence for a bifurcation between the authorial voices of such alienation for Mark, even before we see that Mark's reasoning and polemic introduce us to an original world of creativity.

Leaving Romantic causality aside, this area needs quite fresh research: what are the psychodynamics of original causality concerning the embedding of controversial rationality in a new narrative? Here linguistics, literary theory and logic should be integrated in quests for answers. Within this priority is an abstract multiple question for applied narrative analysis: if there are universal necessary conditions of consequence expressible in a formal universe of discourse, and if Aristotle exposed properties of them, then would they appear manifested in some form in a diachronically unrelated narrative if that narrative succeeded in creatively expressing other universal qualities?

APPENDIX:
False Metaphor in Rhetorical Scholarship

The above sections (2) *Argumentum ad hominem* and (3) *Aristotle's Dialectic, Syllogistic and Rhetoric* require a bridging premise on the representation of confusions in some rhetoric scholarship and the identity of 'logic' terms interior to such confusion. So this Appendix formulates the outline of a theory for this situation, in particular with an eye to some biblical scholarship, and depicts the misuse of 'logic' terminology in this arena of activity as an inadvertent metaphorizing of logic terms.

There are some problematic questions as to what counts towards an inference being valid in deep areas of logic; yet a number of types of cases are certainly fallacious as they appear in some studies. It assists us to list some types of examples relevant to issues in rhetoric's relations to logic, though since the priority is conceptual, I have not troubled to cite the contemporary research studies which manifest these errors, though A. Gibson (1981/2001) is a resource for some earlier examples.

Fallacy is a helpful mapping device with which to isolate some of the problems of interpretation in rhetoric. 'Fallacy' is a metonymy metaphor. That is to say, its mapping facility is not an exhaustive function of the subject which it represents. Explaining an undetected fallacious move in terms of fallacy confers a clarity and visibility on the unsuspected usage which was not even noticed to be a problem prior to this depiction. Such confusion is alien to relevant logic, and logical representation of confusion leaves out some of the qualitative disorder on which it operates. This recasting into logical form improves the unsuspecting user's formulation. Such presentational clarification may obscure, to the unsuspecting user of fallacy, the extent and extremity of the error which the fallacy displays, which needs further exposure in the unwitting metaphorical use of logic terminology. This way of posing the problem is itself unexpected to those whom it characterizes. Of course someone may want to discount this type of approach as an in-house irrelevant game. He may retort, as he embraces a project which interprets a particular ancient Greek text:

(1) 'Have any rules you want; anything goes; therefore rules are outlawed'.

Apart from reminding him that this itself is a use of the deduction which he denies, we might respond, using his own criteria, that:

(2) '(1) means the falsehood of (1)'.

Attempts to interpret logic need to be reducible to the theorems, axioms or presuppositions of inferences that constitute implication. Sure, the criteria for determining these properties may be recondite or problematic in certain respects, though the present comments here are not to be deflected by such difficulties. Quite apart from the issue of whether one invents or discovers further extensions for logic, classical and current logics have determinate identities which place what should be evident limits on a rhetorician's, linguist's and logician's imaginative contribution to extending or retrieving a hitherto unknown property of a logic's identity.

It would not be a successful way of discounting the present points to suggest that they merely fail to recognize conditions facilitating the extension of logic by foreclosing on the possibility of furnishing fresh results that are invisibly 'contained in the premises' of a pioneering inference. If such invisibility resists attempts to expose it as an actual property, then it has to be deemed at most a possible, not a bivalent actual, property. If this is the case, then modal logic will have to be brought to structure the premises, and this downgraded version will have a deductive logical form. But often assertions about a thing being contained in the premises remain just a foggy notion used to encourage imaginative prose ornamented with a few unmeasured (metaphorical) logic terms (as in [1] above). This perhaps becomes a vogue because literary style is also a feature of rhetoric and the emotive psychology associated with it. Just as there has been false science and prescientific culture paraded as science, so there is some bad logic. There is a genuine uncertainty as to what counts as a feature of logic; but this is hardly a relevant or a valid objection to the fallacies described here.

So if one were to put the best spin on these mistakes or fallacies, what is it to come to the nub of the point? It may be helpful to introduce the concept of the, possibly unwitting, uncontrolled metaphorization of logical and rhetorical terminology, to account for the phenomenon I wish here to encapsulate. (This unconscious or muddled use of metaphor is different from explicitly recognized controlled live metaphor, for which see A. Gibson 1997b.) In contrast, I have argued that logic, pure mathematics, and, for example, the languages of astrophysical cosmology are an unusual species of live metaphor (and in a fundamentally different sense, creativity itself may also be anchored to one's capacity to compose live metaphors). Clearly, this live metaphor is distinct from dead metaphor. One would be involved in committing modal segmentation and quantifier shift to purport that this technical use of live metaphor invariantly ranges over the domain of ad hoc dead metaphor fallacies.[79] In effect, the systematic development of such uses of logic terminology produces a hybrid pattern composed of words like 'premise' which are homonyms of the same logical grapheme 'premise'. This situation is quite different from the way in which a term is, in the present perspective concerning logical theory, a live metaphorized use[80] of 7^2 which is derived from the type x^2. If a reader dislikes this original use of live metaphor, it is quite easy to paraphrase the position into some other way of expressing the idea, such as a token/type relation attached to a notion of logical paraphrase.

Such a procedure implements a number of fallacies.[81] First, a modal fallacy[82] of confusing a possible, yet not actually expressed, form with the actual use in the narrative under investigation. Second, a segmentation fallacy, of recombining occurring expressions as functions which they do not have in the analyzed context; this is similar to the false hypostatization in diachronic morphology, for example, in some Semitic studies.[83] Third, a genetic fallacy in retrojective form, of conflating a narrative effect with a purported original ground.[84] Since the literary effect in the narrative has been reformulated in a style which it does not have in use, such a fallacy conflates historical origin with logical nature, precisely in the way W.F. Albright did with his generalized approach to ancient language and logic.[85]

79. For further analysis, see A. Gibson 1981.

80. It is worth noting for the above context that a live metaphor itself may be derived from another live metaphor, and it does not have to be a product of a dead metaphor. A visual example is apt: we may see a re-interpreting film shot (a complex live metaphor) of a photograph or montage (a group of live metaphors); the latter is a live metaphorization of the latter, as 7^2 is a live metaphor of x^2. Obviously this way of speaking is stereotypical, and requires adumbration and expansion for uses other than this illustrative purpose. (For some theory of the logic of live metaphor, see A. Gibson 1997, and forthcoming works.)

81. Some of the formal work for stipulating these fallacies is to be found in A. Gibson 1981b.

82. A. Gibson 1981: 37-39.

83. A. Gibson 1981: 21-24.

84. A. Gibson 1981: 193.

85. A. Gibson 1981: 229-31.

Some speculative rhetorical analysis displays a related confusion, that of merging logic and subjective use of mental experience; this is parallel with a pattern manifested in some Old Testament study, for example in Dahood's work.[86] On occasions such as the above type of scenario where a modal fallacy is a foundation for theorizing, an implication fallacy[87] may be employed to achieve or justify an approach. To isolate fallacies as the above gives errors a certain retrospective clarity which was invisible to the unsuspecting user; this retrospection renders them evident in the way they were not in use—they are usually unconsciously disguised in obscure prose. So, for example, a scholar may argue that, though an instance he is examining does not fit the usual logical or rhetorical canon, then the scholar can still assume or assert that he is using logic or a certain category of it. This is a mistake about intentionality. the mere fact of someone's believing a statement obviously does not make it correct—this is as true for the mind as it is for logic.[88]

Whether or not we adopt Frege as the foundation to document the mistakes in this situation, or appeal to antirealist and irrealist logics such as those devised by Tennant[89] and Boghossian,[90] they all entail that there is sufficient relevant asymmetry between mentality and logics to map confusion between these two phenomena. There are many disagreements amongst logicians; but the foregoing types of fallacies do not even come near nor are salvaged by logical disputes. Such cases may exemplify Geach's[91] view that there is a general tendency to implant bad logic in some twentieth-century didactic cultures.

BIBLIOGRAPHY

Altham, J.E.J.
> 1971 *The Logic of Plurality* (Cambridge: Cambridge University Press).
> 1991 'Plural and Pleonetetic Quantification', in Lewis: 105-19.

Anderson, A.R., and N.F. Belnap
> 1975, 1992 *The Logic of Relevance and Necessity* (2 vols.; Princeton, NJ: Princeton University Press).

Boethius, A.M.S.
> 1998 *Anicii Manlii Sereini Boethii: De Divison Liber* (ed. J. Magee; Philosophia Antique, 77; Leiden: E.J. Brill).

86. A. Gibson 1981: 83-84. This is illustrated by Dahood's rhetorical style in analysis of Hebrew. Here the subjective feature of mental patterns is thereby taken to be causal evidence of external linguistic reasoning.

87. A. Gibson 1981: 201.

88. An obvious case is an apt illustration here: 'If you want some poison, then it is on the table' employs 'if' in a non-truth-functional use, since it is not on the table if you do not want it.

89. Tennant 1997.

90. Boghossian 1989, 1990a, 1990b.

91. Cf. Geach 1972; 1991: 45-48.

Boghossian, P.
    1989   'The Rule-Following Consideration', *Mind* 98: 507-49.
    1990a   'The Status of Content', *Philosophical Review* 99: 157-84.
    1990b   'The Status of Content Revisited', *Pacific Philosophical Quarterly* 71: 264-
                78.
Bolzano, B.
    1837   *Wissenschaftslehre* (4 vols.; Prague: Sulzbach; Theory of Science; Oxford:
                Basil Blackwell, 1972 [trans. R. George]).
Bowie, M.
    1993   *Psychoanalysis and the Future of Theory* (Oxford: Basil Blackwell).
Burnyeat, M.F.
    1994   'Enthymeme: Aristotle on the Logic of Persuasion', in D.J. Furley and
                A. Nehamas (eds.), *Aristotle's Rhetoric* (Princeton, NJ: Princeton University
                Press): 3-55.
    1995   *The Semantic Foundations of Propositional Logics* (New York: Oxford Uni-
                versity Press, 2nd edn).
Dalley, S., and A.T. Reyes
    1998   'Mesopotamian Contact and Influence in the Greek World', in S. Dalley
                (ed.), *The Legacy of Mesopotamia* (Oxford: Oxford University Press): 107-
                24.
Dummett, M.
    1981   *Frege: Philosophy of Language* (London: Gerald Duckworth, 2nd edn).
Epstein, R.L.
    1995   *The Semantic Foundations of Propositional Logic* (Oxford: Oxford Univer-
                sity Press, 2nd edn).
Frege, G.
    1977   *Logical Investigations* (trans. and ed. P.T. Geach and M. Black; Oxford:
                Basil Blackwell).
Garver, N.
    1996   'Philosophy as Grammar', in H. Sluga and D.G. Stern (eds.), *The Cambridge
                Companion to Wittgenstein* (Cambridge: Cambridge University Press): 139-
                70.
Geach, P.T.
    1971   *Mental Acts* (London: Routledge, amended edn).
    1972   *Logic Matters* (Oxford: Basil Blackwell).
    1981   *Reference and Generality* (Ithaca, NY: Cornell University Press, 3rd edn).
    1989   'On Modal syllogisms', in P.A. Schilpp and L.E. Hahn (eds.), *The Philo-
                sophy of Georg Henrik von Wright* (La Salle, IL: Open Court): 557-80.
    1991   'Whatever Happened to Deontic Logic?', in P.T. Geach (ed.), *Logic and
                Ethics* (Dodrecht: Kluwer Academic Publishers): 33-48.
Gibson, A.
    1981/2001   *Biblical Semantic Logic* (Oxford: Basil Blackwell; Sheffield: Sheffield Aca-
                demic Press).
    1987   *Boundless Function* (Newcastle, UK: Bloodaxe Books).
    1997a   'Archetypal Site Poetry', Foreword to J. Milbank, *The Mercurial Wood:
                Sites, Tales, Qualities* (Salzburg Studies in English Literature, Poetic Drama
                and Poetic Theory; Salzburg, Austria: University of Salzburg): vii-xi.

| 1997b | 'God's Semantic Logic: Some Functions in the Dead Sea Scrolls', in S.E. Porter and C.A. Evans (eds.), *The Scrolls and the Scriptures* (RILP, 3; JSPSup, 26; Sheffield: Sheffield Academic Press, 1997): 68-106. |

2000a   *God and the Universe* (London: Routledge).
2000b   *Text and Tablet* (Aldershot: Ashgate).

Gibson, J.C.L.
1978   *Canaanite Myths and Legend* (Edinburgh: T. & T. Clark).

Haack, S.A.
1971   *Deviant Logic* (Cambridge: Cambridge University Press).

Hacking, I.
1975   *The Emergence of Probability* (Cambridge: Cambridge University Press).

Hintikka, J.J.
1996   'The Development of Aristotle's Ideas of Scientific Method', in W. Willians (ed.), *Aristotle's Philosophical Development* (Lanham, MD: Rowman & Littlefield): 83-104.

Kneale, W., and M. Kneale
1984   *The Development of Logic* (Oxford: Clarendon Press, corr. edn).

Lear, J.
1980   *Aristotle and Logical Theory* (Cambridge: Cambridge University Press).

Levi, I.
1967   *Gambling with Truth* (New York: Alfred A. Knopf; London: Routledge).

Lewis, D.
1976   'Probabilities of Conditionals and Conditional Probabilities', *Philosophical Review* 85: 297-315.

Lewis, H.A. (ed.)
1991   *Peter Geach: Philosophical Encounters* (Dordrecht: Kluwer Academic Publishers).

Lewy, C.
1976   *Meaning and Modality* (Cambridge: Cambridge University Press).

Locke, J.
1997   *Essay concerning Human Understanding* (ed. R. Woolhouse; Harmondsworth: Penguin Books).

Magee, J.
1998   *Anicii Manlii Severini Boethii: De Divisone Liber* (Philosophia Antiqua, 77; eds. J. Mansfield, D.T. Runia, and J.C.M. van Winden; Leiden: E.J. Brill).

Popper, K.R.
1972   *Objective Knowledge* (Oxford: Oxford University Press).

Rees, M.
1997   *Before the Beginning* (London: Simon & Schuster).

Ross, W.D. (ed.)
1965   *Aristotle's Prior and Posterior Analytics* (Oxford: Clarendon Press).

Sainsbury, M.
1991   *Logical Forms* (Oxford: Basil Blackwell).

Salvesen, A.
1998   'The Legacy of Babylon and Nineveh in Aramaic Sources', in S. Dalley (ed.), *The Legacy of Mesopotamia* (Oxford: Oxford University Press): 139-61.

Schutrumpf, E.
    1994   'Some Observations on the Introduction to Aristotle's *Rhetoric*' (eds. D.J.
                Furley and A. Nehamas; Princeton: Princeton University Press).
Shoesmith, D.J., and T.J. Smiley
    1978   *Multiple-Conclusion Logic* (Cambridge: Cambridge University Press).
Smiley, T.J.
    1995   'A Tale of Two Tortoises', *Mind* 104, 416: 725-36.
    1998   'Conceptions of Consequences', in E.J. Cronj (ed.), *Routledge Encyclo-
                paedia of Philosophy* (London: Routledge): 599-602.
Sorensen, R.A.
    1998   'Logical Luck', *Philosophical Quarterly* 48: 319-34.
Tennant, N.
    1997   *The Taming of the True* (Oxford: Oxford University Press).
Wallies, M.
    1909   *Ioannis Philoponi in Anitotelis posteriora commentaria cum anonymo im
                librum II*, XIII/13 (Berlin: Georg Reimer).
Wittgenstein, L.
    1996   'Notes on Logic', in M.A.R. Biggs (ed.), *Editing Wittgenstein's 'Notes on
                Logic'* (2 vols.; Working Papers from the Wittgenstein Archives at the Uni-
                versity of Bergen, No. 11).

Why We Need Socio-Rhetorical Commentary and What It Might Look Like

Duane F. Watson

1. *The Challenge that Current Methodologies Pose to the Commentary Genre*

Several years ago I signed a contract to write a socio-rhetorical commentary on a Pauline epistle. At that time I was not quite sure how to proceed
to write such a new type of commentary. I began by looking at the commentary genre itself and was surprised at how little purposeful examination of the genre has occurred in biblical studies. Terence Fretheim wrote,
'It is striking that method in the writing of commentaries is one of the least
explored of the biblical disciplines' (1982: 356-57; cf. Krentz 1982: 373).
The literature on this subject is sparse, often anecdotal. When looking at
socio-rhetorical criticism, there were a number of articles by Vernon
Robbins that were working out the method of socio-rhetorical analysis,
and a few other articles and dissertations by those working with his
proposals, but the method was not spelled out completely and in great
detail in any publication (for the best summaries, see Robbins 1992a: xix-
xliv; 1992d; 1995a; Gowler 1994). Two commentaries claiming to be
socio-rhetorical, although excellent as commentaries, did not move
beyond traditional historical-critical methods of interpretation with an
emphasis in social history (Witherington 1995, 1998). How to write a
socio-rhetorical commentary remained unclear.

Fortunately two recent books by Robbins systematically introduce
socio-rhetorical criticism as an interpretive analytics: *Exploring the Texture of Texts: A Guide to Socio-Rhetorical Interpretation* (1996b) and *The
Tapestry of Early Christian Discourse: Rhetoric, Society and Ideology*
(1996c). These books provide a detailed and workable approach for implementing socio-rhetorical criticism and have provided the needed direction
for my commentary project and other such commentaries in the publishing
pipeline. They discuss how socio-rhetorical criticism interprets a text as

composed of five textures: inner texture, intertexture, social and cultural texture, ideological texture, and sacred texture.[1]

Socio-rhetorical criticism is an interpretive analytics rather than a method in the usual sense. 'An interpretive analytics approaches texts as discourses and "sees discourse as part of a larger field of power and practice whose relations are articulated in different ways by different paradigms" ' (Robbins 1996c: 12, quoting Dreyfus and Rabinow 1983: 199).

> As I understand it, an interpretive analytics uses the strategies and insights of both theory and method, but it uses these strategies and insights in a manner that perpetually deconstructs its own boundaries and generates new ones in the ongoing process of interpretation. The stance of the interpreter is to 'take seriously the problems and conceptual tools of the past, but not the solutions and conclusions based on them'. The goal is to replace 'ontology with a special kind of history that focuses on the cultural practices that have made us what we are'. The task of investigation is 'to find the rules which determined or controlled the discourse that there was' (Robbins 1997a: 29, quoting Dreyfus and Rabinow 1983: 122-23).

Socio-rhetorical criticism has enormous implications for many areas of New Testament study. One implication that concerns us in this study is the need to rethink and redesign the commentary genre. I cannot envision the typical commentary format accommodating socio-rhetorical criticism, but rather I see socio-rhetorical criticism forcing the New Testament guild to look at the commentary genre anew and make significant modifications to accommodate it.

Why will modifications be necessary? Socio-rhetorical criticism moves beyond the boundaries established by the historical-critical methodologies usually used in the composition of commentaries. Socio-rhetorical criticism explores a wide range of issues concerning language, texts, society, culture, ideology, and theology. As the name 'socio-rhetorical' indicates, the criticism utilizes all the resources of anthropology and sociology, as well as rhetoric and communication theory and introduces them in the context of detailed exegesis. In the process, socio-rhetorical criticism brings all the typical biblical criticisms into dialogue and integrated interpretation by focusing upon texts as performances of language; upon literary, social, cultural, and ideological issues central to language as a part of

---

1.   *Tapestry* describes four textures: inner texture, intertexture, social and cultural texture, and ideological texture, whereas *Exploring* adds sacred texture to the list. As the method of socio-rhetorical criticism develops, other textures may be added (e.g. psychological).

society. It contributes to the interdisciplinary paradigm emerging in biblical studies (Robbins 1996b: 1). It acknowledges and examines the text as language performance and understands a text as a tapestry of inter-woven textures, including the inner texture, intertexture, social and cul-tural texture, ideological texture, and sacred texture. It generates multiple strategies for engaging the text and its textures.

> Socio-rhetorical critics, perceiving texts to be 'richly textured' with simul-taneously interacting networks of signification, reinvent rhetoric by reading and rereading, interpreting and reinterpreting texts 'as forms of *activity* inseparable from the wider social relations between writers and readers, orators and audiences' (Robbins 1994d: 165, quoting Eagleton 1983: 206).

Socio-rhetorical interpretation is interactionist. It seeks to integrate the study of religion and humanistic, theological, and socio-scientific disci-plines. It places dialogue at the center of reading and interpreting a text. It generates dialogical interaction between multiple disciplinary strategies for reading and interpreting a text. Socio-rhetorical hermeneutics is also grounded in an ethnography of orality, writing, and reading. The content of the text is not the subject of interpretation per se, but the interaction between the content and its mode of production. 'Interpreters who enact socio-rhetorical hermeneutics will investigate the historical, linguistic, social, cultural, ideological, and theological phenomena that, working together, function as the material, means, and mode of production of the discourse' (Robbins 1998: 289).

Clearly the current form of the commentary genre cannot accommodate the program of socio-rhetorical criticism. Fortunately, the challenge that the proliferation of new methods of interpretation is posing to the com-mentary genre has begun to receive needed discussion. Serious concerns are being raised about the broader issue of the industry of commentary writing as a whole, like this one from Bernard Anderson: 'many people are haunted by uncertainty about the purpose of a commentary and even wonder whether this tool, once useful, has become obsolete and should be discarded in favor of something better' (1982: 341). It is sensed that the commentary will be significantly altered if commentators truly recognize the challenge posed by new methods.

> The genre of the biblical commentary is in the process of being creatively extended. It is being remodeled to accommodate new questions, methods, and emphases—so much so as to force us to ask what the minimal defining characteristics of a commentary are. The transformation is still an incipient one—a series of independent experiments in biblical commentary, inspired by nonbiblical literary criticism (Moore 1987: 29).

While consenting that the commentary will remain a widely used genre in biblical studies, Leslie Houlden notes the growing difficulties of writing commentaries. He remarks,

> Yet so wide and diverse is the range of methods now brought to the study of the biblical books   that it is hard to unify them in a presentable way in relation to a text followed loyally, one section after another. Nowadays, the tangle of issues is so complex that it is virtually impossible to encompass them satisfactorily in the discussion of passages seriatim. Indeed, to work in commentary form may be to be misled (1990: 131).

One future Houlden sees for the commentary is the commentary devoted to one method of approach, such as narrative criticism (as Moore 1987 suggests) or structuralism (Houlden 1990: 131).

Since it utilizes all the new methodologies in New Testament studies, socio-rhetorical criticism brings the challenge posed by these methodologies to the commentary genre to a point of decision. The present form of the commentary cannot easily accommodate the many-voiced dialogue generated by socio-rhetorical criticism and its investigations. The dialogue will necessitate a redesign of the commentary. However, socio-rhetorical criticism does not have the luxury of adopting just one method of interpretation as has been proposed as one solution to the current crisis in commentary writing. In fact it has the initial difficulty of adopting a multitude of approaches which compounds the difficulty already faced by commentary writing. Before we decide what a socio-rhetorical commentary might look like, we need to investigate changes being suggested for the current form of the commentary genre.

2. Current Calls for Change in the Commentary Genre and the Promise of Socio-Rhetorical Criticism to Answer Those Calls

Critique of current commentaries usually includes those features that any serious reader of a commentary will note: poor writing style, too much or too little detail frustrating a simple inquiry, skirting the difficult issues raised by specific pericopes, not taking a clear stand on larger hermeneutical issues, and debating with scholars rather than with the biblical text. However, some critique hits at the heart of commentary writing and calls for significant change. This second part of the paper reviews these calls for change and notes how socio-rhetorical criticism can answer these calls.

a. *Eliminate the Typical Division of Commentaries into 'Academic' and 'Popular'*

One standard complaint about commentaries is the bifurcation in the genre between those that are for the academy or the New Testament guild and those that are for the pastor and educated laity; those that are critical, technical, and historically oriented and those that are devotional and expository; those used for exegesis and research and those used for preaching and Bible study in the church. The author of a socio-rhetorical commentary still has to make the initial decision about the audience and purpose that the commentary will serve. Here is an opportunity to demonstrate that this interactionist commentary is very flexible and can begin to break down the typical bifurcation in the genre. The level of dialogue that it engenders when discussing a texture, the textures that it emphasizes, and the readings of the text that it provides are all managed by the commentator for any audience. In fact, the interdisciplinary nature of the commentary and its awareness of social, cultural, and ideological issues and textures in the text allow it to be tailored to specific audiences determined by educational level, faith commitment, gender, race, ethnicity, and so on, as well as by purposes of research, ideological issues, and private devotion. Socio-rhetorical commentary can be a great tool to let many new voices be heard in interpretation that have been stifled by the very narrow and typical description of the commentary market as envisioned in the bifurcation described above. It will foster commentaries not divided primarily as 'academic' and 'lay' but rather by stated social, cultural, and ideological differences, as these relate to specific audiences.

b. *Move beyond Commentaries as 'Information Retrieval Systems' to Interdisciplinary Commentaries*

In the discussion of commentary writing it is usually remarked that a variety of disciplines and methods needs to be used to provide a comprehensive exegesis of the text (Wenham 1990: 1-12). Disciplines typically used in commentary writing include archaeology, comparative ancient literature, epigraphy, history, and philology. Methodologies typically used include text, form, source, redaction, tradition history, rhetorical, canonical, and literary criticism. More and more information is being amassed for retrieval as the growing length of commentaries attests very well.

However, *multi-disciplinary* efforts are not necessarily *interdisciplinary* efforts. Some use of the disciplines typically employed in commentary writing are interdisciplinary, but often they are used independently. The call has gone out for truly interdisciplinary commentaries. As a highly interdisciplinary method, socio-rhetorical criticism can utilize a host of disciplines or methodologies within, ancillary to, or usually not associated with New Testament study to examine one or more of the textures of the New Testament texts and produce a truly interdisciplinary commentary.

As those calling for an interdisciplinary commentary have warned, there is a potential danger here that an interdisciplinary commentary, like a socio-rhetorical commentary, can become nothing more than a larger amassing of yet more information from more avenues of investigation without any reinterpretation of material or dialogue between the findings of each discipline employed. There is the related danger that one discipline and its categories and interests will dominate the commentary to the detriment of the other disciplines. T. Conley warns,

> Interdisciplinary projects have become rather fashionable lately, with some justification. But lest it seem that interdisciplinary commentaries are what commentaries should be, let us consider for a moment the possibility that an interdisciplinary commentary might simply magnify the problems which crop up around the notion of commentary-as 'information retrieval system'. It seems to me that in the present circumstances interdisciplinary comment-aries can succeed only in juxtaposing or adding 'facts' to one another. Unless one of the disciplines should be raised to the status of architectonic to produce unified information concerning the facts and analyses of different kinds of data and experience, the interdisciplinary commentary can only be a jumble of reported facts which cannot without re-interpreta-tion be made relevant to one another. Of course, what really happens is that the assertion of the priority of one discipline tends to eliminate the 'facts' of the others in order to make them fit the prior discipline's categories and interests, and what you get is usually not *inter*disciplinary at all (1978: 7).

Socio-rhetorical criticism can avoid these possible dangers. The criticism is multidisciplinary and interdisciplinary. As an interpretative analytics, many disciplines are encouraged to dialogue. Each discipline used to investigate each texture is encouraged to talk to the other disciplines investigating the same texture. Also, the disciplines are encouraged to talk to one another among textures as the insights gained from each texture are constantly brought into the discussion of the other textures. For example, the presuppositions of the author found in the exploration of the argumentative inner texture forms the basis of the exploration of the social and cultural texture. In socio-rhetorical criticism no discipline necessarily dominates. A discipline may be predominant in the discussion of a particular texture, but no single discipline guides the process overall. There is the danger that within textures disciplines will be used to perform their functions in isolation, and textures will be analyzed in isolation from one another, but this may be due to the lack of skill of the commentator rather than spell a fault of socio-rhetorical criticism.

c. *Incorporate the History of Interpretation*
The historical-critical method is wedded to historicism and tries to find one plain and literal meaning of a text. Commentaries written primarily with historical-critical methodologies often assume that the ancient text has a univocal meaning, and the purpose of the commentary is to recover that meaning and provide a univocal meaning for today. Thus historical-critical methodologies have been suspicious of 'pre-critical' exegesis of the Bible which perceived several levels of meaning in a biblical text, but this can no longer be the case. Historical criticism in its many manifestations (e.g. form, source, redaction) demonstrates that a text does not have a single meaning, but levels of meaning, and has reminded us of pre-critical exegesis (Anderson 1982: 348-50). Biblical interpretation is part of a history of interpretation (including the pre-critical) and commentators need to be aware of the history of interpretation (*Auslegungsgeschichte*) and the history of the impact that the text makes on later generations using the text (*Wirkungsgeschichte*) (Anderson 1982: 345, 348-50; Coggins 1993: 172-73; Greenburg 1990: 33-36; Keller 1995: 168-69).

> A commentary that aims to represent the nature and stature of any classical work must describe not only how the work came into being and its significance for its original milieu, but how it interacted with subsequent milieux through the witness of later readings. How, in other words, it retained its vitality and meaningfulness through its conversation with the ages. Only by undertaking such a task can a commentary have a chance to become one more bridge between the foundation text and the generations whose identity was shaped by it (Greenburg 1990: 36).

To use the history of interpretation is to recognize that interpreters are not only part of a current faith community, but also the communities that preceded them in the faith. These communities determined the canon and their interpretation has influenced the interpreter through authoritative traditions.

> The history of interpretation of the canonical text is very significant for an exegete who is committed to that text as canonical. In such a situation the history of the text can be considered to be a part or aspect of the text itself.

> For the text as canonical is not simply the 'original' text in the exact same form in which it was first written, but rather the text as it existed at the time the community accepted it as canonical, and as it has existed ever since. By reason of its history the text has become multiform, through copying, translating, exegeting. The 'canonical' interpreter associates himself not only with the present-day community (whose canon-designating authority he accepts), but with that community throughout its history. Thus his concern for the meaning of the text includes concern for the history of the text and its interpretation (Leahy 1978: 27).

Socio-rhetorical criticism fully recognizes the role of the history of interpretation. The history of interpretation is understood to be an essential part of the analysis of the ideological texture of the text. The history of interpretation has made an important contribution to the ideology of commentators, the authoritative traditions with which they identify, and the modes of intellectual discourse that they privilege in interpretation. To take ideology seriously in interpretation, as socio-rhetorical criticism does, the history of interpretation is crucial. This history helps explain what aspects of the text are privileged or reinscribed in interpretation and what aspects of the text are ignored by commentators and their ideologies.

d. *Acknowledge the Role of Faith and Ideology*
Another criticism of commentary writing is that commentators often are not explicit about the assumptions, intentions, and methods that govern their commentaries. Commentary writing is governed by the trends in interpretation, exegesis, and theology of the era of their composition (Houlden 1990: 129-31). There is a call to know the 'orientation and stance of the commentator' (Shepherd 1978: 2; cf. Deist 1997; Edwards 1995: 67; Krentz 1982: 379). 'Almost every feature of every commentary will be value-laden' (Coggins 1993: 166). K. Froehlich writes that it would be helpful 'to focus not on scholarly hermeneutics as such but on the scholars who formulate its theories, not on interpretation but on the interpreters to whose professional work the exegetical consumer looks for guidance'. He calls for a 'sociology of professional exegesis'—an investigation of the sociological setting in which biblical interpreters are writing (1981: 144; cf. Anderson 1982: 347).

One distinction among commentators is whether or not they are attempting to write the commentary with purely historical interests or from the perspective of the Christian faith. This dichotomy is somewhat artificial as R. Coggins rightly remarks about commentary writing: 'I am skeptical as to whether faith, in that sense, has ever left this process'

(1993: 170). He points out that the accepted ideologies which dominate both the Old and New Testaments have shaped our agenda as commentators (1993: 168-69). Houlden remarks that a commentary would be more theologically significant if it took 'an approach which abandons the uncommitted neutrality of the historian and reintroduces faith into the process of apprehending the text' (1990: 131).

Socio-rhetorical criticism encourages commentators to be explicit about their social and cultural identity, and individual and group location and ideology. It is from within this identity and location that interpreters read the text and this makes a commentary a rhetorical move, an expression of argumentation. As G. Wenham says about commentary writing, 'So having argued that presuppositions do make a difference to the ultimate product, I am duty bound to admit my own!' (1990: 9). In addition, socio-rhetorical criticism encourages commentators to make known what methodologies and streams of authoritative tradition they will be using since these also have their own ideologies. The interpretations of the commentators will be an extension of the threads of methods and tradition with which the commentators weave their own contributions. This emphasis in socio-rhetorical criticism on ideological disclosure answers another critique of commentary writing that commentators do not make explicit the disciplines they employ or the theological tradition (or lack thereof) out of which they work.

> In any commentary the commentator's choice of what information to include and of what texts or passages to comment upon is guided by his [and her] interpretation of the work. Since that is usually the case, a commentary really ought to begin with an exposition of the interpretation and of the principles of the disciplines being employed, and ought to present each 'fact' generated by each discipline in such a way as to make the *issues* in the interpretation clear (Conley 1978: 8).

The commentator, the methods and modes of intellectual discourse chosen for the commentary, and the traditions out of which the commentary is written all have their own ideologies. Ideology is responsible for some elements being emphasized or reinscribed and some being ignored in interpretation. Commentary discourse needs to be analyzed with the same tools as the ancient texts they seek to analyze.

> Ancient texts are richly textured environments of analysis and interpretation. Twentieth-century commentaries on these texts adopt various locations in various twentieth-century modes of intellectual discourse. From these locations, twentieth-century commentary discourse re-enacts highly

different aspects of ancient texts… This means that rhetorical critics need to analyze commentary discourse with the same range of resources with which they analyze and interpret ancient texts or texts in any era (Robbins 1997a: 47-48).

e. *Incorporate Theology and Ethics*

One critique of commentary writing stands above all else—the failure to provide theological and ethical dimensions (Fee 1989–90: 389-90; Fretheim 1982: 358; Keck 1994: 2-3; Keller 1995: 169). Commentaries often provide no theological reflection at all or do not move beyond a summation of the exegesis into true theological reflection. In his review of the Word Biblical Commentary series, G. Knoppers states,

> Theological reflection can take many forms and one can only wonder why commentators did not pursue the diverse possibilities. Why is there no more discussion of the theological meaning of a passage, and allusions in that passage to other texts, the citation of that passage in the New Testament, the relevance of the text for religious experience, or a discussion of how the pericope has been used both in Judaism and in the history of the church? (1990: 23).

It is the last point of the contextualization of theology by the faith communities of the Bible that underscores the reasoning that commentaries must be theological (and in fact cannot help but be). Fretheim makes the very crucial point about theology that 'it remains of critical importance to recognize that even then *the theological material is contextual*, forever tied to the experience of specific communities of faith. In any case, theological reflection ought never be an "add-on" or second step to other aspects of exegetical work' (1982: 364). Pheme Perkins makes a similar point about ethics—the commentator needs to ask about the social and communal implications of texts in light of their original social world (1989–90: 394).

In recent times, the Interpreter's Bible perpetuated this bifurcation between commentary and theology-ethics by placing the exegesis and exposition in separate sections and assigning the writing of them to different scholars for the same biblical book. The conviction now is, in league with the adoption of the German practice of combining exegesis with theological inquiry, that commentary and theology-ethics need to be seen as parts of a single venture. The New Interpreter's Bible corrects this bifurcation by assigning exegesis and theological reflection to the same commentator (Keck 1994: 2-3; Keller 1995: 166).

It is to this issue that socio-rhetorical criticism can make a significant contribution. Answering Knopper's critique above, socio-rhetorical critic-ism explores the diverse possibilities for theology. It discusses the sacred meaning of the text, allusions to other texts, citation within the canon if any, and the relevance of the text for the religious experience of different Christian communities as the pericope was used in the history of the Church in different social and cultural locations (cf. Robbins 1996c: 10-11). Commentators will be interdisciplinary in the very use of socio-rhetorical criticism and one of the textures that it examines is the sacred texture which examines the relation of humanity to the divine in the text. The result can be a theology and ethics that are truly contextual. It is a theology and ethics derived from the dialogue between the linguistic, historical, social, cultural, ideological, and theological phenomena of the text which are the material, means, and mode of its production: a dialogue involving commentators and the linguistic, historical, social, cultural, ideological, and theological phenomena they bring to the text.

Regarding theology, this theology would be biblical theology since it involves a careful reading of the biblical text, yet no theology is derived from the Bible without the help of theological and ethical training that the commentator brings to the interpretation. Theology derived from socio-rhetorical criticism is not biblical theology or systematic theology, yet it is derived from the biblical text and informed by systematic theology. It is also informed by social, cultural, and ideological study. This theology is the result of a dialogue with a multitude of disciplines. Socio-rhetorical commentary can be a rich theological and ethical commentary.

3. Constructing a Socio-Rhetorical Commentary

As discussed in the first part of this paper, a socio-rhetorical commentary cannot have the luxury of adopting only one method of approach. Rather, it compounds the problem of using multiple methods in commentary writing. It is too rich to be impoverished by the commentary genre in its current form. As S. Moore remarks, one problem in designing a comment-ary series is 'taming possibilities: definition, delimitation, organization' (1987: 30). This is certainly true of socio-rhetorical commentary. This third part of the paper offers some preliminary ideas on how a socio-rhetorical commentary is distinctive from other commentaries and the format that such a commentary might adopt. Let me stress that these thoughts are preliminary and are likely to change in the process of writing a socio-rhetorical commentary and as socio-rhetorical criticism continues to develop.

a. *The Typical Contents and Format of a Commentary*
It is generally agreed that a commentary should provide a detailed introduction dealing with the issues of authorship, date, provenance, purpose, content, use of sources, influence, and manuscripts and editions of the text; place the text in its historical and literary context; offer textual, grammatical, syntactical, lexical, and philological notes; provide a translation; give a readable commentary without technical jargon; divide the text into sections and provide subtitles for each section; compare each section with other scripture, as well as antecedent and contemporary literature; demonstrate the plan of the text and how it unfolds at the verse and paragraph levels, as well as how each verse and paragraph relates to the overall plan of the book; clarify ambiguities of social, cultural, political, and religious conventions and structures; locate the original author and readers in space and time within the early Church and the world of their day; draw the reader into the context of the text; interact with scholarship; illumine the theology or the relevance of the text for doctrine and practice; contain addenda to discuss special topics; and provide a bibliography and indices (Fee 1989–90: 389; Houlden 1990: 131; Krentz 1982: 374-77; Shepherd 1978: 1; Wenham 1990: 2-7).

Since it is working with all the usual disciplines and methodologies of New Testament studies, socio-rhetorical commentary can provide all these elements. It is my purpose to demonstrate throughout this section how socio-rhetorical commentary will provide these elements. Here I will affirm that socio-rhetorical commentary will reconfigure these elements, looking at them from different perspectives, placing them in different relationships to one another and to other disciplines, and in many cases will provide these elements more fully than traditional commentaries. For a glimpse of the promise of socio-rhetorical criticism for interpretation, see the few existing studies using this criticism in both its more formative and more recent stages: Robbins 1987, 1991, 1992a, 1992b, 1992d, 1994b, 1994d; Hester 1992; Webber 1992; Wachob 1993; Blount 1994; Huie-Jolly 1994, 1997; Sisson 1994; Czachesz 1995.

We begin our investigation with the question, 'What makes a socio-rhetorical commentary distinctive?' The answer lies in part in its distinctions from historical, literary, and social-scientific interpretation. Historical-critical methods view the text as a document and source of data, while socio-rhetorical criticism views the text as a work, a social-cultural-ideological construct, an act of communication with many contexts. The former sees its mission as explanation, while the latter sees it as interpretation, as setting up multiple readings and rereadings. Like socio-rhetorical criticism, literary criticism sees the text as a construct, as an act of communication. However, sometimes it perceives the text as a creation of the author which generates a world of the text that has no reliable relation to the socio-cultural-ideological world outside the text. Literary criticism is not interested in the environment of the implied author, whereas socio-rhetorical criticism argues that the implied author is situated in a social system and we need to explore that system. Social-scientific interpretation emphasizes that meaning comes with social systems and the goal is to present the interpreter with the social system out of which the meaning of the text came. Texts are not world producing, but rather it is interpreters who produce their own world of reality as they interpret a text. Socio-rhetorical criticism assumes that texts produce meaning and meaning is produced by the social system out of which the text and interpreter come (Robbins 1994d: 164-65; 1995b; Seminar 1997).

Socio-rhetorical criticism investigates Christianity as a cultural pheno-menon. It treats canonical texts as ideological constructs and explores the relation of texts to society and culture. It understands that 'language itself is a rich and thickly configured historical, social, cultural and ideological phenomenon' (Robbins 1996c: 2). An interpreter can move from the literary and rhetorical features into a social and cultural interpretation of the discourse of a New Testament text within the context of the first-century Mediterranean world and back again. The interpreter can move from text to society and culture and from society and culture to texts. Overall,

> Socio-rhetorical interpretation is 'interactionist'. It places 'social explana-tion' in an interactional relation to 'textual understanding' (hermeneutical interpretation). The goal is to create a level playing field between 'under-standing' literature and 'explaining' social systems with a presupposition that both social systems and texts are 'contexts from which meaning comes' (Seminar 1997).

The primary difficulty one immediately faces in writing any comment-ary is determining the overall format to be adopted. This difficulty is amplified by an interactionist commentary like socio-rhetorical comment-ary. One highly praised format belongs to the Word Biblical Commentary: bibliography, translation, notes, form/structure/ setting, comment, and explanation. However, this and many other current formats that are structured with combinations of these elements will not suffice for socio-rhetorical commentary. These formats are compartmentalized and conducive to commentaries in the 'information retrieval' mode. However, they are not conducive to commentaries in the interactionist mode like a socio-rhetorical commentary that encourages dialogue between methodologies used and textures explored. The following is a proposal for an interactionist, distinctively socio-rhetorical commentary.

b. *Introduction*

A socio-rhetorical commentary is interested in placing a New Testament book in its Jewish and Greco-Roman Mediterranean context and thus will still have to address the traditional introductory issues. There is still a place for the typical issues of commentary introduction: authorship, date, provenance, purpose, content, use of sources, influence, and manuscripts and editions of the text. However, discussion of these issues will be reconfigured by socio-rhetorical criticism. I suggest that the main content of the introduction of a socio-rhetorical commentary will be five sections devoted to the textures examined by the method: inner texture, intertexture, social and cultural texture, ideological texture, and sacred texture. For the sake of continuity these textures should be discussed as they pertain to the entire New Testament book under consideration. These five introductory sections would not give every detail of the analysis of each texture, but a thorough summary of the textures as determined by the interpretation of the entire book. These summaries would serve as an informed guide for the discussion of the texture within each section of the body of the commentary. They would serve as reference points, preventing the interpreter from having to discuss a texture in detail for each section examined. Virtually all the traditional introductory issues would be addressed by such an introduction, as well as a few more. Let me illustrate what an introduction to a socio-rhetorical commentary in five sections might look like and how it would address topics typically found in the introduction of a commentary.

1. *Inner Texture.* 'Inner texture concerns relationships among word-phrase and narrational patterns that produce argumentative and aesthetic patterns in texts. These intermingling patterns are the context for the "networks of signification" in a text' (Robbins 1996c: 46; cf. Robbins 1996b: 7). 'The purpose of this analysis is to gain an intimate knowledge of words, word patterns, voices, structures, devices, and modes in the text, which are the context for meanings and meaning-effects that an interpreter analyzes with the other readings of the text' (Robbins 1996b: 7). The discussion of inner

texture would replace the introductory discussions of structure and style. It would provide a fuller analysis of each because socio-rhetorical criticism uses rhetorical theory for its principle of organization and application. It recognizes that speaker, speech, and audience are the constituents of a communication situation. This fuller analysis includes discussion of the repetitive, progressive, opening-middle-closing, narrational, argument-ative, and sensory-aesthetic textures (Robbins 1994d: 171-79; 1996b: 7-39; 1996c: 44-95; 1997a: 32-41 on argumentation).[2] Virtually any method that reveals structure and style can be employed to discuss inner texture, including the more commonly used and related disciplines of epistolary analysis, rhetorical analysis, and discourse analysis. Discipline(s) chosen would be determined by such factors as expertise of the commentator, genre of the biblical book in question, and ultimate aim of the commentary.

This rich approach to the inner texture of a text will have implications for the analysis of other textures (and their analysis in turn will impact the analysis of inner texture). For example, study of the argumentative texture of the New Testament books uncovers their social and cultural presup-positions and networks of reasoning that reveal their participation in Mediterranean society and culture (Robbins 1996c: 64). This is an impor-tant starting point for the analysis of the social and cultural and ideological textures.

2. *Intertexture*

> Intertexture is a text's representation of, reference to, and use of phenomena in the 'world' outside the text being interpreted. In other words, the inter-texture of a text is the interaction of the language in the text with 'outside' material and physical 'objects', historical events, texts, customs, values, roles, institutions, and systems (Robbins 1996b: 40; cf. 1992b: 1161; 1996c: 96).

2. In *Exploring* six types of inner textures are sequenced as repetitive, progressive, narrational, open-middle-closing, argumentative, and sensory-aesthetic (Robbins 1996b: 7-8). In *Tapestry* five inner textures are sequenced as repetitive-progressive, opening-middle-closing, narrational, argumentative, and aesthetic (Robbins 1996c: 53). The latter sequence seems to work better for presentation because the last three textures are more complicated than the preceding two and follow more naturally after them. Also, the separation of the repetitive-progressive texture in the former sequence seems prudent. Thus I would argue for six inner textures arranged as repetitive, pro-gressive, opening-middle-closing, narrational, argumentative, and sensory-aesthetic.

'A major goal of intertextual analysis is to ascertain the nature and result of processes of configuration and reconfiguration of phenomena in the world outside the text' (Robbins 1996b: 40; cf. 1996c: 96-97). The discussion of intertexture would replace the typical listing of sources used by the author of a biblical book with a vastly richer discussion of sources, both written and oral, using the oral-scribal, cultural, social, and historical intertextures (Robbins 1992b; 1994d: 179-85; 1996b: 40-70; 1996c: 96-143).

Often commentary introductions simply list the sources that were used in composing the text. These sources are usually written sources and drawn from the Old Testament and Old Testament Apocrypha or Pseudepigrapha. *Oral-scribal intertexture* also determines sources used, but looks at oral as well as written sources, canonical as well as non-canonical, Jewish as well as Greco-Roman. In addition it examines how these sources were utilized, whether by recitation, recontextualization, reconfiguration, narrative amplification, or thematic elaboration (Robbins 1992b: 1161-63; 1994c: 81-88; 1996b: 40-58; 1996c: 97-108; 1997b). It advances typical commentary writing by broadening the focus of intertextural study from canonical (Old Testament) and Jewish sources to include non-canonical and Greco-Roman sources. This widening of the sources analyzed in intertextual study avoids the risk of treating the New Testament as if it were unique in Mediterranean society from which it sprang (Robbins 1992b: 1163). Also, examining how these texts were used is important for the social and cultural and ideological textures.

Cultural intertexture is a text's interaction with culture through direct reference or allusion and echo, to word and concept patterns, values and codes, and myths (Robbins 1996b: 58-62; 1996c: 108-15). Examination of this interaction with culture helps to determine the self-understanding and stance toward culture reflected in the text—whether affirming, challenging, reconfiguring, etc. Often material usually associated with cultural intertexture is partially discussed in the introduction of a commentary in a section on historical or cultural background, as well as piecemeal within the commentary when such background must be given to illumine the text. However, it usually does not receive a systematic presentation or illumine how the text interacts with culture and positions itself toward it. In addition, socio-rhetorical criticism does not limit the exploration of cultural connections to solely Jewish or perhaps Greco-Roman, but broadens it to include both.

Social intertexture concerns social knowledge.

> Social knowledge is commonly held by all persons of a region, no matter
> what their particular 'cultural location' may be... In other words, social
> knowledge is readily accessible to all people through general interaction, in
> contrast to cultural knowledge, which must be taught with careful use of
> language and transmission of specific traditions (Robbins 1996b: 62).

Social knowledge includes social roles, social institutions, social codes,
and social relationships (Robbins 1996b: 62-63; 1996c: 115-18). The
meanings of these are investigated by texts, inscriptions, archaeological
data, etc. Like cultural intertexture, social intertexture does not often
receive systematic treatment, but only occasional discussion when a commentator assumes that a social facet of a text needs explanation. Systematic analysis would enhance the typical introductory discussion of the
relationship between author and audience, why a particular argumentative
approach was chosen, and the dynamics of the occasion and purpose of the
biblical book involved.

Historical intertexture concerns events that have occurred at specific
times and locations. Knowledge of the social, cultural, and ideological
phenomenon within an event is needed to interpret the event (Robbins
1996b: 63-68; 1996c: 118-20). This material is already typically gathered
in the introductory discussion of the occasion and purpose of a biblical
text (e.g. events leading to the conflict at Corinth).

3. *Social and Cultural Texture*. The social and cultural texture of a text is
discovered by using sociology and anthropology to explore the nature of
the social and cultural voices in the text. The issue for this texture is the
social and cultural nature of a text as a text. This texture explores the
social and cultural location of the language of the text and the social and
cultural world the language creates (Robbins 1994d: 185-94; 1996b: 71-
72; 1996c: 144-47). According to Robbins, the social and cultural texture
of the text emerges by exploring its use of specific social topics, common
social and cultural topics, and final cultural categories. The *specific social
topics* pertain to the religious posture or social response of the text to the
world which it hopes to evoke in its audience.

> Specific social topics in the text exhibit resources for changing people or
> social practices, for destroying and re-creating social order, for withdrawing
> from present society to create one's own social world, or for coping with
> the world by transforming one's own perceptions of it (Robbins 1996b: 3).

Adapting Bryan Wilson's typology of sects, Robbins identifies specific
social topics as conversionist, revolutionist, introversionist, gnostic-

manipulationist, thaumaturgical, reformist, and utopian (Robbins 1993; 1994a; 1994d: 185-94; 1996b: 72-75; 1996c: 147-59; cf. 1991).

Common social and cultural topics pertain to the perception of the text of the way that people live in the world. They pertain to 'the range of customary practices, central values, modes of relationship and exchange, perceptions about resources for life and well-being, and presuppositions about purity and taboo the text embodies' (Robbins 1996b: 3). They provide the environment for the specific social topics. According to Robbins and others studying the social and cultural systems and institutions of the first-century Mediterranean world, common social and cultural topics include honor–guilt, dyadic and individualist personalities, dyadic and legal contracts and agreements, challenge–response (riposte); agriculturally based, industrial, and technological economic exchange systems; peasants, laborers, craftspeople, and entrepreneurs; limited, insufficient, and overabundant goods; and purity codes (Robbins 1996b: 75-86; 1996c: 159-66).

Final cultural categories exhibit the values emphasized in the text and the priority among them. They are negotiated priorities usually found in the presuppositions and arguments in the text, and include such topics as what is lawful, holy, true, and necessary. These priorities indicate the cultural location of the text and its orientation to other cultures since these priorities are negotiated differently by different cultures. Robbins identifies the following types of cultural rhetoric that emerge from the use of final cultural categories: dominant culture, subculture, counterculture or alternative culture, contraculture or oppositional culture, and liminal culture (Robbins 1996b: 86-89; 1996c: 167-74).

A systematic discussion of the social and cultural texture would be a welcomed addition to the usual commentary introduction. Often a commentary contains information on aspects of the social and cultural texture of a text, but it is scattered throughout the commentary wherever it illumines the text through explanation of unknown or obscure social and cultural beliefs and practices. Socio-rhetorical criticism goes further by placing the text in its social and cultural location in the first-century Mediterranean world. Social and cultural data are not used simply to explain textual background, but to illumine the religious posture and social response to the world that the text is seeking from the audience, the text's perception of how people live in the world, or the values and priority of values that the text is presupposing or promoting. It moves beyond explaining the text from the perspective of the first-century Mediterranean to placing the text in its first-century Mediterranean world. By so locating the text, socio-rhetorical commentary is better able to avoid anachronistic and ethno-centric interpretation that arises when commentators impose their modern social and cultural values on the biblical text. Also, a socio-rhetorical commentary will be naturally forced to contribute to the construction of the history of early Christianity as it works to determine the text's and its community's social response to the world, its perception of how people live in the world, and its social and cultural location in first-century Mediterranean society (Robbins 1992c; 1997a: 41-42).

4. *Ideological Texture*. Ideology is 'an integrated system of beliefs, assumptions and values, not necessarily true or false, which reflects the needs and interests of a group or class at a particular time in history' (Robbins 1995a: 143, quoting Davis 1975: 14).

> This integrated system proceeds from the need to understand, to interpret to self and others, to justify, and to control one's place in the world. Ideologies are shaped by specific views of reality shared by groups—specific perspectives on the world, society, and humanity, and on the limitations and potentialities of human existence (Robbins 1995a: 143).

'Ideological texture concerns the way the text itself and interpreters of the text position themselves in relation to other individuals and groups' (Robbins 1996b: 4). For Robbins, 'the spectrum of ideology for socio-rhetorical criticism occurs in four special locations: (a) in texts; (b) in authoritative traditions of interpretation; (c) in intellectual discourse; and (d) in individuals and groups' (1996c: 193; see 1994d: 195-99; 1995a: 143-45; 1996b: 95-119; 1996c: 192-236; 1997a: 42-48).[3] Regarding *ideology in texts* 'the task is to explore the manner in which the discourse of a text presents comprehensive patterns of cognitive and moral beliefs about humans, society and the universe that are intended to function in the social order. The investigation especially seeks to identify the intersection of ideas, ideals and social action and to detect the collective needs and interests the patterns represent' (Robbins 1996c: 193). Three ways to analyze the ideology of the texture of the text are through analyzing the social and cultural location of the implied author through social and cultural data built into the language of the text, analyzing the ideology of

---

3.   *Exploring* does not discuss ideology in authoritative traditions of interpretation and splits the discussion of ideology in individuals and groups into two separate categories.

power in the text, and analyzing the ideology in the mode of intellectual discourse in the text (Robbins 1996b: 110-15; 1996c: 193-99).

Regarding *ideology in authoritative traditions of interpretation*, interpreters need to be aware that discourse generates a world of meaning and symbolic universes and thus has power. The interpreter may be working from the perspective of western or eastern Christianity, Protestant or Catholic, and a host of other major authoritative traditions (Robbins 1996c: 200-207). Regarding *modes of intellectual discourse*, every form of intellectual discourse has its own ideology. We need to identify our mode of intellectual discourse because discourse is a social production from a particular ideology. 'Ideological interpretation features an interplay between the selection of a particular ideology to enact intellectual dimensions evoked by the biblical text and the selection of particular intellectual modes of discourse to enact the ideological dimensions of the interpretation' (Robbins 1996c: 214, see 207-15; 1996b: 105-10).

Regarding *ideology in individuals and groups*, ideological texture concerns primarily the social, cultural, and individual location and perspective of the writers and readers of a text and the groups with which they are associated (Robbins 1996b: 96-105; 1996c: 215-20). It 'concerns the biases, opinions, preferences, and stereotypes of a particular writer and a particular reader' (Robbins 1996b: 95). Individual location is important to assess because, 'Only if you have significant insight into the ideological texture of your own presuppositions, dispositions, and values will you be able to analyze the ideological texture both of other people's interpretations of a text and of a text that is the mutual interest of you and another person who has interpreted it' (Robbins 1996b: 96). Individual location can be determined in part by using the special social topics and final cultural categories used in determining social and cultural texture, and by the individual's relation to groups. Borrowing from Boissevain, Robbins suggests determining how individuals are related to one or more groups by the classifications of clique, gang, action set, faction, corporate group, historic tradition, and multiple historic traditions (1996b: 100-105).

The ideological texture is not typically discussed by the historical-critical methods and thus is an addition to the typical commentary using those methods, but it is an addition that those calling for change in the commentary genre have requested. Commentators need to begin their commentaries with a preface placing themselves in their ideological location. Interpreters will identify their ideology, the groups to which they belong and whose values and perspectives they hold, and the ideology of the authoritative traditions they respect and the modes of intellectual discourse they use. Ordinarily the ideological background of a commentary can only be gleaned subjectively from the assumptions and approach of the commentary, or the nature of the institution of the author or the publisher. Commentators aware of their own ideologies and the ideologies of their methodologies and traditions are more aware of what aspects of the text they are privileging and what aspects they are ignoring. They are more aware of what other commentators with different ideologies may find in the text that can enter into their own interpretation. Commentators can overcome a fallacy of historical-critical methods—the claim that they are above ideology because they are working with factual data. In the interpretation of what those data mean, ideology comes into play (Robbins 1995a: 128).

Examination of the ideological texture of the text itself will bring into focus the comprehensive patterns of beliefs that it is affirming to its readers and the collective interests that these patterns indicate for the author and community affirming these patterns. The typical concern of the introduction about authorship can be expanded as the social and cultural location of the implied author can be surmised through the social and cultural data that this author has built into the text. Such language includes references to previous events, natural environment and resources, population structure, technology, socialization and personality, culture, foreign affairs, belief systems and ideologies, and the political-military-legal system (Robbins 1996b: 111-13). Overall, examination of the ideological texture of a text will add to our knowledge of the text itself and its place in early Christianity.

5. *Sacred Texture.* The sacred texture is the way the text speaks about God or the gods and religious life, the relation of humans to the divine. Robbins suggests the following categories to guide an investigation of the sacred aspects of a text, regardless of religion: deity, holy person, spirit being, divine history, human redemption, human commitment, religious community, and ethics. These are often embedded in the inner, inter-, social and cultural, and ideological textures (Robbins 1996b: 120-31; 1996c: 10-11).

A systematic analysis of sacred texture can replace the brief theological points usually made in the introduction of a commentary. Exploration of sacred texture has the potential to restore theology to commentary writing. It will derive the theology of the text from what the text says about God and religious life. In other words, theology would be contextual—what the text assumes about the sacred. Categories of systematic theology are not imposed, but theological assumptions and statements are gathered under the categories applicable to all religions. The interpreter is still free to use the categories of systematic theology if more applicable to his or her ideology. In any case, returning theology to commentary writing is a major advance and a distinctive of socio-rhetorical commentary.

Study of sacred texture also allows the commentator to address current concerns to bridge the Christian faith and other faiths through the analysis of commonalities among the texture of sacred texts. Currently commentaries are unable or unwilling to add this dialogue with other religions. Socio-rhetorical commentary hopes to change this situation.

> A major goal in the coming years must be to introduce a method of analysis that encourages people of faith to compare their own sacred texts with other people's sacred texts and to dialogue peaceably with other people about their beliefs. Any method that does not do this will be a highly deficient form of analysis and interpretation during the third millennium of our Western calendar (Robbins 1995a: 125).

As we have seen, the introduction to the socio-rhetorical commentary will address the more traditional introductory issues, but within the new context of the five textures and in many cases more fully than the traditional commentary. Also, these introductory issues are often discussed within the attempt to demonstrate the text's social, cultural, and ideological location—a very important addition of socio-rhetorical commentary to the commentary genre.

c. *The Body of the Commentary*
The body of the commentary will provide the exegetical detail that supports the summary discussions of the five textures in the introduction. To write the body of the commentary using socio-rhetorical analysis poses a great challenge due to its rich, interactionist nature, yet also offers the greatest possibilities for truly creative work. The following are some preliminary thoughts on the direction this creative work might take.

1. *Structure and Titles.* Almost all the literature on commentary writing agrees that the body of the commentary needs to be a verse-by-verse, section-by-section analysis. By its more integrative nature, both within the analysis of each texture and as a whole, socio-rhetorical commentary does not lend itself to a verse-by-verse analysis. Rather a section-by-section

analysis seems warranted. It might seem most natural to determine these sections according to inner textual analysis. However, this approach would not move beyond the format of current commentaries that embed social and cultural data within the structure as determined by various methods that are also used in socio-rhetorical criticism (e.g. epistolary, rhetorical, topical). Using inner texture to structure the text is to look at it purely for structure rather than for what it tells us about the social, cultural, and ideological textures. For example, an elaborated argument may be made a section of the text without any effort made to see what the assumed or unassumed premises of the argument say about the social and cultural texture. A major contribution and distinction of socio-rhetorical comment- ary may be to structure a commentary according to the interplay of the textures studied. Socio-rhetorical commentary can be structured by explor- ing social, cultural, and ideological textures prior to exploring the inner texture and intertexture. In this way the social, cultural, and ideological aspects of the text are not embedded in the structural study of the text as determined by inner texture and intertexture. Rather the inner texture and intertexture are explored for their contribution to the social, cultural, and ideological textures of the text and what clues they give to the social, cultural, and ideological location of the text (Seminar 1997).

Sectional titles and subtitles can be derived from each of the textures. It may be well to highlight a title derived from the dominant texture as the main heading to each section, but follow it in parentheses by titles derived from other textures in a fashion that reflects the way the section has uti- lized the textures. For example, a title for Phil. 1.3-11 could be 'Thanks- giving for Participation in an Alternative Culture of Righteousness' and the title for Phil. 1.12-30 could be 'The Imprisoned Hero Elicits Allegiance' (Seminar 1997).

2. *Approaches to Analysis*. As indicated above, within each section the commentator can examine each of the five textures, but not necessarily in some mechanical way so that each section is analyzed with all the textures beginning with inner texture and ending with sacred texture. The starting point in socio-rhetorical criticism is not fixed, but depends upon many factors. Several different starting points and their justification come to mind, and these are not necessary mutually exclusive.

One approach is to let the discussion of each section be guided by the analysis of the texture(s) that dominates the section. Commentators can weave the analysis of the other textures into the discussion guided by the dominant texture. For example, in one section the social and cultural texture may be dominant and the argumentation of the inner texture may be best discussed within the context of social and cultural conventions. This approach will avoid the very real pitfall of merely amassing information pertaining to each texture without allowing the different textures to dialogue with one another.

Another related approach is for commentators to begin with the texture that is the most comfortable for them due to their training or interest and discuss the other textures from that context. This approach recognizes that commentators come to the text with different ideological locations, academic training, and authoritative traditions. For example, a commentator interested in theological implications of the text may begin with sacred texture and work from there.

Yet another approach is for commentators to offer multiple readings of each texture, although this approach will probably prove to be impractical. An alternative would be for commentators to tie other readings into their own that are the natural extensions of their reading which give others a way to relate to the text and begin their own reading (Seminar 1998). This would be a natural extension of the program of socio-rhetorical criticism in offering multiple readings and strategies for reading. Socio-rhetorical commentators will be creating their own reading, but can also be indicating where other readings can begin or what readings may be fruitful to pursue.

It is important to note that socio-rhetorical commentators will be creating their own approach or reading(s) within the confines of socio-rhetorical criticism. These commentators must make their approach clear. Their commentaries will not be comprehensive since, like any other commentary, they are offering a reading or multiple readings out of many possible readings.

3. *Particulars.* The ideological texture, the new addition to the commentary genre in socio-rhetorical commentary, provides a new context for some of the more traditional subjects of commentary writing. With the interest in ideology and the history of interpretation within socio-rhetorical criticism, text-critical matters and the streams of tradition generated by different textual readings can receive more discussion than in current commentaries. Debates among scholars within the history of interpretation and authoritative traditions (which in turn affect the commentator) can be discussed as part of the ideological texture. Thus through the ideological

texture, textual criticism and scholarly debates are brought into the dialogue among textures rather than being relegated to notes or sections with little connection to the remainder of the discussion.

Socio-rhetorical commentary offers an alternative to the more literal translation traditionally provided by the commentary. In light of its interactionist nature and the wealth of connections that it uncovers between the five textures that it analyzes, an amplified translation that brings out some of these connections seems most fitting. The translation becomes a summary of the reading of the text that the commentary is offering.

In conclusion, along with the profusion of new methodologies in New Testament studies as a whole, socio-rhetorical criticism requires changes in the commentary genre. Its interdisciplinary and interactionist nature cannot work within the boundaries of the genre as currently drawn. In the redefinition of the genre, socio-rhetorical criticism offers the opportunity to address previous calls for change in the commentary genre successfully, including eliminating the division of commentaries into academic and popular, making commentaries interdisciplinary, incorporating the history of interpretation, acknowledging the role of faith and ideology, and incorporating theology and ethics. The form that the socio-rhetorical commentary will take, like socio-rhetorical criticism itself, is evolving, but some of the key elements are clear. It will reconfigure the typical discussions of introductory issues and provide a creative dialogue between textures within the body of the commentary. It promises to broaden intertextual analysis to include Greco-Roman sources, bring social and cultural data center stage, and bring ideology into the commentary genre as a major element for the first time.

BIBLIOGRAPHY

Anderson, B.W.
    1982   'The Problem and Promise of Commentary', *Int* 36: 341-54.
Boissevain, J.
    1974   *Friends of Friends: Networks, Manipulators and Coalitions* (Oxford: Basil Blackwell).
Blount, B.K.
    1994   'A Socio-Rhetorical Analysis of Simon of Cyrene: Mark 15.21 and Its Parallels', *Semeia* 64: 171-98.
Brown, M.
    1978   'The Commentary in Biblical Hermeneutics', in Hobbs 1978: 10-13.
Bruner, F.D.
    1989–90   'The Why and How of Commentary', *TTod* 46: 399-404.

Coggins, R.J.
1993   'A Future for the Commentary?', in F. Watson (ed.), *The Open Text: New Directions for Biblical Studies* (London: SCM Press): 163-75.
Conley, T.
1978   'Of Commentaries, Good and Bad', in Hobbs 1978: 5-9.
Czachesz, I.
1995   'Socio-Rhetorical Exegesis of Acts 9.1-30', *Communio Viatorum* (Prague) 37: 5-32.
Davis, D.
1975   *The Problem of Slavery in the Age of Revolution, 1770–1823* (Ithaca, NY: Cornell University Press).
Deist, F.
1997   'Inside a Commentary: Reflections on the Writing of Bible Commentaries', *Old Testament Essays* 10: 369-86.
Dillon, J.
1978   'Some Thoughts on the Commentary', in Hobbs 1978: 15-18.
Dreyfus, H.L., and P. Rabinow
1983   *Michael Foucault: Beyond Structuralism and Hermeneutics* (Chicago: University of Chicago Press).
Eagleton, T.
1983   *Literary Theory: An Introduction* (Minneapolis: University of Minnesota Press).
Edwards, O.C., Jr
1995   'Review Article: A First Look at *The New Interpreter's Bible*', *Sewanee Theological Review* 39: 65-74.
Fee, G.D.
1989–90   'Reflections on Commentary Writing', *TTod* 46: 386-92.
Fretheim, T.E.G.
1982   'Old Testament Commentaries: Their Selection and Use', *Int* 36: 356-71.
Froehlich, K.
1981   'Biblical Hermeneutics on the Move', *WE* 1: 140-52.
1987   'Bibelkommentare—zur Krise einer Gattung', *ZTK* 84: 465-92.
Gowler, D.B.
1994   'Introduction', in D.B. Gowler (ed.), *New Boundaries in Old Territory: Form and Social Rhetoric in Mark* (Emory Studies in Early Christianity, 3; New York: Peter Lang): 1-36.
Greenberg, M.
1990   'To Whom and for What Should a Bible Commentator Be Responsible?', in D. Assaf (ed.), *Proceedings of the 10th World Congress of Jewish Studies (Jerusalem, 16-24 August, 1989)* (Jerusalem: World Union of Jewish Studies): 29-38.
Hester, J.D.
1992   'Socio-Rhetorical Criticism and the Parable of the Tenants', *JSNT* 45: 27-57.
Hobbs, E.C. (ed.)
1978   *The Commentary Hermeneutically Considered* (Colloquy 31 of the Center for Hermeneutical Studies in Hellenistic and Modern Culture [Berkeley, 11 December 1977]; Berkeley: The Center for Hermeneutical Studies).

Houlden, J.L.
1990 'Commentary (New Testament)', in R.J. Coggins and J.L. Houlden (eds.), *Dictionary of Biblical Interpretation* (London: SCM Press; Philadelphia: Trinity Press International): 129-32.

Huie-Jolly, M.R.
1994 'The Son Enthroned in Conflict: A Socio-Rhetorical Analysis of John 5.17-23' (PhD dissertation, University of Otago, New Zealand).
1997 'Like Father, like Son, Absolute Case, Mythic Authority: Constructing Ideology in John 5.17-23', *Society of Biblical Literature 1997 Seminar Papers* (Atlanta: Scholars Press): 567-95.

Keck, L.E.
1994 'Introduction to the New Interpreter's Bible', in L.E. Keck *et al.* (eds.), *The New Interpreter's Bible* (8 vols.; Abingdon: Nashville, 1994–): I, 1-6.

Keller, J.A., Jr.
1995 'Of Making Many Books There Is No End: The Making of the *New Interpreter's Bible*', *American Theological Library Association: Summary of Proceedings* 49: 165-72.

Kieffer, R.
1976 'Kleinere Beiträge: Was heisst das, einen Text zu kommentieren?', *BZ* 20: 212-16.

Knoppers, G.N.
1990 'Unfinished Business: A Review Article', *Reformed Journal* 40/9: 20-23.

Krentz, E.
1982 'New Testament Commentaries: Their Selection and Use', *Int* 36: 372-81.

Leahy, T.
1978 Remarks from the Discussion within 'Minutes of the Colloquy of 11 December 1977: The Discussion' summarized by Irene Lawrence, in Hobbs 1978: 27.

Lohfink, G.
1974 'Kommentar als Gattung. Rudolf Schanckenburg zum 60. Geburtstag', *BibLeb* 15: 1-16.

Mays, J.L. (ed.)
1982 'Bible Commentaries', *Int* 36: 339-93.

Moore, S.D.
1987 'Narrative Commentary on the Bible: Context, Roots, and Prospects', *FFF* 3/3: 29-62.

Perkins, P.
1989–90 'Commentaries: Windows to the Text', *TTod* 46: 393-98.

Peterson, E.H. (ed.)
1990 'Symposium: On Writing Commentaries', *TTod* 46: 386-410.

Robbins, V.K.
1987 'The Woman who Touched Jesus' Garment: Socio-Rhetorical Analysis of the Synoptic Accounts', *NTS* 33: 502-15.
1991 'Beelzebul Controversy in Mark and Luke: Rhetorical and Social Analysis', *FFF* 7/3-4: 261-77.
1992a *Jesus the Teacher: A Socio-Rhetorical Interpretation of Mark* (Minneapolis: Fortress Press [1984]).

1992b   'The Reversed Contextualization of Psalm 22 in the Markan Crucifixion: A Socio-Rhetorical Analysis', in F. van Segbroeck *et al.* (eds.), *The Four Gospels 1992: Festschrift Frans Neirynck* (BETL, 100; Leuven: Leuven University Press): 1161-83.

1992c   'A Socio-Rhetorical Look at the Work of John Knox on Luke–Acts', in M.C. Parsons and J.B. Tyson (eds.), *Cadbury, Knox, and Talbert: American Contributions to the Study of Acts* (SBLBSNA; Atlanta: Scholars Press): 91-105.

1992d   'Using a Socio-Rhetorical Poetics to Develop a Unified Method: The Woman who Anointed Jesus as a Test Case', in E. Lovering (ed.), *Society of Biblical Literature 1992 Seminar Papers* (Atlanta: Scholars Press): 302-19.

1993   'Rhetoric and Culture: Exploring Types of Cultural Rhetoric in a Text', in S.E. Porter and T.H. Olbricht (eds.), *Rhetoric and the New Testament: Essays from the 1992 Heidelberg Conference* (JSNTSup, 90; Sheffield: Sheffield Academic Press): 443-63.

1994a   'Interpreting Miracle Culture and Parable Culture in Mark 4–11', *SEÅ* 59: 59-81.

1994b   *New Boundaries in Old Territory: Form and Social Rhetoric in Mark* (ed. D.B. Gowler; Emory Studies in Early Christianity, 3; New York: Peter Lang).

1994c   'Oral, Rhetorical, and Literary Cultures: A Response', *Semeia* 65: 75-91.

1994d   'Socio-Rhetorical Criticism: Mary, Elizabeth and the Magnificat as a Test Case', in E.S. Malbon and E.V. McKnight (eds.), *The New Literary Criticism and the New Testament* (JSNTSup, 109; Sheffield: Sheffield Academic Press; Valley Forge, PA: Trinity Press International): 164-209.

1995a   'Divine Dialogue and the Lord's Prayer: Socio-Rhetorical Interpretation of Sacred Texts', *Dialogue: A Journal of Mormon Thought* 28/3: 118-45.

1995b   'Social-Scientific Criticism and Literary Studies: Prospects for Cooperation in Biblical Interpretation', in P.F. Esler (ed.), *Modelling Early Christianity: Social-Scientific Studies of the New Testament in its Context* (London: Routledge): 274-89.

1996a   'The Dialectical Nature of Early Christian Discourse', *Scriptura* 59: 353-62.

1996b   *Exploring the Texture of Texts: A Guide to Socio-Rhetorical Interpretation* (Valley Forge, PA: Trinity Press International).

1996c   *The Tapestry of Early Christian Discourse: Rhetoric, Society and Ideology* (London: Routledge).

1997a   'The Present and Future of Rhetorical Analysis', in S.E. Porter and T.H. Olbricht (eds.), *The Rhetorical Analysis of Scripture: Essays from the 1995 London Conference* (JSNTSup, 146; Sheffield: Sheffield Academic Press): 24-52.

1997b   'Rhetorical Composition and Sources in the Gospel of Thomas', in *SBL 1997 Seminar Papers* (Atlanta: Scholars Press): 86-114.

1998   'Socio-Rhetorical Hermeneutics and Commentary', in J. Mrazek, R. Dvorakova and S.Brodsky (eds.), *EPITOAYTO: Essays in Honour of Petr Pokorný—on his Sixty-Fifth Birthday* (Prague-Trebenice: Mln): 284-97.

Seminar on Socio-Rhetorical Commentary, 22–23 May, 1997

1997   Vernon Robbins, David deSilva, Bernard Combrink and Duane Watson (and Gregory Bloomquist via the internet) met at Ashland Theological Seminary.

Seminar on Socio-Rhetorical Commentary, 16–17 April, 1998

    1998   Vernon Robbins, David deSilva, Gregory Bloomquist, Glenn Holland and Duane Watson met at Pittsburgh Theological Seminary in the context of the Eastern Great Lakes Biblical Society Annual Meeting.

Shepherd, M.H.

    1978   'What Should a Commentary Be or Do?', in Hobbs 1978: 1-4.

Sisson, R.B.

    1994   'The Apostle as Athlete: A Socio-Rhetorical Interpretation of 1 Corinthians 9' (PhD dissertation, Emory University).

Terrien, S.L.

    1951   'The Interpreter's Bible', *USQR* 6 (June): 3-6.

Wachob, W.H.

    1993   '"The Rich in Faith" and "The Poor in Spirit": The Socio-Rhetorical Function of a Saying of Jesus in the Epistle of James' (PhD dissertation, Emory University).

Webber, R.C.

    1992   '"Why Were the Heathen so Arrogant": The Socio-Rhetorical Strategy of Acts 3–4', *BTB* 22: 19-25.

Wenham, G.J.

    1990   'Contemporary Bible Commentary: The Primacy of Exegesis and the Religious Dimension', in D. Assaf (ed.), *Proceedings of the 10th World Congress of Jewish Studies (Jerusalem, 16–24 August, 1989)* (Jerusalem: World Union of Jewish Studies): 1-12.

Wilson, B.

    1969   'A Typology of Sects', in R. Robertson (ed.), *Sociology of Religion* (Baltimore: Penguin Books): 361-83.

Witherington, B.

    1995   *Conflict and Community in Corinth: A Socio-Rhetorical Commentary on 1 and 2 Corinthians* (Grand Rapids: Eerdmans; Carlisle: Paternoster).

    1998   *The Acts of the Apostles: A Socio-Rhetorical Commentary on 1 and 2 Corinthians* (Grand Rapids: Eerdmans; Carlisle: Paternoster).

Part II

R̲HETORICAL C̲RITICISM OF THE O̲LD T̲ESTAMENT

IDENTIFICATION AND THE DISCOURSE OF FUNDAMENTALISM:
REFLECTIONS ON A READING OF THE BOOK OF ESTHER

Gerrie Snyman

1. *Identification and Socialization*

The present quest for an ethics of reading is an honest attempt at socialization within the academic society. By explaining one's reading conduct,
by laying bare those motives that once led a reader to find a particular
appeal in a specific text, people try to overcome divisions in society (cf.
Meadows 1957: 84). An ethics of reading aspires to lay bare those strategies, influences, frameworks, and ideologies that result in a particular
reading. It is a project that specifically originated in those circles where a
particular kind of reading was felt to be oppressive and not open to
differing interpretations. This is especially the case within poor communities, racially oppressed circles and groups where gender is a disempower-
ing factor.

Ethics of reading deals with division in society. To Kenneth Burke,
division in society is the pillar of rhetoric: if there were no division, absolute communication would have been possible and there would not have
been a thing called 'rhetoric'. But since division is part of life, it has to be
overcome. This is where rhetoric and the project of 'ethics of reading'
meet: both deal with ways in which individuals are at odds with one
another. To overcome the 'odds', Burke (1969a) introduced the notion of
'identification'. Identification means to become *consubstantially one* with
something or someone else; it is an acting 'together', having common sensations, common concepts, images, ideas, and attitudes (Burke 1969a: 21).
Identification is an attempt to find a common source for the resolution of
conflicts (Kirk 1961: 415).

As an emerging nation, present-day post-apartheid South Africa surely
struggles to find its own identity. In trying to resolve the conflict of the
past 300 years, the country is in a process of discovering a larger generalization that will encompass both sides of the conflict. It is not easy, and

sometimes we still find ourselves ignoring the other side of the conflict in order to enable us to 'survive'. Surely, only the bravest and the most stupid and insensitive person would proclaim the theological correctness and legitimacy of apartheid. Worldwide apartheid is condemned as a heresy, but it is fascinating that those reading practices with which it was once biblically justified are now very active in condemning apartheid! Already in 1984 the late Willem Vorster, the doyen of New Testament studies in South Africa, claimed there was no difference between apartheid and liberationist readings of the Bible. Both seek to justify political practices within the same hermeneutical frame of mind. Subsequently we face this very odd moment in our history where church officials not only confess their complicity (or rather that of their predecessors) in the biblical justification of apartheid, but also their conversion from this heresy, yet without retracting any of their hermeneutical practices.[1]

No wonder that people ask whether history has not taught us anything.[2] In my opinion, the problem lies in an urge that springs forth from orthodox or fundamentalistic hermeneutical practices to *identify* with situations or characters in the Bible and a complete inability to question the practices, customs and morals emanating from the biblical text. Religious communities with a deep respect for the biblical text as infallible Word of God will find this critical stance impossible. The examples of Esther and Mordecai can be followed, but not that of Haman, despite his correct observation of Jewish 'apartheid' when, in front of King Ahasuerus, he argues that the Jews are separate and follow their own customs (Est. 3.8-9).

The inability to acknowledge the limits of the biblical text, or to realize that it should not be read only as a light on the believer's way, derives from a consumer-orientated approach towards the biblical text by which readers perpetuate the reading practices they were taught in their

---

1. This is the problem one of my colleagues, Izak Spangenberg, expressed at an annual meeting of the Old Testament Society of South Africa. He asked serious questions about the Dutch Reformed Church's view on Scripture (1996). In his mind the DRC had changed front twice in his lifetime: first over apartheid and then over women in the ministry. When reported in the Afrikaans daily newspapers and the Sunday newspaper, his remarks unleashed a flood of criticism. It was as if he had come up against a brick wall of fundamentalism, requesting believers either to imitate the creeds or keep quiet.

2. Pieter Craffert (1998: 76) closes his article on the ethics of an apartheid reading and an ordinary reading amid the poor and oppressed with the following desperate question: 'Have we learned anything from the fallacious practice of the scriptural support for apartheid?'

respective religious communities (cf. Craffert 1998: 76). In this regard, Quentin Skinner (1988: 272) argues that a consumer approach boils down to an abandonment of authorial intention in favour of an explanation of what the text means to people today. In other words, the text is read as if it were written for the readers who are reading it at this very moment. In this approach the otherness of the text is not respected, in order to render the text true according to the current beliefs of the reader (cf. Craffert 1996: 66-68). In Craffert's mind (1998: 76) it boils down to an oracular use of the biblical text.

Strangely, Kenneth Burke (1969a) uses the following terms in his deliberations on rhetoric and identification: *ritual, magic* and *literature for use*. His concern is Milton's poem *Samson Agonistes* where he finds what he calls an *individual identification* in as much as Milton identifies himself with Samson's blindness and problem with his wife (1969a: 4). He also distinguishes a *factional identification* where the references to the Philistines and Israelites are thought to stand respectively for the Royalists who have regained power in England and the Puritans of Cromwell. The effect of this correspondence, according to Burke (1969a: 5), is the following:

> In saying, with fervor, that a blind Biblical hero *did* conquer, the poet is 'substantially' saying that he in his blindness *will* conquer. This is moralistic prophecy, and is thus also a kind of 'literature for use', use at one remove, though of a sort that the technologically-minded would consider the very opposite of use, since it is wholly in the order of ritual and magic.

In Milton's poem, Burke sees an identification between Samson and the poet himself. Samson is an allegory for the life of the poet, and what Samson did, the poet still has to do. In a way, the biblical figure gives the poet or reader of the story a *grip on how to handle life*. Milton does not say that people should behave like Samson, but he uses the story to illustrate how Samson's behaviour can be observed in his world. He sees in Samson a re-enactment of a role that is inadmissible in his own society: Samson can commit suicide, but in Milton's England it is frowned upon.[3]

---

3.   I would rather refrain from evaluating Milton's identification with Samson, because I am not that knowledgable about either Milton, Samson or Burke. Milton's identification of Samson does not serve to persuade the audience to follow the morals or principles emanating from Samson, but rather to question contemporary behaviour in his own society. Perhaps the difference is that Milton is playful in his identification with Samson, leaving his options open. Identification with a biblical text or characters within fundamentalism does not leave any option. Perhaps this is the difference between Milton's use of a biblical figure and a pious believer's use: to the latter there

Burke (1969a: 5) says that the poetic re-enactment of Samson's role could give pretexts for admitting a motive which would have been inadmissible had it not been clothed or complicated.

The problem I want to put on the table is the way readers identify with characters in the Bible. By turning identification into an equation between the reader and the character, the opposition of apartheid readings by liberationist readings remains a storm in a teacup as long as the inherent relationship with fundamentalism is not recognized and addressed. A liberationist reading may have the moral high ground, but ultimately it is subjected to the same dangers which apartheid readings fell prey to: by ignoring the otherness of the ancient biblical text, it can be as oppressive as its counterpart.

Thus, my humble contention is that the rhetorical notion of 'identification' may be helpful in explaining why a new look at South African hermeneutics is extremely necessary. I start the discussion with the situation that triggered my dilemma: a liberationist reading of Esther 9 that condones the liberation struggle completely and vilifies those who did not participate in the struggle. After having described that reading, I will present you with four factors that influence my thinking at the moment and have perhaps provided grounds for what I am about to say. Then I will lay out some theory of identification based on Kenneth Burke's idea of identification that is a cornerstone of his rhetoric, and Hans-Robert Jauss's programme of aesthetic identification that I wish to (ab)use as a counter measure in those instances of what I would call 'equating identification'. Having outlined my understanding of identification, I will proceed with a discussion of the book of Esther with special focus on ch. 9, which has proven problematic in the history of the book's reception. On the basis of the liberationist reading that triggered my thinking and the way the book of Esther seems to operate in some feminist readings, I explain some hermeneutical aspects within fundamentalism that inevitably lead to an equating identification. Because this kind of identification was one of the driving factors behind a biblical sanctioning of a political system, I am compelled to indicate how Afrikaner civil religion justified apartheid on the basis of their identification with the destiny of ancient Israel.

is a religious imperative to consume the text, to the former the text simply addresses an issue that his community struggles with. By referring to the biblical figure, he tries to come to terms with it. He could have used any other text.

2. *The Problem: A Peculiar Reading of Esther 9*

The reason for discussing identification as a rhetorical strategy used to induce a certain behaviour in an audience, is found in a reading of Esther 9 I received from two male theological students training for the ministry. Their reading formed part of an elaborate assignment in which the students were requested to do a narratological exegesis of Esther 9, to reflect on the context of their reception of the narrative and finally to devise a sermon or meditation on this text addressing some kind of problem they had perceived within their community.[4]

The world of production of the first reading was the Northern Province, the poorest province in the country. The audience for whom the student wrote his meditation ranged from adults with only primary education to some with tertiary education. These people could be found in teaching jobs, piece jobs, professionals, politicians, unemployed and pensioners. They were all bound by their fundamentalist view on Scripture. They obeyed and respected authority, they cared for one another, and they strived to make the country a better place to live in. My student wanted to use Esther 9 to address his audience's attitude towards the former struggle for liberation from apartheid and towards the Truth and Reconciliation Commission. He wanted to compare the struggle for freedom with the killing of the Persians by the Jews in Esther 9, seeking an answer to the question of Christian participation in such a struggle.

He answered this question in the affirmative, referring to people such as Desmond Tutu, Beyers Naudé and Trevor Huddleston. He actually

---

4.   I had posed a similar assignment the previous year, with a similar result from a student from the African community. Of the 14-18 students in this course, only 2 were from an indigenous African background. Both presented me with a reading I would call a fundamentalist-liberationist reading. I am not sure whether the 'rhetoric' of the assignment induced the response I received, because a fundamentalist reading was not that common, especially after the students were required to work through a workbook on a narrative approach to the book of Esther. My first reaction to this kind of reading is embodied in a paper (cf. Snyman 1998) I delivered at the annual meeting of the New Testament Society of South Africa in April 1998, titled: '"Ilahle elinothuthu"? The Lay Reader and/or the Critical Reader: Some Remarks on Africanisation'. In that paper the focus fell on the ethics of such a reading and its value for post-apartheid South Africa. My conclusion was that this kind of reading is rhetorically similar to readings that gave birth to a theological justification to apartheid. In the present essay I explore this idea by undertaking to lay bare the hermeneutics of such a reading in order to indicate why such a reading is not really helpful.

lamented the anti-struggle view's questioning of the 'saintity' [*sic*] of these people, but stated he could not blame them. People questioned these heroes amid petrol bombs, necklacing and the burning of buildings. He asked whether the Jews were to blame in their struggle against the Persians. In his mind, the oppressed in South Africa cannot be blamed for their struggle and its violent consequences: when people were innocently struck, they would inevitably devise a defence mechanism—kill the adversary before he or she kills you.

The latter happened in the story of Esther, he said. Haman and the Persians manipulated or influenced the king to issue a decree to have the Jews killed. Esther and Mordecai had no choice but to defend their people against such a forthcoming massacre. There was no other way out than meeting violence with violence. It is on these grounds that the Jews killed their enemies. After all, the situation was provoked by the Persians.

Inevitably, he regarded the violence of the struggle as justified and in effect a kind of counter-violence against the violence instituted by the apartheid state: teargas, sjambokking, detention without trial, tortures and disappearance of soldiers, which constituted a situation not unlike that of King Ahasuerus who issued a decree that the Jews be massacred. The apartheid system was likened to the Persians and the Jews' fight was likened to the liberation struggle of the ANC. For this reason he felt that now that the battle has been won, Freedom Day (27 April) should be observed just as the Jews observed the Feast of Purim.

The second student was perhaps more crude in his reception of the story, by explicitly likening South African blacks to the Jews and South African whites to Haman and the Persians. The problem this student wanted to address by means of Esther 9 was that of liberation from oppression. The book of Esther, in his mind, presented a circumstance similar to those his community had been subjected to. The book related directly to his social and religious experience, which he thought was similar to that of the Jews in the time of Mordecai. He was of the opinion that the book of Esther would bring hope to those in despair and courage to the weak. The book illustrated the fact that God is always involved in history, even when unacknowledged. He is always working for justice.

How did he address the problem in his community? He saw the characters in terms of race: as black and white. The blacks were seen as the poor and the oppressed and the whites were regarded as the oppressors and the wealthy. In terms of wealth and power, the blacks were the have-nots and the whites the haves. The blacks would regard the whites as enjoying the favour of God. It is for this reason that they would want to liberate themselves, whereas the whites would defend their wealth and dominance as the chosen race.

The extermination of the Jews brought the second student face to face with the reality of his community as the once oppressed and now liberated people. He saw God as standing directly behind the liberation of the black people. He had the open-mindedness to accept that God would, in future, not necessarily be with the blacks, but with all those who are oppressed. The fact that the Jews did not plunder or destroy property served as a warning that the newly achieved democratic rights should not be used to destroy others.

Although he might have realized the limits of his metaphor, his identification of black people with the oppressed Jews, and the inevitable identification of the whites with Haman and his ilk, suddenly made me think about our own situation. The ease with which he identified his community with the Jews and the white people with Haman indicated to me a mindset with which certain communities justified or sanctioned their opposition to the system of apartheid. By stereotyping your adversaries in your stories, it becomes easier to dehumanize them in real life.

The question I would like to answer is whether this kind of identification is a *valid identification*: are there 'good reasons' to identify black people with Esther, Mordecai and the Jews, and white people with Haman and the Persians? In other words, should my student preachers be believed because they have the Bible on their side?[5]

But let me first try to put my good reasons for this essay on the table, so that you may perhaps understand my reception of my students' reading of Esther better.

3. *Narrative Rationality and Good Reasons (for my essay, of course!)*

A recurring theme in Walter Fisher's rhetorical model for studying a narrative in his book *Human Communication as Narration: Toward a*

---

5.   A similar question was posed by J.A. Loader (1987) to liberation theologians in general. His point was that liberation theologians used the Exodus motif as a point of comparison with the South African apartheid situation: if God can side with the slaves in Egypt, he can side with the blacks. According to Loader (1987: 9) these theologians tried to establish the credibility of libertation theology by 'proving' it biblically. Loader's question is the following: but what does one then do with the book of Joshua where God's underdogs became the upperdogs and the Canaanites those with whom God should side?

Philosophy of Reason, Value, and Action (1987) is that human beings in their role as storytellers have a natural capacity to recognize the coherence (probability) and fidelity (truthfulness) of stories they tell and experience (1987: 24). Under coherence I understand the way the arguments fit together and under fidelity whether the story provides good reasons to be believed and whether it will be eventually capable of inducing a desired action within its recipients. The structure of my arguments will become clear in due course.

In the meantime, however, I do feel the need to elucidate some aspects of the reasons for my present deliberations. It is not meant as a confession, but rather as an effort to contextualize and reveal as far as possible the ethics behind my reading.[6] The baring of my soul, if you wish, has a twofold purpose:

a. On the one hand, to account for human behaviour that is not formally logical, yet can be expressed in terms of stories, or the interpretation of things in a sequence.

b. On the other hand, to unmask the hidden ethics of the significant other with which this essay is in dialogue, namely fundamentalism, whose lack of a historical consciousness enables readers to equate the biblical text with their own lives, in many cases reproducing uncritically the values of the story world as well as the world of production of the text.

There are at least four contexts that I want to make explicit.[7] The first context is one that lies uneasy on my mind because of its potential to explode, neutering me as a citizen able to make a contribution to a country

---

6. Fisher (1987: 48) argues that in narratives it is not only the individual form of the arguments that makes a story persuasive, but the values embedded in the story as well. Thus, 'good reasons' are elements that provide warrants for accepting or adhering to the advice promoted in a particular story. I realize that, although I may name a few contexts as having a bearing on my mind while I am writing this essay, it does not necessarily constitute a direct line between the context, my thoughts and this essay. The coherence or structure is to be verified by my audience wherever they are and whoever they might be.

7. My choice is directed at what is currently on my mind, in other words, my academic interests as related to the socio-political problems in South Africa as they unfold in the newspapers and television. Obviously, there would be contexts left behind, contexts that are still implicit, unrecognized and even not consciously taken account of. Perhaps it would be the task of my audience, now and later, to indicate those hidden resources I am not aware of, but hopefully not in the same way meaning

trying to redress a destructive past. At present, the entire picture of the extent of the apartheid regimes's 'antics' is unfolding on our television screens as the Truth and Reconciliation Commission (TRC), a compromise between the National Party's (as the previous apartheid government) and the African National Congress's negotiations in the early nineties. Apartheid was not merely a case of dividing ethnic groups and prohibiting interracial relationships. It was a full-fledged destabilizing force in the community and Southern African region. Recently, in the inquiry into our country's chemical warfare abilities, it came to light that the previous government sanctioned research into racially engineered pharmaceutical manipulation by trying to either devise drugs that would sterilize only black women, or kill black men. In a separate inquiry it was suggested that the Helderberg aeroplane crash in the Indian Ocean in the late eighties was caused by an illegal and highly inflammable substance that exploded in midair. Although the evidence was not tested in a court of law, it is nevertheless unsettling to take note of the possibility of a governmental refusal to have this plane make an emergency landing in the East out of fear for embarrassment or scandal. If true, it was more appropriate to have the people plunge to their death. In a (third) inquiry into the death of the former president of Mozambique (Samora Machel) on South African soil, it was suggested that a beacon in Maputo was switched off and a roving one switched on on the South African side of the border, causing the plane to fly off course. It does not matter that Renamo-rebels were supposed to shoot down the plane. What matters is that, with South African complicity, the plane was driven off course and crashed in South African mountains.

The second context relates to the one just mentioned. Given the depth of corruption and the violation of human rights in the apartheid system, some church groupings decided to provide the TRC with a confession of their complicity in apartheid in the past. However, what was not put on the table were the hermeneutic practices of these churches. Some of these churches provided the National Party with theological justifications of apartheid, and although these fraudulent readings are now rejected and frowned upon, the hermeneutics that gave birth to them remain intact.[8] In its

has been ascribed to the biblical texts in the past, as if the authors spoke about things they did not even know exist!

8.   This is the problem I have with a submission from four members of my own church denomination. Our church (*Die Gereformeerde Kerke in Suid-Afrika*) refused any participation in the reconciliation process before the TRC, claiming that the church never supported apartheid and was critical of the system in the past (cf. Spoelstra 1997:

complete disregard for the human context of the reading and writing processes, the resulting literal reading enables readers to regard the ancient biblical text as a late twentieth-century text whose ethics and morals can be followed without any reflection. The same disregard for the historical, cultural and political distance between late twentieth-century readers and the ancient biblical text is observed within certain circles of liberation theology, especially where the biblical text is the sole focus and the audience, due to their education and skills, receive the text in a naive realist manner. A choice between these two kinds of readings is not hermeneutical in nature, but political. A liberationist reading would be as prone to seek theological justification of political practices as an apartheid reading (cf. Willem Vorster 1984). We are already seeing religious communities scrambling to catch the big fishes of the present political powers. This is the third context I wish to refer to.

At the moment, so it seems, the race is on to get prominent political figures (read ANC members of one of the several legislatures) to enter particular faith communities. Recently, the premier of the Gauteng Province, Mathole Motshekga, joined the Rhema ministries, a vociferous fundamentalist Pentecostal group. This received prominence in a Sunday newspaper very sympathetic towards the ANC: a quarter-page-sized photo with a report on page 3 (cf. Makoe 1998: 3)![9] The value of this catch for

10). Although this may be true (cf. Eloff 1997: 9), the church's members undeniably supported the National Party in the elections. In fact, the person who finally negotiated a settlement with the ANC (former president F.W. de Klerk) is a member of this church. And it should be borne in mind that one of the apologists of apartheid in 1930–50 came from their midst, namely, J.D. du Toit who wrote extensively in defence of apartheid (cf. Snyman 1997b: 8). He was a theologian, a professor at the church's theological seminary in Potchefstroom. Bearing these aspects in mind, I truly admire the four prominent members' submission as individuals before the TRC (Snyman 1997a: 8). However, in their submission, they have not broken with the reading practices with which J.D. du Toit arduously defended apartheid. (See Du Plessis, van der Walt and van Wyk 1997:16-17 and van Wyk 1997: 10). I have to admit that my evaluation might be too harsh. It is quite an emotionally draining (yet brave) experience to say that one is sorry (cf. Serfontein 1998: 4). To simultaneously expect a rejection of the reading practices of the past might be to kick someone already lying down.

9.   A week later, another reporter of *The Sunday Independent*, Maureen Isaacson (1998: 17) wrote: 'One million people cannot be wrong, including Gauteng's premier, Mathole Motshekga, who visited the Rhema church last month but was apparently not born again.' This time, the tongue-in-cheek article and two photos took about two-thirds of the page.

this community of believers is immeasurable: not only have they increased their membership, but also for the prosperity of the individual members they have found a direct link to the political leadership of the country on whom their wealth now depends.[10] I am wondering whether this incident does not testify to a new civil religion in the making now that the previous civil religion has been destroyed. But this one does not seem to sprout from a liberationist grass-roots level. It concerns suburban middle-class citizens uncritically enjoying their wealth in the new ethos of the global-ized market place.

The fourth context relates to the environment with which I am consider-ing these other three contexts, namely my academic environment in which I try to carve out a living and be socially responsible by taking a leaf from an objective of the now defunct Reconstruction and Development Pro-gramme (cf. ANC 1994: 59-60):

> Human resource development must address the development of human capabilities, abilities, knowledge and knowhow to meet the people's ever-growing needs for goods and services, to improve their standard of living and quality of life. It is a process in which the citizens of a nation acquire and develop the knowledge and skill necessary for occupational tasks and for other social, cultural, intellectual, and political roles that are part and parcel of a vibrant democratic society.

At present, the entire education system is in turmoil. Not only do schools face a change in curricula without any proper funding, but our universities face a radical transformation that will introduce new syllabi as well as new faces to lecture them. Undeniably, our role as social labora-tories, where the attitudes and outlooks of the new millennium's intel-lectuals are being moulded, makes it vital for us to transform (cf. Baukney 1998: 8). For this reason, religious education has come under particular scrutiny, especially the role of 'Christian National' education in the past as one of the pillars of apartheid's education system.[11] Of this system, the

---

10.   The significance of Motshega's entrance to this faith community is perhaps best formulated by one of the critics of this move. A United Reform Church minister is reported to have said the following: 'Initially I thought it was a good idea. But when you say Rhema, I have a problem. In my opinion that's not a church; it is a cult where religion is being abused to support typical capitalist ideology. It is a place of profit-making orientation. Go to Rhema and listen for yourself. They think if you are poor it is a curse of God. Anybody who wants to get rich goes to Rhema. It is a prosperity cult' (Makoe 1998: 3).

11.   That system saw the training of thousands of teachers in Biblical Studies,

principal of the University of Fort Hare in the Eastern Cape, Professor Mbulelo Mzamane (1998: 4), said the following:

> In our religious studies programmes, the absence of an African or comparative folkloric studies privileges Jewish folklore, which is then erroneously passed on as *revealed* truth. What emerges is bigotry outrageously parading as religious education.

He wants to bring religious education closer to the humanizing history, culture and social experience of the (oppressed) communities. He privileges a people-centred approach that would open up the rich variety of human experience. He regards the past system as a process of proselytizing people into Christianity. What would he have said about Mathole Motshekga's[12] entrance into a Pentecostal fundamentalist church? I don't know, but Mzamane (1998: 4) said the following about the imperialist tendency of Christianity as he perceives it:

> Many of you from the established (read 'Western') churches see yourselves as religious aristocrats and look down upon the syncretic practices of your counterparts, who have actually succeeded in the most interesting ways to fuse 'Paganism' with Christianity.

making the Department of Old Testament and the Department of New Testament at the University of South Africa the biggest in the world with about 20 lecturers and 5,000 students each. This over production and governmental policies have now led to a decrease in student numbers, leaving the departments in dire straits as they struggle to formulate a new role for themselves in a secular society.

12. Motshekga's family attended the Lutheran church. His grandfather was the first to embrace Christianity. His father was religious, but not very fond of the institution of the church. He would pay his dues, but on a Sunday he would rather work in his vegetable garden, claiming the situation of the day demanded them to have food on the table. Motshekga himself is reported to have said the following about his conversion: 'Inevitably before there is light there is darkness. Non-believers should be allowed to go through that darkness before they discover the light—as I have done. In my early years I doubted Christianity and God' (cf. Makoe 1998: 3). Motshekga's emphasis of darkness and light is characteristic of the psychodynamics of fundamentalism. Ostow (1990: 104) understands these dynamics in terms of the death–rebirth pattern: the possibility of misadventure, illness and death are replaced by certainty, reassurance, that is offered by the guidelines of an inerrant Scripture which is equivalent to the revelation of a classical apocalypse. The world outside becomes the target of God's wrath from which the converted are saved. To this end, the fundamentalist separates him/herself from the world. The fundamentalist cannot live in that world, because he or she is uncomfortable with that world's uncertainty, competitiveness, frustrations and disappointments (Ostow 1990: 107). Furthermore, the world they left behind threatens the absolute system the fundamentalist has constructed.

Well, the way in which this episode received prominence in a Sunday newspaper reveals just this aristocratic moment, with the main 'aristocrat', Pastor Ray McCauley, the founding head of Rhema ministries, claiming the following: 'We are happy to have people accepting Jesus Christ as their saviour. It gives us hope about the future. And for the premier to be leading by example is a great thing. I think other premiers and public figures should take after our premier. But at Rhema everybody is equal' (cf. Makoe 1998: 3).

The 'golden' thread that constitutes the logic of these four reasons is fundamentalism. Apartheid found a religious sanction within Christianity among a group of pious believers who felt threatened, not only by British imperialism but also by what they perceived as African barbarity.[13] The religious sanction they received was unable to reflect on the ethics of the entire enterprise, resulting in a governmental structure that could practically commit murder in the face of a church blinded by her own hermeneutic! My belief is that, first, the hermeneutics of fundamentalism enabled apartheid to prosper, and second, if fundamentalism is not curtailed in some manner, it will not stop any other unjust system either, because of its inherent tendency to co-opt power and its inability to keep that power in check.

4. *Identification*

Of identification, Burke (1969a: 20) says the following:

> A is not identical with his colleague, B. But insofar as their interests are joined, A is *identified* with B. Or he may *identify himself* with B even when their interests are not joined, even if he assumes that they are, and is persuaded to believe so.

---

13. The Anglo-Boer War of 1899–1902 saw the British promising African indigenous inhabitants of the previous ZAR and Free State farms and other privileges when they terrorized the women and children of the Boers, who remained on the farms while the male population fought their 'liberation' war. The British also followed a scorched earth policy, linked with concentration camps. Not only were the homesteads and barnyards burnt down and farmlands destroyed, but the women and children in the conquered territory were rounded up and transported like cattle to adverse concentration camps where they were barely kept alive. These events were burnt into the psyche of the Afrikaner to the extent that a regime legitimizing their claim to power on the traditions and history of these people ended up (without realizing it) doing to others what was done to them.

How does this identification work in the case of Jews and Persians in the set example? By identifying blacks with the Jews and whites with Haman. However, blacks are not identical with the Jews, nor are whites identical with Haman. In the first case, one may present the race argument: colour of skin just might exclude them. More importantly, the two are separated by time as well as culture. But they are joined by their *interests* (cf. Burke 1969a: 20), not merely because they are joined in real life, but because they are assumed to be, or people are persuaded to believe that they are. By identification, the black people are thought to be 'substantially one' with the Jews and the whites with Haman. They are consubstantial with the Jews and Haman because they share some principle: in the case of the blacks, they share the bleakness of the situation and eventual salvation; in the case of the whites, they share with Haman the evil of the system and plans.

In the process of identification there is a move from the narrative to some kind of generalization. Once this generalization is achieved, the matter is turned around: there is a move from the generalities to the narrative as if the narrative is a translation of the generalization originally extracted from the narrative.[14] In Bible reading, readers extract motives from the narratives in a positivistic sense since the text is regarded as a deposit of meaning to be tapped by readers. Once these motives are extracted, the story is explained in a way which illustrates them. A reader respecting the textuality and the historicity of the text will try to find the motive behind the text within its original world of production. But readers not well versed in these matters simply interpret the text as illustrating those motives they see in the text.

In the set example of the Haman–whites identification, the story of Esther becomes (in Burkean terms) the formulation of an essence of a motive in the student's personal context, and not the story's. But the motive is brought back to the story as if the story illustrates that particular motive. The end of Haman illustrates his 'essence': he ends up on the gallows, making him a criminal. The direct identification of people in the readers' community with that figure suggests the fruition or fulfilment of that motive in real life. By implicating white people by identifying them

---

14. I find a parallel situation in what is called 'rigid wisdom'. Traditional wisdom said that a certain kind of deed would result in a certain kind of outcome. Rigid wisdom makes the outcome dependent on the deed itself, so that the outcome suggests what kind of deed it was.

with Haman, their 'timeless essence' is implied in the fate of Haman. We are dealing here with what Burke calls the 'scene-agent' ratio (Burke 1969a: 16) whereby someone is identified with the character of the surrounding situation, whereby the trait of the context is translated into a trait of a character: context = apartheid = evil; whites = voting for the National Party = apartheid = evil.

Rhetoric as identification should be placed within the context of motives. The basic function of rhetoric is the use of words by human agents to form attitudes or to induce actions in other human agents (Burke 1969a: 41). It is a question about the motives of people when they say and do something (Burke 1969b: xv). Any statement about motives offers some kind of answer to the question of what was done (act), when and where it was done (scene), who did it (agent), why it was done (purpose) and how it was executed (agency). When Burke talks about motives, he expects that the *act* should be named, in other words, what took place in thought and in deed. Second, he expects the *scene* to be named: the background of the act, the situation in which it occurred. The person or the kind of person who performed the act must also be made explicit (*agent*) as well as the means or instruments that person used (*agency*). Lastly, the reasons why the act was done or the *purpose* for what it was supposed to achieve, must also be looked into.

In the story of Esther, I have to reckon with the following:

> Mordecai (agent) with the help of Esther (co-agent) thwarts Haman's plan (counter-agent) to commit genocide by using Esther's position as queen (agency) to reveal Haman as an evil person (act) in order to change the decree of the king (purpose) so that the Jews can stay alive in Susa (scene).

When someone makes a sermon on the book of Esther, I have to reckon with the following:

> A student preacher (agent) with the help of his or her lecturer (co-agent and, in some instances, counter-agent) uses the story of Esther (agency) to address a problem (act) in his or her society (scene) in order to change the society for the better (purpose).

Identification with the different aspects of a story rests upon the communicative function of the story. Identification relates to the effects a story has on a reader. I wish to explore these effects according to the aesthetics of Hans-Robert Jauss in his book *Ästhetische Erfahrung und literarische Hermeneutik* (1982). He calls the communicative function of a text *katharsis*, which he defines as:

Enjoyment that originates from either peculiar rational or emotional affects that result in a change of belief as well as a liberation of the spirit within the hearer or spectator.

Genuß der durch Rede oder Dichtung erregten eigenen Affekte, der beim Zuhörer oder Zuschauer sowohl zur Umstimmung seiner Überzeugung wie zur Befreiung seines Gemüts führen kann (1982: 166).

The precondition of this effect is the fluctuation of *Selbstgenuss im Fremdgenuss* ('enjoyment of the self in the enjoyment of what is strange'), the experience of a reader in the experience of another. In other words, the reader must be able to put him or herself in the shoes of a character in the story, behind the pen of the author or behind the eyes of the narrator in the story world.

Distance and bridging the distance are the key features in Jauss's concept of identification or *katharsis*. When prejudices and interests are suspended in an objectivist manner, a distance might have been created between the reader and the text, but there is nothing in place to bridge that distance. Second, when the text is enjoyed without acknowledging any distance (Jauss talks of 'sentimental self-enjoyment'), the aesthetic experience is turned into an ideological reception and premanufactured consumption instead of a cathartic experience. In the end, the text loses its communicative function.

Aesthetic identification is not the same as a passive taking over of an idealized example of behaviour. It consists of a double movement whereby the first one is relativized by the second:

    a.   First of all, readers in the act of reading enter the story world in order to identify with the trials and tribulations of the hero or heroine in the story, forgetting their own world with its problems, interests and bondage.

    b.   Second, readers realize that they have entered the story world and that the story world is not the real world.

I think that people are sometimes so taken up with the persuasive appeal of the biblical text that they completely ignore the second aspect, namely, that they have entered a story world in which certain morals and customs are no longer valid. Or their hermeneutical assumptions do not allow them to recognize the story nature of the text, as is the case in fundamentalism's naive realism which overtook the platonistic critique of the poet as liar and introduced an experience contrasting with what they thought of as a heathen antiquity (Jauss 1982: 171):

> The aesthetic-contemplating distance becomes an apprehension in devotion
> and edification, the purification through catharsis becomes actual transcend-
> ing compassion, the fruitless enjoyment of the imaginary becomes the pro-
> ductive power of the exemplary and the aesthetic amusement of imitation
> becomes the appellative principle of following.

> der ästhetisch-kontemplativen Distanz wird das Ergriffensein in Andacht
> und Erbauung, der Reinigung durch Katharsis das in die Tat überleitende
> Mitleid, dem folgenlose Genuß des Imaginären die fortzeugende Kraft des
> Exemplarischen und dem ästhetischen Vergnügen der nachahmung das
> appellative Prinzip der Nachfolge.

In other words, reading the Bible no longer entails an aesthetic joy in
the development of the Bible story. There is a very strong appeal to
readers' emotions to follow Christ. It follows that everything one wishes
to justify should find some sanction in the Bible: by claiming biblical
sanction, one neutralizes beforehand any criticism as an example of
unbelief. By appealing to the emotions and the moral identification with
Christ, the aesthetic contemplative distance with the story is removed. In
fundamentalism, enjoyment in the imaginary world becomes problematical, because only the factual event or action possesses proof. The joy of
the imaginary can only provide possibilities, whereas joy in the exemplary
provides proof of truth. After all, the exemplary is based on that which
really happened.

The relation of the exemplary to the factual enables moral identification
(Jauss 1982: 187), which is always completed between two poles: a free
following (*Nachfolge*) or a mechanical *Nachahmung* ('das freie, lernende
Begreifen am Beispiel wie auch das unfreie mechanische Befolgen einer
Regel'; 'the free, learning comprehension by way of example as well as
the unfree mechanical following of a rule [Jauss 1982: 190]). In the
church, with its moral appeal, communication is aimed at persuasion to
follow a certain set of behaviour or rules. These rules or behaviour are not
generally formulated, but rather specifically determined.

It is for this reason that my students' identification with the story of
Esther becomes problematical: did the religious power attached to the text
and the subsequent appeal or persuasive force poured into the text not
force these students to identify associatively with the heroes in the story,
simply because they (the heroic characters) enjoy divine sanction? Rhetoric enters the scene as soon as an appeal is made to God and used for
their own moral position: my students correctly questioned the manner in
which Afrikaner civil religion co-opted God for their cause but, by identifying themselves with the cause of the Jews, I think they did the same.

To Jauss an aesthetic reading entails a lesser 'persuasion': the example is much more indeterminate, in that it is further determined by each concretization. Thus, the appeal of the text is not of a forceful prescriptive nature, in that the readers are obliged to do what the text makes its characters do. It seems to me that the exemplary, as opposed to the moral, identification allows for different possible concretizations of the readers' perception of the appeal of the text. The problem with identification in the Bible is that it recounts the extraordinary deeds of people in a divinely sanctioned version of their history, a sacred history as opposed to a secular one. No distinction is made between deeds done on a character's own merit and deeds done in the power of God.

The precondition for the aesthetic experience Jauss wishes to introduce is 'distancing'. Someone reading the text should be able to recognize himself or herself[15] in the text, yet see a difference between himself or herself and the object of identification. There must be some *Spielraum*. The latter is guaranteed in a fictional text because at the last page the story world ends. Obviously, such *Spielraum* ('room to play') is not possible as long as the text is chained in the shackles of fundamentalism.

Jauss (1982) distinguishes between five modes of identification. The first one is *associative identification* whose origins can be traced back to cultic participation of the Middle Ages. *Admirative* and *sympathetic identification* can be traced back to the Aristotelian comparison with the painter: *better than us* or *the same as us*. Admiration is seen as distance creating effect and sympathetic identification is regarded as distance suspending effect. The audience admires that which lies outside their scope of possibilities. In contrast to admiration and sympathetic identification is the *cathartic identification* that highlights the gap between aesthetic identification and moral practice. In the latter identification the audience tries to put themselves into the position of the hero or heroine in order to free themselves from their own feelings, either by tragic shock or comic relief, so that they can be free to form a judgment without didactic urge or imaginary suggestion. *Ironic identification* is a norm-breaking example, illustrating the social function of the aesthetic experience.

Associative identification involves a reader imagining himself or herself in the roles of the characters of a story. It entails either trying to follow the

---

15. The drive for inclusive language use at the Faculty of Theology and Science of Religion of the University of South Africa in Pretoria results in talking about readers either in the plural, or in their respective gender: he or she. But here I am faced with a dilemma: which sex should I put first?

behaviour of the character as a free being, imagining what the character would have done in certain situations, or merely imitating the character as one imitates certain acts in a ritual (Jauss 1982: 252). I understand it as an act in which the readers take part as if they were the characters in the story. The movement is from the reader to the story in that the reader enters the world of the story, not a case of the reader trying to conform his or her life world to that of the story. In other words, the reader tries to find out what a person following a certain set of rules could be like given a certain set of circumstances. This seems to me very much like those games in which a murder takes place and you have to figure out who committed the murder. It is playful, because no one is really murdered, but you have to follow the rules of the game by picking up the clues and investigating them. It works, as long as there is no real murder!

Given the distance between the text of Esther and the late twentieth century, I am not sure that there is much to associate with. The entire lifestyle and social order are strange. The sexual politics are deplorable and indicate an archaic situation. Associative identification with Esther in its entirety cannot take place, but functions only in bits and pieces. One associates with certain actions, but other actions make these actions questionable. In the story world, one can be playful: on the one hand identify with Esther's heroism and determination to set the score once and for all, yet on the other hand be critical of her actions as seen from a twentieth-century human rights perspective. The moment the story world is intruded by the real world, the identification process loses its play-fulness, and it turns into ritual and unfree collective identity where an audience is requested to identify with Esther in general as if all her actions could be taken as normative. What if the character's behaviour is regulated by norms and values of the time of the production of the story, not fit for a later historical period?

Admirative identification (Jauss 1982: 265) indicates that aesthetic experience is constituted in view of the perfection of an example, beyond tragic shock or comic relief. This perfection surpasses any human expect-ation, effecting an admiration that does not cease or weaken as soon as the novelty wears off. It is not 'Staunen', but a perception that leads to the taking over of an example. It is not a mere imitation whereby the model is replicated by minute observation, but rather an emulation (*aemulatio*).

Jauss (1982: 266) ascribes to aesthetic identification a social role which surfaces historically each time new tastes or norms are in the offing, or when societies undergo widespread changes. These changes are reflected in literature when characters symbolize specific group identities. South Africa is experiencing such a transformative stage consisting of a reversal of roles and fortunes. The two readings of Esther 9 I received reflect this period in a very disturbing way. Haman becomes the symbol of white people and Mordecai or Esther the symbol of black people. Yet it is not the book of Esther that says so, but the 'literature' that uses the book. Esther and Mordecai as the heroes in the book are regarded as prime examples of wisdom: by doing the right thing at the right time, they succeed in becoming queen and second in command in the Persian empire.

However, I am not so sure they are that admirable. They conquered the heathen like the Crusaders in order to bring about their Jewish paradise. But similar to the Crusaders in the Middle Ages, Esther and Mordecai left behind a trail of blood. The atrocities of the Crusaders made it possible for political systems such as colonial imperialism and apartheid to suppress people.

Sympathetic identification means having compassion with a character. According to Jauss (1982: 271) the admirative distance is raised so that the audience is led to have solidarity with the character. In contrast to admiration where the hero is placed on a throne, completely out of reach, sympathetic identification allows the audience to see in a character their own imperfection and ordinariness. In such a character, the audience can explore their own possibilities and find solidarity with someone *von gleichen Schrot und Brot* ('a chip off the old block').

Sympathetic identification, in contrast to admirative identification, places the characters on equal footing with the readers. The problem with the book of Esther is that these characters are not on an equal footing with the readers. They are people in powerful positions. They exercise power and it is difficult for people without that kind of power to identify with these figures.[16]

16. In a Bible study in the magazine *Challenge* (Feb./March 1998) I encountered the following reading of the book of Esther by Revd Lehlohonolo Bookholane, where he draws a direct link between Esther and Mordecai and those with political power in the country: 'There is nothing wrong with taking a political position in exile. Nor is there anything wrong with getting married to a king of a foreign land and being part of the palace. The challenge is to keep the faith.

I am reminded of South Africa, where our people moved between pulpits, pews and prison cells depending on the authorities. People went into exile to advance the liberation struggle.

As we begin a new year, we need to remember that former exiles, political prisoners and priests are now in Parliament.

Granted the story leaves the reader with very little compassion with Haman, however, insight into political power may help one understand Esther's and Mordecai's actions. Mordecai blackmails Esther, but when one takes Esther's recalcitrance into account, one wonders whether he has a choice. Esther's request for another day of violence seems bloodthirsty but, given the religious framework of the story, she has to finish what her ancestor, Saul, did not. There are good reasons for their behaviour, yet the outcome raises questions about the morality of these two figures. Again, if the reception of these two characters overlooks the particularity of their situation, identification is based on an 'a-historical' reading of the text that ignores the logic between the action of the character and the event itself. It then becomes easy to legitimize certain forms of behaviour and reject without recognizing that both modes of behaviour may stem from the same acting motive! As will be seen later on, for example, the Jews in the story of Esther came to emulate the Persians more and more: they received power; they did to others what others had intended to do to them; they even used the Persian communication system to expand their own ideologies!

Cathartic identification suddenly confronts me with my own reception of the book of Esther as well as that of my students. I am constantly reminded of what Molière said in 1664 in his preface to his play *Le Tartuffe*. The play offended the piety of the orthodox religion of the time. Molière argued that comedy was an excellent mode to correct the vice of humankind (1971: 29):

> One suffers gladly reprehensions, but one never suffers bantering. One can very well be mischievous, but will nto at all be ludicrous.

> On souffre aisément des répréhensions; mais on ne souffre point la raillerie. On veut bien être méchant; mais on ne veut point être ridicule.

Perhaps I, in my reception of my students' reading of Esther, am the one unable to be rebuked! By being pinpointed by the identification in these two responses, I felt that my own free judgment was curtailed. By being prescriptive, these two responses suspended the free disposition necessary for an aesthetic experience. Or is my deliberation on these two receptions of Esther not an indication of a cathartic experience on my part?

Many of us cherish the memory of the liberating acts of God which kept us alive from losing hope during the struggle. This is the memory we have to keep alive especially when we are in the palace or Parliament. Falling prey to power struggles and privileges are easy, therefore, we need to strengthen our faith.'

Jauss (1982: 277) regards cathartic identification in Aristotelian terms: the readers are transported from the trappings and intrigues of their ordinary life world to the beleaguered position of the hero, so that they may be led by either tragic shock or comic relief to a release of their feelings. Cathartic identification implies an extra step: after identification, reflection on the proposed identification is required. Haman may have been accused of murderous plans, but Esther with the Jews instituted a kind of apartheid. This was what angered Haman. A cathartic identification would imply what Stan Goldman (1990) says about the book of Esther: it illustrates both the dark and light sides of the human heart; it tells us that all are capable of evil and violence.

Recognizing Haman's powerlessness against Mordecai's intransigence, one can understand his anger and frustration. His actions do not differ very much from those plans devised by the former security police and agents to get rid of anti-apartheid activists or liberationists.

In *ironic identification* the hero is portrayed in such a way that his or her heroism is questioned because it does not conform to the structure of the traditional hero in a narrative (Jauss 1982: 283). Reinhard the Fox and Don Quixote are examples of the hero who is ironized in such a way that the audience can recognize the ideal norms of heroism. Irony plays an important role in the book of Esther, but the king whose behaviour is ironized is not the hero. He is portrayed as a fickle, incompetent despot unable to control his wife or any other woman, for that matter. As a powerful king he orders his wife to appear before him, but he cannot make a decision without counselling his male cohort. Although he has power over life and death, and Esther trembles with fear at the thought of appearing before him unannounced, he is like putty in the hands of others, including Esther. Mordecai is usually regarded as the epitome of wisdom, but his open disobedience to a royal command is described by Russel Edwards (1990: 37) as 'monumental stupidity and political madness shown by a Jewish leader, bereft of any form of political sagacity and unable to foresee the logical consequences of his egotistical behavior'!

5. *Some Deliberations on Esther 9*

In Esther 9 the long-dreaded day arrived when the king's proclamation was to be carried out. But instead of a day of the exertion of bloody Persian power over a minority living in exile, far from their homeland or Yahweh, this became a day when this minority overpowered the Persians.

The story would have it that the Jews were invincible: no one could stand before them, not even the leaders of the different provinces! Initially a few people were killed, *inter alia* the ten sons of Haman. It is said that the Persians were so overcome with fear that they summarily supported Mordecai in his new powerful position—a position that was orchestrated by Esther in what amounted to nothing less than a palace coup (Bronner 1998: 8). It is as if the Persians converted to Judaism!

Unlike the past, when Esther was excluded from the king's presence and had to present herself unannounced, the two are now found together with Esther requesting another day to continue the killing and to have Haman's sons hanged. It is as if she wants to make sure that the Persians realize the cost of Jewish life. Esther's request is put forth more boldly than the two previous ones. It is granted, and results in more deaths. In the meantime, Mordecai has grown in power, and ordains a feast to celebrate their victory over the Persians.

In the light of the worldwide focus on human rights and the squirming caused by a certain holiday within apartheid South Africa that was thought vindictive and racist,[17] two questions concerning the morality of the two main characters arise which problematize identification with them: Does anything in the story warrant Esther's request, namely, to kill more people? What kind of feast is instituted that celebrates victory in the face of the conquered?

Susan Niditch (1995: 45) argues that liberation from oppression is a favourite and central literary topos in Hebrew literature. The work acquires meaning for readers whose particular historical and sociological setting finds a structural resonance in the story. Two possible, though obvious, groups of readers who might feel an affinity with the book of Esther are feminists and racially oppressed groups.

Beal (1995: 110) appropriately observes that in the reception of the book of Esther most readers are positioned on the side of women in a male-dominated society. Vashti is a heroine in a gender-based conflict,

---

17. In apartheid South Africa 16 December was celebrated as the 'Day of the Covenant'. It commemorated a covenant with God the Boers had made, just as the ancient Israelites are perceived to have done. On this day in 1838, they promised God that they would celebrate the day as a Sunday if God granted them victory over the Zulus at Blood River. On that day, they drove away the Zulu. The uneasiness of the Zulu people regarding this day now comes over me when Freedom Day (27 April) is celebrated as a day of black victory over whites. Somehow, amid these identifications we need a larger generalization.

making it difficult for the reader to identify with the men in the book (Beal 1995: 107). In fact, Vashti prejudices readers against the male Persian characters. Appreciated in this way, siding with the women in the text turns the book into a gender conflict where female sexuality questions male authority (Brenner 1995a: 12). At first this gender conflict appears to entail mortal danger for the women (Vashti was banned and Esther feared she might die if she went to the king without being summoned). In the end, the gender conflict turns out to have been deadly to some of those who formed part of the Persian male structure. Five hundred men were killed on the first day, including Haman's sons. His wife (and daughters, if he had any) seems to have been spared. In the end, Haman's wife distanced herself from her husband by declaring that he would certainly be killed! Brenner (1995a: 12) suggests that the story of Esther proclaims the moral superiority of the females above the subverted male figures in the story. She is a 'notable success' amid the male-oriented Persian court governed by an autocratic king and the patriarchal social order of Jewish life in the Diaspora, delivering her people from their enemies (cf. Bronner 1998: 9). Siding with her means to perceive her as acting wisely.

Bea Wyler (1995: 120), trying to do justice to the ethnic and gender issues, argues that an ethnic drama unfolds against a sexist backdrop. Against the background of male power a woman tries to ward off a threat to her people posed by a male in a powerful position. Esther experiences what Vashti went through. Wyler (1995: 126) says that when Mordecai asks Esther to intervene (Est. 4.13-14), he practises male power by practically pronouncing a ban on her in saying she will disappear if she does not help. Esther had to do what Vashti had refused in the face of male power! Both experienced the violence of the ruling male class against women. Esther survives because she complies. Her submission causes the gender issue to remain unresolved, whereas the violence of the Persian ruling class against the Jews is solved.

The racial issue is resolved by what Klein (1995: 149) calls the 'shame' that is put on the Persians. She says that Esther and Mordecai, as Jews, live in a dependent position associated with women, whereas autonomy and power are reserved for men. Autonomy and power entail honour, whereas dependence implies shame. Shameless behaviour would be ascribed to someone failing to recognize the rules of human interaction or social boundaries: for a woman it would mean not submitting herself to male power, and for a man it would be failing to remain separate from the women, living in separate quarters, or keeping the women veiled in public and restricting their social interaction to women spaces (cf. Klein 1995: 151)—in other words, not maintaining his autonomy. In the story, the king in all his power does not act in an autonomous way. He is continuously in need of advice: Memuchan, Haman and then Mordecai. Mordecai is the only male in the story keeping his autonomy. Klein argues (1995: 174) that Esther knows when to protect her shame and when to act shamelessly. She is intelligent and resourceful in her use and abuse of the system to achieve her aims.

From a wisdom perspective, one can argue that she acts wisely, because she does and says the right thing at the right time. But shame and honour do not solve the moral problem of her second request, namely, to continue with the killing and have Haman's sons hanged. Goodnick (1997: 103) suggests that the Jews' civil accommodation, resolute self-determination and peaceful negotiation did not bear any fruit so that they had to resort to direct confrontation.

According to Hebrew wisdom, one can argue that the exile which saw people being sent away from Jerusalem implies a group of people living far from Yahweh, that is, in a chaotic world where his order does not prevail. In terms of honour and shame my guess is that this position would amount to living in shame, without any autonomy, because they had lost their homeland and were now forced to observe the customs and laws of the host country.

I base these remarks on one of the intrigue patterns in Old Testament stories and on the traditional and rigid wisdom perspectives. The world in which a story can take place is either a chaotic world from which God is absent, or an ordered world where his creation order prevails without any disturbance. The intrigue of the story then concerns a movement between these two worlds. In wisdom literature, in terms of the doctrine of retribution, those people who do not disturb the order of Yahweh are rewarded with success. In rigid wisdom, their success in life is used as an indication of their wisdom. Those who disturb the order of Yahweh, thus creating disharmony, are rewarded with failure. Similarly, in rigid wisdom any misfortune people experienced was regarded as an indication of some foolish action they once committed.

But what happens in the story of Esther? It is as if the misfortunes of the Jews in exile do not cease: being far from Jerusalem is not enough; in a foreign country they face total annihilation. What happens is that the people of the foreign country are regarded in terms of foolishness, making Esther and Mordecai the wise guys. Haman is the one who disturbs the order of Yahweh by expecting all to bow before him. In his pride he even proposes to annihilate God's people. From a wisdom perspective, his success will depend on whether he abides by wisdom's rules. If he does so, he acknowledges the authority of Yahweh and becomes part of the divine order. If he breaks the rules, he defies God's authority, disrupts the order of creation and will become a fool, whose punishment will take the form of failure and misfortune. The foolish behaviour of Haman is obvious, even to his wife. Readers see his foolishness in his actions, such as verbosity and pride that comes to a fall. Klein (1995: 149) is correct when she argues that the minority culture of the Jews ridicules the dominant culture of the ruling Persians.

The predominant reception of the character of Esther is one favourable to her. I am not sure whether it is due to the partiality towards her as a celebrity which Leila Bronner (1995: 177) finds in the Jewish rabbinical reception of her character, but perhaps it is due to a clear symmetry observed between the main characters: Haman (and the king) as Persians are evil and Esther and Mordecai (as Jews) are good people. But Brenner (1995b: 75) argues these contrasts are not so unsophisticated in terms of good and evil, moral and amoral. She says:

> Mordecai and Haman are paired-off competitors, but neither is an 'either/ or' figure: each mirrors the other's ambitions and intrigues; if the one triumphs and the other loses, this does not qualify either loser or victor as 'evil' or 'great'.

Esther's counter-image in the looking glass is not the king, but Vashti. Brenner argues (1995b: 75) that Esther does what her predecessor refused to do, and her later remarks (1995b: 79) in her article are very significant:

> Nobody is wholly evil in mirrorland, although the reds are ultimately inferior and losers, as preordained by the symbolism of 'white'. Similarly, no one is wholly evil (Haman) or good (Mordecai) in Esther, although Mordecai is 'ours', and thus superior. A non-simplistic tale of mirrors excludes simplistic morality. Thus, an ideo-moralistic reading of Esther can be rejected in favour of a phenomenological or political reading. The winners are those whose side we are on, not necessarily saintly but our favourites. Thus read, Esther is not a morality tale. It can be read as a politico-philosophical guide to life and survival. What does it take, in a diaspora framework, to survive and succeed as a Jew?

Perhaps this is my problem with my students' reading of Esther 9: they have turned a political reading into a simplistic moral tale where characters are either good or evil. Instead of identification one should talk about *equation* in their case. If I look at what it took to survive and succeed as a Jew in exile, then surely moral character was not one of the necessary traits! Neither Esther nor Mordecai can claim moral worthiness. But I suspect that one can read the story as a moral tale if the focus is only on the story, as if its production had not been influenced by the world in which it was produced. Although a classic is a classic because readers feel it addresses issues in their own societies, it is still in need of a reading expounding its historical position.

How does one avoid a simplistic equation between an ancient story and a present situation? Perhaps by trying to find out in which situation the story would have made sense, such as how to survive as a Jew in the Diaspora amidst foreign laws and customs. The book bears no evidence of those issues that characterize the books of Chronicles, Ezra or Nehemiah. Those issues, so it seems, centre around a return to Jerusalem and managing the society of the returnees vis-à-vis those who did not go into exile (cf. Snyman 1997c). In the book of Esther the house of Israel and its members are not the issue. The answer in terms of survival techniques is not very comforting (according to Brenner 1995b: 79): 'you have to mutate into your former adversary, or nearly that'.

But who, then, were the Persians?

The story was designed to reflect the ideology and feelings of the Jews in the Diaspora. The Old Testament provides conflicting reports about the Persians. On the one hand, Chronicles, Ezra and Nehemiah would have us believe that the Persian Period was benign, but the book of Esther suggests that the sojourn was not so amicable.[18] On the other hand, if the situation was as disastrous as depicted by the book of Esther, why did the Persian authority resort to forceful deportations within the kingdom?

Unfortunately, what we know about the Persians is what we glean from non-Persian texts.[19] The depiction of the Persians in the book of Esther

18. I would not claim that the situation in the book of Esther represents a historical situation. But I wonder how this book's negative portrayal of Persian authority would have been received by Persian powers.

19. Pierre Briant (1990: 167) says in this regard: 'Dans ces conditions, l'historiens d'aujourd'hui est dépendant pour une très large part des visions de l'Empire développées dans l'Antiquité par les peuples sujets du Grand Rois (Grecs, Egyptiens, Judéens, Babyloniens). Or, ces écrits ne sont pas neutres, et ils ne présentent d'ailleurs pas généralement comme tels.' The picture of the Persians depends on the group who reports on them. A positive report about them is found regarding their intervention for the Jews in Elephantine in relation to Egyptian hostility (cf. Briant 1988: 146).

would be biased in favour of the Jews. But we do know a few things about the Persians. Pierre Briant (1988) suggests the presence of an 'ethno-classe dominante'[20] as the group with the power to rule. They were an aristocracy around the king, bent on preserving their privileges regarding the politics and the economy. They did not participate in the melting pot of cultures that came into being with the vast deportations and movements of people. However, the expansion of the Persian empire necessitated the incorporation of the conquered people (Sancisi-Weerdenburg 1990: 265). Therefore, it was not strange that the Persian administration allowed the aristocracy of the conquered people in their midst. Stolper (1990: 200) refers to Belsunu, a Babylonian official who became part of the Persian administration of Babylon.

Although this 'ethno-classe dominante' incorporated the ruling elite of the conquered nations, it did not assimilate with these people. The lack of archaeological evidence in the conquered territories testifying to a Persian cultural influence suggests the Persian aristocracy kept to themselves, maintaining their privileges and culture. When a Persian official was sent to one of the colonies, he went with his wife, family, and servants as well as his beliefs, customs, and language. Once in the colony, he would attach himself to those Persians already there and in the service of the Persian satrapy. His allegiance to the Persian throne would allow him to send his children to the Persian court in the province where they could receive instruction in Persian customs (cf. Briant 1987: 12). The safeguarding of the traditions and the purity of the community is one of the conditions sine qua non to maintaining the status and power of this ruling elite.

The Persians were forced to use the existing infrastructures in the provinces, resulting in several kinds of trade-offs between them and the local ruling elite. They would absorb those infrastructures that could pose a threat to their control of the province, but they would also make certain concessions. In some provinces (e.g. Babylon) certain concessions regarding taxes were made. In turn, the local ruling elite would acknowledge Persian control. They would serve the Persian administration in terms of their local customs and the Persian king, in turn, would restore to the local elite their privileges (Briant 1987: 14). In the provinces, this situation

---

20. Briant (1988: 137) defines it as 'l'aristocratie perse unie autour du Grand Roi par des valeurs communes cimentées par l'histoire et une éducation loyaliste, par des rapports fondés sur l'échange services/dons/services; intérêts communs aussi car cette petite couche dominante (qui domine également la société perse) se partage les hauts postes de direction à la cour, à l'armée et dans les satrapies'.

could lead to a solidarity between the local elite and the Persian representative, inducing an autonomy that could endanger the position of the king
in the empire.

Briant (1987: 25) acknowledges certain contradictions in this depiction
of Persian power. One of them is the contradiction between royal power
that tended to become absolute and the maintaining of the privileges of the
main ruling families. The Persian aristocracy tended to define themselves
in relation to royal power as well as to their clan or tribe. But it is
important to notice that position in the royal court did not belong to a
certain member of the tribe, but to the entire tribe. Anyone in the family
could take his place.[21] Briant concludes that in this way the absolute power
of the king was counterbalanced by the cohesion of the family structure.
For the king it meant enduring loyalty and for the family it meant that
certain positions could be kept within the family. Furthermore, the king
would not easily dispose of someone once given this stature, because it
might lead to a palace revolution. When that happened, the entire family
was disposed of.

Briant's and Sancisi-Weerdenburg's remarks pertain to the role of the
Persians in the provinces. But what about the exiles or dislocated people
living in other parts of the empire, especially in the vicinity of the king's
palace? If one accepts that the Persian societal structure in the provinces
was a replica of that found in the king's court, there may not have been
any significant differences. In any case, my concern here is with the
Jewish view of the Persians, which perhaps tells us more about Jewish
ideas concerning power than about the Persians themselves!

The story of Esther and Mordecai deals with two families competing for
the favour of the king, a reality of life at the court. When the narrator
makes ethnicity a problem, it reflects on Jewish racism rather than on
Persian intolerance. Although the Persians did not really mix with other
groups, the story denies this aspect in favour of the Jews' separateness as
particularized by Haman in ch. 3. It seems as if their 'apartheid' is the
spark in the powder keg. But if that was a Persian custom as well, why
would it have been a problem to Haman or Ahasuerus? It was, in fact,
Persian policy not to destroy the cultures of conquered peoples. For this
reason the Persians as a ruling elite kept themselves 'apart' from the local
inhabitants. Should the focus on Jewish separateness not make it difficult

---

21. Briant (1987: 26) refers to the case of Vidranga in Elephantine who became the
Satrap there. But he did not go, and sent his son Nafaina instead. In Babylon Gubaru
was assisted by his son Nabfanga.

for black South Africans to identify with the Jews? Their white compatriots based their apartheid ideology on Jewish separateness with disastrous results. Furthermore, if one wishes to force an identification (as was done in Afrikaner civil religion, see below), one can even suggest that the rise of Afrikaner power in the twentieth century compares well with the Jewish exile and struggle under foreign superpowers!

Given the social milieu in which the book of Esther originated and functioned, Jewish identity would have been a problem. One aspect of the story focuses on the Jews maintaining their Jewishness. This is alluded to in Mordecai's genealogy in Esther 2, although at that stage in the story the Jews still seemed as Haman described them in 3.8: scattered and dispersed. However, the moment they were threatened, all the Jews acted in concert (4.3, 16; 8.17; 9.27-28). One gets the impression of collective action, experience and memory (cf. Clines 1990: 47).

Ironically, the effort to obtain deliverance from the Persians seems to deny the Jewish identity. Esther marries a Gentile, and she is asked to keep her identity secret. Only by denying it can she become powerful. The threat of the genocide arises from Mordecai's divulging of his identity in his open rebellion against Haman. In fact, Mordecai can be accused of endangering the lives of his fellow-people (Edwards 1990: 35). As Clines suggests (1990: 48), the Jewish people were landed in this situation because one Jew acted like a Jew and told people he was a Jew; they escaped only through the work of another Jew who pretended not to be a Jew. Thus, if being Jewish means acting like Esther, no tragedy need be expected, but if it means acting like Mordecai, heaven knows where deliverance will come from!

Be that as it may, what seems to be real is the struggle for the favour of the king between two families, Haman versus Mordecai. And in this struggle, no stone is left unturned! Mordecai receives the Jewish cloak and Haman the Persian one. The struggle is given a religious colour by the allusion to the Amelekites and Saul. Again, if Mordecai and Esther are the heroes, what does one do with the baggage of Saul in the Jewish tradition? He was not a favourite of Yahweh! The heroes in the story are not wholly good. They form part of a past where things did not go well, at least in the eyes of the Jewish tradition that won the day after the exile.

Focusing on the morality of the characters also appears problematical. The story narrates a powerful official's wish to have an entire population annihilated. The allusion is that this problem exists because the Jews did not annihilate that man's ancestors at previous occasions! Saul, the family member Esther and Mordecai are explicitly linked to, did not kill Agag when he should have (1 Sam. 15). With the overdrawn revenge scene in ch. 9, this conflict is resolved once and for all with the killing of Haman's sons and their public hanging/disgracing.

Why were Haman's sons killed along with him? Obviously to indicate the finality of the end of the feud between Israel and 'Canaan'. It also fitted the Persian way of life: if an official got out of favour with the ruling power, not only he but also his entire family suffered. One should notice, however, that it was the Jewish heroine who was enforcing Persian custom. Haman might have been evil, but so were his adversaries, who became more and more like him as they grew in power. If the story is about becoming like the adversary, identification with the heroes is in fact problematic.

Assimilation certainly was a strategy of survival: initially in Est. 3.8 the Jews are depicted as scattered, but in ch. 9 Mordecai is described as ranking next to the Persian king. The Jews end up having dual loyalties: to the Persian government and to their Jewish culture. Even the author took up the Persian style of communication, by writing a Persian chronicle without any explicit reference to Yahweh. The author did not regard the Jews as a kingdom of priests, but as a nation just as any other. In the end, the book provides a picture of the human capacity for evil and violence, regardless of ethnic background (cf. Goldman 1990: 27).

In this light, associative identification with the characters of Esther and Mordecai implies no longer accepting only their morality and courage. It also implies taking responsibility for their violent actions. In this sense, the story is not merely about tolerance of Persian power, seeking its accommodation and co-operation, or infiltrating the Persian court by means of a Jewish woman in order to sway Persian power in Jewish favour (cf. Clines 1990: 46). Survival (or assimilation) means doing what your adversary does. And the moment one starts doing what the adversary does, moral high ground disappears.

Concerning my students' case I would suggest that having survived an evil system, do they seek biblical justification for their liberative deeds? If so, what do they do with their adversaries? The text says they should be killed. Here it becomes important to understand the story within the context of its production: if the story had been written while the Jews were still in exile, telling them how to survive amidst hostile circumstances, the philosophy emanating from this book could be interpreted as 'the end justifying the means'. Violence would then become a strong possibility.

In the fourth century BCE, the story of Esther had serious consequences for Jewish identity. Goldman (1990: 25) sees in the story Jewish self-criticism in the sense of an absence of a superior race, which meant that Jews in the Diaspora were to accommodate themselves in Persian society. In other words, they were to assimilate, yet retain Jewish identity. This seems paradoxical though possible, as illustrated by Mordecai's position in the Persian kingdom (10.3). The Persians, in any case, seem to have been quite positive towards the Jews: the inhabitants of Susa were not hostile towards the Jews. After all, the conflict concerned Haman and Mordecai, not the Persians and the Jews. When the king and Haman threw a party after having condemned certain people to death, the entire city of Susa was in confusion and dumbfounded. Haman's wife also realized the strength of the Jews (6.13). When Mordecai issued a new decree rendering the first one ineffective, the entire city rejoiced. It is ironical that Haman's attempt to stamp out the Jews turned into a massive conversion of Persians to early post-exilic Judaism (8.17).

The paradox of Jewish identity and Persian assimilation can also be seen in the Jewish adoption of Persian writing. From the Persian point of view only that which had been written was valid and permanent. Vashti's deposal was not merely orally decreed (1.19), but written as a law. It is as if writing creates a particular social order: a written law orders the power structure within a family (1.22). The planned genocide of the Jews could only be effected once it was written down as a law.

The infiltration of the Persian system and assimilation to Persian culture reached a climax in Esther 9. By adopting the less charming manners of the Persian court, the Jews set about killing those who wanted to hurt them, doing with them as they pleased (9.5), a sign of godless licence! They did not seek to change the society, but to position themselves at the centre of power.

6. Identification and Fundamentalism

Which kind of identification should one reckon with here, as contrasted to the identification of my students? Timothy Beal talks of 'siding with' the characters. The gender conflict implied in the book allows readers sensitive to gender issues to have sympathy with the women in the story (Brenner, Niditch, Wyler). Concepts of modern-day life are used to explain the conflicts and actions in the story, such as honour, shame and autonomy (Klein). The predominant reception of Esther is favourable, although Brenner argues that no one in the story is wholly good or evil. No one seems to argue that present-day readers should act like Esther or Mordecai. They tend to explain the text in its ancientness, albeit with critical apparatus stemming from the late twentieth century. They seem to realize that there is a distance between them and the text.

Craig (1995: 132-33) mentions a few examples of uneasiness caused by the book among Christian and Jewish readers. This uneasiness is based upon the perceived cruelty and vengeance in ch. 9, rendering Esther and Mordecai less than proper models of character, integrity or piety.

Bearing in mind the need for role models, Walter Fisher (1987: 18) makes an interesting remark about Burke's rhetoric:

> Burke's dramatism *implies* that people function according to prescribed roles; they are actors performing roles constrained or determined by scripts provided by existing institutions.

In Burkean terms, the book of Esther can indeed be regarded as a script providing a few people with prescribed roles. The issue is whether these roles equate those played by Esther and Mordecai, or whether their roles provide what Fisher calls a plot that is always in the process of being recreated, rather than being established once and for all. Do the roles of Esther and Mordecai provide late twentieth-century readers with an example of behaviour, or do they rather help one to understand life? There is a subtle difference. Exemplary behaviour suggests a standard according to which behaviour can be assessed. The question then concerns how well you perform your role. In this instance, the biblical text is used as a kind of law or measuring instance whereas it presents us with heroes. But, as Fisher correctly argues, successful identification does not always result in humane, reasonable action.

Josef Wiesehöfer (1988: 2-3) warns against three dangers when dealing with narratives about legendary figures of the past. He says there is a tendency among historians to typify the character of a nation or a group of people using certain morals in order to legitimize the legends of the archenemy.[22] Second, people tend to regard the history of a people in terms of a history of wars and heroes, a very typical characterization of

---

22. I am not so sure how much our reading of the book of Esther is influenced by the events of the Second World War. When reading Russel Edwards's (1990: 37) reference to a Persian Wansee Conference when Haman persuaded the king to agree to the destruction of the Jews, I think the Holocaust has undeniably influenced our understanding of the book.

ancient Israelite history! In this sense, history is about great people whose behaviour possesses the power of example. Lastly, there is the tendency to use the history of Antiquity as an analogy for contemporary events, not merely as a comparison but as an *equation*. This tendency surfaces in times of national weaknesses or is used to legitimize certain actions. What the text indicates, is how the Jews assumed their powerful position. When it argues that power can only be obtained by emulating those who wanted to kill the Jews, it means that those who take this story as their example would be justified in doing likewise. I would add the following: *because the Bible told them so!*

This is the dilemma I experience with the kind of identification my students came up with: an equation of their situation with that found in the story world. Let me call it an 'equating identification'. In Jauss's terms, the move into the story world should be counterbalanced by a move from that story world into the immediate reading context. Jauss adds something extra: the recognition that it is an unbalanced manoeuvre, since readers realize they are dealing with an ancient text that is strange to their own immediate context. A pious eagerness to honour the religious appeal of the biblical text may cause readers searching for those aspects they have in common with the text to ignore the distance between them and the text. Then the text acquires a privileged position.

The privileged status of the text ensures a process similar to that found in (Scottish) common-sense realism, namely an immediacy of perception which ignores the distance between a text and its readers. There is a single physical world common to the reader and all other people, alive or dead (Forguson 1989: 14-15). The commonality of this world enables late twentieth-century readers to be 'one' with people of 400 to 100 before the Common Era. It is assumed that humankind shares a network of beliefs and that the common nature of these beliefs enables communication and reasoning (Forguson 1989: 104).[23] It is within such a framework that

---

23. One of the conditions for present-day cross-cultural anthropological (comparative) inquiry is the assumption that, in the words of Howard Eilberg-Schwartz (1990: 102), 'although different people have different histories and live in different contexts, cultures always have features that resemble those of others'. I agree that different cultures have a certain level of convergence regarding human activity. One needs only to look at ancient Israel's rituals regarding sexuality and sexual organs in comparison to some African traditions to see some correspondence. But I am not sure whether one can read into this kind of commonality the principled view of common sense.

identification with ancient characters like Esther, Mordecai and Haman makes sense.

Common-sense realism is an important angle from which Christian fundamentalism can be understood (cf. Vorster 1988: 159). Its view of reality constitutes a naive realism, which one can define as the assumption that scientific theories are accurate descriptions of the world as it is (cf. Van Huyssteen 1987: 19). In other words, models of the world are taken literally, as direct replicas of that which they refer to. In terms of Christian fundamentalism the question would be whether the description of God in the Bible reflects his existence in the world. In other words, is the way God is depicted in the biblical texts the way God acts in the world? The way characters are portrayed in the stories of the Bible is regarded as the way Christians should understand humanity. The naive realist would regard the biblical text as a direct replica of the world it refers to. In other words, the woman called Esther, said to have married a Persian king, was indeed his wife and queen of the Persian empire.

The fundamental constituent of common-sense realism is that those things which one perceives with one's senses really exist and that they are indeed what one perceives them to be. In other words, reality is knowable: objects can be observed objectively. Facts exist independently from the observer. What is observed is not ideas about physical objects, things, articles, or facts, but articles you can grasp with your hands, things, objects, or facts you know that have happened or that are true (cf. Vorster 1988: 157). It is in this sense that one can say fundamentalists read the biblical text literally (in the words of Boone [1989: 40]: sensibly, reason-ably, apprehended by the senses). Thus, when the biblical text narrates a historical event and presents readers with a description of that event, it is argued that the event really happened as described in the text. The notion of truth acquires the sense of factuality. Because things happened, they are true. Because they are reported in the Bible and have therefore been inspired, they ought to have a bearing on the readers in informing and/or shaping their lives. There is no regard for the circumstances in which a story referring to a historical event once originated. There is no regard for any interpretative strategies used by an author to present a story to readers. What counts is the story world as the real (historical) world, because it is in history that God revealed himself and it is in history that people learn their lessons.

In the process of acquiring knowledge, it is assumed that religious knowledge is based solely on the biblical text, ignoring the (philosophical) nature of the way in which that knowledge was generated and acquired, the context of the persons acquiring that knowledge, the political situation of the readers as well as the author(s) of the biblical text, their cultures and even their education. If nothing but the biblical text is important in the reading process, the text becomes 'sacrosanct': it is beyond reproach, inviolable and intact, thereby securing for the biblical text an absoluteness in its truth claims while simultaneously emanating a sense of flawlessness. And, reciprocally, the very idea of flawlessness and inviolability feed the privileged status attributed to the biblical text: because nothing can be said against the biblical text, it assumes a favoured position in the hierarchy of factors generating knowledge.

Any distinction between text and interpretation is erased, because the interpreter does nothing more than to expound the plain sense of the biblical text (cf. Boone 1989: 78). And the plain sense is nothing else than what one thinks the biblical text is saying (without inquiring why one has read the text in a particular way) because the text is inspired by God. Inspiration guarantees the flawlessness of the biblical text: if God is omniscient the text cannot contain any mistake. Moreover, reading an inerrant text requires an inerrant reader (Boone 1989: 73), which is found in the authority of the brotherhood[24] of fundamentalism.

Nowadays fundamentalism is a label designating any kind of orthodoxy within world religions. To many it is a quick and effective description, of an unfriendly[25] nature, of someone more orthodox than oneself, while others regard fundamentalists as people out of touch with present-day culture. However, a common feature of all fundamentalisms is their proclivity to base religious authority upon a literal reading of scriptural texts.

---

24. The gathering in fraternities can be psychologically explained, according to Ostow (1990: 116) who finds the sense of belonging to a group essential to the phenomenon of fundamentalism. Fundamentalists protect themselves from danger by moving to smaller fraternal worlds, where by proper behaviour and worship they obtain security and protection through divine providence. The individual who is anxious and discontent in the larger group would experience a rebirth when entering a smaller fraternal group (Ostow 1990: 118). To Ostow (1990: 120) fundamentalism's intolerance of uncertainty and risk testifies to timidity and fearfulness amid its followers. By forming a fraternity, the individual can borrow courage or at least self-respect from the group.

25. To many, the label of fundamentalism is an abusive term smacking of religious imperialism and a shorthand for a hostility toward religion itself, especially when used within Christianity to portray Islam or Judaism (cf. Hassan 1990: 154; Wieseltier 1990: 192).

The text becomes the source of all religious and moral authority and at the same time establishes clear and certain absolute standards for life and thought (cf. Hunter 1990: 68).

Religious fundamentalism, with its emphasis on absolutes, is worlds apart from rhetoric and its relativizing implications. But let us not be misled! Fundamentalism has a powerful rhetoric, especially as it is presented in Christianity. By describing the inner discourse of fundamentalism, by exposing the *hidden authority*, one can hope to defuse its power (cf. Boone 1989: 111). The rhetoric of Fundamentalism boils down to this single concept: *authority* (cf. Sharpe 1983). It is an authority that is disguised to the unsophisticated reader, because the role of the interpreter in the reading process is concealed in the *privileged epistemological position* attributed to the biblical text as a 'sacred' text. Given the privileged status of the biblical text, one can garner support for a particular reading of the biblical text simply by *claiming to be merely saying what the Bible is telling one*, a situation that has proved disastrous within civil religion.

7. *Identification, Fundamentalism and Civil Religion*

Fundamentalism may be a religious phenomenon designating any kind of orthodoxy within world religions, yet its influence stretches far deeper and wider than religion. Ultimately, it influences the choices one makes in life. For example, it has a principled problem with democracy, because anyone representing God speaks to his or her audience with a perspective on authority that is hierarchical in nature (Borowitz 1990: 237). Thus it was possible to proclaim apartheid the will of God without really giving those suffering under it a chance to voice their disapproval. Furthermore, if apartheid was the will of God, any dissenting voice would be regarded as disobedience to that will. Fundamentalism's discomfort concerning sinners and evildoers caused the next logical step into ethnocentrism: the supporters of apartheid became *the* faithful community of God, and the rest the perverts.

In a contrasting mirror image, my students' reception of Esther and Mordecai reflects the same position: via the book of Esther those who participated in the struggle receive divine sanction for their deeds, whereas those who supported apartheid and thus oppressed their fellow-citizens become the perverts who deserve Haman's fate. Whether concerning apartheid or liberation, there is a link between the Bible story and the struggle for a political order. That link becomes very clear once the cosy relationship between civil religion and politics is exposed. The system of apartheid and its religious justification bear witness to the destruction which one can follow when story world is identified with the real world. It appears to me that, apart from providing theological sanction, religious fundamentalism[26] is linked to apartheid in a logical way.

Under the notion of 'civil religion'[27] is usually understood a religion existing alongside and differentiated from that of the churches, suggestive of deep-seated values and commitments that are not explicit in the course of everyday life, a vehicle of national religious self-understanding, and a heritage of moral and religious experience (cf. Bellah 1975). Civil religion is not a substitute for what is called 'revealed religion', but it provides a picture of the religious dimension of everyday life, drawing upon religious ideologies and common historical experiences of people within a nation state in order to unify them (cf. Cristi and Dawson 1996: 321).

Whereas Bellah and Cristi and Dawson provide us with a relatively tame definition of civil religion, its inner workings and influence are not that innocent. From the (little) literature I have read thus far, civil religion can sprout forth from grass-roots level (Durkheimian sense) or it can be imposed from the top as an artificial source of civic virtue (in the sense in which Jean-Jaques Rousseau viewed it). Given our present constitution and the secular nature of the new state, my students' effort to link religion and certain civil values is representative of the Durkheimian sense in that religion is used as an integrating factor in society—in the words of Christi and Dawson (1996: 322), 'lending its sacred rituals to reinforce identification with, and commitment to, the symbol system of the polity and national goals'. In these terms, religion is used to foster shared beliefs, sentiments and values (a new common sense?) necessary for stability.

---

26. Apartheid could have been a form of religious fundamentalism, but I am not sure whether religious fundamentalism always boils down to apartheid. There were religious groupings that criticized apartheid vehemently. However, to Kobus Krüger in his book *Along Edges: Religion in South Africa* (1995: 258) these critiques reveal a weakness, namely the failure to extend their criticisms to religious apartheid. Krüger says the following: 'Mostly the social and political critiques were launched from theologically conservative foundations, ranging from near-fundamentalism or even fundamentalism to varieties of middle-orthodoxy…but without overhauling those doctrinal positions.'

27. I use the notion of civil religion as a device to comprehend the merging of political and religious horizons in modern nation states (cf. Cristi and Dawson 1996: 320).

In what way can the former civil religion of apartheid be characterized? Louw (1989: 49) suggests that there was a close link between civil religion, state theology and church theology.[28] Louw sees civil religion as a set of symbols of religious power playing an essential role in the expression of political positions and the church's power within a certain social context and cultural environment (1989: 47). He regards it as a situation where there is a congruence between religious attitudes encouraged by the church on the one hand and nationalism on the other (1989: 48). This leads to a situation where the church exercises its power over groups, leaving the impression that the laws of the state are safeguarded by church authority. In this way, domination and supremacy could be upheld by a civil religion unable to criticize state theology—as exemplified by the office of the chaplain-general in the previous South African Defence Force—and sterile on grass-roots level.

I am not sure in what way we can talk of a civil religion as being explicitly state-sponsored in South Africa prior to 1994. The interpretation of the Afrikaner experience in terms of a civil religious discourse was done primarily by theologians in the three Afrikaans Calvinistic churches. For example, young ministers were admonished not to limit their efforts to religious needs of their congregations, but to extend them to the needs of society (cf. Thom 1993: 154). What renders this a sad situation is the fact that these churches were in alliance with the state and actually provided the theological basis for the apartheid state without the state explicitly demanding it.

However, I doubt it that any of the former Prime Ministers[29] presented himself as a divinely appointed Moses, as Pinochet of Chile once did. In

---

28. This link reminds me of the narrow relationship between the National Party government and the three Calvinist-orientated churches (Dutch Reformed, 'Hervormd' and 'Gereformeerd') between 1948 and 1994 and their supply of a 'civil religion' that could keep that government in place. It was this civil religion that provided the necessary theological justification of the political system of apartheid. It is as if the tables are now turned, with elements now trying to have the new status quo supported by some kind of theological claim.

29. Moodie (1978: 204) refers to D.F. Malan, a former 'dominee' (cleric) of the DRC who became Prime Minister after the 1948 elections won by the National Party, as saying about the Afrikaner: 'Afrikaner history reveals a firm resolve and purposiveness which makes one feel that Afrikanerdom is not the work of men, but the creation of God... Throughout our history, God's plan for our People is clear, we have a divine right to be because God created our People.' I am not sure in what way the fact that a prime minister who had formerly been a cleric can constitute state-sponsored civil

their discussion of Chilean civil religion under Pinochet, Cristi and Dawson (1996: 326) refer to a caption underneath a photograph of a soldier with a machine gun, guided by a bright star, that appeared in the army newspaper:

> Just like the star that guided the wise men of the east to Bethlehem, today the Chilean soldier looks to the pure sky of his Homeland and listens to the always renewed Biblical image—'I am the root and the lineage of David, the resplendent star of the morning'.

In this way, the Bible became an important motivating factor in Pinochet's design to keep his regime in place.

In South Africa, Afrikaner civil religion found a counter-reaction in black theology. Similarly, in the United States an alternative civil religion was formed in the black community, vis-à-vis Bellah's definition which implies a monolithic view of the American experience: this civil religion was very predisposed towards a 'white' analysis of a perceived universal and transcendental religious reality as revealed in the experience of the American people (cf. Poole 1991: 28). Poole argues that civil religion is not universal, but rather the formulations of those who represent the people who benefit the most from the system and who subscribe to the predominant mytho-cultural hermeneutic (Poole 1991: 39). He says that white theologians relate the problem of faith and history to social interests rather than to the quality of life lived by those victimized by the status quo. He is of the opinion that racism is included in the white American theological enterprise as part and parcel of life. In the face of this situation, he seeks a black civil religion that will articulate a longing for freedom, and an emancipation of black people from white oppression by whatever means black people deem necessary (Poole 1991: 38).

In South Africa this kind of civil religion was in the offing since 1930. The only difference was that it was not black! When one looks at the roots of Afrikaner civil religion, one finds a strong identification between the fortunes of the Jewish people as described in the Old Testament and the weals and woes of a group of people who called themselves 'Afrikaners'. Dunbar Moodie (1978: 302) describes this movement as 'the appeal of the Judaeo-Christian model of salvation history for a group who see themselves as persecuted'. There was a very particular bond between God and these people: 'the history of the Afrikaner shows God's particular will in

religion, though such a person may make the connection between religion and politics less problematical.

the special election of his Afrikaner People as a racial and/or cultural (ethnic) group, with its own God-given language and its own divine destiny' (Moodie 1978: 204).

Between the Anglo–Boer War of 1899–1902 which left the Afrikaner destitute and powerless, and the climax of Afrikaner nationalism (1948), the image of Israel as elected people provided some solace to a rejected group of people ill at ease with their political future in communion with the English. One of the main proponents was J.D. du Toit (in common parlance Totius). The Afrikaner desire to break away from the British led to some interesting readings of the Bible. Differentiation in creation was interpreted as separation of the Afrikaner from the English as well as from the African people (Du Toit 1977: 330). The Great Trek was seen as an obedient response to the call of God not to stay with the unifying forces of the Cape as was the case with the Tower of Babel. The laws of Moses directly commanding Israel not to mix with the Canaanites (Deut. 22.9-11) became divine law for the Afrikaner, imploring them not to mix with other population groups, especially Blacks who became associated with the sons of Ham (cf. Hamerton-Kelly 1993: 169). The time before 1948, which resulted in a victory for the National Party, was identified as the exilic period of the Afrikaner. The Afrikaner could associatively identify with ancient Israel, empowering them to implement some of the Jewish laws in their own social order.

In some cases the Great Trek was compared to Abraham's trek from Ur and to the Exodus from Egyptian bondage (Hamerton-Kelly 1993: 164). In other cases, the suffering and death experienced in Natal (in their con- frontation with the Zulu nation which culminated in the Battle of Blood River) was described as a *via dolorosa*. To Moodie (1978: 205) death and suffering had a special connotation in the Afrikaner civil religion: they led to the first two Boer republics and later to the constitution of the present Republic of South Africa. All these events were filled with biblical images and actions. In the first Anglo–Boer War, for example, the Boers renewed their covenant with God at Paardekraal, where they brought stones from wherever they had come and piled them on a heap. A reminiscence of Joshua at Gilgal (Josh. 4)? A monument was erected over that heap! In fact, the history of Afrikaner civil religion can be traced by its monuments strewn over the country.

In the case of Afrikaner civil religion, civil religion was a faction or a highly sectarian faith and definitely not a canopy of common values fostering social integration. It functioned as a legitimating authority for political ideologies: reconciling groups outside Afrikanerdom to their subservient status to the Afrikaner people and assuring the ruling elite[30] of Afrikanerdom of the righteousness of their rule and privileges. This civil religion was very particularistic and reserved for a certain group of people. Such a civil religion is self-limiting and very episodic in nature. Moreover, it was too closely associated with a political agenda masked by religious symbolism, tarnishing the symbols themselves! These symbols lacked independent validity, failing to evoke deep and lasting commitments. They were not perceived to be rooted in the very nature of reality (cf. Cristi and Dawson 1996: 331-32).

Afrikaner civil religion never constituted a widely held set of fundamental political and social principles concerning the history and destiny of a state that kept that state together, as Linder (1996: 734) describes the phenomenon of civil religion in the United States. My students' responses to Esther 9 which I read, cannot constitute a new civil religion either, because they still divide a nation instead of binding it together. But, I guess, such readings resemble what John de Gruchy (1994: 53) calls 'the slippery slope towards a seedy civil religion of national self-interest, false pride, jingoism, and the domination of others'.[31]

I have to admit that the entire notion of civil religion appears rather problematical at this stage, because in some way or the other it rests on an identification that equates a country's (or nation's) actions (historical as well as proposed ones) with those found in the Bible. Afrikaner politicians were not the only ones equating their own people with Israel. American presidents such as Washington and Jefferson compared the Americans with Israel not infrequently (cf. Lott 1994)! Bill Clinton's inaugural

---

30. According to Dunbar Moodie (1978: 212) there was always the distinction between a small but relatively well-educated and wealthy elite, and the poor white masses. The elite regarded themselves as the protectors, overseers and fathers of the People. This attitude was accepted by the poor, and their subjugation led to an oligarchy at several levels of society, of which the former Broederbond was the most influential.

31. De Gruchy utters these words in connection with the flag as national symbol which he would not want to have in a church. But what about our national anthem? He has no problem singing *Nkosi sikelel' iAfrika* in church, because it is a hymn written a hundred years ago by a Methodist minister. He says (1994: 52) that it may awaken national pride, but its substance is prayer to the Holy Spirit so that the nation may be blessed. Ironically, a state with the most liberal constitution, expressly proclaiming its secular nature, has a hymn as part of its national anthem.

address in 1993 was even more inclined to civil religion than John F. Kennedy's, so much so that fundamentalists such as Jerry Falwell and Pat Robertson accused him of manipulating the Bible and introducing pseudo-Christianity (cf. Linder 1996: 733).

8. *Concluding Remarks: Is Reading the Bible Possible?*

Am I too sensitive towards my students' remarks? I am associated with apartheid because of my birth as a white male Calvinist Protestant of Huguenot and maybe Indonesian descent. My being born into an Afrikaans-speaking family and a church that supported Afrikaner civil religion made these students' remarks have a big impact on me. I am not sure whether my reaction is part of what James Statman, a US political psychologist (1998: 11), would call 'amnesia' and 'denial'. Perhaps I protest too much. But what I have encountered is a civil religion at grass-roots level that legitimizes the new political dispensation theologically by means of a naive realist identification with biblical characters. Peter Clarke (1996: 13) argues that civil religion has a right of existence to the extent that it is able to make a positive contribution to the nation, upholding national values and interests, operating as a unifying force. But who determines these values and interests? During Afrikaner rule from 1948 to 1994 they were determined by politicians and then proclaimed by the church! We now have a secular parliament with quite a few clerics, some even in ministerial positions. Many of the former liberation theologians (at least those who are not accused of abusing European donor money!) have acquired plush positions in the new political landscape.

The rhetorical approach of Kenneth Burke, using identification as one of its cornerstones, indicates that identification takes place when readers have the same interests as the characters. Identification based on shared interests may become frightening when those characters plan death and destruction. Having all white people lumped together under the label of Haman leaves one feeling uncomfortable, to say the least. But, furthermore being confronted with 'Jewish ire', leaves one threatened and fearful, and one actually starts to sympathize with the Persians. Somehow we have reached the thin blue line separating the justified anger of the oppressed from the vindictiveness of a victorious ruling class.

The aesthetic identification of Hans-Robert Jauss leaves much more *Spielraum* for the identification process. It enables readers to enter the story world, and succeeds in reminding readers of the distance and difference between them and the story world, so that identification never becomes an equation. Within this framework I can accept people's identification with heroes such as Esther and Mordecai, because the identification is not fixed. There is always the possibility of deconstructing that identification, simply because joint interest is never reached. I can always question Esther's initial reluctance to intervene for her people or her later abuse of power to get her way with Haman's sons. I know that the story provides good reasons for her actions, but from a different point of view its probability is questionable. The few feminist readings I have referred to never argue that readers should copy Esther and Mordecai. They find their strength in the way Esther appears to conduct her business in a male-dominated world. Indeed *Selbstgenuss in Fremdgenuss*! They are critical enough of the distance between them and the text to realize that no character is wholly good or wholly evil.

Fundamentalism provides a breeding ground for identification based on joint interests. The twentieth-century reader regards the ancient biblical text as a 'modern' text, without any recognition of its otherness or historicalness. Surely, Burke's notion of identification as a search for common sensations, common concepts, images, ideas and attitudes will find willing imitators among a fundamentalist audience whom the biblical text furnishes with role models. Then Burkean identification becomes 'literature for use'. But Burke (1969b: xix) also says:

> Since no two things or acts or situations are exactly alike, you cannot apply the same term to both of them without introducing a certain margin of ambiguity, an ambiguity as great as the difference between the two subjects that are given the identical title.

Without these ambiguities, there is no *Fremdgenuss*. The reception of the biblical text is turned into an ideological reception and constitutes a pre-manufactured consumption embodied in a civil religion seeing no difference between the historical experience of Israel and the historical experience of those who proclaim this civil religion. In this case, religion is used to foster a 'shared' belief system that underlies a particular political ideology. Without effective criticism of the actions or behaviour of biblical characters the Bible becomes an important motivating factor in political life, with the perilous possibility that the dark side of these stories will also be deemed exemplary.

9. *'Identification' with Other Scholars**

ANC (African National Congress)
  1994   *The Reconstruction and Development Programme: A Policy Framework*
            (Johannesburg: Umanyano Publications).
Baukney, H.
  1998   'Universities Find Grail of Transformation Elusive', *Sunday Independent*,
            28 June: 8.
Beal, T.K.
  1995   'Tracing Esther's Beginnings', in Brenner (ed.) 1995: 85-110.
Bellah, R.N.
  1975   'Civil Religion in America', *Daedalus* 96/1: 1-21.
Boone, H.C.
  1989   *The Bible Tells Them So: The Discourse of Protestant Fundamentalism*
            (New York: State University of New York Press).
Borowitz, E.B.
  1990   'The Enduring Truth of Religious Liberalism', in N.J. Cohen (ed.), *The
            Fundamentalist Phenomenon: A View from Within; a Response from Without*
            (Grand Rapids: Eerdmans): 230-47.
Brenner, A.
  1995a   'Introduction', in Brenner (ed.) 1995: 11-25.
  1995b   'Looking at Esther through the Looking Glass', in Brenner (ed.) 1995: 71-80
Brenner, A. (ed.)
  1995   *A Feminist Companion to Esther, Judith and Susanna* (Sheffield: Sheffield
            Academic Press).
Briant, P.
  1987   'Pouvoir central et polycentrisme culturel dans l'Empire Achemenide:
            Quelques réflexions et suggestions', in H. Sancisi-Weerdenburg (ed.),
            Achaemenid History. I. *Sources, Structures and Synthesis* (Leiden: Neder-
            lands Instituut voor het Nabije Oosten): 1-32.
  1988   'Ethno-classe dominante et populations soumises dans l'Empire Ache-
            menide: Le cas de l'Egypte', in A. Kuhrt and H. Sancisi-Weerdenburg
            (eds.), *Achaemenid History*. III. *Method and Theory* (Leiden: Nederlands
            Instituut voor het Nabije Oosten): 137-74.
  1990   'Groningen 1987: Libres réflexions', in H. Sancisi-Weerdenburg and J.W.
            Drijvers (eds.), *Achaemenid History*. V. *The Roots of the European Tradi-
            tion* (Leiden: Nederlands Instituut voor het Nabije Oosten): 167-70.
Bronner, L.L.
  1995   'Esther Revisited: An Aggadic Approach', in Brenner (ed.) 1995: 176-97.
  1998   'Reclaiming Esther: From Sex Object to Sage', *Jewish Biblical Quarterly*
            26.1: 3-16.

*   The fidelity and probability of my narrative lie in my identification with the sources. It is for the readers to decide whether I treated my sources as literature for use…

Burke, K.

    1969a   *The Rhetoric of Motives* (Berkeley: University of California Press).

    1969b   *A Grammar of Motives* (Berkeley: University of California Press).

Clarke, P.

    1996   'Christianity and Nation Building in West Africa (c. 1880–c. 1980)', *Scriptura* 56: 1-14.

Clines, D.J.A.

    1990   'Reading Esther from Left to Right: Contemporary Strategies for Reading a Biblical Text', in D.J.A. Clines, S. Fowl and S.E. Porter (eds.), *The Bible in Three Dimensions* (Sheffield: Sheffield Academic Press): 31-52.

Craffert, P.F.

    1996   'Reading and Divine Sanction: The Ethics of Interpreting the New Testament in the New South Africa', in S.E. Porter and T.H. Olbricht (eds.), *Rhetoric, Scripture and Theology: Essays from the 1994 Pretoria Conference* (JSNTSup, 131; Sheffield: Sheffield Academic Press): 54-71.

    1998   'From Apartheid Readings to Ordinary Readings of the Bible: Has the Ethics of Interpretation Changed?', *Scriptura* 64: 65-79.

Craig, K.

    1995   *Reading Esther: A Case for the Literary Carnivalesque* (Louisville, KY: Westminister/John Knox Press).

Cristi, M., and L.L. Dawson

    1996   'Civil Religion in Comparative Perspective: Chile under Pinochet (1973–1989)', *Social Compass* 43/3: 319-38.

De Gruchy, J.W.

    1994   'Civil Religion in the New South Africa', *South African Outlook* (May): 51-53.

Du Plessis, A., B. Van der Walt, P. Venter and A. van Wyk

    1997   ''n Openbare Belydenis (Uit Potchefstroom)', *Woord en Daad / Word and Action* Spring 361: 16-17.

Du Toit, J.D.

    1977   *Totius: Versamelde Werke: Deel 7* (Kaapstad: Tafelberg).

Edwards, R.K.

    1990   '"Ahasuerus the Villain"—a Reply', *Jewish Biblical Quarterly* 19/1: 34-39.

Eilberg-Schwartz, H.

    1990   *The Savage in Judaism: An Anthropology of Israelite Religion and Ancient Judaism* (Bloomington: Indiana University Press).

Eloff, T.

    1997   'Wat Het die Gereformeerde Kerk Met Apartheid "Gedoen"?', *Beeld* 15 (January): 9.

Fisher, W.

    1987   *Human Communication as Narration: Toward a Philosophy of Reason, Value, and Action* (Columbia: University of South Carolina Press).

Forguson, L.

    1989   *Common Sense* (London: Routledge).

Goldman, S.

    1990   'Narrative and Ethical Ironies in Esther', *JSOT* 47: 15-31.

Goodnick, B.
  1997   'The Book of Esther and its Motifs', *Jewish Biblical Quarterly* 25/2: 101-
              107.
Hamerton-Kelly, R.
  1993   'Biblical Justification of Apartheid in Afrikaner Civil Religion', in K. Keul-
              man (ed.), *Critical Moments in Religious History* (Macon, GA: Mercer
              University Press): 161-72.
Hassan, R.
  1990   'The Burgeoning of Islamic Fundamentalism: Toward an Understanding of
              the Phenomenon', in N.J. Cohen (ed.), *The Fundamentalist Phenomenon: A
              View from Within; a Response from Without* (Grand Rapids: Eerdmans):
              151-71.
Hunter, J.D.
  1990   'Fundamentalism in Its Global Contours', in N.J. Cohen (ed.), *The Funda-
              mentalist Phenomenon: A View from Within; a Response from Without*
              (Grand Rapids: Eerdmans): 57- 72.
Isaacson, M.
  1998   'Swooning in the Aisles for Rhema's Instant Salvation', *Sunday Independent*
              (5 July): 18.
Jauss, H.-R.
  1982   *Ästetische Erfahrung und literarische Hermeneutik* (Frankfurt am Main:
              Suhrkamp).
Kirk, J.W.
  1961   'The Forum: Kenneth Burk and Identification', *Quarterly Journal of Speech*
              47: 414-15.
Klein, L.R.
  1995   'Honor and Shame in Esther', in Brenner (ed.) 1995: 149-75.
Krüger, K.S.
  1995   *Along Edges: Religion in South Africa: Bushman, Christian, Buddhist* (Pre-
              toria: University of South Africa Press).
Linder, R.D.
  1996   'Universal Pastor: President Bill Clinton's Civil Religion', *Journal of
              Church and State* 38/4: 733-49.
Loader, J.A.
  1987   'Exodus, Liberation Theology and Theological Argument', *Journal of Theo-
              logy for Southern Africa* 59: 3-18.
Lott, D.N. (ed.)
  1994   *The Presidents Speak: The Inaugural Addresses of the American Presidents,
              from Washington to Clinton* (New York: Henry Holt).
Louw, D.J.
  1989   'Omnipotence (Force) or Vulnerability (Defencelessness)? The Significance
              of a Theological Interpretation of the Category of Power on an Ethic of
              Conflict Management', *Scriptura* 18: 41-58.
Makoe, A.
  1998   'Motshega Moves from Darkness to Light and Is Reborn', *Sunday Inde-
              pendent* (21 June): 3.

Marty, M., and R.S. Appleby
 1993 *Fundamentalisms and Society: Reclaiming the Sciences, the Family and Education* (Chicago: University of Chicago Press).

Meadows, P.
 1957 'The Semiotic of Kenneth Burke', *Philosophy and Phenomenological Research* 18: 80-87.

Molière, J.-B.
 1971 *Le Tartuffe* (Paris: Librairie Larousse).

Moodie, T.D.
 1978 'The Afrikaner Civil Religion', in A. Mol (ed.), *Identity and Religion: International, Cross-Cultural Approaches* (London: Sage Publications): 203-28.

Mzamane, M.V.
 1998 'Crisis in Religious Education: The HDU Experience'. Unpublished paper, University of Fort Hare.

Niditch, S.
 1995 'Esther: Folklore, Wisdom, Feminism and Authority', in Brenner (ed.) 1995: 28-46.

Ostow, M.
 1990 'The Fundamentalist Phenomenon: A Psychological Approach', in N.J. Cohen (ed.), *The Fundamentalist Phenomenon: A View from Within; a Response from Without* (Grand Rapids: Eerdmans): 99-125.

Poole, T.G.
 1991 'Black Religion and Civil Religion: African-American Voices in America's "Third Time Trial" ', *Journal of Theology for Southern Africa* 77: 27-46.

Sancisi-Weerdenburg, H.
 1990 'The Quest for the Elusive Empire', in H. Sancisi-Weerdenburg and J.W. Drijvers (eds.), *Achaemenid History. V. The Roots of the European Tradition* (Leiden: Nederlands Instituut voor het Nabije Oosten): 263-74.

Serfontein, H.
 1998 'Apartheid's Church Starts to See the Light', *Sunday Independent* (21 June): 4.

Sharpe, E.
 1983 *Understanding Fundamentalism* (London: Gerald Duckworth).

Skinner, Q.
 1988 'Afterword: A Reply to My Critics', in J. Tully (ed.), *Meaning and Context: Quentin Skinner and his Critics* (Princeton: Princeton University Press): 231-88.

Snyman, G.F.
 1997a 'Dit is Tyd Dat GKSA Besef Kritiese Teologie Het 'n Rol', *Beeld* (10 October): 8.
 1997b 'Stel Rassevooroordele Van Totius Aan die Kaak', *Beeld* (24 January): 8.
 1997c 'Wanneer die Appels Ver Van die Boom Val—Juda Se Geslagsregister in 1 Kronieke 2.3–4.23', *In die Skriflig* 31/4: 347-74.
 1998 ' "Ilahle Elinothuthu?" The Lay Reader and/or the Critical Reader: Some Remarks on Africanisation', Paper read at Annual Meeting of the New Testament Society of South Africa, University of South Africa, Pretoria, 15 April.

Spangenberg, I.J.J.
1996   'Die NG Kerk, die Jona-Verhaal en Religieuse Praktyk', Paper delivered at
        the Annual Meeting of the Old Testament Society of South Africa, Stellen-
        bosch, 3–5 September.

Spoelstra, B.
1997   'Bely Vir Apartheid: Dis Vorm, Mense Soek Godsdiens', *Beeld* (14
        January): 10.

Statman, J.
1998   'Whites Are Living in Cloud-Cuckooland', *Sunday Independent* (5 July): 11.

Stolper, M.W.
1990   'The KASR-Archive', in H. Sancisi-Weerdenburg and A. Kuhrt (eds.),
        Achaemenid History. IV. *Centre and Periphery. Proceedings of the Gronin-
        gen 1986 Achaemenid History Workshop* (Leiden: Nederlands Instituut voor
        het Nabije Oosten): 195-205.

Thom, G.
1992   'Between Priestly Identification and Prophetic Confrontation: The Roots of
        the Volkskerk in Afrikaner History', *Studia Historiae Ecclesiasticae* 18/2:
        149-61.

Van Huyssteen, W.
1987   *The Realism of the Text: A Perspective on Biblical Authority* (Pretoria: Uni-
        versity of South Africa Press).

Van Wyk, A.
1997   'Nasionalistiese Politiek Ook Van Liberale Teologie', *Beeld* (20 October):
        10.

Vorster, J.N.
1988   'The Use of Scripture in Fundamentalism', in J. Mouton, A.G. Van Aarde
        and J.N. Vorster (eds.), *Paradigms and Progress in Theology: HRSC Studies
        in Research Methodology*, IV (Pretoria: Human Sciences Research Council):
        155-75.

Vorster, W.S.
1984   'The Use of Scripture and the NG Kerk: A Shift of Paradigm or of Values?',
        in L.J.W. Hofmeyer and W.S. Vorster (eds.), *New Faces of Africa: Essays in
        Honour of Ben Marais* (Pretoria: University of South Africa Press): 204-19.

Wiesehöfer, J.
1988   'Das Bild der Achaimeniden in der Zeit Des Nationalsozialismus', in A.
        Kuhrt and H. Sancisi-Weerdenburg (eds.), *Achaemenid History*. III. *Method
        and Theory* (Leiden: Nederlands Instituut voor het Nabije Oosten): 1-4.

Wieseltier, L.
1990   'The Jewish Face of Fundamentalism', in N.J. Cohen (ed.), *The Funda-
        mentalist Phenomenon: A View from Within; a Response from Without*
        (Grand Rapids: Eerdmans): 192- 96.

Wyler, B.
1995   'Esther: The Incomplete Emancipation of a Queen', in Brenner (ed.) 1995:
        111-35.

Politeness Strategies in the So-called 'Enemy Psalms': An Inquiry into Israelite Prayer Rhetoric

Johan H. Coetzee

1. *Introduction*

The aim of this paper is to identify *politeness strategies* in a few prayers of Ancient Israel in order to determine their rhetorical and social function. Numerous instances of politeness occur in the Psalter of the First Testament. We will, however, confine ourselves to only a few prayers in which direct words are attributed to the enemies of the petitioners, viz. Psalms 2, 3, 13, 41 and 42/43. Politeness as a specific kind of speech-act functions within each prayer in interrelated conversational structures aiming at influencing the audience, in particular God to whom the prayers are normally addressed.

The prayers discussed below are approached with the assumption that they were all *prayed aloud in public*.[1] The implication of this is that the audience of each prayer should be taken seriously. On the one hand, the petitioners take a socio-political risk of response from their enemies who might overhear, or hear about, their prayers.[2] On the other hand, the petitioners rely on God and those present, who are all involved in the rhetorical situations when the prayers are spoken out loud in public, to respond to the benefit of the supplicants.

Hopefully this socio-rhetorical investigation into prayer-politeness, which can be taken as part of cultic politeness in the broader sense, will

---

1. G.T. Sheppard, '"Enemies" and the Politics of Prayer in the Book of Psalms', in D. Jobling, P.L. Day, and G.T. Sheppard (eds.), *The Bible and the Politics of Exegesis: Essays in Honour of Norman K. Gottwald on his Sixty-Fifth Birthday* (Cleveland: Pilgrim Press, 1991), pp. 61-82. Sheppard's theory that 'these prayers were traditionally spoken out loud and intended to be overheard by friends and enemies alike' (p. 64) is based on firm ground.

2. Sheppard, 'Enemies', p. 69.

5

broaden our understanding of the functioning of argumentation strategies implemented in Ancient Israelite cultic prayers.

For the sake of our discussion we will primarily pay attention to the functioning of *rhetorical strategies.* Figures of style will be dealt with if and when they serve the argumentation. The argumentative and therefore persuasive function of prayers is indisputable.[3] The identification of politeness strategies in this paper is based on the model developed by Brown and Levinson.[4] The New International Version is used as a translation of the Hebrew text.

2. A Survey of the Psalms

2.1. Psalm 2

Psalm 2 is a 'royal psalm' which reflects the king's reception of the royal charisma and the concrete commissions he had to carry out. The psalm was recited during the enthronement ceremony.

---

3.   E. Wendland, 'Introit "into the Sanctuary of God" (Psalm 73:17): Entering the Theological "Heart" of the Psalm at the Centre of the Psalter', *OTE* 11/1 (1998), pp. 128-53 (143-44).

4.   P. Brown and S. Levinson, 'Universals in Language Usage: Politeness Phenomena', in E.N. Goody (ed.), *Questions and Politeness: Strategies in Social Interaction* (Cambridge Papers in Social Anthropology, 8; Cambridge: Cambridge University Press, 1978), pp. 56-289. In short, Brown and Levinson (p. 60) are of the opinion that 'patterns of message construction, or "ways of putting things", or simply language usage, are part of the very stuff that social relationships are made of...' They developed a model person (MP) endowed with rationality and face (p. 63). 'By rationality we mean something very specific—the availability to our MP of a precisely definable mode of reasoning from ends to the means that will achieve those ends. By "face" we mean something quite specific again: our MP is endowed with two wants—roughly, the want to be unimpeded and the want to be approved of in certain respects... In particular, caught between the want to satisfy another MP's face wants and the want to say things that infringe those wants...', the MP implements various 'linguistic strategies as *means* satisfying communicative and face-oriented *ends*, in a strictly formal system of rational "practical reasoning"' (p. 63). Brown and Levinson have basically compiled their data from 'first-hand usage for three languages: English (from both sides of the Atlantic); Tzeltal, a Mayan language spoken in the community of Tenejapa in Chiapas, Mexico; and South Indian Tamil from a village in the Coimbatore District of Tamilnadu' (p. 64). They believe 'it is legitimate to project from a careful three-way experiment in three unrelated cultures to hypotheses about universals in verbal interaction because...the degree of detail in convergence lies far beyond the realm of chance' (p. 64).

2.1.1. *Argumentation Strategies.* The chiastically arranged introductory question reports[5] on the conduct of the nations. Not only does this question attract the attention of the audience, but also its argumentative function is to compel response from them with reference to the immediate problem or exigency.[6] The question is put forward in order to articulate the exigency of the rhetorical situation. The stating of the problem (vv. 1-3) and the persuasive solution to the problem (vv. 10-12) frame the rest of the prayer (vv. 4-6, 7-9).

A value judgment is built into the question by means of the noun 'vanity' (v. 1). It is evident that an argument by ridicule is implemented and, mentioning Yahweh's laughter (v. 4), corroborates it.[7] The question argues against the stupidity of the revolt of the nations against Yahweh and his anointed one. The argument by ridicule therefore aims at putting the enemies to shame, serving as a strong bald-on-record[8] face-threatening[9] speech-act.

Tension between the nations of the world and their leaders on the one hand and Yahweh and his anointed one on the other hand is the problem of immediate concern, as illustrated in vv. 2-3. The supplicant sides with

---

5.   See E.N. Goody, 'Towards a Theory of Questions', in Goody (ed.), *Questions and Politeness*, pp. 17-43 (19), for the report function of questions as indirect speech-acts.

6.   These, according to E.O. Keenan, B.B. Schieffelin and M. Platt, 'Questions of Immediate Concern', in Goody (ed.), *Questions and Politeness*, pp. 44-55 (52), are the two basic functions of the interrogative.

7.   In this regard, C.H. Perelman and L. Olbrechts-Tyteca, *The New Rhetoric: A Treatise on Argumentation* (London: University of Notre Dame Press, 1971), pp. 205-206, state that 'Exclusive laughter is the response to the breaking of an accepted rule, a way of condemning eccentric behavior which is not deemed sufficiently important or dangerous to be repressed by more violent means'.

8.   The bald-on-record strategy is used when something is said or done 'straight in the face' of somebody else without trying to save the face of the recipient, e.g. a demand. Maximum efficiency, great urgency or desperation is normally the motive behind the bald-on-record strategy. Redress or politeness is avoided in such a case. See Brown and Levinson, 'Universals', pp. 74, 99-106.

9.   Brown and Levinson, 'Universals', p. 66, define 'face' as 'the public self-image that every member wants to claim for himself'. 'Face' involves two related aspects: '(a) negative face: the basic claim to territories, personal preserves, rights to non-distraction—i.e. to freedom of action and freedom from imposition (b) positive face: the positive consistent self-image or "personality" (crucially including the desire that this self-image be appreciated and approved of) claimed by interactants.'

Yahweh, and in doing so he implements arguments from authority. With reference to Yahweh the supplicant's claiming of common ground is a positive politeness strategy[10] and it is corroborated by the decree of Yahweh mentioned in vv. 7-9. It holds negative implications for the enemies. The tension culminates in v. 3 where words are put in the mouth of the enemies, 'Let us break their chains...and throw off their fetters'. Yahweh's reaction to the revolt of the nations is given in vv. 4-6. This reaction is paralleled with vv. 1-3, illustrating part of the argumentation structure of the prayer.[11]

- In v. 1 // 4 the self-deliberative actions of the two main rivals, the nations and Yahweh, are mentioned, viz. the planning activities of the nations and Yahweh's laughter. The contrast illustrated by the kings *of the earth* (v. 2) and Yahweh *in heaven* (v. 4) corroborates the argument by ridicule. It is ridiculous that earthly beings can revolt against Yahweh in heaven.
- In v. 2 // 5 preparatory actions of the characters are mentioned.
- In v. 3 // 6 we come across the direct speeches of the rivals. Words are attributed to both the enemies and Yahweh. The concern of the kings and nations of the earth is to be released from their submissiveness to Yahweh and his anointed. Yahweh who is in heaven, on the other hand, is concerned about his empowerment of his anointed one 'on Zion, my holy hill', pointing towards heavenly rule initiated from Zion by Yahweh[12] in order to control the rioting nations. The words attributed to Yahweh (6) are meant to be an argument from authority. The authority invoked is emphasized by the pronoun וַאֲנִי, referring to Yahweh.

In the second stanza (vv. 7-9) the king proclaims the decree of Yahweh in Yahweh's own words.[13] During the inauguration procedures the king is

---

10. Positive politeness is oriented towards the positive self-image the recipient claims for him-/herself. See Brown and Levinson, 'Universals', pp. 75, 108.

11. According to Brown and Levinson, 'Universals', p. 237, 'conversational location, both in terms of "local turn-by-turn organization"...and in terms of overall conversational structure...is a crucial determinant of how an utterance is understood'.

12. Typical temple theology is met here. The relationship between heaven and earth is introduced dialectically without identifying the one with the other neither separating them. See H. Spieckermann, *Heilsgegenwart: Eine Theologie der Psalmen* (Göttingen: Vandenhoeck & Ruprecht, 1989), pp. 219-20.

13. חֹק (7a) is a political concept (a proclaimed decree) referring to 'Königs-

declared to be 'son of God' by adoption through a prophetic announcement of a legal act.[14] This prophetic announcement is now repeated aloud in the prayer by the king himself. In this way a very close reciprocal relationship is established between Yahweh and his anointed one, viz. that of *Father* and *son*. The rhetorician who wrote the prayer implemented these two 'in-group identity markers'[15] in the form of a reciprocal positive politeness strategy in order to establish common ground between Yahweh and the king. Yahweh proclaims the king to be his son, which is positive politeness by Yahweh towards the king. Simultaneously, however, the king, by announcing this decree of Yahweh in public prayer, is confessing that he belongs to Yahweh, which is an expression of positive politeness by the king towards Yahweh.

The result is that the king can 'feel good' about his association with Yahweh. This positive politeness strategy, therefore, also serves as an empowerment of the king by Yahweh. His honour and power are based on this sonship.

It is, however, important to look at the proclamation of the decree from another angle as well, namely, as simultaneously serving as a negative politeness strategy.[16] The moment that the king utters the words of the decree ('You are my son...', v. 7) he places Yahweh under the obligation of supporting him in his office as the king of Judah. The expansion of the basic decree ('today I have become your Father. Ask of me, and I will make the nations your inheritance...', v. 8) should be taken as an amplification of this negative politeness strategy.

To my mind this twofold functioning of the same speech-act (as both positive and negative politeness) is characteristic of cultic politeness, especially prayer politeness. This will become more evident when I deal with the other prayers in this paper.

This strategy is implemented by the rhetorician to the benefit of the king and to the detriment of the enemies. This brings a third dimension into the

protokoll'. See H.-J. Kraus, *Theologie der Psalmen* (BKAT, 15/3; Neukirchen–Vluyn: Neukirchener Verlag, 1979), p. 141.

    14. Kraus, *Theologie*, p. 142.

    15. Brown and Levinson, 'Universals', pp. 112-13.

    16. Negative politeness is oriented mainly towards partially satisfying (redressing) the recipient's basic want to maintain claims of territory and self-determination, i.e. freedom of action and freedom from imposition. It is a strategy for approaching the recipient indirectly in order to persuade him/her to react. See Brown and Levinson, 'Universals', pp. 75, 134-35.

picture, namely, that the announcement of the decree also serves as a face-threatening speech-act[17] directed at the hostile nations. As a result of the decree the king will inherit the nations and he will forcefully rule over them. Therefore the announcement of the decree also serves as an argument from authority which is corroborated by the threat in vv. 10-12.

The whole of the third stanza (vv. 10-12) is an argument from authority based on Yahweh as the universal ruler on whom the king's honour is based. By virtue of the authority bestowed upon him the king, from a position of power, delivers an ultimatum in the form of a threat to the rulers of the earth. They must serve Yahweh with fear.[18] This is a bald-on-record face-threatening act aimed at the enemies' negative face want.[19] They have to serve Yahweh or else be destroyed.

2.1.2. *The Audience and Rhetorical Situation.* In this section a hypothetical creation process of the rhetorical situation and of the prayer is sketched. It is done in detail with reference to this psalm only in order to illustrate the interplay between politics and religion in the formative process of the rhetoric of this prayer. Something similar could have happened between the initial petitioners of other cultic prayers and the cult personnel who, as rhetoricians, prepared the prayers for general cultic use. One should also keep in mind that some of the prayers could have been the work of cultic personnel right from the start without any involvement of other so-called 'initial petitioners'.[20]

Both the initial question (v. 1) and the solution (vv. 10-12) involve the world nations and their rulers as part of the audience. They represent the entire political *Umwelt* that could possibly be a threat to Judah and her king. The characters 'Yahweh' and 'his anointed one' also participate in the audience, thereby defining the rhetorical event as cultic-political.

---

17. See Brown and Levinson, 'Universals', pp. 70-76.

18. The emendation to the text proposed by H.-J. Kraus, *Psalmen* (BKAT, 15/1; Neukirchen–Vluyn: Neukirchener Verlag, 1972), pp. 12, 20, reads as follows: נַשְּׁקוּ בְרַגְלָיו בִּרְעָדָה—literally: 'Kiss his feet with trembling'. The kissing of Yahweh's feet is a token of obedience (Isa. 49.23).

19. See Brown and Levinson, 'Universals', pp. 70-71. They define 'negative face' as 'the want of every "competent adult member" that his actions be unimpeded by others' (p. 67). 'Bald-on-record' means direct, without any redress (p. 74).

20. Although the origin of the prayers presently included in the Psalter is a complicated matter, one can at least accept that some of them were initially prayed in some form by 'initial petitioners' and later on cast in their present form by cultic personnel. Others were prepared from scratch by cultic personnel to fit general cultic use.

Initially the rhetorician had probably aimed at influencing the king, the speaker to be, by the prayer that he was composing. The rhetorician had a prayer-event in mind during which the king of Judah would recite aloud in public from the protocol during his inauguration ceremony as part of the process of taking up his office. During the creation process of this psalm, therefore, the rhetorician probably had in mind that the king would first read the prayer, then internalize the content and only then utter it audibly in public. This makes the king the first implied reader. The implied audience for this prayer-event would then be the cultic community, Yahweh and the nations, including their rulers. During the event of uttering the prayer the king, of course, steps down as implied reader and becomes the new rhetorician.

Medhurst[21] provides us with an interesting modern example of the process of development of an inaugural prayer during the history of the United States of America. In 1965 Lyndon Baines Johnson's inauguration as president took place and various clergymen each had to submit a prayer to be prayed during the occasion. With the assistance of his speechwriting staff Johnson proposed deletions and additions to the prayers. He gave his final approval to the prayers before they could be uttered in public. In this instance prayers had therefore been prepared for the inaugural setting by order of the president and he himself thoroughly considered the strategic advantages for himself and the country to be gained through these prayers. Medhurst even demonstrates the strife between the various clergymen during this process. He draws the following conclusions with regard to the pragmatic and functional forces behind the whole process.

> For *inaugural planners and political strategists*, prayer functioned rhetorically to identify the incoming leader with goodness and righteousness. It was an explicit sign that the president believed in God, prayer, and institutionalized religion. It was an implicit testimony to the rapprochement that occurred between civil and religious authorities shortly after the official separation of church and state. It was, in short, good politics.
>
> For the *clergymen* who participated in events of state, prayers functioned to remind the civil authorities of their exercise of power *under* God.

21. M.J. Medhurst, 'The Politics of Prayer: A Case Study in Configurational Interpretation', in T.W. Benson (ed.), *American Rhetoric: Context and Criticism* (Carbondale: Southern Illinois University Press, 1989), pp. 267-92. According to Medhurst (pp. 284, 287) the rhetoric of inaugural prayer functions as rhetorical legitimator of state myths, e.g., that the leader was blessed by God and that the nation is God's people.

Participation was a way of redeeming, if only symbolically, the power and prestige that once accompanied high ecclesiastical office. Though personal power was often highly circumscribed, clerical participation functioned to remind the *audience*, both political and lay, of the institutional importance of organized religion.

For the *audience members* the prayers functioned as rhetorical legitimators of American myths of state, of uncontested propositions to which Americans had traditionally paid obeisance: that the leader was blessed by God; that American ideals were lofty and unblemished; that Americans were God's people; that America had a responsibility to provide moral leadership to the world. These were propositions to be honored and remembered, not debated, for such is the nature of epideictic discourse.[22]

Although no direct conclusions with reference to Psalm 2 as an 'inaugural prayer' may be drawn from this example, the process of development of such a prayer is of importance, and in an attempt to reconstruct a rhetorical situation for Psalm 2 the above illustration can be kept in mind. It is important to remember that this psalm is not a typical 'prayer' directed towards Yahweh. It should rather be classified as an epideictic admonition[23] based on a prophetic decree which had been issued concerning the relationship between a Judean king and Yahweh.

It is also important to keep in mind that the rhetorical situation 'only comes into existence when the "exigence" of the situation comes into relationship with the "interest" of the rhetor'.[24] The rhetorician, therefore, creates a rhetorical situation in relation to historical facts, but in itself the rhetorical situation is not historical and cannot be equated with the historical situation. According to Kraus[25] the historical situation of this prayer is to be found in the enthronement festival of the Judean king and it can be dated during the pre-exilic period of the Judean monarchy.[26]

The rhetorician probably was an official (Levitical priest?) of the Jerusalem temple. By means of the prayer he created interaction between spoken word and ritual within the cult.[27] During the inauguration

22. Medhurst, 'Politics of Prayer', p. 287 (my italics).
23. See Perelman and Olbrechts-Tyteca, *New Rhetoric*, pp. 49-51, for their important view on the persuasive function of epideictic oratory.
24. J.N. Vorster, 'The Rhetorical Situation of the Letter to the Romans: An Integral Approach' (DD Thesis, University of Pretoria, 1991), p. 30.
25. Kraus, *Theologie*, pp. 139-50.
26. Spieckermann, *Heilsgegenwart*, p. 217.
27. D.F. O'Kennedy, 'Prayer: An Integral Part of the Old Testament', *Scriptura* 59 (1996), pp. 421-33.

ceremony of the Judean king or during the annual royal Zion festival[28] various rituals took place in the sanctuary as well as in the palace. With reference to one of these rituals Kraus[29] says, '*Per adoptionem* wird der Regent durch einen prophetisch deklarierten Rechtsakt zum Sohn Gottes erklärt' ('By adoption, the ruler is declared, through a prophetic announcement of a legal text, to be the son of God'). This took place in the sanctuary. The king had to respond to this decree of adoption, and the prayer was probably composed for this specific moment.[30] The prayer or epideictic admonition is therefore 'a carefully prescribed act'[31] and the involvement of the royalties can probably not be excluded or denied, as in the case of the modern example mentioned earlier on. The strong political influence inherent in this poem is proof of royal influence in the process of its development.

The exigency or problem created for the rhetorical situation by the rhetorician is the threat of hostile world nations and rulers to Yahweh and his anointed one. By means of argumentation this exigency must be removed in an attempt to persuade the audience of the universal empowerment of the king by Yahweh.[32] The rhetorical situation and the resulting poem, therefore, relate to the cultic-political sphere and form part of the complex process of development of the Zion theology[33] in Judah. The intention of the rhetorician was *inter alia* to support the king in his religious-political duty as 'son of God' who has to reign in the midst of a hostile world. Nel[34] is correct in saying that the primary concern of the royal psalms 'is to afford legitimacy to the Davidic dynasty and its ruling monarch in a comprehensive relationship with Yahweh, who has previously been recognized as a God of deliverance and not as a national God'. The rhetorician is here partaking in the process of development of a distinctive concept of the king of Judah. The king is put on the world map

---

28. Kraus, *Theologie*, p. 139.

29. Kraus, *Theologie*, p. 142.

30. P.J. Nel, 'The Theology of the Royal Psalms', *OTE* 11/1 (1998), p. 73.

31. G.A. Anderson, quoted by O'Kennedy, 'Prayer', p. 428.

32. Although no proof exists of the presence of diplomats or royalties from neighbouring countries during a ceremony like this in the Old Testament, it cannot be excluded as a possibility. The creation of a rhetorical situation, however, is not historically bound but historically related.

33. See in particular vv. 6, 10-12. Kraus, *Theologie*, pp. 94-103, discusses in detail the various aspects of the Zion theology.

34. Nel, 'Royal Psalms', p. 72.

as the mighty one, appointed by Yahweh, a display of power in the form of argumentation by authority.

In the end the world rulers and nations as part of the audience must be persuaded from the Judean cultic-political point of view to accept the Judean king as empowered by Yahweh, ruling on his behalf over the entire world. This epideictic discourse 'sets out to increase the intensity of adherence to certain values'[35] which the rhetorician wishes to emphasize. Therefore the cultic audience must be persuaded to accept their king as 'the son of God' who must be obeyed. For both the nations and the people of God blessing is promised if they take refuge in God and his 'son'. Yahweh must be convinced of the willingness of the appointed king to take up office. He must, however, also be persuaded to guide the king in performing his duty at both international and national levels.

2.2. Psalm 3
This prayer of lament reflects the experience of the supplicant living through a crisis in which he is isolated and under attack by many foes.

2.2.1. *Argumentation Strategies.* Right from the start an attention-seeking device is implemented by calling upon the name of Yahweh. Both the vocative and the two questions in v. 2[36] are attention-getting strategies.[37] The questions also articulate the immediate concern or exigency of the rhetorician, viz. the threat of his enemies.

In v. 3 the immediate concern is intensified by means of the words attributed to the enemies, 'God will not deliver him', which create 'a vividness and specificity that encourages the reader to accept the "reality" of this person in the world outside the text'.[38]

These words attributed to the enemies serve as a face-threatening act directed at the supplicant (by implication uttered by the enemies) in order to gain Yahweh's sympathy. Duplication and exaggeration in v. 2 (מה־רבו and רבים), v. 3 (רבים) and v. 7 (מרבבות עם) corroborate this face-

---

35. Perelman and Olbrechts-Tyteca, *New Rhetoric*, p. 51.

36. In all the subsequent references to verses in Psalms 3, 13, 41 and 42/43 the versification of the Hebrew Bible (Stuttgartensia) will be followed. The verse numbers of the English translation of these psalms are in each instance one less than that of the Hebrew text.

37. The מה־ in the first semicolon is assumed in the second semicolon as well.

38. V.K. Robbins, *Exploring the Texture of Texts: A Guide to Socio-Rhetorical Interpretation* (Valley Forge, PA: Trinity Press International, 1996), p. 32.

threatening act. He is experiencing humiliation or 'loss of face' instigated by this vast number of enemies. But the attributed words also serve as a negative politeness strategy directed at Yahweh to put the pressure on him to respond. The supplicant does not coerce Yahweh, but by putting these negative words in the mouth of the enemies he introduces some doubt (pessimism) as to whether Yahweh will deliver him or not.[39] Indirectly he is saying, 'God will not deliver me, will he?'

In v. 4 the mood of the psalm changes from complaint to that of trust. This mood is maintained up to v. 7 and it is strengthened by the final expression of trust in Yahweh in v. 9a. By calling Yahweh 'a shield around me', 'my glory' and 'the one who lifts up my head',[40] the supplicant seeks common ground with him, which is positive politeness.[41] However, these designations are simultaneously strong expressions of trust in Yahweh. Expressions of trust act as strong face-threatening speech-acts threatening Yahweh's negative face by putting pressure on him to respond.[42] The intention is to get Yahweh involved to save his honour. The supplicant's honour, which rests in Yahweh ('my glory'), is at stake. Therefore only Yahweh can lift up his head[43] again.

By mentioning 'his holy hill' as a symbol of God's presence in this expression of trust (v. 5), the rhetorician is communicating religious language familiar to at least part of the audience (God and his people).[44] God reigns from Zion, therefore he also answers (delivers) from Zion. This symbol, therefore, carries a strong redemptive connotation for those familiar with it and plays an important role in the argumentation.

The positive politeness strategy, 'From the LORD comes deliverance' (v. 9), is a merit attributed by the rhetorician to God in a timeless way, an argument which confirms God's stability as the one who always delivers.[45]

---

39. Brown and Levinson, 'Universals', pp. 178-81.

40. Translated literally.

41. Brown and Levinson, 'Universals', pp. 108, 112-13.

42. Expressions of trust can simultaneously serve as positive politeness and face-threatening acts depending on the intention of the rhetorician as well as the interpretation of the recipient. They can aim at pleasing God, but also at persuading him to respond. See Brown and Levinson, 'Universals', p. 71.

43. The position of the head is often associated with honour or shame. See J. Pitt-Rivers, 'Honour and Social Status', in J.G. Peristiany (ed.), *Honour and Shame: The Values of Mediterranean Society* (Chicago: University of Chicago Press, 1966), pp. 9-77 (25).

44. See Perelman and Olbrechts-Tyteca, *New Rhetoric*, p. 335.

45. Perelman and Olbrechts-Tyteca, *New Rhetoric*, p. 294.

It stresses God's good reputation as the deliverer of his people. As a negative politeness strategy, however, it implies the act of deliverance by Yahweh. The aim behind this politeness argument (either positive or negative) is to counteract the provocative statement that 'God will not deliver him' which the rhetorician has put in the mouth of the enemies (v. 3).

The appeals for God's deliverance and for his blessings in vv. 8-9 are bald-on-record speech-acts that threaten Yahweh's negative face. The ultimate vindication of honour lies in physical violence,[46] hence the appeal that God must strike his enemies on the jaw in order to close the mouths that utter such a provocative statement. By addressing God with the in-group identity marker אלהי (v. 8), an attempt is made to claim common ground with him, which is a positive politeness strategy. Tension is, however, created when a positive politeness strategy is used as part of a face-threatening act. The function of this tension is probably to strengthen the appeal and therefore the attempt of persuading God. The utterances of confidence in Yahweh (vv. 4-5) and the resulting peacefulness in vv. 4-5 are contrasted with the words that have been put in the mouth of the enemies (v. 3). This contrast acts as basis for the appeal for deliverance in v. 8.

2.2.2. *Audience and Rhetorical Situation.* Involved in the rhetorical situation are Yahweh who is addressed directly in vv. 1-4, 8 and 9b, the enemies (vv. 2, 3, 7, 8), and God's people (v. 9b). The exigency of the rhetorical situation is the enemies' threat that God will not deliver the supplicant. The vagueness and exaggeration with regard to the enemies as audience clearly illustrate the fact that this is a *creation* of the rhetorician in order to bring about a rhetorical situation related to but not exactly similar to his physical situation.

The prayer is primarily addressed to Yahweh in order to persuade him to deliver the supplicant. This Yahweh will do 'from his holy hill', Zion (v. 5). It is intended to be used in the cult for private purposes by an individual when in distress and to be prayed aloud in public. The people of God as audience should therefore be persuaded by the argumentation to use the psalm as a prayer. The enemies must be persuaded to terminate their threatening conduct. Their violence is made public and Yahweh is invoked to strike them and to deliver him. He sides himself with Yahweh.

---

46. Pitt-Rivers, 'Honour and Social Status', p. 29.

2.3. *Psalm 13*
This short prayer is acknowledged by most scholars as a classic example of the individual lament. The supplicant describes the crisis, makes his petition to God, and concludes by rejoicing and praising God in an atmosphere of trust.

2.3.1. *Argumentation Strategies.* The psalm commences with four questions addressed to Yahweh. The interrogative is a modality of considerable rhetorical importance, because it 'presupposes an object to which it relates and suggests that there is agreement on the existence of this object'.[47] The repetition of the interrogatives and the progressive shortening of the sentences in which they occur, as well as the decreasing frequency of the עד־אנה in vv. 2-3 all feature to intensify and stress the supplicant's questioning of Yahweh. The questions culminate in the words, 'How long will my enemy triumph over me?'

These four questions are attention-getting strategies which also bring the immediate concern of the rhetorical situation to the attention of the audience. The immediate concern of the prayer is a threefold life-threatening experience comprising Yahweh forgetting him and hiding his face from him (v. 2); his anxiety and struggling with his own thoughts (v. 3a); and his enemies triumphing over him (v. 3b). The latter aspect is probably his main problem from which the other two emanate. To the petitioner his immediate concern is a large social problem threatening his honour.

Two people in interlocution sharing a positive rhetorical situation normally attempt to apply politeness strategies in order to save each other's face. The same phenomenon also appears in prayers, which are actually monologues directed at Yahweh who is the primary exponent of the audience. The four questions in this prayer, therefore, are negative politeness strategies,[48] indirectly pleading with Yahweh to respond in favour of the supplicant. Indirectly the petitioner begs Yahweh not to forget him any more, not to let him worry any more, not to let his enemies triumph over him any more. The questions therefore serve as persuasion strategies for Yahweh's response. Should he respond to the supplicant's questions he would redress the face-threatening acts. His response would then be an indication of his acknowledgment of the exigency of the rhetorical situation. It is exactly this point the petitioner is driving at.

47. Perelman and Olbrechts-Tyteca, *New Rhetoric*, p. 159.
48. See n. 16.

The imperatives in v. 4 may be interpreted as bald-on-record strategies[49] threatening Yahweh's negative face. These imperatives, however, are not commands, but take on the form of supplications because of the lack of force on the supplicant's side.[50] This lack of force is due not only to the circumstances experienced by the supplicant, but also because of the unequal relationship between God and himself. The supplicant is not in a position to demand anything from God, therefore he 'speaks up' to Yahweh.[51] As argumentation strategies these imperatives have a strong persuasive function.

Should Yahweh not respond in favour of the petitioner, three alternative things could happen. These are being argued in vv. 4b and 5a. Two of the alternatives are introduced by פֶּן (or, or else, lest), while in v. 5b it is assumed. These alternatives form the motives for the imperatives. It could happen that the petitioner would die (v. 4b), or that the enemy would say, 'I have overcome him' (v. 5a), and that his foes will rejoice when he falls (v. 5b).

The words, 'I have overcome him', are attributed to the enemy by the petitioner, and relate to the question in v. 3b, 'How long will my enemy triumph over me?' To put words in the mouth of someone is to create 'a vividness and specificity that encourages the reader to accept the "reality" of this person in the world outside the text'.[52] Coming from the enemy this expression is a bald-on-record speech-act threatening the positive face of the supplicant.[53] It implies the triumph of the enemy over the supplicant putting his honour in jeopardy. It is therefore a strong rhetorical persuasion strategy in his argumentation with Yahweh in order to present himself as the injured party. In this way he wishes to gain sympathy from his audience and to persuade Yahweh to remove the threefold exigency.

The rhetorician creates an incompatibility[54] between God's assumed act of redemption and the enemy's triumph, thereby putting Yahweh before a choice or ultimatum: 'Save me, lest I will die and my enemy will say "I have overcome him".' Similar is the case when on the one hand the

---

49. Brown and Levinson, 'Universals', pp. 99-106.

50. Perelman and Olbrechts-Tyteca, *New Rhetoric*, p. 158.

51. See Brown and Levinson, 'Universals', p. 255, (dyad I), for the kind of relationship that exists between the petitioner and Yahweh.

52. Robbins, *Exploring*, p. 32.

53. Brown and Levinson, 'Universals', p. 67, define 'positive face' as 'the want of every member that his wants be desirable to at least some others'.

54. Perelman and Olbrechts-Tyteca, *New Rhetoric*, pp. 195-205.

question is put, 'How long will you hide your face from me?' (v. 2), and on the other hand he appeals to Yahweh, 'Look on me and answer' (v. 4). Yahweh cannot simultaneously forever forget and save the petitioner. He is put before a choice. The final motivation behind these arguments from incompatibility is to save the supplicant's face and to recover his honour.

By addressing God as יהוה אלהי (v. 4) the rhetorician directs the appeal at Yahweh, the God of the covenant, who is also the supplicant's 'personal' God. In this way common ground is claimed. This way of addressing God can, in the context of this prayer, be classified as an in-group identity marker claiming in-group solidarity with Yahweh and the religious community.[55] The enemy is excluded from this in-group solidarity. It is this in-group solidarity that gives the petitioner the confidence to appeal to Yahweh.

The expressions of trust and praise in v. 6 are an indication of the covenant relationship between the supplicant and Yahweh and are as such positive politeness strategies for seeking common ground. Yahweh would be pleased to be trusted and would receive the songs of the supplicant with delight. These expressions of trust can, however, also be classified as face-threatening acts or negative politeness strategies that threaten Yahweh's negative face by putting pressure on him to respond.[56]

2.3.2. *Audience and Rhetorical Situation.* The immediate concern or exigency of the rhetorical situation, as stated above, is the threatening enemies (v. 3b) causing the supplicant daily sorrow and grief (v. 3a), which is experienced as the hiding of God's face from him (v. 2).

The first question that can be asked with reference to the rhetorical situation is who is praying this prayer. The Old Testament person, like the New Testament person, is a dyadic personality, a group-oriented person. The language being used in the prayer is typical of the dyadic person.[57] Although the petitioner is perceived as very individualistic because of the exclusive use of the first person singular, the in-group identity markers mentioned above betray his dyadic personality. He is serious in associating with Yahweh and the religious community. As a dyadic person his honour

---

55. Brown and Levinson, 'Universals', pp. 112-13.

56. Brown and Levinson, 'Universals', pp. 70-71.

57. B.J. Malina, *The New Testament World: Insights from Cultural Anthropology* (Louisville, KY: Westminster/John Knox Press, rev. edn, 1993), pp. 73-81. Note the three-zone model describing the manner in which personality perception is articulated and the way it is then related to how God functions.

is very important,[58] underlying his argumentation in the prayer. The exigency of the rhetorical situation puts his honour at stake. It is therefore important for him to be saved by Yahweh and to be recognized by the community in which he lives.

From the analysis of the argumentation it is evident that the prayer is primarily addressed to Yahweh, which is characteristic of a prayer. The enemies are also included in the audience, although they are not addressed directly. The aim of the petitioner is to reveal his problem in public by means of public prayer. He wrestles and argues with Yahweh because he believes that he is the only one who can really solve his problem.

But his intention goes further. Seeing that these prayers were usually said aloud in public[59] as part of the daily cultic activities, it implies that the audience should be taken as much wider than those directly addressed. The general public present at the sanctuary during the prayer is also drawn into the rhetorical situation. Among them, one can assume, are supporters of the petitioner as well as possible supporters of the enemies and/or the enemies themselves.[60]

The aim of praying aloud in public is to be overheard by the enemies, their friends, the cultic personnel and the general public. Those who sympathize with him should be stimulated in their conduct. Others should be persuaded to pity him and to stand by him. They should all turn their back on the enemies and their allies. In this way the prayer becomes a socio-rhetorical speech-act. Malina[61] calls it a 'challenge and response' situation forming part of 'a sort of constant social tug of war, a game of social push and shove'. The petitioner therefore seeks sympathy from Yahweh and his supporters in the community and tries to persuade as many of them as possible to take his side. The prayer is thus a socio-rhetorical strategy to redress his shame and to expose the enemies in public.

---

58. See Malina, *New Testament World*, pp. 28-62, who identifies honour and shame as characteristics of the Mediterranean person during New Testament times. A. Abou-Zeid, 'Honour and Shame among the Bedouins of Egypt', in Peristiany, *Honour and Shame*, pp. 243-59, identifies a nuanced form of honour and shame in present-day Bedouin communities in the Western Desert of Egypt, people relying strongly on paternalism and group orientation.

59. See Sheppard, 'Enemies', pp. 61-82, as well as Malina, *New Testament World*, pp. 34-38.

60. Sheppard, 'Enemies', p. 71.

61. Malina, *New Testament World*, p. 34.

Praying aloud in public with such intentions, prayer becomes a public argument from authority against the enemies. By invoking the aid of Yahweh, the cultic personnel as well as the community, the prayer itself becomes an authoritative tool. Especially the Godhead serves as the authoritative person on whom the arguments are based. The enemies should know that Yahweh will preserve the honour of the petitioner and that he will break down their hold on him. In this way the petitioner takes a socio-political risk that his enemies might respond to his prayer.[62] Their response might be either positive or negative. This calculated risk might just persuade them to let go their grip, which will restore his honour.

Over and above the socio-rhetorical persuasive function of the prayer, it primarily remains a religious-rhetorical instrument. Yahweh is the first addressee and from him the petitioner expects real redemption. The culminating verse (6) overwhelmingly confirms this. Speech-act coincides with act of faith in this prayer.

2.4. *Psalm 41*

This prayer probably fits into a life-situation where the supplicant comes to the temple for healing.

2.4.1. *Argumentation Strategies.* The structure of the psalm takes on a concentric pattern, which is vital to the argumentation.

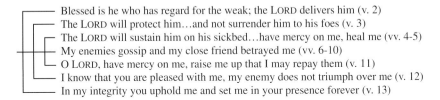

Blessed is he who has regard for the weak; the LORD delivers him (v. 2)
The LORD will protect him…and not surrender him to his foes (v. 3)
The LORD will sustain him on his sickbed…have mercy on me, heal me (vv. 4-5)
My enemies gossip and my close friend betrayed me (vv. 6-10)
O LORD, have mercy on me, raise me up that I may repay them (v. 11)
I know that you are pleased with me, my enemy does not triumph over me (v. 12)
In my integrity you uphold me and set me in your presence forever (v. 13)

The pivot of the structure features as the exigency or problem put forward by the rhetorician. The gossip of the enemies about his illness and the betrayal of his best friend are the main threats experienced by the supplicant.

The prayer commences in an interesting and subtle manner in the sense that the petitioner holds up a model.[63] It is evident, however, that the main

---

62. Sheppard, 'Enemies', p. 69.

63. A model is normally held up to be imitated and can be a pattern to be followed, according to Perelman and Olbrechts-Tyteca, *New Rhetoric*, p. 364. In this instance the pattern to be followed is to behave like 'he who has regard for the weak'.

emphasis is on the fortune aspect attached to the model, viz. 'to be blessed', as is indicated by the prominent placing of the word אשרי (blessed) (v. 2) in the argument. This emphasis on the fortune aspect rather than on the model itself has a persuasive function in that the rule of justice is introduced into the argumentation.[64] The argument is expanded in more detail in vv. 3-4 where it is explained what would happen to 'one who has regard for the weak'. The aim of this expanded argumentation is to bring the model closer to the petitioner's own distressful situation (v. 5). The petitioner equals himself to the model whom 'the LORD delivers in times of trouble'. According to the rule of justice he is entitled to the same treatment by Yahweh as the model. As a face-threatening speech-act this argument puts Yahweh under pressure to bless, heal and deliver the petitioner.

The face-threatening speech-acts in the form of requests in v. 5a and v. 11, urging Yahweh to have mercy on him and to heal him, corroborate the arguments from the model and the rule of justice. To strengthen the argument even further, the supplicant utters a confession of sin (v. 5b), which threatens his own positive face[65] while serving as a negative polite-ness strategy[66] which puts pressure on Yahweh to forgive his sin. By means of the confession of sin the supplicant puts himself baldly on record, expecting credit for his honesty.[67] The confession only implies and does not state directly that his illness is a result of his sin. The implication, therefore, is that forgiveness of sin would bring about physical healing.

The model serves an additional function in the argumentation. By means of this model the supplicant illustrates the connection between his speech-act and himself as a person by identifying himself with the model. In this way the *person* of the supplicant provides a context for the subsequent argumentation found in the prayer. The model enables him to sing his own praises in a very subtle way (vv. 2, 12-13). Although self-praise can be out of place, in this instance the supplicant does not put himself baldly on record. Subtle self-praise is functioning here as 'an indispensable means to attain a legitimate end',[68] the end being the supplicant's healing from his illness, the deliverance from the gossip of his adversaries and the restora-tion of his honour.

64. Perelman and Olbrechts-Tyteca, *New Rhetoric*, pp. 218-20.
65. Brown and Levinson, 'Universals', p. 73.
66. Brown and Levinson, 'Universals', pp. 192-95.
67. Brown and Levinson, 'Universals', p. 76.
68. Perelman and Olbrechts-Tyteca, *New Rhetoric*, p. 319.

The centre part of the argumentation (vv. 6-10), which has been identified as the exigency of the rhetorical situation, deals with the conduct of the enemy. These arguments, therefore, relate to the model in the sense that an anti-model is created. While the model is someone who has regard for the weak, the anti-model implies that the enemies of the supplicant have no regard for the weak. Therefore they cannot share in God's blessing. And this is what the petitioner wishes to prove. With the cultic audience and the enemies themselves as part of the audience in mind (remember the prayer is said aloud in public), this anti-model could serve as a warning to the enemies and as a pattern not to be followed by the cultic community.

The 'fortune' aspect (or blessing) of the model implies Yahweh's deliverance of the one who has regard for the weak in times of trouble (v. 3). The 'times of trouble' relate to the centre part of the argumentation (vv. 6-10) where the anti-model is depicted in detail. The 'trouble' aspect is enclosed by two requests put to Yahweh: to be merciful and to heal the supplicant (v. 5 and v. 11). The 'trouble' aspect and the anti-model thus form the extensive reason for the requests for help in the argument.

The 'trouble' aspect also serves as a strong threat to the supplicant's positive face, initiated by the enemies. The supplicant is humiliated by the enemies' words and conduct and thus put to shame. The words that have been put in the mouth of the enemies in v. 6 and v. 9, as well as the conduct attributed to them, are as such extremely face threatening to the supplicant. The supplicant in this way is baldly putting the enemies on record. Their direct words encourage the audience to accept the 'reality' of the enemies in the world outside the text.[69]

But by attributing these words to the enemies and describing their threatening conduct in detail, the supplicant is actually seeking sympathy from Yahweh, thereby threatening Yahweh's negative face by putting pressure on him to meet his needs.[70] This goes hand in hand with the supplicant's requests for mercy and healing (vv. 5, 11), which are also speech-acts threatening Yahweh's negative face.

The words, 'I know that you are pleased with me' (v. 12) are not only mild self-praise in the context of the model/anti-model argumentation, but also serve as an expression of trust. As such it is a face-threatening speech-act directed at Yahweh in order to persuade him to get involved in the situation of the supplicant. This also applies to the announcements in

69. Robbins, *Exploring*, p. 32.
70. Brown and Levinson, 'Universals', pp. 70-71.

v. 13. By mentioning his 'integrity' in v. 13 the supplicant is referring to his living up to the model of v. 2, which is his claim to honour.

The praise in v. 14 furnishes the prayer with a very positive ending. Although it could be interpreted as a kind of gift-giving[71] and would as such be a positive politeness strategy satisfying Yahweh's positive-face-want, namely to be admired, praise in the context of lamentation also serves as a negative politeness strategy. It is a technique implemented to redress Yahweh's negative-face-want, minimizing the face-threatening acts in the argumentation. The supplicant is toning down his appeal for deliverance by praising Yahweh, showing that he cannot coerce Yahweh to respond to his appeal. In this sense the negative politeness strategy is a technique to acknowledge Yahweh's superiority and his immunity from imposition.[72]

2.4.2. *Audience and Rhetorical Situation.* The audience consists of Yahweh, the enemies and the supplicant's close friend. As a cultic prayer the cultic community is also included in the audience. The exigency is the threat by the supplicant's enemies uttering slander about him in his state of illness, and the dishonouring conduct of his friend. Yahweh is invoked to cure him in order to remove his shame.

Assuming that the prayer was meant to be prayed aloud in public, the intention was that both the enemies and the close friend (or their allies) should overhear.[73] The conduct of the close friend brings shame upon the friend himself:[74] therefore he is perceived as an enemy by the petitioner. He is an unreliable friend who is unfaithful to the supplicant. The conduct of the friend also intensifies the shame experienced by the supplicant. The enemies and the best friend are indirectly addressed in the prayer, and therefore exposed in public. It is also important for the supplicant that his enemies should take notice of his trust in Yahweh and of the fact that he would repay them after his recovery. By exposing the enemies in public the supplicant expects to receive protection in the sense that the prayer might stop their slanderous talk and that the cultic community would turn against them.

This prayer is intended to become 'a significant alternative to gossip because, unlike gossip, it makes God the primary listener, maintains the

71. Brown and Levinson, 'Universals', p. 134.
72. Brown and Levinson, 'Universals', pp. 177, 183.
73. Sheppard, 'Enemies', p. 72.
74. Abou-Zeid, 'Honour and Shame', p. 245.

intimacy of that discourse by not naming the enemy, and directly asks God, rather than neighbors, to respond in word and deed in behalf of the petitioner'.[75]

2.5. *Psalm 42/43*

Psalms 42 and 43 are taken as a single prayer for the obvious reason of the appearance of the refrain in 42.6, 12 and in 43.5. Characteristic of the first section, viz. Psalm 42, is its politeness mode. Never is any direct pressure put on God to get involved by means of bald-on-record imperatives. Imperatives only occur in Psalm 43.

2.5.1. *Argumentation Strategies.* The supplicant commences his prayer with a positive politeness strategy in the form of an argument by comparison in 42.2-3 ('My soul pants for God as the deer pants for streams of water'). By means of this positive politeness strategy he seeks common ground with God. His desire is to be in God's presence and to praise him. לאלהים לאל חי (v. 3) is an exaggeration. It is not only 'God', but 'the *living* God' or 'the God of life' whom he longs for. The exaggeration is also a positive politeness technique for seeking common ground with God.[76] His suffering and the taunting of the enemies put him in remembrance of the leading role he used to play in leading the joyful procession to the house of God (v. 5).

The motive behind this positive politeness, however, is to be relieved by God from his distressful situation. This can be seen in the utterances of self-deliberation in vv. 6, 12 and 43.5 where God is called 'my Saviour'. In the broader context of the prayer, therefore, his desire to be in God's presence happens to be negative politeness, urging God to restore his former position of joy and temple visiting.

The incomplete question in 42.3b requires an answer,[77] a response from God, and is a negative politeness strategy. The supplicant indirectly expresses the desire that God should change his circumstances in such a way that he could meet with him again in the temple. In this sense the question takes on the form of a request putting pressure on God to comply with the plea. Simultaneously the question serves as a device to put forward the real and immediate concern of the supplicant, namely, his

---

75. Sheppard, 'Enemies', p. 74.
76. Brown and Levinson, 'Universals', pp. 109-11.
77. Goody, 'Theory of Questions', pp. 22-23.

separation from God and the taunting of his enemies ('Where is your God?', vv. 4b, 11b).

The taunting of the enemies causes continuous weeping (v. 4), and much pain (v. 11). They ask this question from a superior position in the control mode,[78] challenging the supplicant in public to explain where his God is. The foundation of his honour is questioned, therefore this speech-act threatens the supplicant's positive face. But it is also a dismissal of God and an assertion of self-sufficiency similar to that of the enemies in Psalm 9/10.[79] They deny God's involvement in the life of the supplicant, at least in the situation of distress that he is experiencing. In that sense these words also threaten God's positive face (his honour).

Self-deliberation plays an important role in this prayer. The entire first stanza (42.1-6) can be taken as a direct address to God. The switch to self-deliberation is made in v. 6 and repeated as a refrain in v. 12 and in 43.5. Through self-deliberation the supplicant convinces himself[80] that there is no apparent reason for his despondency. 'Hope in God' is the only means to restore his previous situation of praising God (at the temple). All his arguments in the prayer emanate from this conviction and drive at strengthening this conviction.[81] This is probably the reason why the self-deliberation refrain occurs three times in the prayer.

Keeping in mind that this prayer was prayed in public, the self-deliberation also has a persuasive function not only with regard to God, but also with regard to the cultic audience and the enemies. With reference to God the following positive and negative politeness strategies are encountered in the self-deliberation sections (42.6, 12 and 43.5):

a.	Positive politeness in the self-deliberation
'I will yet praise him, my Savior and my God' could be interpreted as a kind of gift giving[82] and would as such be a positive politeness strategy satisfying Yahweh's positive-face-want-to-be-admired. As a promise it also satisfies God's positive-face-

78.	Control questions are normally asked by a person in a dominant position to test, challenge, control and to hold the inferior accountable for something (see Goody, 'Theory of Questions', pp. 30-31).

79.	W. Brueggemann, 'Psalm 9–10: A Counter to Conventional Social Reality', in Jobling, Day and Sheppard (eds.), *The Bible and the Politics of Exegesis*, pp. 3-16 (8).

80.	According to Perelman and Olbrechts-Tyteca, *New Rhetoric*, p. 41, self-deliberation has a convincing function.

81.	See Perelman and Olbrechts-Tyteca, *New Rhetoric*, p. 44.

82.	Brown and Levinson, 'Universals', p. 134.

wants.[83] He knows that his praises afford God great pleasure. By calling God the names 'my Savior' and 'my God' the supplicant seeks common ground with him. These names are in-group identity markers acting as positive politeness strategies.

b.   Negative politeness

The questions 'Why are you downcast, O my soul? Why so disturbed within me?' can either be interpreted as indirect, non-polite, off-record speech-acts,[84] or they can serve as negative politeness strategies. As off-record speech-acts they transmit an association clue or hint to God that the supplicant is in need of help.[85] The hint leaves it up to God to respond or not. In combination with the subsequent utterance of hope, 'Put your hope in God', the function of the questions becomes that of negative politeness, urging God indirectly to remove the despondency.

In the broader context of the prayer the utterances of praise and hope in 42.5b, 12b and 43.5b serve as negative politeness strategies. The supplicant is toning down his appeal for deliverance by praising Yahweh, showing that he cannot coerce him to respond to his appeal.[86] The utterances of hope are indirect ways of requesting God for help.

As claimed above, the utterances of self-deliberation are primarily intended to convince the supplicant himself that only hope in God can change his circumstances. But because the prayer is intended to be uttered aloud in public, even the self-deliberation arguments obtain persuasive status during the process of overhearing.

The three imperatives in 43.1 and 3 are bald-on-record face-threatening speech-acts addressed to God's negative face. These imperatives, however, are not commands. They rather serve as supplications because of the lack of force on the supplicant's side.[87] As argumentation strategies these imperatives have a strong persuasive function.

The tagging of the enemies as 'ungodly nation' and 'deceitful and

83. Brown and Levinson, 'Universals', p. 130.

84. Off-record utterances are 'indirect uses of language…that is either more general…or actually different from what one means… In either case, H [the recipient—my insertion] must make some inference to recover what was in fact intended' (Brown and Levinson, 'Universals', p. 216).

85. Brown and Levinson, 'Universals', pp. 216-21.

86. Brown and Levinson, 'Universals', pp. 177, 183.

87. See nn. 48-50 above.

wicked men' is a value judgment made by the supplicant aiming at convincing God of the wickedness of his enemies. In contrast to this the conduct of the supplicant (v. 4) reflects reverence for the sacred. Ultimately the supplicant wishes to convey the message that he sides himself with God, which is a positive politeness strategy. In public prayer this is a strong persuasive argument in favour of the supplicant.

The questions in v. 2 are both negative politeness strategies. God is indirectly requested not to reject the supplicant and to remove the cause of his mourning, viz. the oppression of the enemies. The mode of *urgency* in which these questions are spoken out should not be confused with questions in the control mode,[88] because the supplicant finds himself in an inferior position to God.

The promises in v. 4 are positive politeness strategies demonstrating the supplicant's good intentions in satisfying God's positive face wants. 'Holy mountain' (v. 3) and 'altar of God' are both symbols of God's presence and have the function of exciting the feeling of mutual love and constitute a bond of participation,[89] which corroborates the positive politeness reflected by the promises.

2.5.2. *Audience and Rhetorical Situation.* What the physical circumstances of the supplicant were is not clear, apart from the fact that he was separated from the temple, therefore also from God. He found himself at a spot (probably in the open air) somewhere in the northern part of the country of Israel (42.7-8). He was a religious leader who was used to 'leading the multitude to the house of God' (v. 5).

With God, the enemies and the cultic community in mind as elements of the audience, a rhetorical situation is created within which the supplicant's separation from God and the taunting of the enemies on this matter form the exigency. A variety of argumentation strategies that have been identified are implemented in order to remove the exigency so that the supplicant can experience God's presence in the temple again.

3. Concluding Remarks

3.1. *Characteristic Implementation of Argumentation Strategies*
Although a small sample of prayers in which the enemies feature prominently is investigated here, certain patterns of implementation of

---

88. See Goody, 'Theory of Questions', pp. 30-32.
89. Perelman and Olbrechts-Tyteca, *New Rhetoric*, p. 332.

argumentation strategies, especially politeness strategies, have become evident.

1. Owing to the begging nature ('speaking up') of a prayer a high occurrence of negative politeness can be expected which is indeed the case.

2. Arguments of trust and praise can have a positive politeness function, but are often implemented as negative politeness, putting pressure on God to respond. They can also be classified as face-threatening acts. The effect they have on the recipient, which is always Yahweh in these prayers, depends on the recipient's interpretation, which of course is not possible to determine if no real response is reported. Response implied by the supplicant is no indication of real response by the recipient. There is no set pattern in the occurrence of either arguments of trust, praise or lamentation, and they seem to serve the argumentation at random. This might be a reflection of the arbitrary nature of the emotions of the supplicants.

3. Bald-on-record face-threatening speech-acts in the form of direct appeals (imperatives) to God are characteristic of the prayers that have been examined. These imperatives, however, are not commands. They take on the form of supplications because of the petitioners' lack of power. They 'speak up' to God.

4. Questions normally serve as attention-getting devices, highlighting the immediate concern or problem of the supplicants. These questions often occur at the beginning of the prayers (Pss. 2; 3; 13; 42/43), but are also implemented randomly (cf. Ps. 42/43). Many of these questions seem to be in the control mode as if the supplicants were in a position of superiority in their relationship with God. Such questions often occur in conjunction with bald-on-record appeals and have an urging function. These questions, however, rather reflect the urgency of the appeals for help (speak up from an inferior position) than act as demands from a control mode position.

5. It is interesting to note that the words attributed to the enemies often occur in the form of questions to draw attention to the main problem. Whether in question form or not, they always serve as face-threatening speech-acts directed at the supplicant. They have the function of invoking God's sympathy for the supplicant. In the overall argumentation these words are, however, implemented to put the enemies in a bad light to the benefit of the supplicants.

6. By calling the adversaries 'enemies' the supplicants perform strong face-threatening speech-acts towards the enemies. These are distributed randomly in the prayers, serving the argumentation.

3.2. *Sociological Implications*

The formative processes of the cultic prayers of Israel were quite complicated. Apart from their religious function, the argumentation of most of these prayers was initiated by socio-political reasons.

1. The investigation of a political-cultic 'inaugural prayer' like Psalm 2 has shown that the cult was probably strongly influenced by politics.

2. Typical of a dyadic culture the prayers under discussion were prayed aloud in public, whether in the open air (Ps. 42/43), at the Jerusalem temple, or at the royal palace (Ps. 2). This rhetorical technique forms part of the challenge and response type of social communication where the community at large is also drawn into the rhetorical situation in order to regain and reaffirm honour lost.[90]

3. This has certain implications for the socio-political relations between the characters involved in the prayer-acts. Social relations are reflected by the role of *intention* in conveying meaning in verbal interaction.[91] This can be observed in the intentions of the supplicants. Very positive relationships between the petitioners and God counteract the detrimental effect the enemies have on the petitioners. The reciprocal negative intentions between the enemies and the petitioners are portrayed by means of the words attributed to the enemies as well as descriptions of their detrimental conduct. The fact that the supplicants react to a slight upon the honour of the enemies indicates that their own honour is involved.[92] The intentions of the supplicants, therefore, are for the most part primarily to persuade God to come to their deliverance in order to restore their honour (or as the endower of honour in Ps. 2) and to put the enemies to shame. In this way human relationships are intended to be influenced by the invocation of God and by praying aloud in public.

4. When praying is done in public the enemies are in a sense put on trial. Especially the words attributed to them serve the purpose of exposing them in public. During the prayer-act the enemies cannot control their own words and the prayer-act is used as a manipulative tool. The prayer becomes an odd court case[93] during which the supplicant holds power and acts as plaintiff, while the enemies find themselves in the dock.

---

90. Malina, *New Testament World*, pp. 34-37. See also pp. 67-73 for a discussion of the dyadic personality.

91. Goody, 'Introduction', in Goody, *Questions and Politeness*, pp. 1-16 (10).

92. Pitt-Rivers, 'Honour and Social Status', p. 28.

93. Brueggemann, 'Psalm 9–10', p. 5.

5. The honour of the supplicants is not only socially related, but also expresses their close relationship with God. The invocation of violence by God against the enemies is an indication that the supplicants have reached their last resort in order to save their honour. This, in turn, is an indication of the strong social and religious role honour and shame played in their society.

6. Socio-religious conflict between the powerful enemies and the power-less petitioners is portrayed especially when the petitioners put words with reference to the reality of God in the mouth of the enemies (e.g. Pss. 3; 42/43). The dispute about God in these prayers is actually a dispute about life and death, a dispute about social power.

7. The communication in the prayers can be seen as 'upward speech', meaning that it is speech from a powerless speaker to a powerful one. It is therefore likely for the speaker to choose an indirect strategy,[94] as reflected in the predominant occurrence of positive and negative politeness strategies in these prayers.

8. The supplicants avoid threatening their own face. That is why apologies or confessions and begging for forgiveness are so scarce.[95] Only once does an apology of this nature occur in the prayers under discussion (41.5). In this instance one gets the impression that emphasis is rather put on the plea for healing and that sin is only mentioned incidentally and disguised as the reason for the supplicant's illness. Could it be that a confession of sin would derogate the reputation of the supplicant once it was done aloud in public, seeing that he found himself in an honour–shame struggle with his enemies?

9. It is impossible to draw final conclusions from such a small sample of prayers as to whether they reflect a *general* Israelite culture of negative or positive politeness. What has become evident, however, is that supplications, in which the enemies play a prominent role, predominantly portray negative politeness.

10. In addition to the predominant negative politeness in these prayers a mode of bald-on-record face-threatening speech-acts occurs regularly, not only with the enemies as recipients, but also with Yahweh as the recipient. With reference to the enemies this is comprehensible. With reference to

94. S. Blum-Kulka, B. Danet and R. Gherson, 'The Language of Requesting in Israeli Society', in J.P. Forgas (ed.), *Language and Social Situations* (New York: Springer-Verlag, 1985), pp. 113-39 (128).

95. This is also applicable to the Psalter as a whole, although confessions of sin do occur here and there, e.g. Pss. 25.7; 38.3; 41.4; 69.5; 143.2.

God, however, it seems to be contradictory to the more indirect polite 'upward speech' mode for redressing the face-threatening speech-acts of the supplicants. The directness and harshness of some of the pleas can be explained by the urgency of the exigencies. It can, however, also be a reflection of the supplicants' intimate relationships with Yahweh. The closer the social and religious distance between speaker and recipient, the easier the outspokenness. The need for efficiency can also be a further reason for the directness.[96] It is still to be examined whether 'bald-on-recordness' has anything to do with the sexuality of the supplicants in the case of cultic prayers.[97]

11. In these prayers praise can serve as a positive politeness strategy satisfying Yahweh's positive face want to be admired. In the context of lamentation, however, praise can also and does rather serve as a negative politeness strategy. The supplicant is toning down his appeal for deliverance by praising Yahweh, showing that he cannot coerce Yahweh to respond to his appeal. In this sense the negative politeness strategy is a technique for acknowledging Yahweh's superiority and his immunity from imposition.

12. Whether social rules applicable to human relations could be directly applied to the relationship between the Godhead and human beings remains an open question and should be further explored in future. The approach that I have followed in this paper is to my mind sufficient proof that normal rhetorical and social rules were indeed to a large extent applicable to public prayer in Ancient Israelite times.

96. Blum-Kulka, Danet and Gherson, 'Language of Requesting', p. 129.
97. See Brown and Levinson, 'Universals', pp. 256-57, for an interesting probe into this matter.

THE RHETORICITY OF THE 'BODY' IN THE SONG OF SONGS

Hendrik Viviers

1. *Introduction*

a. *Problem*

The Song of Songs is well known for having evoked the most diverse reactions among its readers. As early as the second century CE Rabbi Akiba protested the profanation of the Song in the so-called 'banquet houses'. 'Profanation' pointed to the literal understanding thereof as an erotic love song between a man and a woman. This was taboo in Akiba's eyes who viewed the Song allegorically as portraying the love between Yahweh and Israel. He accordingly called the Song of Songs the 'Holy of Holies' (Pope 1977: 19). A similar reaction can be noted in Protestant circles in the seventeenth century: 'The Westminster Assembly…censured blasphemous Presbyterians who "received it as a hot carnal pamphlet formed by some loose Apollo or Cupid"' (Davidson 1989: 3). The allegorists' negative rhetoric 'profanation' and 'carnal pamphlet' clearly illustrate their hierarchical assessment stance of 'spirit' being good and 'flesh' being bad. At the same time it acknowledges the 'bodily interpretation' of the Song.

In regard to the last-mentioned, the 'bodily' or literal interpretation of the Song, some recent interesting studies have appeared. Although all depart from a natural understanding of the Song they differ markedly. Goulder (1986: 77) states that the 'Song is a fourth-century liberal tract, whose purpose is to win acceptance for foreign marriages…the Song is the most ambitiously anti-racialist document in the Bible'. The heroine is probably a dark Arabian princess being courted by Solomon. Clines (1994: 8, 21-22) views the implied material cause of the Song as '…the need of a male public for erotic literature…that verges on soft pornography… Deep down…the Song…is escapist literature…which…envisages an alternative reality'. From feminist circles Trible appreciates the liberation of the woman of the Song: 'In this setting, there is no male dominance, no female subordination, and no stereotyping of either sex' (Trible 1993: 119). Polaski (1997: 81), however, views the Shulammite as controlled by the panoptical male gaze and the consequences: 'While the female figure is the Subject of the Song, this status does not mean that the Song must be heard as liberating for women. Indeed just the opposite may be true'.

In the light of the above, it is necessary to have another look at the Song, especially from a 'bodily' perspective. The rhetoricity of the body in the Song could add an interesting voice to those already in existence and hopefully provide an epistemological tool to appreciate divergent views. It could also help explain the absence of the divine name from the Song of Songs.

b. *Aim*
Utilizing some of the insights on the 'body' by Leder (1990) and Vorster (1997) the Song will be analysed.

Drew Leder's *The Absent Body* (1990) represents an important phenomenological study on the 'body', to challenge the Cartesian dichotomy of mind/spirit: body/flesh. The thrust of Leder's study can be described as 'I am a body, therefore I am' in opposition to Descartes' 'I think, therefore I am'. He distinguishes three aspects of the body, namely, the ecstatic body, the recessive body and the dys-appearing body. The *ecstatic body* points to the surface body, the sensorimotor part of our body. Our bodies are physically designed with the senses on the outside to open up to stimuli from the outside. This part of the body is overwhelmingly foregrounded in the Song as the two lovers delight (with all senses) in each other's bodies.

The *recessive body* focuses on our viscerality we possess as human beings, our internal organs and the way they function. In opposition to our surface body we are mostly unaware of the workings of the interior body. We cannot, however, exist without energy-releasing digestive processes or a properly functioning cardiovascular system. Emotions affect the viscera and vice versa. The Song refers only in passing to the visceral aspect of our embodiment (e.g. 2.5; 5.2, 4, 8). The *dys-appearing body* refers to a disfunctional body either through pain, disease (cf. dysentery, dyslexia, etc.) or death. The dys-appearing body should be distinguished from the disappearing or absent body (cf. title of book). The last-mentioned implies a healthy, well-adapted body, which is not aware of itself, just as the eye when seeing doesn't see itself or when your legs are walking you aren't really aware of them. The moment, however, the legs cramp we are painfully aware of them, through pain the dys-appearing body surfaces. Now I am not a living body anymore, but have a body (a thing). Just as the disappearing body has fed Cartesian dualism by falsely creating the impression that some actions are immaterial (e.g. the seeing eye not seeing itself physically [in other words 'bodiless' means good]), so has the dys-appearing body. Because we are painfully aware of it when malfunction-ing, body means 'bad'. Very importantly, having a body is a profoundly social thing: 'my self-understanding always involves the seeing of what others see in me' (Leder 1990: 92; cf. also Vorster 1997: 456). Social dys-appearance then implies dehumanizing a person, against which the Song undoubtedly reacts (cf. 3. 'Threatened Bodies' below). Leder's solution in the end is 'to form one body'. This is inspired by Neo-Confucianism that teaches the embodied unity of all things. This is achieved through com-passion (Leder 1990: 161; emphatic identification), absorption (Leder 1990: 165; 'absorb the world and become absorbed in it') and communion (Leder 1990: 168; 'with the All'). The Song naturally realizes Leder's ideal of 'one body'.

Language is never innocent, it is an act that wants to accomplish some-thing. This most certainly also applies to the body-talk in the Song of Songs, even though at first glance, owing to the lyrical and playful nature of the Song, one is tempted to think otherwise. Vorster's illuminating study 'Construction of Culture through the Construction of Person: The *Acts of Thecla* as an Example' (1997) proves to be of great help to under-stand the alternative culture the Song is persuading its readers to adhere to. It also complements Leder's ideas on *social dys-appearance*. Vorster states that the body produces language, but is at the same time constructed by (cultural) language. The symbolization of the body (which crystallizes in the notion of person) can be seen as a rhetorical strategy (Vorster 1997: 446): 'Putting the body into discourse does not reveal, expose or reflect what the body is, but incarcerates the body in the value-system of a society' (Vorster 1997: 450). He convincingly shows how the ascetic discourse of the *Acts of Thecla* (second century CE) marks it as a sub-versive writing, idealizing an alternative society. The construction of person (through the ascetic body) of Thecla points to the social empower-ment of women independent of male control. To what kind of social empowerment does the discursive, erotic body in the Song point?

2. Uninhibited Bodies

In what follows the focus will be mainly on the *descriptions* of the lovers of the Song as well as their *acts*.

The Song contains a rather unique feature in regard to a specific genre, namely, the so-called (Arabic) *wasf* or description song. Although the beauty of bodily physique is described elsewhere in the Hebrew Bible (Sarah—Gen. 12.11, 14; Rebecca—Gen. 24.16; David—1 Sam. 16.18; Bathsheba—2 Sam. 11.2, etc.), the elaborate *wasf* is only found in the Song. We have three descriptions of the woman (4.1-7; 6.4-7; 7.2-8) and one of the man (5.10-16). The description of the man, very similar to that of a statue, probably bears traces of the origin of this form as being hymns dedicated to the gods, describing their statuary (Munro 1995: 60). Soulen (1993: 216 n. 1) downplays this description of the man through the eyes of a woman as 'Less sensuous and imaginative' (women don't have good erotic imaginations?) and is rightly criticized by Falk (1993: 231; cf. also Clines 1994: 13 n. 20). Some even see in 5.14 a subtle reference to the man's phallus. Although Soulen (1993: 219) is correct in interpreting the bodily metaphors of the lovers as presentational rather than represent-ational, he limits their effects only to the emotions of the readers. Again Falk (1993: 230) is correct to view these descriptive metaphors in terms of nonliteralistic visualization (cf. also Munro 1995: 17-18).

Conspicuous is the description of the lovers' *uncovered* to partly covered *bodies* in the first three *wasfs* (two of the women and one of the man) describing them from the head downwards: the women's loose hair (very sensual—cf. Eilberg-Schwartz 1994: 191), oval-shaped eyes, even teeth, rosy lips and cheeks, slender neck and soft, full breasts catch the eye. The man's facial features are described in similar terms, but instead of stopping at the torso, his full body is described. The fourth *wasf*, 'the dancing Shulammite' (7.2-8), is described from toe to head, completely naked and very sensual. Brenner (1993a) convincingly argues that this *wasf* does not only portray an innocent perspective from bottom to top, but indeed a parodying of the *wasf* genre. It protests against congenital, idolized, idealized images of love as found in the first three *wasfs* (Brenner 1993a: 255), this probably being because of the constraints of chastity (Brenner 1993a: 241). What we have in the last *wasf* is a lighter mood (Brenner 1993a: 243), with the 'tone of this poem…ribald and the humour sexual…' (Brenner 1993a: 237). The dancing Shulammite is portrayed as being fat, big and quivering (Brenner 1993a: 248), but nevertheless very sensual. Notice the effect of this dance on the male (7.8-9): 'Your stature is like that of the palm, and your breasts like clusters of fruit. I said: "I will climb the palm tree, I will take hold of its fruit".' This body speaks of earthiness, of real 'flesh-and-blood' (Brenner 1993a: 253), in comparison to the previous ones. Brenner (1993a: 257) concludes from a feminist perspective: 'It is possible to be an attractive female without becoming or pretending to become an idol or a statue; it should be possible for males to desire without putting their women on pedestals (thus conforming to convention) or denigrating their appearance (by resorting to sexual humour).'

These explicit erotic descriptions of the two lovers' bodies confirm Leder's (1990: 137) phenomenological description of sexuality: 'while a mode of sensorimotor relation to the world, it exhibits a visceral autonomy'. The two ecstatic bodies in the Song are extremely, fondly aware of each other through vision, smell, sound, taste and touch which, like other pleasurable sensations, stir up the visceral parts of our body. The viscera are to a certain extent uncontrollable as also the sexual drive. Therefore the urge of the lover to grab his mistress (7.8-9)! And therefore also the proverb-like acknowledgment towards the end of the Song (8.6): 'love is strong as death...it burns like blazing fire, like a mighty flame'. To a certain extent the acute awareness of the body through sexual desire creates the impression of *dys-appearance* (malfunctioning) of which the Song is also aware (2.5): 'Strengthen me with raisin cakes, revive me with apples, for I am sick with love.' But pleasure does not require corporeal hermeneutics (Leder 1990: 78, the 'why' of Job for instance): it soon focuses away from the visceral body to the outer world, to the 'other' to be gratified—'One simply "enjoys" pleasure' (Leder 1990: 78). When Krondorfer (1992: 8, 12, following Schiller) states that in play humans experience freedom from physical and moral constraints to become fully human, this most certainly applies also to erotic play between humans. The 'playfulness' of the dancing Shulammite not only portrays 'freedom' but also creates a 'world' wherein the sexes can find each other (cf. Brenner's conclusion above).

Within a culture where nudity is not the norm, but 'shame about nakedness as a foundational moment in the emergence of human culture' (via Adam and Eve; cf. Eilberg-Schwartz 1994: 91), the spontaneous, uninhibited depiction of nudity in the Song is quite remarkable. One could argue that the privacy of eroticism within the Song (e.g. bedroom scenes) makes it rather natural. Brenner, however, points out an 'active and noisy, slightly drunk perhaps' (public) audience for the Shulammite dance (Brenner 1993a: 245). Can one blame Clines then for stating that the Song is about the 'very stuff of pornography' (Clines 1994: 24)? Male and female nudity are appreciated and enjoyed alike (Falk 1993: 232).

Apart from the frankness of the portrayal of these nude bodies, nudity is also an important equalizer. Brenner has touched on this above already and it is especially Whedbee (1993) that elaborates on this further. He is prepared to extend Brenner's comic (parodying) reading of the 'dancing Shulammite' also to the *wasf* of the man (5.10-15) and other parts of the Song (e.g. the royal wedding procession 3.7-11, the 'royal' Shulammite 6.8-9). Whether one in all cases agrees with him or not, he aptly demonstrates that comedy not only entertains, but also undercuts and subverts (Whedbee 1993: 276). It levels class distinctions (1993: 270) and unites opposites—city and country (Song 1.5-6), king (man—fictional) and commoner (woman) and especially man and woman (Whedbee 1993: 277). Both are equal in their 'essential naked humanness' (1993: 277). Both man and woman are nakedly exposed and vulnerable, of the same 'bone and flesh'.

The descriptions of the lovers by means of *regal imagery* and *nature imagery* especially throw further light on the uninhibited bodily experiences of the lovers. Munro (1995: 48) interestingly points out how fragrance is associated with life, actually a metaphor for life. It is easy to make sense of this if one thinks of the opposite, namely, the stench of death (a decaying body). Fragrance also conveys the innermost essence of a person (Munro 1995: 48). You not only pamper and cherish your body with cosmetics, but you 'become them' as well. A few examples will suffice. Of the man: 'your love is more delightful than wine, pleasing is the fragrance of your perfumes, your name is like perfume poured out' (1.2b-3); 'His cheeks are like beds of spice yielding perfume. His lips are like lilies dripping with myrrh' (5.13). Of the woman: 'How much more pleasing is your love than wine and the fragrance of your perfume than any spice' (4.10). The woman as garden (4.12–5.1) contains the most exotic and aromatic spices imaginable (henna, nard, saffron, myrrh, cinnamon, etc.), which create the impression of 'heady luxuriance' (Munro 1995: 57). These exotic oils and spices reflect both the abundance of the courtly milieu and of nature (Munro 1995: 49). Likewise the descriptions of jewels and precious metals (e.g. 1.9-11; 5.14-15) also portray the splendour of the man and woman (Munro 1995: 67-68). These two 'bodies' are very much alive and indulge in each other's delectable attractiveness. Love is not stingy, it does not hold back but it spontaneously and abundantly gives and enjoys the other.

If regal imagery pictures the two lovers very much alive, even more so the *nature imagery*. Flora, fauna, pastoral imagery, water, all form the natural and 'majestic backdrop to their love' (Munro 1995: 92). They aren't only in nature, but both form part and parcel of nature. In the beautiful spring song (2.8-17) the man is compared to a muscular, agile and virile gazelle (2.8-9), the woman to a dove (2.14). Both animals in particular are associated with love (Keel 1986: 89-94). The framing invitation (2.10, 13) to come and enjoy springtime together with new life beckons the woman to come and enjoy nature and love—'everything in nature mates, why not us?' (Burden 1987: 59).

The lovers are not only in 'paradise', but the woman is 'paradise' (*pardes*; 4.12–5.1), an exotic, desirable garden. Munro (1995: 103) aptly describes lush gardens in the dry ancient Near East as 'symbols of life and hope'. The woman, a 'locked garden' and 'fountain sealed' (4.12), signals that she wants to burst with the abundant life in her (Munro 1995: 107). Not only is nature utilized to 'language' her, but also nature itself becomes 'embodied' through personification (cf. Vorster 1997: 452): 'Wake up North wind. South wind blow on my garden; fill the air with fragrance' (4.16). This garden with all its delicacies is 'incorporated' by the lover into his own body: 'I have gathered my myrrh with my spice, I have eaten my honeycomb and my honey, I have drunk my wine and my milk' (5.1). He becomes 'one body', one flesh with her!

The effortless ease with which the Song naturally realizes the 'forming of one body', Leder's ideal, is conspicuous. The 'universal interconnected-ness' (Leder 1990: 159) or embodied 'unity of all things' (Leder 1990: 156) is beautifully portrayed especially by the nature imagery. The spring song and garden metaphor above aptly portray Leder's notion of *absorption* (Leder 1990: 165): 'when we become deeply absorbed, as in a natural landscape, it is as if we were swallowed into a larger body. At the same time this landscape is swallowed into our embodiment, transforming it from within'. Absorption is very tacitly actualized in sexuality (Leder 1990: 167), when two people become 'one body'. Absorption also has a social dimension, which Leder calls *mutual incorporation* (Leder 1990: 94). Two subjects become 'one body' to perceive and enjoy the world: 'I come to see the forest not only through my own eyes, but as the other sees it' (Leder 1990: 94; cf. spring song above); 'We supplement our embod-iment through the other' (Leder 1990: 94). And implied especially in the nature imagery is Leder's notion of *communion* with the All (cf. below).

The Western dualism of linking woman, nature, and sexuality with the 'lower despicable body' and men with the sublime, rational mind (Leder 1990: 54) is absent in the Song (cf. also Rudolph 1962: 108-109). Instead, the bodies of man and woman blend, and decidedly also blend with body nature. When Munro (1995: 81), in passing, interestingly points out *paronomasia* between nature, love and lovers: *haddûdāîm* (mandrakes = nature), *dôdî* (lover), and *doday* (love), it subtly points to the interconnectedness of everything Leder so strongly advocates.

When it comes to the *acts* of the two uninhibited lovers it is especially the initiative-taking woman who catches the eye and this is noticed by the majority of scholars. Acts here focus more on spontaneous acts rather than dissident acts, although her acts cannot be so sharply separated. The 'dance' above is spontaneous, but most certainly also titillating-rebellious (cf. 3. 'Threatened Bodies' below). Although often confined to 'inside' spaces which signal stability and interiority (Munro 1995: 135), the woman is very much 'outgoing', the initiator and even 'aggressor' when it comes to love. The man, in contrast, is associated with freedom and open spaces (Munro 1995: 137) and is rather passive (cf. Clines 1994: 25, for opposite nuances). She is prepared to follow her 'shepherd' into the male domain of the grazing fields (1.7-8) or to go impulsively and look for him at night in the city streets where respectable women don't belong (3.1-5; 5.2-8). Her commanding voice also frames the Song when she invites the 'king' to kiss her (1.2-4) and to return (against Whedbee) to her as swift as a gazelle, for more love (Whedbee 1993: 268). She indeed is the central protagonist (Whedbee 1993: 269) and is therefore understandably compared to the *iššāh zārāh*, the 'strange woman' of Proverbs 7 (cf. Clines 1994: 14; Bekkenkamp and Van Dijk 1993: 82). Her assertiveness leads to equality and mutuality (Trible 1993: 117): it balances male power. This is beautifully illustrated in the 'duet' of 1.15–2.3 where the two lovers 'echo' each other's compliments, by taking the words from each other's mouths: (man, 1.15) 'How beautiful you are, my darling' (woman, 1.16), 'How handsome you are my lover' (man, 2.2), 'Like a lily among thorns is my darling among the maids' (woman, 2.3) 'Like an apple tree among the trees of the forest is my lover among the young men'. They are indeed 'toe to toe' (Gottwald 1985: 549). Leder's ideal of mutual incorporation and absorption (cf. above) is again aptly illustrated.

The sexual acts in the Song are similarly characterized by spontaneity and mutuality (1.12-14; 2.6-7, 16; 3.4-5; 4.6; 5.1; 6.2; 7.13-14; 8.3-4). Most commentators recognize that the Paradise lost in Genesis is again found in the Song: 'In Eden, the yearning of the woman for harmony with her man continued after disobedience. Yet the man did not reciprocate; instead, he reeled over her to destroy unity and pervert sexuality. Her desire became his dominion. But in the Song male power vanishes. His desire becomes her delight. Another consequence of disobedience is thus redeemed through the recovery of mutuality in the garden of eroticism' (Trible 1993: 117). Mutuality is emphasized explicitly by the refrain of 'mutual belonging' spoken by the woman: 'My beloved is mine and I am his' (2.16; 6.3; 7.11). Of the nine text references referred to above the woman is the speaker in seven instances. The refrain of 'mutual belonging' is in each case uttered when the two lovers' bodies unite to become 'one flesh'. The becoming 'one flesh', the consummation of their love-play, is also never forced, otherwise only half of the refrain would be possible. Their love-play comes spontaneously and naturally. Importantly, Paradise rediscovered according to the Song is not found in some sort of immaterial, spiritual realm, but through the cherishing of our bodies.

Bodily descriptions and bodily experiences speak of uninhibited, paradise-like freedom. There should be no societal hindrances when it comes to the enjoyment of each other and of body nature. There should be no holding back when it comes to giving and receiving love. Bodily play, and erotic play as essential part of it, help people to become fully human, to be fully alive. It equalizes and realizes (creates) a better world through the embodiment of the other.

3. Threatened Bodies

The uninhibited bodies above already reflect subtle dissidence from the dominant Israelite social conventions and norms. In what follows dissidence clearly comes to the fore.

The two lovers live in a patriarchal society. This obviously explains why the man's body (person) is nearly never threatened, but the woman very much so. And it is mostly men, 'patriarchs', that threaten the woman. Even when the 'daughters of Jerusalem' look down upon her because of her darker beauty (1.5-6), they look with the eyes of men who would normally cherish light-skinned beauty (Munro 1995: 43; Hostetter 1996: 36; cf. Lam. 4.7; 1 Sam. 16.12). The so-called 'racialist interpretation' of 1.5 'black am I…and [but?] beautiful' (cf. e.g. Goulder 1986: 12-13, 74-86) does not hold. The woman herself explains the reason for her 'blackness' or swarthiness, namely, sunburn whilst tending the vineyards. Hostetter (1996: 36) rightly points out that the racialist explanation is nothing else than 'the incorporation of a social problem from the twentieth century AD into a text from the first millenium BC'. What we obviously have here is rather a class struggle between country and city, peasantry and elite (aristocracy). The brothers, representing the 'male headed household' (*bet 'āb*; cf. Bird 1992: 952), angrily ordered her (v. 6) to tend to the vineyards. Women's labour in the domestic sphere (Bird 1992: 952) and also as part of the labour force within subsistence agriculture (Bird 1992: 953-54) was quite normal. However, the brothers' anger towards her (not explained) could point to keeping her away from the eager eyes of men in the city streets (cf. 8.8-9; cf. also Munro 1995: 76). They (men) control her, construct her as marginalized, nearly to the extent of being non-existent! Ironically, however, she asserts herself. She is dark, but beautiful! She has a strange beauty, but beauty that smacks even of royalty. She turns embarrassment into opportunity, she won't be intimidated by the depersonalizing actions of either brothers or (male-conditioned) insulting stares of city girls.

Her rebelliousness against patriarchy surfaces even clearer in 8.8-9. What Vorster (1997: 462 n. 16) says of women in the ancient world 'perceived as more susceptible to loss of bodily control and therefore more exposed to seduction. Therefore, they had to be "protected" by seclusion', is aptly exemplified in the above-mentioned text. When she is 'spoken for' (by men; 8.8), her brothers will 'if she is a wall…build towers of silver on her', 'if a door…enclose her with panels of cedar' (cf. also Hos. 2.8-9). This forced spatial restriction of the female body (Vorster 1997: 462) is obviously something completely different than the deliberate, wilful seclusion of the two lovers' bodies in sexual union in the security and privacy of the 'mothers house' (8.2-4; cf. also 3.4). Interestingly, the seclusion to the 'mother's house' and not the 'father's house' as would be expected within Israelite society is another subtle pointer to the subversiveness of the Song (cf. Meyers 1993: 209). Men controlled females' sexuality, a man his wife's and the father the daughter's (Deut. 22.13-21, 28-29; Gen. 34.5-7). In the Song the brothers represent the absent patriarch father. But as in the case of the brothers marginalizing her into the vineyard, she doesn't take it. She challenges them and overtly rebels (8.10): 'I am a wall and my breasts are like towers… I have become in his (*lover*, my insertion) eyes like one bringing contentment.' The little sister is indeed a full-fledged woman, a person in her own right. She obviously is not prepared to live the 'body of her culture' (Vorster 1997: 150).

The woman is threatened and inhibited not only by her family males, but also by other males in the Song, namely the lover's fellow 'shepherds' and also the watchmen of the city. In all her acquaintances with these males she is perceived (cf. 'dreams' in 3.1-5 and 5.2-8) or could be perceived (1.7-8; 8.1) as a *iššāh zārāh* or 'strange' woman. This is the woman the book of Proverbs warns against—'the symbol for the immoral...an embodiment of evil' (Bird 1992: 953)—the one that subverts the moral and religious values of the dominant society. Although she is adventurous and an active, initiative-taking woman, and therefore portrays something of the 'wildness' of the 'strange' woman, it is perhaps an over-statement to regard her so (cf. Clines 1994: 14 and Bekkenkamp and Van Dijk 1993: 82). She is liberated, but not an evil predator. The narrative development of this rural girl to 'queenly status' (Munro 1995: 145) also speaks against this. She is very much aware (and reluctant) of such a stigma by going about the shepherds' tents as a harlot looking for men (1.7-8), or of openly and publicly kissing her lover as such a 'loose woman' would do (8.1). But she is perceived as one for going about in the streets at night, looking for her lover. Obviously the watchmen do not consider (or are unaware) that this is a spontaneous, impulsive love-driven act. She is perceived to be hunting for men and they treat her as they are used to treating such a type—they beat her and wound her, humiliate her as if she is an 'out of control' animal. In contrast to the brothers who control her by indirectly 'encamping' her, the watchmen brutally assault her body. In this way they gain near complete and direct control over her. She is no subject any more, but has been depersonalized to a despicable object. But she survives. Love becomes the motivational force to keep on looking for her lover (5.8): 'Daughters of Jerusalem...if you find my lover...tell him I am faint with love'.

Both lovers also experience threat from other lovers, but then not from a patriarchal source only and obviously also not so seriously. It is not their 'persona' that is threatened as above, but rather their love-play. The other competitors, the 'daughters of Jerusalem' and the 'little foxes' (2.15), are playfully scared away so as not to interrupt their physical intimacy (cf. TEV for translation of the 'refrain of adjuration'; 2.7; 3.5; 8.4).

What is actually happening to the woman's stared at, sexually con-trolled, 'encamped' and beaten body? According to Leder (1990: 97) she becomes a *dys-appearing* body, a dysfunctional body both physically as well as socially. A dys-appearing, malfunctioning body is very acutely experienced when physical disease strikes for instance. Social *dys-appearance* not only affects the sociality of a person, but his/her body as well: 'Dys-appearance on the organic and social level...intertwine' (Leder 1990: 98). For example, if the Western body society constitutes the 'ideal' female body as slim, then obviously overweight women will feel marginalized and become a-social and might even become physically dysfunctional (e.g. anorexic). The woman's body in the Song has indeed become 'a place of vulnerability...to sociopolitical forces' (Leder 1990: 98). She is deliberately made an object, an alien thing. This happens through the 'objectifying gaze' being 'highly distanced' and 'antagonistic', of the daughters of Jerusalem. If one's body looks and acts like everyone else's then you're not aware of it (Leder 1990: 97). But if it looks different, 'swarthy' in the woman's case, then self-consciousness surfaces (Leder 1990: 97). As has been seen above she has also been objectified, thematized as 'thing' both by the treatment of her brothers and the watchmen of the city. They alienate her socially and inflict pain on her body (1.6; 5.7) to control her. This could happen because of the 'discrepancy of power' (Leder 1990: 98) between males and females within Israelite patriarchal society. In such a situation there is no possibility of *cosubjectivity*. It is impossible for her brothers and the watchmen to help her look for her lover. What does all this lead to? What Leder says of the body society's construction of prostitutes, tortured humans, the assembly line worker, that 'their bodies have been taken away from them through the alienating projects of the other', squarely fits the beloved of the Song. The threatening acts to her body, her 'dis-embodiment' burns down to depersonalizing her, dehumanizing her, making her a lesser or even a non-person.

But, as has become clear, she resists and challenges these onslaughts. Indeed, this is not strange for someone who is very much aware of the worth of 'one-bodiness' ('to form one body'), who as a living body actualizes her personhood through love. Love in the Song powerfully withstands the socio-political efforts to fragment the lovers' bodies and personhood.

4. *Confused Bodies*

Two things in the Song especially contribute to the confusion of the bodily portrayal of the lovers. Is their personhood, especially that of the woman, so complete? First, there is the captivity of the woman by the male gaze and, second, the absence of any God-talk in the Song. Admittedly, these might be more confusing to the modern reader of the Song than to its author(s), but they nevertheless question the idyllic, paradised world of the Song.

It has been pointed out above that the Song is indeed feminine biased. Although this seems to balance the scale within patriarchal society to that of equality and the mutuality of the sexes, Brenner is prepared to go much further by emphasizing female superiority (Brenner 1993b: 273). This stance is challenged very convincingly by Polaski (1997: 76-77) who states that 'the female Subject may be understood as the result of the internalization of the *male gaze* (my emphasis) and the adoption of disciplinary practices which assume the presence of "a panoptical male connoisseur"' (quoting Sandra L. Bartky). Polaski develops the ideas of Foucault on Jeremy Bentham's 'Panoptican', a utopian vision of what prisons could be like. In this doughnut-shaped prison, prisoners are being lit up from windows from the outside, but subject to constant observation from observers from the inside. The prisoners cannot see their observers, but are so aware of them that they constitute their own selves according to the perceived gazes focused on them. According to Polaski the same happens in the Song. The woman is constituted by the male gaze to whom she is constantly exposed. This becomes very clear especially in the *wasfs*. Clines has noted the same (1994: 26), but Polaski goes further by pointing out how she internalizes the male gaze, and in this way constitutes her own subjectivity. She becomes 'her own watchman' (Polaski 1997: 79), or in the words of Eilberg-Schwartz (1994: 96) 'the surveyor of woman in herself is male'. The moment this happens women start disciplining themselves, policing their 'make-up...hairdo...if her stockings have bagged...feeling fat' (Polaski 1997: 70-71, quoting Bartky). The internalized male gaze controls them, captivates them. This does not happen to the male in the Song who is able to evade the woman's gaze (Polaski 1997: 76). Although the woman rejects the gazes of some men (her brothers 8.8-10; night watchmen 5.7), she finds her security within the male gaze of her beloved (8.10): 'I was in his eyes as one who finds peace' (Polaski 1997: 80). Vorster (1997: 460) also points out how in antiquity status was conferred upon women by the consistent and regular impregnation and insemination by their men. Therefore a barren woman was 'shameful', a widow who had no man had no status. Impregnation is absent from the Song, but the constant yearning of the beloved for her lover to visit her again and again intimately, even risking her dignity to go and find him, confirms her finding her status and security through the man. Polaski (1997: 81) rightly concludes that the Song might not be so liberating for women. The opposite might be true.

From a bodily phenomenological perspective Leder aptly links up with the views of Polaski. He points out that women might be more aware of their bodies because of the biological changes, owing to pregnancy or menstruation for instance. Men experience their bodies as 'unchanging'. He follows Simoné de Beauvior, who, like Bartky above, states that women assume the social role of the Other (Leder 1990: 99), the 'second sex'. Leder likewise concludes as above that then, 'It is the gaze, the projects of men that are culturally definitive. Hence women are not full cosubjectivities, free to experience from a tacit body'. They live their bodies as men would like to see them. And this, Leder convincingly concludes, amounts to the principle of *social dys-appearance*, bodily (person) malfunctioning. Women become less, the clay in the hands of the modelling man. They are not really liberated, but captivated by the controlling power of the male gaze.

But is it only women's bodies that are thematized in this way? Are not men also very much aware of how they 'look' in women's eyes? Why else are body-building, face-lifts, hair-implantation, and so on, so important to modern men also? Perhaps the sexes experience it as 'natural' to 'stare' at each other. But admittedly, women are being stared at more than men, in the Song and also in modern films, for instance. Female nudity is much more common than male nudity.

The two lovers in the Song share so many things, but there is a conspicuous silence on *religion*. Goulder, not correct in viewing the woman as a black Arabic princess, nevertheless notices the 'heroine never mentions religion' (Goulder 1986: 76). The absence of the divine name in the Song has likewise been noticed. Why is this so?

Many reasons for the absence of the divine from the Song have been offered. The name might be absent, but the background presence of the divine, the All, the Creator is acknowledged *ipso facto*, as the two lovers enjoy their bodies in harmony with body nature. Müller (1994: 376) says the 'ästhetisch sublimierte Natur' ('aesthetic, sublime nature') becomes a 'Maske Gottes' ('Mask of God'). Davidson (1989: 7) represents the consensus among scholars 'that sexuality is assumed to be a creation ordinance, given by God for man to enjoy'.

God's absence or lurking behind the curtains could be not to confuse him with the fertility gods of the neighbours (Viviers 1990: 245). This might be the case when one views especially the prophetic aversion to the fertility cults. Religion might also be absent from the Song, seeing that it can be considered wisdom literature which is not really interested in religious ritual.

The Song, however, viewed from a bodily perspective highlights the direct absence of the divine quite interestingly. Brenner (1993b: 273) has noted that where strong women are present God is absent (e.g. Esther, Judg. 4). In the Song we have indeed met with a 'women's world'. Just as the father figure is absent in the Song, so also is God who represents patriarchy (cf. Landy 1987: 314). One can understand the avoidance of religious ritual especially, because it controls societies and especially women's bodies through its male (priestly) discursive practices. Eilberg-Schwartz (1990: 191) says it aptly: 'The priestly regulations governing bodily emissions (e.g. menstruation, my insertion) clearly exploit associations of masculinity, fertility, and control and contrast these with femininity, death and disorder, in a way that symbolically suppresses women.' The human body in Israelite religion becomes a scene for cultural representations and a place for the display of power (Eilberg-Schwartz 1990: 193). Women, more than men, are regarded inferior and impure (Vorster 1997: 451). It would then make no sense for this strong, liberated woman of the Song even to consider religion in this way. It is not only cold water on hot passion, but decidedly sabotages her body and the wholeness of her personhood.

Apart from patriarchy, God himself is the reason for this absence. In the Song where bodies feature so centrally, the absence of God can be naturally explained by the Israelite God not having a body (unlike the neighbouring gods). God was attributed a limited number of human functions such as speech, jealously and anger. He does not have 'lower' human functions such as hunger, thirst and sexual activity (Eilberg-Schwartz 1990: 138, 193-94; early traces of the 'spirit–flesh' dichotomy?). If God is a no-body (Eilberg-Schwartz 1990: 193), this is rather confusing for his embodied creatures. Humans are made in the image and likeness of God (Gen. 1.26-27), they have to be holy as he is holy (Lev. 11.45), but 'being Godlike and being human were incompatible in certain fundamental ways' (Eilberg-Schwartz 1990: 193): 'the divine realm served as much as an anti-image for the human realm as a mirror of it' (p. 217). Israelites married, procreated and had children, but their God did not. Procreation is a covenantal obligation, but at the same time the source of (religious) contamination: 'While the penis is the symbol of fertility and the covenant it is also the source of semen, which is polluting. From the priests' perspective, Israelites are damned if they do and damned if they don't. There is no escaping the cultural conflict that surrounds sexuality' (Eilberg-Schwartz 1990: 193). It is clear that all this is rather confusing. God and religion are to a certain extent 'written out' of the Song of Songs story.

The male gaze and absence of God-talk that bother and confuse us today did not seem to pose serious problems in the Song. What male and female had in each other in the Song seems to be enough. Their love-play takes up the whole agenda. Clines (1994: 20) says it strikingly: 'That is all ye know on earth and all ye need to know.'

5. *Conclusion*

The Song's rhetoricity of the body creates a world of uninhibited freedom. It speaks openly and freely of nudity, sexuality and the equality of the sexes. The Song's erotic discourse portrays a liberated picture of how the sexes should be able to enjoy their bodies. The 'naturalness' of their bodily and especially sexual experiences indeed marks the Song as 'Paradise regained'. It, however, represents a narrow, small world where nothing else than love really matters (Clines 1994: 21). But it still is a rather unblemished world.

Where this freedom is jeopardized, the Song strongly reacts. It combats hindrances laid in the path of love, especially from the dominant patriarchal society. It subverts patriarchy by showing its readers an alternative world of how things ought to be. Bird (1992: 955) summarizes excellently: 'In the love poetry of the Song of Songs sex is free and freely given; but in Israelite society, as every society, it was not free.' To create this utopian world the Song becomes escapist literature, a wishful dream or fantasy (Clines 1994: 21-22).

Whether this 'wish-fulfillment dream' was created by a man for a male audience (Clines 1994: 7, 13-14), or by a woman (feminist circles), it did not turn the patriarchal world upside down. It did not create an alternative gender-equal society, not then and not later on. Instead 'patriarchy… supressed its subversiveness by recourse to…allegorical interpretation' (Clines 1994: 22). Clines (p. 23), not so convinced of the Song's reforming/revolutionary potential to promote gender equality today, admits that it could be a liberative force in a conservative, patriarchal society (e.g. South Africa).

Apart from the Song's subversive potential, its rhetoricity of the body has an important contribution to make to the well-being of humans. The Song spontaneously establishes Leder's conviction: 'To be human is to be a living body.' Not to have a body, but to be one! The way the body is cherished all along in the Song instinctively combats all dis-embodying practices. It opposes the fragmentation of personhood and therefore the two lovers are so 'alive'. Likewise, all dys-appearing (malfunctioning) bodily practices, physically as well as socially, should be withstood so as to 'form one body'. Then only does a human become a cosubjective with fellow-humans, and through our shared 'one-bodiness' the world is experienced a better place to live in. And life becomes meaningful.

BIBLIOGRAPHY

Bekkenkamp, J., and F. Van Dijk
    1993   'The Canon of the Old Testament and Women's Cultural Traditions', in Brenner (ed.) 1993: 67-85.

Bird, P.A.
    1992   'Women: Old Testament', in *ABD*, VI: 951-57.

Brenner, A.
    1993a   '"Come back, come back the Shulammite" (Song of Songs 7.1-10): A Parody of the *wasf* Genre', in A. Brenner (ed.) 1993: 234-57.
    1993b   'To See Is to Assume: Whose Love Is Celebrated in the Song of Songs?', *BibInt* 1: 265-84.

Brenner, A. (ed.)
    1993   *A Feminist Companion to the Song of Songs* (Sheffield: Sheffield Academic Press).

Burden, J.J.
    1987   'The Song of Songs', in J.J. Burden and W.S. Prinsloo (eds.), *Dialogue with God: Preachers, Poets and Philosophers* (LOT, 3; Cape Town: Tafelberg Publishers): 56-81.

Clines, D.J.A.
    1994   'Why Is There a Song of Songs and What Does It Do to You if You Read It?', *Jian Dao* 1: 3-27.

Davidson, R.M.
    1989   'Theology of Sexuality in the Song of Songs: Return to Eden', *AUSS* 27: 1-19.

Eilberg-Schwartz, H.
    1994   *God's Phallus: And Other Problems for Men and Monotheism* (Boston: Beacon Press).
    1990   *The Savage in Judaism: An Anthropology of Israelite Religion and Ancient Judaism* (Bloomington: Indiana University Press).

Falk, M.
    1993   'The *wasf*', in Brenner (ed.) 1993: 225-33.

Gottwald, N.K.
    1985   *The Hebrew Bible: A Socio-Literary Introduction* (Philadelphia: Fortress Press).

Goulder, M.D.
    1986   *The Song of Fourteen Songs* (JSOTSup, 36; Sheffield: Sheffield Academic Press).

Hostetter, E.C.
    1996   'Mistranslation in Cant 1.5', *AUSS* 34: 35-36.
Keel, O.
    1986   *Das Hohelied* (Zürcher Bibelkommentare AT, 18; Zürich: Theologischer
                Verlag).
Krondorfer, B.
    1992   'The Whole Gamut of Experience: Historical and Theoretical Reflections on
                Play', in B. Krondorfer (ed.), *Body and Bible: Interpreting and Experiencing
                Biblical Narratives* (Philadelphia: Trinity Press International): 5-26.
Landy, F.
    1987   'The Song of Songs', in R. Alter and F. Kermode (eds.), *The Literary Guide
                to the Bible* (Cambridge, MA: Harvard University Press): 305-19.
Leder, D.
    1990   *The Absent Body* (Chicago: University of Chicago Press).
Meyers, C.
    1993   'Gender Imagery in the Song of Songs', in Brenner (ed.) 1993: 197-212.
Müller, H.-P.
    1994   'Menschen, Landschaften und religiöse Erinnerungsreste: Anschlußerörter-
                ungen zum Hohenlied', *ZTK* 91: 375-95.
Munro, J.M.
    1995   *Spikenard and Saffron: A Study in the Poetic Language of the Song of Songs*
                (JSOTSup, 203; Sheffield: Sheffield Academic Press).
Polaski, D.C.
    1997   'What Will Ye See in the Shulammite? Women, Power and Panopticism in
                the Song of Songs', *BibInt* 5: 64-81.
Pope, M.H.
    1977   *Song of Songs* (AB, 7C; New York: Doubleday).
Rudolph, W.
    1962   *Das Buch Ruth. Das Hohelied. Die Klagelieder* (KAT, 17.1-3; Gütersloh:
                Gütersloher Verlaghaus Gerd Mohn).
Soulen, R.N.
    1993   'The *wasfs* in the Song of Songs and Hermeneutic', in Brenner (ed.) 1993:
                214-24.
Trible, P.
    1993   'Love's Lyrics Redeemed', in Brenner (ed.) 1993: 100-20.
Viviers, H.
    1990   'Hooglied: 'n Lied met goddelike klanke', in J.H. Coetzee, S.J. Nortjé and
                H. Viviers (eds.), *'n Vriend in ons poorte: Studies opgedra aan prof Paul du
                Plessis* (Johannesburg: Department Bybelkunde, Randse Afrikaanse
                Universiteit): 235-47.
Vorster, J.N.
    1997   'Construction of Culture through the Construction of Person: "The Acts of
                Thecla" as an Example', in S.E. Porter and T.H. Olbricht (eds.), *The
                Rhetorical Analysis of Scripture: Essays from the 1995 London Conference*
                (JSNTSup, 146; Sheffield: Sheffield Academic Press): 445-73.
Whedbee, J.W.
    1993   'Paradox and Parody in the Song of Solomon: Towards a Comic Reading of
                the Most Sublime Song', in Brenner (ed.) 1993: 266-78.

Part III

RHETORICAL CRITICISM OF THE GOSPELS

Jesus' Rhetoric of Criticism:
The Parables against his Friends and Critics

Craig A. Evans

1. *Introduction*

Popularly regarded as the 'bedrock' of the dominical tradition, the parables of Jesus have for more than a century been at the center of attention in Jesus research.[1] They are, the Markan evangelist tells us, the principal mode of his teaching style (cf. Mk 4.33-34). This claim appears to be borne out, for the Synoptic Gospels record some 45 parables, which account for approximately one-third of his teaching. About half of these parables describe the kingdom of God, the basic element of Jesus' message. Many of the remainder also clarify Jesus' ideas about the kingdom (e.g. who qualifies for entry into it), if only implicitly.

Besides advancing ideas about the kingdom and related topics, many of the parables direct criticism, even threats, against a variety of competitors and opponents. The manner in which Jesus mounts this criticism, or in some instances forms of admonition aiming at conciliation, by means of the rhetoric of his parables is quite interesting. It is in fact often at this point that Jesus' parables differ in function and purpose from those of the later Tannaitic rabbis.

The present study investigates the nature of Jesus' rhetoric of criticism as it is deployed in his parables. This criticism falls into two broad categories: (1) a conciliatory criticism, whereby Jesus' competitors and critics are invited to rethink their positions and conceivably side with Jesus and

---

1. For recent assessments, see B.B. Scott, *Hear Then the Parable: A Commentary on the Parables of Jesus* (Minneapolis: Fortress Press, 1989); C.L. Blomberg, 'The Parables of Jesus: Current Trends and Needs in Research', in B.D. Chilton and C.A. Evans (eds.), *Studying the Historical Jesus: Evaluations of the State of Current Research* (NTTS, 19; Leiden: E.J. Brill, 1994), pp. 231-54; C.W. Hedrick, *Parables as Poetic Fictions: The Creative Voice of Jesus* (Peabody: Hendrickson, 1994).

his movement, and (2) a threatening criticism, whereby Jesus predicts dire consequences for those who do not hear the word of God (cf. Mk 3.35). The first form of criticism is usually directed against scribes and Pharisees. Although later Christian polemic tended to demonize the Pharisees, for they and their successors became the principal competitors and opponents of early Christianity, much of Jesus' criticism of them is more of a collegial, admonitory nature. This stands in contrast to the second form of criticism, which is sometimes directed against the power brokers of Israel. Some of this criticism targeted the Herodian dynasty, but Jesus saves his harshest rhetoric for the ruling priests who, in his opinion, are the most culpable and responsible for Israel's plight. Alluding to or at least pre-supposing Scripture Jesus warns of judgment and destruction. The second form of criticism may also have been leveled at others—of whatever social class—who chose to pay no heed to Jesus' prophetic call.

Comparative study of the rabbinic parables sheds light on aspects of Jesus' parables and in some instances calls into question some modern interpretation. Jesus' rhetoric is, in contrast to the Greco-Roman theories and practitioners of rhetoric, of a distinctly proto-rabbinic cast.[2] This observation stands in tension with the proposals currently in vogue in some circles in North America that Jesus is best compared to Cynicism.[3]

2. For bibliography, see P. Fiebig, *Die Gleichnisreden Jesu im Lichte der rab-binischen Gleichnisse des neutestamentlichen Zeitalters* (Tübingen: Mohr [Siebeck], 1912); W.O.E. Oesterley, *The Gospel Parables in the Light of their Jewish Back-ground* (New York: Macmillan, 1936); D. Flusser, *Die rabbinischen Gleichnisse und der Gleichniserzähler Jesus* (Judaica et Christiana, 4; Frankfurt am Main: Peter Lang, 1981); B. Gerhardsson, 'The Narrative Meshalim in the Synoptic Gospels: A Com-parison with the Narrative Meshalim in the Old Testament', *NTS* 34 (1988), pp. 339-63; B.H. Young, *Jesus and his Jewish Parables: Rediscovering the Roots of Jesus' Teaching* (Theological Inquiries; New York: Paulist Press, 1989); H.K. McArthur and R.M. Johnston, *They also Taught in Parables: Rabbinic Parables from the First Cen-turies of the Christian Era* (Grand Rapids: Zondervan, 1990); P. Dschulnigg, 'Rabbinische Gleichnisse und Gleichnisse Jesu', *Judaica* 47 (1991), pp. 185-97; D. Stern, *Parables in Midrash: Narrative and Exegesis in Rabbinic Literature* (Cambridge, MA: Harvard University Press, 1991); T.P. D'Angelo, 'The Rabbinic Background of the Parables of Jesus', *Catholic World* 235 (1992), pp. 63-67; B. Kowalski, 'Die Wertung von Versagen und Unheil der Geschichte', *Judaica* 50 (1994), pp. 18-23; C.A. Evans, 'Jesus and Rabbinic Parables, Proverbs, and Prayers', in C.A. Evans, *Jesus and his Contemporaries: Comparative Studies* (AGJU, 25; Leiden: E.J. Brill, 1995), pp. 251-97.

3. I have in mind the more extreme views, whereby Jesus' Jewishness is mini-mized; cf. B.L. Mack, *A Myth of Innocence: Mark and Christian Origins* (Philadel-

This is not to say, however, that early rabbinic exegesis and argumentation show no signs of Greek rhetorical influence, or for that matter that the Gospels themselves do not. On the contrary, as David Daube and Saul Lieberman have shown, many of the exegetical rules of the Tannaim (including those attributed to Hillel himself) reflect aspects of Greek rhetoric and logic,[4] while elements of rhetoric may be observed in the New Testament Gospels.[5] Rhetoric in some Cynic traditions may shed light in a general sense on Jesus' stye of teaching and stance over against the power structure that he faced.[6] F.G. Downing offers numerous parallels,[7] usually quite general, between utterances of Jesus and those attributed to Cynics or to sources thought to reflect Cynic ideas. But closer examination shows that the closest and most significant parallels are with proto-rabbinic exegesis and argumentation, not Cynic. Indeed, the parallels with Cynicism, which are not impressive, are probably best explained as the natural

phia: Fortress Press, 1988); J.D. Crossan, *The Historical Jesus: The Life of a Mediterranean Jewish Peasant* (San Francisco: HarperCollins, 1991).

4.   D. Daube, 'Rabbinic Methods of Interpretation and Hellenistic Rhetoric', *HUCA* 22 (1949), pp. 239-64; *idem*, 'Alexandrian Methods of Interpretation and the Rabbis', in M. Gerwig *et al.* (eds.), *Festschrift Hans Lewald* (Basel: Helbing und Lichtenhahn, 1953), pp. 27-44; repr. in H.A. Fischel (ed.), *Essays in Greco-Roman and Related Talmudic Literature* (New York: Ktav, 1977), pp. 164-82; *idem*, *The New Testament and Rabbinic Judaism* (Jordan Lectures in Comparative Religion, 2; London: Athlone, 1956), pp. 151-57; S. Lieberman, *Hellenism in Jewish Palestine* (TSJTSA, 18; New York: JTSA, 1962). Daube ('Alexandrian Methods', p. 44) remarks that the 'whole Rabbinic system of exegesis initiated by Hillel about 30 B.C.E. and elaborated by the following generations was essentially Hellenistic...' Elsewhere he adds (*New Testament*, pp. 156-57): 'In that period, much of Hellenistic rhetoric was the common property of the civilized Mediterranean world. Its effects are hardly less noticeable in Rabbinic literature than in Greek or Roman.' H.L. Strack and G. Stemberger (*Introduction to the Talmud and Midrash* [Edinburgh: T. & T. Clark, 1991; Minneapolis: Fortress Press, 1992], p. 20) are in essential agreement, but caution that the 'direct adoption of the rules from the Hellenistic world cannot be established, even if the correlation and terminology of the rules [of Hillel] go back to Hellenistic influence'.

5.   See R.A. Burridge, 'The Gospels and Acts', in S.E. Porter (ed.), *Handbook of Classical Rhetoric in the Hellenistic Period 330 B.C.–A.D. 400* (Leiden: E.J. Brill, 1997), pp. 507-32.

6.   For a current assessment of rhetoric and Cynicism, see R.F. Hock, 'Cynics and Rhetoric', in Porter (ed.), *Handbook of Classical Rhetoric*, pp. 755-73.

7.   F.G. Downing, *Christ and the Cynics: Jesus and Other Radical Preachers in First-Century Tradition* (JSOT Manuals, 4; Sheffield: JSOT Press, 1988); *idem*, *Cynics and Christian Origins* (Edinburgh: T. & T. Clark, 1992).

overlap one should expect in a common time and region, that is, the natural exchange of words, turns of phrases, and styles that takes place among groups of people who live together. Thus, when Jesus says, 'Physician, heal yourself' (Lk. 4.23), it is not necessary to conclude that Jesus has consciously quoted a Greek source (as seen in Euripides, *Fragments* 1086). This proverbial saying was floating around among the rabbis as well (as seen in *Gen. R.* 23.4 [on Gen. 4.23]).

Perhaps Gregory Bloomquist's appeal to rhetoric in Jesus' teaching style accounts for the Cynic-like appearance of this teaching in places.[8] Bloomquist maintains that 'the presupposition of a rhetoric-less Jesus is both historically improbable and ideologically motivated'.[9] He is surely correct, for we find examples of humor, sarcasm, and parody.[10] Some of this rhetoric finds parallels in Cynic rhetoric.[11] Bloomquist scores points in my opinion by rightly arguing that Jesus' 'counterculturalism' or 'subversiveness' was not intended to overthrow Jewish tradition, but to restore Israelite culture in what was imagined to be the ideal state.[12]

Another recent and important study comes from the late Ben Meyer. He focuses on verbal, poetic, and phonetic features of Jesus' discourse, relying on retroversion of the Greek into Aramaic.[13] Meyer finds numerous

---

8. L.G. Bloomquist, 'Methodological Considerations in the Determination of the Social Context of Cynic Rhetorical Practice: Implications for our Present Studies of the Jesus Traditions', in S.E. Porter and T.H. Olbricht (eds.), *Rhetorical Analysis of Scripture: Essays from the 1995 London Conference* (JSNTSup, 146; Sheffield: Sheffield Academic Press, 1997), pp. 200-31; *idem*, 'The Rhetoric of the Historical Jesus', in *Whose Historical Jesus?* (Studies in Christianity and Judaism, 7; Waterloo: Wilfrid Laurier Press, 1997), pp. 98-117.

9. Bloomquist, 'Methodological Considerations', p. 221.

10. Bloomquist, 'Methodological Considerations', pp. 207-208.

11. Bloomquist, 'Methodological Considerations', p. 222. I think, however, the parallels between Jesus and his earliest followers and Cynicism have been greatly overdrawn in some work, especially that emanating from the North American Jesus Seminar. For criticism, see D.E. Aune, 'Jesus and Cynics in First-Century Palestine: Some Critical Considerations', in J.H. Charlesworth and L.L. Johns (eds.), *Hillel and Jesus: Comparisons of Two Major Religious Leaders* (Minneapolis: Fortress Press, 1997), pp. 176-92; H.D. Betz, 'Jesus and the Cynics: Survey and Analysis of a Hypothesis', *JR* 74 (1994), pp. 453-75; C.M. Tuckett, 'A Cynic Q?', *Bib* 70 (1989), pp. 349-76; *idem*, *Q and the History of Early Christianity: Studies on Q* (Edinburgh: T. & T. Clark, 1996), pp. 368-91; B. Witherington, *Jesus the Sage: The Pilgrimage of Wisdom* (Minneapolis: Fortress Press, 1994), pp. 123-43.

12. Bloomquist, 'Methodological Considerations', pp. 229-30.

13. B.F. Meyer, 'How Jesus Charged Language with Meaning: A Study in Rhet-

examples of visual images (*phanopoeia*), orchestration of sound (*melo-poeia*), and allusive language (*logopoeia*), concluding that as a 'rhetoric-ian, Jesus was a moderate'.[14] Jesus' rhetoric, Meyer avers, was to serve his 'mission of a prince sent to his people in the guise of a commoner commissioned to fire their allegiances against the day when he would be revealed and enthroned as their rightful king'.[15]

In a recent study Richard Burridge surveys the presence and function of rhetoric in the Gospels and Acts.[16] He believes that the first five writings of the New Testament are primarily *bioi* with rhetorical influences.[17] Rhetorical elements are seen in the Gospels' arrangement, the 'discovery' of important facts about the principal subject, style, and memorable quality. The latter point is interesting, for the effort to make the material memorable probably originated with Jesus himself, who, in the style of Jewish teachers of his day, expected his disciples to learn and pass on his teaching.[18]

The present study focuses on features of Jesus' style of argument and prophetic criticism, with special attention given to the parables as vehicles by which Jesus made his criticisms felt. Underlying the usage of the parable seems to be the assumption that one's argument gains strength if it can be illustrated by nature or human conduct. Persuasion, more than illu-stration, appears to be the function and purpose of the parable. The critical dimension of Jesus' parables should in most cases be viewed in this light. The audiences to whom the parables were uttered (as judged by the con-texts supplied by the evangelists, but also as judged by the contents of the parables themselves) fall into four general groups: (1) sympathetic crowds and following, (2) scribes and Pharisees, (3) ruling priests and 'elders of the people', and (4) the Herodian dynasty.

oric', *SR* 19 (1990), pp. 273-85; rev. and repr. in B.D. Chilton and C.A. Evans (eds.), *Authenticating the Words of Jesus* (NTTS, 28.1; Leiden: E.J. Brill, 1998), pp. 81-96.

14. Meyer, 'How Jesus Charged Language with Meaning', p. 285.

15. Meyer, 'How Jesus Charged Language with Meaning', p. 285.

16. R.A. Burridge, 'The Gospels and Acts', in Porter (ed.), *Handbook of Classical Rhetoric*, pp. 507-32.

17. See R.A. Burridge, *What Are the Gospels? A Comparison with Graeco-Roman Biography* (SNTSMS, 70; Cambridge: Cambridge University Press, 1992).

18. One thinks here of B. Gerhardsson's *Memory and Manuscript: Oral Tradition and Written Transmission in Rabbinic Judaism and Early Christianity* (Lund: Gleerup, 1961) and the criticisms that have been leveled against it. However, to say that Jesus expected his disciples (i.e. 'learners') to learn his teaching and be able to repeat it is not necessarily to import into the first century later principles of rabbinic pedagogy.

2. *Directed to Sympathetic Crowds and Following*

Jesus' comments to the crowd following the departure of John's messengers (Mt. 11.7-9 = Lk. 7.24-26) border on sarcasm. What is interesting is that these words were addressed to his sympathizers:

> What did you go out into the wilderness to look at? A reed shaken by the wind? What then did you go out to see? Someone dressed in soft robes? Look, those who wear soft robes are in royal palaces. What then did you go out to see? A prophet? Yes, I tell you, and more than a prophet.

Jesus' comments here, which are metaphorical but do not constitute a parable proper, are offered in defense of John. (In the preceding verses Jesus defended himself.) With a series of rhetorical questions Jesus puts to his hearers, most if not all of whom were sympathetic, a set of contrasting, false alternatives.

'What did you go out into the wilderness to look at? A reed shaken by the wind [κάλαμον ὑπὸ ἀνέμου σαλευόμενον]?' Commentators have been uncertain how to understand this metaphor. In what sense can John be compared to a 'reed shaken by the wind'? Daniel Harrington has suggested that the point of the comparison lies in the contrast between the flexible reeds, which lean in whichever direction the wind is blowing, and the resolute and unbending John.[19] Harrington thinks that the comparison is thus between Herod Antipas, who had imprisoned John (cf. Mk 6.17-29 = Mt. 14.3-12; Lk. 3.19-20; 9.19; Mt. 11.2-3 = Lk. 7.19) and who had used the reed as a symbol on coins he minted on the occasion of the founding of Tiberias, and John the Baptist who without flinching dared to criticize the ethnarc for putting away his wife and marrying his sister-in-law.[20] This interpretation is probably correct, for the only other reference

19. D.J. Harrington, *The Gospel of Matthew* (Sacra Pagina, 1; Collegeville, MN: Liturgical Press, 1991), p. 156. Reeds make frequent appearances in Aesop's Fables. The Fable of the Oak and Reed (Fable 71) may illustrate the contrast assumed in Jesus statement: 'An oak and a reed were disputing concerning strength. When a great wind (ἀνέμου) arose, the reed, being shaken [κάλαμος σαλευόμενος] and leveled by the winds, escaped the uprooting; but the oak, standing against it all, was brought down by the roots.' The language and imagery superficially seem to parallel the dominical tradition. However, in Aesop's fable it is the shaken reed that is prudent, not the unbending, stubborn oak. One might also see Aesop's Fable of the Trees and the Reed (Fable 239). On the relevance of fables for study of Jesus' parables, see M.A. Beavis, 'Parable and Fable', *CBQ* 52 (1990), pp. 473-98.

20. Harrington draws our attention to G. Theissen, 'Das "schwankende Rohr" in

to a 'reed shaken by the wind' is found in *3 Macc.* 2.22, a passage that describes how God prevented the impious Ptolemy from entering the Jewish sanctuary and offering sacrifice. This passage reads: 'He shook him on this side and that as a reed is shaken by the wind [ὡς κάλαμον ὑπο ἀνέμου], so that he lay helpless on the ground and, besides being paralyzed in his limbs, was unable even to speak, since he was smitten by a righteous judgment' (*3 Macc.* 2.22). Jesus' use of the epithet 'reed shaken by the wind' might have been a deliberate allusion to this story, implying that Herod, who has opposed God's messenger, compares to Ptolemy, who also had opposed God. (One should recall the New Testament's implied comparison between Herod Agrippa, grandson of Herod the Great, and Antiochus IV, both of whom were believed to have been struck down by God and to have died similar, painful deaths [Acts 12.20-24; 2 Macc. 9.5-9].) The judgmental sense of being a shaken reed is present also in 1 Kgs 14.15, where the prophet tells the king, 'The LORD will smite Israel, as a reed is shaken in the water, and root up Israel out of this good land which he gave to their fathers, and scatter them beyond the Euphrates, because they have made their Asherim, provoking the LORD to anger' (no parallel in the LXX). Although here the reed is shaken 'in the water', not shaken 'by the wind', the idea is essentially the same.[21]

The other description, 'someone dressed in soft robes', also alludes to Herod.[22] Thus, the two sets of rhetorical questions are synonymous, not antithetical. Did the people go out into the wilderness to see Herod, the

---

Mt. 11, 7 und die Gründungsmünzen von Tiberias', *ZDPV* 101 (1985), pp. 43-55. Theissen argues that the 'shaking reed' alludes to Herod. The shaken reed does not refer to weakness or fickleness, as is rightly stated by J. Nolland, *Luke 1–9.20* (WBC, 35A; Dallas: Word Books, 1989), p. 336.

21. In *b. Ta'an.* 20a the Rabbis appeal to 1 Kgs 14.15, but as in Aesop find in the shaken reed hope that, although Israel will bend, the nation will not be broken.

22. Elsewhere Jesus refers to Herod. In Mk 8.15 Jesus warns his disciples to 'beware of the leaven of the Pharisees and the leaven of Herod'. In Lk. 13.31-33 we have an interesting exchange between Jesus and some Pharisees: 'Just at that time some Pharisees came up, saying to Him, "Go away and depart from here, for Herod wants to kill You." And He said to them, "Go and tell that fox, 'Behold, I cast out demons and perform cures today and tomorrow, and the third day I reach My goal'. Nevertheless I must journey on today and tomorrow and the next day; for it cannot be that a prophet should perish outside of Jerusalem".' Whatever the precise meaning of 'that fox', it conveys no compliment. Finally, the Parable of the Minas (Lk. 19.11-27) and the Parable of the Rich Man and the Poor Man (Lk. 16.19-31) may also allude to the Herods; they will be discussed below.

reed shaken by the wind and the one dressed in soft robes, or did they go out into the wilderness to see John, the one who dared to criticize Herod? The anticipated reply to these rhetorical questions is, 'No, we have not gone out into the wilderness to see Herod'. Jesus anticipates his audience's reply with yet another rhetorical question: 'What then did you go out to see? A prophet? Yes, I tell you, and more than a prophet…' John is a prophet to be sure, for he has criticized the ethnarch in the style of the classic prophet. But John is 'more than a prophet' because he heralds the eschatological hour, performing the preparatory work described in Mal. 3.1 ('Behold, I send my messenger to prepare the way before me…').

The purpose of Jesus' words here was not so much to defend John (and for Jesus this was important, for John's reputation as a genuine prophet and his endorsement of Jesus were very important to Jesus) as it was to criticize his audience. In effect, he has asked the crowd: what did you expect to find in the wilderness, a supporter of Herod, or a critic of Herod? What do you expect? What will satisfy you? The point of these questions is to make the crowd take John's (and Jesus') eschatological message more seriously. The parable that follows elaborates on this point.

The Parable of the Children in the Marketplace (Mt. 11.16-19 = Lk. 7.31-35) continues the train of thought of the preceding material. Its close association with the exchange with John and with the rhetorical questions put to the audience is attested in Q. Even if the parable was uttered on a different occasion, it does appear to be thematically related, in that this tradition is concerned with John and how the people of Israel have responded to his message. The parable reads:

> But to what will I compare this generation? It is like children sitting in the marketplaces and calling to one another, 'We played the flute for you, and you did not dance; we wailed, and you did not mourn.' For John came neither eating nor drinking, and they say, 'He has a demon'; the Son of Man came eating and drinking, and they say, 'Look, a glutton and a drunkard, a friend of tax collectors and sinners!' Yet wisdom is vindicated by her deeds.

Jesus' impatience with the crowds is here more pronounced than in the previous material. The crowds have gone out into the wilderness to hear John and to be baptized by him. But they seem susceptible to critics of John and Jesus. Evidently they have been put off by John's asceticism, on the one hand, and Jesus' openness to association with all types of people, on the other. In behaving this way, they are like children who refuse to participate, no matter what the tune. In essence Jesus is asking them what will it take to get a response from them? The final statement, 'Yet wisdom is vindicated by her deeds', adds rhetorical flourish to the line of argument. Whether or not the people respond, God's wisdom (or possibly God himself) will be vindicated by what he accomplishes through John and Jesus. (Luke makes this point clearer by editing the saying to read, 'by her children'.)

The Parable of the Generous Employer (Mt. 20.1-16) clarifies Jesus' understanding of God's grace as seen in his liberal rewarding of those who heed the summons to submit to his authority. Although the Matthean evangelist edits and contextualizes the parable so that it illustrates Jesus' teaching that 'the last will be first, and the first will be last' (v. 16; cf. Mt. 19.30 = Mk 10.31),[23] the principal point of the parable is that God responds with as much generosity to those who enter the kingdom lately as he does to those who enter it much earlier. The point is thus similar to the point made in the Parable of the Prodigal Son (Lk. 15.11-32), although in that case the parable is directed against Jesus' critics. The Parable of the Generous Employer reads:

> For the kingdom of heaven is like a landowner who went out early in the morning to hire laborers for his vineyard. After agreeing with the laborers for the usual daily wage, he sent them into his vineyard. When he went out about nine o'clock, he saw others standing idle in the marketplace; and he said to them, 'You also go into the vineyard, and I will pay you whatever is right.' So they went. When he went out again about noon and about three o'clock, he did the same. And about five o'clock he went out and found others standing around; and he said to them, 'Why are you standing here idle all day?' They said to him, 'Because no one has hired us.' He said to them, 'You also go into the vineyard.' When evening came, the owner of the vineyard said to his manager, 'Call the laborers and give them their pay, beginning with the last and then going to the first'. When those hired about five o'clock came, each of them received the usual daily wage. Now when the first came, they thought they would receive more; but each of them also received the usual daily wage. And when they received it, they grumbled against the landowner, saying, 'These last worked only one hour, and you have made them equal to us who have borne the burden of the day and the scorching heat.' But he replied to one of them, 'Friend, I am doing you no wrong; did you not agree with me for the usual daily wage? Take what belongs to you and go; I choose to give to this last the same as I give to

23. See E. Linnemann, *Parables of Jesus: Introduction and Exposition* (SPCK Large Paperbacks, 25; London SPCK, 1966), pp. 85-86; Harrington, *Matthew*, p. 283.

you. Am I not allowed to do what I choose with what belongs to me? Or are you envious because I am generous?' So the last will be first, and the first will be last.

It is difficult to determine the original setting and recipients of this parable. It is possible that the parable attempted to justify to the Pharisees Jesus' understanding of the kingdom, much as the Parable of the Prodigal Son seems to have. But whereas the latter parable seems clearly intended to answer Pharisaic (or at least Torah-observant) criticism (as is indicated by the role played by the older son who has faithfully served his father), the Parable of the Generous Employer seems to have had a more universal application. I suspect that the first ears to hear it were sympathetic to Jesus' message; many hearers probably thought of themselves as among Jesus' followers.[24]

Two other parables warn the crowds that God's patience is running out and that the opportunity to enter the kingdom may not be available for much longer. The Parable of the Tree (Lk. 13.6-9; cf. Mk 11.12-14) illustrates this point clearly:

> Then he told this parable: 'A man had a tree planted in his vineyard; and he came looking for fruit on it and found none. So he said to the gardener, "See here! For three years I have come looking for fruit on this tree, and still I find none. Cut it down! Why should it be wasting the soil?" He replied, "Sir, let it alone for one more year, until I dig around it and put manure on it. If it bears fruit next year, well and good; but if not, you can cut it down".'

The Narrow Door saying that prefaces the Parable of the Closed Door (Lk. 13.24-30) does not so much impress urgency on Jesus' hearers as it warns people that there is only one entry into the kingdom of God. This saying, drawn from Q (cf. Mt. 7.13-14), is a common topos in Scripture (Prov. 28.6, 18; Wis. 5.6-7; *4 Ezra* 7.3-15), sectarian writings (1QS 3.18–4.26; *Didache* 1–6; *Barnabas* 18–20), and later rabbinic writings (*Sifre Deut.* §53 [on Deut. 11.26]; *Ab.* 2.12-23). The evangelist has used this saying to introduce the parable proper (note the catchword 'door' in v. 25), which, however, does express urgency. When the door is shut, there will no longer be opportunity to gain entry into the kingdom. The parable reads:

24. Linnemann (*Parables of Jesus*, p. 86) regards the parable as authentic, but thinks that it, like the Parable of the Prodigal Son, was told to counter Pharisaic and scribal criticism of Jesus' table-fellowship with tax collectors and sinners.

> Strive to enter through the narrow door; for many, I tell you, will try to
> enter and will not be able. When once the owner of the house has got up
> and shut the door, and you begin to stand outside and to knock at the door,
> saying, 'Lord, open to us', then in reply he will say to you, 'I do not know
> where you come from.' Then you will begin to say, 'We ate and drank with
> you, and you taught in our streets.' But he will say, 'I do not know where
> you come from; go away from me, all you evildoers!' There will be
> weeping and gnashing of teeth when you see Abraham and Isaac and Jacob
> and all the prophets in the kingdom of God, and you yourselves thrown out.
> Then people will come from east and west, from north and south, and will
> eat in the kingdom of God. Indeed, some are last who will be first, and
> some are first who will be last.

The history of this parable is complex; it evinces Christian editing. But
some of this material probably derives from Jesus (e.g. 'Strive to enter
through the narrow door; for many, I tell you, will try to enter and will not
be able'). The parable probably originally had to do with Jesus' summons
to enter the kingdom, but in its later usage has come to be understood as a
summons to believe in Jesus. In the pre-Easter setting the parable envisions a person who has arrived late and can no longer enter the house. His
cries are to no avail; his prior acquaintance with the owner of the house
cannot open the door. Jesus probably meant the parable to teach that
acquaintance with him (and/or with John) will not guarantee admission
into the kingdom at some later date. If one fails to enter now, there may
not be another opportunity.

Summary
Jesus' parables that warn or criticize the crowds and/or his following teach
a variety of loosely related lessons. The people of Jesus' generation are
fickle and feckless, unable to perceive the signs of their times. They are
unresponsive to any and all overtures, unable to appreciate God's grace,
but foolishly think it is owed them. Jesus' contemporaries, moreover, fail
to recognize God's patience, which is intended to give them time to
repent. Instead, people presume on God and assume that acquaintance
with Jesus or familiarity with the Jewish religion will of itself guarantee
them a place in the kingdom.

3. *Directed to the Scribes and Pharisees*

The Parable of the Great Banquet (Lk. 14.16-24; cf. Mt. 22.1-10) offers a
provocative criticism of election assumptions, a criticism to which most
scribes and Pharisees would have taken exception:

Someone gave a great dinner and invited many. At the time for the dinner he sent his slave to say to those who had been invited, 'Come; for everything is ready now.' But they all alike began to make excuses. The first said to him, 'I have bought a piece of land, and I must go out and see it; please accept my regrets.' Another said, 'I have bought five yoke of oxen, and I am going to try them out; please accept my regrets.' Another said, 'I have just been married, and therefore I cannot come.' So the slave returned and reported this to his master. Then the owner of the house became angry and said to his slave, 'Go out at once into the streets and lanes of the town and bring in the poor, the crippled, the blind, and the lame.' And the slave said, 'Sir, what you ordered has been done, and there is still room.' Then the master said to the slave, 'Go out into the roads and lanes, and compel people to come in, so that my house may be filled. For I tell you, none of those who were invited will taste my dinner.'

The 'great dinner' (δεῖπνον μέγα) suits the present context (cf. v. 1, φαγεῖν ἄρτον; v. 12, ἄριστον ἢ δεῖπνον) and presupposes the eschatological tradition of a great banquet that will take place 'in the kingdom of God' (v. 15). Hope of the eschatological banquet is rooted in Isa. 25.6: 'On this mountain the LORD of hosts will make for all peoples a feast of fat things, a feast of wine on the lees, of fat things full of marrow, of wine on the lees well refined'. This passage and related traditions are what lie behind Qumran's expectations of a messianic banquet (1QSa 2.11-22) and the Enochic banquet attended by the Son of Man: 'They shall rejoice… because the wrath of the Lord of the Spirits shall rest upon them and his sword (shall obtain) from them a memorial feast…they shall eat and rest and rise with that Son of Man forever and ever' (*1 En.* 62.12, 14).

Jesus' recommendation that his companions invite to feasts and dinner parties the poor and the sick (Lk. 14.12-14) occasions the beatitude uttered by an enthusiastic guest: 'Blessed is he who shall eat bread in the kingdom of God!' (v. 15). This makarism undoubtedly reflects conventional wisdom in pious Jewish circles. Unspoken, but probably assumed, is that material blessings are signs of God's blessing. But contrary to this wisdom, Jesus' parable teaches that the material blessings of those initially invited prove not to be sure indicators of divine election. They may have the resources to purchase land, acquire five yoke of oxen, and take a one-year marriage exemption from civic responsibilities[25]—all of which could be taken as signs of divine blessings, in keeping with covenant blessings—

25. These excuses appear to be loosely based on the legislation concerning exemption from holy war (cf. Deut. 20.5-7).

but as it turns out, none of them will taste the dinner. Equally contrary to conventional wisdom, the very ones who appear unblessed, perhaps even cursed—that is, the poor and sick—are ushered into the banquet hall. It is they who will enjoy the kingdom feast, not their wealthier and healthier neighbors.[26] At issue, once again, is the failure to heed the call of the kingdom.

The Matthean version seems to reflect the destruction of Jerusalem and interprets it as divine judgment upon the religious leaders. An element of Christology is also present, as seen in the introduction of the 'son' of the 'king who gave a marriage feast for his son'. The addendum (Mt. 22.11-14) is illustrative of the Matthean interest in two types of people: those who will be saved and those who will be condemned.

In the Parable of the Two Debtors (Lk. 7.41-43) a critical Pharisee is forced grudgingly to concede Jesus' point about forgiveness and gratitude:

> 'A certain creditor had two debtors; one owed five hundred denarii, and the other fifty. When they could not pay, he canceled the debts for both of them. Now which of them will love him more?' Simon answered, 'I suppose the one for whom he canceled the greater debt'. And Jesus said to him, 'You have judged rightly.'

There is nothing in this parable, or in its larger context (Lk. 7.36-50), that suggests that Simon the Pharisee is non-elect or reprobate. His only error is his failure to appreciate the grace that has overtaken the woman and her subsequent, commensurate gratitude. Implicit in Jesus' pronouncement is a recommendation that Simon take stock of himself (i.e. 'You have judged rightly, so do some more of it'). Indeed, the implication is that Simon has little sin for which forgiveness is required.[27] The intention of the parable, as well as the commentary that accompanies it,[28] is in every sense redemptive, even if it evinces a degree of criticism (i.e. Simon only has *little* love).

What has often not been properly recognized is the degree to which many of Jesus' sayings and parables are conciliatory and constructive in

---

26. For a study of the election hermeneutics at work in this parable, see J.A. Sanders, 'The Ethic of Election in Luke's Great Banquet Parable', in C.A. Evans and J.A. Sanders, *Luke and Scripture: The Function of Sacred Tradition in Luke–Acts* (Minneapolis: Fortress Press, 1993), pp. 106-20.

27. And here we must guard against viewing Simon against a backdrop of Pauline hamartiology (as in Rom. 1–3).

28. It is not clear that vv. 48-50 were part of the original exchange.

their criticisms of the scribes and Pharisees. The Parable of the Good Samaritan (Lk. 10.30-37) attempts to provide a definition of neighbor. This definition is important, given the stated requirement to 'love (one's) neighbor as one's self', if one is to fulfill the Law and so gain eternal life (Lk. 10.25-30). The parable reads:

> But wanting to justify himself, he asked Jesus, 'And who is my neighbor?' Jesus replied, 'A man was going down from Jerusalem to Jericho, and fell into the hands of robbers, who stripped him, beat him, and went away, leaving him half dead. Now by chance a priest was going down that road; and when he saw him, he passed by on the other side. So likewise a Levite, when he came to the place and saw him, passed by on the other side. But a Samaritan while traveling came near him; and when he saw him, he was moved with pity. He went to him and bandaged his wounds, having poured oil and wine on them. Then he put him on his own animal, brought him to an inn, and took care of him. The next day he took out two denarii, gave them to the innkeeper, and said, "Take care of him; and when I come back, I will repay you whatever more you spend." Which of these three, do you think, was a neighbor to the man who fell into the hands of the robbers?' He said, 'The one who showed him mercy'. Jesus said to him, 'Go and do likewise.'

The failure of the priest and Levite to offer aid to the stricken man may imply a measure of criticism, but that is hardly the point of the parable. The compassion and mercy of the Samaritan, who has fulfilled the Law's requirements, are the point. There is no hint that the legal expert is to be identified with the priest and Levite. Jesus does not directly answer the legist's question, 'Who is my neighbor?' He invites him, at the conclusion of the parable, to anwer it himself: 'Which of these three, do you think, was a neighbor...?' What is of interest in this parable, like the one above, is the juridical element, in which the hearer is invited to pass judgment on the actions, or lack of actions, of the persons in the parable, and in so doing to pass judgment upon himself. This judgment, however, has a constructive, redemptive goal.

Perhaps the most conciliatory of the parables directed to the scribes and Pharisees is the Parable of the Prodigal Son (Lk. 15.11-32). The parable falls into two parts, with the first part treating the recovery of the younger son (vv. 11-24), and the second part urging the older son to be reconciled to his brother (vv. 25-32). The parable reads:

> Then Jesus said, 'There was a man who had two sons. The younger of them said to his father, "Father, give me the share of the property that will belong to me". So he divided his property between them. A few days later the

younger son gathered all he had and traveled to a distant country, and there
he squandered his property in dissolute living. When he had spent everything, a severe famine took place throughout that country, and he began to
be in need. So he went and hired himself out to one of the citizens of that
country, who sent him to his fields to feed the pigs. He would gladly have
filled himself with the pods that the pigs were eating; and no one gave him
anything. But when he came to himself he said, "How many of my father's
hired hands have bread enough and to spare, but here I am dying of hunger!
I will get up and go to my father, and I will say to him, 'Father, I have
sinned against heaven and before you; I am no longer worthy to be called
your son; treat me like one of your hired hands'." So he set off and went to
his father. But while he was still far off, his father saw him and was filled
with compassion; he ran and put his arms around him and kissed him. Then
the son said to him, "Father, I have sinned against heaven and before you; I
am no longer worthy to be called your son." But the father said to his
slaves, "Quickly, bring out a robe—the best one—and put it on him; put a
ring on his finger and sandals on his feet. And get the fatted calf and kill it,
and let us eat and celebrate; for this son of mine was dead and is alive
again; he was lost and is found!" And they began to celebrate. Now his
elder son was in the field; and when he came and approached the house, he
heard music and dancing. He called one of the slaves and asked what was
going on. He replied, "Your brother has come, and your father has killed
the fatted calf, because he has got him back safe and sound." Then he
became angry and refused to go in. His father came out and began to plead
with him. But he answered his father, "Listen! For all these years I have
been working like a slave for you, and I have never disobeyed your
command; yet you have never given me even a young goat so that I might
celebrate with my friends. But when this son of yours came back, who has
devoured your property with prostitutes, you killed the fatted calf for him!"
Then the father said to him, "Son, you are always with me, and all that is
mine is yours. But we had to celebrate and rejoice, because this brother of
yours was dead and has come to life; he was lost and has been found".'

Far from teaching that the Gentile church has displaced Israel,[29] the
Parable of the Prodigal Son is remarkably conciliatory toward the Phari-

29. L. Schottroff ('Das Gleichnis vom verlorenen Sohn', *ZTK* 68 [1971], pp. 27-52)
has argued that the parable as a whole is a Lukan creation, while E. Schweizer ('Zur
Frage der Lukasquellen: Analyse von Lukas 15,11-32', *TZ* 4 [1948], pp. 469-71) and
J.T. Sanders ('Tradition and Redaction in Luke xv.11-32', *NTS* 15 [1969], pp. 433-38)
have argued that the second half of the parable (vv. 25-32) is Lukan. J. Jeremias ('Zum
Gleichnis vom verlorenen Sohn: Lukas 15,11-32', *TZ* 5 [1949], pp. 228-31), C.E. Carlston ('Reminiscence and Redaction in Luke 15.11-32', *JBL* 94 [1975], pp. 368-90),
and B.B. Scott ('The Prodigal Son: A Stucturalist Interpretation', in G.W. MacRae
[ed.], *Society of Biblical Literature 1975 Seminar Papers* [2 vols.; SBLSP, 14;

sees,[30] whose criticism of Jesus for associating with 'sinners' occasioned the telling of the parable. That the elder son acts out the views of the scribes and Pharisees seems evident and that his attitude toward the restoration of his brother deserves criticism is clear, but the concluding affirmation of the father tells against any notion that the older son has lost his place in the family. He has 'slaved' away (δουλεύω) for his father and has 'never disobeyed' his commands. There is no criticism here.[31] The father assures him that he is 'always with' him and that 'all' that is his is still his son's. Jesus has recognized the Torah-obedience of the Pharisees and approves of it. His only criticism is that they are unwilling to rejoice over the repentance of their less responsible, non-Torah-obedient brothers and sisters.

Summary
Implicit in most of the parables thus far reviewed is the possibility, if not anticipation, that many scribes and Pharisees will eventually come to repentance and enter the kingdom that Jesus proclaims. Some of these parables are juridical in function, inviting the hearer to assess critically his or her own behavior and motives. All of these parables are admonitory and restorative in purpose. Most of those that are considered next are much more threatening and judgmental; hopes of restoration have grown dim.

4. *Directed to the Ruling Priests and Elders of the People*

The Parable of the Two Sons (Mt. 21.28-32) is unique to Matthew and has been deliberately inserted between the Question of Authority (Mt. 21.23-27 = Mk 11.27-33 = Lk. 20.1-8) and the Parable of the Wicked Vineyard Tenants (Mt. 21.33-46 = Mk 12.1-12 = Lk. 20.9-19).[32] In its present

Missoula, MT: Scholars Press, 1975], II, pp. 185-205; *idem, Hear Then the Parable*, pp. 102-105) have argued for the authenticity and unity of the parable, though recognizing that the Lukan evangelist has edited and contextualized the parable. The latter position is accepted here.

30. Linnemann, *Parables of Jesus*, p. 80.

31. L.T. Johnson (*The Gospel of Luke* [Sacra Pagina, 3; Collegeville, MN: Liturgical Press, 1991], pp. 241-42) is correct to sense a note of sadness here. The elder son has worked as a slave for his heavenly father and has never perceived any reward for his faithfulness. But even so, the standing of the elder son is not in any way diminished. He remains the faithful, elder son, even if he is in need of instruction.

32. The exchange between Jesus and the ruling priests in the Question of Authority itself reveals Jesus' skill in argumentation, for he has forced an awkward set of alter-

context it is directed against the ruling priests and elders of the people (cf. Mt. 21.23). The addition of the 'Pharisees' in v. 45 is clearly Matthean redaction, in keeping with his polemic against this religious party. However, it is probable that the Parable of the Two Sons was originally directed to the ruling priests and elders, for the discussion of John coheres with the debate that develops in the Question of Authority.[33]

> 'What do you think? A man had two sons; he went to the first and said, "Son, go and work in the vineyard today." He answered, "I will not"; but later he changed his mind and went. The father went to the second and said the same; and he answered, "I go, sir"; but he did not go. Which of the two did the will of his father?' They said, 'The first.' Jesus said to them, 'Truly I tell you, the tax collectors and the prostitutes are going into the kingdom of God ahead of you. For John came to you in the way of righteousness and you did not believe him, but the tax collectors and the prostitutes believed him; and even after you saw it, you did not change your minds and believe him.'

The order of the sons—the first ultimately obeys, the second does not— supports the authenticity of the parable, for had the parable been composed by the early Church we should have expected the first son to agree to his father's commands and then fail to carry them out, while the second would initially refuse but later comply.[34] This then would correspond to the floating topos 'the first will be last and the last will be first' (Mk 10.31 = Mt. 19.30; cf. *Gos. Thom.* §4), though this topos also appears in the reverse form (Mt. 20.16; Lk. 13.30).

natives upon his antagonists. Countering their question with a question of his own by itself is a skilful move, throwing the burden of the argument back onto his opponents. But the nature of Jesus' question proved to be impossible for the ruling priests and elders to answer. Their inability to answer and therefore Jesus' rhetorical right to refuse to answer the question that had been put to him constitute for him a victory in this exchange, which in a culture very cognizant of honor and shame would only further amplify the triumph.

33. M.-J. Lagrange, *Evangile selon Saint Matthieu* (Paris: J. Gabalda, 1948), pp. 410-11.

34. This in fact is probably what lies behind the scribal activity seen in some MSS, in which the order of the sons has been reversed; cf. Lagrange, *Matthieu*, pp. 409-10; Harrington, *Matthew*, p. 299. For a full discussion of the MS tradition, the options, and a recommendation that the text read as presented above, see B.M. Metzger, *A Textual Commentary on the Greek New Testament* (New York: United Bible Societies, 1971), pp. 55-56.

What is interesting about the Parable of the Two Sons is that although it ends on a critical note, 'Truly I tell you, the tax collectors and the prostitutes are going into the kingdom of God ahead of you' (v. 31), the possibility remains that the ruling priests and elders will follow these repentant sinners into the kingdom. However, the requirement of repentance is still in force: 'For John came to you in the way of righteousness and you did not believe him, but the tax collectors and the prostitutes believed him; and even after you saw it, you did not change your minds and believe him' (v. 33). If they 'change' their minds, there is still hope, even if expectation of repentance is faint.

The Parable of the Wicked Vineyard Tenants (Mk 12.1-11 = Mt. 21.33-43 = Lk. 20.9-18) is a masterpiece of hermeneutical strategy. The parable is widely accepted as authentic, but too often the context in which it is found is treated as late and secondary.[35] The presupposition of Aramaic interpretive tradition, in both the allusion to Isa. 5.1-7 and in the formal citation of Ps. 118.22-23, makes alleged late Christian adaptation and allegorization of the parable unnecessary and doubtful.[36] The coherence of this Aramaic tradition with the Gospels' context of polemic leveled against the Temple establishment places a heavy burden of proof on those who claim that the original context and point of the parable were significantly different.[37] The parable reads:

35. For attempts to understand this parable in contexts other than that provided by the Synoptic Gospels, see J.D. Crossan, 'The Parable of the Wicked Husbandmen', *JBL* 90 (1971), pp. 451-65; *idem, In Parables: The Challenge of the Historical Jesus* (New York: Harper & Row, 1973), pp. 86-96; *idem, The Historical Jesus*, pp. 351-52; Scott, *Hear Then the Parable*, pp. 237-53.

36. *Pace* W.G. Kümmel, 'Das Gleichnis von den bösen Weingärtnern (Mk 12,1-12)', in O. Cullmann and P.H. Menaud (eds.), *Aux Sources de la Tradition Chrétienne: Mélanges offerts à Maurice Goguel* (Bibliothèque Théologique; Paris: Delachaux & Niestlé, 1950), pp. 120-31; repr. in W.G. Kümmel, *Heilsgeschehen und Geschichte: Gesammelte Aufsätze 1933–1964* (MTS, 3; ed. E. Grässer, O. Merk, A. Fritz; Marburg: Elwert, 1965), pp. 207-17; C.E. Carlston, *The Parables of the Triple Tradition* (Philadelphia: Fortress Press, 1975), pp. 178-90.

37. Evans, *Jesus and his Contemporaries*, pp. 381-407; G.J. Brooke, '4Q500 1 and the Use of Scripture in the Parable of the Vineyard', *DSD* 2 (1995), pp. 268-94. The inner consistency of this parable, including the concluding quotation of Ps. 118.22-23, is one reason for rejecting claims that the version preserved in *Thomas* is older and perhaps closer to the original form. Another reason for rejecting this fashionable claim is that there is a sufficient number of Lukanisms in much of the dominical tradition of *Thomas*, including the Parable of the Vineyard Tenants. I argue for this view in J.M. Charlesworth and C.A. Evans, 'Jesus in the Agrapha and Apocryphal Gospels', in

A man planted a vineyard, put a fence around it, dug a pit for the wine press, and built a watchtower; then he leased it to tenants and went to another country. When the season came, he sent a slave to the tenants to collect from them his share of the produce of the vineyard. But they seized him, and beat him, and sent him away empty-handed. And again he sent another slave to them; this one they beat over the head and insulted. Then he sent another, and that one they killed. And so it was with many others; some they beat, and others they killed. He had still one other, a beloved son. Finally he sent him to them, saying, 'They will respect my son.' But those tenants said to one another, 'This is the heir; come, let us kill him, and the inheritance will be ours.' So they seized him, killed him, and threw him out of the vineyard. What then will the owner of the vineyard do? He will come and destroy the tenants and give the vineyard to others. Have you not read this scripture: 'The stone that the builders rejected has become the corner-stone; this was the Lord's doing, and it is amazing in our eyes?'

Jesus' implicit threat is unmistakable and, in light of the parable's context, it provides an answer to the preceding question of authority: 'By what authority are you doing these things?' (Mk 11.27a); in effect, Jesus answers: 'By the authority of the Master of the Vineyard—God'. This parable entertains no hope for Jesus' opponents; their fate is sealed. They have rejected those sent to them, and now they are contemplating murder.[38]

Another curious saying might be considered briefly. In the Lesson of the Fig Tree (Mk 11.20-25) Jesus illustrates the power of faith by saying, 'Whoever says to this mountain, "Be taken up and cast into the sea", and does not doubt in his heart, but believes that what he says will come to pass, it will be done for him' (v. 23). Although in its present form this utterance is not a parable, in its fuller form (if there was a fuller form), it may have been. It is possible that this saying (or parable) originally was a word of judgment directed against the Temple Mount, as has been suggested.[39] If so, then its judgmental perspective would have been

Chilton and Evans (eds.), *Studying the Historical Jesus*, pp. 479-533 (496-503).

38. The murder of the beloved son adds an important rhetorical flourish to the parable, in the form of something approaching a dare. Israel's leaders have historically persecuted the prophets and those sent to her by God (cf. Mt. 23.37 = Lk. 13.34; cf. Lk. 13.33). Now they are contemplating the murder of God's beloved eschatological agent—a high crime indeed! The parable envisions this grievous act as a fait accompli, and thus as unavoidable.

39. W.R. Telford, *The Barren Temple and the Withered Tree: A Redaction-Critical Analysis of the Cursing of the Fig-Tree Episode in Mark's Gospel and its Relation to the Cleansing of the Temple* (JSNTSup, 1; Sheffield: JSOT Press, 1980), pp. 109-17.

essentially the same as that seen in the Parable of the Vineyard Tenants: the ruling priests, who have betrayed their trust, will be dispossessed.

Summary

As in his criticism directed against the scribes and Pharisees, Jesus also ridicules the ruling priests and Sadducees with rhetorical questions, such as: 'Have you not read this scripture?' (Mk 12.10); and 'Is not this the reason you are wrong, that you know neither the scriptures nor the power of God?' (Mk 12.24). Jesus also states flatly: 'You are quite wrong' (v. 27). Jesus has unleased his harshest rhetoric for the ruling priests who, in his opinion, are the most culpable and responsible for Israel's plight. There is an element of political criticism in Jesus' parables as well, as the final two examples should make clear.

5. *Against the Herodian Dynasty: 'Tell that Fox'*

There are two parables which in their original setting may have been directed against the Herodian dynasty. This is suggested because the villains in both parables parallel closely certain details of the Herodian rulers that would have been public knowledge.

The Parable of the Minas/Talents (Lk. 19.12-27; cf. Mt. 25.14-30) reads:

> So he said, 'A nobleman went to a distant country to get royal power for himself and then return. He summoned ten of his slaves, and gave them ten minas, and said to them, "Do business with these until I come back." But the citizens of his country hated him and sent a delegation after him, saying, "We do not want this man to rule over us." When he returned, having received royal power, he ordered these slaves, to whom he had given the money, to be summoned so that he might find out what they had gained by trading. The first came forward and said, "Lord, your mina has made ten more minas." He said to him, "Well done, good slave! Because you have been trustworthy in a very small thing, take charge of ten cities." Then the second came, saying, "Lord, your mina has made five minas." He said to him, "And you, rule over five cities." Then the other came, saying, "Lord, here is your mina. I wrapped it up in a piece of cloth, for I was afraid of you, because you are a harsh man; you take what you did not deposit, and reap what you did not sow." He said to him, "I will judge you by your own words, you wicked slave! You knew, did you, that I was a harsh man,

Others, such as R.H. Gundry (*Mark: A Commentary on his Apology for the Cross* [Grand Rapids: Eerdmans, 1993], p. 649), think 'this mountain' refers to the Mount of Olives.

taking what I did not deposit and reaping what I did not sow? Why then did you not put my money into the bank? Then when I returned, I could have collected it with interest".' He said to the bystanders, 'Take the mina from him and give it to the one who has ten minas'. (And they said to him, 'Lord, he has ten minas!') 'I tell you, to all those who have, more will be given; but from those who have nothing, even what they have will be taken away. But as for these enemies of mine who did not want me to be king over them—bring them here and slaughter them in my presence'.

The parable is not anti-Semitic;[40] far from it. Richard Rohrbaugh has made a compelling case that when audience criticism is taken into account and the peasant following of Jesus is remembered, it is probable that this parable originally did not intend to portray the ruthless noble man as a positive example, as someone who perhaps exemplified Jesus. As Rohrbaugh and Bruce Malina have said,

> if the parable is taken as a description of the way the kingdom of God functions, it is bitter news indeed for peasant hearers. It would confirm all of their worst fears: that God (and Jesus) operates in exactly the same demanding, exploitive, grasping manner as the overlords who daily forced them to produce more and more for elite coffers—rewarding those who did so (thereby exploiting their neighbors) and taking away the livelihood of those who did not.[41]

When the parallels between this parable and the events surrounding Archelaus's bid for his father's kingdom are taken into account,[42] it

40. As has been wrongly argued by J.T. Sanders, 'The Parable of the Pounds and Lucan Anti-Semitism', *TS* 42 (1981), pp. 660-68. The Lukan evangelist engages in polemic, to be sure, but it goes too far to describe it as anti-Semitism. See C.A. Evans, 'Is Luke's View of the Jewish Rejection of Jesus Anti-Semitic?', in D.D. Sylva (ed.), *Reimaging the Death of the Lukan Jesus* (BBB, 73; Frankfurt am Main: Anton Hain, 1990), pp. 29-56, 174-83.

41. B.J. Malina and R.L. Rohrbaugh, *Social-Science Commentary on the Synoptic Gospels* (Minneapolis: Fortress Press, 1992), p. 389.

42. The nobleman went to a far country (v. 12), just as Archelaus went to Rome (*Ant.* 17.9.3 §219); the nobleman hoped to receive a kingdom (βασιλεία) and to return (v. 12), just as Archelaus hoped (*Ant.* 17.9.3 §220: βασιλεία); the nobleman left household instructions to his servants (v. 13), just as Archelaus did (*War* 2.2.1 §14, §19; *Ant.* 17.9.3 §§219, 223); the nobleman's citizens hated (μισεῖν) him (v. 14), just as Archelaus's subjects hated him (*War* 2.2.3 §22; *Ant.* 17.9.4 §227: μῖσος); an embassy (πρεσβεία) is sent after the nobleman (v. 14), as one was sent after Archelaus (*Ant.* 17.11.1 §300: πρεσβεία); the citizens petitioned the foreign country against the nobleman's rule (v. 14), just as the envoys petitioned against Archelaus (*Ant.* 17.11.1 §302); the nobleman slaughtered (κατασφάζειν) his citizens who opposed him (v. 27), just as

becomes all the more improbable that the nobleman was intended to be a positive figure.

The parallels with Archelaus may in fact provide us with an important clue as to the parable's original intention. Jesus may have originally told his parable to illustrate how *not* to be a master and how *not* to be servants. The Archelaus-like figure, who is hated and merciless, may not have been intended to model Jesus, but to *contrast* with Jesus. In other words, in their original context, again remembering the world-view and assumptions of an agrarian peasant society, this parable may very well have underscored grim realities of the present world, *in contrast to the kingdom whose approach Jesus has announced.* This contrast may have offered an implicit criticism of the Herodian dynasty, especially in reference to Archelaus, who tried to gain his father's kingdom and who after a decade of ruthless and incompetent rule was deposed, and Herod Antipas ('that fox!'), who murdered John the Baptist and expressed a (malevolent) interest in seeing Jesus.

The principal lesson of the Parable of the Rich Man and the Poor Man (Lk. 16.19-31) is obvious enough, but the incidental details used in describing the rich man may in fact intentionally allude to Herod. The parable reads:

> There was a rich man who was dressed in purple and fine linen and who feasted sumptuously every day. And at his gate lay a poor man named Lazarus, covered with sores, who longed to satisfy his hunger with what fell from the rich man's table; even the dogs would come and lick his sores. The poor man died and was carried away by the angels to be with Abraham. The rich man also died and was buried. In Hades, where he was being tormented, he looked up and saw Abraham far away with Lazarus by his side. He called out, 'Father Abraham, have mercy on me, and send Lazarus to dip the tip of his finger in water and cool my tongue; for I am in agony in these flames.' But Abraham said, 'Child, remember that during your lifetime you received your good things, and Lazarus in like manner evil

Archelaus had done before his journey (*Ant.* 17.9.5 §§237, 239: σφάζειν); the noble-man received the kingdom (v. 15), just as Archelaus was given half of his father's kingdom (*War* 2.6.3. §93; βασιλεία); when the nobleman returned as ruler (v. 15; *Ant.* 17.13.1 §339), he collected his revenues (vv. 15-19), just as Josephus notes that Archelaus was to receive 600 talents as his yearly tribute (*Ant.* 17.11.4 §320); and finally, when the nobleman returned, he settled accounts with those who had opposed him (v. 27), just as Archelaus 'did not forget old feuds' (*War* 2.7.3 §111), but settled with his opponents, such as Joazar the High Priest, for having supported the rebels (*Ant.* 17.13.1 §339).

things; but now he is comforted here, and you are in agony. Besides all this, between you and us a great chasm has been fixed, so that those who might want to pass from here to you cannot do so, and no one can cross from there to us.' He said, 'Then, father, I beg you to send him to my father's house—for I have five brothers—that he may warn them, so that they will not also come into this place of torment.' Abraham replied, 'They have Moses and the prophets; they should listen to them.' He said, 'No, father Abraham; but if someone goes to them from the dead, they will repent.' He said to him, 'If they do not listen to Moses and the prophets, neither will they be convinced even if someone rises from the dead.'

The description of the rich man, who 'was dressed in purple and fine linen and who feasted sumptuously every day', is consistent with royalty (cf. Prov. 31.22),[43] while reference to his 'five brothers' (v. 28) parallels Herod Antipas exactly, for he had five brothers when this parable would have been spoken.[44] If the rich man does indeed allude to Herod Antipas, then we have here a bit of ironical and theological sedition.

Summary
In what may have been parables directed against the Herodian dynasty we find unflattering descriptions. The royal family is described as avaricious, oppressive, cruel, and lacking compassion for the poor. In the end, they face hell in the life to come, for they do not heed 'Moses and the prophets'.

6. *Conclusion*

One of the interesting features of Jesus' rhetoric of criticism is that it is often leveled against the general public and sometimes against his own followers. Given the polemics that emerged in the post-Easter setting, it is probable that many critical sayings and critical parables were recontextualized so as to target the opponents of the Church. This editorial recontextualization should not, however, deter us from unpacking the original thrust of the material, nor should it lead us to conclude that much of the material originated with the Church and not with Jesus.

The employment of parables as a vehicle of criticism would have cast Jesus' proclamation into a more visibly prophetic mode. Here one thinks

43. See J.A. Fitzmyer, *The Gospel according to Luke X–XXIV* (AB, 24A; Garden City, NY: Doubleday, 1985), p. 1130.
44. The observation has been made by A.R.C. Leaney, *A Commentary on the Gospel according to Luke* (HNTC; New York: Harper & Brothers, 1966), pp. 225-26.

especially of the parables of Ezekiel, though parables are attributed to many other Old Testament prophets. That these Old Testament parables often conveyed prophetic criticism against the nation of Israel, as well as against particular individuals (such as rulers) and groups (such as the aristocracy or ruling priesthood), is surely significant for understanding the rhetorical effects Jesus' parables would have had on his contemporaries. This dimension of the problem will have to be explored in another context.[45]

45. A preliminary investigation of this question will be found in C.A. Evans, 'Parables in Early Judaism', in R.N. Longenecker (ed.), *The Challenge of Jesus' Parables* (MNTS, 4; Grand Rapids: Eerdmans, 2000), pp. 51-75. In my opinion, the closest parallels to Jesus' *use* of parables are found in the prophets of the Old Testament, while the closest parallels to the *form* of Jesus' parables are found in the subsequent rabbinic literature. When taken up in the Gospels the parables of Jesus are often edited and recontextualized and sometimes made to address ecclesiastical issues (though this point is frequently exaggerated in modern scholarship). Finally, in the context of the *Gospel of Thomas*, which is content to present them in a non-Jewish context, the parables are given a timeless, gnomic quality.

A Rhetorical Analysis of Mark's Construction of Discipleship

Paul Danove

This paper investigates the inner textual and ideological textual rhetoric of Mark's presentation of Jesus' disciples.[1] A brief methodological introduction considers the nature and significance of narrative frames for analysis, the construct of the implied reader assumed in the investigation, and the rhetorical use of repetition in the narrative. The analysis of the inner texture examines the use of narrative frames in the characterization of the disciples. This discussion first inquires into the nature of the implied reader's pre-existent beliefs about Jesus' disciples and then analyzes the modifications the narration attempts to introduce into these beliefs. This investigation reveals that the author builds on the reader's pre-existing positive esteem for the disciples by encouraging certain positive aspects of their presentation while introducing negative elements into other aspects of their presentation. The discussion then examines the manner in which the narrative rhetoric maintains the creative tension between the positive and negative aspects of the disciples' presentation. The paper concludes with a discussion of the narrative function of the disciples' presentation and considerations of the ideological and sacred textures of the text.

1. The Method of Analysis

The method of inner textual analysis presumes as its rhetorical unit the entire narration (1.1–16.8) and investigates how and to which end the

---

1.   This analysis seeks to enter into dialogue with the discussion of the various textures of texts developed in V.K. Robbins, *The Tapestry of Early Christian Discourse: Rhetoric, Society and Ideology* (London: Routledge, 1996) and *Exploring the Texture of Texts: A Guide to Socio-Rhetorical Interpretation* (Valley Forge, PA: Trinity Press International, 1996). Elements of the analysis receive alternative development in P. Danove, 'The Narrative Rhetoric of Mark's Ambiguous Characterization of the Disciples', *JSNT* 70 (1998), pp. 21-38.

narration develops specialized connotations for particular words and phrases within this rhetorical unit. An example of such specialization appears in the Markan usage of 'seek' (ζητέω) which, in its initial appearance, 'Everyone is seeking you' (1.37), offers no indication that the verb is being used with any distinctive connotation.[2] The remaining occurrences, however, develop narratively specific information about, relationships among, and negative valuations for those who seek: Jesus' mother, brothers, and sisters who seek Jesus are superseded by those doing the will of God (3.32-35); the Pharisees/this generation who seek a sign will be given none (8.11-12); the chief priests and scribes who seek how to destroy Jesus (11.18); the chief priests, scribes, and elders who seek to arrest Jesus (12.12; cf. 11.27); the chief priests and scribes who seek to arrest and kill Jesus (14.1); Judas who seeks how he may hand over Jesus (14.11); and the chief priests and the entire Sanhedrin who seek testimony against Jesus to kill him (14.55). The final occurrence in the young man's statement, 'You seek Jesus the Nazarene, the crucified' (16.6), places the women into a narratively developed class of characters opposed to Jesus and contributes to their concluding negative valuation in 16.8.[3]

The method accounts for the cultivation of such specialized connotations in terms of the narrative modification of semantic frames that make available to interpreters: (1) points of information about the particular words, (2) relationships among words and references to other frames containing them, and (3) perspectives for apprehending and (e)valuating their function and expectations for their content.[4] In the example of 'seek',

2. *TDNT*, II, pp. 892-93.

3. P. Danove, 'The Characterization and Narrative Function of the Women at the Tomb (Mark 15, 40-41, 47; 16, 1-8)', *Bib* 77 (1996), pp. 374-97. This investigation assumes that Mark ends at 16.8 based on textual (K. Aland, 'Bemerkungen zum Schluss des Markusevangeliums', in E.E. Ellis and M. Wilcox [eds.], *Neotestamentica et Semitica: Studies in Honour of Matthew Black* [Edinburgh: T. & T. Clark, 1969], pp. 157-80, and B.M. Metzger, *A Textual Commentary on the Greek New Testament* [Stuttgart: United Bible Societies, 1975], pp. 122-28) and literary (T.E. Boomershine and G.L. Bartholomew, 'The Narrative Technique of Mark 16.8', *JBL* 100 [1981], pp. 213-23) considerations.

4. C.J. Fillmore, 'Frame Semantics and the Nature of Language', *Annals of the New York Academy of Sciences: Conference on the Origin and Development of Language and Speech* 280 (1976), pp. 20-32 (23): cf. C.J. Fillmore, 'The Need for a Frame Semantics within Linguistics', *Statistical Methods in Linguistics* (1976), pp. 5-29 (20). The concept of semantic frames recognizes all communication as rhetorical. For communication to succeed, speakers/writers must impose certain perspectives; and

the original encounter in 1.37 evokes for the audience pre-existent points of information, relationships, and perspectives for valuation; and the narration then specializes the word's connotation through the repeated evocation of frames and their modification along specific lines. In this way repetition takes on a rhetorical function by raising particular points of information, relationships and perspectives for valuation to prominence. Such narratively modified frames or narrative frames then may be evoked for the audience whenever these words appear in the subsequent narration. At that time their points of information, relationships, and perspectives for valuation establish a narratively specific basis of interpreting, relating, and valuating (positively, negatively, or neutrally) particular concepts and events.[5]

The distinction between the pre-existent content of frames and their narratively generated content engenders a distinction of two different aspects of the implied reader: the authorial audience and the narrative audience. The authorial audience is the audience for which the real author designs a work by making assumptions about the original real audience's pre-existent beliefs, knowledge, and familiarity with literary conventions.[6] The narrative audience in contrast possesses particular beliefs, knowledge, and literary competence developed by the text.[7]

interpreters/readers must recognize these: there is no perspective-free communication. Though interpreters/readers may reconceptualize the content of a communication employing alternative perspectives, every communication presupposes the evocation of particular frames and appeals to particular perspectives: cf. Paul Danove, *The End of Mark's Story: A Methodological Study* (Leiden: E.J. Brill, 1993), p. 81.

5.   The concept of the narrative frame receives development in the writings of Menakhem Perry ('Literary Dynamics: How the Order of a Text Creates its Meanings', *Poetics Today* 1.1-2 [1979], pp. 35-64 [36]), Umberto Eco (*The Role of the Reader: Explorations in the Semiotics of Texts* [Bloomington: Indiana University Press, 1979], pp. 20-21, 37), and Robert Alter (*The Pleasures of Reading in an Ideological Age* [New York: Simon & Schuster, 1989], p. 122). Particular words and phrases have only a potential to evoke the noted frames; and their actual evocation depends on a number of extrinsic and intrinsic factors. My contention is that a close reading of Mark would establish adequate grounds for evoking the frames that receive attention.

6.   P.J. Rabinowitz, 'Truth in Fiction: A Reexamination of Audiences', *Critical Inquiry* 4 (1974), pp. 121-41 (126-27). Discussion of the authorial audience's beliefs, knowledge and familiarity with conventions appears in E. Best, 'Mark's Readers: A Profile', in F. Van Segbroeck *et. al.* (eds.), *The Four Gospels 1992* (Festschrift F. Neirynck; Leuven: Leuven University Press, 1992), pp. 839-55.

7.   Rabinowitz, 'Truth', pp. 127-33. A third aspect of the implied reader, the ideal narrative audience, which arises in the context of unreliable narration (pp. 127-28), is

The authorial and narrative audiences are characterized by distinctive systems of beliefs, knowledge, and literary competence or, hereafter, beliefs.[8] Since the authorial audience's beliefs represent those assumed for Mark's real audience, the narration may appeal to these beliefs in a straightforward manner without the use of verbal repetition. The beliefs of the narrative audience in contrast must be cultivated by the narration and require redundant intensification. Thus verbal repetition is taken to indicate a rhetorical strategy used to cultivate beliefs of the narrative audience.

Repetition may cultivate beliefs for the narrative audience by developing or by undercutting particular aspects of pre-existing beliefs. When the resulting beliefs of the narrative audience do not challenge those of the authorial audience, repetition serves as a sophisticating strategy. However, when the resulting beliefs of the narrative audience are contrary to those of the authorial audience, repetition serves as a deconstructive strategy.[9] Thus, this analysis distinguishes three categories of rhetorical strategies: neutral (no repetition), sophisticating (repetition that builds on pre-existent beliefs), and deconstructive (repetition that undercuts pre-existent beliefs).

The concluding investigation of the ideological and sacred textures of the text examines the contrasting beliefs of the authorial and narrative audiences as representative of the competing ideologies of the original real audience and author.[10] This analysis discusses the original real audience

omitted; for there is significant scholarly consensus that the narrator of Mark is reliable: cf. R. Fowler, *Loaves and Fishes: The Function of the Feeding Stories in the Gospel of Mark* (Chico, CA: Scholars Press, 1981), p. 229; D. Rhoads and D. Michie, *Mark as Story: An Introduction to the Narrative of a Gospel* (Philadelphia: Fortress Press, 1988), p. 39.

8. 'Beliefs' designate the totality of the authorial or narrative audience's system of beliefs, knowledge, and literary competence and not solely religious faith. Their significance for interpretation receives respective attention in W. Booth, *The Rhetoric of Fiction* (Chicago: University of Chicago Press, 2nd edn, 1983), pp. 157, 177; Eco, *Role of the Reader*, pp. 7-8; and Rabinowitz, 'Truth', pp. 125-33.

9. Sophistication of pre-existent beliefs requires less narrative preparation and reinforcement than deconstruction of pre-existent beliefs; cf. Perry, 'Literary Dynamics', p. 37.

10. The method of analysis privileges a first-century community of faith, the Markan *ecclesia* (Robbins, *Exploring the Texture of Texts*, pp. 127-29), whose religious beliefs and language are distinct from that of the rest of the first-century Mediterranean world. Thus, the model of narrative communication employed in the analysis coheres with that presented in Robbins, *Tapestry*, pp. 18-43, but introduces a distinction between Mark's community and the rest of the first-century Mediterranean world: cf. Danove, *The End of Mark's Story*, pp. 56-64.

before considering possible implications for a contemporary believing real audience.

2. *The Pre-existent Beliefs of the Authorial Audience*

The pre-existing beliefs of the authorial audience become apparent in straightforward narration that does not employ explanations, definitions, or redundant attempts to modify the pre-existing content of the frames evoked by particular words.[11] The use of neutral strategies indicates that central elements of the authorial audience's pre-existing beliefs include a familiarity with much of the narrative content of Mark including particular allusions to the Septuagint and a knowledge of and positive esteem for Jesus, John the Baptist, and Jesus' disciples. These beliefs are especially apparent in the opening narration concerning Jesus and John the Baptist. For this narration to be meaningful, the authorial audience must be characterized by pre-existing beliefs that Jesus is the Christ and Son of God (1.1), that the Septuagintal citation is taken to indicate that John is the referent of the angel and Jesus is the referent of 'you' (1.2), that John's and Jesus' activity may be summarized through the word, 'baptize' (βαπτίζω), that John's clothing portrays him as Elijah (1.6; cf. 2 Kgs 1.8), God's authoritative precursor of the great and terrible day of the Lord (Mal. 4.5), and that Jesus is the referent of the more powerful one (1.7).[12] The straightforward presentation of the positive relationship of Jesus with God (1.1, 11) and of John with Jesus (1.2-9) and God (1.2-3; cf. 6.18) indicates a very positive pre-existent esteem for both Jesus and John.

The authorial audience's pre-existent knowledge of and positive esteem for the disciples becomes apparent in the straightforward narration of the immediate response of Simon, Andrew, James, and John to Jesus' call to leave work and family and follow him (1.18, 20), the designation of the twelve as apostles who are to preach and have authority to cast out demons

11. Fowler, *Loaves and Fishes*, pp. 161-62, discusses the use of explanations and definitions in the construction of the narrative audience; and Rhoads and Michie, *Mark as Story*, pp. 46-47, investigate the role of repetition in this process.

12. Mark 1.2-3 also presumes familiarity with who Isaiah is, why he is authoritative, and what is written in the book of Isaiah (and Malachi); and βαπτίζω (1.8) presumes familiarity with the word's theological use and a recognition that being baptized with the Holy Spirit has greater significance than being baptized with water. C. Bryan, *A Preface to Mark: Notes on the Gospel in its Literary and Cultural Settings* (New York: Oxford University Press, 1993), p. 138, deems the conflation of Exod. 23.20 and Mal. 3.1 to be traditional.

(3.14-15), the special name given to Simon (3.16), and the twelve's successful mission to proclaim, cast out demons and heal (6.12-13).[13] Neutral rhetorical strategies also indicate beliefs that the disciples of Jesus witnessed Jesus' resurrection as Jesus said they would (16.7; cf. 14.28) and proclaimed the gospel (13.10). The introduction of this information without attempts to explain or justify the positive implications for the disciples, especially in the first three chapters of Mark, indicates a significant pre-existing knowledge and positive valuation of them by the authorial audience.

3. *The Cultivated Beliefs of the Narrative Audience*

Cultivation of the beliefs of the narrative audience concerning the disciples proceeds in the context of the authorial audience's positive valuation of them. The use of repetition indicates that the narration attempts to sophisticate aspects of these pre-existing beliefs even as it undercuts or deconstructs other aspects. The following analysis isolates examples of the use of sophisticating and deconstructive strategies in the cultivation of the beliefs of the narrative audience.

a. *The Use of Repetition as a Sophisticating Strategy*

The sophistication of beliefs occurs through redundant evocation and development of particular pre-existing points of information, relationships, and perspectives for valuation associated with the disciples. The use of sophisticating strategies to develop pre-existing positive information about the disciples appears in the repetition and coordination of 'proclaim' (κηρύσσω), 'hand over' (παραδίδωμι), and 'baptize' (βαπτίζω).

Proclaiming (κηρύσσω) is the first action predicated of John (1.4) and Jesus (1.14) and the first narrated action of the twelve on mission (6.12; cf. 3.14).[14] This relates John, Jesus, and the twelve, stresses the twelve's role of proclaiming repentance (6.12) and the gospel (13.10) on the pattern of

---

13. Information about the twelve is taken to apply to the disciples at least with respect to the more general elements of discipleship: cf. E. Best, 'The Role of the Disciples in Mark', *NTS* 23 (1976–77), pp. 377-401 (380-381), who notes that, although Mark distinguishes to a limited extent between the disciples and the twelve, narratively the two groups are used similarly.

14. When not used intransitively (1.38, 39; 3.14; 7.36), the content of the proclamation is the gospel (1.14; 13.10; 14.9)/the word (1.45), repentance (6.12), the baptism of John (1.4, 8)/Jesus (1.8) or 'what Jesus did for him' (5.20).

Jesus (1.14-15), and extends the narration's previously established positive valuation of John and Jesus to the twelve when they are first named apostles (3.14) and sent (6.7-12).[15]

Being handed over (παραδίδωμι) is predicated of John (1.14), Jesus (3.19; 14.10, 11, 18, 42, 44; 15.1, 10, 15), the Son of Man (9.31; 10.33a, 33b; 14.21, 41) and Peter, James, John, and Andrew (13.9, 11).[16] Since the context relates the handing over of John and Jesus to their deaths (John, 1.14; cf. 6.14-29; Jesus, 9.31; 10.33), the disciples who will be handed over (13.9, 11) because of Jesus (13.9; cf. 8.35), possibly to their deaths (13.12), receive close identification with John and Jesus and share in their positive valuation. The narration further relates proclaiming and being handed over to death by evoking frames associated with κηρύσσω and παραδίδωμι in the same narrative contexts (1.2-15; 3.13-19; 6.6b-32; 10.32-45; 13.5-13; 14.1-11).[17]

Baptizing (βαπτίζω) is predicated of John (1.4, 5, 8, 9; 6.14, 24), Jesus (1.8) and, by implication, God (10.38, 39).[18] Those baptized include people of Judea and Jerusalem (1.5, 8), Jesus (1.9), and Jesus, James, and John (10.38-39). Baptizing serves as the defining activity of John and is related to his being handed over, ultimately to death (1.14; cf. 6.14-29).[19] Since speaking God's words (6.18) is related to proclaiming (1.14-15), the narration of 6.14-29 relates baptizing and death and correlatively links both to proclaiming. This relationship is strengthened by Jesus' statements

15. Since the notice that Judas betrayed (παρέδωκεν, 3.19) Jesus appears at the end of 3.13-19, the positive valuation associated with δώδεκα in fact is limited to the other eleven.

16. Of the three remaining occurrences of this verb, that in 4.29 is intransitive; that in 7.13 has a non-human object; and that in 13.12 has unnamed referents.

17. E.J. Pryke, *Redactional Style in the Marcan Gospel: A Study of Syntax and Vocabulary as Guides to Redaction in Mark* (Cambridge: Cambridge University Press, 1978), pp. 136-37, attributes the majority of the occurrences of κηρύσσω and παρα-δίδωμι in these contexts to Markan redactional activity. This supports a determination that the linkage of these words is directed to the generation of beliefs of the narrative audience.

18. The verb βαπτίζω has one connotation (1.4, 5, 8a, 8b, 9; 6.14, 24; 10.38, 39) associated with baptism (βάπτισμα, 1.4; 10.38, 39; 11.30) and another (7.4) associated with immersion (βαπτισμός, 7.4). The former occurrences are the focus of this investigation.

19. Baptizing (6.14, 24) and speaking God's words (6.18) are the only actions predicated of John in 6.14-29; and John, in the only statement summarizing his activity, identifies both his ministry and that of the one coming after him (Jesus) as 'baptizing' (1.8).

to James and John concerning the baptism (whose contextual connotation is 'being handed over' and 'being killed') with which both he and they will be baptized (10.38-39; cf. 10.32-33). The frames evoked by βαπτίζω contribute to the disciples' positive valuation by relating James and John (and, through them, other members of the twelve) to Jesus with whom they will share a common baptism and, through Jesus, a correlative link to John the Baptist and God. Again, the narration relates the frames associated with proclaim, be handed over, and baptize/be baptized by evoking them almost exclusively in the same narrative contexts.

The generation of the relationships linking κηρύσσω, παραδίδωμι, and βαπτίζω brings the activity of Jesus, John, and members of the twelve into parallel and extends the very positive valuation of Jesus and John to the twelve. Since the authorial audience has a pre-existent positive valuation of these characters, this repetition engenders a sophistication of beliefs through the generation of narrative frames linking the disciples' activity and fate to that of Jesus (and John).

Sophisticating strategies augment pre-existing negative information about the disciples through repetition of understand (συνίημι) and discuss (διαλογίζομαι), both of which evoke pre-existing frames indicating that the disciples did not always understand Jesus' teachings and actions. The straightforward notice that those around Jesus with the twelve asked Jesus about his parables (4.10) and Jesus' statement that those who do not understand are outsiders for whom everything is in parables (παραβολαῖς, 4.11) set the stage for cultivating a specialized negative valuation for those who do not understand (συνίημι, 4.12; cf. Isa. 6.9).[20] The presence of παραβολή in 4.13 then engenders an ambiguous impact for Jesus' questions, 'You don't know this parable; how then will you know all the parables?'[21] The next occurrence of συνίημι (6.52) resolves any initial

20. Pryke, *Redactional Style*, p. 137, attributes all but one occurrence of συνίημι to authorial composition.

21. M.A. Tolbert, *Sowing the Gospel: Mark's World in Literary-Historical Perspective* (Minneapolis: Fortress Press, 1989), pp. 195-98, would locate a negative valuation of the disciples in Simon's pursuit of Jesus (κατεδίωξεν, 1.36) and the notice about Judas the betrayer (3.19). Attributing a negative connotation to καταδιώκω is dubious; for this word receives no further development. Examination of the Markan connotation of 'seek' (ζητέω), however, did establish, at least in hindsight, a basis for a negative valuation of Simon's statement in 1.37. The straightforward notice about Judas (3.19) indicates that this information is part of the pre-existent beliefs of the authorial audience. Though Judas' designation as one of the twelve is reintroduced twice elsewhere in relation to his betraying Jesus (14.10, 43), the narration offers no

ambiguity through a clear statement that the disciples lack understanding. The intervening narration prepares for this statement through Jesus' assertions that the disciples are cowardly and do not yet have faith (4.40), are afraid (4.41; 6.51), and are amazed (6.51).[22] The occurrence in 6.52 relates a lack of understanding to a hardened (πωρόω) heart and ties both words to 'bread' (ἄρτος). The conjunction of παραβολή (7.17) and 'not understanding' (ἀσύνετοι, 7.18) from the root of συνίημι strengthens the disciples' negative valuation. This negative valuation receives definitive confirmation in Jesus' statement (8.17-18) that repeats ἄρτος (8.16, 17; cf. 8.20), συνίημι (8.17, 21), and πωρόω (8.17) and alludes to a Scripture quotation (8.18; cf. Jer. 5.21; Ezek. 12.2) containing much of the same vocabulary as the quotation from Isaiah in 4.12. In this, Jesus' most lengthy and explicitly negative address to the disciples in the narrative, the frames evoked by συνίημι impose a very negative valuation on the disciples.

Intensification of pre-existing negative information about the disciples also centers on the repetition of discuss (διαλογίζομαι, 2.6, 8a, 8b; 8.16, 17; 9.33; 11.31) with characters whose private discussion results in their negative valuation. The scribes discussing in their hearts that Jesus is blaspheming (2.6) are countered by Jesus' statements and action (2.8-12). The disciples discussing with one another that they have no bread (8.16; cf. 8.10) are depicted as not understanding Jesus' statements and having a hardened heart (8.17).[23] The twelve discussing with one another who is greatest (9.33-34; cf. 9.36) are corrected in Jesus' teaching about being last and servant of all (9.36); and the chief priests, scribes, and elders discussing the origins of John's baptism (11.31; cf. 11.27) are revealed as lacking faith and fearing the crowd (11.31-32) that esteems Jesus (11.18). In each case, those discussing are portrayed negatively as having a faulty understanding of Jesus' statements/teaching (the disciples/twelve) or in

---

direct association of Judas with the term 'disciple' (μαθητής), indicating that developments concerning Judas play only an indirect role in the characterization of the disciples as a group. The implications for the characterization of the twelve explicitly are one of contrast between Judas and the other eleven who never receive direct association with the action of handing over (παραδίδωμι) Jesus.

22. The increasingly negative portrayal of the disciples receives discussion in M.A. Tolbert, 'How the Gospel of Mark Builds Character', *Int* 47 (1993), pp. 347-57 (353) and R.C. Tannehill, 'The Disciples of Jesus: The Function of a Narrative Role', *JR* 57 (1977), pp. 386-405 (398).

23. Note the linkage of συνίημι, ἄρτος and πωρόω to διαλογίζομαι in 8.16-17.

conflict with Jesus (some of the scribes/the chief priests, scribes, and elders).

b. *The Use of Repetition as a Deconstructive Strategy*
The deconstruction of the pre-existent (authorial audience) and recently cultivated (narrative audience) positively valued aspects of the disciples' presentation occurs through the redundant intensification of a negative interpretation of the formerly ambiguous word 'fear' and through the introduction of new negative information about the disciples centered on the phrase 'say to no one' that directly contradicts the pre-existing beliefs of the authorial audience.[24]

Fear (φοβέομαι) may have either a positive or a negative connotation in Koine usage and a positive connotation of 'holy awe' in the presence of divine activity.[25] Within Mark, however, the verb has a consistently negative connotation and imposes a very negative valuation on those who fear. The disciples' fear is related to their lack of faith (4.40-41). The Gerasenes' fear (5.15) leads them to ask that Jesus go from their region, indicating that they do not want to be with Jesus, a central theme of 3.13–6.6a.[26] The fear of the woman with the flow of blood (5.33) initially prevents her from responding to Jesus. Jesus commands first Jairus (5.36) and then the disciples (6.50) not to fear, indicating that this response is inappropriate.[27] Herod's fear (6.20) of the positively valued John the Baptist occurs in the context of his statements that he had John imprisoned for speaking God's word (6.17-18; cf. Lev. 18.16) and then beheaded (6.16). The disciples' fear is coordinated with their lack of understanding (9.32). The fear of those following Jesus (10.32) contradicts Jesus' command to the disciples (6.50) whose defining quality is following Jesus (1.18; cf. 9.34). Various religious authorities fear Jesus (11.18) or the

24. The authorial and narrative audiences have an overwhelmingly positive valuation of the disciples prior to the first use of deconstructive strategies whose use is directed solely to the cultivation of frames imposing a negative valuation on the disciples.

25. *TDNT*, IX, pp. 189-97.

26. The significance of 'being with Jesus' receives extended development in K. Stock, *Die Boten aus dem Mit-Ihm-Sein: Das Verhältnis zwischen Jesus und der Zwölf nach Markus* (AnBib, 70; Rome: Biblical Institute, 1975), pp. 7-70.

27. In 6.52 the narrator advises that the disciples' fear stems from a lack of understanding and hardness of heart, thus relating the developments centering on φοβέομαι and συνίημι.

crowd (11.32; 12.12) that esteems Jesus (11.18) and John (11.32).[28] The women's fear (16.8) in response to the young man's statement prevents them from passing on the message entrusted to them and imposes a negative valuation on them.[29] The related word 'fearful' (ἔκφοβος, 9.6) appears immediately after the narrator's statement that Peter does not know what to say.[30]

Deconstructive strategies introduce new negative information about the disciples through the phrase 'say to no one' (λέγειν μηδενί/οὐδενί, 1.44; 7.36/16.8). This phrase receives parallel development in 1.40-45 and 7.31-37 which begin with a healing (leper, 1.40-42; blind man, 7.32-36), continue to Jesus' command not to speak about the event to anyone (μηδενὶ μηδὲν εἴπῃς, 1.44; ἵνα μηδενὶ λέγωσιν, 7.36), and conclude with the healed disregarding Jesus' command and proclaiming (1.45; 7.36).[31] The failure of the leper and blind man to obey Jesus' command results in their negative valuation.[32] The phrase next appears in 16.8 in the notice that the women said nothing to anyone (οὐδενὶ οὐδὲν εἶπαν) after being told of Jesus' resurrection (16.6) and being ordered to speak (εἴπατε, 16.7).[33] The women's failure to speak makes them the brunt of irony and results in their negative valuation, for this command to speak fails after previous commands not to speak were unable to achieve silence. The women's failure impacts the disciples; for Jesus stated in 9.9 that Peter, James, and John were not to narrate (διηγέομαι) the event of his transfiguration to anyone (μηδενί) except when he is raised from the dead. The women's failure to speak, however, removes the possibility within the narrative for Peter, James, and John to narrate the events of the transfiguration. This

---

28. Developments centered on φοβέομαι and διαλογίζομαι are related in 11.31-32.

29. G. O'Collins, 'The Fearful Silence of Three Women (Mark, 16.8c)', *Greg* 69 (1988), pp. 489-503 and R.H. Lightfoot, *The Gospel Message of St Mark* (Oxford: Clarendon Press, 1950), pp. 88-91, assert that the occurrence of φοβέομαι in 16.8 indicates a positive reaction to the divine and would limit this positive connotation to this one occurrence. The introduction of such a singular connotation in the last verse of the narrative, however, is untenable. Since φοβέομαι has a consistently negative connotation in its earlier occurrences, the frames evoked by its appearance here impose valuations highly resistant to a positive interpretation.

30. Danove, 'Women at the Tomb', pp. 391-92.

31. Pryke, *Redactional Style*, p. 37, attributes the occurrences of this word in the indicated texts to authorial composition.

32. The narrator indicates that an implication of the former leper's disobedience is to hamper Jesus' open movement (1.45).

33. Developments on φοβέομαι and λέγειν μηδενί are related in 16.8.

extends the apprehension of irony to the disciples and Peter and contributes to the disciples' concluding negative valuation.

4. *The Narrative Rhetoric*

The narrative rhetoric maintains the creative tension between the positive
and negative aspects of the disciples' characterization through the ordering, frequency, and distribution of neutral, sophisticating, and deconstructive strategies. Neutral strategies evoking pre-existent frames that impose a
positive valuation on the disciples establish the initial characterization of
the disciples beginning in 1.16-20. To the explicitly treated examples of
neutral strategies could be added numerous others to establish that neutral
strategies are both the most frequently employed and widely distributed
(consistently throughout Mk 1–14) in the narration.[34]

Second in ordering, frequency and distribution are sophisticating
strategies cultivating a positive valuation of the disciples. Developments
concerning 'proclaim', 'hand over' and 'baptize' are first linked to the
disciples in 3.14 (κηρύσσω, cf. 6.12; παραδίδωμι, 13.9, 11; βαπτίζω,
10.38, 39). To these could be added other words and phrases that were not
developed.[35] The distribution of such strategies for the noted examples
spans four chapters (Mk 3; 6; 10; 13), and the noted but undeveloped
examples would grant a significantly wider distribution.

Third in ordering, frequency, and distribution are sophisticating strategies cultivating a negative valuation of the disciples. These begin in 4.12
(συνίημι, cf. 6.52; διαλογίζομαι, 8.16, 17). Inclusion of a few other phrases
associated with not knowing grants only a limited frequency and expands
somewhat the distribution for the noted examples (Mk 4; 6; 7; 8; 9).

---

34. Such examples include every occasion of the introduction of positive information about the disciples that does not receive concerted development or cultivation,
references to the disciples coming, going, entering and departing with Jesus, and the
use of plural verbs and participles in reference to Jesus and the disciples, especially at
the beginning of narrative scenes.

35. To the noted examples could be added the further positive linkage of Jesus,
John and the disciples developed through the repetition of 'desert/wilderness' (ἔρημος,
of John, 1.3-4; of Jesus, 1.12, 13, 35, 45; and of Jesus and the disciples, 6.31, 32, 35),
and the positive linkage of Jesus/the disciples through the repetition of 'cast out
demons' (ἐκβάλλειν δαιμόνια, 1.34, 39; 3.22; 7.26/3.15; 6.13), 'teach' (διδάσκω, 1.21,
22; 2.13; 4.1, 2; 6.2, 6, 34; 8.31; 9.31; 10.1; 11.17; 12.14, 35; 14.49/6.30), 'authority'
(ἐξουσία, 1.22, 27; 2.10 [Son of Man]; 11.28a, 28b, 29, 33/3.15; 6.7; 13.34 [slaves, cf.
10.44], and 'heal' (θεραπεύω, 1.34; 3.2, 10; 6.5/6.13).

Fourth in ordering, frequency, and distribution are deconstructive strategies cultivating a negative valuation of the disciples. These begin in 4.41
(φοβέομαι, cf. 6.50), are limited to 'fear' (φοβέομαι) and 'say to no one'
(λέγειν μηδενί), and appear only in Mark 4, 6, 7, 8, 9, 16.[36]

These findings reveal parallels in the sequence of first occurrence,
frequency, and distribution of the use of strategies:

> neutral (+) > sophisticating (+) > sophisticating (-) > deconstructive (-)

This analysis indicates that the direct characterization of the disciples in
Mk 1.16–3.13 depends solely on the use of neutral strategies that appeal to
the authorial (and real) audience's pre-existent beliefs about and overwhelmingly positive valuation of the disciples. This establishes the initial
credibility of the content of the narration for the authorial (and real)
audience.

The use of sophisticating strategies that cultivate for the narrative audience a positive estimation of the disciples begins in 3.14 (κηρύσσω) and
continues through 13.9-11 (κηρύσσω, παραδίδωμι). The cultivation of
positive aspects of the disciples' presentation prior to negative aspects
establishes initial beliefs of the narrative audience in keeping with those of
the authorial (and real) audience, ensuring the initial credibility of this
construct for the authorial audience.

The use of sophisticating strategies to cultivate a negative presentation
of the disciples relies on appeals to pre-existent knowledge of problematic
aspects of the disciples' history (συνίημι, διαλογίζομαι) and so does not
involve direct assaults on the beliefs of the authorial audience. The
redundant intensification of negative points of information about the
disciples beginning in 4.13 is interlaced with ongoing appeals to the pre-
existent and narratively cultivated positive valuation of the disciples,
ensuring continued credibility. The use of deconstructive strategies to
cultivate a negative interpretation for φοβέομαι relies on the reinterpretation of traditional information and occurs indirectly.[37] This indicates that
the authorial audience's high esteem for the disciples accommodates the
fact that the disciples' reactions to Jesus' deeds at times produced fear.
Redactional activity in the context of 6.50 also suggests at most a neutral

36. My analysis elsewhere has indicated no other independent example of the use
of this strategy: cf. Danove, *The End of Mark's Story*, pp. 191-92.

37. Studies of Markan redactional activity indicate that at least one occurrence of
φοβέομαι (6.50) with respect to the disciples is traditional: cf. Pryke, *Redactional Style*,
p. 15.

or ambiguous interpretation of the disciples' fear within the tradition.[38] The narrative developments centering on this verb also are indirect: though the disciples are the most frequent referents of those who fear (4.41; 6.50; 9.32; 10.32; cf. 16.8 for the women who also follow Jesus), the majority of the development of a negative connotation (5.15, 33, 36; 6.20; 11.18, 32; 12.12) involves characters other than the disciples. The use of φοβέομαι with the very negatively portrayed Herod (6.20) and religious authorities (11.18, 22; 12.12) establishes for the disciples strong relationships with these characters precisely in the midst of their evil machinations against John and Jesus without ascribing equally overt evil actions directly to the disciples.[39]

The use of deconstructive strategies that introduce the only noted example of new negative information that directly contradicts the pre-existent beliefs of the authorial (and real) audience (λέγειν μηδενί) centers almost exclusively on other characters and is not realized with respect to the disciples until 16.8. Prior to this, the narration maintains its foundation in a presumed (authorial audience) and cultivated (narrative audience) positive valuation of the disciples.[40]

The narrative rhetoric maintains the viability of the cultivated negative aspects of the disciples' presentation through prior and continuing appeals to the pre-existent and cultivated positive estimation of the disciples. Thus the narratively cultivated negative estimation of the disciples is deemed a parasitic development whose viability depends on the continuing vitality of the presumed and cultivated positive estimation of the disciples. With the notice that the women never delivered the message and the implication that the disciples never became faithful proclaimers of that message, the parasite kills the host!

38. In isolation from the overall Markan development concerning φοβέομαι and the very negative narratorial comments, especially in 6.52, a range of possible pre-existent interpretations ranging from holy awe to negative fear is possible in 6.50. The authorial audience's very positive pre-existing estimation of the disciples despite knowledge of their occasional fear would grant a strong impetus to garner the most positive interpretation of 'fear' possible in this instance.

39. Tolbert, 'How the Gospel of Mark Builds Character', p. 354.

40. The simultaneous operation of contrary strategies accounts for the observation of R.C. Tannehill, 'The Gospel of Mark as Narrative Christology', *Semeia* 16 (1979), pp. 57-95 (69-70), that the narration simultaneously draws the implied reader to identify with the disciples and to judge them negatively.

5. *The Narrative Function of the Ambiguous Characterization of the Disciples*

The contrary elements of the characterization of the disciples engendered by the operation of sophisticating and deconstructive strategies produces what may be called a profoundly ambivalent estimation of the disciples for the narrative audience. The more positive aspects of the disciples' characterization ensure the continuing credibility of the narration for the authorial audience and establish the context for maintaining the viability of the negative aspects of the disciples' presentation for the narrative audience. The ending at 16.8, however, engenders a crisis of interpretation for the authorial audience which, as a narrative construct of the believing real audience, must reject the content of the ending. Thus the coherence of the narrative world for the authorial (and real) audience crumbles at 16.8. In contrast, the narrative audience, whose beliefs are generated by sophisticating and deconstructive strategies, has a profoundly ambivalent estimation of the disciples and must accept that the disciples never really understood, continued to fear, and never proclaimed the gospel. The narrative audience also recognizes that the outcome of the narrative is not a necessary one but could be rectified by even one disciple who understands, does not fear, and proclaims the gospel. Tragically, the narrative indicates no such disciple.[41]

The ending at 16.8 demands review and reconsideration on the part of the real audience. By maintaining the credibility of the narration for the real audience, the narrative rhetoric encouraged the real audience's identification with the disciples even as it brought the more negative aspects of their presentation to prominence. This afforded the real audience the opportunity to identify related negative aspects of its own story as a disciple. The plausibility of the ending at 16.8 for the narrative audience also encourages the real audience to recognize that its own lack of understanding, fear, and failure to proclaim the gospel may result in its own negative valuation. The narrative withholds from the disciples the message that should lead to proclamation even as it reveals that message to the real audience. The disciples are narratively constrained from undertaking the required action, but the real audience is not. At this point, the real

---

41. A review of the major characters of the story world reveals no other positively valued disciples who are appropriate bearers of the message: cf. Danove, 'Women at the Tomb', p. 396.

audience may recognize the operation of a rhetorical strategy that transforms a story about Jesus into an invitation for a response of understanding, fearlessness, and proclamation of the gospel. If this occurs, the real audience experiences a call to become a faithful disciple; and the Gospel becomes gospel.

6. *The Ideological Texture of the Text*

The contrasting beliefs of the authorial and narrative audiences imply a significant contrast in ideologies between the original real audience and author. The authorial audience, the real author's construct of the original real audience, esteems the original disciples and identifies them with many aspects of the community's ideal of discipleship. The narrative audience, the real author's narratively cultivated alternative to the original real audience, has beliefs that augment the community's ideal of discipleship and, through the characterization of the disciples, recognize the possibility of discipleship failure.[42] In the process of developing this possibility, however, the narration redundantly cultivates for the narrative audience beliefs offering hope: no matter how abject the disciples' failure to do and think the things of God, Jesus remains faithful and continues to call them to follow him (8.32-33).[43] These developments are taken to indicate that the ideology of the authorial audience, the construct of the original real audience, is portrayed as deficient in not giving appropriate significance to the newly emphasized aspects of ideal discipleship (proclaiming, being handed over, and being baptized on the pattern of Jesus) and in not providing for the possibility of discipleship failure and subsequent renewal. The beliefs of the narrative audience, which undergird the real author's proffered alternative ideology, correct these deficiencies.

As a communication between a real author and reader, the narrative constitutes a proclamation about Jesus (and his disciples!) that demands a response; and the rhetorical exigency of Mark's communication is the real author's perceived need to correct a deficient model of discipleship on the part of the original real audience. The narration's emphasis on proclaiming, being handed over, and being baptized (unto death) would indicate a contemporary historical exigency of persecution in proclamation that, for

42. The distinction between the pre-existent and narratively cultivated aspects of discipleship receive development in Danove, *The End of Mark's Story*, pp. 210-21.

43. The pattern of discipleship misapprehension followed by corrective teaching by Jesus receives special repetitive development in 8.32b–9.1, 9.33-37, and 10.35-45.

some at least, issues in discipleship failure for which the community lacks theological resources to make such failure intelligible or to provide remedy. The ideology of the narrative audience addresses this situation with an invitation of hope and a sophisticated model of ideal discipleship as a guiding goal.

7. *The Sacred Texture of the Text*:

Within the framework established by the narration, the authorial audience, the construct of the original real audience, must reject the ending of Mark and embrace the position that the message was delivered and that the disciples and Peter saw the resurrected Jesus in order to assert the existence of the Markan community. In contrast, the narrative audience, the construct representing the real author's ideological alternative, recognizes that the formation of the believing community envisioned by the narration is frustrated.[44] The Gospel as gospel seeks to persuade the original believing community to assume the ideology of the narrative audience and become the believing community proposed by the narration. Whether or not the original real audience or a contemporary real audience will be persuaded to do so cannot be determined from narrative analysis. However, the narration may continue to function as gospel for any believer who experiences persecution, shares an ideology similar to that of authorial audience, or finds in the negative presentation of the disciples resonance with their own, sometimes imperfect, conduct of discipleship. For such Christians the narration may provide a similar hope and goal.

---

44. Robbins, *Exploring the Texture of Texts*, p. 128.

'FROM THE PRAGMATICS OF TEXTURES TO A CHRISTIAN UTOPIA': THE CASE OF THE GOSPEL OF JOHN

Gerhard van den Heever

> In my view, to meet the tasks that lie before it now, rhetorical criticism needs to move beyond the traditional interplay of method and theory into the mode of a comprehensive interpretive analytics (Robbins 1996b: 25).

1. *The Nature of the Beast: Where it Comes Together Is Where It Starts*

Exegetes will differ as to the nature of the beast that needs to be tamed, but if we take seriously the challenge of Vernon Robbins to 'reinvent rhetorical criticism into a new *modus operandi*', as an interpretative analytics (Robbins 1996b: 20), it should be clear that the 'taming' of biblical interpretation, and our evaluative interpretation of our own praxis of biblical interpretation, requires a different way of conversing with the past (and with the textual tradition that serves as the fount from which it springs, a conversation which includes all the history of commentary on that tradition). It is this sense that I understand Robbins's call for 'an interpretive analytics' (a term derived from Dreyfus and Rabinow's discussions of the work of Michel Foucault). Everything comes into play: the society and its practices that shape its discourse, its talking about and conceiving of itself, the pragmatics of its (textual) self-representations, the readers as products of this self-representation, and, one could add, the pragmatics of keeping alive this event or process of self-representation by canonizing these interpretations in an authoritative textual tradition.

A 'different way of conversing with the past' would entail a breaking-out of our conversational conventions. A few such conventions can be pointed out, namely, the limitation of interpretive strategies to one level or texture of a text, the facility with which an author is taken at his word (a product of the exegetes' uncritical acceptance of the presuppositions embedded in the exegetical methods used: 'they have not re-valued or

reinvented our approach to the wily ways of speaker-authors or the selective ways of audience-readers' [Robbins 1996b: 27]), the focus on the time
of the text/the time of reading to the exclusion of what comes before and
after (Wuellner 1991), the neat demarcation of exegetical methods, and the
drawing of boundaries between theological and non-theological disciplines. In this regard it is salutary to be reminded of the words of Jonathan
Z. Smith (with reference to the use of the term 'trajectories' by Helmut
Koester and James Robinson): 'I have come to insist that it is not sufficient
to merely name a text; rather, it is necessary both to locate a text within a
history of tradition and to provide some sort of explanation for the processes of continuity and change' (Smith 1978: xi). This reading of (an
aspect of) the rhetoric of John's Gospel concerns itself, therefore, with the
trajectory of imperial language in the first-century Greco-Roman world:
how John's Gospel picks it up, transforms it, and eventually contributes to
its becoming the foundation of the dominant world-view or religious
superstructure of an empire that has become Christian by the early fourth
century CE.

In a reconfiguring of these conversational conventions into a comprehensive interpretive analytics, a number of boundaries need to be trans-
gressed. First is the boundary between the text and 'what lies outside it'.[1]
The 'outside' of a text is both spatial and temporal. The 'spatial outside'
concerns the text's ability to refer distortingly to other texts and to phenomena in its surrounding world (on the issue of 'distortion', see van den
Heever 1998). Because of the gap between the event and its (final) textual

---

1.   I do not wish to enter into a debate on the issue of the 'inside' or 'outside' of a
text. Ever since Jacques Derrida's now famous statement *Il n'y a pas d'hors texte*:
'there is nothing outside the text', the issue of the textuality of being and existence and
the thorny issues of epistemology, reference and reality, the relationships between texts
oral or written (intertextuality of co-texts), have been at the forefront of post-modern
interpretation theory (Moore 1989: 121-30; see his comments on p. 28: 'It should be
remembered that this chapter is a debunking exercise designed to exorcise whatever
vestiges of naïve realism cling to our collective exegetical psyche. Epistemologically
the text is an abyss but praxically it spills over with properties, as noted earlier. Such
debunking does, however, have undeniable implications for religious faith.'). Of
course, there is a variety of post-modern interpretations of biblical texts, but in general
it is safe to say that it was only with the advent of postmodernism that the acceptance
took root that there is not necessarily one correct reading of a text, also that all readings
are rhetorical in nature, just as the texts themselves are. This opened up the possibility
in the first place for interdisciplinary approaches.

record, and because all ancient communication was highly rhetorical in nature, the issue of an ideologically informed presentation of events constantly raises its spectre (see Sanders' [1998: 1] comment on this issue with regard to the hermeneutics of translation). The temporal outside concerns the discourse preceding the text and into which it speaks even as it strikes up a dialogue with the tradition of which it is part, as well as the effects and traces left by the discourse of the text through our intellectual history (the 'trajectory' referred to by J.Z. Smith).

The second is the boundary between theological and non-theological disciplines. Robbins advocates the use of new resources for developing categories of interpretation and reading strategies and so the fields of rhetorical criticism, communication theory, literary theory (including narratology), post-modern theory, critical theory, the social sciences, text linguistics, pragmatics, and so on make their presence felt in our approaches to biblical texts and infuse our reading praxis with their various vocabularies (Robbins 1996b: 27).

The third boundary is that between the reader as observer and the text as observed object. It has become a fundamental presupposition of the family of reader response theories that the reader is *in* the text. But a reconfigured analytics in the Foucaultian sense will make explicit the way the reader/interpreter rhetorically configures the elements of the texts, or, in Robbins' terminology, the relationships between the various textures, in order to construct its meaning-for-him/her-in-his/her-social situation, to construct a meaning-constellation useful to a desired purpose. Keywords in this regard are 'usefulness' and 'purpose' with the added implication of 'construction of reality' (Berger and Luckmann 1967).

And there is yet a fourth boundary that needs to be collapsed. That is the boundary separating the various textures or layers or aspects of a text. It is quite common in exegetical praxis to reify one such perspective on the text to the extent of remaining captive within that perspective. A few examples will illustrate the point. Most standard commentaries on the Gospel of John are captive to the historical mode of explaining the text, from R. Schnackenburg and R. Brown's magisterial commentaries to the more recent from G.R. Beasley-Murray and L. Morris. 'Historical' in this sense means determining the fit between the reality projected by the text and reality *wie es eigentlich gewesen ist*. The text is taken at face value and used as a window on the historical situation. As Robbins put it:

> Historical criticism regularly begins with the presupposition that the narrator of a New Testament text is right, and others in the historical context

were wrong. In other words, it begins with a presupposition that 'those who were victorious were right' (Robbins 1996b: 235).

Although one does encounter references to the 'purpose of the author', or the meaning of the narrative for the situation of the Johannine community, the assumption that one deals here with real history dominates. At least, the commentaries create the impression of a one-to-one relationship between the gospel narrative and the history it speaks about.[2] Then again a reading may be captive to the textual or narrative level. The most influential of such readings was surely C.H. Dodd's *The Interpretation of the Fourth Gospel.* This seminal work has much akin to more modern narrative critical or structural or discourse analytical readings. Although the book starts with a discussion of the possible 'backgrounds' to Johannine language (which in essence amounts to a discussion of the relevant co-texts or intertextual relations of Johannine language), historical questions are absent when the explication of the structure of the narrative begins. Mark Stibbe's *John's Gospel* and Elizabeth Harris's *The Prologue of the Fourth Gospel* both work with aspects of narrative critical theory (albeit to a far lesser extent in the case of Harris), but in essence both readings stay on the level of the text's 'saying' with little or no integration of historical questions such as historical 'distortions', or any references to the rhetoric of the text. Another reading in the same vein that does deal with the rhetoric of the Johannine narrative, but does not deal with historical questions at all, is Martin Warner's 'The Fourth Gospel's Art of Rational Persuasion'. In this rhetorical reading there is likewise no mention of historical questions or of narrative theory. And lastly, one may point to interpretations of John of a more social, socio-historical or social-scientific character. In this regard one can mention Wayne Meeks's now famous essay, 'The Man from Heaven in Johannine Sectarianism' and his 'Breaking Away: Three New Testament Pictures of Christianity's Separation from the Jewish Communities', as well as to the works of Jerome Neyrey, *An Ideology of Revolt: John's Christology in Social-Scientific Perspective*, and Richard Cassidy, *John's Gospel in New Perspective*.[3] In general these

---

2.   See the apology for historical trustworthiness of the Gospel of John in Robinson 1985, by far, to my mind, the most eloquent and elegant statement of this position.

3.   In the recently published Malina and Rohrbaugh, 1998, as was the case with *Social-Scientific Commentary on the Synoptic Gospels*, there is no integration of historical and, more importantly, literary issues. However, it is only fair to point out that they explicitly present the commentary as a supplement to other (literary and historical) commentaries on the Gospel (1998: 21). Their commentary is about the social values

works deal with the narrative as a window on social history and the social processes evinced by the text, but with little awareness of the narrativity and rhetoricity of the narrative's projection of these purported 'events'.

From what I have described it can be concluded that the text is a junction of three processes, the first being the way the text speaks (the materiality of the text, its configurations of words and phrases, its manipulations and distortions), the second is the nexus of author-and-audience, rhetorical situation and the complex world in which the communication event took place, and the third is the present reader him/herself as part of a social location, espousing ideologies at a remove from the biblical world. A 'comprehensive interpretive analytic' strives to take the concept of junction seriously, weaving to and fro through the three text-processes, letting them interact in order to destabilize each, negating the possibility of an objective, separate existence for each.

The ideology of the text-and-its-interpretation is the knot that ties it all together. If all interpretation is guided by presuppositions and ideologies, and is by its very nature ideological, then it is the ideology of the reader/ interpreter that steers the way the various textures are configured, navigated, conceived in their mutually determining relations (Robbins 1996b: 212-16). Socio-rhetorical interpretation comes together in the interplay of the four textures of inner, inter-, social and cultural, and ideological texture. Necessarily so because:

> New Testament texts are not simply historical, theological or linguistic treatises. Rather, their written discourse is a highly interactive and complex environment. Interpreting a biblical text is an act of entering a world where body and mind, interacting with one another, create and evoke highly complex patterns and configurations of meanings in historical, social, cultural and ideological contexts of religious belief. Rhetorical argument, social act and religious belief intertwine in them like threads and yarn in a richly textured tapestry (Robbins 1996b: 14).

A rhetorical analysis is the interpretation of how the interplay of textures aids or constructs the persuasive strategy and it is about how we consciously configure phenomena inside and outside the text to construct its meaning-for-us.[4] It is all about construed webs of data.

---

espoused by John's narrative and the social meaning of the way the narrative speaks. By their own admission, this commentary which is informed by sociological and anthropological studies on language and values should in its turn inform readings of John from literary and historical perspectives.

4.   Since this study started with a reference to Michel Foucault, I need at this point

2. *Ideology, Communication and Rhetoric*

Textures do not have an objective existence in themselves. Neither do the relationships between text parts and textures exist objectively. They are created archaeologically (to stay with Foucault's metaphor) in the act of 'making sense and meaning'. And while on the subject of 'construction', ideology has everything to do with the generation, construction, or invention of reality (Robbins 1996b: 200, a reference to Elisabeth Schüssler Fiorenza), hence the now popular phrase derived from the title of Berger and Luckmann's book *The Social Construction of Reality*, but one could also refer to the theory of radical constructivism as elucidated in P. Watzlawick (ed.) (1984).[5] What Schüssler-Fiorenza says about the ideology inherent in the discourse of historical interpretation, namely, that not only is information provided but that the meaning of the given information is also interpreted and explained and amplified with directives how to react to this given information, is also borne out by studies in the theory of communication.

> If a computer is to multiply two figures, it must be fed this information (the two figures) *and* information about this information: the command 'multiply them' (Watzlawick *et al.* 1967: 52).

to explicate the indebtedness to his thinking of the approach taken in this paper. Foucault (1982: 6-7) argues that the status of the document as the material remains of earlier actions, events or discourses is questioned at this junction in time in the history of knowledge and inquiry. The 'documents' perused by inquiry are not permeated with objectively given meanings. When we deal with artifactual remains of an earlier era, as in the case of literature from the New Testament era, it is us, the present readers, who construe relationships between the various remains in order to design a world of meaning. 'The document, then, is no longer for history an inert material through which it tries to reconstitute what men have done or said, the events of which only the trace remains; history is now trying to define within the documentary material itself unities, totalities, series, relations…history is the work expended on material documentation (books, texts, accounts, registers, acts, buildings, institutions, laws, techniques, objects, customs, etc.) that exists, in every time and place, in every society, either in a spontaneous or in a consciously organized form. The document is not the fortunate tool of a history that is primarily and fundamentally *memory*; history is one way in which a society recognizes and develops a mass of documentation with which it is inextricably linked' (p. 7).

    5.   One of the chapters in the book is titled 'On Constructing a Reality'.

This simple statement brings to the fore the issue of the relation between the content (report) and the relationship (command) aspects of communication (Watzlawick *et al.* 1967: 52). The report conveys the data of the communication, the command or the instruction as to how it is to be taken, and what to do with it. Communication and meta-communication go hand in hand and are essentially sides of the same coin. This is the domain of the pragmatics of communication. This fairly innocuous statement (the quotation above) has a number of important implications for our understanding of communication, ideology and rhetoric.

First, it implies the continuing valuing (i.e. the imbuing with values) of our projections of reality. Each presented fiction-as-fact implies by virtue of its being selected, manipulated and projected (that is, being 'shown in this way' with a 'vocabulary that activates the following possibilities of meaning construction'), a command to see thus, believe that and do the other. Every so often this 'hidden' and 'unconscious' process surfaces when it becomes explicit. That is when reasons are offered for why the stated case and projected reality should be so.

Second, there is the warning not to take any communicated content at face value. The 'why' and the 'to what end' are inextricably bound to the 'what'. Facts are never neutral and being so are fictions, hence the phrase 'fiction-as-fact'.

The third implication has to do with the presence of the other in communication, or the social value of communicating. In communication studies feedback experiments have shown how in a complex system elements of a chain of events can impact back to earlier elements in the chain, effecting changes in the causal communication. In the case of human communication and interpersonal systems we speak of 'feedback loops' which means that the behaviour of each person affects and is affected by the behaviour of every other person (Watzlawick *et al.* 1967: 28-32). The concept of redundancy takes this one step further. With regard to human interaction, 'redundancy' refers to the effect B has on A's communicative interaction with B because of the *expected* effect of A's interaction, an expected effect that is governed by the rules and codes of communication and the context in which the communication is effected (Watzlawick *et al.* 1967: 34-39). Furthermore, human communication is the only communication that operates two parallel systems of communication, namely, digital and analogic (Watzlawick *et al.* 1967: 60-67). By 'digital' is meant verbal communication, whereas 'analogic' refers to all non-verbal communication, including gesture, posture, facial expression, voice inflection, as well as the context in which the interaction is played out (Watzlawick *et al.* 1967: 62). And then again, communicative interaction can be either symmetrical (where equality is the guiding principle) or complementary (where the process of communication involves partners that are unequal in status in the relationship binding them together as communication partners).

The point of the pragmatics of communication needs to be belaboured. Why proceed at such length about communication? Simply because rhetorical strategies remain for all practical purposes non-existent until they are voiced or signed. Rhetoric and all its 'symptoms', like valuing, world creation and projection, interaction and persuasion, are dependent upon coming to language (however widely one dares to conceive this) since ideologies are betrayed by the way people talk (Candlin 1983: ix). Pragmatics, as one perspective on linguistic communication, has the potential to rise above being merely descriptive and to become an explanatory art. What can be explained in a pragmatic account is how in a specific society and culture, in various speech acts and activities, participants to communicative interaction value their utterances and have their utterances valued by others (Candlin 1983: ix). The 'what' is there for all to see, but why people mean x by saying y, that is the investigative function of an explanatory pragmatics which connect this saying with participant ideologies, value systems and beliefs.

> This view will involve the analyst in explaining the occurrence of certain forms of talk in particular activity types in terms of the communicative strategies they realize, and, ultimately the social purposes of the inter-actants. Insofar as particular discoursal routines are naturalized and taken-for-granted, and, we may infer, certain inferential schemata and outcomes equally predictable in particular situations, such explanatory analysis offers powerful insights into the complex systems of beliefs and actions which constitute a society and, ultimately, a culture (Candlin 1983: ix).

Paying keen attention to what is communicated will provide a key to a society and culture's inner workings. In the context of theological or sacred texts one might put it like this: how a text speaks reveals how it conceives of the universe, how the cosmos and a cosmic orientation is taken to be.

The fourth implication has to do with the special case of narratives. Whereas argumentative literature (such as the letters of the New Testament) openly addresses the situation it speaks to, narratives, especially ancient narratives, do not so easily give away their ideological point. With regard to ancient narratives one may suspect the presence of feedback loops, or redundancy or analogic communication. But none of it is explicitly there. Ostensibly the narratives about the life history of a man, Jesus of Nazareth, the Gospels address their own situations at a temporal and spatial distance from the time of Jesus. Yet they are not explicitly about the situation they speak to. And this is our dilemma, namely, their world does not exist, it has to be created. The interplay of the three text-processes mentioned earlier has to be put in motion by the interpreter, with imagination and guesswork! Let alone the fact that a complex narrative does not freely give its ideology and rhetorical aim away ('it is embedded in the totality of the text…it is only verbalised in bits and pieces' [Van Tilborg 1989: 27]), narratives have unique communicative characteristics.

On the one hand, a reader is easily misled by the mimetic quality of the work into thinking that it describes reality as it is. On the other, one has to keep in mind the distinction between story (the story facts) and discourse (how the story is told),[6] or the distinction by Genette, Bal and Rimmon-Kenan (with differing terms) between story (story facts), narrative (story facts-as-presented) and narration (as the act that produces the narrative as well as the context in which the narrative action took place). Understanding a narrative is trying to understand the relationship between these three aspects. Our only access to the rhetorical event is the material remains of it, namely, the narrative as story facts-as-presented. Everything else is gone. In the light of this it seems a too facile solution to claim, as does Fraser (1983: 31), that communication only succeeds when 'the speaker has an attitude which he *intends* to convey to the hearer in using language, and the hearer recognizes this attitude'. Authorial intention is a notoriously slippery concept, even more so in the case of ancient texts like the Gospels when there is nothing else apart from the materiality of the content to guide the reader in deciding on the intention of the text. And what about the (original) readers? Did they recognize the intention and act accordingly? We simply do not know. We can guess from the way their options are presented in the text what their situation *could have been like*. But the traces left by the Gospel of John in our intellectual history might furnish clues to a duality of possibilities of meaning construction furnished by the Gospel text. But more on that later.

To fathom what a text does/can do is to enter into a very complex set of relationships and web of data. No reader can exhaust the meaning

6. Derived from Chatman 1978.

potentials of a narrative text. My own attempt at aspects of the rhetoric and communication processes in John's Gospel is of necessity a modest attempt. It proceeds from a single perspective on textual communication, namely, from the point of view of what happens in communication processes and within that ambit tries to bring the various textures of the Gospel of John into an interplay with one another, with the ideology of the text as the organizing principle.

3. *Speaking of Utopias*

As stated at the outset with the reference to Foucault and the comprehensive interpretive analytic, the ideology of the interpreter is part of the subject under review. What is mine? Why my interest in rhetoric and terms like 'distortion', 'projection', 'manipulation' and 'world creation'?

I live in a country that is trying to reinvent itself as a new nation, a New South Africa. Terms such as 'rainbow nation', 'nation building', 'simunye' (= 'we are one'), 'affirmative action', 'redressing the wrongs of the past', 'historically disadvantaged', 'Masakhane' (= 'let us build together'), are all buzzwords giving content to the rhetoric of creation of a new identity and a new understanding of our world. As I wrote this I saw on the SABC television news during one of the news items in the background a poster of the ANC (the ruling party since the 'first democratic election' in 1994) which read, 'The Government that brings you Paradise'. That is a utopian claim. But more, it is a utopian claim with a veritable ancestry. It reminds one of the hymnic praises of Augustus as inaugurator of Paradise and has, arguably, a similar rhetorical and propagandistic intent to Virgil's *Fourth Eclogue* (which already in late antiquity was interpreted to be a foretelling of the birth of Christ, by the first Christian emperor, Constantine, in a speech delivered on one Good Friday of the second decade of the fourth century), and his *Aen.* 6.791-95.[7] Constantine's interpretation marks this expectation of a ruler-saviour inaugurating Paradise (or the Golden Age if you wish) as more than just

---

7.   'This, this is he, whom thou so oft hearest promised to thee, Augustus Caesar, son of a god, whom shall again set up the Golden Age in Latium' (Giamatti 1989: 25). The Golden Age of the Latin poets (Vergil, Ovid, Horace) and the Paradise of the Christian Fathers (e.g. Lactantius, Prudentius) and the Christian Sibyllists (*Sib. Or.* 2.313-38; 3.767-95; 8.205-12) have a remarkably similar content: political peace, economic security, harmony between all living creatures, agricultural fecundity.

political propaganda; it is imbued with a religious valuation of the highest order. The passion for Paradise was an essential feature of religion during the first few centuries of the Christian era and remained a constant part of Christianity as world-view.

This is a mentality that crops up time and again in South African political discourse. Not long ago the songwriter Mbongeni Ngema (now implicated in the Sarafina 2 financial scandal) produced a music video where the chorus in a cathedral-like setting hailed (the then) President Nelson Mandela as 'Our Saviour/Messiah'. This emerging civil religion bears an uncanny resemblance to the emperor cult of the first centuries of the Christian era. It is my contention that the Gospel of John mirrors this language to create an anti-Caesar out of Jesus of Nazareth, but, what is more, in the history of the Christian tradition this language went on to justify the evolution of mainstream Christianity into a world-view and political system every bit as oppressive and paranoid as that of the Roman empire.

But let me begin by defining what I mean by ideology in the words of Paul Watzlawick (1984: 206):

> The term *ideology* permits a multitude of definitions, but two elements are common to most of them: the basic supposition that the thought system (the 'doctrine') explains the world in its suchness, and, second, the fundamental, all-encompassing (and therefore generally binding) character of ideology.

How is this relevant to a study of the rhetoric of John's Gospel? One should recognize that the gospel is not about all sorts of bagatelles. It deals with life and death issues, with time and eternity, with judgment and deliverance; in short it deals with an understanding of how the world is. And this is where the communication processes of the Gospel of John start, with an assumption about how the world is. This base sentence can be formulated as follows: Jesus of Nazareth is the centre of the universe.

The name-phrase 'Jesus of Nazareth' stands here for the whole life story or *bios* of an individual who lived in the first third of the first century of the Christian era in Palestine. The phrase 'centre of the universe' indicates the function of the life story as myth. Myth or mythology should be understood here not as narratives about the origin of the gods or the world, but in the sense of identity-giving narratives. The emplotment of a new understanding of human being, world and cosmos and the relationship to fate and the gods in the emerging genre of the Greco-Roman novel serves as an indication of the emergence of a new outlook on the world given symbolic form in a new 'mythology', an 'anthropologized cosmos' as

J.Z. Smith once called it.[8] In essence it entails the entwining of ordinary human lives with the life of the divine, sometimes to the point of viewing human life as the embodiment of divinity.

An assumption such as the one above is not in itself a rhetorical statement. It becomes such when it is offered as an explanation to an other, when it is projected on an audience with a view to persuade them to 'see this, believe that and do the other'. We can now expand the base sentence to show the communicative and rhetorical aspects of this world-view:

> Jesus of Nazareth/this life story/this *bios* must be/become the centre of your universe.

8.   See J.Z. Smith (1978: 172-98). On the whole issue of the rise of the genre of the Greco-Roman novel and the rise of a new mythology, see, e.g., the discussion in Hägg (1983: 101-104), also the relevant chapter in Cameron (1991: 89-119). Much work has already been done in this field: see the overview in Tiede (1984: 1705-29) and Talbert (1978: 1619-51). Whether or not one wants to follow Reinhold Merkelbach in his thesis that the ancient Greek novel is a disguised 'showing' and explication of the ancient mysteries (and I personally have now much sympathy with his thesis) at least one should concede that if one views the problem from the perspective of text-linguistics, especially from the perspective of frame or script theories, then it must be assumed that there exists a much closer relation between the content of the story and recognizable reality for the readers. Newer studies in the rhetoric of communication, especially the field of fantasy theme analysis (Bormann 1989: 210-22), can help explain how fiction can be the vehicle of a shared understanding of the world (a 'fantasy'), how this vision of the world is legitimated when people lock into it ('fantasy chain') and how this becomes a larger rhetorical vision when more groups continue to lock into this shared vision of how things are, of how the world is. In the light of this it might be called for to return to Merkelbach's thesis, this time more sympathetically. It remains a fact that the various plots of the Greco-Roman novels mirror the plot of the myths of Isis and Osiris, Mithras or Helios. The point is not which was first, the myth and ritual or the novel, but the rhetorical effect of the literary genre. How is the self-projection of a generation(s) created and sustained in this literary genre? That is the question. Of course, it has been noted that the later Christian apocryphal acts bear a close family resemblance to the Greco-Roman novel (Hägg 1983: 154-65; also Pervo 1994: 239-54; Perkins 1994: 255-71; and with regard to Jewish literature, the 'Jewish novella', Wills 1994: 223-38). This is the point that Cameron makes, namely that Christianity grew to become the dominant ideology because its rhetorical vision of 'how the world is' picked up on the 'stories people wanted'. She also argues that it is exactly the character of early Christian literature self-expression as biographical narrative that gave it the appearance of divinely ordained historical truth (Cameron 1991: 92).

One can recognize behind this rhetorical statement the stated intent of the author of the Gospel (Jn 20.30-31). This vision serves either to lock an audience into the rhetorical vision or to keep them within the rhetorical vision. However one wants to understand the tense of the verb ('must be' or 'must become'), it should be clear that a social reality is indicated, namely, the sharing of a world, and this specific showing of 'how things are' depends on the social location of the participants in this communication event, as I will indicate shortly: that this showing is not free from rhetorical argument was shown by Warner (1990: 153-77). According to Warner, the Gospel of John is an intricate weaving together of narrative and argument or judgment. Many text phenomena (quotations, narrated direct speech, narration as in the Prologue, choice of metaphors, and the like) serve as witnesses to the God-relatedness of the story. The net effect is to make of the narrative less of a story about a historical person, than to make it a story about God. Then the base sentence can be amplified as follows:

> Because Jesus of Nazareth/this life story/this *bios* is the epiphany of the true God of whose tradition I/we are the custodians, it must be/become the centre of your universe.

Here a life story is given the highest valuation possible. It is also very easy due to theological bias to miss the rhetorical importance of this juxtaposition of life story and story about God. It assumes the ability to judge correctly how things really are and what lies behind everything. This is a powerful rhetorical ploy, especially when viewed in the context of Greco-Roman magic and Hellenistic philosophies (Stoicism, Epicureanism and Cynicism).[9] Hellenistic philosophy was characterized by an 'ethical bias'

---

9.   I deal in this discussion only with Stoicism since Epicureanism, Cynicism and magic traditionally did not receive any attention as possible 'backgrounds' to the Gospel of John. Suffice it to say that whereas Stoicism was society-affirming in its efforts to guide engagement in civic life, Epicureanism and Cynicism were society-negating in their propagation of withdrawal from and reversal of social values respectively (so Green 1990: 633 on Stoicism, 'the attempt to work out a creed that would enable men to come to terms with the world as it was, to operate successfully in it while at the same time retaining some kind of spiritual balance and moral self-respect'). In my construal of the 'political' meaning of John's Gospel this aspect of Stoic thought becomes important. Magic functioned according to the same logic underlying Stoic thought, namely, on the assumption of a sympathetic connectedness between all phenomena. Whereas Stoic philosophy had as its purpose to understand, know and predict the workings of reality in order to live according to it, magic had as

(Walbank 1992: 178) and was preoccupied with the question: what is the best way to live? (Sharples 1996: 3)[10] According to Stoic thinking, 'the most popular philosophy during the first two centuries of the Roman Empire' (Walbank 1992: 180), virtue was the only good, and virtue meant living in accordance with the will of god or nature, in essence, to fit in with how things are and how things work. Underlying this is the assumption that the organizing principle of the human psyche, *logos*, is consubstantial with the organizing principle of the whole universe, the divine *logos*. Human life as rational life should be in tune with the divinely ordained 'order of things'.[11] From here it was but a small logical leap for the Greco-Roman world to portray the emperor as *logos*, ordainer or organizer of the physical world (Chesnut 1978: 1310-32). This philosophical underpinning of imperial ideology was necessitated by the new situation of an all-powerful princeps, upon whose whims and paranoias depended, literally, the fate and welfare of states, cities and whole populations of nations. The idea, fundamental to Roman imperial ideology, of the ruler as embodiment of the Law, Reason or Logos of God, found expression not only in Roman political philosophy (Seneca and Plutarch) but also in Jewish thought (Philo of Alexandria),[12] even into the Christian empire of the fourth century as Eusebius of Caesarea[13] still proclaimed the

its purpose to manipulate reality to conform to the practitioner's expectations from life. Of course, knowledge was also essential for magical practices and perhaps because of this (assuming a similar understanding of the workings of the cosmos as in Stoic thought) Stoic thinking was also able to give a place to magical practices, especially divination and astrology.

10. In Stoicism the study of philosophy, physics and logic serve to shed light on ethics (Colish 1990: 23).

11. This is so movingly hymned by Cleanthes in his Hymn to Zeus (ll. 15-25):

> Nothing occurs on the earth apart from you, O God,
> Nor in the heavenly regions nor on the sea,
> Except what bad men do in their folly;
> But you know how to make the odd even,
> And so you have wrought together into one all things that are good and bad,
> So that there arises one eternal rationale (*logos*) of all things,
> Which all bad mortals shun and ignore,
> Unhappy wretches, ever seeking the possession of good things
> They neither see nor hear the universal law of God,
> By obeying which they might enjoy a happy life (Walbank 1992: 181).

12. *De vita Mosis*; *De Josepho*.

13. *Vit. Const.* 1.5; *De laudibus Constantini* 1.

emperor to be the 'image on earth of the heavenly rulership of the divine Logos, which had now, of course, become the second person of the Christian Trinity' (Chesnut 1978: 1311).

When the narrative of the Gospel of John starts with the *logos* who proceeded from God it leaves no doubt in the mind of the reader that here is presented the secret to a new divinely ordained 'order of things'. None of the Gospels merely contains the facts or life history of the main character, Jesus of Nazareth. The ritual life of the cult community is projected backwards into the history of the cult hero and narrativized into the foundational story of the cult community.[14] As myth and as narrativized and inscribed ritual, the narrative of the Gospel of John itself becomes the groundwork or constitution of a new society, a *thiasos* or *collegium* whose symbolic universe revolves around a different axis, the cult hero Jesus of Nazareth, their new *logos*, God manifest and anti-emperor.

Pretensions to privileged insight into the divinely ordained 'order of things' function rhetorically to overpower the partners in conversation, here, the audience. There is a curious story about an experiment recounted by Bavelas (Watzlawick *et al.* 1967: 39) where each subject was told he was participating in an investigation of how concepts were formed ('concept formation') and was given the same grey, textured card about which they had to formulate concepts. Two subjects were seen simultaneously, but separately. The one was told he was correct in 80 per cent of his formulations and the other told he was correct in only 50 per cent of what he said regarding the card. The ideas of those whose ideas were 'rewarded' with an 80 per cent correct mark remained at a fairly simple level, while those persons who were 'rewarded' with a frequency of only 50 per cent evolved complex, subtle and abstruse theories about the card, taking account of even the smallest detail of the card's composition. When

14. Ever since the advent of *Formgeschichte* this insight has determined the way we look at the Gospel narratives. The Gospels are therefore as much stories about the character of certain early Christian communities (those who 'locked into the fantasy') as they are narratives about the hero of the cult. Any socio-rhetorical cum literary reading of these texts will of necessity ask questions such as, why were these stories told like this, and why in these terms and with these vocabularies? (Again, the distinction between story, narrative and narration, or story facts, story facts-as-presented, and context- and intent-of-presentation.) That necessitates some thought to be given to the basic question of how the base story was manipulated in order to communicate in a specific context somewhere at some point in time. Ergo, 'the reader is in the text'! It is this insight that permits the narratives about Jesus to be read also as windows onto the world and specific context of the first audience(s) of these narratives.

brought together and asked to discuss their findings the persons with the
'simpler' ideas immediately succumbed to the 'brilliance' of the other's
concepts and conceded that the other had analysed the card accurately!

Gnostic speculations like those found in the *Apocryphon of John*, the
Gospel of Truth, *On the Origin of the World*, the *Gospel of the Egyptians*
or the great magical papyri are usually written off as purely fanciful
gobbledegook because it is so difficult to make sense of them. I now begin
to wonder whether that was not precisely the point, an intricate explanation of the world so as to dazzle the audience with its intellectual
brilliance. Consider the case of John's Gospel. Jesus is not just a man. He
is the Logos, co-creator; he has an indwelling alter ego; he traverses the
domains of heaven and earth; he is the same as God. He is the centre of the
universe. He is light; he is bread; he is life; he is the entrance; he is the
true vine; he is the true way. Much has been written on the symbolism of
John, or the metaphorical language of John's Gospel. Apart from symbols
or metaphors, it is perhaps called for in the light of our perspective here in
order to understand these word pictures of Jesus as mystifying explanations.[15] John made his point powerfully.

Viewed historically (i.e. from the perspective of the social and historical
texture of the text) this base sentence performs two actions. On the one
hand it relates the life story it narrates to the language of the other human
gods of its time, and it takes up the values of surrounding society and
comments on them (the aspect of similarity). At the same time, on the

---

15. Malina and Rohrbaugh (1998: 4-11) note a number of features of Johannine
language use that are useful to consider in this regard. First is the issue of relexical-
ization. This entails the development of a distinctive set of vocabulary to replace a
section of regular language use, basically amounting to new in-group slang for well-
known concepts. The new vocabulary marks the group as socially set apart. The second
is overlexicalization. A number of different terms, metaphors and phrases is used with
regard to Jesus, without any real progression in the depiction of Jesus; they represent,
rather, variations on one theme. Both these aspects imply an interpersonal side to this
language use. This language can only be understood by those on the 'inside', those
who have already committed themselves to be followers of Jesus of Nazareth. A third
feature I want to highlight is the function of John's language as anti-language. To
support this they quote Halliday, '"Antilanguage" is the language of an "antisociety",
that is "a society that is set up within another society as a conscious alternative to it"'
(p. 7). In the case of the Gospel of John, this would mean that the way the text speaks
marks the Johannine community as a group set apart, dissociating themselves from
mainstream civic life.

other hand, a disruption emerges, a jostling for the position of truth. This is the area of the polemics of the text: against the 'Jews', against the Romans, against anyone not holding the correct values and beliefs. Who represents the truth? Obviously, in retrospect, for so it shimmers through, the author as the voice that narrates the story, he is privy to privileged information; he knows what Jesus thinks; he knows what 'makes Jesus tick'; he is adopted as Jesus' son and successor to headship of Jesus' school.[16] Which reality is to be believed on which the society of truthful believers is to build their social organization?

But one could expand the base sentence once more. This time to give recognition to the fact that the narrative is not at home in a purely transcendental philosophy. It deals with concrete human beings living their concrete lives in a concrete society, making a living, socializing and experiencing the stresses and burdens of living under the yoke of the Roman empire. It can read as follows:

> Because Jesus of Nazareth/this life story/this *bios* is the epiphany of the true God of whose tradition I/we are the custodians, it must be/become the centre of your universe…because of the benefits you will derive from living thus.

At this point, three aspects of the discourse of John's story meet, namely, the text as narrative (*bios*), the rhetoric of the text (as its persuasive world projection) and its utopian vision. In the narrative of the Gospel of John we experience an emerging utopian vision that would later play out on a grand scale with the Christianization of the Roman empire.

---

16. I follow here Sjef van Tilborg's identification of the so-called Beloved Disciple with the author/narrator. The Beloved Disciple appears at the end of the story, from ch. 13 onwards, and in the way his privileged position vis-à-vis Jesus at the symposion table (the intimacy of leaning into his breast), Jesus' love towards him and his adoption as son to take care of Jesus' house (the episode at the cross of Jesus entrusting his mother to this disciple) are portrayed evoke the institution of school succession after the departure of the rabbi or philosopher. These practices were known from the Hellenistic world but also in the world of early Judaism. Similar tales of love preferences towards a special disciple were known with regard to Jochanan and his disciple Eliezer, Eliezer and his disciple Aqiba, Elisha and his disciple Meir, and Jochanan and his disciple Resh Laqish. Where this disciple appears in the narrative we find the 'testament of Jesus' , the farewell discourse and his dying words on the cross. The genre of the 'testament' in Greco-Roman literature had as its function to speak directly to the community hearing/reading the text. In this way the narrator/author is enshrined as the authoritative locus of the true tradition.

It would now be opportune to consider the components of ideological realities. I will summarize the theses put forward by Watzlawick (1984: 206-47):

> Because the cosmic order is incomprehensible to the average person, an ideology is all the more convincing the more it relies upon an unusual, superhuman or at least brilliant originator. Closely related to this is the thesis that the more it allies itself with a preferred mode of explanation like making claims to scientificity, the more convincing it is.[17]

> Because it is impossible to survive in a universe without meaning and order, an ideology as explanation of the world is psychologically (and with regard to the ancient world I would add, socially) necessary. Such an explanation of the world must be invulnerable and not leave any questions unanswered.

> Once a world-view is imbued with totalizing, eternal values, an ideology easily evolves into its opposite. And at this level it does not matter whether the content of ideologies differ: they evince a tyrannical stereotypy.

> It cannot demonstrate its truth from within. No matter how many witnesses to or proofs of Jesus' divine origins are given in the narrative, in the end they have to be believed, and coming to the truth is part of a mysterious process of being called by the Father as his children, given to Jesus by the Father. The counterproposal would run like this: those who refuse to believe, who oppose Jesus and the world-view espoused by John, are children of the Devil.[18]

> If an ideology is to be universally valid, it follows that only one position can be true. All others are heresy. The word *hairesis* originally meant choice, a condition in which one can choose. But not so in the view of John. The stark contrasts drawn between truth and untruth, light and darkness, life and death permit no freedom of choice. There is only one option, John's.

4. *Rhythms, Frames and Outlook*

We can move closer into the narrative of John to pick up the threads of his utopian vision. Since the rhetoric of the narrative can only be disclosed through a close attention paid to the interplay of textures, and since no single reading can grasp all the possible angles to a narrative text, I will be

17. Witness the revelatory character of John's narrative: the coming of God's envoy from God's world, the many identifications of Jesus as God's agent through the use of a variety of 'titles' for Jesus, the miracles as signs of God's presence, the disputes with the 'Jews' about Jesus' origins and authority.

18. E.g. Jn 8.42-47.

very selective in my configuration of textual phenomena in order to illustrate the points I made above. There are many possible angles to John's narrative but I have selected as a thread with which to unravel the knot the political language of John, the way he narrated the life story of Jesus in terms of the language of the imperium. Once we are able to see how the political language of imperium and emperor cult intrudes on the narrative, we will begin to see the social and ideological ramifications of the story.

As a guiding principle I have used the triad rhythms, frames and outlook. 'Rhythms' refers to what is repeated, what is returned to in new connections and configurations constantly creating new frameworks and contexts for the interpretation of text phenomena. 'Frames' refers to the evocations and resonances of social reality, both in the sense of tools in the hands of the author who deliberately slips in words and descriptions that will call up the correct mind-picture in the minds of the audience, and in the sense of keys that will enable the audience to recognize that it is their social situation which is being addressed.[19] And 'outlook', that slippery and elusive world-view that took symbolic form in the narrative, is the projected created world held out for the readers to share in.[20]

a. *Frames of Imperial Language*

In reading a narrative it is always necessary to refer back to the threefold distinction of story (story facts), narrative (story facts-as-presented) and narration (the act and its communication context that produces the act). It is on the level of story facts-as-presented that the language of the imperium intrudes as the way the story of Jesus is told, as the way in which Jesus' *bios* is presented *in the terms of* the political reality of the imperium.

19. I adhere to the 'conservative view' that the Gospel of John is to be located in Ephesus/Asia Minor, at the very least in the eastern provinces of the Roman empire. I cannot prove this provenance, I accept it. But the language of the text does make eminent sense when read in this context. It is because of its traditional identification with the city of Ephesus that I think the language of the imperium is such an appropriate key to the ideology of the Gospel, as the emperor cult had a very special meaning in the Roman province of Asia (i.e. Asia Minor). It was in this area where it grew strongest (see Price 1984). For the inbedding of John in an Ephesian context, see Van Tilborg 1996.

20. I am assuming some of the earlier work I have done on John and the emperor cult, see my forthcoming 'John and the Imperial Persona: Divine Redeemers and the Conflict of Utopias', so I will only shortly summarize.

As at the beginning of this essay, we should start at the end of John's narrative. From Jesus' triumphal entry into Jerusalem to his execution, the mood that prevails is shot through with political realities an Ephesian audience would have been well acquainted with. Jesus' triumphal entry in Jn 12.12-19 is portrayed in the same fashion as the *adventus* or *triumphus* with a description of the festive procession, the decoration of the scenery and the songs of praises (MacCormack 1972: 721-52). Jesus is hailed as the coming King of Israel. In the context of Ephesus this was a well-known phenomenon ever since the triumphal entry of Mark Anthony as 'New Dionysus' in 38 BCE and the *adventus* of Hadrian as 'New Dionysus' in 129 CE; the latter event marks the outer limit of the time frame under consideration. The religious roots of the *adventus* or *triumphus* never became extinct. The point that John is making through the portrayal of Jesus' entry is that this is the advent of a conquering god.

This line of portraying by means of political language is taken up again in the passion narrative from 18.28–19.27, especially from 19.1. In an ironical portrayal (perhaps an example of Johannine irony!) Jesus' trial is presented as the installation of a Roman imperial pretender. The scenes that follow one another are reminiscent of usurpation of power by an imperial pretender (Van Tilborg 1996: 110-11). In 19.1-3 the soldiers acclaim Jesus as king and invest him with the 'symbols of power': 'crown' and 'purple toga'. Then follows the epiphany before the people 19.4-7, where Pilate's function in the narrative is to be the herald who announces Jesus to the populace. This is followed in 19.8-12 by a discussion with a member of the senate about power during which the point is made that God is the source of power and that Jesus has a unique relation to that source of power. All are subject to it, even the emperor.

These scenes are significant because they highlight the tensions running deep between the Johannine community (in Ephesus?) and the Roman authorities and Jewish leadership as these tensions are narrativized into the Jesus life story. Jesus is received into the city as 'King of Israel', a judgment with which the Jewish leaders do not concur. It is they who deliver him over to the Roman governor on a charge of sedition, vying to be king in Caesar's place. Jesus' defence is that he is not that type of a king (18.36). Nevertheless, the Romans make him king (see the inscription on the cross 19.19-22) but the Jewish leaders refuse to have him foisted on them and they demand his crucifixion for Jesus made himself a son of god, meaning by that (if one heeds the context) that he made himself emperor, for they shout that they have no king except Caesar.

This depiction of Jesus' career as king is symptomatic of Rome's dealings with its client kings.[21] The Jewish reaction to the phenomenon of client kingdoms is well illustrated by the episode of the deliberation of the Jewish council in 11.45-53. According to the reported perspective of the Jewish leadership, the quality of their relations with Rome will determine the relative freedom they will enjoy. Loyalty to Rome would hold many benefits such as 'restored freedom and independence' (so inscriptions attest, of course purely nonsense since real freedom had long ceased to exist. This is just rhetorical freedom), alleviation of tax burdens and so on. In this context 'being a friend of Caesar' becomes relevant. The Romans made kings and deposed kings. According to the perspective of the text the Jews buy into imperial ideology and opt for loyalty to the Roman emperor. John's narrative portrays the Jewish leadership as negating the messianic expectations inherent in the kingship claims and royal titles used in the narrative to depict Jesus. For John, the Jewish leaders opt for the Roman utopia.

b. *The Benefits of Utopian Existence*
We can move back and forth through the narrative as we reconfigure the ratios between the various textures. The phenomenon of public benefactions provides one more nexus between the reality of the imperium and social reality or public life in Ephesus.[22] This is another instance where, for the Johannine community, reality meets language. Inscriptions testify to the fact that (next to public building works or the funding of games) feasting was counted as one of the most important expressions of euergetism.

It is sufficient to mention a single example that is of importance for a reading of the 'feasting scenes' of John. In an inscription from Kyme (some distance north of Ephesus), roughly contemporaneous to the New Testament era, Kleanax, priest of Dionysos Pandemos, is honoured for his generous distribution of food and wine.[23] Six times in the text it is mentioned that Kleanax provided for sumptuous public feasting on various

---

21. See the many examples in what is still a masterful exposition of the history of Roman rule in Asia Minor (Magie 1950).

22. Skillfully manipulated by the hands of the author. At the end of the episode of the miraculous feeding, he has the crowd chasing after Jesus to make him king by force. John knew what he was talking about. That is what kings are supposed to do, distribute food.

23. See the text in Kearsley 1994: 233-41.

occasions.[24] In the description of Kleanax's benefactions we find a direct imitation of Roman ethos, especially in the description of throwing food to the crowd (l. 38) (Kearsley 1994: 239). Under the Romans, most notably since Augustus, this was taken to new heights with regard to both the boasting phraseology and the size of the benefactions (*Res Gestai Divi Augusti* 15-16). The abundance of inscriptions that attest to the proliferation of epithets like 'saviour', 'benefactor' and the combination 'saviour and benefactor' enables us to see what an important feature such benefactions were for civic life in Asia Minor. That these benefactions were not just secular meals is demonstrated by the way in which the Kleanax inscription places the food and wine in relation to the gods (l. 18, the sanctuary of Dionysos; l. 31, New Years Day with sacrifices to the gods; l. 36, the Festival of the Lark; l. 41, Games of Augustus).

A further consideration will help us to see the links between benefactions such as these and utopian expectations. The combination of the gift of abundant wine (the wine miracle at Cana, Jn 2) and the dispensing of bread (the miraculous multiplication of Jn 6) find their counterpart in the combination of the cultic associations of Dionysus (provider of wine) and Demeter (provider of grain) in Ephesus. An inscription attests to the 'pro poleos Demetriastai kai Dionysou Fleo mystai' ('the Demetrios of the city and the initiates of bountiful Dionysus'). The connection is provided by the bounty and fruitfulness associated with both Demeter and Dionysus. 'Bounty' and 'fruitfulness' are essential descriptors of the returned Golden Age in utopian expectations. This is what we see in John 2 and 6, a generous dispensing of an overabundant supply of wine, food and bread.

In this context we should realize that a different understanding of what it means to be saved emerges. To be saved means to be relieved from the stresses and burdens of the everyday struggle to make a living. In a world constantly on the brink of famine an overabundant supply of food and wine is the very stuff of fantasy and utopian dreams.[25] The earliest

---

24. Lines 17-19 (to the 'citizens and Romans and nearby residents and foreigners'…'a crowd'), ll. 31-34 ('everyone in the city'…'many of the citizens and Romans'), l. 36 ('all the freedmen and slaves in the city'), l. 38 ('citizens, Romans, residents and foreigners'), l. 40 ('victorious athletes, magistrates and many of the citizens'), ll. 41-44 ('Greeks and Romans, and nearby residents and foreigners').

25. This was an old dream of a Golden Age where, as Hesiod, put it, men lived like gods without toil or grief (Green 1990: 392). In the comic poets we find tales of self-functioning utensils and rivers which ran with wine and gravy, fish baked themselves,

depictions of the Christian vision of utopia are (remarkably often) banquet scenes.[26] It can be argued that the many references to 'life' in John's narrative should be understood also in this domain of meaning.[27]

There is another point to this portrayal of the benefaction feeding in John 6 that is not without social relevance. It concerns the way the 'eucharistic' scene is narrated. Accounts of the assemblies of religious associations in the Greco-Roman world show that the usual fare at their banquets was bread and fish (as in Jn 6) and this accords with the earliest pictorial depictions of the Eucharist. So the effect of this narrated scene is to place the divine benefaction in the private sphere where the Johannine community gathers, withdrawn from public life.

Here too we encounter that strange character of ancient society as praise and honour culture. Because of his great and many benefactions Augustus let himself be labelled 'the one and only', 'first and foremost'. Functionally, this is not far removed from epithets for Jesus in John like *monogenes* ('unique', 'the one and only'), a description that harmonizes well with the description of the bread as divine food and the wine of the Cana miracle as unsurpassed wine.

c. *Framed Rhythms of Repetition: The Names of Jesus*
Once we understand how the author narrativizes his social context into the Jesus life story, we may begin to configure the relations between different text parts differently. In the context of the portrayal of Jesus as anti-emperor, we may rethink the many 'names' for Jesus in John. The portrayal of Jesus via naming is one of the outstanding features of John's Jesus *bios*. The variety is remarkable. There is Word/Logos (and creator),[28] Lamb of God (and if you accept, as I do, that this refers to the apocalyptic ram, then Son of Man belongs to this domain as well),[29]

---

trees bore roast birds that flew into the diner's mouth, kitchens did their own cooking and dishes were washed without human aid (Green 1990: 392). Later in the Middle Ages and early Modern period one can detect the effects of regular famines on the almost magical qualities with which foodstuffs like white bread came to be surrounded (see Camporesi 1989 and 1993).

26. See Snyder 1985 on early Christian art and what it says about how early Christians understood themselves. For the portrayal of the multiplication of the bread and its interpretation, see Schiller 1971: 164-67 and Grabar 1969: 8-9.

27. On 'life' as an organizing metaphor in John, see van den Heever 1992: 89-100.

28. Jn 1.1, 14.

29. Jn 1.29, 36 (Lamb of God), 51; 3.13, 14; 6.27, 53, 62; 8.28; 9.35-37; 12.23, 34; 13.31 (Son of Man).

Prophet/the One who was to come,[30] Rabbi (and Teacher),[31] Messiah (= Christ),[32] Son/only son/Son of God,[33] King of Israel/King of the Jews,[34] Lord/Teacher and Lord/Lord and God,[35] God's Holy One,[36] and Saviour of the world.[37] If we read the Gospel of John as a direct conversation between John and his Ephesian audience we may assume that the names and titles used for Jesus in the narrative 'explain' the main character to the audience in terms familiar to them. From the many narrated scenes in which the crowds or Jesus' opponents voice the question 'Who is he?'[38] it is clear that the identity of Jesus and the attitude towards him formed a central concern of the narrative. Called forth by these questions the names and titles for Jesus in the narrative function as answers to these questions but also suggest the meaning he has/should have for people. Again one is confronted with the question as to which would be the correct frame to fit to each of the titles. If we read them in an Ephesian context another pattern emerges.

The question of Jesus' identity which runs throughout the Gospel narrative is first explicitly voiced in 1.19-23. In the Andrew/Simon and Nathaniel scene, Jesus is identified as Messiah (= Christ), Son of God and King of Israel. At the end of the narrative the circle is closed again with Jesus identified as Christ, Son of God. In between Jesus is executed as King of Israel/King of the Jews and is acclaimed Lord and God. Again, theological bias might cause us to overlook the political dimension given to the narrative by these titles.

This titularization had special significance for the Roman province of Asia in the first century CE. It was here that the emperor cult really took off as a way of dealing with the hitherto unknown phenomenon (to the

30. Jn 4.44; 6.14; 7.40; 9.17; 12.13.
31. Jn 1.38, 49; 3.2; 6.25; 9.1; 11.8, 29; 13.13, 14; 20.16.
32. Jn 1.41; 4.25, 26; 7.26, 27, 31, 41; 9.22; 10.24, 25; 11.27; 20.31.
33. Jn 1.14, 18, 34 (= Lamb of God), 49; 3.17, 18, 35, 36; 5.18-29; 6.40; 8.28, 29-38 (implied equality with God); 10.33-38 (accusation that he makes himself God); 10.36; 11.4, 27 (the combination Lord + Christ + Son of God + One who has to come); 14.13; 19.7; 20.31.
34. Jn 1.49; 12.13, 15 (implied in 18.19-24, 37); 18.39; 19.3, 12 (King = Son of God), 19.
35. Jn 6.68; 9.38; 11.3, 11, 12, 21, 27, 32; 13.9, 13, 14, 36, 37; 14.5, 8; 20.28; 21.7, 15, 17, 21.
36. Jn 6.69.
37. Jn 4.42.
38. Jn 1.19, 21, 22; 7.26-31, 40-52; 8.25.

Greeks) of such absolute power (Price 1984). As a first-century papyrus phrased it: 'What is a god? [Answer] That which exercises power.' From the first tentative applications of the title 'god' and 'son of god' the use drastically increased by the halfway mark of the first century so that by the end of the century Domitian could insist on being called *dominus et deus*, 'lord and god'.[39] The title *kyrios*, 'lord', occurs in this 'political' sense and its use escalates throughout the first century. *Kyrios* becomes an important indication of the divine character of the one so named (Van Tilborg 1996: 41).

Other names fit into this political-divine pattern as well. Son of Man, for instance, stems from the apocalyptic tradition and indicates a figure that traverses the realms of heaven and earth, conversing with God, who will appear again as end-time saviour (Schnackenburg 1968: 529-42). And here one should realize that eschatology is not innocent. A quick perusal of apocalyptic material will establish how thickly utopian expectations of the reversal of fortunes are laid on. John's narrative, therefore, one must accept, is a portrayal of God's man as revolutionary warrior.

Consonant with this repetitive manner of expressing Jesus' identity is the use of the 'I am' sayings.[40] They take their form from the Isis areta-logies found around the region of the Aegian Sea especially Asia Minor. As self-promotions they tell of the benefits to be derived from the god, but in their grammatical form as demonstratives, the emphasis is placed on the *who*: 'it is I who will give'. Therein lies a polemic element. Jesus is thereby marked off against the other pretenders to the crown of centre of the universe. Furthermore, in putting Isiac self-revelatory language on Jesus' lips, John still moves within the ambit of imperial ideology. The Hellenized Egyptian goddess Isis was known, next to Dionysus, as a conquering god.[41] In the most complete Isis aretalogy, the one found in Kyme, Asia Minor, and dated to the first century BCE to first century CE, we read:

> l. 1   I am Isis, tyrant of every land…
> l. 25 I broke down the government of tyrants…
> l. 40 I am the Queen of war…
> l. 48 I set free those in bonds…

39. See Magie 1950: I, 405-629, Price 1984, and Van Tilborg 1996: 25-58 for the history of progressive divinization of the emperors.
40. See again van den Heever 1992 for a discussion of these sayings as metaphors.
41. For a fuller discussion of Isis as conquering tyrant, see Versnel 1990: 35-95.

Isis is here portrayed as liberating goddess. In this aspect she embodies the old Greek idea of the gods as destroyers of tyrants. However, Isis is simultaneously 'tyrant of every land' and it is this double play on Isis as tyrant and destroyer of tyrants which reflects accurately the double role of Rome as conquering empire and its self-promotion as upholder and restorer of early freedoms and constitutions (cf. Magie 1950: I). Her cult having been proscribed at Rome in the course of the second and first centuries BCE, she nevertheless endeared herself to the Flavians to become, eventually, the representation of Roman power at the borders of the empire in Europe from the second century CE onwards.

The significant point about both Dionysus and Isis is that, as conquering deities, they demand complete loyalty. Regularly occurring acclamations such as *heis Dionysos* ('Dionysus is one') or *Isis, una quae es omnia* ('Isis, you are the one and only') provide an insight into the mentality in operation in the Roman imperial ideology. Total allegiance is what is at stake. One might further surmise that the appellation of Jesus as *monogenes, unicus*, 'one of a kind' (Jn 1.14) should be understood in this context, especially if read in conjunction with the polemical character of the metaphors in John (the '*true* light', the '*true* vine', '*good* shepherd', the '*only true* way to life', '*true* vine'). He is the one and only, perhaps in conscious opposition of the *monos kai protos*, 'first and foremost', of Augustus's benefactions as promoted in the *Res Gestai* 16.1. Here again, in the exclusive perspective on the 'order of things' we see the ideology of utopian thinking in operation.

Utopian visions do not permit democratic dissent. Even as these visions conjure up dreams of egality and egalitarian societies existing in harmony, peace and prosperity, the reality is a very harsh contradiction to the dream. Those who dream the utopian dream are every inch as paranoid and intolerant of dissension from the dream as those who propagate the imperial ideology as the utopian vision. So it has been through history from the first recorded tyrants in Athens, to the Hellenistic tyrants, to the emperors in Rome, to the Christian empire and church, to the early modern period (for example Savonarola's Florence), to the Third Reich and Stalinist Russia and the Cambodia of Pol Pot.

d. *Outlook: Who is Right? John against the 'Jews'*
The pragmatic force of John's narrative is such as to dissociate it from the social reality evoked by his language use. It is closely allied to the question as to who represents the truth. John's language presents the

reader with a polemic against and dissociation from the (social) reality of imperial ideology, but no account of the polemics in John can leave unaccounted for the importance of the polemics against 'the Jews'. It is of the utmost importance for an understanding of John's rhetoric as well as for an understanding of the social context of this communicative text to consider the relation between John's anti-imperial rhetoric and the polemics against 'the Jews'.[42] I propose that the anti-imperial rhetoric of John sets the mood of his communication and relates it to the general political discourse of the day, while the anti-'Jewish' rhetoric localizes the communication event, namely, John's narrative, in a specific context and a more narrowly understood social setting where buying into imperial discourse was at issue.

The polemics in chs. 4 to 11 raise various issues, which can arguably be condensed to the following two questions. Who represents the true Jewish/Israelite tradition? And, are the Jews really free?[43]

If one takes John's narrative to be sympathetic to the Samaritans (see below), then it is possible to read the episode recounted in 4.27-42 as an implied criticism of the 'Jews' for it is the Samaritans who recognize Jesus as 'Saviour of the world' (another imperial title!).[44] According to the perspective of the text, the Samaritans buy into the ideology of Jesus as anti-emperor in contrast to the 'Jews' who are happy to be 'friends of Caesar'. One might surmise, therefore, that there were groups in the Mediterranean world who saw themselves as the true Israel. I take the inscriptions found at the synagogue of the Samaritans on Delos to mean exactly that (Llewelyn 1997: 148-51). The two Delian inscriptions (dated 250–175 BCE and 150–50 BCE respectively) attest to the presence of an association of schismatic Jews who designated themselves as *Israelitai*,

---

42. Most modern studies on John have made much about the aspect of the breaking away from early Judaism of the Johannine community. To remain with that line of questioning, however, is to remain in what is basically still a theological or christological questioning, even though one might emphasize the social matrix of such a separation of Church and synagogue. Reading the polemics against the 'Jews' in conjunction with the anti-imperial ideology allows one to construct the context of communication of John's narrative much more precisely, and what is more, so I believe, one can gain a clearer understanding of the origins of Christianity, at least with regard to a specific, albeit very important, locale.

43. I leave out of consideration for the purposes of this paper the polemics against (followers of) John the Baptist in Jn 1 and 3.22-26.

44. For a discussion of this episode in the light of imperial language, see Koester 1990: 665-80.

rather than *Ioudaioi*. The mention in the inscriptions of their contributions towards the temple cult at Mount Gerizim shows them to be Samaritans. Their self-appellation of 'Israelites' proclaims a descent from Jacob-Israel, which title lays claim to be in direct succession to Jewish tradition of an even greater antiquity than is implied by the *Ioudaioi* of contemporary Judaism. If one takes into account the positive evaluation of the term 'Israel' in John, the presence of Jesus' ministry in Samaria (the only Gospel to devote any attention to Samaria) and the known presence of Samaritan interests in Ephesus,[45] it could be ventured as an opinion that the Johannine community stood in some kind of close relationship with the Samaritan community.[46]

The Johannine polemics against the 'Jews' occupy a substantial section of the first part of the Gospel. In 5.1-17 Jesus encounters opposition from the 'Jews' for the healing on the Sabbath. At issue is whence his authority to do what he is doing. The ensuing reported discussion has Jesus answer to the charge that he healed on a Sabbath and that he is continuing the actions of the Father, and doing so with an authority derived from God himself. The ensuing discussion in 5.18-47 centres on Jesus' appropriation of divinity for himself. Again, the issue is whence his authority to claim filial intimacy with God the Father. And the answer provided is that had they understood the Jewish Scriptures and tradition, they would have realized that he is God incarnate (5.36-40); hence the reference to Moses in 5.46, 47. According to John, Jesus represents the true essence of Jewish tradition.

The narrated scenes of 7.10-31 (Jesus teaching the crowds and their conflicting opinions about him) and 7.45–8.59 (the unbelief of the Jewish leaders) thematize the unwillingness and inability of the Jewish leaders to see God in action in Jesus' actions. This opposition results eventually in the severance of the link of the Jesus-followers with the synagogue. According to the way it is portrayed in John, this is no peaceful parting, rather, it is the result of persecution, a 'putting out of' the synagogue. The last polemical episode that needs to be mentioned is 10.22-42. The essence

---

45. I refer here to the inscription erected c. 129 CE in honour of the proconsul Falco by Samaritans from Neapolis (Sebaste) (Van Tilborg 1992: 105).

46. But not quite (still?) part of the Samaritan community. The narrated conversation in 4.21-26 ('not in Jerusalem, nor on Gerizim...the Messiah who will reveal the real way to God is Jesus himself') serves to offer a 'third way', namely, in close proximity to the Samaritans, but unlike them who are still bound to their temple and traditions, centered on the worship of a human mediator of divinity.

of the conflict between Jesus and the 'Jews' is found in 10.33, namely the accusation that he 'makes himself God'.

When one takes a synoptic view of the polemical passages in John mentioned above, it is clear that they essentially centre on the question: Who is Jesus? Who stands behind him? How should one judge him? These are the questions that John is answering directly in the narrative (compare 7.40-42, 'He is the Prophet...he is the Christ', and 10.24-38, 'if you are the Christ, say it openly'). Jesus is, in John's perspective, the one speaking on God's behalf and occupies, because of this, the position of summation of Israelite/Jewish religious tradition and Scriptures as they are understood by (at least a part of) contemporary early Judaism.

The second big question touches on the issue of Jewish at-home-ness in the world. Jesus' opponents are quick to react to his accusation that being in untruth they are not free, that they have never been slaves (8.31-33). While at the time of writing of the Gospel this cannot have been true for the Jews in Palestine, this is true for the situation of Jews in Asia during the first century. Herod (later the Great) played an important role in procuring political rights and favours for Jews (especially from Ephesus) when he and Agrippa, the son-in-law of Augustus, toured the eastern Roman provinces (Magie 1950: I, 478-79). His own clan, the Herodians, extended their presence far beyond the boundaries of Palestine. A large group lived in Rome and Antioch (Hengel and Schwemer 1997: 229-30). But, even more, the Herodian clan was linked by blood to all the ruling families of the client kingdoms of Rome in the region, from Armenia, Pontus, Commagene, Emesa, Galatia and Parthia to minor aristocratic houses in Arabia and west to Pergamon and Ephesus (Hengel and Schwemer 1997: 454 n. 1178). The Herodians were politically open to Roman rule and viewed the rule of Rome as ordained by God's will, just as Josephus would later justify Roman rule (*War* 3.400-402).

It is in this sense, I think, that the 'not of this world' of John should be understood. Jesus' kingdom is 'not of this world' (19.36), quite literally. His kingdom is a counter-society in the hands of John.[47]

---

47. At this point the political dissociation implied by the phrase 'my kingdom is not of this world' is only the culminating point of a whole ensemble of oppositions running through the narrative from beginning to end: spirit/flesh, above/below, life/death, light/darkness, not of the world/the world, freedom/slavery, truth/lie, love/hate (Malina and Rohrbaugh 1998: 5). 'John's Gospel reflects the alternate reality John's group set up in opposition to its opponents, notably "this world" and "the Judaeans"' (Malina and Rohrbaugh 1998: 9).

5. *Cometh the man…*
(…cometh the church and the Christian empire)

Let us, now almost at the end of my argument, make a short digression through the thought world surrounding the narrative of the Gospel of John. I do this in order to demonstrate that John's Gospel fits into a larger pattern of utopian expectations. It is part of a utopian trajectory that visualizes the return of a golden age in conjunction with the coming of a saviour-figure who is the inaugurator of the 'golden age'. And this is my contention, namely, that John's Gospel emulates (consciously?) the imperial ideology which made Augustus out to be bringer of the utopian pax. It is to the Roman poets that we return.[48]

There comes a boy, says Virgil in his *Fourth Eclogue*, born from a virgin, who will inaugurate again the Golden Age:

> the great line of the centuries begins anew. Now the Virgin returns, the reign of Saturn returns; now a new generation descends from heaven on high. Only do thou, pure Lucina, smile on the birth of the child under whom the iron brood shall first cease, and a golden race spring up throughout the world! Thine own Apollo now is king! (ll. 5-10; Giamatti 1989: 23).

Then Virgil goes on to spell out the characteristics of Golden Age existence: the earth will give her bounty, animals will live in harmony with one another and man will not feel the strain of hard work (Giamatti 1992: 24). In his foundational mythology of the Julian dynasty, the *Aeneid*, Virgil makes explicit who the recipient of the adulation is:

> This, this is he, whom thou so oft hearest promised to thee, Augustus Caesar, son of a god, whom shall again set up the Golden Age in Latium (*Aeneid* 6.791-95; Giamatti 1989: 25).

Horace, in the *Sixteenth Epode*, a vision of peace and refuge after the ravages of the civil war, presents a similar picture of Golden Age existence, namely beautiful nature, fecund earth, ideal weather, harmony among all living creatures (Giamatti 1989: 28). According to Ovid's *Metamorphoses* 1.89-112, the essence of the Golden Age is social harmony,

---

48. Of course, the idea of a Golden Age is far older. The first mention of it occurs in Hesiod's *Works and Days*, and it appears again in Homer's *Odyssey* Book 6, then also in the Homeric Hymns and Pindar (Giamatti 1989: 11-23). I limit myself to literature from the same time-frame as the Gospel of John and other early Christian literature.

natural fecundity, political peace, economic security, personal happiness, a time noble and simple, rustic and blissful (Giamatti 1989: 30).

We can compare this to other utopian visions. I would mention only one example, *Sibylline Oracles* 3.[49] In between various oracles of judgment we find references to the coming of a saviour king and to a restored Golden Age:

> And then God will give great joy to men,
> for earth and trees and countless flocks of sheep
> will give to men the true fruit
> of wine, sweet honey and white milk
> and corn, which is the best of all for mortals
>
> (*Sib. Or.* 3.619-23).

> And then God will send a King from the sun
> who will stop the entire earth from evil war,
> killing some, imposing oaths of loyalty on others;
> and he will not do all these things by his private plans
> but in obedience to the noble teachings of the great God
>
> (*Sib. Or.* 3.652-56).

> And then, indeed, he will raise up a kingdom for all
> ages among men, he who once gave the holy Law
> to the pious, to all of whom he promised to open the earth
> and the world and the gates of the blessed and all joys
> and immortal intellect and eternal cheer.
> From every land they will bring incense and gifts
> to the house of the great God. There will be no other
> house among men, even for future generations to know,
> except the one which God gave to faithful men to honor
> (for mortals will invoke the son of the great God).
> All the paths of the plain and rugged cliffs,
> lofty mountains, and wild waves of the sea
> will be easy to climb or sail in those days,
> for all peace will come upon the land of the good.
> Prophets of the great God will take away the sword
> for they themselves are judges of men and righteous kings.
> There will also be just wealth among men
> for this is the judgement and dominion of the great God.

49. The endorsement of Cleopatra in this text should probably cause the text to be read as a Jewish oracle originating in Egypt. However, since there are many echoes of this oracle in Christian literature (especially Lactantius's *Divine Institutes*) and since the Pseudepigrapha were only preserved in Christian circles, we may take this text as indicative of early Christian values. See n. 7 above for references to other *Sibylline Oracles*.

Rejoice, maiden, and be glad, for to you the one
who created heaven and earth has given the joy of the age.
He will dwell in you. You will have immortal light.
Wolves and lambs will eat grass together in the mountains.
Leopards will feed together with kids.
Roving bears will spend the night with calves.
The flesh-eating lion will eat husks at the manger
like an ox, and mere infant children will lead them
with ropes. For he will make the beasts on earth harmless.
Serpents and asps will sleep with babies
and will not harm them, for the hand of God will be upon them
                                (*Sib. Or.* 3.767-95).[50]

While this example may suffer from the fact that it essentially represents a dream, the realization of which can only be hoped for, there was at least one attempt to put utopian ideas into practice in the Jewish world, and that was the Qumran community of Essenes. Doron Mendels (1979: 207-22) has compared the features of the Qumran community as they are presented especially in the *Community Rule* (1QS and 1QSa). He has demonstrated (convincingly to me) that the Essenes exhibited the same type of social organization as the ideal and utopian societies written about by Iamboulos and Euhemeros. Some of the features the Essenes have in common with these utopian communities are: strict isolation from the outside world, internal harmony, small community led by elders, community of goods, cooperation and equality, common meals, asceticism and special diet, uniformity of dress, antithesis to city life, a concern with purity and baptisms, opposition to marriage, the absence of a temple and a stark dualism. This self-representation of the Essenes as a utopian society came at a time when the ideal of a socially dissociated utopia became popular in the Hellenistic world (Mendels 1979: 221).

If our localizing of John's narrative is correct, then one may read John's rhetoric as creating a similar dissociated group (sect?) as the Essene community and one which is also utopian in character.

6. *Concluding Remarks*

This is what John does, he creates a counter-world in which to live, but one that demands complete loyalty. It is a utopian vision that assumes a reversal of fortunes. But what happened after the text?

50. Translation from Charlesworth 1983: 376-79.

The utopian vision persisted into the Christian empire and later. The Virgilian vision of a utopian Golden Age was kept alive in Lactantius's *Divine Institutes*, Book 5, and also in Prudentius's Book 2 of the *Contra Symmachus* (Giamatti 1989: 30-31). In their hands the Islands of the Blessed of the classical Golden Age visions became the Christian paradise. But apart from this, the imperial imagery was also retained in the Christian vision. E.A. Leach (1983: 67-88) has demonstrated how the iconography of post-Nicene Christian orthodoxy employed imperial symbols to suggest the hierarchy of divine mediation that was characteristic of the orthodox theology of a Trinity removed far beyond human reach and experience. This was characteristic of a millennial movement that had itself become imperial and hence, unmillennial, as it established itself in the mainstream of political life of the late Roman period. Millenarianism is an option for those who join new cults because they experience themselves as politically disenfranchised and millenarian cults mostly start life as egalitarian groups (Leach 1983: 72). The Gospel of John has had a life in both worlds, millenarian and anti-millenarian.

Epiphanius's discussion of the Nazoraeans in the *Panarion*, or *Medicine Chest against the Heresies* 2.29 provides a clue to the development of imperial mentality in the post-Nicene church. Answering the question as to why Jesus, if he was a descendant of David, did not occupy the throne in Judaea, Epiphanius put it thus (2.29.4.8-9; my emphasis):

> For he who is always king did not come to achieve sovereignty. Lest it be thought that he advanced from a lower estate to a higher, he granted the crown to those whom he appointed. For his throne endures, and there will be no end of his kingdom. And he sits on the throne of David, and has *transferred David's crown and granted it, with the high priesthood, to his own servants, the high priests of the catholic church.*

The Gospel of John was arguably the most important source document for christological thought in the first few Christian centuries and not only for the christological controversies which led to the ecumenical councils of the fourth and fifth centuries CE (witness the important role ascribed to the Gospels of Matthew and John by Eusebius in his *Church History*, as well as the importance attached to John by Irenaeus in his *Adversus Haereseis*). Christian discourse from the third century onwards was dominated by considerations of the incarnation of God: How is God mediated? How does God appear in human history? As Leach has argued, incarnation is not an innocent issue; it touches on matters of great importance, which have severe social and political ramifications.[51] In the case of the early Roman empire as well as the later Roman empire, the incarnation of divinity is at the centre of its symbolic universe. Its symbols and meta-phors justify a hierarchical and tyrannical empire. So we read in that great apologist of the first 'Christian' emperor, Eusebius's *Church History*:

> [to free those subject to tyranny at Rome, Constantine and Licinius]...were stirred up by the King of kings, God of the universe and Saviour (9.9.1)

> ...calling in prayer upon God who is in heaven, and his Word, even Jesus Christ, the *Saviour of all*, as his ally (9.9.2; my emphasis)

> [After the victory over Maxentius] Constantine by his very deeds sang to *God the Ruler of all* and Author of the victory; then he entered Rome with hymns of triumph, and all the senators and other persons of great note, together with women and quite young children and all the Roman people, received him in a body with beaming countenances to their very heart as a *ransomer*, *saviour* and *benefactor*, with praises and insatiable joy (9.9.9; my emphasis).

It should be quite clear what it is that has happened here. The old imperial titles and epithets have been transferred to God, who is now conceived in imperial terms. There is, however, a simultaneous transferral back to his earthly representative, who appears in his stead as saviour and benefactor, also imperial honorific epithets. When one keeps in mind that the narrative of John's Gospel portrays Jesus as saviour and benefactor, as earthly epiphany and representative of the God whose programme is the agenda for his actions, one can see that a structural parallel exists between John's Jesus//God, and Eusebius's Constantine//God. Constantine has de facto become a 'son of God'-like emperor. The language of John created the Christian church-empire.

This is perhaps the biggest Johannine irony: even as John creates an audience dissociated from the world, his later readership would be very much at home in the world. His ideology of opting out could later revert into its opposite after the Christianization of the empire with disastrous effects for those who 'did not make it'. The Christian empire did not come into existence as if in one short moment and by universal consent. It was constructed. Every century of the crucial growth phase, the second, third

---

51. '[I]n what sense was early Christian doctrine intermeshed with its social context?... As a result, the seemingly endless debate about the nature of the Trinity and the limits of Christ's humanity continues to be treated as if it were part of an ongoing seminar continued over centuries within the closed doors of a University Faculty of Theology' (Leach 1983: 69). I could not have put it better.

and fourth centuries saw progressively more comprehensive heresiologies published. The second century saw Irenaeus' *Adversus Haereseis*. The third century, Hippolytus's *Refutatio omnium haeresium*, and the fourth century, Epiphanius's *Panarion* or *Medicine Chest against the Heresies*. The bulk of the contents of these heresiologies did not consist of the descriptions of the heretical sects themselves. The description of the heresies is in each case followed by a voluminous exposition of the true and orthodox faith.

Thus, by chipping away at the Right and the Left was the Christian centre created. But the way it came into being, more often than not through coercion, pogrom and sword, was not necessarily good news for those who did not make it, the Gnostics, Manichees, Jewish Christians or Arians.

BIBLIOGRAPHY

Beasley-Murray, G.R.
    1987   *John* (WBC, 36; Waco: Word Books).
Berger, P.L., and T. Luckmann
    1967   *The Social Construction of Reality: A Treatise in the Sociology of Knowledge* (Harmondsworth: Penguin Books).
Bormann, E.G.
    1989   'Fantasy and Rhetorical Vision: The Rhetorical Criticism of Social Reality', in B.L. Brock, R.L. Scott and J.W. Chesebro (eds.), *Methods of Rhetorical Criticism: A Twentieth Century Perspective* (Detroit: Wayne State University Press): 210-22.
Cameron, A.
    1991   *Christianity and the Rhetoric of Empire: The Development of Christian Discourse* (Sather Classical Lectures, 52; Berkeley: University of California Press).
Camporesi, P.
    1989   *Bread of Dreams: Food and Fantasy in Early Modern Europe* (Oxford: Polity Press).
    1993   *The Magic Harvest: Food, Folklore and Society* (Oxford: Polity Press).
Candlin, C.N.
    1983   'Preface', in Richards and Schmidt (eds.) 1983: vii-x.
Cassidy, R.
    1983   *John's Gospel in New Perspective* (Maryknoll: Orbis Books).
Charlesworth, J.M. (ed.)
    1983   *Old Testament Pseudepigrapha*, I (London: Darton, Longman & Todd).
Chatman, S.
    1978   *Story and Discourse: Narrative Structure in Fiction and Film* (Ithaca, NY: Cornell University Press).

Chesnut, G.F.
    1978   'The Ruler and the Logos in Neopythagorean, Middle Platonic, and Late
                Stoic Political Philosophy', in *ANRW*, II.16.2: 1310-32.
Colish, M.L.
    1990   *The Stoic Tradition from Antiquity to the Early Middle Ages*. I. *Stoicism in
                Classical Latin Literature* (Leiden: E.J. Brill).
Dodd, C.H.
    1978   *The Interpretation of the Fourth Gospel* (Cambridge: Cambridge University
                Press).
Foucault, M.
    1982   *The Archaeology of Knowledge* (London: Tavistock).
Fraser, B.
    1983   'The Domain of Pragmatics', in Richards and Schmidt (eds.) 1983: 29-60.
Giamatti, A.B.
    1989   *The Earthly Paradise and the Renaissance Epic* (New York: Norton [1996]).
Grabar, A.
    1969   *Christian Iconography: A Study of its Origins* (London: Routledge & Kegan
                Paul).
Green, P.
    1990   *Alexander to Actium: The Hellenistic Age* (London: Thames & Hudson).
Hägg, T.
    1983   *The Novel in Antiquity* (Berkeley: University of California Press).
Harris, E.
    1994   *The Prologue of the Fourth Gospel* (Sheffield: Sheffield Academic Press).
Hengel, M., and A.M. Schwemer
    1997   *Paul between Damascus and Antioch: The Unknown Years* (London: SCM
                Press).
Kearsley, R.A.
    1994   'New Testament and Other Studies §10: A Civic Benefactor of the First
                Century in Asia Minor', in S.R. Llewelyn and R.A. Kearsley (eds.), *New
                Documents Illustrating Early Christianity*, VII (Grand Rapids: Eerdmans).
Koester, C.R.
    1990   '"The Saviour of the World" (John 4.42)', *JBL* 109.4: 665-80.
Leach, E.A.
    1983   'Melchisedech and the Emperor: Icons of Subversion and Orthodoxy', in
                E.A. Leach and D.A. Aycock (eds.), *Structuralist Interpretations of Biblical
                Myth* (Cambridge: Cambridge University Press): 67-88.
Llewelyn, S.R.
    1997   'An Association of Samaritans at Delos', in S.R. Llewelyn (ed.), *New Docu-
                ments Illustrating Early Christianity*, VIII (Grand Rapids: Eerdmans).
MacCormack, S.
    1972   'Change and Continuity in Late Antiquity: The Ceremony of *Adventus*',
                Historia 21: 721-52.
Magie, D.
    1950   *Roman Rule in Asia Minor* (2 vols.; Princeton: Princeton University Press).
Malina, B., and R. Rohrbaugh
    1998   *Social-Science Commentary on the Gospel of John* (Minneapolis: Fortress
                Press).

Meeks, W.
    1972   'The Man from Heaven in Johannine Sectarianism', *JBL* 91: 44-72.
    1985   'Breaking Away: Three New Testament Pictures of Christianity's Separation from the Jewish Communities', in J. Neusner and E.S. Frerichs (eds.), *'To See Ourselves as Others See Us': Christians, Jews, 'Others' in Late Antiquity* (Chico, CA: Scholars Press): 93-116.

Mendels, D.
    1979   'Hellenistic Utopia and the Essenes', *HTR* 72: 207-22.

Morgan, J.R., and R. Stoneman (eds.)
    1994   *Greek Fiction: The Greek Novels in Context* (London: Routledge).

Morris, L.
    1971   *The Gospel according to John* (NICNT; Grand Rapids: Eerdmans).

Moore, S.D.
    1989   *Literary Criticism of the Gospels: The Theoretical Challenge* (New Haven: Yale University Press).

Neyrey, J.H.
    1988   *Ideology of Revolt: John's Christology in Social Science Perspective* (Philadelphia: Fortress Press).

Perkins, J.
    1994   'Representation in Greek Saints' Lives', in Morgan and Stoneman (eds.) 1994: 255-71.

Pervo, R.I.
    1994   'Early Christian Fiction', in Morgan and Stoneman (eds.) 1994: 239-54.

Price, S.R.F.
    1984   *Rituals and Power: The Roman Imperial Cult in Asia Minor* (Cambridge: Cambridge University Press).

Richards, J.C., and R.W. Schmidt (eds.)
    1983   *Language and Communication* (London: Routledge).

Robbins, V.K.
    1996a   *Exploring the Texture of Texts: A Guide to Socio-Rhetorical Interpretation* (Valley Forge, PA: Trinity Press International).
    1996b   *The Tapestry of Early Christian Discourse: Rhetoric, Society and Ideology* (London: Routledge).

Robinson, J.A.T.
    1985   *The Priority of John* (London: SCM Press).

Sanders, J.A.
    1998   'The Hermeneutics of Translation', *Explorations* 12.2: 1.

Schiller, G.
    1971   *Iconography of Christian Art*, I (London: Lund Humphries).

Schnackenburg, R.
    1968   *The Gospel of John* (2 vols; London: Burnes & Oates).

Sharples, R.W.
    1996   *Stoics, Epicureans and Sceptics: An Introduction to Hellenistic Philosophy* (London: Routledge).

Smith, J.Z.
    1978   *Map Is Not Territory* (Leiden: E.J. Brill).

Snyder, G.F.
 1985   *Ante Pacem: Archaeological Evidence of Church Life before Constantine* (Macon, GA: Mercer University Press).
Stibbe, M.
 1994   *John's Gospel* (New Testament Readings; London: Routledge).
Talbert, C.H.
 1978   'Biographies of Philosophers and Rulers as Instruments in Religious Propaganda in Mediterranean Antiquity', in *ANRW*, II.16.2: 1619-51.
Tiede, D.
 1984   'Religious Propaganda and Gospel Literature of the Early Christian Mission', in *ANRW*, II.25.2: 1705-29.
van den Heever, G.A.
 1992   'Theological Metaphorics and the Metaphors of John's Gospel', *Neot* 26.1: 89-100.
 1998   'Finding Data in Unexpected Places: A Socio-Rhetorical Reading of John's Gospel', *Neot* 33.2: 343-64.
Van Tilborg, S.
 1989   'The Gospel of John: Communicative Processes in a Narrative Text', *Neot* 23.1: 19-32.
 1992   'Efese en het Johannesevangelie', *Schrift* 141: 79-111.
 1996   *Reading John in Ephesus* (NovTSup, 83; Leiden: E.J. Brill).
Versnel, H.S.
 1990   *Inconsistencies in Greek and Roman Religion. I. Ter Unus. Isis, Dionysos, Hermes: Three Studies in Henotheism* (Studies in Greek and Roman Religion, 6; Leiden: E.J. Brill).
Walbank, F.W.
 1992   *The Hellenistic World* (London: Fontana).
Warner, M.
 1990   'The Fourth Gospel's Art of Rational Persuasion', in M. Warner (ed.), *The Bible as Rhetoric: Studies in Biblical Persuasion and Credibility* (Warwick Studies in Philosophy and Literature; London: Routledge): 153-77.
Watzlawick, P., J.B. Bavelas and D.D. Jackson
 1967   *The Pragmatics of Human Communication: A Study of Interactional Patterns, Pathologies and Paradoxes* (New York: Norton).
Watzlawick, P. (ed.)
 1984   *The Invented Reality* (New York: Norton).
Wills, L.M.
 1994   'The Jewish Novellas', in Morgan and Stoneman (eds.) 1994: 223-38.
Wuellner, W.
 1991   'Rhetorical Criticism and its Theory in Culture-Critical Perspective: The Narrative Rhetoric of John 11', in P.J. Hartin and J.H. Petzer (eds.), *Text and Interpretation: New Approaches in the Criticism of the New Testament* (NTTS, 15; Leiden: E.J. Brill): 171-86.

Part IV

RHETORICAL CRITICISM OF THE PAULINE LETTERS

Contrary Arguments in Paul's Letters

Anders Eriksson

One of the basic tenets of classical rhetorical theory is that the speaker should always keep the opposing viewpoint in mind. Remembering the opposite side was essential in actual oratory when the opposing party was present, especially since both sides were trying to win the favor of the hearers. The rhetorical training was geared at winning the favorable verdict from the judges in the courtcase, obtaining the assent of the people in a political speech, and securing the admiration of the audience in the festive oration. To accomplish this goal the speaker was taught how to twist and turn the facts of his own case to make the case more worthy of commendation, as well as how to discredit the opposing viewpoint.

A review of the rhetorical handbooks shows how closely connected these two aspects were in the teaching of rhetoric. Not only did the speaker need to be able to present his own case favorably and to support it with arguments, but he also had to be able to discredit the opponent's case as well. In rhetorical theory confirmation and refutation are simply seen as opposite sides of the same coin, praise is the opposite of blame, the just the opposite of the unjust, the advantageous the opposite of the disadvantageous. The use of polarity is indeed one of the central features of classical rhetorical theory.

Not surprisingly, this polarity is also found in the *progymnasmata*, the preliminary rhetorical exercises. In the elaboration of the chreia, the argument from the contrary was designed to engage the student in oppositional discourse. The contrary argument is one of the four basic categories used to support a thesis in argumentation; the other three are the arguments from analogy, example and ancient testimony.[1] It achieves its

---

1.   This paper is an initial report from the project Early Christian Letters in the Light of Classical Rhetoric and Epistolography sponsored by the Swedish Research Council for the Humanities. My part of the project is to review Paul's letters from the perspective of contemporary rhetoric. I am especially interested in analyzing Paul's

supporting role in an indirect fashion by disproving, or at least putting in doubt, the opposing alternative.

The purpose of this paper is to investigate to what extent Paul uses arguments from the contrary in his letters. To achieve this purpose we first need to look at the description of the argument from the contrary in the rhetorical handbooks.[2] With that clearer definition in mind we can then return to Paul's letters and determine if Paul uses contrary arguments and, if he does, what they look like.

1. *Contrary Arguments in Rhetorical Theory*

In the elaboration of the chreia, the contrary argument is that type of argument which engages in deductive logical argumentation. The argument from analogy is based on everyday occurrences and typically involves farmers and imagery taken from nature. The argument from example adduces a pertinent parallel from history or literature to prove a point. The argument from ancient testimony supports the case by invoking statements from the canon considered authoritative by the audience.[3] As a school exercise, the contrary argument draws upon the students' previously completed studies in logic. It reminds the becoming orator that a speech must be related to an opposing viewpoint.

According to Aristotle's *Topica* there are four kinds of opposites or ἀντικείμενα.[4] A statement can stand in opposition to another statement by being: (1) a direct contradiction of terms (ἀντίφασις), like 'affirmation' and 'negation', or 'to be' and 'not to be'; (2) a relative opposite (τὰ πρός τι), such as 'double' and 'half', and 'master' and 'servant'; (3) the opposites of state and privation (ἕξις and στέρησις), that is, the possession of

argumentation in light of these four basic categories. My colleague Walter Übelacker will look at the importance of letter conventions for the analysis of New Testament letters.

2.   The study of the handbooks helps us understand what the argument is. Whether Paul was influenced by handbook rhetoric and whether he used the argument consciously is another issue.

3.   The best presentation of the different types of arguments in the *chreia*-elaboration is by B. Mack, 'Elaboration of the Chreia in the Hellenistic School', in B. Mack and V.K. Robbins, *Patterns of Persuasion in the Gospels* (Sonoma, CA: Polebridge Press, 1989), pp. 31-67. See especially the section on the elaboration in Hermogenes, pp. 57-63.

4.   *Top.* 2.2 (109b17-23); 2.8 (113b15); 5.6 (135b8-136b14). Cf. Cicero, *Top.* 11.47-49. Translations, unless otherwise noted, are from the LCL.

something and the privation of it, such as sight and blindness; or finally (4) a statement can be opposed to another statement by being its contrary. Aristotle's *Topica* treats these possible types of arguments, and all four types of opposites are successively treated as well. In his *Rhetoric*, however, Aristotle limits his instruction to the contrary type of opposition. Contraries are appropriately regarded as the most useful kind of opposites in actual discourse.

a. *Contraries*

What then are contraries? Contraries (τὰ ἐναντία) are defined as 'extreme opposites under the same genus...which cannot reside in the same subject together'.[5] In *Rhetoric* (2.23.1) Aristotle mentions self-control and lack of self-control as typical contraries. They are the two extremes of virtue and vice, under the genus ἦθος or moral character. Some contraries are logical opposites, like 'good' and 'bad', 'black' and 'white', 'long' and 'short', 'quick' and 'slow'. In dialectics and rhetoric the contraries used are not necessarily true, but, just like the other persuasive probabilities, they are based on assumptions that most people would accept and which do not require further demonstration. They are dependent on ἔνδοξα.[6]

Aristotle gives the following example which shows that contraries are dependent on the opinions shared by the audience:

> The possibility of anything, in respect of their being or coming to be, implies the possibility of the contrary: as for example, if it be possible for a man to be cured, it is possible for him also to fall ill: for there is the same power, faculty, potentiality, i.e. possibility of affecting a subject, in the two contraries, in so far as they are contrary one to another.[7]

In this case the existence of 'health' implies the existence of its contrary 'illness', because the existence of something also implies its non-existence. This contrariety is not phrased in a strictly logical fashion as it

5. E.M. Cope, *Commentary on the Rhetoric of Aristotle*, II (ed. J.H. Sandys; Cambridge: Cambridge University Press, 1877), p. 179.

6. In the first chapter of the *Topica* Aristotle distinguishes between scientific demonstration, which proceeds from premises that are necessarily true, and dialectical reasoning, which proceeds from generally accepted opinions. He defines the latter ἔνδοξα as opinions 'which commend themselves to all or to the majority or to the wise—that is, to all of the wise or to the majority or to the most famous and distinguished of them', *Top.* 1.1 (100b22-24).

7. Aristotle, *Rhet.* 2.19.1 [1392a]. G.A. Kennedy (trans.), *Aristotle on Rhetoric: A Theory of Civic Discourse* (New York: Oxford University Press, 1991).

is derived from the experience of ordinary people who know that they can be healthy as well as sick.

Contraries can be used for a variety of purposes. One purpose is to understand the distinctions being made in an argumentation when a particular expression is used. This is valuable since such an exercise helps one detect ambiguities in meaning. How these ambiguities can be found by looking at contraries is described by Aristotle:

> First, examine the case of its contrary and see if it is used in several senses, whether the difference be one of kind or in the use of a word. For in some cases a difference is immediately apparent in the words used. For example, the contrary of 'sharp' [ὀξύς] when used of a note is 'flat' [βαρύ], when it is used of a material substance, it is 'dull' [ἀμβλύ]. The contrary of 'sharp', therefore, obviously has several meanings, and, this being so, so also has 'sharp'; for the contrary will have different meanings, corresponding to each of those meanings. For 'sharp' will not be the same when it is the contrary of 'blunt' and when it is the contrary of 'flat', though 'sharp' is the contrary in both cases.[8]

As this example with the word 'sharp' illustrates, the search for contraries becomes an analytical tool which ensures that propositions are correctly defined and will hold up under the opponent's scrutiny. Conversely, analyzing the opponent's use of contraries helps the orator see the opponent's inconsistencies.

Earlier in the *Topica*, Aristotle has already pointed out that contraries can be used to secure propositions. When a speaker knows the opinions of the listeners, he can appropriately make use of the contrary opinion:

> In like manner, also, propositions made by way of contradicting the contrary of received opinions [τὰ τοῖς ἐνδόξοις ἐναντία] will seem to be received opinions; for if it is a received opinion that one ought to do good to one's friends, it will also be a received opinion that one ought not to do them harm. Now that we ought to harm our friends is contrary to the received opinion, and this stated in a contradictory form is that we ought not to harm our friends. Likewise also, if we ought to do good to our friends, we ought not do good to our enemies; this also takes the form of a contradiction of contraries, for the contrary is that we ought to do good to our enemies. The same is true of all the other cases.[9]

Thus the contradiction of the contrary is another way of phrasing the original statement. The usefulness of contraries is obvious in that they

---

8. Aristotle, *Top.* 1.15 (106a10-20).
9. Aristotle, *Top.* 1.10 (104a20-24).

allow the speaker to vary his propositions and make them stronger by exploring the opposite side of the issue.

Not all uses of contraries result in a contrariety. Aristotle mentions six ways in which contraries may be combined, but only the last four contraries actually result in a contrariety:

> That there are six kinds of combinations is obvious; for either (a) each of the contrary verbs will be combined with each of the contrary objects, and this in two ways, for example, 'to do good to friends and to do harm to enemies', or, conversely, 'to do harm to friends and to do good to enemies'; or (b) both verbs may be used with one object, and this also in two ways, for example, 'to do good to friends and to do harm to friends', or, 'to do good to enemies and to do harm to enemies'; or (c) one verb may be used with both objects, and this also in two ways, for example, 'to do good to friends and to do good to enemies', or, 'to do harm to friends and to do harm to enemies'.[10]

These combinations of contraries also illustrate that each proposition can have more than one contrary. Aristotle comments: 'For "to do good to friends" has, as its contrary, both "to do good to enemies" and "to do harm to friends".'[11] The whole purpose of the combination exercise is to find the particular contrary which is useful for dealing with the thesis.

b. *Contrary Arguments*

A contrary argument is an enthymeme where the relationship between two contraries functions as an argumentative link between an assertion and a rationale. Thomas Conley defines the enthymeme as a claim supported by evidence which has a *protasis* that provides argumentative links between the claim and the available data.[12] The argumentative link is a rule which functions as a major premise in a syllogism. This major premise is often unexpressed, and is dependent on the implicit knowledge the hearers have of the subject matter, that is, the special topics, or on their acceptance of various strategies of reasoning, that is, the common topics. Now the topos ἐκ τῶν ἐναντίων is a common topic which provides an argumentative link between an assertion and a rationale.

That the contrary argument is an enthymeme which uses the common topic of the contrary is explicitly stated by Aristotle in the latter part of the

10. Aristotle, *Top.* 2.7 (112b27-40).
11. Aristotle, *Top.* 2.7 (113a15-17).
12. T. Conley, *Rhetoric in the European Tradition* (Chicago: University of Chicago Press, 1990), p. 15.

second book of *Rhetoric*, where Aristotle lists 28 common topics which can be used in the construction of demonstrative and refutative enthymemes. The first example of these common topics is the topos ἐκ τῶν ἐναντίων:

> One topos of demonstrative [enthymemes] is that from opposites [ἐκ τῶν ἐναντίων]; for one should look to see if the opposite [predicate] is true of the opposite [subject], [thus] refuting the argument if it is not, confirming it if it is.[13]

Cope explains the inference drawn in this case as 'from the correctness or incorrectness, the truth or falsehood, of the assertion of compatibility or coexistence in the opposites, or that one *can* be predicated of the other'.[14]

The first illustration Aristotle uses exemplifies this: 'Saying that to be temperate is a good thing, for to lack self-control is harmful.' The two contraries here are temperance (τὸ σωφρονεῖν) and lack of self-control (τὸ ἀκολασταίνειν). Their contrary nature excludes qualities inherent in the one from the qualities inherent in the other. This is the unexpressed premise or rule derived from the topos of contraries. The minor premise is the well-known case that lack of self-control is harmful, both for the individual himself and his surroundings. This case can be regarded as evidence since most hearers could assent to the trueness of the premise on the grounds of their own personal experience. The resulting conclusion would necessarily be that temperance is a good thing.

Aristotle's second illustration of a demonstrative enthymeme derived from contraries is from *Messeniacus*: 'If the war is the cause of present evils, things should be set right again by making peace.' The contraries in this illustration are war and peace. The predicates associated with them are 'present evils' and 'setting things right again'. In this argument the opposite predicate 'setting things right' is true of the opposite subject 'peace', and therefore the contraries confirm the argument. The argument could be analyzed as consisting of the rule which says that war and peace are contraries, which means that the predicates of the war exclude the predicates of peace. The actual case which forms the minor premise is the fact that war is the cause of the present evils. This evidence can be regarded as self-evident by hearers troubled by the consequences of war. The resulting conclusion is that peace will set things right again. The contrary to war will alleviate the pains of war.

---

13. Aristotle, *Rhet.* 2.23.1 (Kennedy's translation).
14. Cope, *Commentary*, II, p. 238.

c. *Constructive and Destructive Arguments from the Contrary*

The arguments that are formed from contraries can be both destructive and constructive. In the fifth book of the *Topica*, Aristotle discusses the rules drawn from different modes of opposition which can be used for the formation of propositions:

> Next, you must examine on the basis of opposites and, in the first place, of *contraries* and, for destructive criticism, see whether the contrary of the term fails to be a property of the contrary subject; for then neither will the contrary of the former be a property of the contrary of the latter. For example, since injustice is the contrary to justice, and the greatest evil is contrary to the greatest good, but it is not a property of 'justice' to be 'the greatest good', then the 'greatest evil' would not be a property of 'injustice'.[15]

This example is a kind of destructive argument in which the speaker makes use of the incompatibility between two sets of alleged contraries, denying that they are true contraries.[16] Finding this incompatibility serves to establish the invalidity of the argument. Aristotle continues his illustration with a constructive argument:

> For constructive argument, on the other hand, you must see whether the contrary is a property of the contrary; for then the contrary too of the former will be a property of the contrary of the latter. For example, since 'evil' is contrary to 'good' and 'object of avoidance' contrary to 'object of choice' and 'object of choice' is a property of 'good', 'object of avoidance' would be a property of 'evil'.

In this constructive argument the terms involved are true contraries and they can therefore be used to make a valid argument.[17]

Cicero mentions constructive arguments from the contrary like the following: 'If we shun folly (as of course we do), let us pursue Wisdom;

---

15.   Aristotle, *Top.* 5.6 (135b7).

16.   This destructive argument can be analyzed in syllogistic form as follows:

Rule: Injustice is the contrary to justice, and the greatest evil is contrary to the greatest good;

Case: but it is not a property of 'justice' to be 'the greatest good';

Result: therefore the 'greatest evil' is not a property of 'injustice'.

17.   This constructive argument can be analyzed in the following syllogistic form:

Rule: 'Evil' is contrary to 'good'; and 'object of avoidance' is contrary to 'object of choice';

Case: 'Object of choice' is a property of 'good';

Result: 'Object of avoidance' is a property of 'evil'.

and kindness if we shun malice.'[18] Here wisdom and folly are the terms posited as contraries. The topos of contraries gives the rule that what is predicated of the one should have the contrary predicate for the contrary term. The case is that we of course shun folly. This evidence from experience forms the rationale for the assertion that we should pursue wisdom.

One common form of the constructive argument from contraries is the contradiction of the contrary which results in a rephrasing of the original proposition. The illustration of the contradiction of a contrary that was previously cited can thus be analyzed as an enthymeme: 'If it is a received opinion that one ought to do good to one's friends, it will also be a received opinion that one ought not to do them harm.'[19] The terms posited as contraries here are 'do good' and 'do harm'. The rule from the topos of contraries is that doing good to someone excludes doing harm to the same person. The well-known case is that 'one ought to do good to one's friends'. The conclusion that results from the argumentative link formed by the topos of the contrary is that one ought not to harm friends. The contradiction of the contrary is one way of reformulating the proposition by means of a constructive enthymeme.

It seems, however, that the rhetorical tradition developed a certain proclivity for the destructive forms of the argument from the contrary. *Rhet. ad Her.* 4.18.25 defines the *contrarium* or reasoning by contraries as 'the figure (of diction) which, of two opposite statements, uses one so as neatly and directly to prove the other'. The six illustrations given of this figure invariably introduce opposite statements where a particular case conflicts with a general rule. The first illustration is the following: 'Now how should you expect one who has ever been hostile to his own interests to be friendly to another's?'[20] The contraries are the two pairs 'hostile' and

---

18. Cicero, *Top.* 11.47. Cf. Quintilian 5.10.73.

19. Aristotle, *Top.* 1.10, (104a20-24).

20. Ps-Cicero, *Rhet. ad Her.* 4.18.25. The other five illustrations are the following: 'Now why should you think that one who is, as you have learned, a faithless friend, can be an honourable enemy? Or how should you expect a person whose arrogance has been insufferable in private life, to be agreeable and not forget himself when in power, and one who in ordinary conversation and among friends has never spoken the truth, to refrain from lies before public assemblies?' Again: 'Do we fear to fight them on the level plain when we have hurled them down from the hills? When they outnumbered us, they were no match for us; now that we outnumber them, do we fear that they will conquer us?'

'friendly', and 'one's own interests' and 'another persons interests'. The rule from the topos of contraries is that the qualities associated with one's own interests are opposite to the qualities associated with another person's interests, that is, selfishness is assumed. We would expect a person to be more friendly to his own interests than to another's interests.[21] In the actual case the person under consideration is not even friendly to his own interests. On the contrary, the idiot is hostile to his own best interests. Therefore, one cannot expect him to be friendly to another's interests. This type of contrary argument is a particular case contradicting a commonly accepted rule.

In rhetorical speech, it was considered very effective to show that the words or deeds of the opponent in fact contradicted a commonly accepted rule. Anaximenes in *Rhetorica ad Alexandrum* recommends:

> The investigator must try to find some point in which either the speech that he is investigating is self-contradictory or the actions or the intentions of the person under investigation run counter to another. This is the procedure—to consider whether perhaps in the past after having first been a friend of somebody he afterwards became his enemy and then became the same man's friend again; or committed some other inconsistent action indicating depravity; or is likely in the future, should opportunities befall him, to act in a manner contrary to his previous conduct. Similarly observe whether something that he says when speaking now is contrary to what he has said before; and likewise also whether he has ever adopted a policy contrary to his previous professions, or would do so if opportunities offered.[22]

The case that contradicts the commonly accepted rule forms an enthymeme where the rule is the major premise, the contradicting case the minor premise, and where the resulting conclusion is that the opponent is contradicting himself, either by word or deed. In fact, when Anaximenes discusses different kinds of proofs he mentions the enthymemes:

> Enthymemes [ἐνθυμήματα] are (1) facts that run counter to the speech or action in question, and also (2) those that run counter to anything else. You will obtain a good supply of them by pursuing the method described under the investigatory species of oratory, and by considering whether the speech contradicts itself in any way, or the actions committed run counter to the principles of justice, law, expediency, honour, feasibility, facility or

---

21. This introduces an *a maiore ad minus* line of reasoning.
22. Aristotle, *Rhet. ad Alex.* 5.1427b15-27. Cf. the discussion on τεκμήρια, 'previous facts running counter to the fact asserted in the speech', in 9.1430a14-22. I am grateful to Manfred Kraus for pointing this parallel out to me.

probability, or to the character of the speaker or the usual course of events. This is the sort of enthymemes to be chosen as a point to use against our opponents.[23]

Quintilian seems to share the view that the most common form of the contrary argument is the destructive kind where two conflicting premises result in a negative conclusion, such as when the particular case contradicts the general rule. He mentions 'arguments from opposites', using the Greek term ἐναντιότης 'from which we get enthymemes styled κατ' ἐναντίωσιν'.[24] In a previous passage he claims that 'the majority hold the view that an *enthymeme* is a conclusion from incompatibilities: wherefore Cornificus styles it a *contrarium* or argument from contraries'.[25]

d. *Contrary Arguments in the Elaboration of a Chreia*

The contrary arguments used in the elaboration of *chreiai* in the *progymnasmata* are both constructive and destructive in type.[26] Hermogenes gives an example of a constructive argument. The thesis of the chreia is 'Isocrates said that education's root is bitter, its fruit is sweet'. The statement from the opposite that supports this thesis is: 'For ordinary affairs do not need toil, and they have an outcome that is entirely without pleasure; but serious affairs have the opposite outcome'.[27] The two sets of contraries here are: 'ordinary affairs' and 'serious affairs'; 'pleasurable outcome' and 'unpleasurable outcome'. Since these are contraries they exclude one another, and if a quality like unpleasurable outcome belongs to the one, it cannot belong to the other. The well-known case is that ordinary affairs need no toil and have an outcome without pleasure. The conclusion to this contrary argument thus is that serious affairs have a pleasurable outcome. This conclusion is now used to support the thesis of the chreia. Since education is a serious affair it has a pleasurable outcome, that is, it produces a sweet fruit.

---

23. Aristotle, *Rhet. ad Alex.* 10.1430a23-31. Cf. the distinctions between contraries, enthymemes and τεκμήρια in 14.1431a29-35. I have translated ἐνθυμήματα with enthymemes, instead of the translation 'considerations' chosen by Rackham in the LCL.

24. Quintilian 9.2.106.

25. Quintilian 5.10.2.

26. The earliest extant elaboration of the *chreia* is found in *Rhet. ad Her.* 4.44.56-58. The contrary argument is of the same constructive type as the one in Hermogenes below.

27. Hermogenes, 'On the Chreia', in R.F. Hock and E.N. O'Neil (eds.), *The Chreia in Ancient Rhetoric. I. The Progymnasmata* (Atlanta: Scholars Press, 1986), p. 177.

Aphthonius's elaboration of the same chreia, which is attributed to Isocrates, also contains a constructive argument from the contrary:

> If, however, anyone in fear of all this avoids his teachers, avoids his parents
> by running away, avoids his paedogogi because of his aversion to them, he
> comes to be completely without their guidance and in ridding himself of his
> apprehension also rids himself of their guidance. All these things then
> influenced Isocrates' decision to call education's root bitter.[28]

This statement ἐκ τοῦ ἐναντίου elaborates the contrary to the thesis of the
chreia. It amplifies the bitter fruit and unpleasurable outcome for the one
who does not work seriously with his education. The contradiction of the
contrary thus becomes a reformulation of the positive thesis that education
is serious business which produces sweet fruit.[29]

In contrast to these constructive arguments, Theon in his *progymnasmata* gives an example of a destructive argument from the contrary:

> We also object to *chreiai* from the opposite points of view [ἐκ τῶν
> ἐναντίων], as, for example against Isocrates' saying that one should honor
> teachers before parents, since the latter have offered us the chance to live
> but teachers the chance to live nobly. We say in objecting to this idea that it
> is impossible to live nobly, unless our parents have given us the chance to
> live.[30]

The contraries in Isocrates's saying are 'living a [mere] life' and 'living
nobly'. He associates parents with the former and teachers with the latter,
and adds the value judgment that noble is better than ignoble. Theon turns
the table on Isocrates by questioning his description of the parents' contribution as less noble than the teachers'. Theon claims that the contrary is
the true case and therefore parents should be honored above teachers.

This contrary argument is an example of cunning or μῆτις, 'the kind of
wisdom appropriate to the contingent and threatening situations of life
where survival depends upon clever sagacity'.[31] Cunning is contrasted to
σοφία, which is the kind of wisdom appropriate to the orders of reality
understood as stable systems. When a contrary argument shows the case
which contradicts the reasoning of the opponent, whether that case is

28. Aphthonius of Anthioch, 'On the Chreia', in Hock and O'Neil (eds.), *The
Chreia in Ancient Rhetoric*, p. 227.

29. Cf. The argument from the contrary in the elaboration of the maxim in
Aphthonius's *progymnasmata*.

30. Theon of Alexandria, 'On the Chreia', in Hock and O'Neil (eds.), *The Chreia
in Ancient Rhetoric*, p. 101.

31. Mack, 'Elaboration of the *Chreia*', p. 47.

found in the opponent's word or deed or in another exception to the rule, the contrary argument forms a clever rejoinder against the opponent's claim.

Summary
Contrary arguments are enthymemes. They are arguments in which the posited contrariety between two terms, or two sets of terms, functions as an argumentative link between an assertion and a rationale, between a result and a case. That the contrary relationship between two terms can function as an implied major premise, or a rule, is one of the common topics of rhetorical theory.

There are two kinds of contrary arguments, the constructive and the destructive kind. In the constructive argument the case supports the rule and the resulting conclusion therefore serves to establish the thesis. In the destructive argument from the contrary, the case contradicts the rule. The contradicting case can either be a word or deed made by the opponent or a more general conflict between two premises. The contradicted rule can be either a statement of the opponent or a more general principle. In either case, the enthymeme which is based on contraries 'seems the most pointed form of argument'.[32]

2. *Paul's Use of Contrary Arguments*

Paul's letters are filled with antithetical expressions like 'heaven' and 'earth', 'flesh' and 'spirit', 'circumcision' and 'uncircumcision', and 'grace' and 'works'. In as far as these contrasts are mutually exclusive they are contraries, that is, 'the extreme opposites under the same genus... which cannot reside in the same subject together'. With this abundance of contraries in Paul's letters it is no surprise that he also uses them to make contrary arguments.

a. *Paul's Constructive Arguments from the Contrary*
As explained previously, the constructive contrary argument is often in the form of a contradiction of a contrary. If the contrariety between the two terms is conventional the argument from the contrary can be viewed as a rhetorical figure. Colossians 3.2 can be seen as an example: 'Set your minds on things that are above, not on things that are on earth.' In this case

---

32. Cicero, *Top.* 13.55.

the possibilities inherent in the contrary 'on earth' are not explored and the statement functions more or less like a stylistic device. Nevertheless, even figures of speech have a rhetorical function and this contradiction of the contrary can be analyzed as an enthymeme where 'above' and 'earth' are contraries which mutually exclude one another. From this rule it is deduced that if one sets one's mind on the things above (case), one cannot set one's mind on the things on earth (result). The enthymeme in this rhetorical figure is brief indeed and expressed in one sentence.

Similar contradictions of the contrary are found in many places in Paul's letters where an action is combined with contrary objects and the latter object is contradicted. In Phil. 2.21, 'All of them are seeking their own interests, not those of Jesus Christ', the action 'seeking' is combined with the contrary objects 'one's own interests' and 'the interests of Jesus Christ'. The contrariety posited between the terms gives the rule that they are mutually exclusive. If the case is that these persons seek their own interests, it therefore follows that they are not seeking the interests of Jesus Christ.[33]

Another example of a contradiction of a contrary is Gal. 5.16: 'Walk in the Spirit, and do not follow the lusts of the flesh.' Here the contraries are 'flesh' and 'Spirit'. Following the Spirit thus excludes following the flesh. The opposition between flesh and Spirit is elaborated in the following verses, where 5.19-21 is an amplification of the term 'flesh' and 5.22 an amplification of 'Spirit'. Here we can see how Paul fully exploits the possibilities inherent in the contrary to the initial proposition.

The contradiction of a contrary is often more than mere ornamentation. When Paul in 1 Thess. 4.7 claims that 'God did not call us to impurity, but in holiness', the contraries 'impurity' and 'holiness' express the extremes of vice and virtue. Being contraries they are mutually exclusive: this is the rule or unexpressed major premise derived from the common topic of contraries. Since God's calling was to holiness, it cannot have been to impurity (case). Therefore the Thessalonians should flee impurity and seek holiness (result). This constructive argument from the contrary thus becomes a supportive argument to the admonition in the previous verses to live a life pleasing to God.

The contrary arguments which contradict a contrary often have the rhetorical function that they create a dissociation between the two terms posited as contraries. This is seen in the following verse, which amplifies

---

33. In criticism of this argument it could be questioned whether 'one's own interests' and 'the interests of Jesus Christ' are really mutually exclusive.

the distinction between those who live a life worthy of God and those who do not: 'Therefore whoever rejects this rejects not human authority but God' (1 Thess. 4.8). The contraries here are 'human authority' and 'God'. Paul claims that rejecting his admonition is the same as rejecting God (result), since his admonition to flee impurity and seek holiness is congruent with God's calling (case). The contraries thus aid in establishing an opposition between those who live a life worthy of God and those who oppose Paul's admonition.

This dissociation is continued in the next chapter with the help of the two sets of contraries 'darkness' and 'light', and 'night' and 'day'. 'But you, beloved, are not in darkness, for that day to surprise you like a thief; for you are all children of light and children of the day; we are not of the night or of darkness' (1 Thess. 5.4-5). Night and day are mutually exclusive (rule), therefore the one who belongs to the day (case), cannot belong to the night (result). The claim that the Thessalonians are 'children of the light and children of the day' dissociates them from those others who are 'children of the darkness' and 'children of the night'. In this case the contraries 'light' and 'darkness' are conventional, but their important rhetorical function comes from the way Paul associates some people with the one and other people with the other.

The rhetorician who is planning an argument from the contrary must carefully plan what terms he should posit as contraries. As Aristotle reminds, 'For "to do good to friends" has as its contrary both "to do good to enemies" and "to do harm to friends".'[34] The contrary chosen should serve the purpose of the speaker. Especially in those cases when the contrariety posited between the terms is unconventional, it is easy to see the argumentative function.

In 1 Cor. 15.39-41 there is an argument from the contrary which serves to support the restated theme of 15.38: 'But God gives it (the sown body) a body as he has chosen, and to each kind of seed its own body'. The thesis here is diversity. The contrary argument in 15.39, 'Not all flesh is the same flesh', is a contradiction of the contrary to this thesis. The contraries are 'all flesh is the same flesh' and 'each seed has its own body', that is, uniformity versus diversity. The well-known case is that 'not all flesh is the same flesh'. The conclusion is that God gives 'each kind of seed its own body'. This conclusion is elaborated in an amplification where the aim is to stress the difference between different types of bodies. The

---

34. Aristotle, *Top.* 2.7 (113a15-17).

rhetorical function of this contrary argument is to introduce the distinction between different kinds of bodies which Paul will use in his attempt to prove that the resurrection body is different from the natural body.[35] It is interesting to note that this argument from the contrary is preceded by a thesis, a rationale, a restatement of the thesis, and is followed by an analogy, an example, and a conclusion, that is, the same argumentative sequence as was recommended in the *progymnasmata* for the elaboration of the *chreia*.[36]

In Gal. 1.11-12 Paul claims that the gospel he has preached to the Galatians is not from men, but from God. The contraries here are 'God' and 'men'. The positive thesis is first stated in 1.11a as 'the gospel that was proclaimed by me'. This thesis is restated in 1.12c as the Gospel which Paul has received 'through a revelation of Jesus Christ'. In the intervening lines Paul explores the possibilities inherent in the contrary to this thesis. The contrary to a divine message is a human message. Paul expresses this in three ways, each time contradicting the contrary. His gospel is 'not of human origin', Paul 'did not receive it from a human source', nor was he 'taught it'.

This contrariety between a gospel from God and a gospel from men is not something that Paul has inherited from contemporary sources. It is Paul's construction in the particular rhetorical situation which the letter to the Galatians seeks to address. What Paul accomplishes by this argument from the contrary is that he creates a dissociation between two types of 'gospels' where he is aligned with God and where some unspecified others by implication are aligned with the not-God. Since these verses function as the *propositio* for the whole letter, the symbolic universe created by the argument from the contrary is basic to the rest of the letter. Subsequently Paul will elaborate in what way his gospel is from God, and identify those on the other side and their teaching.

It must be noted that the law of contradiction in rhetoric is something quite different than in logic. In logic, the law of contradiction says that A is not non-A. In rhetoric, the terms A and non-A are not clearly defined. The terms posited as contraries can be terms usually accepted as con-

---

35. My observation in this case thus corroborates the finding by Mack and Robbins, *Patterns of Persuasion*, pp. 198-99, that the rhetorical function of the contrary in the elaboration of the *chreia* is to clarify the proposition.

36. See my fuller treatment in A. Eriksson, *Traditions as Rhetorical Proof: Pauline Argumentation in 1 Corinthians* (ConBNT, 29; Stockholm: Almqvist & Wiksell, 1998), pp. 267-72, 312.

traries, but they can also be an innovation by the speaker. Some of the most well-known theological statements in the New Testament are of this latter category. Take, for example, the claim in Gal. 2.16 that justification is not by works of the law but through faith in Jesus Christ. Not many Christians before Paul would have seen 'works of the law' and 'faith in Christ' as mutually excluding alternatives. Most would probably have combined the terms which Paul posits as extreme ends under the genus 'ways of justification'. It is thus Paul's creative argument from the contrary in a specific rhetorical situation which has given Christianity one of its most pointed theological statements.

Thus, the constructive argument from contraries serves not just to support a thesis, but also to provide that thesis with an opposing alternative. This opposing alternative can then be used as the dark background against which the speaker's thesis is presented. The way the speaker associates persons, qualities, and things, with the opposing contraries can then be used for the construction of a whole ideological landscape, or theology.

b. *Paul's Destructive Arguments from the Contrary*

The destructive argument from the contrary is also found in Paul. As previously explained, in its simplest form it is a claim that a case contradicts a rule, where the contradicted rule can be either a statement of the opponent or a more general principle. In Rom. 2.1 Paul claims that the actions of the interlocutor contradict his words: 'Therefore you have no excuse, whoever you are, when you judge others; for in passing judgment on another you condemn yourself, because you, the judge, are doing the very same things.' The rule, of course, is that word and deed should be one. The case is that the judge commits condemnable acts. The resulting conclusion is that the acts of the judge contradict the rule and the judge, thereby, stands condemned himself. Paul's argumentative move here is a clever turning of the tables.

Another example of actions contradicting words is found in 1 Cor. 15.29: 'Otherwise, what will those people do who receive baptism on behalf of the dead? If the dead are not raised at all, why are people baptized on their behalf?' This famous *crux interpretum* has occasioned a wealth of writings, most of them devoted to finding the actual practice Paul refers to. Few have seen its rhetorical function as an argument from the contrary. Paul's point in this passage is simply that the very same Corinthians who claim that the dead are not raised still perform a baptism for the dead which presupposes that the dead are actually resurrected. Their actions contradict their words. What the actual practice was is not known. It might be that what Paul calls a 'baptism for the dead' is in fact a label which the Corinthians themselves might not have used. Paul's label might have referred to something as simple as a ritual washing of the corpse. The point is that the expression functions in a contrary argument which contradicts the interlocutors' statement that 'there is no resurrection of the dead', and thereby supports Paul's thesis that there is a resurrection from the dead.[37]

Besides contradicting the words of the opponents themselves, actions can also contradict a principle stated by the speaker. This is the case in 1 Cor. 8.10 where the actions of the Corinthian who has 'knowledge', and sits in an idol's temple eating idol food, contradict the principle of concern for the weaker brother which Paul has formulated in 8.9. The twofold result of this contradiction between actual conduct and formulated rule is explained in 8.11 as the weaker brother being destroyed, and in 8.12 as a charge that those who claim knowledge and eat idol food sin against Christ.[38]

It is important that the case which contradicts the rule is grounded in the shared opinions, or ἔνδοξα, of the audience. Some of the strongest of the audience's opinions are those opinions that are based on their own experience. Consequently in 1 Thess. 2.5 Paul claims that the Thessalonians' own experience of Paul's visit in Thessalonica contradicts the claim that he should have come with words of flattery or with a pretext for greed. In this verse the actions known by the audience contradict a charge made by the opponents. In Gal. 3.5 the Galatians own experience of the reception of the Spirit by faith contradicts the statement that the giving of the Spirit is dependent on works of the law. In this verse the actions known by the audience contradict the principle which Paul ascribes to the opponents.

The contradiction between case and rule, between minor premise and major premise, does not have to be a contradiction between the opponent's words and deeds, but can be a more abstract contradiction between two conflicting principles. In 1 Cor. 10.14-22 Paul elaborates the thesis 'flee idolatry'. The thesis is supported by arguments from example and analogy. First, the tradition of the Lord's Supper in 10.16-17 is used as an example to support the avoidance of idolatry. The unity between the Lord and the

---

37. Cf. Eriksson, *Traditions as Rhetorical Proof*, pp. 264-65.
38. Cf. Eriksson, *Traditions as Rhetorical Proof*, pp. 162-64.

believers which is established through the ritual of eating the bread and drinking the cup excludes any loyalty to any other lord. The analogy made with the priests in the Old Testament (10.18), whose sacrifices established a ritual unity (not only with the altar but also with God to whom the sacrifices were offered), serves to support the thesis that the Corinthians should flee idolatry. The thesis, however, needs more precision in the actual case under discussion, the eating of idol sacrifices. To clarify the thesis, Paul brings in the opposing alternative: 'What do I imply then? That food sacrificed to idols is anything, or that an idol is anything?' The 'no' presupposed as the answer to this rhetorical question has been the contrary alternative to the whole discussion ever since 8.1. The formulation in 10.19 is a reformulation of the opposing viewpoint, which was formulated already in 8.4 as a Corinthian slogan: 'no idol in the world really exists'. Paul has now explicitly formulated the two contrary principles 'flee idolatry' and 'idols don't exist'. Paul's solution to this contradiction is not to claim that idols are anything in themselves. To do so would be to deny his monotheism, but he does claim that the idols have another kind of existence. Behind the idols stand demons, and therefore sacrificing to idols means sacrificing to demons. God and demons are mutually exclusive contraries under the genus divine beings and therefore it is impossible to sacrifice to both. Or as Paul phrases it: 'You cannot drink the cup of the Lord and the cup of demons. You cannot partake of the table of the Lord and the table of demons.'[39]

In the following example it is not only evident how Paul phrases his theology, but it is possible to get a glimpse of how he arrived at his theology. Here I refer to the contrary argument in Gal. 3.21: 'Is the law then opposed to the promises of God? Certainly not! For if a law had been given that could make alive, then righteousness would indeed come through the law.' Paul's previous discussion could have given the impression that the Torah of Moses and the promise to Abraham are mutually exclusive entities. In this destructive argument from the contrary, Paul denies that the two are true contraries. The law and the promise would only contradict one another if the definition of the law given by his opponents holds true, that is, if the Torah could bring life. In that case the law, and not the promise, would be the real life-giver and the two would become contraries. However, the actual case is that the law does not make alive. For Paul the Torah does not retain its traditional Jewish role. The

39. Cf. Eriksson, *Traditions as Rhetorical Proof*, p. 169.

conclusion to this contrary argument is therefore that the redefined law does not contradict the promises of God.[40]

This formulation shows how Paul, in a very particular rhetorical situation, defends himself against charges made by opponents. The theological statement that is derived from the argumentation is an example of a clever rejoinder that redefines the traditional understanding of the law. Here Paul does not so much expound an already established theology as he creates rhetorical arguments by means of established rhetorical topoi, in this case the topos of the argument from the contrary. Here he shows himself to be a rhetorical debater, who uses cunning by means of contrary arguments to prove his point.

3. *Conclusion*

Paul uses many contrary arguments in his letters. He uses the constructive type of contrary argument in which the contrary of a proposition substantiates the original thesis. The terms he posits as contraries can be either conventional or contraries he has created himself. The contrariety posited between the two terms can be used to paint the dark background to the thesis and thereby create an ideological landscape. In several cases it has been shown that the rhetorical function of the constructive argument from the contrary was to create a dissociation between things or people.

The destructive argument from the contrary exploits the incongruence between a case and a rule, often in the form of an opponent's actions contradicting his words. The contradiction can also be between two conflicting principles. Both these forms are found in Paul.

In summary, the analysis of the contrary arguments in Paul gives a view, not only of his finished theological statements, but also of the way in which he goes about construing these statements. We can see Paul the rhetorician at work.

40. I would like to thank Vernon Robbins, Greg Bloomquist and Marc Debanné for a fruitful conversation on the Rhetoric-L concerning the analysis of this contrary argument.

TOWARDS A NEW, RHETORICALLY ASSISTED READING OF ROMANS 3.27–4.25

Douglas A. Campbell

This paper is the first phase in a fourfold re-evaluation of the meaning of Paul's argument in Rom. 3.27–4.25, a re-evaluation taking place self-consciously in a post-Sanders era when many traditional approaches to Paul's texts are appearing increasingly problematic (at least to some interpreters). Rhetoric participates in this re-evaluation at various points although in rather different senses.[1]

In this first phase of the re-evaluation I wish merely to suggest that an important set of textual correlations in this section of the letter seems to have been largely overlooked (and, if valid, these will form the basis for

---

1. The other three phases are: (2) the politics of ecclesial interpretation; (3) a phenomenological, martyrological, and intertextual reading (although undertaken in part here); and (4) appropriate explanation of the discussion's broader function and provenance. Rhetoric as politically influenced interpretation and as argumentation are both important approaches in the following (see Perelman and Olbrechts-Tyteca 1969; Murphy 1994), featuring in addition to the structural and stylistic suggestions that I will utilize below (along with some possible insights from delivery). In addition to these five distinct methodological contributions to this particular investigation I would add possible contributions from rhetoric in more general terms to the interpretation of Paul's letters in terms of memory (a relatively minor area), and the illumination of important aspects of the letters' cultural background, especially in relation to problems at Corinth, Galatia, Thessalonica (there with respect to 1 Thessalonians only), and arguably also Colossae (see in relation to Corinth esp. Litfin 1994). It should be noted further that these seven possible avenues of contribution from rhetoric are partial and indirect as well as differentiated. Moreover, they overlap with related ancient cultural phenomena like theatre, the Sophistical movement, and philosophy. For the student of Paul then—to use a trope that the rhetors themselves would probably have been ashamed of—one might say that 'the rhetorical method' comprises one useful set of tools in the interpretative toolbox, and we can perhaps even speak of seven different drill bits.

my alternative reading). The correlations are important because they offer the novel interpretative possibility in relation to this section of Romans of an argumentatively differentiated reading that can take full account of different argumentative foci and consequent shifts in terminology throughout Paul's discussion; differentiations and shifts that are stumbling blocks for more monolithic (and, often in tandem with this, more programmatic) readings.[2] (This more flexible approach can also then possibly resolve the discussion's nagging ambiguities more effectively.) So the interpretative promise of these perceptions in terms of exegetical accuracy is considerable.

The all-important textual correlations are establishable primarily on internal comparative grounds of style and argument. But rhetoric can play a supporting role for this hypothesis by supplying evidence of similar practice from roughly contemporary sources concerning the structure of discourses, thereby lending indirect support to a suggestion made initially on internal grounds. Consequently, the following discussion attempts to begin to establish this new reading in two phases that correspond to this direct and indirect corroboration—the first phase is, of necessity, rather more detailed.

2.   The consequent configuration of any subsequent debate will also favour the differentiated approach. A traditional (or any alternative) monolithic approach that claims Paul is addressing one primary issue here—and positively—will need to establish that semantic unity through all of Rom. 4, in defiance of the variations in terminology and substance that the differentiated reading will point out are present. In effect, then, the monolithic reading will have to establish its reading, which is generally based on the key ideas and terms of one sub-section of the chapter, over the entire discussion; a very difficult task. Against this, the advocate of semantic differentiation will merely have to point out the particularities of the text that resist this imposition—*and without necessarily denying the validity of the insights of the traditionalist (or their competitor) into one particular sub-section of the chapter*. It is the inappropriate extension of those insights into adjacent material that can be challenged—clearly an easier position to defend. (In addition, underlying the traditional approach and its standard interpretative revision [see n. 12 below] one can detect the assumptions that Abraham is being deployed, first, primarily positively by Paul and, second, also therefore monolithically: of course these crucial assumptions may or may not hold good—they need to be examined critically and established, and in relation to the above reading's detection of multiplicity.)

1. *The Internal Case*

a. *The Problem*

Romans 3.27-31 has in some senses suffered the same fate as the Son of Man; it has nowhere to lay its head. That is, scholars have seldom known how to co-ordinate this section of argument with its context. Some have favoured a link with 3.21-26,[3] a link that in stylistic and substantive terms is awkward. Others have opted for its independent function after that important thesis statement but before the definitive exemplum of Abraham is introduced in 4.1 that supposedly illustrates from that later point the thesis of 3.21-26, an option that inevitably leads to the section's interpretative marginalization between those two more famous discussions. More recently, a few have sought to co-ordinate the section with the following discussion of Abraham, but as yet not with any obvious interpretative success.[4]

The section also does not lack internal problems. It contains two especially unusual statements (in)famous for their supposed attestation to a third use of the law in Paul, namely, νόμος πίστεως in v. 27 (in context διὰ νόμου πίστεως) and νόμον ἱστάνομεν in v. 31 (cf. elsewhere only ἵνα τὸ δικαίωμα τοῦ νόμου πληρωθῇ ἐν ἡμῖν κτλ. in 8.3). There is also a puzzling allusion to the Shema in v. 30. Otherwise the passage seems densely packed with the terminology typical for this section of Romans; an association between πίστις and δικαιο– terms, at times in sharp antithesis to ἔργων.

---

3.   All biblical references are to Romans unless otherwise indicated.

4.   The first option is followed e.g. by Ziesler (1989: 106-20). Against this see my observations (1992: esp. 79-83 but also 22-37 and 51-56). The second, perhaps standard, approach may be represented by Stuhlmacher (1994: 65-68). The third was tabled by Stowers (1994: 227-50) and is much less popular, possibly because as well as flying in the face of traditionalist theological expectations, in Stowers's work the proposal is integrated with several other radical suggestions. There are also other proposed correlations, i.e., some scholars have argued that ch. 4 (in its entirety) picks up only one set of statements from within 3.27-31, generating three further structural possibilities: (4) that ch. 4 elaborates 3.27-28 (a standard Lutheran approach: see e.g. Cranfield); (5) that—conversely—ch. 4 elaborates 3.29-30 (see, e.g., Gaston 1980; Sanders 1983; Hays 1985; Donaldson 1992); and (6) that ch. 4 elaborates 3.31 (see, e.g., Barrett 1957; Rhyne 1981; Siker 1991). We will see much more clearly after the discussion that follows that there is a considerable degree of truth in these last proposals—they are correct in much that they affirm, but wrong I will suggest in what they inferentially deny. (There is a useful summary of views here in Donaldson 1992: 9-10, esp. nn. 25-27.)

We will not consider all the problems of the much longer 4.1-25 here, but it is interesting to note that some of its more famous conundrums parallel exactly the two sets of problems just noted for 3.27-31. At the more localized level, scholars have struggled in particular with the subject of the infinitive εὑρηκέναι in 4.1: do *we* discover something about Abraham or does *he* discover something for himself? The latter would be the more normal grammatical usage, but that apparently defies the overarching function of the passage which seems to deploy an example intended to assist *our* (i.e. the audience of the letter's) understanding of justification. So at the beginning of ch. 4 the problem of compressed and hence enigmatic statements already noted in 3.27-31 seems, at least at this point, to persist. Moreover, various scholars have called into question this traditional construal of the entire passage's function in the aforementioned exemplary role: as Käsemann observes pithily (although not himself finally in opposition to the traditional construal), '[t]he question…inevitably arises how far Paul could establish the existence of Christian faith in the pre-Christian era, and how he was able to get over the apparent contradictions involved'.[5]

So it is well-known that 3.27-31 contains certain enigmatic phrases while its function within the letter's broader argument is also somewhat unclear. Romans 4.1-25 also begins with an enigmatic assertion and is possibly also problematic in terms of its broader argumentative function. I would suggest that the lack of clarity surrounding 3.27-31, and, to a lesser extent, 4.1-25, is in large measure a consequence of their separated structural roles and subsequent interpretation. Correspondingly, a coordinated approach to these two sections will afford considerable gains in interpretative precision. This suggestion is not being posited on these *a priori* grounds, however: it is based on a string of stylistic indicators which imply reasonably strongly that these passages belong together and are meant to be read in integrated terms (hence many of our interpretative problems here may well have been self-inflicted).

b. *Stowers's Suggestion and its Implications*
Stanley Stowers suggested some time ago that the diatribal style evident from 3.27 actually continues seamlessly through 4.1 (he carries the diatribe through to 4.2 [1981, 1994]). That is, in terms of ancient conventions

---

5.   Käsemann 1971: 79. See also the extensive protests of Klein in 1969a, 1969b, and 1969c (to which Käsemann is in part replying): these are briefly canvassed by Gaston 1980: esp. 39 and 60 (n. 2).

of genre, the interposition of a significant break in Paul's argument at the point of 4.1 is unnecessary and prompted on positive grounds by largely artificial considerations (why should chapter divisions be taken seriously without further internal support for their demarcations derived critically?). I believe that this suggestion of Stowers's, although little utilized, is extremely important. Stowers's observation creates the possibility of considering the two sections as a united discussion and also, more specifically, of considering the initial statements of ch. 4—notably those of v. 1—primarily in relation to the diatribal discussion that precedes them rather than in relation to the more discursive material that follows. I do not think that the full implications of Stowers's proposal have yet been grasped, however.

I myself wish to suggest here two further interrelated theses concerning 3.27–4.25: (1) Rom. 3.27–4.1 is best treated initially as a textual unit in its own right largely because, in confirmation of its apparent stylistic unity, it also elaborates an integrated series of issues in substantive terms. In short, it sets out an argumentative agenda (an agenda with four main items). (2) Romans 4.2-25 then comprises a precisely corresponding series of responses to those issues, responses that reprise not merely their substance but in many instances the exact terminology of their initial statement. In sum, my overarching suggestion here, which was catalyzed by Stowers's insights, is that Rom. 3.27–4.25 is a carefully interconnected composition comprising the diatribal announcement of an explicit fourfold agenda in 3.27–4.1, and a set of four corresponding answers deployed seriatim through 4.2-25 that analyse the four issues just tabled in terms of the Abrahamic tradition. (More precisely, it argues in terms of Gen. 15.6 against other readings of Abraham. The entire section also thereby corresponds in general argumentative terms to the extended discussion of 1.18–3.20; see Campbell 1995.)

In order to demonstrate this suggestion I suspect that it is important above all to grasp the neat correlation that exists in the text between the four programmatic issues tabled by 3.27–4.1 and the precisely corresponding discussion of those issues in 4.2-25. If these correlations are deemed valid then everything else largely falls into place, so in what follows I shall focus on the evidence for them. But before doing this I must note briefly how the diatribe of 3.27–4.1 functions to present this argumentative agenda.

c. *The Diatribally Presented Agenda*

The first three issues of the fourfold agenda are tabled in a largely parallel fashion in 3.27-31. A question (or set of questions) is followed in typical diatribal fashion by the customary brief response, usually a contradiction or denial (but on one occasion an affirmation that follows two initial questions). These responses are then reinforced in turn by more programmatic statements that stand over against the initial questions (in the third instance this statement is more abbreviated). In this fashion each of the first three sub-units within the diatribe tables in a typically dialogical fashion an argumentative antinomy—while leaving the letter's audience in no doubt about which side of the dispute Paul will be taking.[6] The fourth issue is tabled within a far more difficult text, 4.1, but I will suggest below that this too is fundamentally antinomous. The unit begins with a typical diatribal formula—'what then shall we say?!' Another question then follows that tables the opposing issue in the form of a question (and as, in fact, the previous three issues have been introduced). But the text falls silent at this point, hence one suspects that the unstated denial and countervailing claim are simply implicit (although we will have to consider the possibility of an affirmative response as in vv. 29-30). Formally then the text reads as follows:

> Is A the case?
> No!
> It is not A but B!
>
> Is C the case? Is it not also D?
> Yes!
> Indeed, it is C *and* D!
>
> Is E the case?
> No!
> It is F! (and—implicitly—not E).
>
> What then shall we say?!
> Did Abraham obtain G in relation to H?
> (Implicitly: absolutely not!)

Following these brief exchanges, the letter's audience should be aware of the existence of certain disputes, namely, A versus B, C's extension to D, E versus F, and the achievement of G in relation to H (or not). Thus the

---

6.   And note the somewhat uncharacteristic series of particles functioning interrogatively: οὖν, ἤ, οὖν and οὖν (3.27, 29, 31; 4.1).

diatribe has in the main dramatized certain antinomous issues, presenting them in terms of a vivid dialogue of contradiction (imagine reconstruing a typical departmental agenda in such terms). The main consequence of this textual strategy is the foregrounding of the specific issues that are being both asserted and denied there in sequence. Hence I would agree almost entirely with Stowers's claim: 'Paul's resumed dialogue with the teacher in 3.27–4.2 establishes the issues for the discussion of Abraham' (1994: 225).

Now this is not what we might ordinarily expect a diatribal discussion to do (although, as we have just seen, Stowers is happy with it). Earlier in the letter Paul seems to have used diatribes in the more typical neo-Socratic fashion to confound an interlocutor's assumptions (see 2.1-5 and 3.1-9). That is, the diatribes there are primarily internally connected, leading an interlocutor from an initially ignorant position to one of (relative) enlightenment, a process preferably effected in terms of their own assumptions. Consequently, those texts traverse something of an argumentative journey, a structure; however, that is not I would suggest present in 3.27–4.1. Against any such general neo-Socratic expectation we should note briefly (1) that Paul is not necessarily bound to observe rules of genre precisely; (2) nor are rules of genre rigid; (3) nor does he seem to observe rules concerning other genres precisely (I am thinking especially of epistolary genres); hence (4) Paul demonstrably uses diatribal and, more generally, dialogical styles in various ways; (5) nor is he completely outside the expectations of a diatribe given that he is ultimately attempting to confound an interlocutor on various points; (6) this particular diatribe is in any case demonstrably difficult in terms of any ostensible neo-Socratic function, that is, it is not obviously internally connected in the manner of 2.1-5 or 3.1-9 (or, at least, not very well); and (7) it will prove in any case to correlate perfectly as an 'agenda' (rather than a neo-Socratic confutation) with the discussion that follows it. Unfortunately, time forbids the detailed justification of all these claims here (and I feel the lack of point 6 especially—although the gist of this contention should be apparent below). We will concentrate largely on point 7 in the belief that this is the best positive evidence for the reading and, if successful, that it is also strong enough to sustain the case in its own right (in order to disprove the reading objectors have to undermine these correlations while demonstrating the diatribe's internal coherence, although this last only as far as v. 31 and offering then a coherent reading of 4.1 as well, interpretative tasks that could prove difficult).

To conclude this phase of discussion, I suggest that the diatribe of 3.27–4.1 tables in dialogical form an argumentative agenda comprising four antinomous assertions along with several minor supporting considerations (denoted below in parentheses):

1. 3.27-28: πίστις and not ἔργων justifies[7] a person and excludes boasting (πίστις is also in some sense a Torah—literally νόμος—like ἔργων);
2. 3.29-30: circumcized Jews *and* uncircumcized Gentiles will be justified through πίστις (God is God of both; and God is one);
3. 3.31: πίστις does not abolish Torah—again literally νόμος—but rather confirms it; and
4. 4.1: Abraham did not obtain forefatherhood of 'us' (i.e. of us Gentiles) according to the flesh (i.e. through the covenant of flesh, circumcision). (For this reading of 4.1 see more below.)

Given time, I would attempt to show that this is an accurate summary of 3.27–4.1, and also that these propositions are not especially comprehensible as consequences of one another in context (something reasonably apparent in a lot of the passage's commentary where, at the least, a great deal of interpretative material must generally be imported in order to generate a consequential reading), but that they read better as related issues within a broader debate. However, the next step in our discussion here is positive rather than this more negative contention, namely, the claim that the ensuing discussion of 4.2-25 matches this construal of 3.27–4.1 in terms of a fourfold argumentative agenda exactly, responding in substantive terms to its queries in terms of the scripturally attested evidence in Gen. 15.6 concerning Abraham. In sum:

1. 3.27-28 is discussed more fully in 4.2-8;
2. 3.29-30 in 4.9-12;
3. 3.31 in 4.13-16a; and
4. 4.1 is elaborated in 4.16b-22.

(Verses 23-25 are a transitional conclusion.)

I shall now discuss this proposed argumentative correlation in more detail.

---

7.   I will use this conventional translation for δικαιόω on occasion merely to avoid confusion. In no sense should this be taken as an endorsement of that translation.

d. *The Evidence of Correlation*

Before addressing the evidence specific to each proposed correlation, three general observations concerning the nature of that evidence are necessary.

1. Two motifs are present throughout the entire discussion, namely, πιστ- and δικαιο- terminology (there are 13 occurrences of δικαιο- terms: 8 of the noun, 4 of the verb and 1 of the rare δικαίωσις; and 21 of πιστ-terms: 15 of the noun and 6 of the verb), and this should not be surprising. There is an evident similarity between the specific issues that Paul raises in 3.27–4.1. Moreover, he addresses them all in terms of Abraham and Gen. 15.6, a text that basically supplies this terminology (or, at least, shares it with other texts like Hab. 2.4). It is also important to note, however, that these motifs grounded in this text alone will not serve in their own right to give a single argumentative focus to the following chapter (a characteristic error of much interpretation at this point): that would be to ignore the other half of the data which is deployed in four distinct stages. Doubtless Paul is asserting something positive with his use of Gen. 15.6 and its particular terms, but I would suggest that this assertion will only be grasped precisely if the text's specific, contingent, and somewhat diversified, argumentative function has first been carefully analysed.

2. The crucial evidence concerning our suggested correlations derives from identifying the more distinctive motifs involved in each specific phase of discussion. We would expect these distinctive motifs to be tabled in the relevant announcement of a particular issue within 3.27–4.1, and then resumed in the later corresponding sub-section of ch. 4. That is, their presence would be expected in both the announcement and the subsequent analysis—and of course they will be a primary indicator of Paul's specific concerns within those particular discussions.

3. But it follows from this that we would also *not* expect the presence of this more specific material in any other announcements or responding sub-units. That is, the presence of specific motifs in one particular announcement and subsequent corresponding discussion should also correlate with the absence of those specific motifs from the other announcements and their discussions or, more accurately, their displacement by the motifs specific to any new issues (although perhaps we should allow a small degree of leeway here given that Paul might both refer to closely related points within discussion elsewhere—syntactical combinations should be especially helpful here).

With these three general observations in place we can now approach the specific suggested correlations (and here I have struggled to render in prose a configuration that is largely self-evident in visual terms).[8]

e. *Roman 3.27-28 and 4.2-8*

> 3.27 Ποῦ οὖν ἡ καύχησις; ἐξεκλείσθη. διὰ ποίου νόμου; τῶν ἔργων; οὐχί, ἀλλὰ διὰ νόμου πίστεως 3.28 λογιζόμεθα γὰρ δικαιοῦσθαι πίστει ἄνθρωπον χωρὶς ἔργων νόμου.
> 4.2 εἰ γὰρ ᾿Αβραὰμ ἐξ ἔργων ἐδικαιώθη, ἔχει *καύχημα*· ἀλλ᾿ οὐ πρὸς θεόν. 4.3 τί γὰρ ἡ γραφὴ λέγει; ἐπίστευσεν δὲ ᾿Αβραὰμ τῷ, θεῷ, καὶ ἐλογίσθη αὐτῷ εἰς δικαιοσύνην. 4.4 τῷ δὲ ἐργαζομένῳ ὁ μισθὸς οὐ λογίζεται κατὰ χάριν ἀλλὰ κατὰ ὀφείλημα· 4.5 τῷ δὲ μὴ ἐργαζομένῳ, πιστεύοντι δὲ ἐπὶ τὸν δικαιοῦντα τὸν ἀσεβῆ, λογίζεται ἡ πίστις αὐτοῦ εἰς δικαιοσύνην, 4.6 καθάπερ καὶ Δαυὶδ λέγει τὸν μακαρισμὸν τοῦ ἀνθρώπου ᾧ ὁ θεὸς λογίζεται δικαιοσύνην χωρὶς ἔργων, 4.7 μακάριοι ὧν ἀφέθησαν αἱ ἀνομίαι καὶ ὧν ἐπεκαλύφθησαν αἱ ἁμαρτίαι· 4.8 μακάριος ἀνὴρ οὗ οὐ μὴ λογίσηται κύριος ἁμαρτίαν.

There are no less than three motifs peculiar to only this sub-section and its announcement (3.27-28 and 4.2-8): boasting, works, and a mutually applicable notion of νόμος, that is, a principle relevant at this point, somewhat unusually, *both* to works and to πίστις (cf. 3.31, along with other unusual but different senses in 13.18 and Gal. 5.14; also Gal. 6.2).[9]

---

8. It is also of course important to consider at some point the extent to which Paul might be reflecting traditional Jewish exegetical argumentative techniques here, although that is really a task for another study. Here it must suffice to suggest that, in terms of Hillel's traditional seven rules of *middoth*, the first sub-unit clearly uses principle 2, *gezerah shawah* (verbal analogy based on a similarity of words—'catchword linkage'), and probably also principle 7, *dabar halamed me'inyano* (meaning established by context). The second sub-unit again uses principle 7. The third possibly utilizes principle 5, *kelal upherat* (the general and the particular), extending a particular rule (concerning Gen. 15.6) into a general principle (concerning scriptural fulfillment versus negation). The fourth sub-section also seems like a slightly tendentious application of principle 5 (although bearing points of similarity to principle 4, *binyan ab mishene kethubim*, building a family or principle from two texts, and/or principle 6, *kayoze bo bemaqom 'aher*, resolving a difficulty in one text by comparing it to another with points of general similarity). But it is difficult to be more precise without further detailed investigation, while Paul's usage at various stages also looks distinctive. A good introductory treatment is Longenecker 1975. A well-known and more recent account influenced by modern literary theory is Hays 1989 (Rom. 4 is treated briefly— and rather conventionally—on pp. 54-57; see also his well-known 1985 study).

9. The two motifs common to the entire discussion occur in this announcement and its correlative sub-section with the presence of πιστ- terminology (one substantive

In slightly more detail: boasting is tabled in 3.27 and is reprised in 4.2, a verse that also explicitly resumes the specific concern of works, a motif tabled in both 3.27 and 28 (and not elsewhere in the preparatory diatribe). So 4.2a signals the uptake of these two motifs from 3.27-28 quite clearly, also grounding both on the verb used in 3.28: εἰ γὰρ Ἀβραὰμ ἐξ ἔργων ἐδικαιώθη, ἔχει καύχημα.[10] It is also reasonable to detect some thematic connection between these two motifs: boasting was linked to works earlier in the argument of Romans (significantly, in 2.17-24; cf. also, inversely, 3.19b), so it is perhaps not surprising to see them treated here in one breath. Works in fact turn out to be the central concern of the sub-section, being referred to three more times, and in 4.4 even elaborated in some detail: τῷ [δὲ] ἐργαζομένῳ ὁ μισθὸς οὐ λογίζεται κατὰ χάριν ἀλλὰ κατὰ ὀφείλημα. Hence in juxtaposition to πίστις and under the overarching consideration of scriptural texts, it dominates the short discussion. Significantly, however, boasting and works disappear completely after this point: they occur nowhere else in ch. 4 (or, as we have said, in 3.29–4.1). This correlation alone should be sufficient to make our case in relation to the first diatribal antinomy and its analysis vis-à-vis Abraham and Gen. 15.6. At this point another motif is also in play, however.

The uptake of the third specific motif of νόμος as applied both to works and to πίστις is a more ambiguous point, but arguably Paul means with his unusual comments in 3.27 the testimony or teaching of Torah (see esp. Davies 1984a, 1984b—this point holds well in retrospect). Certainly that construal makes sense there (and not all the alternatives do), while the signifier has also been used earlier in this sense in Romans (see esp. 2.17-

in 4.5 echoing the wording of 3.27-28, assisted by two participles), and the corresponding event or process denoted by δικαιο– terms (twice the wording of 3.28 is reproduced with the verb and three times the cognate substantive appears, doubtless influenced in the immediate context by Gen. 15.6). The signifier λογίζομαι also recurs in both texts, but it is used in a different sense in 4.3-7 (and elsewhere in ch. 4) from 3.28, hence it might signal the linkage between these two sections at the level of mere pronunciation, but not substantively (it also occurs in vv. 9-10, there also largely under the influence of Gen. 15.6 that has just been cited again, and it occurs again in vv. 22-24 within the entire discussion's conclusion).

10. An important point because on our overall structural reading 4.2 resumes the antinomy tabled in 3.27-28, thereby changing direction from 4.1. Consequently, the resumptive signals need to be quite strong, and they are. (γάρ in v. 2 should then be read in an appropriate explanatory, and not a continuative or connective, sense. Alternatively, it may be a weakened resumption; cf. Rom. 15.27; 1 Cor. 9.19; 2 Cor. 5.4; cf. BAGD 152.)

20; also vv. 21 and 23). If valid, this reading of νόμος *is* taken up by the sub-section, specifically by 4.3 *and* 4.7-8, where the testimony of Scripture in the sense of teaching is tabled decisively as Paul specifically states: τί [γὰρ] ἡ γραφὴ λέγει… and, later, καὶ Δαυὶδ λέγει… In fact, nowhere else in the chapter does Paul either signal the introduction of Scripture so prominently *or* combine two scriptural texts in this positive fashion to address a single point (i.e. Gen. 15.6 and Ps. 32.1-2). Hence it is at least arguable that 4.2-8 also resumes the third unique motif in 3.27-28, specifically, the supplementary contention there in terms of νόμος if that denotes a concern with the authoritative teaching of Scripture. The sub-section is arguably distinctive at this point as well since such scriptural 'flagging' and dual deployment now also cease.

So our first diatribal announcement of an antithetical issue, namely, the elimination of boasting and the simultaneous presence of justification through πίστις, not through works, does indeed seem to be taken up by 4.2-8 *and nowhere else in ch. 4*. Certainly there is no further mention of works in the chapter, which suggests that any further discussion of the concerns of 3.27-28 elsewhere will be difficult. Similarly, the teaching of Scripture is marshalled in a somewhat distinctive fashion in only this sub-section in possible fulfilment of Paul's cryptic earlier remarks concerning νόμος πίστεως and νόμος ἔργων.

Corresponding to these stylistic indicators is an argumentative appropriateness. The diatribal anticipation of 4.2-8 signalled an antinomy between πίστις and works: which of these was the scripturally attested principle that would eliminate boasting and simultaneously justify? Paul's attempted demonstration in 4.2-8 swings off the fortuitous presence in Gen. 15.6 of a term suggestive of free transfer, namely, λογίζομαι. He suggests on this evidence that Abraham was not justified by a meritocratic accumulation of works on analogy to wages, which would both obligate God and allow Abraham to boast—justly!—of his successful efforts. Genesis 15.6 indicates that the whole process responded rather to the single quality of Abraham's πίστις and was a free transfer, κατὰ χάριν (and consequently there was also nothing to boast about). Moreover, Ps. 32.1-2, which shares the same term for transfer as Gen. 15.6 (and can therefore in terms of Jewish exegesis be legitimately tabled), seems to confirm this less calculating manner of divine dealing with humankind, although here it is construed negatively (i.e., instead of the gifting of positive things to Abraham in no relation to merit, negative things due in terms of merit are not reckoned).[11] The principle of desert associated with works and appropriate boasting therefore seems doubly confuted, and—on dual scriptural grounds—the case here seems effectively closed.

But perhaps many scholars would grant this correlation between 3.27-28 and 4.2-8—because v. 28 is held by many to enunciate *the* programmatic principle for the bulk of ch. 4 (if not, as Luther thought, *for the entire gospel*, and hence his emphatic amendment of the text in v. 28 to *sola fides*). So as important as the perhaps uncontentious correlations here are the sudden shifts following both 3.27 and 4.8. Although certain motifs are retained, this particular argument and set of concerns do not in fact continue: another set takes its place that does not so much follow on from this initial set of concerns as view a related problem from the same perspective.[12]

f. *Roman 3.29-30 and 4.9-12*

3.29 ἢ Ἰουδαίων ὁ θεὸς μόνον; οὐχὶ καὶ ἐθνῶν; ναὶ καὶ ἐθνῶν, 3.30 εἴπερ εἷς ὁ θεὸς, ὃς δικαιώσει περιτομὴν ἐκ πίστεως καὶ ἀκροβυστίαν διὰ τῆς πίστεως.

4.9 ὁ μακαρισμὸς οὖν οὗτος ἐπὶ τὴν περιτομὴν ἢ καὶ ἐπὶ τὴν ἀκροβυστίαν; λέγομεν γάρ, ἐλογίσθη τῷ Ἀβραὰμ ἡ πίστις εἰς δικαιοσύνην. 4.10 πῶς οὖν ἐλογίσθη; ἐν περιτομῇ ὄντι ἢ ἐν ἀκροβυστίᾳ; οὐκ ἐν περιτομῇ ἀλλ᾽ ἐν ἀκροβυστίᾳ· 4.11 καὶ σημεῖον ἔλαβεν περιτομῆς σφραγῖδα τῆς δικαιοσύνης τῆς πίστεως τῆς ἐν τῇ ἀκροβυστίᾳ, εἰς τὸ εἶναι αὐτὸν πατέρα πάντων τῶν πιστευόντων δι᾽ ἀκροβυστίας, εἰς τὸ λογισθῆναι αὐτοῖς [τὴν] δικαιοσύνην, 4.12 καὶ πατέρα περιτομῆς τοῖς οὐκ ἐκ περιτομῆς μόνον ἀλλὰ

11. On the precise construal of λογίζομαι, as well as the timing of the 'crediting' of 'righteousness', see Gaston 1980: 50-52, and esp. *Mek.* 4 (on Exod. 4.31).

12. Corroboration of the presence of an argumentative break at this point is found in the assertions of various, generally more revisionist, scholars that 'justification of the ungodly' and a critique of 'works' are not the central concern of ch. 4 because that distinctive argumentation ceases at v. 9, while if those concerns were central that terminology and analysis would have to continue much further into the chapter: see e.g. Hays 1985; Donaldson 1992: 9; Wright 1991: 36, 167-68; 1995: 30-67, esp. 39-42; Stowers 1994: 221-50. Against the traditional approach, such scholars, perceiving (again correctly) the importance of circumcision and promise in what follows, tend to assert more salvation-historical approaches. Such approaches, however, still need to deal themselves with the presence of the traditional reading in vv. 1-8 *and* with the subsequent modulations in the terminology of circumcision and promise; motifs which *do not occur in juxtaposition*, and *both of which* also drop out of sight well before the end of the chapter (which is to ask 'how is the much-maligned sub-section comprising vv. 16b-22 treated?').

καὶ τοῖς στοιχοῦσιν τοῖς ἴχνεσιν τῆς ἐν ἀκροβυστίᾳ πίστεως τοῦ πατρὸς ἡμῶν Ἀβραάμ.

The only motifs retained here in 4.9-12 from vv. 2-8 are δικαιοσύνη (and the closely-associated μακαρισμός, with three and one instance/s respectively; δικαιόω is not used), πίστις (with three instances in addition to one cognate participial occurrence), and the (modified) citation of Gen. 15.6 accompanied by an ensuing use of λογίζομαι (three instances also). But just as the contrasting motif of works and the competition for scriptural attestation have faded, two new motifs within another antinomy suddenly dominate the argument of the sub-section *and both are specifically signalled by 3.29-30*, a sub-section that spoke of 'Jew and Greek' and 'circumcision and uncircumcision' (περιτομὴ καὶ ἀκροβυστία). There is actually no discussion of 'Jew and Greek' in 4.9-12, but both terms of the second antinomy in v. 30, namely, περιτομὴ καὶ ἀκροβυστία, *occur no less than six times each in this sub-section, yet they occur nowhere else in Romans 4* (neither of course do they occur in 3.27-31 outside v. 30).

Thus the stylistic signals at the point are again almost unmistakeable. Paul's concern seems to have shifted in this argumentative sub-section away from meritorious works along with its claim to scriptural attestation to some question concerning circumcision and uncircumcision (as evidenced also by the different use made of Gen. 15.6 and λογίζομαι), a shift precisely signalled by 3.29-30 following on from 3.27-28.

Corresponding to the stylistic shift is an argumentative shift. We no longer consider if Abraham boasted before God because of a meritocratic accumulation of works (to which Paul has already answered negatively in favour of a looser system of transfer), but we build on the point that he trusted God and was given δικαιοσύνη in relation to this. The discussion now focuses, however, *on the precise temporal point when this took place*, observing that this 'blessing' was given to Abraham when he was in his uncircumcized and *not* in his circumcized state (and the events of Gen. 15.1-6 do precede those of Gen. 17 in narrative terms—so Paul makes happy use of the four sources of the Pentateuch here).[13]

As in 4.2-8 with its details concerning works, the concerns of the sub-section are signalled not merely by the high statistical profile of certain new motifs but also by their syntactical elaboration and the presence of

---

13. Scholars evaluate the success of Paul's argument here diversely with opinions ranging from C.H. Dodd's 'a palpable hit' (1932) to Donaldson's judgment that it is 'contratextual' (that is, distinctly dodgy: see 1992).

rarer terms in relation to them. So Paul states here …καὶ σημεῖον ἔλαβεν περιτομῆς σφραγῖδα τῆς δικαιοσύνης τῆς πίστεως τῆς ἐν τῇ ἀκροβυστίᾳ: circumcision is a 'sign' and 'seal' of a state already existent.[14] In fact Paul is probably subordinating the 'sign' of circumcision by equating it with a 'seal', that is, with a stamp of ownership or suchlike that indicates (and authenticates) *a more fundamental prior reality*. Hence the key principle Paul wishes to negate, present within the sub-section in a statistically prominent way, is also characterized in terms of a more unusual—and subordinating—motif.

In sum, the brief discussion of 4.9-12 suggests that Abraham, on the strength of the early temporal placement of the events of Gen. 15.6 in his story, demonstrates justification in an uncircumcized state. Instead, the key principle is (again) πίστις, a motif drawn from that text which uses the cognate verb. By implication God can also justify uncircumcized peoples, as well as the circumcized, on the basis of any πίστις that they might have. And to reiterate, desert is not in view for this particular antinomous thesis and related proof as it was in 4.2-8, so neither is the non-merito-cratic quality of πίστις and its association with λογίζομαι the key argumentative premise for Paul. It is the *temporal* (and narrative) occurrence of Gen. 15.6 that counts in relation to the single ritual act of circumcision (which Paul also does not treat meritocratically here). So a significant argumentative disjunction between 4.2-8 and 4.9-12 is apparent (that will lead to trouble for the traditional reading). However, the discussion of 4.9-12 *does* correspond nicely to the antinomous thesis of 3.29-30 where πίστις somehow embraces the distinction between circumcision and

14. 'Sign' only occurs elsewhere in Romans in 15.19; and elsewhere in Paul largely generic usage in 1 Cor. 1.22; 14.22; 2 Cor. 12.12 (2x), and 2 Thess. 2.9 and 3.17. Paul's usage in Rom. 4.11, however, is probably dictated by Gen. 17.11, where that signifier occurs (although in a different, more important sense), so he seems to qualify its sense further in context by supplying the still more unusual motif (for him) of 'seal' or 'stamp'. Cf. elsewhere in Paul only 1 Cor. 9.2. The possibly related σφραγίζω is used in Rom. 15.28; 2 Cor. 1.22; cf. also Eph. 1.13 and 4.30. A generic seal or stamp marked overtly on an item (or even person) a state of ownership, possession or identification already established on other grounds (usually by the exchange of money; in the case of a letter, by composition). The 'sign' of the covenant has therefore, according to Paul, become instead 'a stamp' signifying the presence of a prior and more fundamental state (that is, of a transaction or event that has already taken place), which Paul suggests is associated with πίστις on the grounds of Gen. 15.6. Of course, something also need not necessarily *bear* a stamp to be owned or possessed (or written) by someone; the stamp is, strictly speaking, optional (so v. 11).

uncircumcision (while, interestingly, the supplementary warrants of vv. 29 and 30 drop from view, which is *not* to say that they are unimportant principles for Paul: he just does not seem to develop them in this particular context).

g. *Romans 3.31 and 4.13-16a*

3.31 νόμον οὖν καταργοῦμεν διὰ τῆς πίστεως; μὴ γένοιτο, ἀλλὰ νόμον ἱστάνομεν.
4.13 Οὐ γὰρ διὰ νόμου ἡ ἐπαγγελία τῷ Ἀβραὰμ ἢ τῷ σπέρματι αὐτοῦ, τὸ κληρονόμον αὐτὸν εἶναι κόσμου, ἀλλὰ διὰ δικαιοσύνης πίστεως. 4.14 εἰ γὰρ οἱ ἐκ νόμου κληρονόμοι, κεκένωται ἡ πίστις καὶ κατήργηται ἡ ἐπαγγελία· 4.15 ὁ γὰρ νόμος ὀργὴν κατεργάζεται· οὗ δὲ οὐκ ἔστιν νόμος, οὐδὲ παράβασις. 4.16a Διὰ τοῦτο ἐκ πίστεως, ἵνα κατὰ χάριν, εἰς τὸ εἶναι βεβαίαν τὴν ἐπαγγελίαν παντὶ τῷ σπέρματι, οὐ τῷ ἐκ τοῦ νόμου μόνον ἀλλὰ καὶ τῷ ἐκ πίστεως Ἀβραάμ...

Romans 3.31 tables the question of whether the principle of πίστις abolishes or affirms Torah (continuing our earlier suggested reading of νόμος). The motif of abolition, suggested by the verb καταργέω in 3.31, is reprised once exactly in the corresponding section of ch. 4 (and nowhere else), while the closely similar κενόω is also used there once (and nowhere else). And probably corresponding to ἱστάνομι, the countervailing verb of establishment used in 3.31 is the closely-related phrase... εἰς τὸ εἶναι βεβαίαν that is used in 4.16 (again, its only occurrence in ch. 4, cf. 15.8). These instances are admittedly not as statistically dense as those of the key motifs in the preceding two sections (perhaps because this sub-section is considerably shorter), but they are present and they are also as distinctive in terms of the adjacent argumentation. I conclude: the notion of negation versus establishment is clearly present in 4.13-16a but not elsewhere in Romans 4. But the section possesses other distinctive motifs as well.

The motif of promise, ἡ ἐπαγγελία, is confined largely to this particular sub-section. There have been no instances of ἡ ἐπαγγελία up to v. 13, but then it occurs in vv. 13, 14 and 16. It recurs again within the chapter only in v. 20 (the cognate verb occurs in v. 21), although in quite different syntactical combinations. This distribution is echoed by that of τὸ κληρονόμον, which occurs in this sub-section twice in a clear and close relation to 'promise', but nowhere else in the chapter. Futhermore, these motifs are said in their five instances here either to be abolished or eva-cuated if the principle of νόμος is followed, while πίστις 'establishes' them. They are both also of course clearly grounded in the Scriptures, hence they do fulfill a certain reading of νόμος.

But for those familiar with Gal. 3.15-20 it should come as no surprise that Paul can play off the set of divine promises made to Abraham in Gen. 15.1-5 against later nomistic arrangements like observance of the full Mosaic legislation (both of which systems can legitimately take the brief descriptor νόμος).[15] Apart from the probable parenthesis of v. 15 (cf. also 3.20b; 5.14, 20; 7.7–8.1), this sub-section seems to recapitulate that argument, supplying in vv. 13 and 16 the further distinctive motif of seed (it recurs here only in the quotation of Gen. 15.5 in Rom. 4.18, but is extremely central to the related discussion in Galatians with four of the five instances of 'seed' in that letter occurring there), while that argument in Galatians even uses the same (crucial) verb as 3.31 and 4.14, κταργέω (see Gal. 3.17). So, once again, small unique details seem to assist the main point of each sub-section and largely if not completely uniquely to that sub-section.

Paul's substantive point seems to be that if inheritance is predicated on law-observance, then the state of πίστις noted in Gen. 15.1-6 would have been effectively overruled. Thus, by this teaching, a declaration of Scripture would have been evacuated or abolished. Conversely, to maintain that declaration in defiance of any modification would be to establish or affirm Scripture (at this particular point of course, although perhaps extendable on grounds of principle 5, *kelal upherat* [see n. 8]). Indeed, perhaps Paul attempts to turn the tables on the antithesis at this point. The more obvious reading for a traditional orthopractic Jew would be of course to take things the other way round, with law-observance fulfilling Torah and Paul's abandonment of that in view of πίστις alone appearing to neutralize or to evacuate a large portion of Scripture. Romans 4.12-14 and 16a are a pithy rejoinder to that expectation and to any criticisms extrapolated from it.

In view of this, it seems fair at least to suggest that 4.13-16a corresponds distinctively to the antinomous concerns of 3.31 with abolition vis-à-vis fulfilment of Torah, concerns apparent in these terms nowhere else in the surrounding diatribe or Romans 4. Paul articulates this antimony in vv. 13-16a in a mode already familiar (to us) from Galatians of promise (ἐπαγγελία), and also inverts a possible charge in these terms. The sub-section and its anticipatory announcement consequently continue exactly the structural and argumentative dynamic that we have already observed for 3.27-28 in relation to 4.2-8 and 3.29-30 for 4.9-12.

---

15. A relationship grasped clearly by Wright (1991: 167-68).

h. *Romans 4.23-25*

4.23 Οὐκ ἐγράφη δὲ δι᾽ αὐτὸν μόνον ὅτι ἐλογίσθη αὐτῷ, 4.24 ἀλλὰ καὶ δι᾽ ἡμᾶς, οἷς μέλλει λογίζεσθαι, τοῖς πιστεύουσιν ἐπὶ τὸν ἐγείραντα Ἰησοῦν τὸν κύριον ἡμῶν ἐκ νεκρῶν 4.25 ὃς παρεδόθη διὰ τὰ παραπτώματα ἡμῶν καὶ ἠγέρθη διὰ τὴν δικαίωσιν ἡμῶν.

Verses 23-25 have been offset at this point because I suspect (like many other interpreters, e.g. Stuhlmacher [1994: 69]) that they constitute a broader conclusion to the discussion as a whole, as well as a transition to the concerns of ch. 5, rather than (in terms of the present analysis) an argumentative sub-section corresponding to specific concerns tabled from 3.27.[16] This concluding and transitional function for vv. 23-25 is signalled in part by the explicit switch in application in vv. 23-24a: Paul places 'us' centrally here, not Abraham. The first-person plural pronoun then occurs *three more times* in the rest of the small sub-section. This is not, however, an occurrence symmetrical to 4.1, 12 and 16, where ἡμῶν qualifies 'father' directly and the question there concerns how Abraham is 'our' father. In vv. 23-25 Paul is simply talking about 'us', that is, the letter's audience, and in general soteriological terms: 'we' are those to whom δικαιοσύνη will also be given, those trusting the one who raised Jesus from the dead. So the argument seems to have moved beyond Abraham's fatherhood at this point and to have returned to 'trust' and λογίζομαι in direct relation to the letter's audience (an important resumption also of the theme of giftedness that Paul wishes to emphasize here; see Gaston 1980: 57). Moreover, and as we have just seen, Jesus is tabled for the first time in the entire discussion, initially as the object of God's resurrection, and then within a cryptic twofold formula embracing his atoning death and resurrection; events applied explicitly to 'us' (there is also the matter of the striking composition of v. 25, usually explained by New Testament scholars form-critically but cf. *paromoeosis* in *Rhetoric to Alexander* 28). In short, this sub-section tables two important new motifs, namely, Jesus (in terms of both his resurrection and atoning death) *and* the letter's audience (in broad soteriological terms), concerns that are clearly taken up in detail by 5.1-11 and the following discussion (see e.g. references to

---

16. Note, the transitional function of vv. 23-25 has been asserted by many scholars not committed to the present structural analysis, so once again certain generalized perceptions from the ongoing scholarly debate over this text confirm to a degree the specific contentions being urged here (cf. n. 12).

Jesus' death in vv. 6, 8, 9 and 10, and possibly also in vv. 1 and 2), but that do not correspond especially tightly to any part of the preceding discussion, or to any prior anticipatory antinomy. Hence the sub-section functions analogously to a *transitus*.

This desire on the part of Paul to push through his initial argumentative conclusions concerning specific technical questions to something with more relevance for his audience is also evident earlier in the letter, notably in 1.16-17, 3.22 and 3.26, where distinctive accusative constructions indicate that an instrumental notion has as its goal the letter's audience, literally, either 'all those who trust' (1.16b and 3.22), or the more generic one who trusts or who lives by means of the faithful one (1.17 and 3.26; cf. also 4.12 and 16—and the point is even made here in similar grammatical terms: cf. the unusual accusative διά in v. 25 [2x] that precisely corresponds to 3.25b). It is therefore entirely plausible to find a similar push towards inclusion at the end of this discussion. In this Paul is signalling—and as we would only expect—that his rather discursive discussion of technical soteriological points in relation to Abraham and the events of Gen. 15.6 that takes place from 3.27–4.22 is meant at some point to apply helpfully and directly to his Gentile audience (cf. 15.4).

The substantive implications of this sub-section beg to be unravelled at this point, but unfortunately that would take me too far from my present concerns which are largely compositional and stylistic. It must suffice for now to claim that vv. 23-25 should not be included directly in the specific agenda and responses of the rest of the section—which does, however, immediately entail that Paul's discussion in the bulk of ch. 4 is quite historical being focused on the case vis-à-vis Abraham himself (so reducing considerably the problems of typology; see Käsemann's difficulties in 1971: 95-99), although the discussion leans heavily on one text (i.e. this would not be considered a 'historical' approach in modern terms but 'proof-texting'). With vv. 23-25 offset, we can turn to our last correlated agenda and sub-section which is now more clearly delineated in 4.1 and vv. 16b-22. (This fourth sub-section is now also approximately the same size as its argumentative siblings—in my text it comprises 9.5 lines as against 8.5, 8.5 and 6.5 respectively, although this is not an argument for this arrangement.) Somewhat to my surprise, commentators have not generally detected a transition in Paul's argument at this point (i.e. between vv. 12-16a and vv. 16b-22), so the case here must be especially detailed.

i. *Romans 4.1 and 4.16b-22*

4.1 Τί οὖν ἐροῦμεν εὑρηκέναι Ἀβραὰμ τὸν προπάτορα ἡμῶν κατὰ σάρκα;
[16b] ...ὅς ἐστιν πατὴρ πάντων ἡμῶν, 4.17 καθὼς γέγραπται ὅτι πατέρα
πολλῶν ἐθνῶν τέθεικά σε, κατέναντι οὗ ἐπίστευσεν θεοῦ τοῦ ζωοποιοῦντος
τοὺς νεκροὺς καὶ καλοῦντος τὰ μὴ ὄντα ὡς ὄντα· 4.18 ὃς παρ᾽ ἐλπίδα ἐπ᾽
ἐλπίδι ἐπίστευσεν, εἰς τὸ γενέσθαι αὐτὸν πατέρα πολλῶν ἐθνῶν κατὰ τὸ
εἰρημένον· οὕτως ἔσται τὸ σπέρμα σου· 4.19 καὶ μὴ ἀσθενήσας τῇ πίστει
κατενόησεν τὸ ἑαυτοῦ σῶμα νενεκρωμένον, ἑκατονταέτής που ὑπάρχων,
καὶ τὴν νέκρωσιν τῆς μήτρας Σάρρας, 4.20 εἰς δὲ τὴν ἐπαγγελίαν τοῦ θεοῦ
οὐ διεκρίθη τῇ ἀπιστίᾳ, ἀλλ᾽ ἐνεδυναμώθη τῇ πίστει, δοὺς δόξαν τῷ θεῷ
4.21 καὶ πληροφορηθεὶς ὅτι ὃ ἐπήγγελται δυνατός ἐστιν καὶ ποιῆσαι. 4.22
διὸ καὶ ἐλογίσθη αὐτῷ εἰς δικαιοσύνην.
[Quotations or direct allusions to the Old Testament underlined: in
sequence, Gen. 17.5; 15.6; 17.5; 15.5; 21.6/17.1; and 15.6.]

The ambiguities of 4.1, as well as the peculiar difficulties evident from
v. 16, require a considerably more detailed engagement with substantive
concerns than was the case for the other sub-sections. As we saw in §a, the
subject of the infinitive is unclear, as is the sense of the verb itself
(εὑρίσκω occurring there as the perfect infinitive εὑρηκέναι). Paul usually
deploys this verb in the sense 'to find';[17] however, it may mean 'to obtain'
(or 'to attain').[18] The verb also does not recur specifically in vv. 16b-22
(unlike every other anticipatory marker). Abraham's (fore)fatherhood of
'us' is undisputed, however, and this alone may generate sufficient interpretative leverage on the sub-section for our present purposes.[19] I would
suggest that two aspects of this fatherhood, although not foregrounded by
much current commentary on the passage, are important for a complete
understanding of Paul's argument at this point: (1) that this fatherhood is,
like most fatherhood, biological, and by extension, generative of kinship,
hence in Abraham's case fatherhood is focused on Isaac, a miraculous
conception by means of whom the family and nation of Israel subsequently came into being in fulfilment of God's original promises to him;
and (2) that the question of Abraham's fatherhood of Isaac and thereby of

17. Cf. Rom. 7.10, 21; 10.20 [Isa. 65.1]; 1 Cor. 4.2; 15.15; 2 Cor. 2.13; 5.3; 9.4;
11.12; 12.20; Gal. 2.17; Phil. 2.8; and 3.9; cf. also LNSM 325-26, 29, §§27.1, 27.

18. Cf. esp. Mt 11.29; Acts 7.46; Heb. 9.12; also Josephus, *Ant.* 5.41 (where
'obtain' seems better than 'find', but the latter is not impossible); cf. also LNSM 151,
807-808, §§13.17 and 90.70.

19. Note, he is not explicitly said here—or anywhere else—to be *the type*/τύπος of
later believers, a general notion Paul is well aware of but does not deploy here: see
5.14b; cf. also 8.29; 1 Cor. 15.49; see also Gaston 1980: 57-58.

Israel is linked by the book of Genesis—problematically for Paul—with the rite of circumcision, the *berith mila* (and *not* with meritorious works *per se*), a connection established especially by Genesis 17, which recounts the giving of the covenant of circumcision to Abraham.

In more detail, admittedly the motif of fatherhood is not limited to the fourth sub-section. It occurs three times in the second sub-section in vv. 11 and 12 (2x), as well as three times in vv. 16b-18 (although not, it should be noted, in the third sub-section). In all these cases it is Abraham's fatherhood 'of us' that is important, that is, Paul is clearly concerned to extend the illustrious Jewish patriarch's paternity over Gentiles in some sense (and the exact method of that extension should not be prematurely assumed). But while vv. 11-12 claim the paternity of Abraham over the uncircumcised and circumcized alike on the basis of Gen. 15.6, that section does not elaborate or prove the claim of fatherhood itself (merely, and as we have seen, the legitimacy of δικαιοσύνη being given within an uncircumcized state in relation to πίστις)—we might say that the motif receives no syntactical development there. Hence I suspect that the motif's occurrence in vv. 11 and 12 only reiterates the claim to Abraham's appropriate 'fatherhood' of Gentiles made by 4.1 (although that Paul mentions this in the context of circumcision will ultimately prove significant). Verses 16b-22, however, grapple directly with the issue of Abraham's paternity ultimately of 'us' Gentiles, and in a much more problematic context. The problem is signalled almost immediately in that sub-section with the citation of Gen. 17.5 in v. 17; a text that explicitly states Abraham's future fatherhood of the Gentiles, πατέρα πολλῶν ἐθνῶν τέθεικά σε. This text occurs twice in the sub-section, providing two of the three instances of πατήρ there (it is cited again in v. 18). I suspect that the presence of this particular text here is very important.

Intriguingly, Paul did not cite Gen. 17.5 in Galatians, although he employed Abrahamic traditions there extensively.[20] Neither does Paul cite

20. He deployed a mixture of Gen. 12.3 and 22.18 (and 26.4: cf. also Sir. 44.21) in 3.8: ἐνευλογηθήσονται ἐν σοὶ πάντα τὰ ἔθνη. The verbs are identical in both texts, and the dative phrases very similar—ἐν σοί in 12.3 and ἐν τῷ σπέρματί σου in 22.18/26.4. The subjects are also close: πᾶσαι αἱ φυλαὶ τῆς γῆς in 12.3 and πάντα τὰ ἔθνη τῆς γῆς in 22.18. So either the dative phrase from 12.3 (i.e. ἐν σοί) has been slipped into 22.18, or the subject of 22.18 has been substituted for that of 12.3. In the context of Galatians, one suspects the former (seed will be a prominent motif in Paul's later argument as will—arguably—the story of Gen. 22). Gen. 18.18 is also very close, using ἐν αὐτῷ instead of ἐν σοί.

Gen. 17.5 anywhere else in Romans,[21] *and for obvious reasons*. Genesis 17 links Abraham's fatherhood of many Gentile nations explicitly with the covenant of circumcision (which, it also says, will be '*a sign*' of 'an everlasting covenant'). Abraham even receives that promise here as his name in the context of undergoing the ritual surgery. It is a short step now to the perception of another argumentative antinomy at this point in the text that aligns nicely with the other problems that Paul has been attempting to resolve in context. The issue concerns Abraham's fatherhood of the many Gentile nations. Is this to be construed as Gen. 17.5 suggests—and as most of traditional Judaism in Paul's day also understood it—and linked with circumcision, literally, the excision of a piece of male flesh, and probably thereby also with broader law-observance? Or, is it to be construed (somehow) differently from this, perhaps as Gen. 15.6 alone might suggest, and therefore independently of circumcision and/or law-observance, as vv. 2-16a have already argued for related matters?[22]

Paul also cites Gen. 15.6 in Gal. 3.6, and a phrase found specifically in Gen. 12.7; 13.15; 17.7-8, 9; and 24.7 in Gal. 3.16: καὶ τῷ σπέρματί σου (cf. also Gen. 22.18, a dative, and vv. 17 and 18a for accusative instances, τὸ σπέρμα σου; only καί is missing from these texts). He also uses the stories of Hagar and Ishmael and Sarah and Isaac as recounted in Gen. 16 and 21 in 4.21-31, citing Gen. 21.9 explicitly in 4.30.

21. In fact, this is the text's sole occurrence in the New Testament. Acts 7.5 cites Gen. 17.8, a reference made to the land in Stephen's speech.

22. This link with circumcision can explain Paul's undeveloped use of 'father' in the chapter's second sub-section, a section also concerned with circumcision. The two motifs are probably linked in his mind by their connection within their original context in Genesis, although they were in any case a standard Jewish association: see *Jub.* 15.9-34; Sir. 44.19-21 (esp. v. 20b: ἐν σαρκὶ αὐτοῦ ἔστησεν διαθήκην); 1QS 16.1, 5-6 (cf. *m. Ned.* 3.11 and *Gen. R.* 46.1: 'Great is circumcision, for despite all the religious duties which Abraham our father fulfilled, he was not called perfect until he was circumcised'; see also *Gen. R.* 2.3; 42.8 and 44.4). I owe the insight that Paul is grappling with circumcision and the awkward implications of Gen. 17 in Rom. 4 originally to Donaldson (1992; see also now his 1997 study), although he would disapprove of the way I have developed this notion. I think that Donaldson is profoundly correct in his claim that Paul is struggling here (at times) with an opposing reading of Abraham based on Gen. 17, but of course in my view this does not explain all this chapter's argumentation; merely that particular announcement and consequent sub-section.

This problem for Paul might also possibly be reinforced by a contemporary Jewish view that truth comes in two forms, elemental then developed, so in this context, Gen. 15.6 *then* 17.5: see Daube (1956: 141-50), taken up by Longenecker in the context of Galatians (1990: 111). This would be entirely appropriate here, but unfortunately I see no explicit evidence that the view is in play.

But one might ask at this point why Paul would table the issue of circumcision again, when he seems already to have dealt with that in vv. 9-12. The problem introduced by Gen. 17.5 from v. 16b onwards is slightly different from that addressed by Rom. 4.9-12, although ultimately it concerns the same religious ritual (i.e. different arguments are being brought to bear on the same basic contention). Genesis 17.5 tables circumcision in the context of Abraham's fatherhood, and so does not consider the ritual as an isolated observance (cf. *y. Bikk.* 1.4; *Tanh. B.* 32a and *Pes. R.* 108a; collected in Hansen 1989: 197). Moreover, and as I shall argue in more detail shortly, both the original story as recounted in Genesis, and Paul's discussion of that story here in Romans 4, assume the fulfilment of that fatherhood in a rather concrete fashion *in the conception and birth of Isaac*, the child of promise.[23] That is, Abraham became the father of Israel, and then somehow of 'many nations', specifically through Isaac, a succession denoted in much Jewish literature merely by the phrase 'the/our fathers' or its equivalent.[24] This event, which fulfilled Abraham's divine promise of fatherhood and blessing, now creates a difficulty for Paul because it occurred well after the events of Gen. 15.6, while the

---

23. A point that, if true, draws Paul's discussion of Abraham here much closer to some of his discussion of Abraham in Galatians. Gentiles enjoy Abraham's fatherhood only when they are grafted into his illustrious son, someone descended from Isaac, and also corresponding to him, that is (of course) Jesus, the miraculously-conceived, crucified and 'on the third day' (cf. Gen 22.4) resurrected one.

24. So we ought to resist spiritualizing the text at this point. I would suggest that it is Abraham's biological fatherhood that is under discussion; cf. esp. Sir. 44.22 following vv. 19-21; *Jub.* 16.12, 16b (cf. 19.16-29, where Abraham also recognizes that God will bless the seed of Jacob rather than Esau, seed meaning descendants); also Isa. 51.2; *2 Bar.* 57.1; see also Boyarin 1994; Stowers 1994: 221-50. Much modern Gentile exegesis passes too easily over the substantial intermediate steps between Abraham, his fatherhood, and 'us', that to a Jewish mind were probably entirely normal and necessary. Abraham's fatherhood of Jews is one of kinship and descent. Conversely, an exemplary spiritualized 'fatherhood' looks suspiciously like a later Christian contribution to the reading of Abraham. So Stowers's pointed observation: 'later Christian readings, with their categories of sin and salvation, have obscured the issues of ethnic lineage and inheritance that would have appeared central to Paul's ancient readers. Paul writes about gentiles who… [are] outside of the fleshly lineage of Abraham and its sonship' (1994: 221). Of course, the spiritualized reading may ultimately prove correct, but it will have to be established in the face of the general exegetical trend contemporary to Paul, and that we must assume, at least at first, that he shared. Indeed, we must find reasonably unambiguous textual indications in support of such a phenomenologically revisionist reading.

covenant of circumcision, established in ch. 17, now stands between them. So Paul must attempt to deal with the argument here that Abraham's paternity of Isaac, and through him his paternity ultimately of 'many nations', occurred only *after* the covenant of circumcision was established and accepted, *and that the latter is therefore the presupposition for the former*. In short, the link between Abraham's later paternity of and through Isaac and circumcision, a link effectively established by Gen. 17.5 but also assumed by much Judaism of the time, is what seems to create the present problem for Paul.

But is Isaac's birth actually a factor in ch. 4? (Certainly much commentary does not seem to emphasize this.)[25] Put slightly differently, is Abraham's paternity (an explicit motif) being considered here in fundamentally realistic terms by Paul, as it was by many of his contemporaries?

As the well-known contexts of Gen. 15.6 and 17.5 suggest, Abraham's paternity was effected there through the miraculous conception and birth of Isaac to Sarah, an event recounted in Genesis 21. This was the specific fulfilment of the earlier divine promises of blessing which were overtly connected—in typical tribal fashion—to progeny and thereby to multiple descendants and their inheritance of that staple of existence, land (Abraham's complaints in chs. 12 and 15 were similarly oriented). Isaac was therefore the first link in the biological and familial chain of paternity that would lead, through Jacob, to the nation of Israel, and also beyond that somehow to the many nations. His creation and birth was consequently the critical event that enabled the fulfilment of the promises made in Gen. 15.1-5 and 17.1-5 (as well as elsewhere), while the bulk of later Jewish consideration of Abraham—although often emphasizing different details in his story—assumes this pragmatic notion of fatherhood. I would suggest that this traditional expectation of Abraham's in Genesis that a son and heir would be born in accordance with God's promises in order to facilitate the blessing of many descendants, an expectation maintained by Abraham's later descendants, namely, the Jews, is imprinted across Paul's narrative as well (after all, he assumes as much in 9.6-13).

---

25. For example, Käsemann's magnificent discussion passes over it in silence (1971). Gaston is a partial exception, noting—intriguingly—the point briefly in his consideration of Gen. 15.6 in its original Hebrew context (1980: 41). The presuppositions and eventual direction of this study are very different from Gaston's, but his sensitivity to Jewish understandings of Abraham, and thereby to previously overlooked nuances in Paul's discussion, is exemplary. Similar considerations apply to Stowers (1994: esp. 225, 229) and Donaldson (1992 and 1997).

In v. 17 Paul speaks of a God who can give life to the dead and who calls things that are not as though they are. This corresponds directly to the statements of v. 19 that *Abraham's loins and Sarah's womb are dead*; something bound up—clearly problematically—with the promises. The problem is of course that the old couple are impossibly past *child-bearing*, and that God must therefore in effect create life from the dead in order to fulfill his promises, an action specifically realized in the conception and birth of Isaac. Hence Isaac is the unstated but necessary focus of v. 17b *and* vv. 19-21.

Verses 24-25 confirm this by briefly supplying an analogy between Christians and Abraham. Christians will be given δικαιοσύνη, like Abraham was, because they trust in the God who raises Jesus from the dead, while v. 25 adds that Jesus himself was delivered over to death as well as raised to life. For this analogy to hold properly, Abraham must trust God *concerning Isaac*, a son conceived in the face of death and thereby in a sense also resurrected (and later on, in Gen. 22, also in effect received back from the dead).[26] That is, Christians trust God 'the father' concerning 'his son', dead and raised, just as Abraham trusted God concerning his son, conceived from the dead and thereby brought to life (and also later raised 'on the third day'). If we drop Isaac from this comparison then all the christological information supplied by Paul in vv. 24b-25 is redundant, while the analogy itself is weaker and less apposite[27] (and why would we resist the full analogy in any case, given the cues already present in context concerning Isaac?).

In support of these two direct textual implications we may note that Gen. 15.5 is quoted in v. 18b, 'thus will be your seed', a text appropriately read in its contexts (i.e. originally in Genesis, elsewhere in Paul, notably in Gal. 3, and here in Romans) as a singular reference to Isaac (so also 4.13). Finally, Paul alludes to Gen. 21.5 in v. 19,[28] a verse drawn from the

26. Jesus of course is also a son: see 1.3, 9 (cf. 1.4); 5.10; and 8.3, 29, 32 (Gen. 22.12/16).

27. Christians, like Abraham, trust in a God who resurrects from the dead (cf. 4.17 and n. 31 below); a 'flatter' reading with no christological rationale or distinctive Christian content.

28. Verse 19b states that Abraham is 'approximately a hundred years old' (ἑκατονταέτης που ὑπάρχων), a statement informed by Gen. 21.6, and more distantly by 17.1, 17 and 24. In Gen. 17.1 he is 'ninety-nine years old', ἐτῶν ἐνενήκοντα ἐννέα, and in Gen. 21.6 'a hundred years old', ἑκατὸν ἐτῶν. Paul's approximate terminology here is therefore deliberate. Isaac has not yet been born but the promise in Gen. 17.5 has already been given. So according to the text he is *almost* a hundred years old.

chapter, and actual pericope, that recounts Isaac's miraculous conception and birth.[29]

Hence it seems reasonably well-attested that behind the question of Abraham's fleshly paternity of 'the many nations' in fulfilment of Gen. 15.6 and 17.5 (etc.) as Paul addresses the issue in Romans 4 is the miraculous birth of Isaac, the son through whom the promises are initially continued in order (later) to be fully realized. Crucially, Gen. 17.5 also seems to suggest that acceptance of the covenant of circumcision was a critical intermediate step on the way to this famous and miraculous fulfilment of those promises.

If we grant that this challenge lies behind Rom. 4.16b-22, a challenge freighted by Gen. 17.5 in relation to Abraham's paternity of Isaac and the intervening step of circumcision, it is important to grasp next that it constitutes a rather peculiar argumentative difficulty for Paul, and will consequently require a slightly different response from his preceding ones. Much of Paul's argumentative leverage in 4.2-16a against the challenges tabled there derived from the early placement of Gen. 15.6 in the overall story of the patriarch. This text was able to trump the matters of meritorious law-observance, circumcision, and the putative negation of scriptural teaching, largely because it occurred earlier than, and hence independently of, those events, as well as being itself a clear scriptural assertion, as well as a rather minimalist one. However, if it is granted that the birth of Isaac is central to the discussion from v. 16b, then Gen. 15.6 is now limited in its argumentative usefulness since Isaac's birth took place in ch. 21 and hence well after 15.6. Any easy temporal trumping or equivalent direct refutation is now precluded. So how does Paul make his case?

In fact, Paul does seem to follow the same basic strategy. That is, he again tries to use Gen. 15.6 to disrupt the challenge, in this case the ostensible connection between circumcision and Abraham's paternity of Isaac. But he has now to broaden the apparent relevance of this text rather than merely table it in its own right, so several new premises must be

---

Paul's chronological accuracy in terms of the text is also apparent in Galatians (see esp. 3.17).

29. And note that the citation of a fragment of Gen. 15.6 in v. 22 following the statement that 'God was able to do what had been promised' is almost certainly also taking its meaning from this divine conception. The giving of δικαιοσύνη to Abraham is indeed the gift of a salvific eschatological event or action that is furthermore, in context, the giving of a miraculous son born of, in procreative terms, dead parents. It is a life-giving resurrecting eschatological action, as v. 17 has already hinted.

supplied to make his case plausible at this point—and a rather cunning piece of argumentation ensues. More specifically, Paul brackets Gen. 17.5 with statements that speak of another story, a story extrapolated from Gen. 15.6, thereby essentially narratively assimilating it. The two key narrative dynamics are, on the one hand (of course), Abraham's πίστις and, on the other, the resurrecting God who gifts salvation. Any protests against this unfolding story will ultimately look unnecessary, and perhaps even impious, even though the distinctive concerns of Gen. 17.5 in its own context have thereby actually been marginalized.

In more detail: the Greek of vv. 16b-22 is complex. In fact, it comprises one sentence that runs from v. 16 to v. 21 being constructed with a series of subordinate clauses using relative pronouns, participles, conjunctions and parentheses (cf. to a degree 3.21-26). The point of transition into the distinctive concerns of the fourth sub-section is marked by the first relative pronoun that co-ordinates 'the fatherhood of all of us' with Abraham (and note the resonance with 4.1), thereby introducing a different subject from vv. 13-16a which was concerned with negation versus fulfillment. Three stages of semantic layering and argumentation are apparent from this point: Paul characterizes Gen. 17.5 itself in a particular fashion in v. 17; Gen. 17.5 is related directly to Gen. 15.6 in v. 18; and then that depiction is embellished dramatically through a distinctive accumulation of clauses in vv. 19-21. The result is that Gen. 17.5 ends up reading like Gen. 15.6. The first stage, v. 17, quotes Gen. 17.5 and attaches a qualifying clause with the phrase κατέναντι οὗ. Hence before progressing further in our general analysis, we must pause to consider in some detail the meaning of this difficult but important phrase.

BDF suggests (§294, esp. [2]) that a switch in word order has taken place, allied with the attraction of the relative to its antecedent (which, as things stand in the text, now follows the relative). That is, Paul intends to say κατέναντι τοῦ θεοῦ ᾧ ἐπίστευσεν, but ends up saying κατέναντι οὗ ἐπίστευσεν θεοῦ...; 'in the sight of God, in whom he trusted' as against 'in the sight of [something], he trusted God' (cf. also 2 Cor. 1.4 and Eph. 1.6). I hesitate to correct BDF, but on this occasion I suspect its recommendations are wrong.

The clause so construed does not integrate easily into its context: '*in the sight of God*, the one who makes alive the dead and calls the non-existent existent, *in whom he trusted*...' This statement supposedly follows the citation of Gen. 17.5 and precedes a new line of thought introduced by a relative pronoun that harks back to 'Abraham' in v. 16a, so it must be relatively self-contained. It can only work in fact if the two clauses concerning fatherhood intervening between τῷ ἐκ πίστεως ᾿Αβραάμ in v. 16a and κατέναντι in v. 17b are themselves marginalized parenthetically (or some such) and the emphasis of the prior phrase on Abraham's πίστις is assumed to be central. Even then, however, it does not make a great deal of sense: 'in the presence of God, Abraham trusted in God'. This seems an odd, if not completely redundant, assertion. Paul does not speak of 'trust' in these terms anywhere else. BDF's suggestion also requires the relative pronoun to have both switched its correct place with the substantive θεός *and* been attracted to its case, a twofold assumption.

The immediate context (i.e. v. 18 and following) suggests rather that the matter of Abraham's paternity is *central* (not marginal) to the following discussion, so to suggest a parenthetical function in vv. 16b-17a looks incorrect. The relative pronoun is also at present in the right case opposite κατέναντι (i.e. the genitive), so there is no need, at least initially, to assume its attraction and relocation. The crucial question then is what other possible antecedents are present in context apart from θεός that could take the appropriate sense of κατέναντι. Hence at this point we must consider what semantic range κατέναντι itself has.

The relevant comparative semantic sample for κατέναντι used in this figurative sense is small: 2 Cor. 2.17, 12.19; also Sir. 28.26, and Jdt. 12.15, 19. In these texts the improper preposition, always taking a genitive, means basically 'in view of' or 'in the presence of' (hence in this sense also 'before')—and so it is understandable that BDF sought to place God here as its object. Paul speaks in Christ and in the presence of (or 'before', or 'in view of') God; Sirach warns against an unguarded tongue allowing exploitation because of statements made in the presence of others; and Judith has her maidservant lay down lambskins for her to sit on, and then eats and drinks her prepared food, in the presence of Holofernes.

But can Abraham stand 'in the presence of' the only other possible antecedent in context, namely, *the saying itself* (i.e. Gen. 17.5), and then, following this, go on to trust in God?[30] Actually the ensuing context states twice that Abraham does orient himself vis-à-vis God's statements (see vv. 18 and 20). Indeed, all of Romans 4 presupposes the argumentative

---

30. LNSM proves that the preposition can take an impersonal object: see Mt. 21.12 (a village opposite), Mk 13.3 (the Mount of Olives), and 15.39 (the cross), although I demur that the sense of 'opposite' is as necessary as their translations here suggest (see 718, §83.42).

implications of Abraham trusting God's promises (in context, the statements of Gen. 15.1-5). So that Abraham would stand 'in the presence of' God's statement of Gen. 17.5, and then go on *to trust* God himself concerning the outcome of that statement, makes excellent sense within our broader construal of the sub-section. I would suggest further that it is Paul's exact intention here to link *the statement* of Gen. 17.5 with *the action* of Gen. 15.6 in terms of trust, hence why that action is stated immediately following the citation of the other text. This also seems possible in the broader context of much Old Testament piety. Moreover, no displacement or attraction of the relative pronoun now needs to be posited.

For these reasons I suggest following that construal here, namely, 'the faithful Abraham, who is the father of us all, just as it is written "the father of many nations I have made you", in the presence of which [i.e. that declaration], *he trusted* the God who makes alive the dead and calls the non-existent existent [i.e. cf. Gen. 15.6]'. In further support, and as we will see shortly, v. 18 makes exactly the same point.

We can now return to Paul's further thematic development at this point. In v. 17, the first stage of the sub-section's argument, God is embellished by Paul distinctively. He 'makes the dead alive' and 'calls the non-existent existent' (the Greek is plural). It seems fair in general terms for Paul to state in v. 17 that God is these things in relation to Gen. 17.5—many Jews believed in a resurrecting God.[31] But the suggestion is even more appropriate given the specific context of Paul's claim. In vv. 19-21 (as we have noted previously) it becomes clear that these attributes pertain specifically in context to the conception of Isaac. Moreover, the conception of Isaac will be an especially life-creating event. Hence Paul foregrounds the twin elements of Abraham's trust and God's life-creating power soon to be focused in Isaac *in relation to Gen. 17.5* (and any concomitants are allowed to slip unmarked into the background).

---

31. Some scholars suggest a scriptural echo, most likely of Isa. 48.13, but these statements looks more like variations on a Jewish theologoumenon. As Burchard comments, '[a]round the beginning of our era "He who gives life to the dead" had become all but a definition of God in Judaism' (*OTP*, I: 234 [n.p.]). See also Hofius (1989: 121, n. 1), who cites in comparison with 'the one who makes alive…', 2 Cor. 1.9, *Jos. Asen.* 8.9 and 20.7, the second of the 18 benedictions, and *b. Ket.* 8b; and in relation to 'the one who calls…', 2 Macc. 7.28 (an important text: cf. also vv. 22-23), *2 Bar.* 21.4 and 48.8b, Philo, *Spec. Leg.* 4.187 (also *Op. Mund.* 81); cf. *2 Clem.* 1.8 and *Apostolic Constitutions* 8.12.7. Cf. also the contextually related notion of giving glory to God, so Mt. 5.16 and 1 Pet. 2.12; also, more generally, Jn 5.21.

Verse 18, reaching back to the antecedent of Abraham in v. 16b with a second relative pronoun, links Gen. 17.5 to Gen. 15.5 explicitly and adds further important qualifying material to the verb πιστεύω which has just been used in v. 17. That is, the second component in the narrative dynamic Paul wishes to establish is now elaborated. Abraham is said specifically to trust (literally) 'from hope to hope'. This again, as a positive claim in context, seems fair. Of course Abraham hoped that God would grant him an heir. Verse 18 also notes, however, that this particular attitude and hope had already been established by Gen. 15.6, because that text also promised Abraham 'seed', that is, both texts spoke of promises and were ultimately focused on Isaac, the heir. In effect, then, this similarity and consequent linkage pushes Abraham's attitude of hopeful trust in God's promise back 13 years. By the time God speaks in Gen. 17.5 Abraham has been trusting in hope for well over a decade. The implication is that he will continue to do so as Gen. 17.5 is spoken to him, that promise adding the further information that he will thereby be the father 'of many nations' (although this was something already apparent to the careful reader of Genesis in 12.3). So Abraham's trust is thereby extended over time *and* a symmetry between Gen. 17.5 and 15.6 is further established.

By this point, then, Paul has introduced the two elements of the resurrecting, life-creating God and Abraham's ongoing hopeful trust in him into the context of Gen. 17.5 on the basis of their general narrative plausibility there and a consequent apparent continuity with Gen. 15.6. Their presence seems entirely natural given the surrounding story of Isaac's promised conception and Abraham's trust in God concerning this. But the fact that they are the only elements which Paul is specifying at this stage *also ineluctably highlights them*. Verses 19-21 now dramatize this suggestion considerably (i.e. Paul doesn't want us to miss the point).

Verses 19-21 uses three conjunctions to add three further verbs and their clauses, along with three more participial clauses, to this unfolding picture (clearly the most complex of the semantic layers Paul crafts in the sub-section). These clauses link the two narrative motifs we have already noted more tightly together, although the focus remains on Abraham's attribute of trust as in v. 18. But Abraham, according to Paul, does not merely trust in God and his promises hopefully and over time in v. 19. He trusts specifically in spite of 'the death' of his loins and 'the death' of Sarah's womb (i.e. their death in procreative terms). And God's life-giving attribute, noted in v. 17, now corresponds precisely to this particular problem, a problem that is, however, again narratively appropriate since the production of a son remains Abraham's central concern. That is, it is again narratively plausible for Paul to emphasize that Abraham's trust at the narrative and temporal point of Gen. 17.5 existed in the context of a struggle between his death in procreative terms and God's promise of an heir. The more elaborate text here states, moreover, that Abraham is not weak or wavering in the face of this knowledge but, rather, his trust waxes in strength and he even glorifies God because of his deep conviction that God is able to do what has been promised (and indeed will do it). In short, the principle of πίστις is massively reified and also connected directly with the story's central concern, namely, God's miraculous creation of Isaac. After this breathless accumulation of clauses dramatizing Abraham's trust it seems entirely plausible for Paul to state '*therefore* (διό) δικαιοσύνη was given to him' (this also is another tacit introduction of Gen. 15.6). Who would deny the appropriateness of God's response to Abraham here in the light of this heroic contest in terms of trust? At the end of a fourteen-year battle with biological realities, Abraham's trust in God's cryptic promises seems to have been vindicated.[32]

32. Paul's development of πίστις here is important (he uses the verb twice and the noun twice). He gives considerable detail concerning his perception of its nature in the context of his argument. It persists over time (technically about 14 years); it does not waver; it hopes; it gives glory; it does not doubt when faced with irrefutable facts concerning death; and so on. It is, in short, a martyrological reading of the signifier denoting a trust so deep and extensive that it slides over into the active quality of faithfulness in terms of perseverance, hope, and steadfast endurance; something denoted in Greek also by πίστις. For speakers of English, the presence of trust *over time* in someone *and under extreme duress* would be regarded as actively pursued and largely identical with faithfulness or fidelity (cf. also loyalty, steadfastness, etc.). Important verbal equivalents for πίστις in Paul are therefore ὑπομονή, ὑπακοή, and ὑπήκοος (see for the first esp. Rom. 8.25 [also perhaps 5.3 and 4], cf. 2.7; 15.4-5; also 2 Cor. 1.6; 6.4; 12.12; Col. 1.11; for the second, Rom. 5.19 [also 1.5 and and perhaps 16.26]; the last, Phil. 2.8; cf. LNSM 307-308, 467-68, §§25.167-78, 36.12-22). This quality is ultimately transferable to Christians, as vv. 23-24 suggest, but in these terms it is also equally transferable to Christ himself in the context of his martyrological death at Easter, and then perhaps makes better sense overall if it is mediated to Christians by and 'in' him (what Christian will attempt this martyrological trust independently of Christ?). Moreover, it would seem that Abraham as attested by Gen. 15.6 and the subsequent story is a paradigm of trust for Paul (viz. 'strong trust'), so Paul seems more than happy to explicate the verb used by the LXX in terms of the cognate substantive (3.27–4.25 has 6 instances of the verb and 15 of the noun). Conversely, 'belief'—that is, the affirmation or certitude of propositional knowledge—is a minor semantic component. It is present, as it has to be, but that is not Paul's concern in

But what has Paul achieved here in argumentative terms? As we have already suggested, the argument is not formal in the sense it has been in his three previous sub-sections—Paul at this point cannot use Gen. 15.6 simply to knock out the opposing contention. Hence he has used a mixture of bombast, pathos and narrative suggestion, so at the end of the sub-section we 'feel' Paul's point as a generally plausible impression more than grasp a clear logical victory (and hence perhaps some of the difficulties various interpreters have grasping and articulating it).[33] Primarily on overarching narrative grounds, Paul has claimed that the promise in Gen. 17.5 to Abraham of fatherhood in the context of circumcision is best understood in terms of the two crucial dynamics set in train by Gen. 15.6, namely, Abraham's unbending trust in God's promise of an heir and God's later life-creating response in terms of Isaac's miraculous conception. That trust is now elaborated in heroic terms, evoking our admiration and sympathy as well as our judgment of general narrative plausibility. During this brief but powerful dramatization Paul simply does not mention the attendant issue of circumcision that Genesis 17 raises. But we tend not to notice this omission—our attention is otherwise engaged. God seems to gift Abraham his paternity in response to his extraordinary fidelity, and Gen. 17.5 has thereby been subsumed within an elaborated Gen. 15.6. Moreover, to add anything to this short story of extraordinary trust and its reward—if we *do* notice its oversimplifications—now seems somewhat gauche. *This would detract from Abraham's heroism* to which God responds graciously as he had promised.[34]

context (cf. Jas 2.19). In essence, the context is personal, hence the emphasis is on 'trust', an interpersonal quality.

33. I do not detect either enthymemic and/or abductive reasoning here.

34. One can imagine Paul retorting, 'Are you really suggesting that the poor man has not done enough yet?!, or that this superhuman contest is in some way inadequate?!' (arguments alternatively in terms of pathos and logos). This is tantamount to saying that a martyr, having just been executed for their confession of the one God, will only be saved if they also kept the Sabbath correctly throughout their life; a not invalid point but an insensitive one in context, and possibly also asking too much—such a suggestion here also belittles the piety of the great Patriarch. I suspect that Paul was well aware of this fall-back position. Furthermore, such a contention integrates with a widespread view in Paul's time of Abraham in heroic terms and as supremely faithful to God more in the manner of a martyr (cf. 1 Macc. 2.52) than someone perfectly law-observant (as in *Jub. passim*; *T. Levi* 9.1-14; *2 Bar.* 57.1-3; 1QS 3.2-4; *m. Qid.* 4.14; *Lev. R.* 2.10 [on Lev. 1.12]); a view generated primarily, but not exclusively, by Abraham's behaviour in Gen. 22 (note also the Jewish tradition of

As stated earlier, Paul's case so construed in vv. 16b-22 is not overly plausible in formal terms (I suspect that it will only persuade those already convinced), but this does nevertheless seem a plausible construal of his argument in context. The reading makes sense of his troublesome and unusual deployment of Gen. 17.5 (otherwise, this is the intertextual equivalent of shooting himself in the foot), and also of the question concerning Abraham's fatherhood 'of us' in terms of kinship (i.e. through actual descent, hence in Abraham's specific case, through Isaac: cf. also 9.6-13 and Gal. 4.21-31), and this in the broadly antinomous terms that characterized the other three issues discussed in context. We can even see why Paul gets himself into trouble at this point and is forced to be uncharacteristically laboured. His favoured proof-text, Gen. 15.6, cannot deal so effectively with this particular challenge and he must resort to drama and bombast.

If this reading of vv. 16b-22 is granted, we can now also perhaps more plausibly resolve some of the ambiguities in the notorious 4.1 and perceive its possible function as the fourth sub-section's compact anticipatory announcement.

The basic issue in the later sub-section as I see it is Abraham's paternity of the Gentile nations, that notion being signalled there three times and most notably by the dual citation of Gen. 17.5. Consequently Abraham is an entirely appropriate subject for the infinitive in 4.1. A case can be made suggesting that Abraham 'discovers' or 'finds' something in vv. 16b-22 (there are several verbs and phrases related to cognition in the passage because of Paul's elaboration there of the motif of trust drawn from Gen. 15.6). But the reading 'obtains' fits so well in context that this is probably unnecessary. Verses 16b-22 revolves around Abraham's receipt of the divine gift of Isaac, and through him the divinely promised inheritance of many nations, so the 'obtaining' of paternity by Abraham seems an excellent reading of 4.1. Furthermore, the salience of Gen. 17.5 in vv. 16b-22 also suggests construing the first-person plural personal pronoun in 4.1 emphatically. It is precisely Abraham's fatherhood '*of us*' ('the many nations') that is ultimately at issue. Hence thus far it seems quite appropriate to understand 4.1b to be asking in some fashion, 'Did Abraham obtain paternity of us, the Gentiles?'

Abraham's faithfulness through ten trials, the last and most important of which was the *Akedah*). Paul does not introduce the *Akedah* here explicitly (unless perhaps it is implied by vv. 24-25), but the general heroic view of Abraham certainly seems operative (see Sandmel 1971; Hansen 1989: 175-99; Longenecker 1990: 110-12).

At this point we must consider the two remaining semantic elements in the verse carefully, namely, the initial diatribal statement τί οὖν ἐροῦμεν and the final phrase κατὰ σάρκα (and the interpretation of these two elements is partly interdependent). Should the diatribal commonplace be rendered as part of a complex sentence, or as a sentence in its own right thereby also setting off the remainder of 4.1 as a self-contained statement? I incline to the latter.

Although the clause τί οὖν ἐροῦμεν can be read as part of a sentence there are only two such instances in Paul, and in Rom. 3.5 it is part of an apodosis while in 8.31 it receives only a very minor addition. Moreover, in all its Pauline occurrences (see also 6.1; 7.7; and 9.14 and 30) the interrogative takes the sense '*what?*' It is now difficult to render the rest of 4.1 as a meaningful complement to this question. More appropriate, and more stylistically comparable, is a rendering of the following words either in terms of a second more detailed question or as a programmatic or countervailing statement.[35] So an integrated function and/or possible variant meaning for τί οὖν ἐροῦμεν should probably be rejected, and a standard independent diatribal rendering followed: 'What shall we say then?'; a rendering that asks for a further following statement, here supplied by the rest of 4.1.

We ought now to render the verse's final—and still problematic—phrase with some emphasis, hence in the sense, 'Did Abraham obtain paternity of us, the Gentiles, *in relation to flesh*?' Read in this manner the phrase κατὰ σάρκα can be understood to be signalling the matter of circumcision (cf. Gen. 17.11, 13, 14, 23-25; Sir. 44.20; Gal. 6.13), and such a reading would also thereby reproduce the adversarial quality of the previous three issues, not to mention a 'hot topic' in context. The prepositional phrase κατὰ σάρκα is consequently quite important, bearing the brunt of Paul's inquiry; something assisted by its placement at the end of

35. A case can be made for rendering τί 'how'; an acceptable, albeit possibly Hebraic, reading of τί presupposing the Hebrew *moh*: see BAGD 819 citing Mt. 7.14 (given that reading) and, more certainly, Lk. 12.49; also Ps. 3.2; Song 1.10; 7.7; 2 Kgs 6.20; cf. also BDF §299 (4); although in these texts in isolation. But in the face of its uniform usage elsewhere and the sense that it is a fixed dialogical *phrase*, this seems unlikely. Yet, as we have just seen, without this slightly altered interrogative meaning it is difficult for it to function effectively within an extended sentence—the question 'what' did Abraham obtain or discover makes little sense, especially given that the answer, 'fatherhood', is immediately present in the same sentence. This consequently counts against rendering the phrase *as* part of a longer sentence.

the sentence. This construal and emphasis seems better than a reading in terms of some sort of response to the inquiry just made in terms of Abraham's actual paternity: 'What will we say (about Abraham's fatherhood of us)?' It seems less likely that Abraham's actual ancestry (in some sense) is in doubt as much as its manner or mode.[36] But how are we to construe this strange sentence constructed with an infinitive in exact grammatical terms, even if we are confident that its general sense has been grasped? Surely Paul could simply have supplied the appropriate verb and given us a question in terms of direct discourse? But this is not what we have to deal with, however much we would prefer it.

Nevertheless, in classical Greek the complements to verbs of perception, saying, and so on, are often given by infinitive constructions, and often also in the form of an indirect question (although participles are another grammatical alternative). Indirect discourse has largely disappeared from the New Testament in favour of direct discourse,[37] and where it does appear distinctive particles tend to signal its presence, namely, ὅτι and/or ὡς.[38] Moreover, Rom. 4.1 begins with a question and no complement is actually necessary. But Paul does wish to supply further information here as he has in the previous three stages of this diatribe, and as he does whenever he uses this particular diatribal phrase (see 3.5; 6.1; 7.7; 8.31; 9.14 and 30). The infinitive in 4.1 *may* then signal the presence of an indirect question which is supplying information complementary to the

36.   Paul does not argue *for* Abraham's fatherhood later on in ch. 4. He struggles with its presuppositions.

37.   'Indirect discourse with (acc. and) infinitive, so strongly developed in classical Greek, is almost entirely wanting in the New Testament; Lk. is probably the only one who retains it to any considerable degree, and even he quickly slides over into the direct form (s. A[cts] 25.4f...)' (BDF §396).

38.   See Moule 1959: 153-54, esp. his examples of Lk. 24.23, Acts 25.4, and 28.6. I doubt the relevance of Rom. 2.18 (*sic*: see v. 19; cf. also v. 17). Most importantly, however, BDF states: '[i]n classical Greek the complement of verbs of (perceiving,) believing, (showing,) and saying which indicate the content of the conception or communication, is formed to a great extent by the infinitive. If the subject of the infinitive is the same as that of the governing verb, it is not expressed...otherwise it is in the acc... In addition, the complement of verbs of perception, showing, saying, but not of believing, is often formed by means of an indirect question' (§396).

The participle is an alternative. BDF cites 2 Cor. 5.19 (which uses a participle; cf. also v. 20), 11.21 (a perfect verb; cf. v. 17) and the possibly useful 2 Thess. 2.2 (a perfect verb).

verb of saying just used. Certainly there is nothing to prevent Paul from slipping into indirect discourse on occasion as Luke does (and cf. LXX). This suggestion works best, however, if we suppose an ellipse of ἐροῦμεν in 4.1b; something that would again be quite in character for Paul as well as for other Greek speakers at the time (so the remainder of the sentence is, strictly speaking, the complement to this verb and not to the initial diatribal question, although the two verbs would be identical). The immediate overt repetition of this verb would be conspicuously clumsy, but its implicit presence creates a grammatically perfect sentence denoting more specifically in an indirect question—in a rather classical manner—the content of Paul's initial generic question in 4.1a: 'What [then] shall we say?—Will we say that Abraham obtained forefatherhood of us [Gentiles] *in relation to flesh*?'[39] At any rate, this is the most elegant solution I know of currently for this rather notorious verse,[40] and it is borne out in detail exactly by my suggested reading of the subsequent correlative argumentative sub-section in vv. 16b-22.

To draw our discussion of this sub-section to a close; again it seems plausible to posit a correlation, on this occasion a fourth one between the last discursive sub-section concerning Abraham and 15.6 in ch. 4 in vv. 16b-22 and an earlier thesis statement in 4.1. Without claiming to have unravelled all the mysteries of Rom. 4.1 and 4.16b-25 I suggest that here Gen. 15.6 confronts Gen. 17.5 antinomously in relation to the scripturally foretold matter of Abraham's paternity of 'the nations of the earth', a text that raises the awkward matter for Paul of the covenant of circumcision in Abraham's flesh and its putative presuppositional role, a problem also signalled precisely by a reasonable reading of 4.1 as a question stated in terms of indirect discourse. And as in the preceding three argumentative sub-sections, Paul asserts here the primacy of Gen. 15.6, although perhaps less convincingly (i.e. his argument is not formally watertight). Rather, his

---

39. Admittedly, this *could* be phrased simply as a statement, but the expectations of the three preceding diatribal issues *and* of the bulk of the other occurrences of this particular question in Romans are of a further inquiry. A flat statement here—subsequently strongly undermined by Paul—would also almost certainly elicit a denial (μὴ γένοιτο), whereas a question is phrased more hypothetically and so does not ask for this negation to such a degree (it carries itself a note of inquiry). For these reasons I favour rendering the sentence interrogatively.

40. It was first suggested to me by Stanley Porter (at the fifth conference on Rhetoric and Scriptural Interpretation, 27-30 July 1998, Florence). Any errors in the brief outworking of that approach here should, however, be attributed to me.

argument here more narratively enfolds the text he is concerned to neutral-ize, a strategy that also explains the distinctive shift in style to a serried accumulation of clauses. The application is then made quickly in v. 22. By v. 23, however, Paul begins to effect a transition to christological concerns that are also more relevant to his audience, thereby leaving the specific agenda of 3.27–4.1 behind.

Hopefully enough has also been said by this point to suggest that the entire case of this paper on internal stylistic and argumentative grounds for a fourfold correlation between the diatribal agenda of 3.27–4.1 and the responding discursive analysis of 4.2-22 is a reasonable one. The theory seems to make sense both on detailed internal grounds and when viewed as a whole. We must turn now to consider briefly the question of the further possible corroboration of this type of composition from elsewhere in Romans, and perhaps also from further afield in the Pauline corpus, before considering any indirect corroboration from contemporary rhetorical sources.

j. *Anticipatory and Summary Sections Elsewhere*
It would be a useful corroboration if the same structural technique could be found elsewhere in Romans. I would suggest that there is one clear instance, along with several other less decisive ones.

Romans 7.5-6 summarizes in two sentences comprising three main propositions the three major thematic concerns of chs. 5–8, namely, life in the flesh (cf. 7.7-25), transition through death thereby leaving behind νόμος (i.e., a participatory death in Christ; cf. 6.1-11; 7.1-4), and new life in the Spirit (cf. 5.1-11; 6.12-21; 8.1-39). Admittedly, this important sum-mation does not precede all the relevant discussion, but it does announce the two longest, most discursive analyses of the two relevant ontologies, and this should suffice to demonstrate clearly that Paul can think and compose in terms of short summary sections that announce his main argumentative concerns in context.

More controvertably, 5.12-21 and 9.30-33 are similar summarizing sections. The implications of 5.12-21 are partly obscured by Paul's evident concern there with theological caveats (specifically, concerning 'non-transgressive sin' in vv. 13-14, and concerning the superiority of Christ over Adam in vv. 15-17, perhaps arguably along with a resumption of the concern over the law's relationship with sin in v. 20). But if these are set to one side, a short programmatic set of statements does emerge, namely, vv. 18-19 and 21 (or alternatively vv. 18-21). These powerful antitheses arguably set the framework in terms of Adam and Christ for the entire analysis of chs. 5–8, also connecting that frame with many of the argument's key terms. Significantly, with the exception of a chiastic anticipation by 5.1-11 of Paul's later eschatological discussion in ch. 8, this set of statements also stands at the head of his discussion.

Romans 9.30-31 also arguably states the central concerns of chs. 9–11—that the Gentiles, evidently not pursuing δικαιοσύνη nevertheless received δικαιοσύνη, but Israel, pursuing δικαιοσύνη and assisted by a Scripture concerning δικαιοσύνη, did not receive it. This contrasting set of salvation-historical anomalies *that clearly reverses the basic expectations of most Jews in Paul's day* is arguably the agenda for all of Paul's layered apologetic from 9.1–11.36. Like 7.5-6, the summary occurs about one-third of the way through the relevant discussion, where it compresses the relevant issues being discussed extensively in context into a couple of compact programmatic statements. (It is also worth emphasizing that these are not 'thesis statements' that announce Paul's main theological goals in Romans and in his gospel as a whole, so much as 'thesis' statements that announce subordinate but important issues currently under vigorous dispute, so perhaps they are more analogous to *causa*, etc.)

Hence 7.6-7, and perhaps also 5.12-21 (specifically 5.18-19 and 21) and 9.30-31, arguably show that Paul in Romans at times *compresses* the issues at hand into compact summary statements, while in the case of 5.18-19 and 21 this occurs almost at the beginning of the relevant discussion. That Paul can *anticipate* his argument should not in any case be doubted. Romans 1.16-17 is a widely-acknowledged anticipation of 3.21-26. More controversially, 3.21-26 can be seen as an anticipation of 5.1-11 (and perhaps also of 6.1-11). Also widely acknowledged, however, is Nils Dahl's suggestion that 5.1-12 accurately anticipates the concerns of ch. 8 (Dahl 1977).

In sum, while the sample could probably be broadened, given time, even our minimal sample supplies evidence sufficient to reinforce our proposed analysis of 3.27–4.25. The key to our proposal is the suggestion that in 3.27–4.1 Paul *compresses* the issues into pithy programmatic statements, using there a dialogical form (as in 9.30-31), and he also thereby *anticipates* the concerns he will shortly address seriatim with the example of Abraham and the help especially of Gen. 15.6. That Paul *could* have operated in this fashion argumentatively seems to me to be corroborated conclusively by these other texts in Romans.

At this point I wish only to note that Galatians is arguably structured in an almost identical manner.[41] I myself would suggest that a thesis statement for the entire letter is found in 1.4. More importantly for our present concerns, however, is the announcement of a series of central concerns or issues in 1.6-9, namely, two gospels and two respective proponents. I would suggest that these are taken up by the body of the letter from 2.15. Meanwhile a related although distinct set of issues is announced in vv. 10-12; issues more of style than substance. These are then taken up directly by the discussion of 1.13–2.14 (connections often overlooked but grasped in part by B.J. Dodd [1996]). Once concluded, Paul's main concerns are resumed from 2.15 but they are complex. So Paul (again arguably) announces in summary form his view of the key issues (2.15–3.1, 3-4), and then proceeds to work through these issues largely in order with an exegetical comparison (3.3, 5-14), an apocalyptic analysis of the coming of πίστις (the heart of the letter: see 3.15–4.10, 21-31, this section being summarized in 5.1-6), an emotive set of appeals to the original arrival of the gospel in Galatia (i.e., arguments from pathos and ethos concerning himself and the Galatians, following arguments in terms of logos: see 4.11-21; 5.7-12), and an analysis of life in the Spirit as against existence in the flesh (5.13–6.10). His argumentative task complete—and largely as announced—the letter then concludes, reverting to an epistolary closing (6.11-18).

If this is the case in Galatians, an angry, possibly quite incomplete, hasty, and even poorly informed letter, how much more would we expect similar structuring techniques in the carefully composed, reflective, better informed, and more systematic Romans (a letter, it should be noted, that nevertheless addresses many of the same issues)? In sum, the comparative evidence from elsewhere in Romans, assisted by a possible analysis of Galatians, to my mind corroborates the proposal here concerning Rom. 3.27–4.25 reasonably strongly: Paul demonstrably anticipates and summarizes his arguments and concerns, and at times seems to combine both these functions in the same short statements. Hence what I would suggest he is attempting in 3.27–4.1, and then following on from that in 4.2-25, is

41. Again time regrettably precludes establishing the following contentions as they deserve although Martyn (1997) and Witherington (1998) are instructive—the latter, however, unwisely follows the forensic hypothesis of Betz. Longenecker is also helpful (1990): see esp. a useful survey of the rhetorical approach in conjunction with epistolary insights on pp. c-cxix, although he is too enamoured of Hansen's distinctive rhetorical and epistolary suggestion (1989). I am encouraged that a very similar case is also made by Anders Eriksson for 1 Corinthians (1998).

not uncharacteristic for him, and especially within a Judaizing context. It is time now to turn to rhetoric, but here our case can be made quite briefly.

2. *The External Evidence from Ancient Rhetorical Theory and Practice*

Anyone familiar with the Greco-Roman handbooks would recognize the foregoing techniques immediately since those theorists dealt explicitly with just these concerns within the model of a generic speech as it was taught to children. The value of summarizing pithily the central concerns of a speech in advance centred in the recommendation, old by the time of Aristotle, to construct a thesis statement to be delivered just after the introduction, the (προ)θέσις or *propositio* (and various techniques existed that could also 'spin' this statement in favour of the speaker).

Related to this was the recommendation at times to summarize in advance within a *partitio* the particular serried arguments that would be made subsequently through the main section of proofs (πίστεις or *probatio*), here not so much to signal the speaker's central concerns as simply to aid clarity (so signalling in fact the speaker's detailed argumentative intentions). Proofs could be extremely complex and if the audience consequently got lost their force, in all pragmatic contexts, was wasted. Hence an enumerative anticipatory summary in both these instances could greatly assist an audience's understanding, and thereby also facilitate the speaker's overarching objective of persuasion.[42]

42. Rhetorical theory is rather diverse in its recommendations here, possibly in part because the dividing line between the *propositio* and the *partitio* could be unclear in practice. A *partitio* (cf. Gk προκατασκευή, προέκθεσις and μερισμός) could introduce a speaker's central point in terms of similarities and differences (in its first sub-section according to the *Rhetoric to Herennius* [c. first century BCE; hereafter *RH*] 1.4 and 17; cf. also 2.2 and the beginning of each subsequent book: Cicero notes that this was often an advantageous manoeuvre, cf. *De Inv.* 1.31-33). Cicero also speaks of an alternative, fully enumerative section called an expository *partitio*, while the *RH* expects this to comprise the second half of the *partitio*, the *distributio*, after the foregoing enumeration of similarities and differences (and breaking that section down as well into an enumeration in terms of number—no more than three, and cf. 1 Cor. 14.27, although Quintilian demurs on this—and a brief exposition of the main points). Quintilian speaks of the technique's flexibility (*Inst.* 4.5.1-25) citing examples from Cicero's *Pro Cluentio* (see §§1-3 and 9; cf. *Pro Murena* 11 and *Pro Milone* 6, 7 [cf. also §§23 and 32]). Intriguingly, we also find this technique in some of Cicero's philosophical writings, for example, *De Senectute* (5.15; cf. also *De Officiis* 1.7-10; cf. also 2.1, 9a; 3.6-8), a possibility he himself notes (*De Inv.* 1.33). See also Martianus

This anticipatory summary could also of course be complemented by short concluding summaries that iterated the main points within a section or division (again with appropriate 'spin') and thereby remind the audience of what had just been covered in detail. But these techniques were not limited to sections of proof. The pedagogical *Rhetoric to Alexander* (c. fourth century BCE; hereafter *RA*) is replete with such summaries—the entire treatise corresponds to an initial *partitio*, while almost every ensuing sub-section (there are 38) is either introduced by a *partitio* (in terms of the *RH* a *divisio*: see below) or corresponds to a discrete element in a preceding one. All are also concluded by an appropriate iteration or summary, as is the entire treatise. In fact this anonymous tract is an excellent example of the ubiquity, the flexibility, and the usefulness of the techniques of anticipation and compression in a discourse followed by orderly exposition and further compressed iteration (and also, it should be noted, in a pedagogical context). In this vein, the *RH* notes under its treatment of style a 'divisio' (4.40.52, and not to be confused with the divisio that enumerates the topics to be discussed throughout the whole discourse: cf. also Quintilian. *Inst.* 9.2.105) that 'separates the alternatives of a question and resolves each by means of a reason subjoined'; something very close to the practice of the *RA* and, at times, Cicero, and also to Paul as I have suggested construing him here.

It should also be recalled that speakers could assist their audience's understanding at these points through intonation and/or gesture (i.e. through aspects of delivery: see e.g. Philodemus, *Rhet.* 4.2 in Hubbell 1920: 300-301; see also *RH* 3.26-27). Quintilian speaks of Cicero's mockery of his rival, Quintus Hortensius (*Inst.* 4.5.24), where the butt of the joke seems to be that Hortensius ticked off the points of his *propositios* on his fingers as he recited them (a gesture still used today, but in Cicero's jaundiced view somewhat childish). In fact, Cicero notes that Hortensius was famous for his carefully constructed *propositios* (*Brutus* 302-303; cf. elsewhere on Hortensius 1-6, 228-30, 279, 301-30; also *Pro Quinctio* 35)—and one can only imagine the assistance the audience of the letter to the Romans might have received thereby from Phoebe if she ticked off Paul's serial points on her fingers as well! Such possible aids from gesture—and the same results could often be achieved by intonation—indicate that paragraphs serializing theses do not necessarily ask too much

Capella, *De nuptiis Philologiae et Mercurii* 5.556, who also (accurately) cites Cicero's *Pro Quinctio* (35-36) as an example of the technique.

of the understanding of an audience. Gesture and/or its equivalent may well have assisted them where modern readers struggle.[43]

That many speakers would have been skilled in the composition of the sort of short summarizing statements which I suggest are operative in Rom. 3.27–4.22 and elsewhere in Paul's writings is further corroborated by the devotion of a considerable part of rhetorical pedagogy in the Hellenistic age to the formulation of short statements of the essential 'issue' under dispute (Greek στάσις; Latin *status* or *constitutio*). The area is notoriously complex, appears rather casuistic, and has consequently been rather neglected by modern students of ancient rhetorical practice (however, see now Heath 1995). But especially since Hermagoras of Temnos's systematic formulations ('probably the most important figure [in Hellenistic rhetoric]', Russell 1996: 1313—he lived c. 150 BCE) this educational approach was largely standard: 'the *stasis* system…enabled a speaker to establish the type of the case…and draw on a check-list of topics appropriate to that type' (Winterbottom 1996: 436; cf. also Russell 1996: 1313; and Eriksson 1998: 43-48), hence it provided formal procedures for the difficult but crucial area of invention (note, not arrangement, within which discussion of broad structural elements like the *propositio* occurs) where a student or speaker had 'to "find" [εὕρεσις] things to say to meet the question at issue' (Russell 1996: 1313).[44]

The reduction of complex problems to a short appropriate summary is a learned skill (although it is assisted by intelligence and clarity of thought), and one that greatly assists effective communication and argument—it is the ancient equivalent of 'asking the right questions' or 'grasping the key points' (one thinks in particular of the modern law student's training to discover a given case's *ratio decidendi*). The central issues are thereby brought into focus so that ensuing composition and argumentation can be brought to bear on them (while without such accurate summarization those crucial subsequent tasks will not function so effectively). Such skills would have informed a great deal of public discourse in Paul's time, and he *might* even have learned something similar himself from a *grammaticus*

43. Stowers also makes much of this dimension in Paul's letters, although he relies more heavily on προσωποποιία than I would (here): see his 1994: 16-21, 232-33, 264-72.

44. Hermagoras's system is not extant except in reported fragments: see, however, discussions in *RH* 1.18-27; 2.2-26; Cicero, *De Inv.* 1.10-17; 2.12-end; Quintilian, *Inst.* 3.5.4–3.6.104; Hermogenes, *On Stases* (c. second century CE) and Sopater, *Division of Problems* (c. fourth century CE); also Mart. Capella, *De Nuptiis* 5.440b-68.

in the context of the gymnasium in Tarsus.[45] Whatever their point of acquisition, I would suggest that he clearly possesses them to some degree by the time he composes his letters to Christians in Galatia and Rome in the 50s CE.[46]

I am not for a moment suggesting that Paul was trained directly in these techniques in an élite fashion by a rhetor using manuals, exercises and published speeches like those noted above, or that his letter to the Romans (or for that matter Galatians) reproduces the structure of a Greco-Roman speech designed for oral delivery to an élite audience. But that these overt theoretical observations concerning argumentative summation, compression, anticipation and iteration exist is to my mind quite significant. They indicate that public speaking in the Greco-Roman world at times self-consciously practised just the techniques that I am suggesting on internal grounds inform the structure of Rom. 3.27–4.22, and this was a world that Paul moved in actively (i.e. publically speaking) for at least 25 years. That this is a coincidence seems to me quite unlikely. More likely is the possibility that this intelligent if unconventionally trained scholar, preacher and teacher absorbed from his milieu various techniques that contributed to more effective communication, and that those techniques are consequently also occasionally evident in his preserved correspondence (in just the manner that perhaps philosophical tropes and motifs are as well), although a basic Hellenistic education in childhood may also have assisted him (see

45. In Acts 21.39 Paul possibly claims citizenship of Tarsus which, if true, almost certainly implies education in that city's ephebate. Acts 22.3 confirms this if the key participle ἀνατεθράμμενος is referred to the preceding 'Tarsus' as against the following 'Jerusalem', but the point is debated. 'Being reared' or 'being nurtured' in Jerusalem does not in any case exclude an education there in stases or, for that matter, an earlier preliminary education in Tarsus before the 'nurturing' of Pharisaic instruction at the feet of Gamaliel in Jerusalem. 23.34 also suggests Paul was 'from the province of Cilicia' (something, if true, dictated by birth, upbringing, education, or affection?). That later education, however, almost certainly displaced a formal rhetorical education for Paul at Tarsus under a ῥήτωρ, although some preliminary exposure to rhetorical exercises may have taken place under a γραμματικός (so Paul's education into texts and memorization, begun at the secondary 'grammatical' level—although there through Homer—would have continued reasonably directly within his Pharisaic training). Hence the disavowals of 1 Cor. 2.4-5 and 2 Cor. 10.3-5, 10.

46. The actual argumentation of Rom. 4 does not, in my opinion, correspond to the technical recommendations of *stasis* theory. It looks closer to forms of contemporary Jewish exegesis (see Longenecker 1975: esp. 32-38, 104-32; and n. 8 above), garnished one suspects with native wit. But the basic approach of isolating key problems in short statements and then focusing on them looks the same.

Heath 1995: 6-7, 11). In short, popular culture was affected by elite culture—as Woody Allen says, 'life imitates art'—and so in the extant testimony to the latter we may detect elements that have trickled down to the extant texts of occupants of the former like Paul.

In sum, the primary corroboration for my overarching suggestion concerning Rom. 3.27–4.22 remains internal, but that suggestion does in my judgment also receive additional indirect confirmation from the ancient rhetorical corpus. In particular, Paul's argumentation in 3.27–4.22 matches in general terms the recommendations found in stasis theory—without reproducing any of them precisely—and this gives me further cause for optimism that the foregoing reading is on the right path.

APPENDIX

In 3.27–4.1 the agenda is set in terms of four antinomous problems or challenges that will be answered in relation to Abraham and Gen. 15.6:

> Question 1:
> Where, then, is boasting?
> It has been excluded.
> Through what kind of Torah [i.e. 'scriptural teaching']?—
> a Torah of works?
> Not at all: but by a Torah of faithfulness.
> For we consider a person to be saved by faithfulness, apart from works of Torah.

> Question 2:
> Is God the God of the Jews only?
> Is s/he not also God of the Gentiles?
> Yes, of course, of the Gentiles as well.
> Indeed, 'God is one', who will save the circumcized through faithfulness and the uncircumcized through faithfulness.

> Question 3:
> Then do we abolish the Torah [the Scriptures] through faithfulness?
> Absolutely not!
> Rather, we confirm the Torah (i.e. [literally] cause it to stand).

> Question 4:
> What then will we say?
> [Will we say that] Abraham obtained forefatherhood of us [Gentiles] in relation to the flesh [i.e. through circumcision]?
> [Absolutely not...]

In 4.2-22 four answers are then given in relation to Abraham:

Answer 1: If indeed Abraham was vindicated by works he had a boast (although not to God him/herself!). But what does the scripture say? 'Abraham trusted in God and salvation was given to him' (Gen. 15.6). Wages are not given to the worker according to grace (or, as a gift) but in accordance with obligation. To the one who does not work but trusts in the one who vindicates the ungodly, however, their trust leads to the giving of salvation, just as David speaks of the blessing of the person to whom God gives salvation apart from works: 'Blessed are those whose transgressions are forgiven, and whose sins have been covered up; blessed is the person to whom the Lord does not account sin' (Ps. 32.1-2).

Answer 2: Is this blessing, then, on the circumcision or also on the uncircumcision?, because we are saying 'Abraham's trust led to the giving of salvation' (Gen. 15.6—modified a little). When then was it given? while in the state of circumcision or in [the state of] uncircumcision? It was not in circumcision, but in uncircumcision!—and he received the sign of circumcision; a seal of the salvation associated with the trust which he had in the uncircumcized state, so that he should be the father of all those who trust within the uncircumcized state, that they should have salvation given to them; and the father of the circumcized—who are not circumcized alone, but are also marching in the footsteps of the trust in the uncircumcized state that our father Abraham had.

Answer 3: Now, it was not through the law that the promise that he should inherit the world came to Abraham or to his seed, but through the salvation associated with trust. For if those of the law are heirs, then that trust has been nullified and the promise abolished (indeed, the law effects wrath—while where there is no law, there is no transgression [see later in my letter...]). Therefore, it is by means of trust, in order that it may be as a gift, so as to establish the promise to every seed/descendant—not to the one who is of the law only, but also to the one who is of the trust of Abraham...

Answer 4: ...Abraham, who is the father of all of us, just as it is written 'I have made you the father of many Gentile nations' (Gen. 17.5); in the presence of which [promise], he 'trusted God', the one who makes alive the dead and who calls that which is non-existent existent; [Abraham] who from hope to hope believed that he would be 'father of many Gentile nations' (Gen. 17.5) according to the statement 'thus will be your seed' (Gen. 15.5) and, not having weakened in trust, he knew that his own body had died being about a hundred years old, also knowing the death of Sarah's womb, however, he did not waver through distrust concerning God's promise but was strengthened in trust giving glory to God and being fully convinced that the one who had promised was capable also of effecting it. Therefore 'salvation was given to him' (Gen. 15.6).

Now, this was not written for him alone—that it was given to him—but also
for our sake, that is, for those to whom it will be given; those who trust in
the one who raised Jesus our lord from the dead, the one who was delivered
for the sake of our reprobations and raised for the sake of our salvation…

BIBLIOGRAPHY

Barrett, C.K.
    1957   *A Commentary on the Epistle to the Romans* (BNTC; London: A. & C.
                Black).
Boyarin, D.
    1994   *A Radical Jew: Paul and the Politics of Identity* (Berkeley: University of
                California Press).
Campbell, D.A.
    1992   *The Rhetoric of Righteousness in Romans 3.21-26* (JSNTSup, 65; Sheffield:
                JSOT Press).
    1995   'A Rhetorical Suggestion concerning Romans 2', in E. Lovering (ed.),
                SBLSP (Atlanta: Scholars Press): 140-64.
Cranfield, C.E.B.
    1975   *A Critical and Exegetical Commentary on the Epistle to the Romans* (2 vols.;
                Edinburgh: T. & T. Clark).
Dahl, N.
    1977   'Appendix I: A Synopsis of Rom. 5.1-11 and 8.1-39', in *idem, Studies in
                Paul: Theology for the Early Christian Mission* (Minneapolis: Augsburg):
                88-90.
Daube, D.
    1956   *The New Testament and Rabbinic Judaism* (London: Athlone).
Davies, W.D.
    1980   *Paul and Rabbinic Judaism: Some Rabbinic Elements in Pauline Theology*
                (London: SPCK, 4th edn [1948]).
    1984a   'Law in First-Century Judaism', in *idem, Jewish and Pauline Studies*
                (London: SPCK): 3-26.
    1984b   'Paul and the Law: Reflections on Pitfalls in Interpretation', in *idem, Jewish
                and Pauline Studies* (London: SPCK): 91-122.
Dodd, B.J.
    1996   'Christ's Slave, People Pleasers and Galatians 1.10', *NTS* 42: 90-104.
Dodd, C.H.
    1932   *The Epistle of Paul to the Romans* (London: Hodder & Stoughton).
Donaldson, T.L.
    1992   'Abraham's Gentile Offspring: Contratextuality and Conviction in Romans
                4'. Unpublished Paper Delivered at AAR/SBL International Meeting, San
                Francisco (24 pp.).
    1997   *Paul and the Gentiles: Remapping the Apostle's Convictional World*
                (Minneapolis: Fortress Press).
Dunn, J.D.G.
    1988   *Romans 1–8* (WBC, 38; Dallas, TX: Word Books).

Eriksson, A.
1998   *Traditions as Rhetorical Proof: Pauline Argumentation in 1 Corinthians* (ConBNT, 29; Stockholm: Almqvist & Wiksell).
Gaston, L.
1980   'Abraham and the Righteousness of God', *Horizons* 2: 39-67.
Hansen, G.W.
1989   *Abraham in Galatians: Epistolary and Rhetorical Contexts* (JSNTSup, 29; Sheffield: JSOT Press).
Hays, R.B.
1985   ' "Have we found Abraham to be our forefather according to the flesh?": A Reconsideration of Rom. 4.1', *NovT* 27: 76-98.
1989   *Echoes of Scripture in the Letters of Paul* (New Haven: Yale University Press).
Heath, M.
1995   *Hermogenes on Issues: Strategies of Argumentation in Later Greek Rhetoric* (Oxford: Clarendon Press).
Hofius, O.
1989   *Paulusstudien* (Tübingen: Mohr [Siebeck]).
Hubbell, H.M.
1920   'The Rhetorica of Philodemus', *Transactions of the Connecticut Academy of Arts and Sciences* 23: 243-382.
Käsemann, E.
1971   'The Faith of Abraham in Romans 4', in *idem*, *Perspectives on Paul* (London: SCM [German edn 1969; lecture delivered 1965–66]): 79-101.
1980   *Commentary on Romans* (trans. G.W. Bromiley; Grand Rapids: Eerdmans, 4th edn).
Klein, G.
1969a   'Römer 4 und die Idee der Heilsgechichte', in *idem*, *Rekonstruktion und Interpretation* (BEvT, 50; Munich: Kaiser [1964]), 145-69.
1969b   'Exegetische Probleme in Römer 3, 21-4, 25', in *idem*, *Rekonstruktion und Interpretation* (BEvT, 50; Munich: Kaiser [1964]), 170-79.
1969c   'Individualgeschichte und Weltgeschichte bei Paulus', in *idem*, *Rekonstruktion und Interpretation* (BEvT, 50; Munich: Kaiser [1964]), 180-224.
Lausberg, H.
1960   *Handbuch der Literarischen Rhetorik* (2 vols.; Munich: Hueber).
Litfin, D.
1994   *St Paul's Theology of Proclamation: 1 Corinthians 1–4 and Greco-Roman Rhetoric* (SNTSMS, 79; Cambridge: Cambridge University Press).
Longenecker, R.N.
1964   *Paul, Apostle of Liberty* (New York: Harper & Row).
1975   *Biblical Exegesis in the Apostolic Period* (Grand Rapids: Eerdmans).
1990   *Galatians* (WBC, 41; Dallas: Word Books).
Martyn, J.L.
1997   *Galatians* (AB, 33A; New York: Doubleday).
Moule, C.F.D.
1959   *An Idiom Book of New Testament Greek* (Cambridge: Cambridge University Press).

Murphy, N.C.
    1994   *Reasoning and Rhetoric in Religion* (Valley Forge, PA: Trinity Press International).
Parker, T.D.
    1997   'Abraham, Father of Us All in Barth's *Epistle to the Romans*'. Unpublished Paper Delivered to S69 ('History of the Reception of Romans and Exegesis Consultation') at the SBL/AAR International Meeting, San Francisco (23 pp.).
Perelman, C., and L. Olbrechts-Tyteca
    1969   *The New Rhetoric: A Treatise on Argumentation* (Notre Dame: University of Notre Dame).
Rhyne, C.T.
    1981   *Faith Establishes the Law* (SBLDS, 55; Chico, CA: Scholars Press).
Russell, D.S.
    1996.   'Rhetoric, Greek', in *OCD*: 1312-14.
Sanders, E.P.
    1983   *Paul, The Law, and the Jewish People* (Philadelphia: Fortress Press).
Sandmel, S.
    1971   *Philo's Place in Judaism: A Study of Conceptions of Abraham in Jewish Literature* (New York: Ktav).
Siker, J.S.
    1991   *Disinheriting the Jews* (Louisville, KY: Westminster/John Knox Press).
Stowers, S.K.
    1981   *The Diatribe and Paul's Letter to the Romans* (Chico, CA: Scholars Press).
    1994   *Rereading Romans: Justice, Jews, and Gentiles* (New Haven: Yale University Press).
Stuhlmacher, P.
    1994   *Paul's Letter to the Romans: A Commentary* (trans. S. Hafemann; Louisville, KY: Westminster/John Knox Press; Edinburgh: T. & T. Clark [1989]).
Winterbottom, M.
    1996   'Declamation', in *OCD*: 436-37.
Witherington, III, B.
    1998   *Grace in Galatia: A Commentary on St Paul's Letter to the Galatians* (Edinburgh: T. & T. Clark).
Wright, N.T.
    1991   *The Climax of the Covenant: Christ and the Law in Pauline Theology* (Minneapolis: Fortress Press).
    1995   'Romans and the Theology of Paul', in D.M. Hay and E.E. Johnson (eds.), *Pauline Theology. III. Romans* (Minneapolis: Augsburg–Fortress Press): 30-67.
Ziesler, J.A.T.
    1989   *Paul's Letter to the Romans* (London: SCM Press; Philadelphia: Trinity Press International).

THE RHETORICAL SCRIBE: TEXTUAL VARIANTS IN ROMANS AND THEIR POSSIBLE RHETORICAL PURPOSE

Stanley E. Porter

1. *Introduction*

In the study of rhetoric as a whole, attention to textual variants has been greatly neglected. For example, there is no single category of entry in the Watson and Hauser bibliography on rhetoric dedicated to entries discussing textual variants.[1] So far as can be determined from the titles of individual entries, within the set of entries devoted to the Pauline letters, none is obviously dedicated to the study of the Pauline textual variants, within a context of their possible rhetorical purpose or impact.[2] To confirm that my initial impression was valid, I have checked several specific works, and have been interested to find that a number of works that address what they see as technical points of argumentation in New Testament passages are apparently unaware of the textual variants that often attend to these passages, and make little or no comment upon them.[3] However, several of the works mentioned by Watson and Hauser do pay *some* attention to textual variants. For example, Douglas Campbell in his study of Rom. 3.21-26 does discuss at a few places textual variants that are to be found within that passage.[4] However, he does not study these

1. D.F. Watson and A.J. Hauser, *Rhetorical Criticism of the Bible: A Comprehensive Bibliography with Notes on History and Method* (BIS, 4; Leiden: E.J. Brill, 1994).

2. There are studies of scribal tendencies, however. See, for example, B.D. Ehrman, *The Orthodox Corruption of Scripture: The Effect of Early Christological Controversies on the Text of the New Testament* (New York: Oxford University Press, 1993).

3. For example, J.D. Moores, *Wrestling with Rationality in Paul: Romans 1–8 in a New Perspective* (SNTSMS, 82; Cambridge: Cambridge University Press, 1995).

4. D.A. Campbell, *The Rhetoric of Righteousness in Romans 3.21-26* (JSNTSup, 65; Sheffield: JSOT Press, 1992), *passim*.

variants in terms of what difference they might make to his rhetorical analysis, but tends to discuss them as isolated incidents of variation that must be decided *before* he proceeds to the task of rhetorical analysis. In an article that appeared in 1990 on Rom. 13.1-7, I argued similarly, rejecting a reading in v. 1 on the basis of its weak attestation,[5] not fully contemplating its potential significance for shifting and changing the argument itself in its rhetorical function, nor asking the question of why, from a rhetorical standpoint, a scribe might have made such a change. In my own defense, I think that I did a better job of appreciating such difficulties in an article that appeared in 1991, where I argued that a crucial textual variant in Rom. 5.1, whether one should read ἔχωμεν or ἔχομεν, and one in 5.6 with a connecting word, had potential to change one's entire understanding of the book of Romans.[6] However, since that time, I have not seen any significant number of articles that devote themselves to the place of textual variants in rhetorical analysis. This is confirmed in the volumes that have come out of the series of conferences of which this paper is a part, as well as in the recently published *Handbook of Classical Rhetoric.*[7]

2. *Why Study Variants? Principles and Practice of Textual Criticism*

The observation that there are not many significant studies devoted to the rhetorical impact of textual variants, especially in terms of New Testament texts, raises the question of the potential worth of such study. If this area has been greatly neglected, perhaps there is a reason for such neglect. In other words, one may well need to justify this as a more sustained and developed area of study.

5.   S.E. Porter, 'Romans 13.1-7 as Pauline Political Rhetoric', *FN* 3 (1990), pp. 115-39, esp. p. 119.
6.   S.E. Porter, 'The Argument of Romans 5: Can a Rhetorical Question Make a Difference?' *JBL* 110 (1991), pp. 655-77.
7.   S.E. Porter and T.H. Olbricht (eds.), *Rhetoric and the New Testament: Essays from the 1992 Heidelberg Conference* (JSNTSup, 90; Sheffield: JSOT Press, 1993); S.E. Porter and T.H. Olbricht (eds.), *Rhetoric, Scripture and Theology: Essays from the 1994 Pretoria Conference* (JSNTSup, 131; Sheffield: Sheffield Academic Press, 1996); S.E. Porter and T.H. Olbricht (eds.), *The Rhetorical Analysis of Scripture: Essays from the 1995 London Conference* (JSNTSup, 146; Sheffield: Sheffield Academic Press, 1997); S.E. Porter and D.L. Stamps (eds.), *The Rhetorical Interpretation of Scripture: Essays from the 1996 Malibu Conference* (JSNTSup, 180; Sheffield: Sheffield Academic Press, 1999); S.E. Porter (ed.), *Handbook of Classical Rhetoric in the Hellenistic Period 330 B.C.–A.D. 400* (Leiden: E.J. Brill, 1997).

I think that there are two useful responses that might be made to such a legitimate question. The first is that the few studies that do exist show that there is at least greater potential insight to be gained in asking such questions of textual variants than has been gained before. This is consonant with an approach that considers it appropriate to analyze the rhetorical purposes of a given author. As we know regarding the history of textual transmission, even though a text was written, it still was transmitted through various manuscripts. In the process of transmission, scribes made changes to the manuscript (see below), some of them accidental and unconscious, but others conscious and intentional. If we use the term 'rhetoric' in the broad sense of describing and explaining the purposes and motivations for presenting as persuasive an argument as one can, it stands to reason that these scribes, rather than being mindless drones, were in a very real sense themselves rhetors. It is their rhetorical practice that I believe is worth examining in more detail. The second response is that I do not believe that the questions have yet been properly formulated to be able to gain the fullest possible insight and benefit for our rhetorical analysis. In other words, we are not in a position to answer the question of the rhetorical benefit of examination of textual variants, since we have not yet really asked the question properly.

In one of the studies that I cited above, I argued that the book of Romans is best seen as, generically, a diatribe. One of the passages that has resisted such analysis, since major features of diatribe had already been identified in earlier and later chapters of the book, has been ch. 5. According to my analysis, however, there are a number of features of diatribe in Romans 5. These include the use of the exemplum in 5.12-21, the chain progression of vv. 3-5, parallelism throughout, and short, crisp balanced sentences (e.g. in v. 12). Two features, however, are the most important, and they focus upon textual variants. The first is whether the subjunctive or the indicative verb forms should be read in v. 1 and v. 2. Although earlier scholars had accepted the subjunctive reading, recent scholarship has rejected the reading ἔχωμεν in favour of ἔχομεν, because of the thought that the subjunctive introduces an element of doubt into Paul's argument. However, two arguments weigh in favour of the subjunctive. One is a revised understanding of the subjunctive that does not imply uncertainty but exhortation, here regarding Christian existence.[8] The second is the overwhelming textual evidence in its favour. If the first

8. See S.E. Porter, *Verbal Aspect in the Greek of the New Testament, with Reference to Tense and Mood* (SBG, 1; New York: Peter Lang, 1989), esp. pp. 167-73.

subjunctive is accepted in v. 1, then the use of καυχώμεθα in v. 2 as subjunctive is to be accepted also. The second variant occurs in v. 6. The problem here has been that the argument of ch. 5 seems to remain intact even if vv. 6-7 are deleted, even though v. 6 seems to anticipate v. 8. In the textual tradition, one finds the repetition of the particle ἔτι. If the first ἔτι came about through contraction, the variant εἰς τί γάρ can be accepted, introducing a rhetorical question that propels the argument into the second part of the section. The result of these two text-critical decisions—the exhortative introduction to the chapter and the rhetorical question as part of the argumentational structure—as well as other observations, was to place Romans 5 firmly within the ambit of dialogical style, unifying the conception of the entire book as a diatribe.

My use of textual criticism in this previous study, however, was some-what piecemeal. I looked at all of the possible variants for a given variant unit, and did not look at larger patterns of variants suggested by a given scribe. As it turns out, I accepted two variants that were, so far as the textual apparatus of the Nestle–Aland text is concerned, not shared by any single manuscript. I would now see this as a serious flaw in my, and any other, text-critical approach. That is, I ended up creating my own eclectic text that does not in fact mirror any extant text. The assumption is that one is working back to a hypothetical original document, but without any means of checking such a hypothesis, apart from whether or not one's final argument is convincing to contemporary scholars. I wish to suggest that a better way forward is to think in terms of extant manuscripts, that is, actual manuscripts that were written by real scribes in the early church, and that we can check. These should provide the basis for our textual criticism, and probably, in fact, for the texts that are used in our study of the Greek New Testament. This approach requires some adjustments to the ways in which textual criticism is currently practiced.

The field of textual criticism has developed a number of criteria for accounting for changes in texts. Some of these alterations are called unintentional scribal alterations, because they result from various acci-dents of seeing or hearing, such as confusing letters, substituting words, omitting words, and repeating letters, words or passages, etc. These are unfortunate, but can often be accounted for on the basis of relatively straightforward criteria. The alterations that are more important for my purposes here, however, are the intentional scribal alterations. These are often described as changes in grammar, spelling and style, harmonization with parallel biblical passages, clarification of difficulties, such as geographical or historical points, conflation of readings for the sake of completeness, addition of appropriate material, such as a full christological title, and theological matters.[9]

There are at least two major problems with this traditional way of approaching textual criticism. The first is that it tends to discuss individual variants in isolation, weighing the manuscripts that attest to a given variant on an ad hoc and instance-by-instance basis. This is not in fact the way that manuscripts were created, nor the way they functioned in the early Church. What is neglected in these criteria is the fact that individual scribes copied these manuscripts. They may have had some reference to a few other manuscripts, and quite possibly the entire Bible for reference (not to mention what they knew by memory, either well or badly), but they were producing a manuscript for use within their Christian community, not going through the scholarly process of adjudicating variants verse by verse. The second neglected feature is that there are other possible motivations for alteration that are not covered by these criteria. One notices that there is no specific place for something that might be called a rhetorical variant, apart possibly from the category of style. But stylistic changes often relate more to phrasing, word choice or morphological changes (such as a more proper Attic construction or spelling—and the manuscripts are full of these changes, unfortunately not noted by modern printed editions). Again, given the environment in which individual scribes were responsible for manuscripts (even such a complex manuscript as Sinaiticus had a finite number of scribes involved in its production), there are a whole host of reasons for changes. Disregarding the unintentional changes, since they are difficult to account for apart from their accidental nature, rhetorical purposes would seem to constitute a basis for a number of the changes consciously introduced. Most of these might also fit within the categories of intentional scribal alterations noted above, but these categories are more descriptive than motivational. What I am saying is that some of these variants may be motivated by the desire to make a more persuasive case for the document concerned, whether it is in terms of a theological or other reason. Of course, the way that I have framed this statement assumes that we have the original with which to compare the variants. This is, as noted above, simply not true. The situation is that we

9. These are discussed in E.J. Epp, 'Textual Criticism in the Exegesis of the New Testament, with an Excursus on Canon', in S.E. Porter (ed.), *Handbook to Exegesis of the New Testament* (NTTS, 25; Leiden: E.J. Brill, 1997), pp. 60-61, and in virtually every other introduction to textual criticism.

have a number of different manuscripts. At a number of different places these manuscripts have different readings. I believe that if we look at given manuscripts in their entirety, we can formulate different reasons for why a given scribe may or may not have retained and/or changed certain readings in the text on the basis of rhetorical purposes, and that when these readings are compared over the whole of the manuscript, certain interesting rhetorically analyzable results come to the fore.

In this paper, I wish to look at the book of Romans in terms of the variants in Codex Alexandrinus when compared to the text of Codex Vaticanus.[10] I have chosen these texts for a good purpose. Codex Vaticanus, along with Codex Sinaiticus, since the time of Westcott and Hort, has constituted the basis of modern textual criticism of the New Testament. Even within the revised criteria of the Alands for constructing the New Testament eclectic text, along with the early papyri (approximately 53 of them), and 4 other majuscule manuscripts, along with Codex Alexandrinus and Codex Washingtonianus,[11] pride of place is still maintained by Codex Vaticanus and Codex Sinaiticus. I have chosen Codex Alexandrinus so that we can establish a precise relationship between two complete manuscripts, one earlier and the other later relative to each other. There are other combinations that could also be used, some of them perhaps even more effectively (e.g. Günther Zuntz used 𝔓46 as his starting point for establishing the Pauline corpus, but that manuscript lacks Rom. 1.1–5.16),[12] but this will serve as a useful starting point. This way I hope to avoid the problem that is encountered in the printed Nestle–Aland[27], that is, the situation with variants is already skewed because they do not include all variants, and the collating base is not a particular manuscript but already an eclectic text. With Codexes Vaticanus and Alexandrinus, we are examining the textual tradition as it was actually used within a specific Christian community, one from the fourth and the other from the fifth centuries. I realize that it is unlikely that Alexandrinus actually used

10. I have used two convenient printed editions. They are: A. Mai, *Novum Testamentum Graece ex Antiquissimo Codice Vaticano* (London: Williams & Norgate, 1859) for Vaticanus; and B.H. Cowper, *Novum Testamentum Graece ex Antiquissimo Codice Alexandrino a C.G. Woide* (London: Williams & Norgate, 1860) for Alexandrinus.

11. Epp, 'Textual Criticism', p. 66. See K. Aland and B. Aland, *The Text of the New Testament* (trans. E.F. Rhodes; Grand Rapids: Eerdmans, 2nd edn, 1989), p. 104.

12. G. Zuntz, *The Text of the Epistles: A Disquisition upon the Corpus Paulinum* (London: British Academy, 1953).

Vaticanus, and that they therefore do not have a direct link, but they are sufficiently related with regard to text-type and date to use them as a starting point for this kind of analysis. When I began, I also thought that examining the book of Romans in these two manuscripts, often linked because of their text-critical importance, would provide a large enough base for gathering samples, but without providing an excessive number of variants with which to contend (I was right). I will also make comparisons with other manuscripts where important, as well as the printed Nestle–Aland[27].

3. *Examples of Variants with Rhetorical Significance in Romans*

There are a number of variants that simply will not be commented upon, although they could prove useful for other kinds of analysis. These include such common features of manuscripts of this time as itacism in spelling, the use of final nu (1.7) or sigma (1.15), or not. These might well prove instructive for establishing provenance of the manuscript, as well as certain Atticistic scribal tendencies, but they do not seem to me to help to get at scribal rhetorical practice. Nevertheless, even discounting these variants, there are still just about 140 textual variants between Vaticanus and Alexandrinus. These cover a wide range of variations and include changes in wording, changes in word order, adding additional words, deleting words, changes in syntax, alterations of a more grammatical sort, such as verbal aspect, mood, and number, and even displacement of chunks of text (such as the doxology of 16.25-27 being placed at the end of ch. 14 in Alexandrinus). Most of these changes can be accounted for on the basis of a number of more straightforward explanations. For example, a number of the changes seem to have been introduced to clarify difficult syntax, others to explicate or more clearly label a construction. However, in the course of examining each of these, it seems that there are a number of these variants that were perhaps introduced for rhetorical reasons. These are the ones that I wish to comment upon.

a. *The Style of the Scribe of Alexandrinus: A Plain Presentation of Details regarding Christian Experience*
If one were so inclined, it would be possible, I suppose, to argue that almost every variant was introduced by our rhetorical scribe to help to make a plain and clear presentation of details regarding Christian experience. Whereas I think that there is some, if not much, intrinsic merit in

such a grand explanation of all text-critical details, here I wish to concentrate upon two particular kinds of changes. The first are alterations in
sentence connectives, and the other are changes in clause structure.

1. *Connectives*. Sentence connectives are an area in which the scribe of
Alexandrinus seems to assert his independence for a purpose. Connectives
have been an area of much discussion in Greek and other linguistic circles
over the years, so there is an established body of thought regarding how
they generally function (even if some recent work has called some of this
into question). There are a number of places where Alexandrinus takes the
more expressive but perhaps ambiguous γάρ found in Vaticanus and
changes it to δέ (Rom. 1.17; 7.14; 8.18, 22; 10.3). The connective word
γάρ is an important one in Greek, and especially widely and well used in
earlier Attic writers. It has the function of indicating a more logical or
supportive discourse function. The connective δέ is part of a more connected and continuative style, not necessarily contrastive but connected,
much in the same way as καί is connective, but with slightly more disjunctive forcefulness.[13] The overall result of the change noted here is to
establish a more forceful and connected, as opposed to more explanatory,
syntax—even if one cannot point to a particular instance of the change and
see this forcefulness or connectedness displayed. The scribe of Alexandrinus also changes one instance of the more peculiar τε, even though it is
an intensive particle, to δέ (Rom. 1.27). This too is consistent with his
more direct and forceful connected style. By contrast, this scribe only
changes one instance of δέ to γάρ (Rom. 11.16), again not wildly inconsistent with his overall style. There is also one instance of the scribe
changing οὖν to γάρ (Rom. 3.28), and one instance of γε to γάρ, although
this is part of a complex of changes (Rom. 5.6, the example I discussed
briefly above; this last example would, I must admit, force me to rethink
how I have previously analyzed this set of variants). Whereas in four
instances the scribe of Alexandrinus eliminates a connective (δέ in Rom.
1.12; καί in 6.6; οὖν in 9.19; ὅτι in 10.9), in six instances he adds a
connective. Of these added connectives, one is to create a μέν...δέ construction where only the δέ was used before (Rom. 2.8), two are instances

13. See M. Thrall, *Greek Particles in the New Testament: Linguistic and Exegetical
Studies* (NTTS, 3; Leiden: E.J. Brill, 1962), pp. 41-63; cf. J. Denniston, *The Greek
Particles* (Oxford: Clarendon Press, 1934), pp. 56-114, 162-203; J. Blomqvist, *Greek
Particles in Hellenistic Prose* (Lund: Gleerup, 1969); S.E. Porter, *Idioms of the Greek
New Testament* (BLG, 2; Sheffield: JSOT Press, 2nd edn, 1994), pp. 204-16.

of adding καί (Rom. 3.8; 11.17), two are of adding γάρ (Rom. 3.2; 14.5), and one is of adding οὖν (Rom. 14.12). There are two general results of these variant changes. The first is an overall reduction in the number of different types of connectives that are used. This is consistent, not with a more primitive style, but with one that is more focused on particular kinds of connectives. The second result is that this particular connective style seems to be more straightforward and direct, having gained in number of instances of connectives used.

2. *Word Order*. Word order has been a neglected area of Greek language discussion.[14] The state of discussion is such that we only have general patterns of usage to rely upon. There are a number of instances where the scribe of Alexandrinus, however, has altered the word order of Vaticanus. The scribe of Alexandrinus tends towards a linear subject–verb–object structure, placing constituents, such as prepositional phrases, together with the words they modify, a tendency consistent with general trends in New Testament Greek syntax. Thus, in three instances, Alexandrinus changes the syntax so that the order is subject–verb–object, with modifiers placed with their respective units (Rom. 8.11; 10.9; 14.11), whereas in two instances Alexandrinus changes word order so that this order is displaced from what it is in Vaticanus (Rom. 12.3; 16.2). This seems balanced in proportions, however, raising the question of whether we have a rhetorical tendency here. When these instances are examined, their importance becomes more noticeable. In two of the instances in which the clausal ordering is changed by the scribe of Alexandrinus, the passages are concerned with God or Christ. Thus, in Rom. 8.11, Alexandrinus changes from a structure that speaks of 'the one who raised Christ from death' (ὁ ἐγείρας Χριστὸν ἐκ νεκρῶν) in Vaticanus to 'the one who raised from death Christ Jesus' (ὁ ἐγείρας ἐκ νεκρῶν Χριστὸν Ἰησοῦν), the result being that raising from death, which is linked through event and sphere, is now syntactically linked, and the object of such a complex act is the closing element of the linear syntactical string. In Rom. 10.9, what Vaticanus says is that 'God him raised' (ὁ θεὸς αὐτὸν ἤγειρεν), reformulated by the scribe of Alexandrinus as 'God raised him' (ὁ θεὸς ἤγειρεν αὐτόν).

These two sets of examples provide sufficient material for stylistic evaluation of the scribe of Alexandrinus. Pauline style has been typified as

14. See S.E. Porter, 'Word Order and Clause Structure in New Testament Greek: An Unexplored Area of Greek Linguistics Using Philippians as a Test Case', *FN* 6 (1993), pp. 177-205.

having elements of all three of the major styles spoken of by the ancient writers—complicated or grand style, running or elegant style, and plain or loose style—as well as elements of a fourth style, suggested by Demetrius, the forcible style.[15] It appears that the scribe of Alexandrinus was one who liked the running or elegant style, typified by parataxis and often associated with narrative. Rather than having displaced structures, typical of the periodic tendencies of the complicated or grand style, this rhetorical scribe tends towards a paratactical arrangement of elements.

b. *Favouritism towards Judaism*

Commentators and textual critics have occasionally identified a bias against the Jews in certain manuscripts. The most notorious perhaps is Codex D (Bezae), which has been identified as reflecting a distinctly anti-Jewish bias.[16] The opposite seems to be the case on the part of the scribe of Alexandrinus. There is an apparent tendency for the scribe of Alexandrinus to bring the place of the Jews to the fore, rather than slighting them. This is seen in a number of important scribal variants.

1. *Jew first and Greek*. Favouritism towards Jews and Judaism is made most evident by the scribe in the way that he makes reference to the Jews. An important phrase in Romans is Paul's statement that God's work in relation to humanity was for both Jews and Greeks. He uses this kind of wording five times, and at several significant junctures. One of the most obvious ways that the scribe of Alexandrinus has of showing his favouritism for the Jews is in the way that he handles this phrase. In two instances where the scribe of Vaticanus simply has 'Jew and Greek', the scribe of Alexandrinus adds the word 'first' (πρῶτος), making the phrase 'Jew first and Greek' (Rom. 1.16; 3.9). It is less important whether the use of 'first' here is temporal or positional (I think that both may be in mind), but more important that the scribe uses the phrase, establishing priority for the Jews in God's salvific plan. As a result, in four of the uses of this phrase in Alexandrinus there is the word 'first'. The only one that does not have

---

15. See S.E. Porter, 'Paul of Tarsus and his Letters', in Porter (ed.), *Handbook of Classical Rhetoric*, pp. 533-85, here p. 577. For a fuller treatment, see Campbell, *Rhetoric of Righteousness*, pp. 79-83.

16. E.J. Epp, *The Theological Tendency of Codex Bezae Cantabrigiensis in Acts* (SNTSMS, 3; Cambridge: Cambridge University Press, 1966); D.C. Parker, *Codex Bezae: An Early Christian Manuscript and its Text* (Cambridge: Cambridge University Press, 1992), esp. pp. 189-91, where he reassesses these conclusions.

'first' is Rom. 10.12, where the point is that there is no distinction between Jew and Greek.

2. *Selected Phrasing.* In a number of other instances, the scribe of Alexandrinus uses particular phrasing in order to emphasize the place of the Jews, and their relationship with Christians. For example, in a number of ways, the author brings out the sacrificial dimension in Christian belief, drawing attention to its roots in earlier Jewish practice. In Rom. 3.25, the scribe changes the wording of the verse so that the phrase with regard to faith is not written. Instead, the phrase reads, not 'ἱλαστήριον through [the] faith in his blood' (Vaticanus), but 'ἱλαστήριον in his blood' (Alexandrinus), textually linking 'blood' directly with ἱλαστήριον. This phrasing would probably have emphasized the sacrificial imagery in the minds of those who thought in this framework, rather than imposing 'faith' as an intermediary.[17] This is an important phrasing, as we will see when we look at another verse in this section below. Romans 11.12, which states 'but if their transgression is the riches of the world and their lacking is riches of nations, how much more their fullness', is not to be found in Alexandrinus. This statement, which could be and has been interpreted as simply reiterating what has been said in the verse before to emphasize Jewish sinfulness further, could have been deleted accidentally, but there is, I think, a more likely rhetorical reason for its deletion. The result of the deletion is that the passage goes from a statement about the salvific purpose of Jewish sinfulness to a note of caution to the nations about God's purpose with regard to his people, the Jews. The result is not to dwell upon division between Jew and Gentile, drawing attention to Jewish sinfulness, but upon unity regarding the common human predicament. Similarly, in Rom. 5.17, the scribe has rephrased statements regarding sin. Vaticanus refers to 'the transgression of the one' (τῷ τοῦ ἑνὸς παραπτώματι), usually interpreted as a direct reference to Adam's sinful act. This is restated by the scribe of Alexandrinus as simply 'one sin' (ἐν ἑνὶ παραπτώματι), without necessarily drawing attention to Adam as the one who committed it.

Even reference to the law comes in for rethinking by the scribe of Alexandrinus. At the end of the notorious ch. 7 of Romans, in v. 23, the

17. See E. Käsemann, *Commentary on Romans* (trans. G.W. Bromiley; Grand Rapids: Eerdmans, 1980), p. 99, who says that it is not accidental that Alexandrinus drops 'through faith'.

scribe of Alexandrinus refers to another law in my members that 'fights and takes captive the law of my mind, the one that is in my members' (ἀντιστρατευόμενον καὶ αἰχμαλωτίζοντα τῷ νόμῳ τοῦ νοός μου, τῷ ὄντι ἐν τοῖς μέλεσίν μου), rather than referring to another law in my members that 'fights with the law of my mind and takes me captive by the law of the sin which is in my members' (ἀντιστρατευόμενον τῷ νόμῳ τοῦ νοός μου, καὶ αἰχμαλωτίζοντά με ἐν τῷ νόμῳ τῆς ἁμαρτίας τῷ ὄντι ἐν τοῖς μέλεσίν μου; Vaticanus). The effect is to conclude this section with a toning down of any emphasis upon the law being sinful, and placing the blame away from the law and firmly within the human being. Instead, the scribe of Alexandrinus has it said in Rom. 10.5 that Moses writes of 'the righteousness from faith' (τὴν δικαιοσύνην τὴν ἐκ πίστεως), not 'from the law' (τὴν δικαιοσύνην τὴν ἐκ νόμου) as Vaticanus writes, which states that if one keeps these things he will live by them. So, when the scribe of Alexandrinus comes to Rom. 11.1, he asks the question of whether God cast aside his people, 'whom he foreknew' (ὃν προέγνω), adding these words to what Vaticanus has. Of course not, Paul responds.

In the light of this evidence, one might wonder why it is that, in Rom. 9.4, the scribe of Alexandrinus leaves out an entire phrase that defines the Israelites, deleting the entire rest of the verse after the word 'Israelites' (it usually reads 'Israelites, to whom belongs the adoption as sons and the glory and the covenants and the giving of the law and the service and the promises'). This appears to offer evidence counter to what I have just introduced, or at the least suggest that scribal practice is not so much rhetorical as haphazard. However, one needs to read Rom. 9.3-5 without the words of v. 4 to appreciate a possible reason for the deletion. Paul states that he would wish to be anathematized for his kinsmen, the Israelites, from whom the fathers and from whom is Christ, who is God over all. In other words, rather than this deletion compromising the scribe's position, it seems to reflect his attempt to link Christ more closely with the Jewish people, one of his key emphases (see also below). A similar inconsistency may be found in Rom. 15.31. When speaking of his upcoming trip to Jerusalem, Paul uses the word 'offering' (ἡ δωροφορία) in Vaticanus, but the word 'service' (ἡ διακονία) in Alexandrinus, when speaking of what he intends to take there. In this instance, the scribe of Alexandrinus seems to be wishing to avoid cultic terminology, possibly in terms of reference to Paul.

c. *Jesus as Jesus and Christ*

The scribe of Alexandrinus also has a keen sense of who Jesus Christ is, especially in terms of his Jewish heritage. He emphasizes this through several means of scribal alteration.

1. *Titles and References*.[18] There are 12 places in these two manuscripts, Vaticanus and Alexandrinus, where titles or personal references regarding Jesus, etc., are written differently. In Rom. 1.1, both Vaticanus and Alexandrinus use 'Jesus Christ', which is a reading rejected by the Nestle–Aland[27] text under the influence of Sinaiticus, which has 'Christ Jesus'. I realize that the critical apparatus of Nestle–Aland and of Tischendorf state that Vaticanus reads 'Christ Jesus', and it may well since I am using Mai's questionable edition. What is important for my purposes here is the realization that Alexandrinus uses 'Jesus Christ', which it does often throughout the book of Romans. For example, 'Jesus Christ' is used in 1.4, 6, 7, 8; 2.16; 5.1, 10, 11, 15, 17, 21; 7.25; 10.9; 13.14; 15.5, 6, 30; 16.20, 25, 27; but not in 3.22 , 24; 6.3, 11, 23; 8.1, 2, 11, 34, 39; 15.16, 17; 16.3, where 'Christ Jesus' is used.

Several of these passages merit further comment. In Rom. 2.16; 5.17; 13.14; and 16.25 and 27, 'Christ Jesus' is read in Vaticanus and Nestle–Aland[27], but becomes 'Jesus Christ' in Alexandrinus. This is the single largest tendency of change regarding titles of Jesus Christ in these two manuscripts. There has, of course, been much debate regarding what the significance of the ordering of these elements is in Paul's writings. A traditional view has been that the ordering 'Jesus Christ' places the emphasis upon the human dimension of this figure, rather than 'Christ Jesus', which emphasizes the divine or messianic.[19] One does not need to go so far as to form a general Pauline tendency to realize that at least the scribe of Alexandrinus seems to have wished to refer to this figure as 'Jesus Christ'. A plausible reason, in conjunction with what we have seen above, especially with regard to his phrasing in Rom. 9.4 and the link to the Jewish sacrificial terminology, is that he fully appreciates the Jewish

18. The use of christological titles has been applied to study of apocryphal gospels. See S.E. Porter, 'The Greek Apocryphal Gospels Papyri: The Need for a Critical Edition', in B. Kramer, W. Luppe, H. Maehler and G. Poethke (eds.), *Akten des 21. Internationalen Papyrologenkongresses Berlin, 13–19.8.1995* (2 vols.; Stuttgart: Teubner, 1997), II, pp. 795-803, esp. pp. 801-802.

19. Some of these issues are discussed in W. Kramer, *Christ, Lord, Son of God* (SBT, 50; trans. B. Hardy; London: SCM Press, 1966), *passim*.

(i.e. human) heritage of this figure at least as much as the divine (note that he also places him in parallel with God in Rom. 9.4). There are several other changes as well that are at least compatible with this dualistic perspective. In Rom. 5.10, 'through the death of his son' (διὰ τοῦ θανάτου τοῦ υἱοῦ αὐτοῦ) in Vaticanus becomes 'through our Lord Jesus Christ' (διὰ τοῦ κυρίου ἡμῶν Ἰησοῦ Χριστοῦ) in Alexandrinus. Rom. 8.35, in which Vaticanus has 'love of God which is in Christ Jesus' (τῆς ἀγάπης τοῦ θεοῦ τῆς ἐν Χριστῷ Ἰησοῦ), reads 'love of [Christ]' (τῆς ἀγάπης τοῦ [Χριστοῦ]) in Alexandrinus;[20] but in Rom. 6.3, where Vaticanus has simply 'Christ', Alexandrinus has 'Christ Jesus'.

2. *Romans 3.22.* One of the most controversial passages in recent discussion in Romans is the phrase found in Rom. 3.22, similarly in v. 26, which uses the wording (in English translation which preserves the debated ambiguity) 'faith of Jesus/Christ' (διὰ/ἐκ πίστεως Ἰησοῦ [Χριστοῦ]) (parallels are also found in Gal. 3.22). Here is not the place to recount the debate over this phrase, but the issue has become one of whether the genitive phrase is meant to be taken as objective, the traditional view (i.e., 'faith directed towards Jesus/Christ'), or subjective (that is, 'faith or faithfulness of Jesus/Christ'), the view that seem to be gaining strength in recent interpretation.[21] In the course of discussing this phrasing, there are a number of types of evidence that are often marshalled. These include grammatical reasons related to Pauline usage, theological and conceptual reasons related to similar or divergent thought on the part of Paul, and extra-biblical evidence related to syntax and word usage among other authors of the Greco-Roman world, including Josephus. I have been surprised to discover that one of the neglected sources in this debate is the

20. There is an apparent lacuna in the manuscript, according to the printed edition, but the editor in his reconstruction seems to think that there is not sufficient space for anything longer than the single word.

21. There is simply too much secondary literature to cite here in this context. Besides commentaries, see the recent debate in R.B. Hays, 'ΠΙΣΤΙΣ and Pauline Christology: What Is at Stake?', pp. 714-29; and J.D.G. Dunn, 'Once More, ΠΙΣΤΙΣ ΧΡΙΣΤΟΥ', pp. 730-44, both in E.H. Lovering, Jr (ed.), *SBLSP* (Atlanta: Scholars Press, 1991). Other bibliography worth examining, among others, includes R.B. Hays, *The Faith of Jesus Christ* (SBLDS, 56; Chico, CA: Scholars Press, 1983), pp. 157-84, with history of discussion; D.M. Hay, 'Pistis as "Ground for Faith" in Hellenized Judaism and Paul', *JBL* 108 (1989), pp. 461-76; Campbell, *Rhetoric of Righteousness*, pp. 58-69; *idem*, 'Romans 1.17—*a Crux Interpretum* for the Πίστις Χριστοῦ Debate', *JBL* 113 (1994), pp. 265-85.

scribe of Alexandrinus. At Rom. 3.22, he writes of 'faith in Christ Jesus' (πίστεως ἐν Χριστῷ ᾿Ιησοῦ), using the preposition ἐν, changing the phrasing from the simple genitive to the dative case. There are several important factors to note here.

The first is that this reference does not simply solve the issue of how to interpret the genitive construction in Rom. 3.22 (or anywhere else), since even the phrase 'in Christ' is highly debated.[22] Nevertheless, this evidence should count for something, at least for determining the rhetorical purposes of the scribe of Alexandrinus. It is surprising that this reading has not entered into the scholarly discussion, since it is at least as relevant as twentieth-century scholars trying to debate ancient Greek syntax and terminology. A brief survey of commentaries reveals that this textual variant has not entered into the discussion in any significant way since Sanday and Headlam's commentary, which merely cites the reference but does not discuss it.[23] Sanday and Headlam probably do not discuss it because most likely it is to be interpreted in harmony with the objective genitive interpretation that they adopt, and that was predominant in interpretation at that time. Most commentaries simply cite the evidence available in the Nestle–Aland edition, and note that there is some disagreement over whether 'Christ' or 'Jesus Christ' should be written (Vaticanus drops 'Jesus'), to my mind a far less important textual variant. To briefly recount the textual state of play regarding Rom. 3.22, however, only three manuscripts probably older than Alexandrinus have this verse, Sinaiticus, Vaticanus and 𝔓40 (third century), so this is the fourth oldest extant interpretation of this verse that we have, and it is one well worth considering. It is clear that this is a conscious change by the scribe (or whoever the scribe was following), since it requires both addition of the preposition and change of the ending of one of the proper names, Χριστῷ (even if a *nomen sacrum* were used, at least the final letter would have been changed from υ to ω). The most likely interpretation of this scribe's use of the phrase is in terms of the understanding of the prepositional phrase. It is not a faith that originates with Christ or his faithfulness, but a faith that resides in Christ. This interpretation by the scribe of Alexandrinus is much more compatible with the traditional objective interpretation of the genitive phrase, it must be admitted.

22. For brief discussion, see Porter, *Idioms of the Greek New Testament*, p. 159.
23. W. Sanday and A.C. Headlam, *A Critical and Exegetical Commentary on the Epistle to the Romans* (ICC; Edinburgh: T. & T. Clark, 1895), p. 84.

There is more to be said about this passage, from the standpoint of the scribe of Alexandrinus, however. First, whereas in Rom. 3.21-26 Vaticanus refers to 'Christ' (v. 22) , 'Christ Jesus' (v. 24), and 'Jesus' (v. 26), and the Nestle–Aland[27] refers to 'Jesus Christ' (v. 22), 'Christ Jesus' (v. 24), and 'Jesus' (v. 26), the scribe of Alexandrinus refers to 'Christ Jesus' (v. 22), 'Christ Jesus' (v. 24), and 'Jesus' (v. 26). The switch from the scribe's more usual 'Jesus Christ' to 'Christ Jesus' is noteworthy, since the focus of the passage for him seems to be upon this figure as the agent of God's work in relation to humanity. The change from 'Jesus Christ' seems to be a conscious one to bring attention to the redemptive actions of Christ. These include being the one in whom faith is placed (v. 22) and whose blood is a ἱλαστήριον (v. 25). Again, note the deletion of reference to faith here, since faith is not in his blood but in his person as the Christ.

4. *Conclusion*

On the basis of these textual variants, relatively few though they may be, perhaps one can be allowed to speculate regarding the origins of Codex Alexandrinus. It would seem consistent with the indications in the manuscript that the scribe had a certain favouritism for the Jews. Whereas one cannot speculate that the scribe himself may have been a Jew, the indication would seem to be that he was at least one who was familiar with a sizable or significant Jewish community. This is consistent with the traditional thought that the manuscript originated in Alexandria, Egypt, which had a sizable Jewish population. In fact, one of the first and earliest Christian communities outside of Palestine may well have been in Egypt, as the result of connections through the Jewish populations of Palestine and Egypt. However, it is also consistent with the recent hypothesis by Scot McKendrick of the Manuscript Room of the British Library that the manuscript originated in Ephesus,[24] another centre of Jewish life in the ancient world. The Jewish favouritism of the scribe would also perhaps be consistent with the scribe's efforts to draw to the fore the human dimension regarding Jesus, but without neglecting what it means for him to be the Christ. This would provide a line of continuity, rather than conflict, between the two communities of faith. Jewish practice, such as sacrifice, is not only retained but emphasized, with faith being located in Jesus

---

24. McKendrick's paper is to appear in S. McKendrick and O. O'Sullivan (eds.), *The Bible as Book: The Transmission of the Greek Text* (London: British Library Publications, in press).

Christ—the person is the object of faith, but the sacrificial dimension, his blood, is the centre of redemptive activity. This would constitute what the scribe of Alexandrinus sees as a persuasive message to deliver to his Christian readers.

Romans 7 Derhetorized

Lauri Thurén

1. *Introduction*

W.G. Kümmel's classical interpretation of ἐγώ in Romans 7 is an early crown jewel of rhetorical criticism. It demonstrates how the interpretation of a crucial theological passage has always been dependent on this discipline. The aim of this article is to highlight, and critically examine, Kümmel's solution.

When interpreting biblical texts, it is important to pay attention to the author's rhetoric inasmuch as he does not always exactly mean what he seems to say. If Paul portrays the Corinthians as kings (1 Cor. 4.8), it would be a serious mistake to use this as material for a historical or sociological reconstruction of the congregation. It is evident that the rhetorical technique of *irony* is utilized.[1] His habit of using *hyperbole* is likewise evident to any reader,[2] and it is easy to perceive the *captatio benevolentiae* at the beginning of most of his letters. A 'literal' interpretation of any of these devices would give rise to far-fetched conclusions.

Our problem with Paul's rhetoric is that not all devices are similarly apparent to us. This is partly due to the failure of many theologians to recognize the persuasive nature of his letters. But even if we are aware that he sought, first and foremost, to influence his readers and not only describe his theology, we may be led astray by the fact that the ancient customs of communication were somewhat different from ours. Hence the need for rhetorical criticism. A careful comparison of Paul's texts and rhetorical customs, both ancient and general, enables identification of many devices, tactics, and strategies, and revelation of their 'true meaning'. Annoying pitfalls of interpretation can be avoided thereby.

---

1.   See Conzelmann 1975: 87.
2.   For example in 1 Cor. 1.4-5, 7; 2.2-3, 9; 6.12; 11.2.

But even this 'derhetorization' is not without its risks. Beside simple fallacies of omitting or misunderstanding rhetorical features, one may be tempted to deliberate misuse. If the aim is to identify theological ideas behind the text, or to reveal the 'true meaning' of what Paul says, it is easy to characterize an offensive Pauline expression as 'mere rhetoric'. Especially when the text seems to be theologically controversial or even contradictory, a reference to rhetoric may provide too facile a solution.

For there are many other possible explanations. We should not be pre-occupied with the idea that Paul was a 'prince of thinkers', producing polished theology—maybe he often contradicts himself.[3] Or maybe he was a poor rhetorician, and expressed his theology so vaguely that it is easily misunderstood.[4] What we assess as an offensive comment in his texts may reveal his actual opinion. But there are even more annoying options: our limited knowledge of rhetoric, or our theological preconceptions, may blur the picture.

Thus, if we would avoid simple misunderstandings, it is necessary to pay attention to the persuasive techniques whereby Paul approaches his audience. However, we should not use rhetorical criticism in order to harmonize his thinking. Actual theological or rhetorical shortcomings may well be present. Or perhaps there is more than meets the eye.

2. Romans 7—The Need for a Rhetorical Solution

Using rhetorical criticism to solve important exegetical and theological problems is not as modern a phenomenon as may be imagined. In his 1929 dissertation, Kümmel applied a rhetorical explanation to a major contro-versial issue, the identity of ἐγώ in Rom. 7. His initiative proved highly successful: only three years later Rudolf Bultmann declared the discussion at an end, and Kümmel's solution has rarely been seriously questioned since.[5] Scholars have reached the final answer.[6] Thus even those modern theologians, who otherwise show remarkable insight in observing weak points in traditional exegetical results, accept the solution with little hesitation.[7] Early rhetorical criticism has proven indisputable, with its

3. Räisänen (1987) is a well-known representative of this view.
4. For evidence of such occasions in Pauline epistles, see Thurén 2000: 29-35.
5. Bultmann 1932. Laato (1991: 139 n. 3), however, cites 14 critical scholars.
6. Hübner 1987: 2668.
7. Cf. Hübner 1982: 69-70; Räisänen 1987: 109. For 13 further examples, see Laato 1991: 138 n. 2.

ability to resolve obvious and abrasive exegetical tensions.

Notwithstanding, this masterpiece of rhetorical criticism requires further consideration. As Kümmel's methodological heirs, modern scholars interested in rhetorical criticism should re-examine the grounds of his solution. We should study how he achieved his results in order to learn something—and even raise some critical questions. One can discern at least four reasons why ἐγώ was interpreted as not meaning Paul.

a. *Contextual and Theological Tensions*

The problem which Kümmel[8] was addressing was not rhetorical, but theological. ἐγώ in Rom. 7.14-25 is described as a hopeless, gloomy character. He is a slave sold under sin and the flesh, lacking the ability to do good. How could such a picture fit in with Paul's teaching about Christians? Not only other epistles, such as Galatians,[9] but even the immediate context contradicts such an assumption. According to 7.1-6 the Christian is absolutely free from the law, and no longer its prisoner. The following 8.1-11 tells the same story. Paul hardly speaks of his own Jewish past in 7.7-13, as if he had sometimes lived without the law. On the contrary, he can boast of having been righteous (Phil. 3.3-8). Likewise, as a Christian, he is not guided by the flesh (2 Cor. 10.3), but is a good example to others. The description in Rom. 7.14-25 is far removed from such a person.[10]

Thus, the extremely pessimistic figure of Rom. 7.14-25 is difficult to combine with Paul's general, simple and optimistic proclamation. Although the Christians in general, or Paul as a model Christian, are not presented as wholly blameless,[11] they are guided by the Spirit and free from the law. Those who are not cannot please God (Rom. 8.8).

Attempts to see ἐγώ as describing Paul are beset by complex philosophical explanations and theological problems. Nor can the Apostle be accused of inconsistency, since the immediate context includes some of the most difficult sentences to be combined with vv. 14-25, if the ἐγώ meant Paul or any other Christian. It is unlikely that he so rapidly forgot what he wrote.

---

8. Kümmel 1974 (originally published 1929): esp. 36-138.

9. In Gal. 5.16-18, which resembles Rom. 7, the Spirit and flesh are presented as mutually exclusive; and the Christians walk in the Spirit. Thus Kümmel 1974: 105-106.

10. Kümmel 1974: 97-119.

11. Kümmel 1974: 101; cf. Westerholm 1988: 62.

The text becomes more coherent, if we explain ἐγώ in another way. The logic of chs. 7–8 then becomes easier to comprehend, and the Pauline theology more straightforward.

b. *Defending Paul's Ethos*

But for the ancient Christians, there was another, more telling reason to find an alternative interpretation. Nilus of Ancyra writes in order to correct another reader, Olympius: 'God forbid! The divine apostle does not say concerning himself that "I see another law in my members taking me captive through sin".'[12]

Nilus, who lived in the first half of the fifth century, is known to have taught an ascetic way of life.[13] For him, it was intolerable to think of the holy Apostle as a miserable sinner. Thus he claims to Olympius that Paul is simply utilizing *ethopoiia*, a rhetorical device. As a pupil of the great orator Chrysostom, he was more familiar with sophisticated rhetorical techniques than his friend, or indeed than Paul.

Nilus was not alone. As Paul was a highly respected saint of the early church, it must have been very perplexing to read the description of a weakling in Romans 7, as referring to Paul, although some obviously did so. The personal *ethos* of Paul is better represented by a reinterpretation of ἐγώ: the Apostle can be seen as an honourable model Christian.

Origen perhaps explained Romans 7 with 1 Cor. 9.22: Paul adapts himself to the addressees.[14] Different stages of a person are depicted, according to the technique of *prosopopoiia*.[15] But he also maintains, for example, that Rom. 7.24 is Paul's own cry.[16] Irenaeus claims that Rom. 7.18 and 24 speak of people unable to attain salvation.[17] Tertullian is against interpreting ἐγώ as Paul;[18] Jerome has different opinions, but can say that 7.19 does not mean Paul.[19]

However, the opposite interpretation is even better attested among the

---

12. *Epist.* 1.152.

13. Hesse 1994: 568-73.

14. Origen, *Com. Rom.* 6.9 (Rufinus) [1086A]; a corresponding interpretation is in *Com. in Evangelium Joannis* 10.5.316-17.

15. Cf. Stowers 1995: 194-96.

16. Origen, *Exhortatio ad Martyrium* 3.565. Schelkle (1959) offers a good perspective on Origen's and other Fathers' different opinions.

17. Irenaeus, *Adv. Haer.* 3.20.3.393.

18. Tertullian, *De Pudicitia* 17.1013.

19. Jerome, *Commentaria in Danielem* 3.29.509.

Fathers. It was obvious that somehow ἐγώ meant more than Paul alone—
'sub sua persona quasi generalem agit causam' ('by means of his person
intends, as it were, a universal reference').[20] Perhaps Paul had in mind all
Christians,[21] but this was usually seen as an additional meaning beside
Paul himself.

Romans 7 is not the only case where the Church Fathers would show
Paul in a good light in order to save his reputation. 1 Corinthians 9.19-23,
where Paul claims to be a kind of religious and theological chameleon,
was also annoying and provoked different explanations. Regarding this
offensive passage too, the main sources for the 'rhetorical' explanation in
the early Church are based on the specialists in rhetoric, Origen and John
Chrysostom![22]

In principle the Early Fathers offer a good source for understanding how
the contemporary addressees might have regarded Paul, since they are so
close to him both culturally and linguistically. However, they ought not to
be used uncritically. When clear and obvious tendencies can be suspected,
their testimony is of little value. I think that when we are dealing with
Paul's ethos, this is the case.

In explaining Romans 7, Nilus and his colleagues are actually defending
Paul's ethos like a Roman defense attorney trying to save his client. They
had four options.[23] Since status number 1, *status coniecturae*, that of
denial, and status number 4, *status translationis* or procedural objection,
are excluded from the outset, the Fathers select number 2, *status
definitionis*, or redefinition. Since the charges could not be denied (*status
coniecturae*), they had to be redefined.

The Fathers' tendency to explain away offensive passages in the Pauline
texts is easy to understand, as the Apostle became a saint in the first

20. Ambrosiaster, *Com. in Epistulam ad Romanos* 114.

21. Eusebius, *Com. in Lucam* 65; 597; *in Psalmos* Ps. 60.2-3; 68.30-31; *Praep. Ev.*
12; 27; 997; Cyril Alexandrinus, *Explanatio in Epistolam ad Romanos* 809-16; Basil,
Regulae brevius tractatae, Interrogatio 16, Responsio 1093; Methodius, *De resur-
rectione* 2.2.7-8; 4.1.5 etc.; Hilarius, e.g. *Tractatus super psalmos*, *Tractatus in 118
psalmum*, Gimel 3, Jod 8.15; Ambrose, e.g. *De Abraham* 2.27; 490-91; *Expositio in
Psalmum* 118.3; 11.20; 46.

22. Cf. quotations from the Church Fathers by Mitchell 2001. Like Stowers, she
uses the Fathers (Tertullian and Clement of Alexandria are discussed, too) as unbiased
witnesses, but aims proper criticism against the tendencies of Philo.

23. Cf. the doctrine of status in Lausberg 1960: §§79-138; J. Martin 1974: 28-44.
The doctrine is often misused in rhetorical criticism. It was designed for the courtroom
and must be applied in other contexts with great care.

Christian centuries, and his image had to be polished as brightly as possible. But from a purely historical point of view, it is obvious that the Fathers are misusing derhetorization.[24]

The readers, whom Paul envisaged in front of him when dictating Romans, hardly saw him as especially venerable. On the contrary, according to a common opinion, one of the purposes of the letter was to introduce Paul to the congregation(s) and perhaps defend his reputation against different rumors.[25] Thus the original readers were unlikely to share the Church Fathers' specific frame of reference for their interpretation. The Fathers' interpretation was obviously suitable for the Church, but it is problematic for historical exegesis.

c. *Liberation from Captivity*

At a later stage, another reason appears. An important task of New Testament scholarship in the 1960s was to liberate Paul from his 'Lutheran captivity'. One of the main figures in this movement was Krister Stendahl.[26] The idea, which rapidly became popular, was hardly inspired by purely exegetical interests. Perhaps it was not per se a reaction against the medieval scholarship of Martin Luther, although Stendahl's *Doctorvater* Anton Fridrichsen promoted traditional Lutheran values in the Church of Sweden. It is more likely that the liberation movement was directed against the popular existentialist reading of Paul by Rudolf Bultmann and his followers, which can be seen as a modern Lutheran-Pietist interpretation.[27] But be that as it may, Stendahl's thesis was clear: Paul should not be seen as an archetype of a medieval introspective Christian nor as a modern existentialist believer.[28] The alleged self-searching in Romans 7 appears to be anachronistic.

d. *Current Trends*

The concerns of perhaps both the Early Fathers and the post-existentialist exegetes are no longer especially cogent nowadays. But already Kümmel had an additional vision when interpreting Romans 7, prompted by the

---

24. According to Stowers (1995: 196), 'Origen shows us how and why an ancient reader would have understood Rom. 7.7-25 as προσωποποιία.' I disagree: most ancient readers did not share his Christian tendencies.

25. For discussion, see Donfried 1991.

26. See especially his hallmark article, Stendahl 1976.

27. Cf. Stendahl 1976: 87-88. But concerning ἐγώ in Rom. 7 Bultmann and Stendahl agree that Paul does not mean himself.

28. Stendahl 1976: 93-96; Stowers 1995: 191.

changed view of Paul's contemporary Pharisaism.[29] Although unpopular at the time, Stendahl could easily accept this view, as a more realistic attitude to Judaism and particularly Pharisaism was popular among Swedish exegetes long before Sanders and Neusner.[30] But after the impetus of these two scholars in the seventies, there is still a current trend to absolve ancient Judaism from the caricature, which has lived too long even in scholarly exegesis. It is obvious that biblical scholarship should be ashamed of this interpretation, not only because it testifies to careless reading of Paul and ancient Jewish sources, but also because it may have contributed to the anti-Jewish attitudes in the Third Reich. According to the new understanding, the law was a source of joy for the Pharisees. They were not hypocritical religious monsters, nor such terrible sinners as was previously thought.[31] Correspondingly, as a former Pharisee, Paul could describe the Gentiles, but hardly himself, in the manner of Romans 7.

e. *Conclusion*

Thus we have at least four reasons which prompt an understanding of ἐγώ, which does not denigrate the Apostle. However, witnesses who can be suspected of all but the first of these motives, in voicing their interpretation must be treated with great suspicion. Neither our search for logical or theological consistency, nor the moral requirements which the early Church imposed on the divine Apostle or those which we set for the historical Paul, not to mention modern exegetical remorse, should guide the interpretation or decide what the text originally meant.[32] If a reader fights for a cult figure created in the first Christian centuries, or against some medieval, or even a twentieth-century theology, we may suspect that such tendencies are present. With the possible exception of the first, these motives were absent in the original situation of Romans.

3. *Derhetorizing the Text*

So what did Paul mean when saying ἐγώ in Romans 7? Whereas the mind of the historical Apostle is beyond our reach, it remains our duty to scrutinize the text and its context.

29. Kümmel 1974: 112-18.

30. See e.g. Lindeskog 1938; Odeberg 1964 (originally published 1943).

31. In fact, such a theory is based on a biased reading of Paul's rhetoric: he never describes what Jews actually were as did later scholars. Caricatures are used for rhetorical purposes only. See Thurén 2000: 68-69.

32. Cf. Stowers 1995: 191.

a. *Mapping the Semantic Field*

The semantic field of the word ἐγώ in Romans 7 can only be defined if we can postulate how it was envisaged to be understood by the original historical readers, viz. the members of the Roman Christian congregation(s), and how it was designed to affect them. The simplest meaning of the word is to be found in the dictionaries. Unfortunately they are unequivocal: ἐγώ is the 'pronoun of the first person'.[33] The English dictionaries can offer little more: 'I' denotes 'the person speaking'.[34] The semantic field of the word seems to be very narrow. At first glance, ἐγώ stands for the Apostle himself.

This is where rhetorical criticism comes into the picture. 'If, however, Paul is not speaking of himself, there remains no other choice, than to search for another subject and to speak whether the I is *somehow a rhetorical means* of expressing his thought.'[35]

It is interesting to note that Kümmel did not begin by performing a rhetorical analysis. Instead, when all other possibilities were excluded and the problem remained insoluble, rhetoric was invoked as a last resort. The same applies to the Fathers: only rhetoric could enable them to escape the semantic boundaries of the word, so that both the *logos* and the *ethos* of the Apostle were saved.

But, according to Kümmel, a rhetorical explanation of Rom. 7.7-13 seems unlikely at first glance. Turning to the more difficult, and awkward, vv. 14-25, where the subject must remain the same, he repeats: 'the most natural and easily available notion is…the assumption that Paul is speaking of himself' (90).

These statements seem to weaken his case inasmuch as the peculiar use of ἐγώ must have been easily understood by the addressees. In other words, if the theologians, whether ancient or modern, arrive after much education and consideration at the result that ἐγώ does not mean Paul, there must be some indication that the original readers, who did not share their knowledge, were nevertheless thought to understand it in the same way easily and immediately. The text was designed for oral delivery; Paul hardly reckoned that a deep scrutiny by some experts in the congregation

33. LSJ, *s.v.*; Bauer, Aland and Aland 1988, *s.v.* The only help we can find is the addition by Bauer, who in the case of ἐγώ in Rom. 7 refers to Kümmel.

34. *Longman Dictionary of Contemporary English* (1978), *s.v.*

35. 'Wenn aber Paulus nicht von sich selber redet, so bleibt nichts anderes übrig, als nach einem andern Subjekt zu suchen und fragen, ob das Ich nicht *irgendwie eine rhetorische Form* zur Ausführung eines Gedankens ist.' Kümmel 1974: 87, my italics.

afterwards corrected the first, natural understanding of the hearers. In other words, unlike Kümmel, the original addressees must have been able immediately to exclude Paul from the semantic field of ἐγώ.

b. *An Ancient Rhetorical Device?*

In practice, the rhetorical use of ἐγώ, where the author himself is excluded, could be best substantiated if we found a suitable, generally known, ancient rhetorical custom or device. Without such external evidence, the rhetorical solution remains too hypothetical. For on the surface level of the text, there are no signs of a change in the identity of the speaker. This, however, does not exclude the possibility that Paul actually used some kind of natural device and expected his addressees to understand it aright.

In search for such a technique, scholars of the eighteenth and nineteenth centuries suggested names like *metaskhematismos*, *koinosis*, or *idiosis*. However, Kümmel admits that such technical terms are not found in ancient literature,[36] and states: 'In der Rhetorik scheint diese Stilform nicht vorzukommen.'[37] Instead, Kümmel only refers to the general flexible use of the first person in the Pauline literature, as well as by ancient Greek, Latin, and Jewish authors.[38]

Stanley Stowers recently revitalized Kümmel's thesis by claiming that Paul uses the ancient technique of *prosopopoiia*.[39] Suddenly there seems to be no doubt: Romans 7 'fits extremely well' with this technique.[40] It was 'almost certain' that Paul was aware of the uses of this device and thus could have employed it in Romans 7. Here Stowers refers especially to Origen and Nilus.[41]

But not only is the testimony of these Fathers problematic. Stowers also presents the device itself in a misleading way. Referring to Martin among others, he defines it as 'a rhetorical technique in which the speaker or

---

36. Kümmel 1974: 120.

37. Kümmel 1974: 132 n. 2. Similarly Michel 1978: 224-25 n. 5: 'Es ist aber nicht möglich, diesen "Ichstil" dem hellenistisch-rhetorischen Material ein- bzw. unterzuordnen.'

38. Kümmel 1974: 121-32. For additional examples from Qumran, see Braun (1959: 4-5).

39. Stowers 1995: 180-202. Already Kümmel considered *prosopopoiia* as a possibility (Kümmel 1974: 132 n. 2).

40. Stowers 1995: 202.

41. Stowers 1995: 182, 188-91, 193-98.

writer produces speech that represents not himself or herself but another person or type of character'.[42] However, in Martin, as well as in other handbooks, the definition is somewhat different: *prosopopoiia* usually referred to the personification of inanimate objects or abstract concepts; moreover it was sometimes used of people who had died or had never lived, but were represented as living.[43]

The ancient specialists could discuss how an actor should present the *prosopopoiia* in Homer and whether an orator should modulate his voice to indicate the device.[44] But Paul was hardly a well-trained actor or orator.[45] If, however, he knew the technique, he must also have been aware of the difficulty of identifying the person discussed in the training.[46] Perhaps he did, for we know that he was aware of the absence of the most powerful means needed: sending a letter excludes *immutatio vocis* (Gal. 4.20)! If *prosopopoiia* was used in a peculiar way which could cause problems, why did he not so indicate?

Another major problem in any rhetorical analysis arises from our view of the original partners in communication and their educational level; viz. not only the author but also the audience. Were they sufficiently conversant with all the rhetorical strategies, tactics and devices, which we find somewhere in the vast ancient literature? How many of these were 'in the air' so that they could be easily utilized and understood by the communicants? For the handbook-rhetoric as we know it was far removed from the public at large. Porter states that rhetorical training 'required years of work and included much theoretizing…and practice…it is difficult to believe that Paul through haphazard means could have acquired a working knowledge of these categories, much less mastery of them, even if they were "in the air"'.[47] The same applies even more to the readers Paul envisages in

42. Stowers 1995: 180.

43. Bühlmann and Scherer 1973: 70; J. Martin 1974: 151, 292-93. For a modern definition, see Nida, Louw, Snyman and Cronje 1983: 186-87. Stowers's translation 'speech-in-character' instead of the standard 'personification' is also peculiar.

44. Stowers 1995: 183-84.

45. Although 2 Cor. 11.6 may be 'mere rhetoric' (see R.P. Martin 1986: 342-43), serious questions concerning Paul's rhetorical education are raised by Porter 1997: 535-38, 562-67. Stowers (1995: 184) claims that Paul had received training in letter-writing. One may ask, why is there so little evidence thereof in his epistles, which, despite some characteristics discussed by modern epistolographers, bear very little resemblance to normal ancient letters.

46. As presented by Stowers 1995: 181-83.

47. Porter 1997: 563-64.

Rome. Even if he knew some peculiar techniques, it is even less plausible that he used them when writing to the complex Roman audience with its various educational abilities.

Summing up, if Paul spoke in first person singular excluding himself, but without giving any sign thereof, he must have assumed that his audience was well aware of such a technique. But evidence from ancient rhetoric shows that no such commonly known device existed. Modern exegetes decided to exclude Paul from Romans 7 only after much theological scrutiny, and at least partly as a reaction against medieval and modern German exegesis. They referred to the reading of some Fathers, which, however, was clearly apologetic. Thus all these interpretations must be treated with great caution. For rhetorical critics, these remarks call for self-criticism. We have to recognize the temptation to eliminate annoying utterances by using rhetoric as a magic key.

c. *A General Rhetorical Device?*

But if, as Kümmel stated, the superficial and the most natural interpretation of ἐγώ in Romans 7 does not exclude Paul, how is the passage to be understood? Fortunately, the rhetorical interpretation does not depend only on the masters of ancient rhetoric. There is another option: the universal, general rhetoric, which is sometimes called 'modern' or 'new' rhetoric. These labels are somewhat misleading, as we are dealing with features of human communication, which are generally known and only loosely connected with the contemporary culture. The use and understanding of such techniques do not require any specific training but only some sensitivity for communication.[48] For example, almost everybody knows that it is advisable to begin a speech or a letter with some friendly words to the addressees; the listeners or readers are well aware that not all the flattery by the orator or author is to be taken literally.

Thus not even the idea of personification by using the first person must be rejected. But instead of considering the specific, sophisticated education of ancient actors or lawyers, a more general understanding and use of the concept are required. Then recent studies of rhetoric may be more illustrative: like any modern scholarship they build upon earlier masters, but can be more useful. Thus Perelman's *New Rhetoric* mentions *prosopopoiia*. This modern view of personification resembles the ancient one: Perelman speaks of personification of an object or a group. It gives

---

48. Cf. Kennedy 1984: 10.

coherence to the group discussed and stabilizes its boundaries.[49] Both modern and ancient general definitions of the device are well suited to the interpretation of many Fathers: in Romans 7 ἐγώ stands for all Christians, Paul included. It is indeed a rhetorical device, but the general use thereof, which can be grasped by anybody, does not allow the exclusion of the speaker himself from the first person singular.

The interpretation of the chapter becomes somewhat easier, if Paul's personal experience is not at stake. Instead of inferring 'Western' intro-spective ideas, which could see Paul as a modern philosopher wrestling with his personal existential anxiety, the collective understanding of ἐγώ in Romans 7 sees him as an example, just as he claims to be in other cases.[50] Paul's goal is not to present the dark side of himself for the Roman Christians, but to discuss the role of the law and sin in the Christians' life. For such a theoretical treatise, personification could bring life and coherence.

But this interpretation also revitalizes the theological problems inherent in the chapter. How could Paul and even other Christians be so totally 'sold under sin', lacking all capacity to do good? Does it not contradict the context, where the Christian is said to be completely free from sin and the law? Could rhetorical criticism shed more light on the question?

d. *Building up Paul's Ethos*

Why does an author choose the first person, when other options exist? In the case of the plural the reason is obvious: the reference to 'us' creates a sense of solidarity and intimacy. Simultaneously the audience is led to think in the way 'we' think. Insofar as *identification* is a basic means of persuasion,[51] the use of first person makes it easy to identify with the author. Such a use of the first person plural is found in Rom. 1.11-12 and in 5.1–7.6.[52] According to Holland, Paul's use of the first person singular in 7.7-25 serves the same purpose, as 'a reiteration and further expansion of ideas introduced and explored in the previous chapters, using the first person singular in place of the first person plural'.[53]

---

49. 'By means of *prosopopoeia*, the thing personified is turned into a speaking and acting subject', Perelman and Olbrechts-Tyteca 1969: 330-31, 294.
50. 1 Thess. 1.6; 1 Cor. 4.16; 11.1; Phil. 3.17; 4.9.
51. Burke 1962: 548, 597-80.
52. Thus both Stowers (1994: 269-70, 292) and Holland (1999: 263).
53. Holland 1999: 263-69.

To be more specific, Paul presents himself as a bad example. According to Holland, this involves subversion of 'the philosophical *topos* of the teacher as a moral example'. In the rhetorical situation of Romans, it would be unwise merely to discuss the sins of the addressees. Instead of claiming apostolic authority, Paul attempts to appear as a sympathetic figure, who shares the past troubles of the addressees, and hopes to be 'mutually encouraged by each other's faith, both yours and mine' (Rom. 1.12).[54] Paul is making his own character sympathetic by *not* being a superman. This technique is typical of him: not only the negative boasting in 2 Cor. 11.23–12.10, but already the beginning of Romans, where Paul presents himself to the addressees as παῦλος δοῦλος, a little slave, may serve as examples. Some Church Fathers of course had difficulties in understanding this tactic.

The rhetoric described here is of a general nature and well suited to the rhetorical situation of the epistle. But there are two inherent problems. First, even if 'I' in Rom. 7.7-13 is so universal as to include Adam,[55] the natural meaning of the text is that 7.14-25 describes the present situation of the author. This, however, is at odds with v. 6, where 'we' are said to be free from the law. Second, Holland's explanation is based on the idea that Paul was once 'at the mercy of the sinful desires evoked by the law in Romans 7.5'.[56] But how does this does accord with Paul's description of his glorious Pharisaic past in Phil. 3.4-8, which partly prompted Kümmel's solution?[57]

Thus, the rhetorical explanations of both Stowers and Holland contain valuable elements, but are not therefore applicable. Ἐγώ in Romans 7 is obviously used as a rhetorical device, as a personification of a group, but its role must not be pressed so hard that the author himself is excluded. A universal function of the technique is more plausible: Paul presents Adam as a prototype and himself as an example of a Christian, thereby hoping to build up his *ethos* and to gain some goodwill among the addressees, who cannot be expected to respect his apostolic authority. But this explanation still assumes Paul's past or present wretchedness, which is a classical problem of interpreting Romans 7.

---

54. Holland 1999: 269-71.
55. For the discussion, see Dunn 1988: 378, 399-402; Laato 1991: 130-32, 168-72.
56. Holland 1999: 269.
57. Kümmel 1974: 111, 117.

4. *Hyperbolical Language*

Instead of resorting to conventional methods, which have too long been applied to the problem, I shall once more ask whether rhetorical criticism still has something to offer. But as stated above, it does not suffice to invent sophisticated techniques. The general characteristics of Pauline rhetoric need to be illuminated.

a. *Exaggeration—A Key Feature in Pauline Rhetoric*

The most striking rhetorical feature in Pauline texts is his habit of exaggeration. No handbooks are needed to perceive this technique. In Corinth, he knows nothing, save Jesus Christ (1 Cor. 2.2); and no one κατὰ σάρκα (2 Cor. 5.16). The Corinthians are kings (1 Cor. 4.8-13), and the faith of the Romans is known throughout the world (Rom. 1.8). Paul works and prays constantly, night and day,[58] whereas the Jews seem just to rob temples (Rom. 2.21-23). This hyperbolical language had its shortcomings, as people could take it too literally.[59]

The tendency to exaggerate is not limited solely to isolated expressions. In Galatians, Paul sees the antagonists' theology as 'yeast', and his mission is to show how it can 'leaven the whole batch of dough, viz. the Christian theology or the addressees' faith (Gal. 5.9). The antagonists' theology is thereby presented as a caricature.[60]

His own proclamation of the gospel and Christian freedom is hardly free from *hyperbole* either. The baptismal proclamation is a good example: baptism means *death* with Christ, perhaps originally also *resurrection* as in Col. 2.12. Whereas in Rom. 6.3-4 the picture of baptism is not in balance—instead of speaking of resurrection with Christ, Paul adds an exhortation to live in Christ—one can assume an earlier, formally balanced formulation behind the Corinthians' troubles. According to many scholars the Corinthians believed in a 'realized eschatology'. They had already risen with Christ in baptism. Therefore there was no death or resurrection to be expected, and there was no more sin.[61] But in support of this thesis, no reference to influence by mystery religions is required, not

---

58. 1 Thess. 1.2-3, 9; 3.10; 1 Cor. 1.4; Rom. 1.9-10; Phil. 1.4.

59. Cf. the question of associating with immoral people in 1 Cor. 5.9-13.

60. See further Thurén 2000: 69.

61. For discussion, see Eriksson 1998: 239-41; cf. also Wilson 1968: 90-107; Thiselton 1978: 523-25; and Tuckett 1996.

to mention an imaginary phenomenon called 'Gnostic libertinism'.[62] In all probability, the source of the addressees' error is again the Apostle himself.[63] When he declared the Christians as free from sin, the law, and death, problems ensued.

b. *1 Corinthians 15.56*
To solve these problems Paul wrote 1 Cor. 15.56, which is an interesting parallel to Romans 7, and surprisingly overlooked by Kümmel: 'The sting of death is sin, and the power of the sin is the law.' In the context (1 Cor. 15.50-57), the physical death of the Corinthian Christians is presented as a result of sin, and consequently of the law, and these forces are *not* conquered until the parousia of Christ, when Paul and the Corinthians are transformed (vv. 52-54).[64]

In this section it is unmistakably implied that even as Christians Paul and the Corinthians still live under the power of the law. Without the law, sin would have no means of causing death. That the cry of triumph over death will one day resound has no meaning, unless the law concerns the Corinthian Christians at the time when the letter was written. This, however, is in diametrical opposition to Rom. 7.6 and 8.1-9, where the Christians are proclaimed free from the law—but fits well with Rom. 7.14-25, if it describes Christians.

It would be too easy a solution to dismiss 1 Cor. 15.56 as a gloss,[65] or an ad hoc rhetorical figure without deeper significance. The awkward metaphor, and the surprising theology therein, have often been ignored or (deliberately?) misrepresented by scholars.[66] In the verse sin is the sting of

62. Cf. Wedderburn 1987: 296-359. The Christian sources reiterate the same stereotypical charges of libertinism which may simply be attributable to standard vilification.

63. Thiselton 1978: 515: 'We may assume that the Corinthians either took up Paul's own words about freedom from law, or more probably that they felt drawn towards a more radical application of Paul's own eschatological dualism than he himself had seemed to allow.'

64. Beker (1980: 229) rightly argues that death cannot be merely a consequence of sin, since then it could not be 'the last enemy' to be defeated before the final triumph of God.

65. The idea is promoted by, e.g., Weiss 1910: 380. For discussion, see Laato 1991: 179 n. 2.

66. Commenting on 1 Cor. 15.56, Fee (1987: 805) explains: 'In Pauline theology sin is the deadly poison' Can a metaphor be more gravely distorted?

a scorpion,[67] and the power of this sting, viz. the poison injected thereby, is the *law*.

Disregarding the crucial role of the law, Beker postulates 'a theological problem, that [Paul] does not resolve consistently', viz. a 'fundamental inconsistency': sin has been overcome by Christ, yet its result, death, remains the last enemy. Thus the Apostle is said to contradict himself.[68] But in 1 Corinthians 15, Paul assumes that the metaphor functions well, probably due to previous oral teaching. Otherwise he would either provide further information or omit the controversial topic when discussing resurrection. Why cloud the sensitive issue of resurrection with a provocative statement about the law?

This brings us back to Romans 7, where the addressees are unaware of Pauline oral teaching. Both sections describe the law's hold on the flesh of the Christians, and end with similar thanksgivings (Rom. 7.25/1 Cor. 15.57). Romans 7 is longer and goes into greater detail, distinguishing between the 'I' who *has* flesh and the 'I' who *is* flesh (7.18). Since the flesh is an integral part of a man, the whole Christian must physically die—thus far he is still under the dominion of the law. But the two previous deaths—the death of Christ and the death of the Christian in baptism—ensure that the controlling part, the spirit, is free from the law and consequently free from the punishment. This principle will then materialize in the resurrection, where the whole man is renewed, and the triumphal cry of 1 Cor. 15.56 is finally relevant both spiritually and physically.

Romans 7–8 thereby displays Paul's solution of the 'continuing dilemma', which scholars have correctly recognized in his theology. The chapters provide us with a fuller explanation of the loaded, somewhat surprising idea that the law still has power over the Christian. In 1 Corinthians 15 the train of thought is taken for granted, whereas in Romans 7 the idea is discussed—probably because the addressees are not expected to know the specific Pauline teaching.

Why and how did Paul arrive at so complex a theory? Would not it have been simpler to abide by the clear message of Galatians: the Christian is totally free from the law? Above we saw that in 1 Corinthians Paul is often fighting against the outcome of his own rhetorically exaggerated teaching.

---

67. LSJ, *s.v.*

68. Beker 1980: 222, 228. To give Paul some credit Beker notes that the problematic relation of suffering and evil to sin and death, dependent on this inconsistency, has 'haunted Christians throughout the ages' (Beker 1980: 232).

This provides a specific challenge: a unilateral powerful attack à la Galatians cannot be attempted; the Apostle has to explain that the situation is more complicated than the addressees realise.

The contrast between Pauline rhetoric and harsh reality was probably intensified when some Christians in Corinth had died (cf. 1 Cor. 15.12). This was a problem for the addressees who believed in the eventual resurrection and final victory over death in baptism, which they had learnt from Paul. Despite the enthusiastic Pauline gospel—freedom from the law, from sin, and therefore from death—death remained a fact. This violated Paul's earlier proclamation; an explanation was essential.[69] Paul has to tell the addressees why the Christians were not actually immortal, despite his theological rhetoric. The least he could do was to explain death as a temporary consequence of the residual power of sin and the law, which, however, was on the wane. Thus Paul needed the idea of the law's continuing hold on the flesh of the Christian in order to explain why the Christians still die and await the resurrection despite their overall freedom from the law and its penalties.

Whereas Galatians only hints (Gal. 5.17), Romans and 1 Corinthians demonstrate that the total freedom from the law and sin propagated in Romans 8 and Galatians is a *rhetorically biased phenomenon*—it is the truth, but not the whole truth—like the idea of the Christian's freedom from death. The Corinthians had misunderstood Paul's rhetoric in both cases by taking his expressions at their face value.

The same pattern can thus be found behind Paul's teaching concerning ethics and the resurrection: an overstated message had resulted in misunderstanding. Freedom from the law and from death was a major topic in the Pauline gospel, and Galatians demonstrates how far he can go in emphasizing this freedom. But in 1 Corinthians he experiences the countereffect: his rhetoric is taken too literally. The issue is particularly delicate, since Paul cannot blame external influences or foreign teachers as in Galatians, and runs the risk of compromising his basic message of freedom. Or at least its persuasive force.[70] Thus in Romans 7–8, both sides are presented—but in an exaggerated, hyperbolical way.

69. Fee (1987: 716) states generally: 'it seems unlikely that an articulated doctrine of resurrection belonged to the earliest Christian preaching, especially among Gentiles'.

70. Although (or simply because) any comparison between Paul and Luther is almost an *anathema* in current exegetical discussion, I would say this: the Reformer too had to fight against people who had taken his rhetorically overstated proclamation

c. *Philippians 3*

Finally we can ask how the idea of sin's general dominion fits with Paul's bold proclamation of his blameless Jewish past in Phil. 3.3-8.

For me it seems likely that even here Paul is exaggerating for the sake of rhetoric. Neither his bold claim to innocence nor the recourse to regarding everything as σκύβαλα describes objectively his thinking. For instance in Romans Paul claims that both Jews and Gentiles are sinners, and he hardly excludes himself. At the same time, Paul's attitude to his Jewish past is not particularly negative: despite all the rhetoric in Phil. 3.3-8 the fact remains that he *is* boasting of it![71]

This piece of pure *epideictic* oratory[72] includes three phases, and one should not overstate the first. First, after a pre-warning, Paul in an astonishing way praises his Jewish past and his achievements (Phil. 3.4-6). In the second phase, the position becomes milder (vv. 7-8a): these gains are too small compared with the major gain in Christ. But not until the third phase is Paul's actual thesis revealed (v. 8b): the glorious Jewish past is nothing but σκύβαλα. The technique can be compared with the three-step tactic in 1 Cor. 8.4/5-6/7-13, where only the third actually describes Paul's standpoint concerning food offered to idols.

5. *Conclusion*

In interpreting the peculiar use of ἐγώ in Romans 7, Kümmel and his followers have made a correct observation: the text cannot be explained only in theological terms; we also have to understand its rhetorical nature; Paul wanted to persuade, not to write dogmatics.

Ἐγώ is indeed used as a rhetorical device, the assumed effect of which on the original addressees, however, cannot be precisely determined. Paul probably spoke of himself as a representative of a larger group. But the most important point in the rhetoric of Romans 7 is his use of *hyperbole*: the Christian is presented as totally free from sin, and yet totally subject to it. This is not a doctrine à la Luther, but a means of persuasion: principles

---

too literally and turned into antinomists. Both preachers faced a difficult rhetorical situation, as they could not deny their own proclamation which the antagonists adduced.

71. Cf. also 1 Cor. 11.22.

72. Hawthorne (1983: 130) remarks that Paul here discusses the typical epideictic *topoi*: descent, education, titles, citizenship, etc.

are expressed in a black-and-white manner in order to affect the addressees with maximum power.

Such simplification of the multifaceted truth is a typical pedagogic technique, but impedes any attempt to create a balanced picture of Paul's
thinking. However, harmonization of these ideological tensions in Paul's
proclamation is not the answer. Rhetorical criticism should not be used to
support contemporary trends, nor as a facile solution to theological
problems.

BIBLIOGRAPHY

Bauer, W., K. Aland and B. Aland
    1988   *Wörterbuch zum Neuen Testament* (Berlin: W. de Gruyter).
Beker, J.C.
    1980   *Paul the Apostle* (Edinburgh: T. & T. Clark).
Braun, H.
    1959   'Römer 7,7-25 und das Selbstverständnis des Qumran-Frommen', *ZTK* 56:
              1-18.
Bühlmann, W., and K. Scherer
    1973   *Stilfiguren der Bibel: Ein kleines Nachschlagewerk* (BibB, 10; Fribourg:
              Schweizerisches Katholisches Bibelwerk).
Bultmann, R.
    1932   'Römer 7 und die Anthropologie des Paulus', in H. Bornkamm (ed.), *Imago
              Dei* (Festschrift S. Gustav Krüger; Giessen: Alfred Töpelmann): 53-62.
Burke, K.
    1962   *A Rhetoric of Motives* (New York: Prentice–Hall).
Conzelmann, H.
    1975   *A Commentary on the First Epistle to the Corinthians* (trans. J.W. Leitch;
              Hermeneia; Philadelphia: Fortress Press).
Donfried, K.P. (ed.)
    1991   *The Romans Debate* (Edinburgh: T. & T. Clark).
Dunn, J.D.G.
    1988   *Romans* (2 vols.; WBC, 38AB; Waco, TX: Word Books).
Eriksson, A.
    1998   *Traditions as Rhetorical Proof: Pauline Argumentation in 1 Corinthians*
              (ConBNT, 29; Stockholm: Almqvist & Wiksell).
Fee, G.
    1987   *The First Epistle to the Corinthians* (NICNT; Grand Rapids: Eerdmans).
Hawthorne, G.F.
    1983   *Philippians* (WBC, 43; Waco, TX: Word Books).
Hesse, O.
    1994   'Nilus von Ancyra', *TRE* 24 (Berlin: W. de Gruyter): 568-73.
Holland, G.
    1999   'The Self against the Self in Romans 7.7-25', in S.E. Porter and D.L. Stamps
              (eds.), *The Rhetorical Interpretation of Scripture: Essays from the 1996*

Malibu Conference (JSNTSup, 180; Sheffield: Sheffield Academic Press): 260-71.

Hübner, H.

1982   *Das Gesetz bei Paulus* (FRLANT, 119; Göttingen: Vandenhoeck & Ruprecht; 3rd edn).

1987   'Paulusforschung seit 1945: Ein kritischer Literaturbericht', in *ANRW*, II.25.4: 2649-2840.

Kennedy, G.

1984   *New Testament Interpretation through Rhetorical Criticism* (Chapel Hill: University of North Carolina Press).

Kümmel, W.G.

1974   *Römer 7 und das Bild des Menschen im Neuen Testament, Zwei Studien* (TB, 53; Munich: Chr. Kaiser Verlag).

Laato, T.

1991   *Paulus und das Judentum: Anthropologische Erwägungen* (Åbo: Åbo Academy).

Lausberg, H.

1960   *Handbuch der literarischen Rhetorik* (2 vols.; Munich: Hueber).

Lindeskog, G.

1938   *Die Jesusfrage im neuzeitlichen Judentum* (Uppsala: Lundequist).

Longman Dictionary of Contemporary English

1978   (Burnt Mill: Longman).

Martin, J.

1974   *Antike Rhetorik: Technik und Methode* (Handbuch der Altertumswissenschaft, 2.3; Munich: Beck).

Martin, R.P.

1986   *2 Corinthians* (WBC, 40; Waco, TX: Word Books).

Michel, O.

1978   *Der Brief an die Römer* (MeyerK, 4; Göttingen: Vandenhoeck & Ruprecht).

Mitchell, M.

2001   'Pauline Accommodation and "Condescension" (συνκατάβασις): 1 Cor. 9.19-23 and the History of Influence', in T. Engberg-Pedersen (ed.), *Paul beyond the Judaism-Hellenism Divide* (Louisville, KY: Westminster/John Knox Press): 192-214.

Nida, E., J. Louw, A. Snyman and J. Cronje

1983   *Style and Discourse with Special Reference to the Text of the Greek New Testament* (Cape Town: Bible Society of South Africa).

Odeberg, H.

1945   *Fariseism och kristendom* (Lund: Gleerup, 2nd edn).

Perelman, Ch., and L. Olbrechts-Tyteca

1969   *The New Rhetoric: A Treatise on Argumentation* (trans. J. Wilkinson and P. Weaver; Notre Dame: University of Notre Dame Press).

Porter, S.E.

1997   'Paul of Tarsus and his Letters', in S. Porter (ed.), *Handbook of Classical Rhetoric in the Hellenistic Period 330 B.C.–A.D. 400* (Leiden: E.J. Brill): 533-85.

Räisänen, H.

1987   *Paul and the Law* (WUNT, 29; Tübingen: Mohr-Siebeck, 2nd edn).

Schelkle, K.H.

1959   *Paulus, Lehrer der Väter, die altkirchliche Auslegug von Römer 1–11*
            (Düsseldorf: Patmos, 2nd edn).

Stendahl, K.

1976   'The Apostle Paul and the Introspective Conscience of the West', in K.
            Stendahl, *Paul among Jews and Gentiles and Other Essays* (Philadelphia:
            Fortress Press): 78-96.

Stowers, S.

1994   *A Rereading of Romans: Justice, Jews, and Gentiles* (New Haven: Yale
            University Press).

1995   'Romans 7.7-25 as a Speech-in-Character (προσωποποιία)', in T.
            Engberg-Pedersen (ed.), *Paul and his Hellenistic Context* (Minneapolis:
            Fortress Press): 180-202.

Thiselton, A.

1978   'Realized Eschatology at Corinth', *NTS* 24: 510-26.

Thurén, L.

2000   *Derhetorizing Paul: A Dynamic Perspective on Pauline Theology* (WUNT,
            124; Tübingen: Mohr-Siebeck).

Tuckett, C.M.

1996   'The Corinthians Who Say 'There is no resurrection of the dead' (1 Cor
            15,12)', in R. Bieringer (ed.), *The Corinthian Correspondence* (Leuven:
            Leuven University Press): 247-75.

Wedderburn, A.J.M.

1987   *Baptism and Resurrection: Studies in Pauline Theology against its Graeco-
            Roman Background* (WUNT, 44; Tübingen: Mohr-Siebeck).

Weiss, J.

1910   *Der erste Korintherbrief* (MeyerK, 5; Göttingen: Vandenhoeck & Ruprecht).

Westerholm, S.

1988   *Israel's Law and the Church's Faith: Paul and his Recent Interpreters*
            (Grand Rapids: Eerdmans).

Wilson, J.H.

1968   'The Corinthians Who Say There Is No Resurrection of the Dead', *ZNW* 59:
            90-107.

The Christological Premise in Pauline Theological Rhetoric: 1 Corinthians 1.4–2.5 as an Example

Dennis L. Stamps

1. *Introduction*

At the Malibu conference in 1996, I offered a paper on the theological rhetoric of the Pauline epistles which was a preliminary and foundational attempt at distinguishing Christian rhetoric, particularly Pauline theological rhetoric, from other forms of rhetoric.[1] By rhetoric, I mean rhetoric as understood in the broadest terms, as the ways and means of persuasion, and the evaluation of the potential effect of the text in defined contexts. That paper noted the development of a concept of Christian rhetoric based particularly on the work of G.A. Kennedy which in essence seems to distinguish Christian rhetoric from classical forms of rational persuasion.[2] The way Kennedy distinguishes Christian rhetoric from a more rational mode of persuasion is very similar to modern understandings of persuasive discourse. In this modern and more general discussion there have developed two distinct rhetorical strands: one which identifies a formal and philosophical method of persuasion labelled 'argumentation' or 'demonstration'; and a second which identifies a more emotive and irrational appeal labelled 'rhetoric'.[3] Religious discourse is most often identified with the latter.

In the end, I identified Christian rhetoric with a different perspective, that of W. Wuellner who sees *all* argumentation as rhetorical, but

---

1. D.L. Stamps, 'The Theological Rhetoric of the Pauline Epistles: Prolegomenon', in S.E. Porter and D.L. Stamps (eds.), *The Rhetorical Interpretation of Scripture: Essays from the 1996 Malibu Conference* (JSNTSup, 180; Sheffield: Sheffield Academic Press, 1999), pp. 249-59.

2. G.A. Kennedy, *New Testament Interpretation through Rhetorical Criticism* (Chapel Hill: University of North Carolina Press, 1984), pp. 6-8.

3. See the fuller discussion in Stamps, 'Theological Rhetoric', pp. 253-54.

distinguishes between modes of argumentation.[4] Wuellner is unwilling to classify a distinctive category of Christian rhetoric over against classical rhetoric along the lines of Kennedy, though he is willing to speak of Christian rhetoric, Jewish rhetoric, Islamic rhetoric, etc., each having distinctive rhetorical patterns. This perspective on rhetoric, which has many tenets of New Rhetoric, questions the assumption that classifying Pauline texts according to the conventions of classical rhetoric or Greco-Roman rhetoric is tantamount to identifying the ways and means of Pauline argumentation. What this suggests, and needs testing out, is that there may be something identifiable as Christian rhetoric (which is not *ipso facto* Greco-Roman rhetoric), but there may also be something distinctive about Pauline Christian rhetoric. To try to conclude a too terse summary of a complex discussion found in the previous paper, I, in the end, suggested a hypothesis that one would suspect that one of the key characteristics of Pauline theological rhetoric, that is its argumentation to persuade, would be an appeal to Christology. It is this thesis which I wish to test out by analyzing the rhetorical argumentation of 1 Cor. 1.4–2.5.

Before looking at this text, I want first to reflect further on what is meant by Pauline argumentation based on some of the suggestions from the 1996 Malibu conference. Second, I want to state more clearly what level and method of analysis I am engaged in at this point in terms of assessing the argumentation. Finally, I want to examine the argumentation in the text itself.

2. *Further Reflections on Pauline Argumentation*

In general, the one distinction which many commentators note with regard to Christian rhetoric is its appeal to authority. This authority has been variously defined: God, Jesus, Holy Spirit, Hebrew Scripture, Christian tradition. B. Mack and A. Eriksson have noted the authoritative appeal to the kerygma or the traditions as a core conviction.[5] Where Mack and Eriksson depart is that Mack sees this appeal as outside the cultural conventions of Greco-Roman rhetoric (i.e. outside the norms of rationality)[6]

---

4.   See particularly, W. Wuellner, 'Paul's Rhetoric of Argumentation in Romans: An Alternative to the Donfried–Karris Debate over Romans', *CBQ* 38 (1976), pp. 330-31.

5.   B.L. Mack, *Rhetoric and the New Testament* (Minneapolis: Fortress Press, 1990), pp. 96-98; A. Eriksson, 'Special Topics in First Corinthians 8–10', in Porter and Stamps (eds.), *Rhetorical Interpretation*, pp. 272-301 (273-76).

6.   Mack, *Rhetoric*, pp. 96-97.

and Eriksson sees this appeal as according to just such a cultural convention, at least in terms of the use of logos, ethos and pathos, and more particularly as appeal to special topics.[7] It is because Eriksson wants to maintain direct links with Aristotelian rhetoric that he is uncomfortable with Olbricht's concept of 'church' rhetoric.[8] But Olbricht is hardly dismissing Aristotelian rhetoric, rather he is asserting that such rhetorical theory is insufficient for fully understanding the nature of Christian rhetoric or Christian discourse as found in the canonical writings of the New Testament, in particular, the Pauline epistles. But Olbricht, like Mack, Eriksson and even Kennedy, notes that Christian rhetoric is distinctive in that it operates within a particular world-view: 'God (through God's son and the Spirit) carries out divine purposes among humans.'[9] Olbricht is happy to use Aristotelian rhetorical theory to dissect Pauline rhetoric, but recognizes it may not be completely sufficient to ascertain Paul's persuasive strategies.[10]

To state more succinctly the three positions noted above:

1. Mack finds Christian rhetoric as non-rational (that is non-Aristotelian) authoritative appeal to core Christian convictions.
2. Eriksson finds Christian rhetoric as Aristotelian argument with appeal to special topics, specifically the kerygma or Christian tradition(s).
3. Olbricht finds Aristotelian rhetoric as a means to begin assessing Christian rhetoric, but Christian rhetoric has a distinctive world-view which distinguishes it from Aristotelian rhetoric and thereby makes Aristotelian rhetorical theory insufficient for a full analysis of Christian rhetorical strategies.

In terms of argumentation we see distinctives emerging. Mack is claiming appeal without proof. Eriksson and Olbricht detect appeal with proof, though they differ as to the degree to which that proof can be fully assessed by Aristotelian categories. Exactly what is being appealed to in each case varies slightly, but generally each sees a measure of

---

7. Eriksson, 'Special Topics', pp. 273-76.
8. T.H. Olbricht, 'An Aristotelian Rhetorical Analysis of 1 Thessalonians', in D.L. Balch, E. Ferguson and W.A. Meeks (eds.), *Greeks, Romans, and Christians: Essays in Honor of Abraham J. Malherbe* (Minneapolis: Fortress Press, 1990), pp. 216-36 (226-27).
9. Olbricht, 'Aristotelian Rhetorical Analysis', p. 226.
10. Olbricht, 'Aristotelian Rhetorical Analysis', p. 236.

foundational Christian convictions or beliefs as the basis of the appeal. So, to conclude, Mack, Eriksson and Olbricht offer different perspectives on the nature of Christian rhetoric, but each confirms that it is at least appropriate that I might begin to read a Pauline text in order to determine its persuasive strategy by assessing the appeal to Christology, since this represents a set of foundational Christian beliefs.

Another matter with regard to argumentation which needs further comment is the Malibu paper by J.D.H. Amador.[11] In this paper he suggests that as rhetorical critics we are very attached to authors in our critical practice.[12] The author becomes a control for the critical method. With regard to rhetorical criticism, preserving the author's reputation as a coherent thinker (arguer) and as an able rhetorician seems to be implicit in the general practice of rhetorical critics. As Amador reads 1 Corinthians 11, he detects a lack of logical reasoning and a lack of consistent rhetorical arrangement.[13] While I may have specific issues with the details of Amador's reading of 1 Corinthians 11, I think he is generally correct in his point about the way a concept of the author influences the practice of rhetorical criticism.

To expand upon Amador's concern, I personally am not concerned to recover the authorial intention, defined in this instance as the mind-set of the author in relation to what the author wrote at the time of writing. I certainly hold to the presupposition that authors intend and that intentionality is inscribed or entextualized in the text an author writes. But critics can only offer an interpretation of the intention which is entextualized. I am more interested in offering a critical analysis of a text which offers a reading of the rhetorical ways and means and their effects. How that critical analysis relates to the authorial intention is an important question, but a secondary matter.

Amador's point about the priority rhetorical critics give to authors is one of the reasons I have my suspicions about the almost formulaic way Greco-Roman rhetorical theory is applied to biblical texts, Pauline texts in particular. While I am willing to recognize that those who were trained in rhetoric would more likely be an able practitioner of rhetoric, I am unsure as to the level of rhetorical training Paul received.[14] While I am willing to

---

11.   J.D.H. Amador, 'Interpretive Unicity: The Drive toward Monological (Monotheistic) Rhetoric', in Porter and Stamps (eds.), *Rhetorical Interpretation*, pp. 48-62.

12.   Amador, 'Interpretive Unicity', pp. 48-55.

13.   Amador, 'Interpretive Unicity', pp. 55-60.

14.   S.E. Porter, 'Paul of Tarsus and his Letters', in S.E. Porter (ed.), *Handbook of*

recognize a degree of universal structures of argumentation in all civilized Western communication (à la Kennedy, Corbett, Vickers, etc.) which can be analyzed according to classical rhetorical theory, I am unsure as to the guarantee that this gives to Paul's rhetoric being wholly coherent and consistent in terms of classical rhetoric.[15] The problem with using forms of ancient rhetorical theory as a critical method is that it can pre-determine what you will find, or, as Olbricht suggests, it can act as a 'levied, controlled stream'.[16]

This brings me to the point where I want to discuss the level and method of analysis which I will use in analyzing the theological argumentation in 1 Cor. 1.4–2.5.

3. *Level and Method of Analysis*

I have two biases. I resist complicated scientific analyses which put the critic in control because only s/he (and possibly a select few) knows and understands the method. This is another reason why I resist some forms of Greco-Roman rhetorical analysis of biblical texts. My second bias is my exegetical training. My exegetical training suggests living with the text first, trying to come to terms with the text on its own terms, not imposing any external system of interpretation until it emerges appropriately from the text. But I am conscious that this is critically naive. To have an exegetical goal is to suggest an exegetical method, and to have an exegetical method is to predetermine, to some extent, what one will find in the text.[17]

Nonetheless, in trying to avoid bringing a predetermined rhetorical theory to the Pauline text, I want to ferret out the pattern of argumentation, the means of persuasion, the theological rhetoric. My premise is that it seems reasonable that one of the distinguishing features of Christian

---

Classical Rhetoric in the Hellenistic Period 330 B.C.–A.D. 400 (Leiden: E.J. Brill, 1997), pp. 533-85 (533-38).

15. This is a very difficult and complex issue. The question is whether all human communication operates according to a theory of rhetoric as established by the classical tradition or whether all human communication is rhetorical. While classical rhetorical theory is a good place to begin as a basis to understand such rhetoric it is not necessary to end with classical rhetorical theory; see T.H. Olbricht, *Informative Speaking* (Chicago: Scott, Foresman, 1968).

16. Olbricht, 'Aristotelian Rhetorical Analysis', p. 236.

17. M.G. Brett, 'Four or Five Things to Do with Texts: A Taxonomy of Interpretive Interests', in D.J.A. Clines, S.E. Fowl and S.E. Porter (eds.), *The Bible in Three Dimensions* (Sheffield: JSOT Press, 1990), pp. 357-77.

rhetoric should be an appeal to Christ—a christological premise. It is quite possible that this is not so. But, if there is a christological premise, the way it is employed needs careful examination. It may or may not be along the lines of Greco-Roman rhetorical cultural convention. I am not assuming an unbiased or objective perspective. I have stated clearly that I am convinced that Pauline theological argumentation is rhetorical, that it is a way and means for persuasion: persuading an audience in a particular situation.[18] Rhetorical criticism is concerned to 'unmask' the ways and means of persuasion and to evaluate the effects of these persuasive strategies.

At this point in my analysis of these texts, I want to examine in very basic literary terms how a christological assumption is present (or not) and deployed. One aspect of this may be what Eriksson calls appeal to Christian traditions or kerygma. Another aspect may be the assumption of a world-view where God acts out divine purposes through an agent, the divine son, Jesus Christ. The level of this analysis at this stage is more identification with some preliminary analysis of how it is used and the effect it creates.[19]

4. *An Analysis of the Use of the Christological Premise in the Theological Rhetoric of 1 Corinthians 1.4–2.5*

The importance of 1 Corinthians 1–4 for understanding Pauline rhetoric is well accepted.[20] However, agreement as to Paul's use of rhetoric in this section of the letter is debated.[21] For the sake of more detailed analysis a smaller section is selected, 1 Cor. 1.4–2.5, yet a long enough section to either substantiate of disprove the importance of a christological premise. The section chosen is also recognized as having more than one type of rhetorical unit. It is important in epistolary terms because the epistolary situation, or the basis upon which the letter parties (the sender[s] and

18. Stamps, 'Theological Rhetoric', pp. 252-59.
19. T.H. Olbricht at the Florence conference suggested that I am actually engaged in rhetorical analysis at the level of topos instead of the more crucial level of the enthymeme. I concur but we differ as to the importance of the enthymeme for understanding Pauline rhetoric.
20. D. Litfin, *St Paul's Theology of Proclamation: 1 Corinthians 1–4 and Greco-Roman Rhetoric* (SNTSMS, 79; Cambridge: Cambridge University Press, 1994).
21. See a survey of the discussion in R.D. Anderson Jr, *Ancient Rhetorical Theory and Paul* (Contributions to Biblical Exegesis and Theology, 17; Kampen: Kok Pharos, 1996), pp. 239-48.

recipients) meet in the letter is established in the letter opening (1 Cor. 1.1-9), and in the transition to the letter body with its preliminary statement of the letter purpose (1.10) together with the preliminary argument to substantiate this purpose.

a. *Identifying the Rhetorical Units*

One of the problems is identifying the extent of the different rhetorical units. Rhetorical critics suggest several hypotheses. M.M. Mitchell classifies 1.4-9 as an epistolary thanksgiving and a rhetorical *prooimion/exordium*; 1.10 as a thesis statement to the deliberative argument; 1.11-17 as *diegesis/narratio* or statement of facts; and 1.18–4.21 as the first section of proof.[22] B. Witherington labels 1.4-9 as thanksgiving and *exordium*; 1.10 as *propositio*; 1.11-17 as *narratio*; 1.18-31 as argument 1, division 1 and 2.1-16 as argument 1, division 2 in the *probatio*.[23] M. Bunker identifies 1.10-17 as *exordium*, 1.18–2.16 as *narratio*.[24] D. Litfin calls 1.4-9 the thanksgiving and 1.10–2.5 the central passage.[25] Traditional biblical critics outline the letter in a similar pattern. G. Fee calls 1.4-9 the thanksgiving, 1.10-17 a statement of the problem, 1.18–2.5 and 2.6-16 as two distinct arguments.[26] H. Conzelmann sees 1.4-9 as a *proemium* (thanksgiving); 1.10-17 survey of the problem; 1.18–2.5 as the first argument.[27] The primary question is whether the section should end at 2.5 or 2.16.

For the sake of this discussion, using an epistolary framework for the analysis, 1.4-9 will be treated as thanksgiving; 1.10-17 as a statement of the letter purpose; 1.18-25, 1.26-31 and 2.1-5 as discrete sections which provide an initial argument. There are distinct transition points at 1.10, 1.18, 1.26, and 2.1. The transition at 2.6 is not as sharp rhetorically, but the adversative, δέ, and the change from first person singular to first person

22. M.M. Mitchell, *Paul and the Rhetoric of Reconciliation: An Exegetical Investigation of the Language and Composition of 1 Corinthians* (Louisville, KY: Westminster/John Knox Press, 1991), pp. 184-86.

23. B. Witherington, III, *Conflict and Community in Corinth: A Socio- Rhetorical Commentary on 1 and 2 Corinthians* (Grand Rapids: Eerdmans, 1995), pp. vi, 76.

24. M. Bunker, *Briefformular und rhetorische Disposition im 1. Korintherbrief* (GTA, 28; Gottingen: Vandenhoeck & Ruprecht, 1983), pp. 52-56.

25. Litfin, *St Paul's Theology*, pp. 178-81.

26. G. Fee, *The First Epistle to the Corinthians* (NICNT; Grand Rapids: Eerdmans, 1987), p. 21.

27. H. Conzelmann, *1 Corinthians: A Commentary on the First Epistle to the Corinthians* (trans. J.W. Leitch; Hermeneia; Philadelphia: Fortress Press, 1975), pp. 25-39.

plural suggests a key transition. So, there appear to be at least three different units: 1.4-9; 1.10-17; 1.18–2.5.

b. *1 Corinthians 1.4-9 and the Epistolary Situation*

The reason I want to begin with 1.4-9 is that it is crucial to establishing the epistolary situation or context. In epistolary terms, it functions as part of the opening.[28] The transition to the letter body at 1.10 is explicit.[29]

In christological terms, the letter opening is crucial. Referring back to the earlier opening elements: sender, addressee and greeting (1.1-3), an overt christological emphasis is established. Paul's status is as an apostle of Jesus Christ; Sosthenes, as a brother; the Corinthians, as the church of God. Paul becomes an apostle by God's will implicitly effected through Jesus Christ. The Corinthians have become the 'called out ones' (*ecclesia*) by the sanctifying work of Christ Jesus: the significance of the Corinthians' new spiritual position, being 'in Christ', is firmly established. Paul was called to be an apostle; the Corinthians were called to be 'holy ones/ saints' along with all the others who call upon the name of *our* Lord Jesus Christ. The unity of the saints is their common confession, 'Jesus is Lord', which even Paul shares.

The thanksgiving maintains this christological emphasis. What the sender gives thanks for is how the recipients have received God's grace by being in Jesus Christ (v. 4). It is significant that the sender does not directly give thanks for the recipients as would be common in Greek family/friendly letters. Rather, Paul gives thanks to God for what God has done through Jesus Christ. The relational implications for the epistolary situation are important. The orientation is not personal, the welfare of the recipients, but spiritual. More significant, it is the sender who in essence discloses and confirms the spiritual status of the recipients through the knowledge he has of what God has done to or for the recipients. The primary disclosure and confirmation is the benefits which the Corinthians receive through their status of being 'in Christ'.

The benefits of being 'in Christ' are enumerated: the Corinthians receive grace, are enriched in all things especially speech and knowledge (v. 5), and are not lacking in any spiritual gift (v. 7). These benefits are not only

---

28. A brief summary of epistolary form is D.E. Aune, *The New Testament in its Literary Environment* (LEC, 8; Philadelphia: Westminster Press, 1987), pp. 183-91.

29. J.L. White, 'Introductory Formulae in the Body of the Pauline Letter', *JBL* 90 (1971), pp. 91-97.

related to being in Christ, they are related to other christological assertions. The witness or testimony (the gospel) about Jesus Christ has been
confirmed in them: that is, they have responded to the kerygma about
Jesus Christ (v. 6). Both the past and the present take on new meaning due
to the Corinthians' spiritual status; because they responded to the gospel
(the past) they are enriched (present). This Christian identity is then
extended into the future: the Corinthians are eagerly awaiting the revelation of Jesus Christ which is still to come and they are being kept strong
so that they can be blameless on the Day of the Lord (vv. 7a-8).

At the end of the thanksgiving, a closure is secured by a repeated
reference to God: God has been referred to only at the beginning and end
of the thanksgiving. But in both cases, at v. 4 and v. 9, the person and
work of God is related to Jesus Christ in some particular way: v. 4, God
has given you grace in Christ Jesus; v. 9, God who has called you into
fellowship with his Son Jesus Christ. The subtle effect establishes a comprehensive deistic world-view which both Jew and Greek could comprehend, but one in which the primary agent of God or the primary locus of
God's action is identified as Christ Jesus. The christological premise is
clearly articulated.

The christological premise is also presented as part of the assumed
shared common reference. The overt way in which this is assumed means
the sender firmly establishes the epistolary situation: to be a recipient of
this letter one assents to the theistic world-view and to the christological
spirituality of this world. Both the commonality of what is true and the
relational mutuality between the letter parties are emphasized in the
thanksgiving. Three times, in vv. 7, 8 and 9, Jesus Christ is identified as
our Lord.

The context for the letter established by the letter opening is spiritual
and based on a shared understanding and experience of spiritual identity
conferred by God in Christ.

c. *1 Corinthians 1.10-17: Statement of the Problem*
Having clearly established the basis for the epistolary situation, the letter
body is opened by a statement of the primary reason for writing. Unlike
Mitchell, Fee and others, I do not see one overarching problem or issue as
the key to understanding every part of the epistle. Rather, I see 1 Corinthians as a 'pastoral' letter which addresses a primary issue and a number
of subsidiary issues, some of which are directly related to the primary
issue and some are not.

The use of παρακαλέω ('appeal, exhort') as an introductory formula to the body of a letter is well established.[30] Epistolary convention is followed. What is unconventional is the stated basis of that appeal, 'in [or through] the name of our Lord Jesus Christ'. The christological emphasis of the letter opening is reiterated and a christological premise is stated as the authority and context of the primary epistolary purpose.[31] The ground of the appeal is both authoritative, invoking a spiritual power, and a recalling to a common understanding, the basis of their spiritual identity. The appeal to Jesus Christ has several rhetorical implications. First, the confession which unites the wider Christian community is recalled from v. 2. Second, the name of Jesus Christ which was the authority for their baptismal ritual is remembered (and anticipates what follows in vv. 13-17). Third, their common spiritual identity of being 'in Christ' is alluded to as a foundation for the appeal to unity (a common motif in this letter). It is the name of Jesus Christ and all that this implies which makes it possible to share 'the same' or unite around the 'same things' (note the use of αὐτός three times in 1.10).

That there is a need to exhort the Corinthians to unity is confirmed by an external report (v. 11) and by the writer's own restatement of the problem (v. 12).[32] The sender continues to clarify and address the problem through three rhetorical questions which reassert the christological foundation (v. 13): 'Is Christ divided? Was Paul crucified on your behalf? and Were you baptized into the name of Paul?'. Of course the reply to all three questions is, 'no'. Christ is not parcelled out to a select few; Christ is the ground which unites all Christians including the Corinthians. The work of Christ on the cross for the benefit of each Christian (i.e. each member of the Corinthian church) also unites them, and their common baptism, confession and experience, which is christocentric, is a basis for unity. The rhetorical use of questions reinforces the context established by the letter opening (1.1-9) and the appeal in the statement of the letter's purpose (1.10).

In 1.14-17, a narrative of the letter writer's past work among the Corinthians particularly in relation to baptism and preaching is rehearsed. Through this narrative, the commonality of the Corinthians in relation to the letter writer(s) is reasserted and also the rhetorical questions are

---

30. C.J. Bjerkelund, *Parakalō: Form, Funktion und Sinn der parakalō-Sätze in den Paulinischen Briefen* (Oslo: Universitetsforlaget, 1967).

31. Fee, *First Corinthians*, p. 53.

32. Mitchell, *Paul*, p. 201.

implicitly answered in the negative. The narrative highlights the absurdity of the division along party lines whatever is the basis for the party splits. The narrative implicity recalls the commonality of baptismal identity no matter who did the baptizing. It also transports the recipients to that which is prior to their baptism, their response to the preaching of the gospel, of the witness about Jesus Christ (cf. 1.6), of the Christian kerygma. The recollection is christocentrically asserted. It was Christ who sent Paul, not to baptize but to preach (compare the apostolic commission in 1.1). The essential content and form of that preaching is christologically focused: it is the cross of Christ and its ongoing effect (power) rather than (human) wisdom of speech. As in the previous unit, notice once again the use of inclusio, but in this section it is christocentric: the appeal to unity in v. 10 is grounded in the name of Christ, and the recall of the Pauline mission which founded the Corinthian church was initiated by Christ and based on the proclamation about the cross of Christ (v. 17).

In 1 Cor. 1.10-17, the epistolary purpose is stated and a statement of the primary problem is provided with sufficient narrative to clarify and substantiate the issue. In this brief section, the christological premise is asserted and utilized in a number of crucial ways which illustrate the essential nature of that premise for the rhetoric of the letter.

d. *1 Corinthians 1.18–2.5: Argument or Proof*

In this section there is a distinctive argument which elucidates the suggestive contrast between (human) wise speech and preaching the cross which concluded the previous unit (1.10-17). However, in this argument there is a slight change in tack. The contrast is not so much (human) wisdom versus preaching the cross, but wisdom versus foolishness. This allows the focus to become an explanation of divine wisdom. It is the cross which becomes the example of this wisdom. In 1.18-25 there is a fundamental discussion of wisdom and foolishness as exemplified in the message of Christ crucified. This contrast is then discussed in relation to the experience of the Corinthians (1.26-31). Then, in 2.1-5, the same contrast is discussed with regard to Paul's practice of preaching when he came to the Corinthians.[33]

---

33. For a three-part analysis of this unit, 1.18–2.5, see Conzelmann, *1 Corinthians*, p. 39; Fee, *First Corinthians*, pp. 66-67; and R.B. Hays, *First Corinthians* (Interpretation; Louisville, KY: John Knox Press, 1997), pp. 26-36.

1. *1 Corinthians 1.18-25.* There are a number of important issues in this text which have potential relevance for understanding Paul and the place of rhetoric, but our focus is limited to the use of the christological premise. From this limited perspective, the word (message) of the cross (v. 18) is the foolishness of the proclamation (v. 21) which relates to Christ crucified (v. 23) and to Christ, the power of God and the wisdom of God (v. 24). The connections between these ideas can be simplified as follows: the word of the cross is the foolishness of what was preached; what was preached was Christ crucified which is the power and wisdom of God. An equation is established between the word of the cross, what is proclaimed, and Christ.

The shift between v. 23 and v. 24 is interesting. In v. 23 there is a more subjective assertion probably based on experience: 'we proclaim'. In v. 24, however, the reflection is more objective. The persons in view are the called ones, an idealized type who are a subset of both racial/cultural groups designated in v. 23. The awkward syntax of v. 24 suggests that v. 24b might read as an ontological statement:[34] Christ is the power and wisdom of God, or, even better, the power and wisdom of God is Christ (Christ crucified is understood). But the focus is soteriology, not Christology per se. Yet the effect is to identify the salvific word of the cross with Christ. The nuance of this section is not to state that Christ personifies wisdom and power, but rather that God's power and wisdom was embodied or on display, even proclaimed in and through, Jesus the Christ (Χριστός in v. 23 is both the person Jesus and the agent of God, the Messiah).

In quite fundamental terms, this argument constructs a closed world-view in which wisdom and power are disclosed or revealed in Christ. This is God's plan. This is contrary to any claim, even boast, that one can access such through human words of wisdom which are limited to this world (vv. 20-21). The plan is revealed in the word of the cross, Christ crucified, which is proclaimed to Jew and Gentile. Those who respond or believe (v. 21), the called ones, are being saved. In christological terms, the word of the cross is identified with the narrative of Christ, specifically the aspect of a crucified Messiah. The Jesus tradition is the assumed historical reality and the revealed divine plan upon which spiritual knowledge and identity are established.

---

34. Conzelmann, *1 Corinthians*, p. 47.

2. *1 Corinthians 1.26-31*. Rhetorically, the move is from the principle to the example. The focus is to illustrate the contrast between the word of the cross and wise speech in the experience of the Corinthian community. This section relates back to 1.10-17 and also exemplifies the fundamental 'truth' of 1.18-25. In v. 26 the radical shift to second person effectively drives the discussion back to the recipients. Dialogically, possibly through a diatribe (note the use of the imperative),[35] the letter recipients are invited to reflect upon their experience: 'Think about (consider) your calling, brothers and sisters.' Note how the recipients are placed among the ideal type as called ones. The assumption is that they have believed the preaching of the cross.

Christologically, there is nothing explicit until v. 30. Verse 29 in a sense is the conclusion of the reflection, a general principle drawn out from the particular experience of the Corinthians. But v. 30 brings the general back to the particular. Conzelmann provides an insightful paraphrase: 'You are, by God's act, in Christ, insofar as salvation has been transmitted to you by the proclamation.'[36] To expand, in the experience of their calling (1.2, 6, 26 [cf. 1.24]), the Corinthians have been given by God a new spiritual identity, being in Christ, by responding to the preaching of the cross. Now this christological concept is expanded so that to be identified in Christ is to be identified with the wisdom of God (v. 30b). The notion of Christ being the wisdom of God is further enlarged so that in Christ is also manifested God's righteousness, sanctification and redemption. It is not that Jesus hypostatically becomes wisdom, but that God's wisdom, etc. can be found by being in Christ. Therefore there is no human glory or boasting as comes from human speculation: if one wants to boast as a called one, such boasting must be of what God has done 'in Christ', in the Lord.

The recipients must consider a world where humans act apart from God versus a world where God acts in Christ. If the Corinthians consider themselves 'in Christ', then, following the argument, all wisdom, power, glory or boasting are to be found in what God has done in Christ. Whether the letter recipients are foolish or wise in the world's system, though most are actually foolish (according to the sender's point of view), it does not really matter. In a world where God acts in Christ, the world's system is potentially reversed and definitely reoriented according to the way God has acted in Christ. 1 Corinthians 1.30 is a crucial text in the christological

---

35. Conzelmann, *1 Corinthians*, p. 49.
36. Conzelmann, *1 Corinthians*, p. 51.

premise, for in this text God's action in Christ is made explicit with regard to the Corinthians; the echoes of 1.4 and 9 are deliberate. The christo-centric spiritual identity of being in Christ established in the thanksgiving, appealed to in 1.10-17 and elaborated in 1.24, is now further expanded in 1.30-31.

3. *1 Corinthians 2.1-5.* Having stated the fundamental idea of the word of the cross, Christ crucified as divine wisdom and worldly foolishness, having shown how the paradox of God's wisdom and folly is borne out in the Corinthian community, the argument moves to the specific practice of the letter sender. It is an appeal to the shared experience of both the sender and recipients but from the speaker's point of view. The rhetoric of this unit operates at several levels. There is a focus on ethos, and there is an apologetic aspect. But essentially it serves to illustrate, from the sender's experience, the topic of 1.18; it also brings this topic to a close.

In clarifying the contrast between wise speech and the word of the cross in his own preaching, deliberate links are made with previously estab-lished concepts. In 2.1 there is a reference to the preacher's style (form), not using eloquence (speech) or wisdom (implicitly human or worldly) in proclaiming the word of God. The distinction between speech and wisdom is interesting and has not been made before. In 1.5, it is speech and knowledge; in 1.17 speech and wisdom are combined into one semantic unit, wise speech. The effect is to distinguish proclamation from human eloquence and wisdom.

A similar semantic shift occurs regarding the content. What is pro-claimed is the 'testimony of God', a direct echo of 1.6 where 'the testi-mony of Christ' is the actual phrase. At this transition to a new section, this phrase deliberately corresponds to the phrase in 1.18, 'the word of the cross'. But as 1.18-25 clarified, the word of the cross is Christ crucified, so 2.2 clarifies that the testimony of God is 'Jesus Christ and him crucified'.

Once again the christological premise is deployed. Once again a theistic perspective is particularized in Jesus Christ. The divine order has expressed itself specifically and uniquely in Jesus Christ. This divine wisdom is in distinction from human eloquence and wisdom. The sender wholly identifies his own practice and perspective with this.

The result of the speaker's orientation to this particular divine order is that the recipients are similarly identified with this divine order: their faith stands on the power of God, not on human wisdom. In 1.18-25 the power of God was identified as the word of the cross (1.18) and even simply

Christ (1.25). The mutuality and commonality between the sender and the recipients and between the recipients themselves is reinforced.

Rhetorically, this unit is quite powerful. By specifying both the manner and message of the Pauline mission to the Corinthians, it explicates and reinforces the theological reference which unites the letter parties. The preacher was solely committed to the word of the cross and so the faith of those who are called rests on Christ crucified.

Throughout the argument of 1.18–2.5 there has been a consistent and constant particularizing of the theological reference to Christ.

5. *Summary*

The use of or appeal to the christological premise in 1 Cor. 1.4–2.5 is overt. Primarily in this text there is the consistent move to particularize the action of God in Christ. But this particularization is comprehensive or overwhelming in that the spiritual identity of anyone who identifies with this world-view is to be in Christ.

The thanksgiving (1.4-9) which is part of the letter opening establishes the basis for the epistolary situation. The basis for the relational interaction in the epistle between the letter parties is spiritual. It is focused on what God has done in Christ and how that has given both the sender and recipients a particular spiritual identity, being in Christ. This identity reorients the temporal understanding of all who are 'called' in that past, present and future are christologically defined. The thanksgiving establishes a shared spirituality which is distinctly christocentric; in so doing, it establishes the basis upon which the sender and recipients relate through the letter.

At the beginning of the body of the letter, the epistolary purpose is stated and substantiated. The primary exhortation is christologically grounded (1.10). In 1.13-17 three rhetorical questions and the rehearsal of the Pauline mission focus the question of unity back on the christological premise established in the opening. The basis for unity is their response to the Christ-initiated mission which preached the cross of Christ and their christocentric experience of baptism.

In 1.18–2.5 a three-pronged argument to substantiate the christocentric unity is provided. First, the gospel which has been confirmed in them is the word of the cross, Christ crucified. Through the preaching of the word of the cross, the wisdom and power of God are revealed as being in Christ. This divine plan is contrary to human wisdom. Second, the experience of the Corinthians also confirms this. Their calling confirms the distinctive wisdom of God and locates them in this divine wisdom, Christ, in whom also is located God's righteousness, sanctification and redemption. Third, the preaching practice of Paul when he came to the Corinthians was to proclaim this divine order so that the faith of the recipients would be in God's power, which is in Christ. In a carefully crafted argument, the christological premise is enlarged. The letter recipients learn that being in Christ means that they are also located in the power, wisdom, righteousness, sanctification, and redemption of God which is particularized in God's action in and through Christ.

6. *Conclusion*

There are several qualifications which need to be mentioned in the review of this study of the christological premise in 1 Cor. 1.4–2.5. This is only one Pauline text. It is possible that a christological premise is crucial to the rhetorical situation of this epistle. In order to test out the importance of a christological premise for Pauline theological rhetoric, several or all of the Pauline letters need analysis. But hopefully this analysis is suggestive. In examining the christological premise in an epistle, it is potentially significant that one analyze both the letter opening which establishes the epistolary context and the letter body, especially the statement of the letter purpose, when given, and the preliminary argument which begins to address the letter purpose. When a christological premise is operative in these parts of the letter, it is reasonable to suggest that it plays a dominant role in the theological rhetoric of the letter.

It is also important that I mention that throughout this analysis little reference was made to either the author or the situation. This is not to deny those historical contingencies—indeed they have not been completely ignored in this analysis—but to focus on the rhetoric as it operates in the text. Once this is examined, rhetorical analysis can move out to the larger rhetorical critical agenda.

Equally, little or no analysis was given with reference to any particular rhetorical theory or convention. This analysis does suggest that such theory might be useful at some points to explicate the ways and means of the rhetoric and its effect. But this is to suggest that such theory functions at a heuristic level, as a critical method for reading the text, and not as the correct method to recover the true form and content of the text. In fact, in terms of Greco-Roman rhetoric as explained in the handbooks, I believe this text might be found wanting (this is another exercise). There is clearly planned and developed argumentation which has potential reflections of classical rhetoric. But there is also a hint of a midrashic method in the use of key words as the basis for expanding and developing the discussion (this too is another paper).[37]

More importantly, while this one analysis does not substantiate my thesis, I believe it is suggestive for the thesis that a christological premise is an essential part of Christian rhetoric, particularly as it is practiced by Paul. I hope that it will be suggestive for further study which tries to understand the rhetoric of the New Testament.

37. But see W. Wuellner, 'Haggadic Homily Genre in 1 Corinthians 1–3', *JBL* 89 (1970), pp. 199-204.

Rhetoric and Metaphor, and the Metaphysical in the Letter to the Ephesians

Richard Lemmer

1. *Setting the Course*

A postmodern approach to literature and rhetoric frees us from the old dichotomy of *form* in contradistinction to *content*, from appending too much to the authenticity of writings based on the availability of certain historical data.

There needs to be an awareness of a different kind or genus of knowledge, to which a postmodern approach sensitizes us. This leads to the possibility of not decrying knowledge of religious belief and experience, often done by modernistic views, operating within positivistic categories only. This awareness leads to an acceptable *epistemic status of religious knowledge*, and opens up the possibility to study a phenomenon such as metaphor, as a mechanism in the communication of the metaphysical.[1]

A holistic approach to writings should be advocated, in which letter and spirit come to us as a unit. This frees one from the endeavour of making the epistemic status and validity of a text's integrity merely dependent on firm knowledge of the historical author and readers, as if one can 'prove' God (or religious reality and verity) thereby.

In order to persuade their readers, writers of the New Testament often cast their thoughts in the form of metaphors. It appears as if in their view there existed a 'meta-rhetoric', and this not only functioned on cognitive and emotional levels, but also pointed to a meta-level of ontology. It is precisely here where a study of metaphor is useful, if not imperative.

Like a number of other books of the New Testament, the letter to the Ephesians is rich in metaphor/ical and also figurative allusions. It is clear

---

1. That obviously does not imply that all metaphors point at metaphysical reality; but that metaphors, given the definition below in 'A Different View of Metaphor', are especially suited to communicate the 'uncommunicable'.

that the appeal of the author to persuade his/her readership points at this meta-level of cognition, in order to confirm the religious status of the readers. This status was under siege, by those holding to previous religious categories, by political authorities exerting pressure, as well as by regression into previously held beliefs in a spirit-world which would inexorably impact on the readers' lives. The author now revolutionizes the readers' viewpoint, by an implementation of new categories infused by means of the use of metaphor.

By way of argument, one may ask: 'Why a postmodern perspective?'[2] I would like to answer in the words of, among others Ward (1996: 132, quoting Bauman): 'Postmodernity, one may as well say, brings "re-enchantment" of the world after the protracted and earnest, though in the end inconclusive, modern struggle to disenchant[3] it.' It is the re-evaluation of ambivalence, mystery, excess and aporia as they adhere to, are constituted by, and disrupt the rational, that lies behind the re-enchantment of

2.   In advocating a postmodern perspective, I suggest neither originality, nor an uncritical stance to everything offered in the name of 'postmodernism'. Devaney (1997), among others, offers a number of very critical and sobering questions with reference to postmodern theory, on anumber of fronts, and one should take notice of these. However, I think his assertion that the bulk of the work produced by scholars and academe from this quarter is in general 'third rate' is presumptious and an overstatement.

I espouse *certain tenets* of this movement, not least its *holism* and attempt at *re-integration* of facets of inquiry, and its advocacy of tolerance and qualitative acceptance of the perception of reality as observed by 'the other'. Furthermore, I espouse a 'truncated' view of the postmodern; the postmodern can and does only exist coterminously as a 'mutation', as well as a cutting off of the moorings of modernism. Ward (1996: 132-33) points out how Lyotard already observed that postmodernism is not a 'period concept'. It is an aspect of modernism itself; this much is clear when one observes Kant's respect for ambiguity and aporia, as already being at work in the Enlightenment project. Ironically, the same could be observed in Descartes, Marx, Nietzsche and Freud. I say 'ironically', because Descartes is usually nominated as the 'father of modernism'. An imperative and valuable shift of emphasis emerges regarding rhetoric, literature, language and also *metaphor* when allowing postmodern perspectives to dominate.

3.   He also refers to Max Weber who declared that the world conjured by technology was a disenchanted world. Ward observes that science, the spirit of *technē*, empiricalism, positivism and materialism offered to explain the world and managed to *erase the mystery*. This observation obviously does not intend wholesale decryal of modernism; it does, however, serve to expose its *hubris*.

the world. Reality is no longer tabulated and evaluated in terms of empirical fact.

The following observation is apropos to this essay: 'The world is multiple worlds; and worlds are created by, and shift within, nets of signs and symbols *pointing beyond themselves* towards other nets of signs and symbols' (Ward 1996: 132; italics mine). In this view there is a new dynamic allowed to serve as means of orientation, in which, 'Temporality rather than spatiality, economies rather than places, narrative rather than nouns are the vehicles for identity and meaning' (Ward 1996: 132-33).

To characterize by way of negation, Ward points out that the philosophy of religion will not be so phallocentric or ethnocentric, nor tied to Enlightenment texts (Descartes, Hume, Kant) and to Enlightenment procedures: the law of non-contradiction, the logic of subject to predicate, and then the law of causality. This is the more valid, when one realizes that rationalities are local, specific and embedded within cultures and language.

This brings about a broadening of the possibilities of 'knowing and understanding', also a broadened understanding of metaphor/s, and the way an author may specifically employ it/them.

Finally, in the nature of postmodernism, it is clear that *nothing measurable nor conclusive* can be achieved by this kind of endeavour. What is presented below about the 'pragmatics' of metaphor is *impressionistic* and suggestive.

2. *Rhetoric as Understanding, Knowing and Communication*

For the purposes of this essay, rhetoric is characterized, not as a single method nor the adherence to one school of analysis, but as the *collection of approaches* that is united by the common assumption that the intentional use of language in communication, and a receiver's response and the situation or context in which communication takes place, all interact to change human thought, feelings, behaviour and action (Goodwin, in Makaryk 1993: 174-75). Thus the phenomenon of communication and its analysis can be characterized as an *interactive process*, between all of the various constituents and determinants within a communicative situation.

a. *Interactive Process*
Studying rhetoric as an *interactive process* is an endeavour to understand how discourse works to bring about and sustain changes within the person who communicates (within the receiver) and, even more widely, within the communicative environment at large. From this viewpoint, rhetorical

analysis does not only involve 'rhetorical discourse'; but all discourse is rhetoric and text—indeed all kinds of texts are rhetorical. Furthermore, the analysis of rhetoric is the description of all elements that are involved in communication, that is the rhetorical dimensions of all discourse, that is involved. In terms of Goodwin's (in Makaryk 1993: 176-77) summary, I would not espouse a *traditionalist*, neither a *transitionalist*, but a *contemporary approach*, which is a multi-faceted (more than a multi-disciplinary) approach. Furthermore, one would take notice of any theory or methodology that can explain and evaluate the motivation of a speaker, the response of an audience, the structure of a discourse and the communication environment as such. By offsetting *rhetorical* from *literary criticism*, one arrives at a somewhat more complex profile (cf. Goodwin, in Makaryk 1993: 177-78). Thus rhetorical criticism analyses any form of communication; it canalizes texts, not for what they are, but *for what they do*, how they change the world outside of that work. In this way each rhetorical 'deconstruction' would describe at least one attempt to understand how a certain text with its co-texts and intertexts endeavours/ed to communicate intentions and change human behaviour. Following this view of rhetoric it would unquestionably elicit the issue as to the kind of knowledge that is attainable by this 'deconstruction'.

This deconstruction takes into account the possible complexity of the event/process of origination and communication of texts; that there is a kind of 'reciprocal osmotic' process taking place between all 'constituents' within a given communication. This renders any finality in deconstructing a given process to be futile.

b. *Once Again, the Epistemic Status of Rhetoric*
Michel Meyer (1994) endeavours to define a move away from modernity to what he terms 'problematology'.[4] I find this discussion of Meyer (1994: 65) rather appealing.[5] The following cognate aspects to rhetorical analysis need to be reflected on (language, literature and communication):[5]

---

4. The extent of 'problem' as common denominator in this understanding of rhetoric is more than a mere 'issue'.

5. He (1994: 65) distinguishes between the classical (and classic) view of argumentation, whereby he means syllogistic inference, alternatives are *ex-hypothesi* excluded: 'A, then B, and not-B is excluded, whereas rhetorical inference, or argumentation, [should] leave[s] several possibilities open most of the time'. In this instance, *rhetoric* obviously refers to a paradigmatic way of understanding; to a

The use of language and rhetoric. It is essential that one should recognize the inevitable and intricate relationship between rhetoric and language as a system of symbols used by human beings. It may be broadly defined as the 'use of words by human agents to form attitudes or to induce actions in other human agents'. Whatever form rhetoric takes, it is 'rooted in an essential function of language itself…the use of language as a symbolic means of inducing cooperation in beings that by nature respond to symbols' (so Burke, as cited by Foss, Foss and Trapp 1985: 157-58).

Rhetoric of literature. Meyer (1994: 59) points out that one should respect the 'problematological difference', which is the phenomenon that the 'text itself does not answer something other than the problem it fictionalizes in some other way. The problematicity of the text calls for an answer that the reader has to give'.

There is an obvious and distinct connection between *everyday reality*[6] and *literature*, and between *literature* and *rhetoric*; thus between everyday life and rhetoric.[7] This observation makes it possible to analyse and interpret everyday realities in rhetorical terms. However, as was pointed out in the above, each attempt to interpret will be tentative.

This is in turn related to the matter of reading, particularly reading of aesthetic texts. Ward (1996: 130) points out (in his discussion of Fish, Lyotard and Cixous) that the body ('the text as tissue') comes before and constitutes knowledge. It is the coterminous relationship between experience and expression which causes all knowledge to be bound to aesthetics. However, this experience, as it emerges in and through expression 'is of the unpresentable, is of an aporia'.[8]

Rhetoric and communication. It was already indicated that classical or old-fashioned views of rhetoric are not only outmoded, they are in fact truncated viewpoints. Far more satisfactory would be a viewpoint that places

---

particular epistemic possibility/impossibility, and not to the classical/classic conceptions of argumentation.

6.   Meyer (1994: 61) remarks that this '[e]verydayness can be described…but as something opaque and rather enigmatic in its subjectively grounded interrelatedness'.

7.   This observation would also be underscored by Meyer (1994: 65), when he observes: 'There is no difference in principle between logical inference, rhetorical inference, and literary interpretation. In all these cases a problem is in question.'

8.   In the sense of Christian theology this 'givenness' would be named 'grace'— the grace of God and its disclosure in revelation.

the notion of rhetoric within the ambit of *communication* (whatever 'texts' are meant, be they oral, written, graphic, painting, drama/acting, etc.). Obviously, much more is meant by *communication* than the mere flow of information by overt means of speaking or writing; this wider notion can be summed up in the concept 'identification' as understood by Burke (Foss, Foss and Trapp 1985: 157). This understanding entails what Burke calls 'consubstantiality' between human agents: 'We form selves or identities through various properties or substances, including physical objects, occupations… beliefs and values' (p. 158). Persuasion takes place as a result of this 'identification'.[9] One will no doubt find that this 'maxim' of identification would also include the use of metaphor as means to bring about the desired effect in readers (or recipients).

3. *A Different View of Metaphor*

Before turning to the interrelatedness of metaphor and rhetoric, it is felicitous to reflect on the phenomenon of metaphor, and to signal a 'more postmodern' understanding. In general, to come to an understanding of metaphor still proves extremely elusive. The following indicates this (Harris 1992: 222, citing from Vico and Eco):

> The 'most luminous and therefore the most necessary and frequent' (Vico) of all tropes, the metaphor, defies every encyclopedic entry. It has been the object of philosophical, linguistic, aesthetic, and psychological reflection since the beginning of time… Although innumerable definitions of metaphor exist… The vast literature on metaphor…reflects the difficulty of explaining the interrelated issues [of recognition, creation, interpretation and their value in communication].

A 'history' of inquiry into metaphor is indicated by Harris (1992: 222), and indicates the following major viewpoints: even by the definition of Aristotle, 'metaphor' has been one of those elusive and enigmatic concepts that defies any conclusive description and understanding. It is interesting though that it appears as if Aristotle saw metaphor as more than mere substitution (indicating something new); also that it is a very effective means of expression. For later authors (e.g. Diomedes and Gregorius Corinthius) the matter of *means of expression* seems to be uppermost. Harris (1992: 223) goes on to describe later developments regarding

---

9.   He does not advocate that this should replace 'persuasion', but that 'identification' *supplements* the aspect of persuasion (Foss, Foss and Trapp 1985: 158).

metaphor, referring to I.A. Richards. The latter challenged Aristotle's view of something special and exceptional in the use of language. Richards observed the process of metaphor in language usage, the process of exchange of meanings, and provided the literary world with the terminology of 'tenor' and 'vehicle'.[10] Finally, Richards did not so much understand metaphor as the bringing together of two words, but as rather 'two associated complexes'.

In the case of Searle (of speech-theory fame), he stresses the process by which metaphors are recognized, such as looking for utterance meaning which differs from sentence meaning.[11] Following this would be Eco's theory of semantic markers: 'Such markers are both connotative and denotative, *the connotative ones representing culturally determined associations*' (Harris 1992: 225; my italics).

Of a more ontological and essential nature is the following discussion by Harris (1992: 225-27): if one negates a strong resemblance between metaphor and simile, then comparison drops away and 'substitution' as the basis of metaphor is stressed. Another question is whether the pragmatic effect of metaphors would be commensurate with the semantic anomalousness. Harris answers this in the negative.[12] On this score (identification and pragmatics) the final point of importance would be that metaphors are culturally related. This does mean that metaphors are quite distinct, even though there may sometimes be 'dead' metaphors.[13] This leads to a more essential question, namely, whether metaphor is 'cognitively, and not simply rhetorically, creative'. Positivistically, the answer would be that metaphors, like metaphysical concepts, can obscure the nature of reality.[14]

The opposite of this *positivist* (or 'anticonstructivist' as some would have called it at the time Harris wrote), the *constructivist* viewpoint, is that

10. 'Tenor' and 'vehicle': the first refers to that which is illuminated, and the 'vehicle' that which illuminates it; also the tenor need not be explicitly named; for example the expression 'narrow fellow in the grass' is the vehicle for the tenor 'snake'.

11. At this point Harris (1992: 225) relates Black's 'associated commonplaces', 'qualities commonly associated with a thing whether or not necessary to its definition or true in fact'.

12. That is, there need not be such significant anomaly to identify metaphor, nor for metaphor to have pragmatic effect; cf. the example: 'Bill is a snake'.

13. This does not imply, however, that all language eventually becomes metaphors; they do remain distinct phenomena.

14. As an example of this view Harris (1992: 226) refers to Rudolph Carnap's 'The Elimination of Metaphysics through the Logical Analysis of Language'. The title speaks for itself.

all human understanding of reality is in any case *interpretive*, and may never be finally known, since it is *constructed*; metaphors play a major role in such construction. The latter viewpoint opens the possibility to advocate that: metaphor *creates* the similarity. 'Paul Ricoeur writes that metaphor "has more than emotive value because it offers new information. A metaphor, in short tells us something new about reality"' (so cited by Harris 1992: 227). It is of course especially Lakoff and Johnson who went yet further,[15] and hold that thought is itself metaphorically structured in that there are large conceptual metaphors; thus they do not simply help construct our understanding of reality. It is especially abstract thought that needs to be understood metaphorically. Nevertheless, there are other dimensions. Metaphors not only give insight, but can equally be sources of confusion and conflict. Part of the solution lies in the *recognition of large-scale conceptual metaphors*.

It is of course an open question whether there can be talk of a particularly 'postmodern understanding of metaphor'. And yet, I think that, following Gordon (1995) in the ensuing discussion, it can be rightly termed a 'postmodern' (and deconstructive) emphasis, which allows for more than mere rationality in the analysis of metaphor.[16]

It was argued in the above that *metaphors* are also vehicles of reflection of everyday realities (and problems) within which ever symbolic universe (e.g. historical, socio-religious, and so on) they are framed, and by means of whatever discourse.[17]

Whereas there are those who would want to move away completely from the notion of metaphor, and replace it with the idea of 'metonomy',[18] there are yet others who would redefine metaphor away from former

---

15. Cf. Harris 1992: 227.

16. In this context 'metaphor' elicits a number of other facets of understanding and cognition, such as language, theory of literature, epistemology, etc., to which some attention has been given in the above, and also in what is to follow.

17. Meyer (1994: 62) appears to endorse this, when he remarks: 'And what is an argument if not a discourse on a given question, whether via subquestions (i.e., a story) or not?' He points out that this goes against the grain of the image that we generally have of argument, since that view has only severed poetics from rhetoric.

18. Although I think the research by Goossens (1996) conclusively indicates that this cannot be the case. In his 1996 article he concludes that metonomy may occur within metaphor (and be so dissolved); but the opposite does not take place. In defining the relationship between these two literary phenomena, Eco argues that metaphors originate when metonymic thought paths are short-circuited, so referred to by Harris (1992: 228).

'models' and 'functions' of understanding, such as that which was proposed by Richards, Black, Lakoff and Johnson. One such is the treatment
by Gordon (1995).

I am rather intrigued[19] by the discussion by Paul Gordon in his *The
Critical Double: Figurative Meaning in Aesthetic Discourse*. He bases his
argumentation on the ancient Protagorean dictum of the *dissoi logoi*: 'On
every question there are two opposing answers, *including this one*'
(Gordon 1995: 1). The purpose of the 'critical double' is to demonstrate
that this Protagorean notion constitutes a fundamental principle of
aesthetic/rhetorical discourse. Thus '[f]rom the opening chapters on
metaphor, rhetoric...the "critical double" is identified with the way all
literary and rhetorical texts utilize structures of meaning to deny the very
structures of meaning on which they are based' (1995: 12). He goes on to
point out that deconstruction has a place still, in spite of the current
popularity of cultural and multicultural, and new historical methodologies
(1995: 13); thus the reputations of the major deconstructivist writers,
Gadamer, Heidegger, Adorno, de Man, Derrida and Miller remain intact.

c. *Excursus: Background to Gordon's View of Metaphor*
It is necessary to sketch the following general tenor of Gordon, in order to
provide a backdrop for perusing his discussion of the vehicle of metaphor.
He suggests that often the 'answer' to any aesthetic question may or may
not be the right one. He refers to the analogy in the *Foot Book*, by Dr
Seuss (which is of course a bit of 'sophistry'), according to which it turns
out that for many 'the left foot may turn out to be the right foot'; thus the
right foot is not the right one, the right answer is not the right answer, but
in either case one must move forward and try to be right. It then involves
the possibility put forward by Derrida, as to whether there is a 'right'
interpretation to a work of art, in reference to the debate between Schapiro
and Heidegger on *Van Gogh's Shoes*: were these Van Gogh's own shoes
or those of a peasant? Gordon goes on to deconstruct Derrida's own
observations on the former two's debate. He evaluates between Derrida
and Heidegger, and concludes with Heidegger that, in the case of a work
of art, *the work is something else over and above the thingly element, and
that that something else in the work constitutes its artistic nature*, in the
words of Heidegger: 'Dies Andere, was daran ist, macht das Künstlerische

---

19. I do not think that I do full justice to this work in this essay, since it may want
to communicate more widely. However, for the purposes of what is advocated here, it
provides an excellent and lucid argument.

aus' (quoted by Gordon 1995: 4)—the artwork is a thing that is made, but it says something other than the mere thing itself is; therefore, *allo agoreuei*. This leads to the notion of the double figurative meaning of all aesthetic objects; in this way art is *double*: 'neither one nor two'. Even though one may not be able to establish the original meaning of the work of art,

> [a]rtistic originality is the revelation of truth as unconcealedness (*aletheia*) that is not at all impaired by the confusion one has in assigning a place of origin to the aesthetic experience…by the lack of 'propositional correctness'…we experience something more, the unconcealed Being of beings which suddenly appears 'springs forth' (Gordon 1995: 4-5).

It is in this aesthetic experience where we come into contact with more than what is known, 'the being of beings'. It is also here that we should experience the doubling of art as 'something else', as a figurative allegorical encounter. Gordon (1995: 8) argues that, analogous to the wrestling of Jacob and being overmastered, and thus mastering by being defeated, in the very process of succumbing to admitting defeat of not knowing, resides the mastery. Moreover, in reference to Heidegger, Gordon points out Heidegger's idea that it is art which reveals the truth of the thing itself and the being of beings by virtue of a double, where essence mysteriously occupies.

In what Gordon calls his 'model of doubling', he follows Gadamer's observations on *Erlebnis*, where, in experience of an artwork, it is experienced on both the inside and the outside as a paradox, which represents ourselves; the true doubling that occurs when a part becomes a whole yet remains but a part. In this 'doubling' there is something of a 'doubt'. He concludes (1995: 18) that:

> [a]pophthatic discourse, the discourse of God and of art, is necessarily double because it must seek to return to a cause or meaning that is not outside the realm of art but nonetheless always beyond it—that is to say always ready in being simultaneously present and absent in referencing back to something contained within the artwork.

It is against the above background that something more is to be said about Gordon's view of metaphor. Gordon (1995: 19) begins by discussing the two notions or different terms used to describe the relationship between the so-called tenor and vehicle. In reference to a quotation from I.A. Richards, Gordon (1995: 19) draws a distinction between 'dual' and 'double': '[T]o be dual is to be *both* the same and different, while to be double is to be different *and* the same.' Metaphoric 'doubling' (rather than dualling) refers to the two distinct units that are one; the A and the B of metaphor become respectively B and A. Because metaphor is double, neither one nor two, a gap in meaning takes place, which now separates the metaphor from itself.[20]

To conclude on this 'doubling' nature of metaphor, Gordon (1995: 20) explains: 'Consequently, any definition of metaphor will, in describing it as something, elide this gap and so on, by offering a partial truth of resemblance, yield metaphors of metaphorization.' He then asks how one can define metaphor when it is nothing by logical terms; when it brings about an identity that is not an identity. Thus (now in reference to Protagoras), we are caught up between the Scylla and the Charybdis of recognizing our inability to understand the phenomenon of metaphor, and the inevitable failure of our every recognition. This leads to the inference that all one can ever do about metaphor is to return to metaphor.

It appears that Aristotle's view of metaphor was remarkably 'postmodern', when one peruses the astute explanation by Gordon (1995: 20),[21] as he discusses Aristotle's remarks (with its usual acuity) about metaphor which also refer to clarity and obscurity (so in the *Rhetoric*, when defining metaphor). Gordon refers to terms of Aristotle such as: 'perspicuity', 'pleasure' and 'foreign air', 'uncanny' and 'foreign', 'cannot be learnt from another'. Aristotle also insists that metaphor *teaches us*.

If espoused, these observations by Gordon open the way to advance matters somewhat, even if it may remain unsatisfactory for the positivist.

d. *'Metaphors' as Heuristic Devices for the Metaphysical*

Thus this 'deconstructive view of metaphor' opens up a particular possibility which may be linked to the metaphysical, to the religious dimension, since in positivist terms there is a commonality between metaphor and the metaphysical, namely, their 'obscurity'.

It is clear that in the phenomenon of *metaphor* we have something which can supersede normal cognition, a device that could elevate thinking and emotions above ordinary natural language. It is this possibility for

---

20.   Vincente (1996: 195) would concur with this, in rejecting a purely semantic analysis in terms of the linguistic meaning of metaphor.

21.   After this (1995: 27) Gordon proceeds to discuss the well-known attempts by Richards, Black and Beardsley and the interaction theory of metaphor. However, Beardsley's attempt could be described as a controversion theory, which is merely a shift of emphasis; however, he does not emphasize the contradictory characteristic of metaphor as primary.

'otherness' that renders metaphor as a device to 'discover'/open up to the dimension of the metaphysical. It is on this 'otherness' that I would like to base my further discussion.

4. *Metaphor as Means of Rhetoric and the Pragmatics of Metaphor*

According to the view of rhetoric advocated above (section 2) metaphor is rhetorical; and rhetoric includes the use of metaphor. However, then there is also the more specific sense in which one may speak of the 'pragmatics of metaphor' (the rhetorical effect of metaphor). Both these dimensions are important.

The importance of metaphor for rhetoric is undeniable. Ward (1996: 18) points out that discussions about metaphor (and also other figurative expressions such as metonomy and allegory) play an important role in the projects of Jacques Lacan, Paul Ricoeur, Jacques Derrida, Paul de Man and Jean-François Lyotard. In fact, it is the emphasis on metaphor in structural linguistics which has fostered the current interest in rhetoric and writing.

There are those (e.g. Vincente 1996: 207), however, who conclude that there is no real difference in the cognitive processing of metaphor (or figurative language) above literal language.[22] Grice[23] maintains that in communicating by means of figurative language a speaker communicates by means of *implicature*.[24] Grice would say: 'In the case of metaphor, he or she says—or makes as if to say—something false, while he or she implies some related proposition which allegedly restores his or her claim to rationality and co-operation' (Vincente 1996: 196). There appears to be a flouting of one of the maxims of conversation, which triggers the calculating of 'implicated' meaning.

Further consideration of the cognitive facets of metaphor in communication should keep in mind that there are definite mechanisms whereby metaphor may operate. Pauwels (1995: 125-58) refers to the matter of 'salience'; the more salient a metaphor within a community, the more effective would be its communication. However, since salience is relative, one should rather speak of 'levels of metaphorization'.

---

22. When it comes to this aspect of metaphor, I would rather side with Grice whom Vincente rejects on this point.

23. As referred to by Vincente 1996: 196.

24. Although not necessarily the same, this notion is reminiscent of Gordon's view of 'doubling' in metaphor (cf. above).

From research done,[25] it has been established that cognitive resources find non-literal messages more difficult to process. This needs to be discussed within the ambit of the *nature of language* as well. Much research has been done on metaphor, both within the 'sciences' as well as in the 'humanities', in which aspects of (meta-) cognition have been investigated. In this research, metaphor as means of cognition has been offset against other language phenomena. So it has been argued that there is a certain *effectiveness*, but also *potential* in metaphor not for instance found in symbol (Sally McFague addresses the reasons for this potential; referred to by Ward 1996: 18-19):

> Metaphors have the ability to speak of that which is unknown or ineffable. Metaphorical thinking is the way we all think—by making comparisons between the known and the unknown. Effective comparisons in metaphorical statements shock or surprise—that is, they have emotional effect upon readers. They are [in fact] transformative... [M]etaphor '[is] the way by which we understand as well as enlarge our world and change it'. They transform our world by replacing the old and the wornout with the new... metaphors comment critically on conceptual idols. Metaphors do not fix meaning and so they cannot, therefore, become the object of idolatry. Their inherent instability of reference keeps meaning open, tentative and iconoclastic. They articulate and generate a surplus of meaning. By calling or interpretation, metaphors draw the reader into an engagement with the world they configure. They draw the reader into a relationship with the text, a world which is other than their world... Metaphors have ontological value, a value which manifests itself when 'the literal sense is left behind so that the metaphorical sense can emerge...'

I find the above helpful for the present discussion, particulary on the notion of metaphor as *heuristic*; to lead onto yet newer ontological (also in a metaphysical sense) discovery and understanding (see below on the metaphors and rhetoric in Ephesians).

However, it is Janet Martin Soskice who concentrates more fully on the *cognitive function* of metaphor. According to Ward (1996: 20) she wants to make epistemological rather than ontological claims for metaphor: 'the reference of metaphor [is] the grounding experience from which the metaphorical articulation arose'.

---

25. E.g. Jaffe 1988. Much research has been done especially since the 1980s on *cognition and metaphor*. I only take partial notice of this research, since it is very much embedded in empiricist approaches. The results are, nevertheless, of some interest for the pragmatic aspects of metaphor, i.e. for the rhetorical.

5. *Rhetoric and Metaphor in the Letter to the Ephesians*

As advocated in the above, the historical is not without significance. However, in the history of its research it was/is especially the historical issues (authorship and *raison d'être*) that purported to jeopardize any authentic understanding of this letter. New Testament scholars would be aware of debates of yesteryear[26] which surrounded the letter to the Ephesians. On the one hand there were those who gathered information ('very empirically') to show by means of word counts, and on the basis of the use and the non-use of 'Pauline' vocabulary and ideas, that this letter was not written by Paul; others wrote tomes to counter this (e.g. Percy 1946 and Van Roon 1974). Since this was done in the heyday of historical criticism, one should understand these endeavours in that light.

Despite the fact that these uncertainties do surround this letter, some socio-cultural background can be assumed, which renders the interpretation of its metaphors possible, even if this cannot be finally established.

There was a process of *interactive communication* taking place, which *supersedes the issues of this letter*. Obviously, underlying the author's rhetoric was a shared universe of supposed meta-realities. Since this letter is so rich in metaphor and figurative language, the success and effectiveness of its communication must have resided in the deployment of these 'realities'.

a. *Metaphor/s in the Letter to the Ephesians*
This letter contains a number of rich metaphors,[27] and the letter constitutes two large complex metaphors, embedded in a 'meta-metaphor' underlying the letter, which emerges as a 'meta-narrative' of God's general and particular history with the readers. I propose that this narrative is told with the following objective in mind (Lemmer 1988: 111-33): that these are Gentile readers, whose adopted *religious identity* as belonging to the entity, God's people, was under siege, whoever and whatever was to be blamed for this exigence. And this situation needed to be remedied.

26. Not much needs to be said here, since it has little relevance for this essay. However, underlying this phase was more than mere idealistic quests: it appears that ecclesiastical politics played a great role in all of this, cf. Lemmer 1988.

27. In the ensuing discussion only a selection will be made, in order to illustrate the argument of the essay.

It should be pointed out that the following description draws from 'clear' metaphors, hidden and suspended metaphors, as well as from the general *figurative* language of the letter. Furthermore, I refrain from discussing these with reference to the Greek (for the various terms there are many sources to consult).[28]

b. *Proposition of What Underlies These Meta-metaphors*
The rhetorical situation/exigence.[29] The proposed meta-metaphors are related to the underlying narrative of this letter, which in turn is indicated by the rhetorical situation (cf. Lemmer 1988: 111-33).[30] As with most writings of the New Testament, a complexity of rhetorical 'situations' is addressed simultaneously in Ephesians. Any close reading of this letter warns one that there is *not just one situation* that is being addressed; for that, the entire argument appears to be too complex and diverse, if not diffuse.

In Ephesians the most salient of these situations addressed appears to be, very simply stated, as follows: (a) *Doubt concerning identity*. It appears as if some[31] of the readers doubted the status of their identity—whether they were truly members of God's people in the sense of the *in-group* notions entertained by Israel, as commonwealth of the God of the universe. This caused them to relapse into certain fears of forces in the universe and certain behaviour patterns. (b) *Fear of extraneous (external) forces*. The other major exigent situation thus involves the threat by

28. Obviously, the non-use of Greek terminology does impair the final effect of a study such as this, and for finer nuances as well as socio-cultural richness embodied in the various metaphors, it would have been apropos to have studied it in that medium. Furthermore, by just referring to the English one may not be sufficiently addressing the issues of what a reader in antiquity would have perceived as metaphor and what not. However, for the sake of the broad argument in this essay, use of a literal translation such as the RSV 1971 should suffice.
Concepts, lexemes and collocations from the text of Ephesians, identified as possible metaphors, will be indicated by means of italics in the text of this essay.
29. To speak of 'one' exigence only is fallacious. Nevertheless, I do think that the various 'exigencies' in this letter are subordinate to the one major issue; that of the *new religious identity* of the readers, and its concomitant effects.
30. I did not use the notion of 'rhetorical' situation there, but referred to it as 'argumentative' situation.
31. I say 'some', since it may be that the author could be addressing a 'peanut gallery' of readers as well; those who could have given rise to this doubt of identity, and which he/she may have hoped would also read this letter.

extraneous 'political' forces. It is conceivable that these *two* situations (a) and (b) could indeed have been related, *doubt of identity* giving rise to *fear of extraneous forces*. There may have been two distinct 'sets' of forces involved here; being also somehow related to each other: (1) political authority/ies and (2) spiritual forces.[32]

The underlying meta-narrative. Some of the textual indicators that seem to indicate this problem of identity can be inferred, not by mirror reading, but by an inversion of the tenor of the indicators. The narrative can among others be assumed from the particular uses of deixis.[33]

It appears that the *Jewish Christians*[34] in this community could have cast doubt on the true new identity of the Gentile readers. In order to allay the above exigencies, the author narrates two narratives intertwined as one or, more probably, *one narrative* with *two* distinct facets. The *essence* of the narrative is that the readers may be well assured that the Gentile readers are in God's ownership, and they are secure in this ownership, as well as that they are in *full participation* in God's benefactions toward them. The distinct facets of the narrative are: (1) God, by primordial decision and later redemptive actions, effected their special belonging to him, and his people. (2) By the latter, the readers may be assured that they are secure against extraneous forces, be they spiritual or material (political).

Given the proposition of the exigencies, the following emerges: the author is obviously at pains to re-establish these readers in their relating to the concept of 'belonging to the people of God'. He begins by telling them a story (providing them with a narrative), a story with universal, cosmological, and 'eternal' intent and extent. In the economy of this story, the readers are a very special denominator. The interesting phenomenon is that the author initially casts his argument from the very point of view from which the readers may experience their threat, namely, the fairly well-established notion that Eph. 1.1-14 receives its mould from the

32. For underpinning textual indicators to these exigencies, see 'The metaphors reciprocal to the underlying narrative', below.

33. Cf. also Lemmer 1988: 116-33. This profuse use of deixis (personal pronoun) clearly constitutes some framework for a narrative.

34. I argue that the 'antagonists' could not have been Judaizers, such as those who may have been involved in the rhetorical situation of the letter to the Galatians (cf. also Lemmer 1988: 121-33). There are only very oblique allusions to such 'antagonists', only to be inferred from the structure of the argument, never clearly indicated.

Jewish synagogal *berakah*. The threat of identity of the readers as to whether they actually belong to the people of God appears to have been from a Jewish origin. Thus the author tackles this problem on this Jewish level. After all, those posing the problem were the original people of God. However, this needs to be qualified: these are not 'purely' Jewish people, but particularly 'Christian-Jewish'.

The author establishes that the readers' identity of belonging to the people of God is beyond cavil; they were after all chosen even before the foundations of the world—their 'election' is thus securely founded even before God chose Israel. But there is more. They have now been *sealed* as the inheritance of God. Moreover, they are incorporated in God's all-time work of bringing everything together in his Messiah (1.10-14). Thus they are incorporated in the Messiah's entire redemptive work, even into the highest heavens (1.19-23). They now belong to a certain special entity called the 'Body of Christ'.

Chapter 2 clearly narrates the story of their former ignominy (2.11-22) as outcasts, but this has now been finally reversed. They actually belong to what was formerly holy ground to Israel only, namely, the *Temple*, and they can actually denominate God, which would be the God of Israel, *Father* (2.18-19).

But the story goes on: this new inclusion has formerly been a 'mystery'. This has now been revealed that already long before God intended them to be part of his new plan. Moreover, this affords these readers access to God himself (3.11-12), a rare and special privilege indeed. The author proceeds to affirm this knowledge for the readers in his plea to the Father that they be may fully understand this.

The narrative continues. This privilege necessitates certain demands, such as walking worthily (4.1-3) of their status. Furthermore, they should take care not to be swayed from this belief (4.13-14), by any threat, be it either fear for the spirit world or political forces.

The metaphors reciprocal to the underlying narrative. Reciprocal to this narrative, or embedded therein, are *two plexes of metaphors* to communicate respectively the realities concerning *security of identity and security against forces*. These plexes are respectively made up and supported by a number of individual cognate metaphors, which support the above macro-metaphorical cast.

Plexus One: securing identity. There are a multiplicity of metaphors that support and explain their secure identity as belonging to God and their participating in his benefactions. The main metaphorical complex here comprises the notion that the new identity of the readers is founded in expressing it in terms of *donata* by God, couched in 'eternal' (1.4, *before the foundation of the world*) and 'metaphysical' (1.3, *in heavenly places*) terms. They are part now, not of something merely natural and physical, but of that which 'predates' everything. Moreover, they share in something ostensibly supraterrestrial, inasmuch as they are elevated into a 'heavenly' existence (2.6, *made to sit with him in heavenly places*).

The stress on *sonship* (1.5) and *heirship* (1.14) and that the readers share *an inheritance in the saints* (1.18)[35] all endorse their undeniable identity—they *are* God's own *workmanship* (2.10). There is reference to the time when the readers had no status with the people (and by inference the God) of Israel; see Eph. 2.11-13, the reference to being *alienated from the commonwealth of Israel, and being strangers to covenants and promise*. Then follows the assurance that the readers are *no longer strangers and sojourners, but fellow citizens with saints and members of the household of God*. Thus this situation has been irrevocably reversed.

And so it goes on and on, also assuring the readers that they are in fact part of that most holy of Israel's symbols, the *Temple of God* (clearly metaphorically intended). And so it continues, until in Ephesians 4 the author appeals to the readers that on the basis of this *identity* they should conform to a lifestyle that evidences their identity.

This complex is constituted by identifying the numerous individual metaphors which cogently argue and underpin the notion of *identity*. Brief attention can be given to some of the explicit and hidden single metaphors which comprise this plexus.

The readers are blessed in Christ (1.3): the idea of *being in a person* (which has been the focus of many an inquiry) clearly marks the use of metaphor and, whatever else, somehow indicates a new sphere of existence. The same in this instance is clear concerning *in heavenly places* (1.3). Even for the ancients, the dualism of being on earth, and at the same time in heaven, must have signalled something greater than they would otherwise have perceived or understood.

These readers are actually *children* of God (1.5). In antiquity is was quite conceivable that humans could be progeny of divine beings. Even so, use of this denomination for human beings would not have been a common occurrence. The *sealing* (1.13) of this sonship would not indicate

---

35. Whether this be understood as God's inheritance, or the saints' inheritance.

an unusual idea, but the *sealing by means of the Holy Spirit* would have indicated something unusual, the linking of two worlds, not commonly associated with one another—the linking of physical with the meta-physical realities. Yet, this *meta*-phor continues, this Holy Spirit is actually the *guarantee* of an inheritance, albeit an inheritance not of this world—guarantee (or engagement ring or first instalment, as some would have it) is clearly from the commercial world, now used to indicate a metaphysical reality.

The creating of a new identity from many is expressed as *one new man* (2.15). The readers are now *citizens* of the *household* of God (2.19) and that this no longer refers to a natural existence only endorses the meta-phorical reference here.

This new entity of God's people is compared to a *building on foundations* (2.20-21), and the process involved to constitute this is a *building activity* which takes place when erecting this edifice, which is actually a *temple* (2.21). This temple obviously supersedes even the Temple in Israel—*the* symbol of Israel's uniqueness as God's people. These readers now are 'co-constituents' of this *temple*.

The author himself plays a key role in all of this since he is a *steward* (a dispenser) (3.2) in the dispensing of this privilege of belonging. Together the various parts constitute a body (3.6 and cf. 1.20-23).[36] God actually *indwells* (3.14-19) this temple. The stability of all this is *grounded* and *rooted* in the 'soil/base of love'.

The challenge to withstand any threat[37] is depicted by a rich set of metaphors (cf. 4.13-14) Those who allow themselves to be swayed are like *children*. Then follows a number of metaphors redolent of seafaring concepts (4.14); being *swayed and tossed by waves*.

There is a return (after 4.12) to the 'body' metaphor, when there is mention in 4.16 to *joined and knit*, every joint, *each part* working properly, this corporately secures their identity.

The reality of the external threats are of course indicated by distinct metaphors (however, there are overlaps between the 'identity metaphors' and the 'threat metaphors').

36. Space and the purview of this essay prohibit the full discussion of the sig-nificance of this metaphor.

37. Clinton E. Arnold's *Ephesians: Power and Magic* (1989) cogently indicates the role that all kinds of forces played in the context of the Ephesian readers. I would not advocate that this could be the only backdrop to the letter.

Plexus Two: securing against forces. A number of figurative descriptions and metaphors underscore the strategic position of strength from which to resist any onslaught. As was argued above, these forces could have been of a twofold nature, namely, (1) political authority/ies[38] and (2) spiritual forces, being somehow related to each other.

This struggle against forces (especially then civil authorities under-pinned by spiritual principalities)[39] seems clear even from the following textual indicators. The stress on an *inheritance* which is *secure* (1.11-14); prayer for knowledge of *wealth* which is *eternal and worthwhile* (1.16-19); and that this is tied up with the supreme rulership of the object of their allegiance, Jesus Christ (1.20-23; cf. 1.22). All other potentates are *under his feet* (1.22). God freed them from these ominous forces when he made them alive (2.1-7); he also took them right out of the sphere of the forces' influence/s. This could imply that the thrust of these metaphors is to indicate a securing in the minds of the readers of their position and posses-sion (which is pre-eminently of a metaphysical nature) against the forces that would threaten their existence.

Finally there is the famous passage (6.10-20) which refers to a combat against such external forces: *we are not contending against flesh and blood, but against the principalities.*[40] This section of the letter, serves to *finally* identify the essential nature of the struggle/battle as ultimately a metaphysical one. The plethora of single metaphors (and figurative lan-guage) which clearly constitute this complex metaphor provides the means whereby the readers themselves should resist these onslaughts by an appeal to their essential position and identity.

c. *Rhetorical Use of Metaphor/s as Heuristic for Religious Truth in Ephesians*

Before perusing the way in which metaphor could serve as 'heuristic for religious truth' attention needs to be given to the notion of *religious truth*

---

38. Thurston Moritz, *A Profound Mystery: The Use of the Old Testament in Ephesians* (1996), clearly indicates the possibility that the struggle indicated by the letter could refer to combat in the arena. Thus the struggle was also against the political authorities.

39. This relationship between two sets of forces could indicate some apocalyptic backdrop to the 'world' of this letter.

40. Yet, once again a relationship between civil (earthly) forces and metaphysical forces are clearly linked here. Cf. again the entire thesis of Moritz (1996), who establishes the link between the set of metaphors (complex battle metaphor) here with battle in the arena.

as such. This once again places one squarely into the ambit of *epistem-ology*, but also requires the defining of the nature of 'religious truth'. To turn to the last facet first.

The epistemic possibility of the numinous, of the metaphysical, is once again opened up by certain tenets of the postmodern. The discussion by Ward (1996: 102-31) on 'Theology and Aesthetics: Religious Experience and the Textual Sublime'[41] offers some reflection in this regard, when he focuses on the experiential aspect in terms of the reading and listening subject. Of course this act of 'transference'[42] in reading is not restricted to the reading of religious texts only, since there is also that side to reading 'where knowledge emerges which is more profound and prior to rational-ity' (Ward 1996: 104). He refers to the coinage by Martha Nussbaum of the concept of 'catalepsis', which refers to being surprised, vivid particu-larity, qualitative intensity, 'in which, with blinding certainty, we gain self-knowledge' (1996: 104). Already on the level of reading,[43] something can take place: '*Aisthesis* itself already reveals and transforms. Aesthetic experience draws this power from the contrast it establishes from the outset in relation to everyday experience' (so Ricoeur,[44] cited by Ward 1996: 106). It is on this level that we have to conceive of the way in which the encounter of metaphor could have enhanced the 'spiritual' cognition of the readers of the Ephesians.

The main reason for the implementation of these metaphors resides in the heuristic they provided for the readers to bring them to discovery. Although these metaphors would obviously have found their roots within the socio-cultural reference, especially the dogmatism of certain schools in ancient Judaism, it is especially because of their *religious* significance and a particular socio-political reality that these metaphors could have been effective.

The density and nature of metaphors used held the potential that they would have lifted the readers quite out of their everydayness of experi-ence, especially given the probable rhetorical situation. In the words of Ward (1996: 13-14): 'There may be religious experience in some micro-second when self-consciousness is silenced and the self dissolves into the transcendent…'

---

41. Ch. 4 of his book: *Theology and Contemporary Critical Theory*.
42. Ward (1996: 104) refers to the use of this notion by Julia Kristeva.
43. That does not imply a discounting of notions of 'revelation' and 'repre-sentation'.
44. To Ricoeur, *aesthetic experience is religious experience*.

It was when the readers were quite compellingly (and probably effectively) made aware by means of the narrative, by means of plexes of metaphors, that *belonging to God*, and the *already secure rule* of Christ over all evil forces (also those dominating the political authority) they could have snapped out of their doubt regarding their *identity* and *their fear* in the face of opposition. This the author endeavours to bring about by means of the sets and subsets of the metaphors. The pragmatic potential of these could have lifted them out of their cognitive uncertainty and spiritual paralysis.

Finally, it is important to return to Gordon's notion of 'the double', which is precisely created by the use of metaphor. To finally understand what these readers could have understood by 'metaphysical' is of course impossible. It may be that in their world the spheres of 'physical' and 'metaphysical' were in any case enmeshed. But this could exactly be what Gordon means by 'doubling'. To these readers,[45] the one world flows into the other: metaphysical and physical (earthly) are different sides of the same reality. And it is the 'metaphorization' of their experience; expressed in other terms by means of metaphors, that existential change was communicated to the situation in which the readers found themselves, by making them aware that their exigent situation was also part of another reality; now expressed in different terms.

More pragmatically formulated (returning to Sally McFague as quoted by Ward 1996: 19; cf. 'Metaphor as Epistemic Means', in the above): 'metaphors draw the reader into an engagement with the world they configure. They draw the reader into a relationship with the text, a world which is other than their world'; and so there was at least the possibility that the author of Ephesians succeeded in changing the exigence of the readers, by changing their cognition of their world. In this way, metaphors have ontological value.

BIBLIOGRAPHY

Arnold, C.E.
    1989   *Ephesians: Power and Magic: The Concept of Power in Ephesians in the Light of its Historical Setting* (Grand Rapids: Baker Book House).

45. And for those who now find their hermeneutical horizons concurring with that of those times.

Devaney, M.J.
    1997   *'Since at least Plato…' and Other Postmodern Myths* (New York: Macmillan Press).
Foss, S.K., K.A. Foss, and R. Trapp
    1985   *Contemporary Perspectives on Rhetoric* (Prospect Heights, IL: Waveland Press).
Goodwin, D.
    1993   'Rhetorical Criticism', in Makaryk (ed.) 1993: 174-78.
Goossens, L.
    1995   'Metaphtonymy: The Interaction of Metaphor and Metonymy in Figurative Expressions for Linguistic Action', in L. Goossens *et al.* (eds.), *By Word of Mouth: Metaphor, Metonomy and Linguistic Action in Cognitive Perspective* (Amsterdam: John Benjamins): 159-74.
Gordon, P.
    1995   *The Critical Double: Figurative Meaning in Aesthetic Discourse* (Tuscaloosa, AL: University of Alabama Press).
Harris, W.V.
    1992   *Dictionary of Concepts in Literary Criticism and Theory* (New York: Greenwood Press).
Jaffe, F.G.
    1988   'Metaphors and Memory: A Study in Persuasion' (PhD thesis, Ann Arbor, MI: University of Michigan).
Lemmer, H.R.
    1988   'Pneumatology and Eschatology in Ephesians: The Role of the Eschatological Spirit in the Church' (DTh thesis, Pretoria: University of South Africa).
Makaryk, I.R. (ed.)
    1993   *Encyclopedia of Contemporary Literary Theory: Approaches, Scholars' Terms* (Toronto: University of Toronto Press).
Meyer, M.
    1994   *Rhetoric, Language, and Reason* (Philadelphia: Pennsylvania State University Press).
Moritz, T.
    1996   *A Profound Mystery: The Use of the Old Testament in Ephesians* (Leiden: E.J. Brill).
Pauwels, P.
    1996   'Levels of Metaphorization: The case of *Put*', in L. Goossens *et al.* (eds.), *By Word of Mouth: Metaphor, Metonomy and Linguistic Action in Cognitive Perspective* (Amsterdam: John Benjamins): 125-58.
Percy, E.
    1946   *Der Probleme der Kolosser und Epheserbriefe* (Lund: Gleerup).
Van Roon, A.
    1974   *The Authenticity of Ephesians* (Leiden: E.J. Brill).
Vincente, B.
    1996   'On the Semantics and Pragmatics of Metaphor: Coming Full Circle', *Language and Literature* 5.3: 195-208.
Ward, G.
    1996   *Theology and Contemporary Critical Theory* (Basingstoke: Macmillan).

An Enthymematic Reading of Philippians: Towards a Typology of Pauline Arguments

Marc J. Debanné

1. *Introduction*

In recent years, a considerable number of rhetorical critics of the New Testament have turned their attention to enthymemes[1] as a fundamental rhetorical device in texts.[2] Expectations are running high as to the possible harvest of information that the analysis of enthymemes may bear. Some scholars hope that it will shed more light on New Testament writers' argumentative technique: after all, the enthymeme is a micro-argument, a building block for larger argumentative schemes. Others expect to open a window on the authors' social world, since the usual understanding of the enthymeme is a step of reasoning depending on one or more silent presuppositions (or premises) for its persuasive force—presuppositions shared by author and addressee, which the critic attempts to 'bring to the surface'.

---

1.   Although the meaning of this term is problematic, as we will soon see, it will be useful to provide the reader with a preliminary and general definition. This one is given by M. Kraus: 'The enthymeme is one of the most important elementary means of persuasion of rhetoric. One understands by this a densely formulated argument which seeks to confirm the truth of a proposition about a particular state of affairs through its deduction from another proposition which is universally recognized or hardly refutable' (M. Kraus, 'Enthymem', in *Historisches Wörterbuch der Rhetorik*, II [Tübingen: Max Niemeyer Verlag, 1994], cols. 1197-1222; translation mine). One classic example of an enthymeme is the following: 'Socrates is mortal, for he is human'.

2.   For instance, by browsing through the entries in the archives of the RHETORIC-L LISTSERV ('Rhetorical Analysis of Jewish and Christian Scriptures' internet mailing list) of the last two years, one will be struck by the importance being placed on this question.

a. *Some Recent Approaches to New Testament Enthymemes*
Current studies display a variety of approaches. Among other things, one
can sense an uncertainty about a working definition of the enthymeme. A
brief consideration of five recent works will not only illustrate the usefulness of the concept as an analytical tool, but will also reveal the particular
issues that still require clarification.

John D. Moores's *Wrestling with Rationality in Paul* [3] studies the argumentation of Romans 1–8 by identifying and analysing the enthymemes,
and then studying the larger argumentative sequences that they form. He
opts for a definition of enthymeme popular since late Antiquity and
predominant in modern times: it is a syllogism where one of the premises
is silent and can be teased out using rules of logic (pp. 33-37). Through his
application of this analytical approach, Moores demonstrates just how
puzzling Paul's method of deduction is. He is particularly helpful in
identifying factors woven into Paul's argumentation which render his
inferential patterns complex: creative theological leaps, metaphors,
eschatological thinking, the paradox of 'the already and the not yet',
among others. Moores is far more speculative (and less clear) when he
appeals to Umberto Eco's semiological theory of sign production to make
sense of Paul's allegedly obscure use of rational discourse for the expression of supernatural matters (pp. 5-10). One of Moores's key hypotheses is
that Paul uses demonstrative language to teach religious truths which do
not really depend on demonstrations (because their reliability is based on
spiritual experience), nor are modified in any way by them (rather, these
truths evolve over time through a somewhat independent process of sign
production). [4] For Paul, the value of argumentation lies not in proof, but
rather in its ability to *encourage* the addressee through an intellectually
positive formulation of the content of the faith (pp. 2, 159-60).

That same year appeared David Hellholm's 'Enthymemic Argumentation in Paul: The Case of Romans 6'. [5] In this highly technical article,

3.   J.D. Moores, *Wrestling with Rationality in Paul: Romans 1–8 in a New Perspective* (Cambridge: Cambridge University Press, 1995).

4.   Moores, *Wrestling with Rationality*, p. 28: 'My primary aim here in discussing
coding *levels* [provided by Eco's theory of sign production] is simply that of making
clearer what is involved in the choice of explanations that presented itself to us as we
reflected on that factor in Paul's discourse which is his confidence in the experiential
proof that his addressees had of the veracity of his doctrine'.

5.   D. Hellholm, 'Enthymemic Argumentation in Paul: The Case of Romans 6', in

tools from analytical philosophy, text-linguistics and Aristotle's theory of rhetorical argument are combined to study a perplexing argumentative passage. Hellholm emphasizes argumentative context: an enthymeme is not recognized first by any characteristic of its own; rather, it is through a detailed analysis of the argumentative structure of the entire passage (using an appropriate model of elaborated argument provided by classical rhetoric) that the position of enthymemes in the text is determined. For the analysis of arguments themselves, Hellholm essentially limits himself to Aristotle's theory of argumentation and typology of arguments and proofs (pp. 127, 132-38). He succeeds in providing an original and compelling understanding of this theologically difficult passage: the tour de force is perhaps the reading of Romans 6 no longer as a theological text about baptism, but as a defense of justification by faith, viewed as the *causa* of the entire epistle (pp. 139-41, 159). Meanwhile, two difficulties linked with Hellholm's methodological choices need to be addressed. For one, Hellholm focuses on a passage that appears to lend itself unusually well to an analysis through strict application of Aristotle's rhetorical theory. The prospect of extending the method to other texts remains problematic.[6] More importantly, the danger of circular reasoning is not fully avoided: Hellholm uses an Aristotelian analysis to prove that Paul uses an Aristotelian method of argumentation. For instance, it is through an application of ancient rhetorical theory that Rom. 6.2 is construed as a *testimonium*. It is then suggested that the warrant of the passage must contain traditional material (pp. 146-47). Later, Hellholm uses the result that Rom. 6.2 embodies an appeal to tradition to conclude that Paul 'adheres fully' to the rules of ancient rhetoric (pp. 176-79).

Others have felt the need to update the definition of the enthymeme. Vernon Robbins's recent 'From Enthymeme to Theology in Luke 11.1-13'[7] uses analytical tools provided by the pragmatist philosopher C.S.

T. Engberg-Pedersen (ed.), *Paul in his Hellenistic Context* (Minneapolis: Fortress Press, 1995), pp. 119-79.

6.   There is an absence of consensus among scholars that Aristotle's rhetorical views were well known in Paul's environment, let alone that Paul knew them well. Hellholm's heavily Aristotelian analysis and his conclusion that Paul followed the philosopher's rhetorical instruction closely ('Argumentation', pp. 176-78) collide with this uncertainty.

7.   V.K. Robbins, 'From Enthymeme to Theology in Luke 11.1-13', in R.P. Thompson and T.E. Phillips (eds.), *Literary Studies in Luke Acts: Essays in Honor of Joseph B. Tyson* (Macon, GA: Mercer University Press, 1998), pp. 191-214.

Peirce (end of the nineteenth century) to better understand the function of enthymemes in texts. This new strategy, which to be fair is still experimental, envisages only three types of enthymemes. They correspond to three types of syllogisms: the deductive, the inductive (these first two modes of reasoning are well known to classical rhetoric), and the abductive syllogism, which corresponds to a hypothetical and creative type of reasoning.[8] This is a welcome development because it surpasses the limited scope of understanding of 'real-life' micro-arguments offered by the simple deductive and inductive schemes. In particular, the concept of abductive enthymeme offers a promising avenue to the analysis of enthymemes which involves a 'creative leap' of reason. But one may wonder whether this new solution widens the scope sufficiently. The apparent assumption underlying the model is that all enthymemes are syllogisms and must be analyzed as such. This appears to preclude the possibility of other types of enthymemes which are not syllogistic, that is, which invite the listener to perform a mental step that is best described neither as a syllogism nor even as logical.

At another pole, voices are heard which either explicitly or implicitly

---

8.   Perhaps the easiest way to understand the difference between these types of argumentative steps is to consider simple examples of scientific reasoning. The *deductive* syllogism presents itself as a direct inference: 'This woman is pregnant, therefore she must have had intercourse with a man'; the conclusion (or *result*) flows out of necessity from the preceding premise, on the basis of an unexpressed universal premise (or *rule*): 'All women who are pregnant have had intercourse with a man'. The *inductive* syllogism reasons in the opposite direction: from a case and observed result (or preferably from a set of cases with identical results), one induces a universal rule: 'Patient A has chicken pox and is highly contagious, patient B also, patients C, D and E as well; therefore, any patient with chicken pox will be highly contagious.' Clearly, an induced conclusion is more probabilistic than a deduced one: the induced 'rule' will need to be confirmed by further tests. Finally, the *abductive* syllogism is hypothetical in nature: by means of an 'educated guess', the scientist will attempt to match an observed result with a known universal rule, in order to 'diagnose' the case which caused the result: 'This woman has stopped having her period; perhaps she is pregnant.' Since the rule is 'All pregnant women stop having their period', and not 'All women who stop having their period are pregnant', a deduction is not possible, but only an abduction which must be confirmed by further data. See Kraus, 'Enthymem', col. 1216; and R.L. Lanigan, 'From Enthymeme to Abduction: The Classical Law of Logic and the Postmodern Rule of Rhetoric', in L. Langsdorf and A.R. Smith (eds.), *Recovering Pragmatism's Voice: The Classical Tradition, Rorty, and the Philosophy of Communication* (Albany: State University of New York Press, 1995), pp. 49-70 (66, 68-69).

discourage the use of the enthymeme as a useful concept in New Testament rhetorical criticism. R. Dean Anderson Jr argues that Paul's micro-arguments are quite unlike those promoted by the rhetorical theories of his time.[9] The apostle's inferential passages are generally authoritarian (his arguments are not 'defended', but 'stated'; p. 252) and suppress too many steps. Thus they cannot be called enthymemes in the classical sense. Anderson's criticism of the too rigid application to the Pauline epistles of ancient rhetorical theories, with their particular understanding of argumentation and of enthymeme, holds something in common with another very different approach developed much earlier by F. Siegert in his *Argumentation bei Paulus*.[10] In this work, the idea that the enthymeme is the basic building block of argumentation is discarded (for reasons quite different than those of Anderson) in favor of a much larger selection of micro-building blocks provided by the contemporary rhetorical theory of the *New Rhetoric.*[11]

b. *Unresolved Issues*

While these studies and numerous others continue to shed light on New Testament argumentation, questions about which criteria to use to identify enthymemes in texts, about proper methods of analysis, and even about the very legitimacy of enthymematic analysis within rhetorical study, remain unanswered. It will be helpful at this point to propose a list of broad issues where considerable diversity or disagreement endures. (1) The *definition* of the enthymeme and its exact contours as a rhetorical and logical concept have varied considerably throughout history, and scholars today are unsure as to which one to opt for, or whether to craft a new definition from synthesis, or to discard the concept altogether. (2) *Identification* of enthymemes in a text struggles with the problem of criteria—are there any formal characteristics (either internal to the enthymeme or within the broader context) which indicate the presence of an enthymeme? Or must one look rather for something more abstract related to argumentative

9. R.D. Anderson, Jr, *Ancient Rhetorical Theory and Paul* (Kampen: Kok Pharos, 1996), pp. 140-41, also p. 202.

10. F. Siegert, *Argumentation bei Paulus: Gezeigt an Röm 9–11* (WUNT, 34; Tübingen: Mohr Siebeck, 1985), p. vii in particular, but also pp. 23-84, 119-80. The notion of enthymeme and closely related concepts are discussed, pp. 191-95.

11. C. Perelman and L. Olbrechts-Tyteca, *Traité de l'argumentation: La nouvelle rhétorique* (Brussels: Institut de Sociologie de L'Université Libre de Bruxelles, 2nd edn, 1970).

content? (3) Once an enthymeme has been pinpointed, what is the correct way to analyze it? There is considerable hesitation regarding *logical content and analysis*, with some scholars holding fast to the popular treatment of enthymemes as truncated categorical syllogisms, while others attempt to integrate other logical schemes.[12] (4) The enthymeme's *relation to argumentative context* may be given a central role in analysis (Hellholm's treatment of Rom. 6 offers a prime example of this; so does Robbins's study of Lk. 11.1-13 which sets the text against the grid of the elaborated *chreia*) or very little if the device is viewed as a micro-argument and building block for larger arguments which stands on its own. (5) What is the nature of the *information* that the unpacking of enthymemes provides to the exegete? Some will see it as a window onto the rhetorical training of the author, others will speak of argumentative technique, and yet others of shared rhetorical conventions and values within the particular speech community of author and audience.[13]

2. *Proposing a Solution*

The object of this study is to suggest a new approach to enthymeme analysis which aims to eliminate some of the problems mentioned above. As a first step, it appears necessary to find a solution to the difficult problem of *definition*. One way to do this is to suspend the question: rather than starting from a definition of enthymeme which defines the logical procedure involved in an exhaustive fashion would it not be preferable to adopt a broad 'rule of thumb' based on criteria of general textual form which says as little as possible about the logical or argumentative pattern

---

12. One example is Robbins's use of the Peircian triad of deduction, induction and abduction (see above). Another is Siegert's replacement of syllogistic analysis with the vast array of universal argument types developed by Perelman and Olbrechts-Tyteca. Yet another interesting approach is that of M. Angenot, *La parole pamphlétaire: Typologie des discours modernes* (Paris: Payot, 1982). For his analysis of nineteenth-century French polemical literature, he develops a new list of common topics (pp. 383-400). He defines the latter as universal patterns from which argumentative steps in discourses—what I am calling enthymemes—are built (pp. 161-62). In virtue of a principle of reciprocity, these topics are also to be used to analyze arguments. Angenot's inclusion of the categorical syllogism in the list of topics is significant (pp. 157-58). So is his view that it is rarely useful in the analysis of an enthymeme (p. 168).

13. Robbins, 'From Enthymeme to Theology', p. 192, for instance, shows how analysis of enthymemes can bring out the way in which the text 'enacts the social, cultural, and ideological context in which it was written'.

'behind' it? Once established, this rule can then be used as a 'net' to identify and gather various specimens of enthymemes in a text.

This 'rule of thumb' is not hard to find: few would disagree with Vernon Robbins's basic description of *the enthymeme as an assertion supported by another statement (or rationale)*.[14] This not only echoes the views of the ancient rhetors such as Quintilian (c. 95 CE),[15] but is also confirmed by the discriminating historical judgment of Kraus.[16]

a. *Advantages of the 'Rule of Thumb'*

The *advantages* of using a broad recognition rule as a 'fishing net', as opposed to a precise logical definition, are manifold. First, we are not permitting any particular understanding of the logical inner structure of the enthymeme (e.g. 'the enthymeme is a truncated categorical syllogism') to limit our catch. Rather, this approach allows the various samples of enthymemes found in the text to inform us of the diversity of possible logical or non-logical argumentative connections that can exist between statement and rationale.[17] This in turn removes the wall that separates the limited notion of enthymeme upheld by 'traditional' textbooks on argumentative logic[18] from the broad spectrum of micro-arguments that

---

14. V.K. Robbins, 'The Present and Future of Rhetorical Analysis', in S.E. Porter and T.H. Olbricht (eds.), *The Rhetorical Analysis of Scripture* (JSNTSup, 126; Sheffield: Sheffield Academic Press, 1997), pp. 24-52 (33). See also Robbins, 'From Enthymeme to Theology', p. 191: 'Rationales in discourse create enthymemes'.

15. One of Quintilian's definitions of enthymeme is a 'proposition with a reason' (*Or.* 5.10.1-2; 5.14.1, 24-25; LCL). There also exists an analogous statement in Aristotle, *Rhet.* 2.21.2: '…if the cause is added [to a maxim] and the reason, the whole is an enthymeme…'; Kennedy).

16. Kraus, 'Enthymem', col. 1197: 'One understands by [enthymeme] a densely formulated argument which seeks to confirm the truth of a proposition about a particular state of affairs through its deduction from another proposition which is universally recognized or hardly refutable.'

17. If the objective involves not only an analysis of enthymemes but also a clarification of the definition, the three steps of recognition, analysis and definition need to be as methodologically independent from one another as possible. Otherwise, the reasoning would become circular. For example, if I recognize as enthymemes only those passages that appear to function as truncated deductive syllogisms, and then, analyze them as such, chances are that my working hypothesis will be conveniently confirmed in the end: all these cases will show that an enthymeme is a truncated deductive syllogism.

18. See for example I.M. Copi, *Introduction to Logic* (New York: Macmillan, 1953), pp. 204-11; and P.J. Hurley, *A Concise Introduction to Logic* (Belmont, CA:

contemporary rhetorical theories are offering in its place.

Second, this rule permits one to look for enthymemes in any text type, and not only in argumentative texts. Intuitively, this makes sense: without contradicting the reality that sustained arguments remain the textual milieu par excellence where statements backed up by other statements can be found in great numbers, no one can deny that rationales exist (and may even abound) in stories, moral literature, poetry, prayers, etc. It is significant, for instance, that one of today's leading scholars in New Testament rhetorical analysis has recently turned to the analysis of enthymematic discourse in the gospel narratives.[19]

Third, this approach in no way betrays the fundamental idea so dear to classical rhetoric that the enthymeme involves something ἐν θυμῷ, 'in the mind'. After identifying an enthymeme using the rule of thumb, the implicit information needed to fill out the argumentative step will remain a central point of interest. The difference with other approaches is that this will be done with more flexibility of method on account of the anticipated diversity in persuasive structures.

b. *Analysis of Enthymemes: A Synthesis of Methods*
Biblical scholars have tended to limit the argumentative analysis of enthymemes to a single logical scheme, the categorical syllogism. What is proposed here is a methodology whereby an identified enthymematic form is studied against the grid of a variety of solution types before one is actually chosen (see Fig. 1).

The first step of the procedure (illustrated in the figure somewhat like a flowchart) is the recognition of an enthymeme within a text using the rule of thumb. Once a potential enthymeme is identified, different attempts at analysis can be undertaken. Attempted solutions can either be 'logical' in nature or related to 'perception of reality'.[20] These two terms will now be explained briefly.

Wadsworth, 5th edn, 1994), pp. 192, 245, 281.

19. Robbins, 'From Enthymeme to Theology', pp. 191-93.

20. The term 'perception of reality' is inspired by Perelman and Olbrechts-Tyteca, *Traité de l'argumentation*, p. 351: 'Les arguments fondés sur la structure du réel se servent de celle-ci pour établir une solidarité entre des jugements admis et d'autres qu'on cherche à promouvoir'. Also, the division of arguments into these two broad groups comes from Perelman and Olbrechts-Tyteca; beyond, I do not follow their typology of arguments closely.

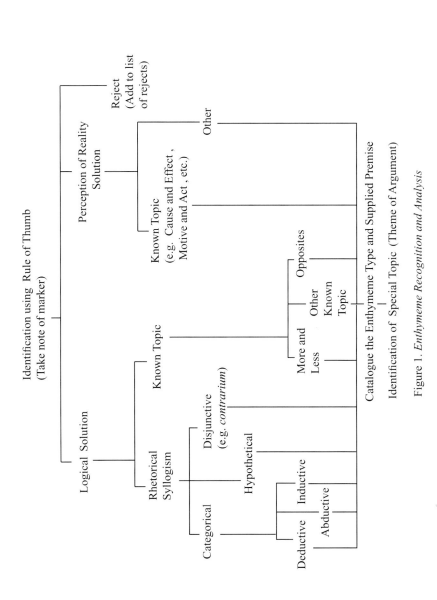

Figure 1. *Enthymeme Recognition and Analysis*

The *logical* solutions are the ones that are described by a logical or mathematical formula.[21] These include the various types of syllogisms: categorical (e.g. *all A are B, and C is A, therefore C is B*);[22] hypothetical (e.g. *if P then Q; now P; therefore Q*), and disjunctive (e.g. *either P or Q; but now P; therefore not Q*).[23] Other logical solutions are based on formulae which are not as logically 'tight' as syllogisms, but which function as 'logical likelihoods'. Two such formulae—or 'topics'[24]—famous for their widespread use in Antiquity and beyond appear in the flowchart of Figure I as examples: the topic *from opposites* (i.e. *if A is B, then presumably the negation/contrary of A is the negation/contrary of B*); and the topic *from the more and less* (i.e. *if A is B, then more of A is more B; or less of A is less B*).[25] This category is labelled 'Known Topic' in Figure 1.

The *perception of reality* solutions are based on formulae which do not embody logical relations, but relations of a looser nature. These relations reflect observations about the structure of reality which have become socially accepted judgments in a particular society, culture or language group, and for this reason can be used to construct arguments. Many are universal, such as the common topic of *cause and effect*: *if cause A is present, then its effect A' will also be present; if cause B does not exist, then there will be no effect*. Another example is the topic of *motive and action*: *if person A had no motive to perform act B, then A probably was not its author* (see Fig. 1). Many of the common topics catalogued in Aristotle's *Rhet.* 2.23 fall into this category. However, if the solution is

---

21. Perelman and Olbrechts-Tyteca, *Traité de l'argumentation*, p. 351, calls this type of argument 'quasi-logical', because its claim to rationality is based on a relation to the descriptive logical formula which is 'more or less strict'.

22. This is an example of a deductive categorical syllogism. For inductive and abductive syllogisms, see the discussion of Robbins's 'From Enthymeme to Theology' above.

23. This particular case of disjunctive syllogism was called a *contrarium* by Cicero (Kraus, 'Enthymem', cols. 1206-1207).

24. It is well known that throughout history the rhetorical term *topic* has been given a number of different definitions, to the point where even an individual author's usage may sway between one or more meanings (Aristotle is a prime example). For convenience, I will limit the use of the term *common topic* to indicate the abstract formula (based either on logic or on perception of reality) upon which an enthymeme's argument is constructed. I will use the term *special topic* for the 'theme' or 'subject matter' of this argument.

25. These two common topics can be found in Aristotle, *Rhet.* 2.23.1, 4.

perceived to be of this group but no previously catalogued form is recognized, the analyst may formulate the solution herself ('Other' under 'Perception of Reality' Solution, Fig. 1). This option is a way of keeping the method 'open': it permits the text itself to inform the analyst of 'unknown' topics that are perhaps rare, or specific to a particular author or group.

The procedure involves attempting a first solution using the most familiar formula, the categorical syllogism, and working one's way 'left' on the chart, to see whether any other description is preferable. One proceeds from the more logical solutions to the 'perception of reality' solutions. Whichever formula is chosen as the most fitting for this particular case is a decision left to the judgment of the analyst. It must be stressed that in analysis of enthymemes, one regularly encounters situations where more than one formula will 'work' in the sense of shedding at least partial light on the argumentative step and providing some form of silent premise needed to complete the thought.[26] The strategy involves opting for the formula which provides the *most satisfactory* missing premise and general solution (i.e. the one where the fourfold combination of statement, rationale, missing premise[27] and formula offers the greatest explanatory scope for the argumentative step within its wider discourse). The subjective element involved in the decision is not to be viewed as a problem but as the necessary reality that accompanies any form of interpretation. Tools (such as the methodological suggestions here) may be offered, but their fruitful use remains an art.[28]

26. For instance, experience shows that almost any enthymematic form can be analyzed as a categorical syllogism where a missing premise (usually the major, universal premise) can be teased out. But the question remains: is this analysis truly satisfactory, or can we do better? The possibility of multiple solutions is mentioned in Perelman and Olbrechts-Tyteca, *Traité de l'argumentation*, p. 307.

27. It must be remembered that part of the objective of enthymematic analysis is to recover silent premises which undergird the argumentation, in order to peer more deeply into the common ethos of author and audience. The logical rules to do this in the case of syllogistic enthymemes are well known; see for instance Copi, *Introduction to Logic*, pp. 187-207. For non-syllogistic enthymemes, the missing premise can be reconstructed by taking the formula (or common topic) and replacing the variables by the terms of the actual argument. It is important to formulate it in such a way that the specificity of the ideological import becomes clear; this process is described by G. Declercq, *L'art d'argumenter: Structures rhétoriques et littéraires* (Paris: Editions Universitaires, 1993), pp. 95-96.

28. Regarding the subjective element in argument analysis, see Hurley, *Concise Introduction to Logic*, pp. 15, 18, 282.

There will be cases where at first glance the rule of thumb will identify a passage that looks like an enthymeme, but no solution for it will be found. Among other possibilities, these situations include inferences which are so direct, so tautological, that there is really no 'in the mind' information that needs to be filled out, and therefore no analysis is necessary. In such cases, the enthymeme is compiled in a list of 'rejects' (see Fig. 1). Since the method is heuristic, there is a possibility that it has been prematurely discarded. The keeping of a list permits a later re-evaluation.[29]

Once an entire portion of text has be scanned and analyzed, the missing premises and argumentative formulae used can then be catalogged. The subject matter of the missing premises (I also call this the theme, or *special topic* of the argument) can be listed and grouped. The objective of these final steps is to generate an organized enthymematic database associated with the text. This database can be viewed as a new text, lying right below the surface of the written text and necessary to it, for it is part of the supporting structure of its argumentative layer.

3. *Philippians 1: An Experiment*

a. *Introduction*

Paul's epistles are an excellent place to test this kind of approach. For one thing, the Pauline letters are argumentative texts,[30] and hence one can expect to find many enthymemes embedded in the discourse. At the same time, any Pauline letter is composed of a variety of text types, some displaying a very strong argumentative component, others less so. The first chapter of the epistle to the Philippians, our sample text, has the advantage of displaying such a variety. The 28 verses following the opening address (vv. 1-2) can be divided into three main sections: the introductory prayer and thanksgiving (vv. 3-11), a theological interpretation of Paul's personal circumstances (vv. 12-26), and a pastoral exhortation (vv. 27-30). While none of these sections are argumentative in their primary intention, they

---

29. An example of this category of argument is Phil. 1.23b: 'My desire is to depart and be with Christ, for that is far better' (NRSV). The silent premise is a tautology: 'Anyone prefers what is preferable.' The absence of a true enthymeme seems to be confirmed by the hesitations of the textual variants, many of which omit the 'for' (γάρ). Alternatively, it could be argued upon re-evaluation that the silent premise, formulated slightly differently, contains a thought worth examining: 'Anyone prefers what is *better* (than their present state).'

30. Hellholm, 'Enthymemic Argumentation in Paul', p. 119.

all contain arguments. The number of enthymemes reflects this reality (I have found 7 in the prayer, 9 in the 'theological' section, and 3 in the exhortation, for a total of 19).

b. *Some Examples of Enthymeme Analysis*
Limitations of space do not permit the presentation of all 19 enthymemes with their analyses. The following is simply an illustration of how the method can be used. It consists of a sample of three studied enthymemes, one from each of the sections of Phil. 1.3-30.

1. The first example appears at the very beginning of Paul's opening prayer for the Philippians. This is an example of a enthymeme that can be analyzed syllogistically in a satisfactory manner:

> I thank my God every time I remember you... because of your sharing in the gospel from the first day until now. [FOR] I am confident of this, that the one who began a good work among you will bring it to completion by the day of Jesus Christ (Phil. 1.3-6; NRSV).

Here the preferred solution is a categorical deductive syllogism:

M   God brings to completion any good work that he begins among you [as believers].[31]

{m   Your sharing in the gospel from the first day until now is [clearly] a good work begun by God among you.}[32]

=>   [God will bring to completion your sharing in the gospel from the first day until now]. I thank my God every time I remember you... because of [it].

While there is nothing exotic about this solution, a few explanatory comments are in order. First, in syllogistic analysis not only does the silent premise have to be worked out (it is between the braces '{}' above), but prior to this the formulation of the expressed premises often needs reworking to bring out the force of the argument.[33] In this solution, both expressed premises are complemented with extra (understood) words in brackets, '[]'. In particular, the conclusion is elliptic and needs

31. Both in the biblical quotations and the solutions to the enthymemes, square brackets '[]' indicate something I felt necessary to add to the NRSV translation for clarity or completion.

32. Braces '{}' indicate the reconstituted suppressed premise.

33. Copi, *Introduction to Logic*, pp. 187-91; Hurley, *Concise Introduction to Logic*, pp. 281-85.

considerable 'filling out'. Second, unlike most enthymemes in ordinary discourse (Paul is no exception), this one is a second order enthymeme and not a first order, that is, it is not the major but the minor premise which is silent. In this particular case, Paul prefers to state the rationale by spelling out a universal principle in the form of a maxim (v. 6) rather than by alluding to this principle through a minor (particular) premise, perhaps because it is not well known to the audience. Third, the silent premise, 'Your sharing in the gospel from the first day until now is [clearly] a good work begun by God among you', powerfully brings together a belief about God's character—God finishes any good work he begins—and the religious experience of the Philippians, elevated to the status of a 'good work of God'. The special topic—or theme—from which Paul constructs the enthymeme is God's character. Fourth, the structural marker which indicated the presence of an enthymeme is the participle πεποιθώς ('For I am confident'), interpreted here as a causal. This illustrates the wide variety of grammatical markers which are used by Paul to introduce rationales. Furthermore, it witnesses to the interpretive component of enthymematic reading. This is a situation where the reader 'creates' the enthymeme by opting for the causal interpretation from a variety of options for participles. It is interesting in this respect that the NRSV chooses to minimize the argumentative element of the passage by omitting the conjunction 'for' in its translation. Fifth, the passage actually contains two 'rejects'. First, the phrase 'because of your sharing in the gospel (ἐπί + dative)' was considered as a possible rationale, but then discarded because its link with the verb 'to thank' is so direct that it functions as an object rather than a rationale. Second, the rationale statement 'the one who began a good work among you will bring it to completion' is actually a Pauline maxim and is itself supported by silent premises.[34] Paul (and probably his Philippian audience) are well aware of these premises, but they are out of our reach because of historical distance.

2. The next passage concludes the second section or 'theological reflection' (Phil. 1.12-26). Here is an example of an enthymeme for which a *topical* solution of the logical type is preferable:

> I know that I will remain and continue with all of you for your progress and joy in faith, SO THAT your boasting in Christ may abound through me when I return to you (Phil. 1.25b-26; NRSV modified).

---

34. Regarding the syllogistic 'filling out' of maxims, see Angenot, *La parole pamphlétaire*, p. 167; and Aristotle, *Rhet.* 2.21.2. For a similar treatment of modern publicity slogans, see Hurley, *Concise Introduction to Logic*, p. 284.

This micro-argument is best described by the common topic *from the more and the less*: if A is B, then 'more A' is 'more B'. In this case, A is the 'boasting in Christ' potentially caused by a future event, and B is God's willingness to make it happen for the sake of encouraging faith. It will be helpful to spell out the argument in a way similar to that of the previous example:

{SILENT PREMISE
    The MORE 'boasting in Christ' will be potentially caused by a future event, the MORE God is inclined to make it happen to encourage the faith of believers.}

m   Paul's return to the Philippians will cause 'boasting in Christ' not only to occur, but to 'abound' (περισσεύω).

=>   God[35] will cause Paul to remain and to return to the Philippians after his captivity.

Two important observations are to be made. First, the structural marker in this case is the conjunction ἵνα which introduces a purpose clause. Because they give the '*why*' of an action, thought, motive, and so on, purpose clauses usually have an *explicative* rather than *argumentative* function.[36] However, they can be re-expressed as arguments—as enthymemes—in some cases where there is an obvious attempt to prove the validity of an action, thought or motive by its purpose.[37] This passage is a case where the reader/listener is led to work out an argumentative connection 'in the mind' between action and purpose. Second, this is a situation where a syllogistic solution 'works', but is not satisfactory. The categorical syllogism which can be generated from this passage would look something like this:

{M   God intends to cause believers' faith to progress through specific joyful occasions which cause 'boasting in Christ' to abound.}

m   Paul's return to the Philippians will cause 'boasting in Christ' to abound among the Philippians.

=>   God intends to cause the Philippians faith to progress through Paul's return to them.

35. Since the purpose clause clearly expresses God's intention and not Paul's, it is imperative to include 'God' in the full argument.
36. Hurley, *Concise Introduction to Logic*, pp. 21-24.
37. Hurley, *Concise Introduction to Logic*, pp. 22-23.

The weakness of this syllogism is that it does not account for the quant-itative element evoked by the verb περισσεύω, which adds a *comparative* component to the argument.

   3. The final example is taken from the exhortative unit of 1.27-30:

> Only, live a life (πολιτεύεσθε) in a manner worthy of the gospel of Christ, SO THAT, whether I come and see you or am absent and hear about you, I will know that you are standing firm in one spirit, striving side by side with one mind for the faith of the gospel, and are in no way intimidated by your opponents (Phil. 1.27; NRSV).

This is an instance of the common topic *from the parts to the whole*, catalogued in *On Rhetoric* 2.23.13 as well as by Perelman and Olbrechts-Tyteca.[38] It can be formulated thus: for a condition X to be true for all of Y, it has to be true for all the parts (Y1, Y2, Y3, etc.) of Y. In this case:

> X is Paul's assurance that the Philippians are standing firm together in the faith;
> Y is the life of the Philippian community as perceived by Paul;
> Y1 is that part of life when Paul is present with the Philippians;
> Y2 is when Paul is absent;
> The argumentative force of the rationale relies on the 'spelling out' by Paul that Y = Y1 + Y2. In other words, Paul discloses the key to providing him with the assurance he seeks by breaking down the apostle/church relationship into its two component parts (or modes).

The following points are significant in terms of the ideological import that Paul brings to the bare formula behind the argument. First, the persuasive force of the rationale comes from Paul's emphasis on his own perception of the Philippians. Second, his perception of the Philippians' existence is *binary*: when he is present, when he is absent. Interestingly, he is inviting the Philippians not only to understand their own existence in such a way, but to consider his own existence in the same way (1.30b). Third, Paul selects the verb πολιτεύομαι ('to live as a citizen') to express a 'way of being' which will cover both these parts of the addressees' religious life. Through this term Paul appears to be borrowing from Greco-Roman moralistic teaching to invite the Philippians to live out their spiritual struggle with a consistency like that of ideal citizens faithful to their state.

---

   38. Perelman and Olbrechts-Tyteca, *Traité de l'argumentation*, pp. 315-25.

4. *Results*

a. *Some General Statistics*

A total of 25 passages in Phil. 1.3-30 were identified by the rule of thumb as potential enthymemes. Of these 25, 19 were 'solved' and 6 were placed in the 'reject' list. Of the 19 solved, 13 were treated as syllogisms of various types, and 6 were solved topically (3 with a 'logical' formula, 3 with 'perception of reality' patterns). Of the 13 syllogisms, 11 were 'categorical deductive', one was treated as an abduction (Phil. 1.22-25), and one as a disjunctive syllogism (Phil. 1.19-20).

Also of interest is the distribution of syntactic markers which triggered the recognition of the rationale statements:

γάρ	3
ὅτι	1
διό	0
οὖν	0
participle	7
relative pronoun	0
ἵνα final/purpose clause	3
ὥστε result clause	1
other preposition	2
infinitive clause	1
other[39]	1
TOTAL	19

For the 'rejected' texts, the distribution of markers is as follows:

γάρ	1
ὅτι	0
διό	0
οὖν	0
participle	0
relative pronoun	1
ἵνα final/purpose clause	1
ὥστε result clause	0
other preposition	1
infinitive clause	0
other	2
TOTAL	6

39. Included in 'other' are enthymemes where there is no obvious syntactic marker. For example, there are enthymemes where the rationale follows an assertion after a punctuation mark (in the modern Greek text).

The various reasons invoked for discarding are listed in the following table:

Argument too unclear	1
Tautological argument	2
Only an apparent rationale	1
Maxim with rationale absent	1
Interpretive option	1
TOTAL	6

b. *The Silent Premises: A Text beneath the Text*
What follows is the collection of silent premises teased out of the enthy-memes of Philippians 1, using the techniques described in Part 2. The nature of this list is ambiguous. On the one hand, it can be viewed as 'another text' since it is composed of material unsaid by the explicit text. On the other hand, because it supports the argumentative strand of the visible text, it does not lie deep below its surface. It is part of the 'literality' of the text, in the sense that the text's intelligibility depends on its component statements.[40] The approach differs then from other herm-eneutical strategies which seek to go *deep* under the surface text to recover a *repressed* sub-text, such as with certain psychoanalytic or political readings.[41] However, compared with such deep readings, it carries the advantage of a higher degree of methodological control.

Unexpressed premises for enthymemes in Philippians 1.3-30:

{m   Your sharing in the gospel from the first day until now is [clearly] a good work begun by God among you} (1.3-6).

{Topical premise:
It is proper to add to the *thought* of thankfulness to God for someone the *action* of prayer for them} (1.7, 9).

{M   It is right (δίκαιον) for me to think this way—that is, thank God for you, pray for you, and be confident that God will complete your salvation—regarding anyone who holds me in his/her heart} (1.7).

40. Angenot, *La parole pamphlétaire*, pp. 183-84.
41. Angenot, *La parole pamphlétaire*, pp. 183-86.

{M   Anyone who shares in God's grace for me, both in my imprison-
        ment and in the defense and confirmation of the gospel, holds me
        in his/her heart} (1.7b).

{Topical premise:
        If God is a witness to what I am telling you, then it is true.} (1.8).

{{M   Anyone who loves Christ wants to be pure and blameless on the
         Day of Christ}} (1.9-10).

{M   All those whose love abounds in knowledge and full insight for
        determining what is best will certainly be pure and blameless for
        the day of Christ} (1.9-10).

{M   Anyone that will have produced the harvest of righteousness that
        comes through Christ for the glory and praise of God will be
        pure and blameless for the day of Christ} (1.10-11).

{M   Anything—even a personal calamity—that becomes widely
        known among outsiders as being 'for Christ' actually helps
        spread the gospel} (1.12-14).

{M   Anything—even a personal calamity—that makes the brothers
        confident to speak the word boldly and without fear actually
        helps the spread of the gospel} (1.12-14).

{Topical premise:
        The action of proclaiming Christ is desirable to such an extent
        that motives for doing it lose their importance} (1.15-18).

{M   All preachers who really believe that I have been appointed by
        God for the defense of the gospel proclaim Christ out of love for
        me (and not with a desire to hurt me) while I am in prison}
        (1.16).

{M   Anyone who proclaims Christ with the intent to hurt me is not
        preaching Christ sincerely but out of selfish ambition} (1.17).

{M   I will rejoice about anything—even bad in appearance—that
        brings about salvation} (1.18b-19).

{Silent premise, disjunctive syllogism:
        An event becomes a channel of salvation when it causes Christ to
        be exalted in one's body, but not when it puts one to shame

(or alternately: Any event which causes Christ to be exalted…is a channel
        of salvation, whereas one that brings shame does not).} (1.19-20).

{M   In any sphere of personal existence which is 'in Christ', Christ will be glorified in the physical body} (1.20-21).

{M   Whatever happens in the future of God's servant is what God deems preferable for the church, not what the servant prefers for himself} (1.22-25).

{Topical premise:
       The MORE 'boasting in Christ' will be potentially caused by a future event, the MORE God is inclined to make it happen to encourage the faith of believers} (1.25b-26).

{Topical premise:
       If Paul is to be assured that the Philippians are standing firm in faith in their *entire* existence, it must be so for its *two moments*: when Paul is present with them, and when he is not} (1.27).

{M   Any situation where the experience of *suffering for Christ* is added to that of *faith in Christ* is God's doing} (1.28b-29).

{Topical premise:
       Your (the Philippians') struggle is similar to mine (Paul's), which is paradigmatic of God's gift of 'suffering for Christ'} (1.29-30).

c. *Common Topics*
I have named *common topics* the formulae (logical or stemming from perception of reality) which describe the inferential step of enthymemes. Outside of those formulae which can be called syllogisms and which have already been described, here are the six other common topics encountered in Philippians 1:

1.   *Properness of matching a thought with a corresponding action*: here the *thought* is thankfulness to God for the Philippians; the *action* is prayer for their spiritual maturation (1.7, 9; 'perception of reality' topic).
2.   *Warrant from Paul's own spiritual authority ('God is my witness')*. Paul is attesting to the sincerity of his expressed feelings and commitment of love by appeal to a testimony of God (1.8; 'perception of reality' topic).
3.   *Relativization of the motive*: if an action Y (with its result Y') is morally desirable, then its motive X becomes a minor concern (1.15-18; 'perception of reality' topic).

4. The *more and the less*: if A is B, then 'more A' is 'more B' (1.25b-26; logical topic).
5. From the *parts to the whole*, catalogued by Aristotle in *On Rhetoric* 2.23.13. It can be formulated thus: for a condition X to be true for all of Y, it has to be true for all the parts (Y1, Y2, Y3, etc.) of Y (1.27; logical topic).
6. The topic *from induction*: X is Y, because in another similar (or paradigmatic) situation X' was Y (1.29-30; logical topic).

d. *Special Topics*
I have linked the term *special topic* to the subject matter (or themes) from which Paul draws the premises of his enthymemes. Here are the special topics of the 19 enthymematic passages considered in Philippians 1:

— God's character (1.3-6)
— proper action (universal ethics) (1.7, 9)
— proper action (universal ethics) (1.7)
— universal proof of friendship (1.7b)
— God's authority (1.8)
— eschatological hopes (1.9-10)
— eschatological hopes (1.10-11)
— Christian worldview—how to view calamities (1.12-14)
— the highest value—the spread of the gospel (1.15-18)
— power hierarchy in the Pauline movement (1.16)
— power hierarchy in the Pauline movement (1.17)
— eschatological hope and its bearing on hierarchy of values (1.18b-19)
— salvation (1.19-20)
— God's faithfulness/eschatological hope (1.20-21)
— God's providence (1.22-25)
— God's character (1.25b-26)
— ways of understanding the apostle/church relationship (1.27)
— legitimation of something through 'divine origin' (1.28b-29)
— the paradigmatic experience of an apostle (1.29-30).

5. *Concluding Remarks*

Obviously, the short length of the sample text makes conclusions about Paul's use of enthymemes seem premature. Nonetheless, the 'test run' provokes reflections on the method itself. In conclusion I should like to mention briefly some of the points that appear important to me.

I will begin with two practical observations: first, when studying enthymemes in a text it quickly becomes obvious that 'logic' is only one component of an enthymeme. Another component fundamental to rhetoric is style. Because of style, which modulates textual form according to its own rules, the direct relation between *form* of an enthymeme and underlying *logic* is a very complex matter which cannot easily be sorted out. For instance, there appears to be little or no correlation between the supporting common topic/formula and the syntactic marker introducing the rationale statement. Second, the exercise inevitably makes one aware of the trade-off between the broadness of the rule of thumb and the vastness of the task: the broader the rule, the more candidate passages there are to examine (I isolated 25 passages in a single, non-argumentative chapter), and the higher the risk of ending up with an unclear profile of what characterizes the group of texts called 'Pauline enthymemes'. Put in different terms, it would be interesting to repeat this study of Philippians 1 using somewhat stricter criteria for recognition, to see what effect this would have on the results.

Finally, two brief theoretical considerations. First, what is the relation of this type of analysis to rhetorical criticism? Certain aspects of the method limit the relation to a tangential one. For one thing, the scope of investigation is limited to a single rhetorical device. Furthermore, if it is compared to other studies where the use of a specific tool, such as rhetorical maxims,[42] is studied, it becomes clear that enthymemes are a rhetorical device of a unique nature. Enthymemes are not only valued by rhetors, but are actually built into the grammatical structure of language. Enthymeme is the rhetorical device lying closest to the hazy border between rhetoric and grammar. For this reason, enthymematic analysis is as syntactic as it is rhetorical. Second, this approach is not per se a rhetorical study of enthymemes (as the two studies of New Testament maxims mentioned in n. 42 are rhetorical analyses of maxims), but rather it proposes a way

---

42. See in particular R.A. Ramsaran, *Liberating Words: Paul's Use of Rhetorical Maxims in 1 Corinthians 1–10* (Valley Forge, PA: Trinity Press International, 1996), who tackles Paul's rhetoric from the particular angle of his use of maxims. Also I.H. Henderson, *Jesus, Rhetoric and Law* (BIS, 20; Leiden: E.J. Brill, 1996), who approaches the historical Jesus by tracing gospel maxims through tradition history. Both these studies have in common the working out of a clear rhetorical definition of maxim before text analysis.

to read texts enthymematically. It permits the reader to go through a discourse looking for possible combinations of affirmations and rationales, and posing the question: would this pair of statements be best understood as an enthymeme? Would their relation be best appreciated as argument-ative? It is only later, when trial and error have led to a clear definition, that confident rhetorical study of enthymemes may be attempted.

A FANTASY THEME ANALYSIS OF 1 THESSALONIANS[*]

James D. Hester

1. *Introduction*

In previous work on 1 Thessalonians, I have analyzed it using, on the one hand, topics from the classical rhetorical genre of the funeral oration and, on the other, a version of Johannes Vorster's 'Interactional Model' (Vorster 1990), which I modified by making more direct use of Bitzer's functionalist criticism and Perelman's concept of the 'universal audience'. (Hester 1996, 1998) In this essay I want to describe the rhetorical-critical method called Fantasy Theme Analysis (FTA), provide a brief account of 1 Thessalonians produced by its application,[1] and finally comment on some specific examples of pragmatic expressions of Paul's *paideia*[2] found in the letter that derive from his rhetorical vision.[3]

---

*   I want to thank Professor Ernest Bormann for careful criticism of an earlier draft of this paper. His comments were very helpful, but I bear responsibility for the analysis and arguments made.

1.   As far as I can determine, this paper represents the first attempt to use this analytical method on a biblical text.

2.   In a series of communications Anders Erikkson has asked me to explain more directly what I mean by 'Christian *paideia*'. In general I mean that body of tradition, and the teaching that derives from it, that defines the topography of the world that Christians created from the experience of belief. *Paideia* is both definitional and contextual. It has heuristic value in that it guides the Christian to new insights into the meaning and function of faith, but that discovery is conditioned by the social world of the believer.

3.   In an essay he wrote for Petr Pokorný's festschrift, Vernon Robbins has pointed out that in 1 Thess. 1–3, Paul seems to be using a story line that has three elements to it: rejection, imitation and glory. I was delighted to encounter this observation because it was analogous to the major fantasy themes that I had identified in work I was doing on a fantasy theme analysis of the letter. It also suggested to me that Robbins's socio-rhetorical analysis and my own work were converging. That was reinforced for me when I read David deSilva's socio-rhetorical study of honor discourse in

2. *Fantasy Theme Analysis (FTA) and*
Symbolic Convergence Theory (SCT)

Fantasy Theme Analysis emerged from a series of seminars conducted by Ernest G. Bormann at the University of Minnesota in which small group communication was studied. It was first described by Bormann in an article published in 1972 and refined over time by him, his students and colleagues. It developed a technical vocabulary, the major terms of which are listed in the glossary below, to help the critic describe analyses of shared fantasies that Bormann claims are embedded in public discourse about experiences or events that some group finds unconventional, chaotic, or otherwise conflicts with their world-view or self-understanding. Ultimately it developed a theoretical model, Symbolic Convergence Theory, to help guide studies of empirical data.

SCT seems to share some conceptual perspectives with Kenneth Burke's 'Dramatistic Criticism'. Burke's rhetorical theory emphasized not the classic canons of rhetoric—invention, arrangement, style, memory and delivery—but the dramatic pentad of 'what' (act), 'where' (scene), 'who' (agent), 'how' (agency), and 'why' (purpose) (Burke 1969: xv). His system is intended to provide a critic with a method for analyzing 'human symbolic interaction', allowing a critic 'to analyze the reality experienced by different rhetors' (Burgchardt 1995: 205).

SCT has concepts analogous to these in that fantasy themes have characters, scenarios, scenes and sanctioning agents (Cragan and Shields 1981: 6-7, 9). But Bormann was influenced in its development by social-scientific research, and in particular the work of Robert Bales who studied the ways in which small groups create 'dramas' that then function as social reality for them. Bormann, modifying Bales's work in part by moving away from its Freudian-based analysis, argued that small group fantasies 'chain out' not just among members of the group but indeed into larger segments of society, modifying their behavior as well (Bormann 1972: 398-99). Proponents claim that SCT is able to provide a kind of explanation of why people behave in the ways they do (Cragan and Shields 1981: 7).

1 Thessalonians, in which he refers to 'the group's counter-definitions of reality (including its evaluation of outsiders)' (deSilva 1996: 57). Throughout the study deSilva refers to Paul's concern for group maintenance, using honor/shame discourse, by defining group boundaries, one of the points FTA also identifies.

SCT is a general theory of communication[4] that provides an account of the formation of group consciousness through the use by the group of imaginative language that creates for it a shared sense of reality. It assumes that rhetoric can be epistemic and that, because it is, it can help an individual make sense of a world that may be for him or her chaotic, even hostile and threatening. It also assumes that the rhetoric of an individual can be shared and 'chained out' in a process of communication within a group that produces a 'convergence' or overlapping of private symbolic worlds so that a common consciousness or a shared reality emerges.[5] A group of individuals finds ways of talking about attitudes or emotions they have shared in response to some person or event. They produce 'fantasies', not figments of imagination but imaginative inter-pretations of events that have occurred in a particular time and place. These fantasies use metaphorical or other forms of 'insider' language that 'interprets events in the past, envisions events in the future, or depicts current events that are removed in time and/or space from the actual activities of the group' (Foss 1989: 290). Fantasy themes constitute the story that is the reality for the group and form the basis for discursive argument.

In SCT, the story is called a 'dramatizing message'. It is possible to understand the dramatizing message as a kind of rhetorical artifact produced by the speaker that is adapted by the audience's experience. Set somewhere other than the here and now, it references people involved in a

---

4.   Bormann is careful to distinguish between 'special theory', which he understands as useful in explaining how to conduct communication within the constraints of a certain time and place, and 'general theory' (Bormann 1990: 3-5). 'General theory' he defines as being able to account for 'broad classes of events' and 'tendencies in human communications events that cannot be ignored or rescinded by the participants' (Bormann, Cragan and Shields 1994: 266). In other words, special theories deal with communication events in which models for communication are mutually agreed upon but could be ignored by some participants; general theories explain what happened in the past; they may have predictive value as well.

5.   Cragan and Shields (1992: 200) list six epistemological assumptions that undergird SCT: 'Meaning, emotions, and motive for action are in the manifest content of a message; Reality is created symbolically; Fantasy theme chaining creates symbolic convergence that is dramatistic in form; Fantasy theme analysis is the basic method to capture symbolic reality; Fantasy themes occur and chainout from all discourse; At least three master analogues—righteous, social, and pragmatic—compete as alternative explanations of symbolic reality.'

dramatic situation. Using metaphors, analogies, puns, allegories, anecdotes, narratives and other imaginative language, it describes some past conflict or envisions some future conflict and interprets them so that they make sense to the group (Bormann 1983a: 434). The message is a possible trigger for the production of fantasy sharing. Hearing the story, group members share their experiences and a common interpretation of what happened emerges.

The content of these messages is made up of fantasy themes. Themes grow out of the phenomenon of group sharing and reflect group consciousness. They are orderly, shared interpretations of an experience that allow members to talk with one another about a shared experience. The language of fantasy themes characterizes the event or experience, giving it a 'spin' that allows members of the group to account for differing perceptions of what happened (Bormann 1990: 107). They use insider references, or 'symbolic cues', that can cause emotional response to that experience. They can also be an inventional source for the group. They can be repeated in a variety of dramatizing messages and function in part to remind the group of its common history, and they allow the group to integrate new experiences into that history. Themes help dramatizing messages refresh group consciousness.

Fantasy themes can be organized under fantasy types, which are general scenarios, reference to which can help explain or interpret new experiences. Stock scenarios and generalized persona are synthesized from various themes shared by the group. Rather than referencing specific actions or experiences of characters, they contain a general plot and tend to depend more heavily on inside cues or symbolic language (Bormann 1986: 227-28). Because they assume familiarity with shared fantasies, types undergird the group culture. In conventional terms, it is within fantasy types that commonplaces are found.

And, finally, fantasy themes and types can be organized into a larger rhetorical vision, a coherent vision of social reality that can be conjured by the use of key words or slogans (Bormann, Cragan, and Shields 1994: 281). A group's rhetorical vision provides a 'common set of assumptions about the nature and reality of proof' that is necessary for discursive argument. Evidence need not be tied to empirical experience, or even dialectic, but can be based on such things as 'revelation', as Bormann has shown was true for the Puritans (Bormann 1985).

SCT moves the locus of invention from an individual speaker, and his or her resources, to the group. While it is true that an individual can be charismatic enough to guide the process of chaining out a group's fantasies through the expression of a single powerful rhetorical vision, one individual's vision will not typically dominate over time if group consciousness is raised high enough (Bormann 1990: 111-12). Furthermore, in SCT the focus of attention moves from the speaker to the message. It is the message, not the messenger, that expresses reality for the group (Cragan 1975: 5). Finally, SCT can help explain the processes of the development of group consciousness and the creation of a rhetorical community whose members share a common rhetorical vision. It can provide an explanation for how a socially constructed view of reality comes to be shared by an ever larger group of people until that view and the rhetorical vision that sustains it adapts or no longer expresses the group's understanding of the world (Bormann 1989: 189; Bormann, Cragan and Shields 1996: 24).

SCT posits that the social reality constructed by the group not only allows for discursive argument within the group but also can be a source of motivation for action (Bormann 1982b: 289, 304). Margaret Duffy's study of the political campaign to get approval for the institution of riverboat gambling in the conservative political environment of the state of Iowa demonstrates how fantasies were used to direct the actions of the competing groups in that campaign (Duffy 1997).

Finally, an FTA of the rhetoric, or public discourse, of a group may allow the critic to anticipate the behavior of a group (Bormann 1982b: 304; Cragan and Shields 1981: 10). For example, an analysis of a group's rhetorical vision could suggest at what stage the social reality of the group finds itself—consciousness creating, consciousness raising or consciousness sustaining—and therefore predict the viability of the vision for maintaining the group's definition of reality and anticipate actions by the group to make changes in the vision in order to cope with new experiences or events (Bormann, Cragan and Shields 1996).

3. *An FTA of 1 Thessalonians*

Because of the focus of this essay, I will not recount generally held scholarly opinions on the occasion and epistolography of the letter, nor will I comment on matters like particular issues of forms or word usage, unless, of course, they bear directly on the development of fantasy themes or dramatizing messages found in the letter. Those kinds of things can be reviewed in the body of literature that uses conventional methods of interpretation to analyze the letter.[6] Reference to representative literature can be found in the bibliography below.

Bormann has argued that there are 'three phases to the development and continuance of a rhetorical vision: (a) consciousness creating, (b) consciousness raising, and (c) consciousness sustaining' (Bormann 1982c: 58). Without summarizing the features of all three, I will focus on the last.

The final stage of the life cycle of a rhetorical vision is a period of consciousness sustaining. This stage deals with keeping those who have been converted to a rhetorical vision committed to that vision. Things have happened in the life of the group that have affected the commitment of its members and may have even caused some to leave the group for another rhetorical vision (Bormann 1982c: 58-59). This is the communications challenge the proponents face. If the rhetorical vision is flexible enough, symbolic fantasies can be reconstructed using new characters, plot lines, and scenes (Bormann, Cragan and Shields 1996: 13). If not, little or no accommodation to change features of the rhetorical vision to deal with changes in the world around a group is made, and the predominant rhetorical strategy is preservation.

It is my contention that in 1 Thessalonians Paul is engaged in sustaining the consciousness of the group by reminding them of his persona while with them and exhorting them to continue their imitative behavior, and by providing them with new details of his fantasy. Exhortation includes appeals to chain out what they already know and integrate the new explanations of certain fantasy themes into their sharing. At the end of the letter, the exhortation to have it read to others serves to enlarge the group through sharing what Paul says in the letter, thus inviting others to respond and contribute to the process of shaping the group's consciousness. There is no indication that Paul has in mind creating a new group consciousness. The explicit references to insider status and persecution by outsiders requires that his intent be understood as keeping the group together and committed to his rhetorical vision.

There appear to be three major fantasy themes in the letter: imitation of persons crucial to the life of the community (1.5-6; 2.4, 14), persecution that resulted from that behavior (1.6; 2.2, 14-16, 18; 3.3, 7), and vindication in the form of glorification that will come if the Thessalonians remain faithful and persist in that behavior (1.10; 3.13; 4.6, 13; 5.1-9, 23).

---

6.   A survey of recent scholarship done by Raymond Collins (Collins 1984: 3-75) was partially updated by Earl Richard in 1990 (Richard 1990).

These three themes converge through the sharing of a dramatizing message that has as its major characters God, Paul, the Thessalonians, and the outsiders who persecute the believers. The rhetorical vision that informs the message is both reviewed and elaborated upon in the first three chapters of the letter.

The rhetorical vision is sketched out in the thanksgiving section (1.2-10).[7] All the fantasy themes are found here, as are references to the sanctioning agent, the important scenes, the major characters, and the important actions of the drama. Found also are the topics[8] of love, faith, hope and knowing, all of which appear, and upon which he elaborates, in the narrative found in chs. 2 and 3. These topics should also be understood as 'inside cues', references to past actions performed by the Thessalonians designed to enable them to recall their responses when they first heard, and then chained out, the drama told to them by Paul. Their function as cues is underlined by Paul's use of the topos of 'remembering' to introduce the past actions of the 'work of faith' and 'labor of love' performed by the Thessalonians.

The topos of 'knowing'[9] is used to indicate to the Thessalonians that Paul recognized their 'election' by God, thus their status as 'insiders'. It is also used to remind the reader of the kind of character Paul manifested while with them, a topic that will become the focus of the narrative later. His character is a reflection of his persona, which is typically created by shared fantasies. The narrative will depend on fantasy sharing to remind them of Paul's persona in the group and not some other persona that might have been created by others.

The 'sanctioning agent' is identified as the 'message' or 'word' which the Thessalonians received 'in power and in the Holy Spirit' (1.5). Its authority is manifest in the character of Paul and those who imitate him, the audience itself! The dramatizing story is set in a general sense within the ministry of Paul, with scenes in this particular 'drama' being set in Philippi and Thessalonica where affliction and persecution have been

---

7.   I do not accept the analysis of those who argue that the thanksgiving period must continue through 3.10 because of the presence of 'thanksgiving' language in 2.13 and 3.9. The function of that language is different from that found in the conventional Pauline thanksgiving, which is quite nicely reflected in 1.2-10.

8.   I am using the word 'topics' here in the sense conventionally understood as those subject matters that will be reviewed in the body of the letter.

9.   Although it might be self-evident, I want to indicate here that I include in this topos references to prior instruction (4.2, 9; 5.1) received by the Thessalonians.

experienced and where, in Thessalonica, the actions of Paul, his companions and the Thessalonian believers have taken place. Furthermore, the goal of the drama, vindication found in glorification, closes out the section.

A narrative is begun at 2.1, and continues through 3.6, describing past experiences. By the use of insider cues, and symbolic words and phrases (gospel, apostles, witness, word of God, kingdom, glory, church, wrath, joy, faith, love), reference to both insiders (Thessalonians, Paul, Timothy, God, Lord) and outsiders (generic 'men', countrymen, Jews, Satan, Gentiles who do not know God), and by use of figures of speech such as analogies (2.3-5, 6-8, 11-12) and anecdotes (3.1-3, 6) Paul's dramatistic rhetoric provided an interpretation for those who shared the fantasy of their shared experiences, and reminded them of that shared reality. A recounting of this shared history is designed to trigger an emotional recall of those times and lay the foundation for further sharing of fantasies and chaining out of group experiences. This would in turn strengthen their faith—that is certainly Paul's expectation as made evident in chs. 4 and 5—and help to sustain group consciousness.

Motives for action embedded in the vision include the receipt by the Thessalonians of the gospel in 'power' and imitation of the ministry of Paul in Macedonia by the Thessalonians in the thanksgiving section. They are illustrated by a narrative portraying Paul's own actions while he ministered to the Thessalonians (2.1-12) and explaining Paul's behavior while absent from them (2.17–3.6). These are all illustrations from the past, based on what the Thessalonians who shared the fantasies comprising the rhetorical vision already 'know' (2.1. 2, 5, 11) and 'remember' (2.9) about the topics of love and faithfulness. They may be designed to illicit from the hearers of the letter additional reports of experiences that would add to the fantasy chain, thus also contributing to his goal of sustaining their group consciousness. In this context 'knowing' is not just a matter of being familiar with the content of the gospel message but, as importantly, with the behavior of those who carried it.[10]

---

10. From the point of view of FTA, there is no need to argue that in 2.1-10 Paul is answering charges made by opponents. He uses his story to dramatize the theme of rejection. The character of his 'insider' persona—courageous, honest, sincere, humble, nurturing, hardworking, blameless—is what the Thessalonians are to imitate regardless of the circumstance of persecution. The narrative of his work among them reinforces the new reality of being chosen and reminds them that the experience of being caricatured, ridiculed, and hampered in the work of the gospel is the lot of Christians.

The topos of thanksgiving found in 2.13 introduces in the midst of the narrative an inside cue triggering the theme of imitation (2.14-16), which in turn serves to reinforce the exhortation to particular kinds of action that will come in the pragmatic expression of the rhetorical vision that is elaborated in chs. 4 and 5. In this section, however, Paul reminds the Thessalonians that the vision they share incorporates the same fantasies that motivated the Judean churches and caused Jesus, them and Paul to be persecuted. The reference to the 'Jews' here should be understood as a personification of the 'outsider' who as such faces the wrath of God. The rhetorical vision that Paul shares, is found in expressions of escape from the wrath to come, from which the outsiders will not escape (2.16), and glorification upon the return of the Lord and the resurrection of believers.

Persecution is the social/political expression of the theme of rejection. One of its consequences has been the enforced separation of Paul from the church. This separation is an aspect of persecution because it has prevented Paul from sharing with them all they need to know of his *paideia*, causing him to send Timothy in his place and leaving him with hope that he can return some day to finish the job (3.10). In 2.18, we find another personification of a persecutor, Satan, who is identified as the one preventing Paul from doing his work, just as the Thessalonians' fellow-countrymen and the Jews had interfered with the spreading of the gospel.

However, this story of separation provides Paul with the opportunity to illustrate the theme of imitation once more. He reminds them in 3.2 that he has not abandoned them but provided for their spiritual welfare by sending Timothy, not only giving Paul the opportunity to check up on them (3.5), but also to give them an example of just how Paul 'abounds' in love for them (3.12). This is another place where Paul uses a narrative to provide background for the pragmatic expression of his rhetorical vision.

The plot line in the narrative deals with the redefinition of Paul's persona. Reference in 2.7 to some sort of rights that he might have exercised as an 'apostle', followed by reminders of his humility and tenderness among them, suggests that he made use of a public persona in his ministry to outsiders but acted differently when he was among them privately. Throughout the narrative he may have been reminding the Thessalonians not to confuse the two persona because it is the private

Best (1972: 16-22) reviews the discussions concerning the presence of opponents in Thessalonica. For recent studies reviewing the arguments for and against understanding 2.1-12 as an apostolic apology and offering alternatives to that understanding, see Walton (1995), Weima (1997), and Winter (1993).

person whom they are to imitate in their dealings with one another. The apostolic persona emerges in the pragmatic teaching in chs. 4 and 5.

By the end of the narrative it is clear that Paul is arguing that the basis of reality for the believer is not found in the world of persecution and death but in the faithfulness of God who empowers the message of Paul and his companions through the power of the Spirit. As will be made clear in the particulars of the pragmatic expression of this vision, the embattled yet faithful and loving believer, who lives with the Lord in the Spirit now, will, at a time known only to God, be joined by other Christians to meet the Lord Jesus and live with him forever. This is the vision that should sustain them.

4. *The Pragmatic Expression of Vision*

The pragmatic dimension of Paul's rhetorical vision is laid out in chs. 4 and 5, typically described as paraenetic in content. It is here that the motives for the rhetorical vision surface most clearly: on the one hand, faithful maintenance of 'insider morality' not only aids in proper personal and interpersonal relations but also prepares the believer to meet the Lord. On the other, understanding of Christian *paideia* arms the believer with the tools for successfully dealing with the outside world.

It is interesting to note that we find in 4.1, for the first time in the letter, an apparent appeal to the authority of the 'Lord Jesus'. This particular deictic reference has been used before only in 2.15, where it is part of the illustration of the theme of persecution. However, the reference to the 'Lord Jesus' in 4.1 appears in what could be understood as an introduction to a chiastic-like structure (4.2-8) in which it is made clear that the instructions that came from Paul to the Thessalonians were derived from the authority of God. The reference in 4.2 is completed thematically in 4.8 by reference to God and the Holy Spirit. In Perelmanian terms, God is the 'universal audience', the guarantor of and authority behind the values that Paul preaches.[11]

11. Although I have found no such reference in descriptions of SCT or FTA, it seems to me that the concept of 'sanctioning agent' shares some conceptual features with Chaim Perelman's concept of Universal Audience. Admittedly Perelman is neither 'dramatistic' nor social-scientific in his theories, but it might be argued that there are values associated with a 'sanctioning agent' and that the Universal Audience has a kind of authority that comes from its ability to 'sanction' the premises used by the speaker. It is also true that the concept of social construction of reality has affinities with situational rhetoric.

It is also interesting to note that the most pragmatic issue of all—acceptable sexual behavior—is the first issue to be addressed (4.3-7). Cultural mores and individual morality have to be redefined on the basis of the new reality constructed by Paul's rhetorical vision, which they already know and which distinguishes them from the outsiders (4.1-2, 5). And Paul speaks not just out of the strength of his own character, reviewed in the narrative passages in chs. 2 and 3, but out of that of God. To reject Paul is to reject divine authority (4.8).

Having established the basis for the authority of his *paideia*, Paul can turn from personal morality and interpersonal relationships to local issues of charity (4.9-12), how to respond to the death of church members (4.13-14), and then to eschatology and its place in informing the activities of believers (4.15-17). In other words, motivation for action moves from the believer outward to the world created by the rhetorical vision and is defined by the believer's status as an insider (4.2, 9, 13; 5.1-2).

In 4.9-12, the insider nature of community life and the importance of its obligations are heightened by two devices. In 4.9 Paul uses a *hapax legomenon*, θεοδίδακτοι, to emphasize the special relationship believers have to God. And, in 4.12 he makes specific reference 'to those outside' and how the Thessalonians are supposed to relate to them. Christians take care of their own and avoid dependence on outsiders!

It would seem that in Paul's initial sharing of his vision, the dramatic portrayal of God raising Jesus from the dead had been picked up and chained out into the fantasy theme of the return of the Lord. The fantasy is referenced by the use of the symbolic phrase, 'we believe that Jesus died and rose again' (4.14a). In 4.13-18 that drama has to be chained out further. The chaining is continued to include reference to the resurrection of the believers who have died before the Lord's return (4.14b). A new drama, based on the 'word of the Lord', that details the process or sequence of experiences that are the destiny of the believer is introduced.

Once the full dramatizing message of resurrection has been told, the two themes—insider morality and resurrection of the believers—and their associated concepts produce an expression of the fantasy type that is dominant throughout the letter, eschatological hope. That type continues through 5.1-10, where Paul reminds the Thessalonians of the fantasy theme of the Day of the Lord that he had already shared with them, using language that is based on both remembering what they have been taught (5.1) and already 'knowing' the fantasy theme and its pragmatic requirements, that is, commitment and vigilance (5.2-8). The consequence of election is salvation, and the believer lives 'with' the Lord no matter what his or her physical condition, dead or alive, or, to use insider terminology, 'awake' or 'asleep' (5.9-10).

From 4.1 on, the motive for action found in the rhetorical vision has been imitation that leads to vindication. Group participants are expected to behave in ways about which they have been told and have had modeled for them in the work of Paul and his companions. They are reminded of past experiences in order to motivate them to continue what they had already begun. This motivation is undergirded not only by the use of the topos of knowing but also by the reference to the activity of instruction, that which came from God (4.9) and Paul (4.11); and that which must be undertaken by believers (4.18). Action will result in escape from the wrath to come (1.10), blamelessness (3.13), and resurrection (4.17).

Beginning with 5.11, we encounter a different motive. Starting with the appeal in 5.11 to continue the process of encouragement and education—in terms suggested by SCT, to continue chaining out the fantasy—in v. 12, Paul turns to the task of ensuring the environment for this action of chaining. He provides a list of practical instructions for stabilizing the community. The list begins with an instruction to respect the leaders of the community and ends with a blueprint of how to maintain the integrity of the process of fantasizing: 'test everything; hold fast to what is good; abstain from every form of evil' (5.21-22). This stabilization is important if the community was to remain firmly in the world created by the vision that Paul had shared with them. The elaborated fantasy theme of resurrection found in 4.13-18 had the potential of being misinterpreted. To forestall at least one potential misinterpretation, Paul follows that elaboration with a reminder in 5.3-5 of what he had already taught them about the timing of the return of the Lord. The entire line of pragmatic instruction is then supported by his exhortation in 5.12-22, for mutual support, education and reliance on the group's leaders, which would, of course, include him. If the group heeds his exhortation, reshaping of the rhetorical vision would be guided by insiders. The new motive is the responsibility of the group to envision the future and develop pragmatic ways to ensure that the group can both sustain the vision and adapt it to new circumstances.

Finally, in 5.27, he makes sure that the rhetorical vision of this letter is shared with an audience larger than those represented in the group of immediate recipients.[12] In some sense the injunction to read the letter to all the 'brethren' reinforces imitative behavior—Paul shared his vision with them in the past and has sent the letter to them by messenger; now they are to be his messengers to others—and implies an attempt to keep the fantasy themes focused. The letter and the authority of its author provide a control mechanism in the communities in which it is read. Other rhetorical visions should be tested against what is found in it, a process already commended to them in 5.20-21. If the recipients of the letter followed through on Paul's instruction, one could anticipate that Paul's rhetorical vision was used to strengthen the resolve of the church and give them new ways to cope with the concerns produced by persecution.

FTA of the letter suggests another way of thinking about how to describe its function. Is it a 'paradoxical encomium' (Wuellner 1990), or a paraenetic letter (Malherbe 1983, 1989), or perhaps a letter of consolation (Chapa 1990; Smith 1995)? Does the search for identification of a letter type as described in the epistolary handbooks by which to classify this or any of Paul's letters really get at the 'function' of his letters? Obviously I would argue that it does not!

The ability of letters in general 'to constitute specific illocutionary acts (such as requests, excuses, promises, commands, etc.) as well as to generate communicative strategies' (Violi 1985: 162) is the phenomenon upon which to focus. For the most part Paul uses the letter genre to communicate his already shared rhetorical vision to a community that needs to remember its founding fantasies and be encouraged to chain them out, thus giving them new sources of motivation. The pragmatic expression of the rhetorical vision reflected in this letter is an integral part of its overall rhetoric. The dramatic message is intended to inspire and/or modify the behavior of the group. Narrative is the motivation for behavior. When the narrative is concluded, what might be called the 'argumentative effect' of the message is suggested by Paul himself. Although imitation has triggered persecution, it is, more importantly, inspiration for successful living. Thus λοιπὸν οὖν in 4.1 should be understood to mean 'then'.[13] The

12. Collins (1984: 366) remarks that the reason for this 'command' from Paul is to guarantee that all the believers in Thessalonica get the benefit of Paul's teaching. He goes on, however, to argue that they had picked up the ancient Jewish practice of reading religious texts out loud to one another and thus were doing with Paul's letter what they did with earlier texts. He is not convincing, in my judgment.

13. LSJ 1061; Bruce (1982: 78) has 'For the rest, then'; Best (1972: 153), 'For our

pragmatic activities, the behavior and beliefs Paul expected of the Thessalonians described in chs. 4 and 5, are derived directly from the dramatizing message told in chs. 1 through 3. Because of the vision embodied in the message, 'then' the Thessalonians are to behave and believe in certain ways in the future.

Given this analysis of the letter, it seems to me that in 1 Thessalonians we find Paul engaged in attempting to sustain community consciousness. That is its function. There is evidence to suggest that the process of fantasy chaining in his absence had created problems, or at least raised questions.[14] Furthermore, the delineation of an insider ethos that was important for future experience, the exhortation to respect their leaders, and the solemn injunction to have his letter read to others strongly implies that the original vision might have been losing its hold on the group. To offset those problems, Paul has to communicate further dramatic messages in order that the group raise its consciousness beyond the here and now and see the full power of his vision. In this effort the predominant principles of his rhetorical strategy seem to be rededication to their ministry in Macedonia and restoration of what they 'know' so that they can engage in community building with the help of their leaders. Furthermore, throughout the letter the principle of conservation is reinforced by reference to imitation, and rededication is implied in the exhortations to encourage and build up each other. Both the identification of the audience and the content of the message make it appear that Paul was not creating consciousness but was trying to direct its future development.[15] Paul seems to believe

last matter, then'; Marshall (1983: 104) 'therefore' or 'and now'; Wanamaker (1990: 147) 'finally now'. Collins (1984: 301) calls λοιπόν a 'somewhat banal transitional term', which 'occurs in the introductions to moral exhortations characteristic of Stoic-Cynic diatribes'.

14. Without elaborating on the evidence in detail, I can quickly point out the conventionally recognized issues of Paul's motives while in Thessalonica (2.4-6); the effects of persecution (3.2-3); his concern for the possible inadequacy of his initial teaching (3.10); and concerns about the fate of members of the group who have died (4.13). Exigences for writing the letter would seem to be based on problems and questions raised by his vision.

15. Bormann, Cragan and Shields (1996: 25) claim to have identified '12 operative rhetorical principles'. Three—novelty, explanatory power and imitation—operate primarily in the consciousness creating stage. Two—critical mass and dedication—during the conscious raising stage. Three—shielding, rededication and reiteration—during consciousness sustaining. Others operate during the decline and terminus state of a vision. 'Conservation' is my term.

that there is a controlling vision that should be used to limit the flexibility of a group to incorporate fantasies imported by other groups.[16] 'Stay the course' seems to be the dominant motive for this letter.

5. *Conclusion*

Keeping in mind the character of the audiences for Paul's letters—believers, insiders whom he believed shared something of his rhetorical vision—it is interesting to speculate on the possibility that all his letters fall somewhere on the spectrum of the life cycle of a rhetorical vision between raising and sustaining group consciousness. An FTA of Romans, for example, might provide an insight into how he went about raising group consciousness or at least influencing it; his comments in Rom. 1.11-12 suggest that motive. What we may be seeing in many of his other letters are attempts to limit the influence of chaining out by groups in his absence, the Corinthian correspondence being perhaps the best example of this effort.

SCT and FTA may also prove to be useful in mapping the topography of the Pauline tradition. An analysis of the rhetorical vision of the Pastorals, for example, would tell us a lot about how Paul's rhetorical vision was adapted to changing circumstances. I use the word 'topography' quite deliberately, because a look at early Christian literature would suggest that there were multiple chains developed from the rhetorical visions found in the undisputed letters of Paul, and that we must, therefore, think of the Pauline tradition as a regional development with a complex variety of features rather than how I have characterized it in the past, as a 'trajectory'.

Symbolic Convergence Theory (SCT) and Fantasy Theme Analysis (FTA): A Glossary

Symbolic Convergence Theory: a general theory of communication that attempts to offer an explanation of the presence of a common consciousness on the part of members of a group. It posits that the sharing of group fantasies and the chaining out of those fantasies is responsible for that consciousness and group cohesiveness. As fantasies are 'dramatized', a convergence of symbols on which participants agree occurs, and fantasy

16. Bormann (1982c: 60) speaks of the use in advertising and political mass media campaigns of adaptation of appeals to already established rhetorical visions.

themes and fantasy types help the group understand unexpected, confusing, or even chaotic events or experiences. The process of convergence creates social reality for the group until new exigences cause new fantasies and moments of sharing, which in turn produce new group realities. These realities provide the underlying assumptions used by the group in discursive argumentation.

Fantasy Theme Analysis: a method of rhetorical criticism designed to analyze and describe the rhetorical artifacts produced by symbolic convergence, not just in small group communication but also in social movements, political campaigns, etc. Analysis focuses on the content of message and the relationship among message elements.

Dramatizing Message (DM): a story that contains a pun, double entendre, personification, figure of speech, analogy, anecdote, allegory, fable or narrative. The story often deals with past conflict or the potential of future conflict and is thus set in time references of somewhere/sometime rather than the here and now. It is based on some original facts. A DM is the basis for group fantasy sharing. If it is accepted by the group and is chained out in a process of elaboration and other responses, then it becomes a group fantasy. Acceptance may be due to the rhetorical skill of the one conveying the message.

Fantasy: 'The creative and imaginative shared interpretation of events that fulfills a group's psychological and rhetorical need to make sense out of its experience and anticipate its future' (Bormann 1990: 104). Fantasies are dramatic reconstructions of past events and experiences that create a social reality for a group and its participants.

Fantasy 'chains' are created when a group member tells about an experience, or event, and others who shared in that experience add their view of it until it becomes the experience of the group.

Fantasy sharing is a means whereby groups establish identity and set boundary conditions for identifying insiders from outsiders. It is also a way in which group history and traditions are developed, thus enabling the group to think of itself as unique (Bormann 1990: 115).

Fantasy Theme: the content of the DM. Themes become part of the group consciousness; are artistic and organized; and are slanted, ordered, and interpretive. As a result, they provide a way for two or more groups of people to explain an event in different ways. An illustration of a fantasy theme is, 'Illegal immigrants consume more in social services that they contribute in taxes'.

Fantasy Type: a general scenario that covers several concrete fantasy themes. This scenario may be repeated with similar characters and may take the same form. It can be generalized so that characters become personas who act in predictable fashion. Rhetors simply make use of a familiar type and the audience fills in the particulars. 'Fantasy types allow a group to fit new events or experiences into familiar patterns' (Foss 1989: 292). An example of a fantasy type is, 'The American Dream', or 'Academic Freedom'.

Rhetorical Vision: a unified construction of themes and types that gives those sharing fantasy types and themes a broader view of things. A rhetorical vision may be indexed by a symbolic cue or key word. A number of rhetorical visions can be integrated by means of a master analogy (Foss 1989: 293). Seven principles apply to all rhetorical visions: novelty, explanatory power, imitation, critical mass, dedication, rededication, and reiteration (Bormann, Cragan and Shields 1996: 25). It is a rhetorical vision that can attract and help integrate larger groups of people into a common symbolic reality (Cragan and Shields 1981: 6).

Sanctioning agent: 'The source which justifies the acceptance and promulgation of a rhetorical drama' (Cragan and Shields 1981: 7). Agent can refer to an external source of authority like God or to a dominant feature of a culture or a moment in history, like a war or the Crucifixion.

FTA Elements in 1 Thessalonians: A Preliminary Taxonomy

Fantasy type: eschatological hope.
Major fantasy themes:

1. Imitation of faithful and reliable persons or groups: 1.5-6; 2.3-13.
2. Persecution experienced by heroes of the faith and by believers who imitate those heroes: 2.1-2, 14-16; 3.1-7.
3. Vindication of the pure and holy in the form of 'escape' from coming wrath, which takes place in the form of resurrection of the dead and ascension of all believers to 'heaven': 4.2–5.10.

Rhetorical vision:

> Present persecution: both Paul and church have suffered it to some degree and Paul's message is and has been that persecution is the lot of the believer.
>
> Praxis: fantasy has a practical side that has to be expressed if vindication is to be experienced. ('You know...' what has to be done.)
>
> Future glory: it is the past that guarantees future outcomes; present events and experiences do not. (All you need is more description of the future so that you can make sense of the present.)

Master analogue for rhetorical vision: resurrection of the dead/ascension of believers.

Goal of rhetorical vision: maintenance of fantasy chain, thereby sustaining group consciousness: 5.11-22.

Dramatizing message: 1.8-10; 2.1-20; 3.1-6.

Major Symbolic Words: Faith, Love, Hope, Knowing, Holiness.

Major Inside Cues: Work of Faith, Labor of Love, Steadfastness of Hope, Wrath.

BIBLIOGRAPHY

Literature on Symbolic Convergence Theory and Fantasy Theme Analysis

Bormann, E.G.
1972	'Fantasy and Rhetorical Vision: The Rhetorical Criticism of Social Reality', *The Quarterly Journal of Speech* 58: 396-407.
1982a	'A Fantasy Theme Analysis of the Television Coverage of the Hostage Release and the Reagan Inaugural', *The Quarterly Journal of Speech* 68: 133-45.
1982b	'Colloquy: I. Fantasy and Rhetorical Vision Ten Years Later', *The Quarterly Journal of Speech* 68: 288-305.
1982c	'The Symbolic Convergence Theory of Communication: Applications and Implications for Teachers and Consultants', *Journal of Applied Communications Research* 10: 50-61.
1983a	'Fantasy Theme Analysis and Rhetorical Theory', in J.L. Golden, G.F. Berquist and W.E. Coleman (eds.), *The Rhetoric of Western Thought* (Dubuque, IA: Kendall/Hunt): 432-49.

1983b   'Symbolic Convergence: Organizational Communication and Culture', in L.L. Putnam and M.E. Pacanowsky (eds.), *Communications and Organizations: An Interpretive Approach* (Beverly Hills, CA: Sage Publications): 99-122.

1985   *The Force of Fantasy: Restoring the American Dream* (Carbondale: Southern Illinois University Press).

1986   'Symbolic Convergence Theory and Communication in Group Decision-Making', in R.Y. Hirokawa and M.S. Poole (eds.), *Communication and Group Decision-Making* (Beverly Hills, CA: Sage Publications): 219-36.

1989   *Communication Theory* (Salem, WI: Sheffield Publishing Co.).

1990   *Small Group Communication: Theory and Practice* (New York: Harper & Row, 3rd edn).

Bormann, E.G., J.F. Cragan, and D.C. Shields

1994   'In Defense of Symbolic Convergence Theory: A Look at the Theory and its Criticisms after Two Decades', *Communications Theory* 4: 259-94.

1996   'An Expansion of the Rhetorical Vision Component of the Symbolic Convergence Theory: The Cold War Paradigm Case', *Communication Monographs* 63: 1-28.

Burgchardt, C. (ed.)

1995   *Readings in Rhetorical Criticism* (State College, PA: Strata).

Burke, K.

1969   *A Grammar of Motives* (Berkeley: University of California Press).

Cragan, J.F.

1975   'Rhetorical Strategy: A Dramatistic Interpretation and Application', *Central States Speech Journal* 26: 4-11.

Cragan, J.F., and D.C. Shields

1981   *Applied Communication Research: A Dramatistic Approach* (Prospect Heights, IL: Waveland Press).

1992   'The Use of Symbolic Convergence Theory in Corporate Strategic Planning: A Case Study', *Journal of Applied Communications Research* 20: 198-218.

Duffy, M.

1997   'High Stakes: A Fantasy Theme Analysis of the Selling of Riverboat Gambling in Iowa', *The Southern Communication Journal* 62: 117-32.

Foss, S.K. (compiler)

1989   *Rhetorical Criticism: Exploration and Practice* (Prospect Heights: Waveland Press).

Mohrmann, G.P.

1982a   'An Essay on Fantasy Theme Criticism', *The Quarterly Journal of Speech* 68: 109-132.

1982b   'II. Fantasy Theme Criticism: A Peroration', *The Quarterly Journal of Speech* 68: 306-313.

Selected Literature on 1 Thessalonians.

Best, E.

1972   *A Commentary on the First and Second Epistles to the Thessalonians* (London: A. & C. Black).

Boers, H.
    1976   'The Form-Critical Study of Paul's Letters: 1 Thessalonians as a Case Study', *NTS* 22: 140-58.
Bruce, F.F.
    1982   *1 & 2 Thessalonians* (WBC, 45; Waco, TX: Word Books).
Chapa, J.
    1990   'Consolatory Patterns? 1 Thess. 4.13, 18; 5.11', in R.F. Collins (ed.), 1990: 220-28.
Collins, R.F.
    1983   'The Unity of Paul's Paraenesis in 1 Thess. 4.3-8, 1 Cor. 7.1-7: A Significant Parallel', *NTS* 29: 420-29.
    1984   *Studies on the First Letter to the Thessalonians* (BETL, 66; Leuven: Leuven University Press).
Collins, R.F. (ed.)
    1990   *The Thessalonian Correspondence* (BETL, 87; Leuven: Leuven University Press).
deSilva, D.A.
    1996   '"Worthy of his honor": Honor Discourse and Social Engineering in 1 Thessalonians', *JSNT* 64: 49-79.
Donfried, K.P.
    1984   'Paul and Judaism: 1 Thessalonians 2.13-16 as a Test Case', *Int* 38: 242-53.
    1985   'The Cults of Thessalonica and the Thessalonian Correspondence', *NTS* 31: 336-56.
    1989   'The Theology of 1 Thessalonians as a Reflection of its Purpose', in M.L. Horgan and P.J. Kobelski (eds.), *To Touch the Text: Biblical and Related Studies in Honor of Joseph A. Fitzmyer* (New York: Crossroad): 243-60.
Fowl, S.
    1990   'A Metaphor in Distress: A Reading of νήπιοι in 1 Thessalonians 2.7', *NTS* 36: 469-73.
Havener, I.
    1981   'The Pre-Pauline Christological Credal Formulas in 1 Thessalonians', in K.H. Richards (ed.), *SBL Seminar Papers* (Chico, CA: Scholars Press): 105-28.
Hays, R.B.
    1988   'Crucified with Christ: A Synthesis of 1 and 2 Thessalonians, Philemon, Philippians and Galatians', in D.J. Lull (ed.), *SBL Seminar Papers* (Atlanta: Scholars Press): 324-32.
Hester, J.D.
    1996   'The Invention of 1 Thessalonians: A Proposal', in S.E. Porter and T.H. Olbricht (eds.), *Rhetoric, Scripture and Theology: Essays from the 1994 Pretoria Conference* (JSNTSup, 131; Sheffield: Sheffield Academic Press): 255-83.
    1998   'Speaker, Audience and Situation: A Modified Interactional Model', *Neot* 32: 75-94.
Hughes, F.W.
    1990   'The Rhetoric of 1 Thessalonians', in Collins (ed.) 1990: 94-116.

Jewett, R.
    1986   *The Thessalonian Correspondence: Pauline Rhetoric and Millenarian Piety*
                (Philadelphia: Fortress Press).
Johanson, B.C.
    1987   *To All the Brethern: A Text-Linguistic and Rhetorical Approach to 1 Thessa-*
                lonians (ConBNT, 16; Uppsala: Almqvist & Wiksell).
Koester, H.
    1979   '1 Thessalonians—Experiment in Christian Writing', in F.F. Church and T.
                George (eds.), *Continuity and Discontinuity in Church History: Essays*
                Presented to George Huntston Williams on the Occasion of his 65th
                Birthday (Leiden: E.J. Brill).
Lambrecht, J.
    1990   'Thanksgivings in 1 Thessalonians 1–3', in Collins (ed.) 1990: 183-205.

Longenecker, R.N.
    1985   'The Nature of Paul's Early Eschatology', *NTS* 31: 85-95.
Louw, J.P., and E.A. Nida
    1988   *Greek–English Lexicon of the New Testament Based on Semantic Domains*
                (New York: United Bible Societies).
Malbon, E.S.
    1983   ' "No Need to Have Anyone Write"?: A Structural Exegesis of 1 Thessa-
                lonians', *Semeia* 26: 301-36.
Malherbe, A.J.
    1983   'Exhortation in First Thessalonians', *NovT* 25: 238-56.
    1986   *Moral Exhortation, a Greco-Roman Sourcebook* (LEC, 4; Philadelphia:
                Westminister Press).
    1987   *Paul and the Thessalonians: The Philosophic Tradition of Pastoral Care*
                (Philadelphia: Fortress Press).
    1989   'Exhortation in 1 Thessalonians', in A.J. Malherbe, *Paul and the Popular*
                Philosophers (Minneapolis: Fortress Press): 49-66.
    1990   ' "Pastoral Care" in the Thessalonian Church', *NTS* 36: 375-91.
Marshall, I.H.
    1983   *1 and 2 Thessalonians* (NCB; Grand Rapids: Eerdmans).
Mearns, C.L.
    1981   'Early Eschatological Development in Paul: The Evidence of 1 and 2
                Thessalonians', *NTS* 27: 137-57.
Neyrey, J.H.
    1980   'Eschatology in 1 Thessalonians: The Theological Factors in 1.9-10; 2.4-5;
                3.11-13; 4.6; 4.13-18', in P.J. Achtemeier (ed.), *SBL Seminar Papers*
                (Atlanta: Scholars Press): 219-29.
Olbricht, T.H.
    1990   'An Aristotelian Rhetorical Analysis of 1 Thessalonians', in D. Balch *et al.*
                (eds.), *Greeks, Romans and Christians: Essays in Honor of Abraham J.*
                Malherbe (Minneapolis: Fortress Press): 216-36.
Palmer, D.W.
    1981   'Thanksgiving, Self-Defense and Exhortation in 1 Thessalonians', *Collo-*
                quium 14: 23-31.

Pearson, B.
    1971   '1 Thessalonians 2.13-16: A Deutero-Pauline Interpolation', *HTR* 64: 79-94.
Richard, E.
    1990   'Contemporary Research on 1 (&2) Thessalonians', *BTB* 20: 107-15.
Russell, R.
    1988   'The Idle in 2 Thess 3.6-12: An Eschatological or a Social Problem?', *NTS* 34: 105-19.
Sanders, J.T.
    1962   'The Transition from Opening Epistolary Thanksgiving to Body in the Letters of the Pauline Corpus', *JBL* 81: 348-62.
Smith, A.
    1995   *Comfort One Another: Reconstructing the Rhetoric and Audience of 1 Thessalonians* (Louisville, KY: Westminster/John Knox Press).
Violi, P.
    1985   'Letters', in T.A. van Dijk (ed.), *Discourse and Literature* (Amsterdam: John Benjamins): 149-67.
Vorster, J.
    1990   'Toward an Interactional Model for the Analysis of Letters', *Neot* 24: 107-130.
Walton, S.
    1995   'What has Aristotle to do with Paul? Rhetorical Criticism and 1 Thessalonians', *TynBul* 46: 229-50.
Wanamaker, C.
    1990   *The Epistles to the Thessalonians* (NIGTC; Grand Rapids: Eerdmans).
Weima, J.A.D.
    1997   'An Apology for the Apologetic Function of 1 Thessalonians 2.1-12', *JSNT* 68: 73-99.
Winter, B.
    1993   'The Entries and Ethics of Orators and Paul (1 Thessalonians 2.1-12)', *TynBul* 44: 55-74.
Wuellner, W.
    1990   'The Argumentative Structure of 1 Thessalonians as Paradoxical Encomium', in Collins (ed.), 1990: 117-36.

THE RHETORIC OF ELECTION AND
CALLING LANGUAGE IN 1 THESSALONIANS

K.K. Yeo

1. *Introduction*

Election and calling language occurs quite frequently in the Pauline corpus, especially in the Thessalonian correspondence (and in Romans).[1] Historically, this study has been taken over by systematic theologians, who are overly concerned with the abstract philosophical categories of the Arminian/Calvinist TULIP controversy.[2] Most unfortunate is the fact that biblical scholars undertaking this study are sometimes also caught in the same posture without first unveiling the contextual meaning of the text. Such examples are *Paul and Perseverance*, the dissertation by Judith Gundry Volf;[3] and to a lesser degree, the writings of I.H. Marshall.[4]

With regard to Paul's intent, Marshall agrees with Volf that election, bolstered by perseverance, serves to prevent the audience from falling away.[5] In other words, they perceive that the election language is used by

---

1.   Cf. Rom. 4.17; 8.30; 9.7, 11, 24, 25, 26; 1 Cor. 1.9; 3.12; 7.15, 17, 18, 20, 21, 22 (2x), 24; 10.27; 15.9; Gal. 1.6, 15; 5.8, 13; Eph. 4.1, 4; Col. 3.15; 1 Thess. 1.4; 2.12; 4.7; 5.9, 23-24; 2 Thess. 1.11; 2.13-14; and if the Pastorals are Pauline, 1 Tim. 6.12; 2 Tim. 1.9.

2.   TULIP is an acronym meaning Total depravity, Unconditional predestination, Limited atonement, Irresistible grace, and Perseverance.

3.   J. Gundry Volf, *Paul and Perseverance* (Tübingen: J.C.B. Mohr, 1990). See also G.C. Berkouwer, *Faith and Perseverance* (trans. R.D. Knudsen; Grand Rapids: Eerdmans, 1986).

4.   I.H. Marshall, 'Election and Calling to Salvation in 1 and 2 Thessalonians', in R.F. Collins (ed.), *The Thessalonian Correspondence* (Leuven: Leuven University Press, 1990), pp. 259-76; *idem*, 'Predestination in the New Testament', in C.H. Pinnock (ed.), *Grace Unlimited* (Minneapolis: Bethany Fellowship, 1975), pp. 127-43. Consult also his commentary, *1 and 2 Thessalonians* (London: Marshall, Morgan & Scott, 1983).

5.   Marshall, 'Election and Calling', p. 275.

Paul to assure the Gentile converts that they belong to God's elect, and that nothing subsequent can overturn God's original plan of pre-destination.[6] Volf sees the dichotomy between divine work and human effort, but Marshall sees no tension between God's spiritual work and human activities of faith and love.[7] Though both correctly perceive a connection between election/calling and staying in the salvation of God in the midst of tribulation, they seem to be preoccupied with their own extra peripheral agenda.

Below is my attempt to use a rhetorical approach[8] to read the calling and election language in 1 Thessalonians in understanding the contextual meaning of such language in the letter. The calling motif in 1 Thessalonians appears (1) in the *exordium* (1.4 of 1.2-10) where the themes are laid out; (2) in the first *narratio* (2.12); (3) in the *probatio* (4.7; 5.9); and (4) in the epistolary closing (5.23, 24) of 1 Thessalonians' demonstrative piece.[9] I will regroup these five pericopae in the following three purposes of Paul's calling language: rhetoric of honor, rhetoric of purpose, and rhetoric of hope.

2. *Rhetoric of Honor in the Context of Suffering*

Paul's calling language is largely situated in the context of the suffering which the congregation faced. A context of affliction and suffering is evidenced in 1 Thess. 1.6 (they 'received the word in much affliction' [θλίψει πολλῇ]); in 2.14 (they 'suffered' [ἐπάθετε]); in 3.3 (where Paul sends Timothy so that no one be moved by 'these afflictions' [θλίψεσιν]); and in 3.4 (where Paul tells them beforehand the 'sufferings' [θλίβεσθαι] they are going to endure). The politically inflammatory connotations of their Christian proclamation, especially their apocalyptic and millennial

6. Marshall, 'Election and Calling', p. 275.

7. Volf, *Paul and Perseverance*, p. 228; Marshall, 'Election and Calling', p. 275.

8. For more on my definition of rhetorical approach, see my two books: *Rhetorical Interaction in 1 Corinthians 8 and 10: A Formal Analysis with Preliminary Suggestions for a Chinese, Cross-Cultural Hermeneutic* (BIS, 9; Leiden: E.J. Brill, 1995), Chapter 4 ('Defining my Approach to Rhetorical Criticism'); *What Has Jerusalem to Do with Beijing? Biblical Interpretation from a Chinese Perspective* (Harrisburg, PA: Trinity Press International, 1998), pp. 165-97.

9. My rhetorical structure of 1 Thessalonians is: Epistolary Prescript (1.1); *Exordium* (1.2-10); *Narratio* (2.1–3.13); *Probatio* (4.1–5.11); *Peroratio* (5.12-22); Epistolary Closing (5.23-28). Cf. C.A. Wanamaker, *The Epistles to the Thessalonians: A Commentary on the Greek Text* (NIGTC; Grand Rapids: Eerdmans, 1990), p. 50.

faith, has brought persecution, a result of their alleged polemic against the civic cult.[10]

The Pauline gospel not only poses a threat to Rome, the gospel also brings social harassment to the new converts for breaking familial and social ties.[11] The turning from 'idols' to the 'true and living God' (1.9) means that Christian converts are living a betraying lifestyle in the eyes of non-Christian friends and family.[12] The conversion to Christianity for the Thessalonians means also that they have abandoned the beneficence and status of the former philia networks altogether.[13]

There is also trauma within the church. The profound perils the congregation face include grief over deceased members (1 Thess. 4.13-18), over-preparedness for the parousia (1 Thess. 5.1-11), resistance by the *ataktoi* to the community's expectation of labor (1 Thess. 5.12-14) and rejection of Paul's traditional ethic (1 Thess. 4.1-12).[14] The problems of 1 Thessalonians are, therefore, grief, perplexity, anxiety, and disappointment in the expected parousia.

In light of the above problems the congregation faced, Paul's first use of the election language in 1 Thess. 1.4 ('we know, brethren beloved by God, the choice of you') is to encourage them. Paul praises the audience unceasingly for their 'faith, love and hope'. 'Brothers beloved by God' is a

10. For example: Jesus Christ as κύριος (1 Thess. 1.1, 3, 6; 2.15, 19; 3.11-13; 4.1, 2, 6, 15; 5.2, 9, 12, 23, 27, 28); the Christians are to wait for the royal arrival (παρουσία) of their Lord (1 Thess. 2.14; 3.13; 4.12; 5.23); and some will be 'crowned' (2.19). Cf. K. Wengst, *Pax Romana and the Peace of Jesus Christ* (trans. John Bowden; Philadelphia: Fortress Press, 1987).

11. See the analysis of J.M.G. Barclay, 'Conflict in Thessalonica', *CBQ* 55 (1993), pp. 512-30.

12. Cf. P. Perkins, '1 Thessalonians and Hellenistic Religious Practices', in M.P. Horgan and P.J. Kobelski (eds.), *To Touch the Text: Biblical and Related Studies in Honor of Joseph A. Fitzmyer* (New York: Crossroad, 1989), pp. 325-34 (326); K.P. Donfried, 'The Theology of 1 Thessalonians as a Reflection of its Purpose', in Morgan and Kobelski (eds.), *To Touch the Text*, pp. 243-60; Barclay, 'Conflict in Thessalonica', pp. 512-30. See also New Testament witnesses in 2 Cor. 8.1-2 and Acts 17.1-9.

13. See A. Smith, *Comfort One Another: Reconstructing the Rhetoric and Audience of 1 Thessalonians* (Louisville, KY: Westminster/John Knox Press, 1995), pp. 98-100.

14. Drawing on the research of C. Spicq, Jewett identifies the problem of the ἄτακτοι as those 'rebellious or insubordinate' resisters of authority in 1 Thess. 5.12-14 (cf. 2 Thess. 3.6-15). Jewett argues that this word should not be translated as 'loafers' or 'idlers'. R. Jewett, *The Thessalonian Correspondence: Pauline Rhetoric and Millenarian Piety* (Philadelphia: Fortress Press, 1986), pp. 104-105.

captatio benevolentiae, not just for the purpose of securing goodwill but also for fostering community spirit, as such the *logos* and *pathos* of Paul's rhetoric are mutually reinforcing.[15] The form of the rhetoric is thanksgiving.[16] The reason for thanksgiving is that Paul knows their relationship with the living God. Paul's thanksgiving is so sure, because he knows the salvation of the audience lies in the family relationship with God and one another: 'we know...brethren...choice' (εἰδότες...ἀδελφοὶ...ἐκλογὴν).[17]

Paul is affirming or assuring the congregation through the rhetoric of thanksgiving prayer which unveils the rhetor's ethos in the transparency of God's discernment, draws the audience's pathos to the realm of the divine, and empowers the logos of persuasion with God's grace. In addressing the stasis of suffering, the rhetoric of prayer and thanksgiving gently yet persuasively gives assurance and comfort.

Two phrases stand out in this assurance: 'brothers beloved by God' and 'your choice/election'. 'Brothers beloved by God' is repeated in 2 Thess. 2.13, a phrase often applied by Deuteronomic writers to God's love for Israel during the captivity.[18] The emphasis here is on the assurance of God's unconditional acceptance and love. This is all the more crucial when the problem the community faces is persecution, which tends to alienate the individual from the larger society. Thus the idea of 'beloved' and 'election'[19] to salvation ought to be understood as the idea of being part of a new family. This understanding is emotionally appealing to the

15. It is important to note that the congregation's behavior and faith are examplary in vv. 7-10 because they first imitate the example of Paul and 'the Lord' in v. 6.

16. J.T. Sanders, 'The Transition from Opening Epistolary Thanksgiving to Body in the Letters of the Pauline Corpus', *JBL* 81 (1962), pp. 348-62.

17. Cf. Wanamaker, *Epistles to the Thessalonians*, pp. 76-77.

18. Deut. 32.15; 33.12; Isa. 44.2; cf. Sir. 45.1. Paul is using this term in Romans (cf. chs. 1, 9 and 11.28) to speak of God's unconditional inclusive love for all humanity, Jews and Gentiles.

19. The word 'call' (ἐκλογή) is completely absent in the LXX, though the verbal form of the word ἐκλέγομαι, which is roughly equivalent to the Hebrew word בחר meaning 'to choose' or 'to select', is common. In the Old Testament, בחר refers to the people of Israel as the people chosen by God. The word is used in the plural or the collective sense in relationship to Yahweh, i.e., those for whom Yahweh cares dearly. In the Apocryphal literature, the term is used to characterize a pious group within Israel, consecrated to Yahweh. If that consecration is linked with purpose, then the word is qualified with εἰς τι or a ἵνα (in order that) clause. Here Paul uses the ὅτι (because) clause in the sense of reason or purpose. See L. Coenen, 'ἐκλέγομαι', *NIDNTT*, I, p. 537; G. Schrenk and G. Quell, 'ἐκλέγομαι', *TDNT*, IV, pp. 144-92 (144-76).

audience in two ways. First, the best solution to suffering is to nurture hope in the context of community. Second, the notion of community-bonding appeals to those long-standing converts who had roots in the city ancestry line. With the immigration of officials and elites, the congregation lost its sense of roots and family. The Pauline message of family and new world reality is affirming and effective rhetorically. This rhetoric is also compatible with laborers who yearn for a new social reality, or utopia. Both 'brothers' and 'election' exemplify family language, which functions as 'language of belonging'.[20] This epideictic language also reinforces the group identity necessary for community continuity and vitality in a hostile world.

Since the word 'chosenness' is not found in the LXX, and since the phrase used here is an abstract noun ('God's choice of you') rather than a verbal phrase, the theological problem of whether Paul meant pre-destination/freewill of a certain people or individuals for salvation/ damnation is not the situational issue, nor is it the primary issue. Rather, Paul seems to emphasize the free will of God, who acts among the Thessalonians with a purpose, as the ὅτι clause in 1 Thess. 1.5 indicates. Furthermore, Schrenk rightly observes that 'this ἐκλογή is manifested in the powerful operation of the Spirit in the community'.[21] This Pauline consolation may be a correction of the audience's radical millenarian idea of realized elect status and elitism.

Paul's calling language takes on political nuances in its second appearance in 1 Thess. 2.12: 'Exhorting you and encouraging and charging to lead life worthy of God who calls you into his own kingdom and glory.' 1 Thessalonians 2.12 is found in the *narratio* of 2.1–3.13, which recounts events that have occurred or are supposed to have occurred,[22] in this case, Paul's past, present, and future ministry in Thessalonica in the similar context of affliction. This is related to the *exordium* in that Paul praises himself and the congregation at great length for past and present endurance of afflictions. What Paul and the congregation have in common is important because it becomes the rhetorical *topos*. In the *exordium*, Paul praises the audience's faith and says that they have become

20. W. Meeks, *First Urban Christians: The Social World of the Apostle Paul* (New Haven: Yale University Press, 1983), p. 85.

21. Schrenk and Quell, 'ἐκλέγομαι', p. 179. This idea of purpose parallels the classical usage of the word ἐκλογή in Plato (*Rep.* 3.414a; 7.535a, 536c; *Leg.* 7.802b) and Aristotle (*Eth. Nic* 10.10, 1181a).

22. Cf. Cicero, *De inventione* 1.

'imitators' (1.6) of him and the Lord. Here Paul illustrates how his own Thessalonian ministry has encountered opposition and hardship.[23] In a sense, both the congregation's and Paul's faith are assured (1.5) despite the tribulation, because God is the God who calls (2.12).

The kingdom and glory language[24] is best understood in the context of the political messianism of the time: Augustan expectation of the new age with a divine ruler.[25] This form of messianism must have appealed to some in the audience when compared to the Pauline message of Christ whose kingdom is yet to come. The present tense of καλοῦντος ('calling') in 1 Thess. 2.12 is atypical. Perhaps, it serves to stress the dynamic progressive and yet-to-be-consummated reality of the kingdom and glory of God.[26]

Calling to kingdom and glory does not mean elimination of affliction. E. Best highlights this point with a radical phrase, 'normality of persecution'.[27] To the Thessalonian Christians who are lower-class handworkers in deprivation,[28] the calling language to kingdom and glory exerts rhetorical power because the language offers hope and prosperity to the deprived, marginalized laborers who yearned for utopia and messianic triumph.

The rhetoric of disassociation between the appearance of paradoxical life and the reality of the gospel is evident: calling with a purpose, and how that purpose can be one of affliction. This is, of course, the primary sense of the purpose clause. Paul has to affirm a more coherent vision of the reality of 'commitment of faith'.[29] More than spelling out the divine

23. Cf. F.W. Hughes, 'The Rhetoric of 1 Thessalonians', in Collins (ed.), *The Thessalonian Correspondence*, pp. 94-116 (101).

24. For 'kingdom', see K.L. Schmidt, 'βασιλεία', *TDNT*, I, p. 579. For 'glory', see G. von Rad and G. Kittel, 'δόξα', *TDNT*, II, pp. 233-35.

25. Cf. Jewett, *The Thessalonian Correspondence*, p. 126.

26. See the aorist tense in 1 Thess. 4.7; 2 Thess. 2.14; Gal. 1.6; 1 Cor. 1.9. 1 Thess. 2.12 has a variant reading of an aorist tense 'who called' (ℵ A syr[p, h] cop), but the present tense (B D G 33 81) is a stronger reading. Cf. E. Best, *A Commentary on the First and Second Epistles to the Thessalonians* (London: A. & C. Black, 1972), p. 108.

27. Best, *1 and 2 Thessalonians*, p. 135; cf. 1 Thess. 3.4, 'we told you...that we were to suffer affliction'. Bruce writes similarly that 'persecution is a natural concomitant of Christian faith' (F.F. Bruce, *1 & 2 Thessalonians* [WBC, 46; Waco, TX: Word Books, 1982], p. 45).

28. R.F. Hock, *The Social Context of Paul's Ministry: Tentmaking and Apostleship* (Philadelphia: Fortress Press, 1980), pp. 34-36.

29. W. Wuellner, 'The Argumentative Structure of 1 Thessalonians as Paradoxical

purpose in the congregation's life, Paul also confers special honor on the congregation, as the classical Greek usage of the words καλέω and κλῆσις ('call') denotes.[30] Furthermore, as Edson shows, there are many cults in Thessalonica which preach the hope of a joyous afterlife, an immunity to pain symbolized by the phallus, the generative and 'life-giving power'.[31] Paul, however, proclaims that the gospel is not without affliction, a sharp contrast to the radical millenarian belief.

The ministry of Paul and his co-workers was considered politically inflammatory to those who sought to enforce the decrees of Caesar. Against such imperial forces, Paul proclaimed another Lord, another good news, another kingdom. In short, the calling language of 1 Thess. 2.12 not only brings hope and comfort, but it also points to the fact that God calls the audience into his *own* kingdom, in contrast to the kingdom of Caesar.

The rhetoric of calling language is therefore couched in the parousia-hope in 1 Thessalonians which makes it more than a praising letter in which 'approval is expressed, encouragement is given, and gratitude is shown'.[32] The honor and shame language used throughout 1 Thessalonians seems to indicate that Paul has a twofold purpose in mind. The first intention is to counter Roman society's domination or pressure on the Thessalonian Christians. The second intention is to form Christian community within a self-defined boundary based on the honorable values of God and the ultimate purpose of history (eschatology).

The first intention of Paul is to clarify the honor and shame value-system of the wider culture of which the Thessalonians were part. The suffering of the Thessalonians is the explicit indication of society's disapproval of the group in the perspectives of both the Christians and non-Christians. However, the dyadic (other-oriented perspective of self-worth) rhetoric works both ways for Paul. The wider culture might manipulate the Thessalonian Christians into believing that their suffering

Encomium', in Collins (ed.), *The Thessalonian Correspondence*, pp. 117-36 (133).

30. Homer, *Od.* 10.231; 17.386; *Iliad* 9, 7, 5; Xenophon, *Symp.* 1.7; Plutarch, *Pericles* 7.5. Cf. L. Coenen, 'καλέω', *NIDNTT*, I, pp. 271-73. In the Old Testament tradition, this divine calling implies claims on humankind which often lead to suffering for God's sake. Cf. 1 Sam. 3.4-10; 2 Kgs 1.3, 9; Exod. 3.4; 5.2.

31. C. Edson, 'Macedonia, III. Cults of Thessalonica', *HTR* 41 (1948), pp. 153-204 (165). Cf. M.P. Nilsson, *The Dionysiac Mysteries of the Hellenistic Age* (Lund: Gleerup, 1957), pp. 44-45. Cf. K.P. Donfried, 'The Cults of Thessalonica and the Thessalonian Correspondence', *NTS* 31 (1985), p. 337.

32. Jewett, *The Thessalonian Correspondence*, p. 71.

and harassment for being Christians are shameful, their loyalty to Jesus is hopeless, and their holy living is ethically binding. Paul in the letter does not agree. In fact, he inverts the same shame and honor language to build his case that values and ideologies from the wider culture is hopeless, without integrity and redemption, and it is his gospel of Jesus Christ that is truthful, redemptive and hopeful.

The rhetoric of calling language in 1 Thessalonians can be read as forming a new system of honor and shame according to the gospel of Jesus Christ. Paul uses the honor and shame language as means of social control in forming or directing the behavior or identity of a group. Honor is a means of approving a certain value and including that person into the community as its own, and it constantly reinforces the group's sense of worthiness as well as direction. Shame itself works just the opposite: it disgraces, alienates, and constantly dismantles the value system of another group.

The language of honor and shame by Paul reverses the source of approval. For Paul, God is the ultimate source of honor. Paul also presents an ironic result because of such reversal of source, viz. the shame and disapproval of the Thessalonian Christians from the society becomes the honor and reputable exemplum among other churches in the neighboring areas. The community is shaken (3.3) by their loss of honor, but society's disapproval is interpreted by Paul to be a shameful act, manipulated by the tempter (3.5). The negative sanctions from society and shameful example from the *ataktoi*'s behavior are interpreted as deceptions and not in accordance with truth. Another reversal example is the mention of a deluded proclaimers of peace (1 Thess. 5.3) in contrast to the God-taught community and Paul's preaching of truth.

The strategy of Paul in using the honor and shame language is to clarify the nature of deviance and normalcy. The Christian 'cult' of Paul might be regarded as deviant by outsiders and their harassment is the best indication of not conforming to the norm of society. But Paul explains to the Christians that their suffering is 'normal'. In fact that is their lot (honorable destiny?), and they have been informed beforehand (3.3-4). Paul then cites various normal examples to prove his case: he himself, other apostles, and Judean Christians all go through suffering.

The second intention of Paul is to define for the Thessalonians a new system of honor and shame. Instead of getting one's self-worth through the dyadic reception from outside culture (see 1 Thess. 4.12), Paul intends to foster the honor language first from the in-group of Thessalonian

Christians. The identity of the group is named in a network of various relationships: related to Son of God (1 Thess.), they are the church of God in Thessalonica (1.1), children of light (5.3-8), brethren (3.1, 7; 4.1, 6; 5.1, 4, 12, 14, 25), and the beloved (1.4; 2.8) ones. The boundary issue between believers and unbelieving world is affirmed. The community is initiated by God through their obedient response to the gospel of Jesus Christ (1 Thess. 5.12-22).

The building up of the community is confirmed by Paul's urgency to visit the Thessalonians. Paul's parousia to see the community 'face to face' (3.10), however, is hindered by Satan—a despicable language of shame rendered on the evil one. In line with an apocalyptic world-view, Satan has no regards for God's standard, Satan confuses shame and honor. Yet, in Paul's rhetoric and theology Satan belongs not to the realm of God but that of darkness, thus Satan is not pleasing God or gaining approval from God. Christians in Thessalonica are called otherwise: to please God and to live a life worthy of God's kingdom (reign). They are God's choice (1.4) as they respond positively to the gospel preached to them (1.5). The election language is essentially an honor language by which the identity of the Thessalonian Christians is now located in the choice of God.

Perhaps the most explicit use of honor language in 1 Thessalonians is Paul's relocation of honor not in the temporal eye of the present but in the eschatological eye of the ultimate, viz. the imminent Day of the Lord: 'For what is our hope or joy or crown of boasting before the Lord Jesus at his coming? Is it not you? For you are our glory and joy' (2.19-20). It is honorable to turn from idols to serve a living and true God, so also to wait for his Son from heaven, whom God raised from dead, Jesus who delivers them from the wrath to come (1.9-10). It is honorable to lead a life worthy of God, who calls them into God's own kingdom and glory (2.11-12). It is honorable to belong to God and Father, who establishes their hearts unblamable in holiness at the coming of the Lord Jesus with all his holy ones (3.12-13). It is honorable to be in the destiny of obtaining salvation rather than wrath (5.9). And it is honorable to trust in the hope that the God of wholeness makes them whole and blameless at the coming of the Lord Jesus Christ (5.23).

3. Rhetoric of Purpose in the Context of Ethical Despair

The second purpose of Paul's calling language is to provide a purpose for the Thessalonians in the context of their ethical despair as seen in some of the *ataktoi* members. The social behavior of the *ataktoi* is caused by the radicalization of the millennial hope into irrational eschatological excitement. The theology of the *ataktoi* is one of eschatological excitement.[33] The word *ataktoi* does not denote laziness but a rebelling against order.[34] The Thessalonian *ataktoi* were not merely lazy or without a job, but were those who refused to work (2 Thess. 3.10), rejecting order in the church (3.6) and thus creating dissonance within the church. The *ataktoi* members of the Thessalonian church are not the authorities or leaders. Had they been, Paul surely would have blasted them with his own critique, just as he did with the Galatian agitators or the super-apostles of 2 Corinthians. Instead, Paul uses encouragement and praise language to correct their mistaken eschatological and ethical assumptions. Paul's tone of speaking as a nursing parent indicates also that these 'enthusiastic' members were not deacons or leaders, but laity whom Paul could restore to community acceptance by reminding them of the traditions he had received and had taught them.

In 1 Thess. 5.13 Paul exhorts his readers to have 'peace among yourselves', possibly referring to the disruptive behavior of the *ataktoi*. The wording of 2 Thess. 3.16 on 'the Lord of peace himself give you peace' might also indicate the church was going through disturbances caused by the *ataktoi* rebelling against Paul's ethics and his attitude toward work. Paul's work-ethic is characterized by peace so that the majority poor would not be burdened by the *ataktoi* who refused to work.

In response to the problem of ethical despair, Paul, in the third appearance of the calling language in 1 Thess. 4.7 ('For God did not call us for wickedness but into holiness'), spells out the ethical purpose of the calling language. 1 Thessalonians 4.7 is found in the *probatio* of 4.1–5.11, where the ethical holiness teaching is expounded. Jewett calls this section 'the divine grounding of the admonition' within the first proof of the

---

33. L. Morris, *The First and Second Epistles to the Thessalonians* (Grand Rapids: Eerdmans, 1991), p. 252; Marshall, *1 and 2 Thessalonians*, p. 219; and Best, *1 and 2 Thessalonians*, pp. 176-78.

34. What kind of order is meant is dependent on the context: Philo refers to matter before creation as ἄτακτος (*Op. Mund.* 22); Josephus uses ἀτάκτως in parallelism with ἀνόμως, 'lawlessly' (*Apion* 2.151), and he characterizes the retreat of an army as ἄτακτος (*War* 3.1113). In papyri, the word refers to lack of discipline (P. Oxy. 275). See also C. Spicq, 'Les Thessaloniciens "inquiets" étaient-ils des paresseux?', *ST* 10 (1956), pp. 1-13; G. Delling, 'Τάσσω κτλ.', *TDNT*, VIII, pp. 27-48.

probatio.[35] Donfried claims that the language of 1 Thess. 4.1-9 is paraenetic.[36] In the entire Pauline corpus, the word 'instructions' (παρεγ–γελίας) as a noun is used here only. The phrase 'the will of God' is used here and in Rom. 8.8, where the calling language also occurs.

The contemporary Pauline usage of this word 'call' (ἐκλογή) is a military-political term, meaning to be chosen for a purpose or to perform a task.[37] Paul's rhetoric here encourages the audience so that they will continue to encourage others, even those Christians in Macedonia. Paul's encouragement does not aim merely at group-sufficiency or maturity, but to the purpose that they will be benefactors to each other. This community building in turn helps them to deal with the problem of persecution. This kind of Pauline reassurance can therefore be categorized as *oxymoron* in a rhetorical form, or as a 'literary mysticism'[38] or a rhetorical 'figure' to re-establish 'a coherent vision of reality…by dissociation'.[39] Granting help to others does not exhaust one's energy; rather, it builds one's stamina to deal with persecution.

The *inventio* of Paul's rhetoric here is not taken from Greco-Roman sources but from a Jewish source, albeit implicitly. The Jewishness of his rhetoric is seen in the rhetorical arrangement.[40] Tomson calls this section (1 Thess. 4.3-7) 'three halakot from what we may call Paul's catechism to the gentile church of Thessalonici'.[41] The first halakha is the prohibition of unchastity, related to the Noachian commandments (in 1 Thess. 4.3). The second commandment is to avoid contracting marriage in an indecorous manner (in 1 Thess. 4.4-5). Tomson specifically mentions that: 'σκεῦος parallels the Hebrew כלי, "vessel" or "wife"' (see Str-B 3,632f),…

---

35. Jewett, *The Thessalonian Correspondence*, p. 75.

36. Donfried, 'Cults of Thessalonica', p. 341.

37. E.g. Plato, *Rep.* 536c; Polybius 6, 10, 9; Plato, *Laws* 802b. Cf. L. Coenen, 'Ἐκλέγομαι', *NIDNTT*, I, pp. 536-43 (536).

38. K. Burke, *A Rhetoric of Motives* (Berkeley: University of California Press, 1969), pp. 324-28.

39. C. Perelman, *The Realm of Rhetoric* (Indianapolis: University of Notre Dame Press, 1982), p. 126.

40. If the Jewish rhetorical reconstruction here is accurate, it is an argument from authority. It is puzzling, though, why Paul would use Jewish material for the Gentile audience.

41. P.J. Tomson, *Paul and the Jewish Law: Halakha in the Letters of the Apostle to the Gentiles* (Assen: Van Gorcum; Minneapolis: Fortress Press, 1990), p. 91. One should probably not take the word 'catechism' literally, because there is no way to show that Paul had that tradition.

κτᾶσθαι corresponds to לקנות, cf mKid 1.1, etc (Str-B)'.[42] The third law is mentioned implicitly in 1 Thess. 4.6 and is against wrongdoing in business. This law parallels the Rabbinic prohibition of הונאה, honaa... (mBM ch 4; tBM 3.13-29).[43]

The meaning of *ataktoi* as 'standing against the order of nature or of God'[44] provides insight into the inappropriate, obstinate behavior of some of the congregation in 1 Thess. 4.5: 'in the passion of lust like heathen who do not know God'.[45] This unholy sexual behavior is not abstinence but libertinism in lust. Those *ataktoi* are rebelling against Paul's teaching (cf. 4.2) and are involved in lustful libertinism.

The intention of God's calling is clear: 1 Thess. 4.7 says God calls the Thessalonian Christians, not for (ἐπί) but in (ἐν) holiness. 'For' (ἐπί) and 'in' (ἐν) can be used interchangeably, but here it highlights the purpose of being called 'into holiness' (ἐν ἁγιασμῷ).[46] Jewish prophets do not use the term 'holiness' (ἁγιασμός) to denote a pure being, a pious essence. For them, it means belonging to the Holy One, Yahweh.[47] Because one belongs to Yahweh, then one is expected to be ethical, just, and morally good.[48] This is the purpose of God's calling: 'the will of God, your sanct-ification'. The one who has been related to God must practically realize God's provision of power over impurity or unholiness. The indicative (seen in the phrase ἐν ἁγιασμῷ in vv. 4, 7) and imperative (seen in the infinitives ἀπεχεσθαι, εἰδέναι, κτᾶσθαι, ὑπερβαίνειν, πλεόεκτεῖν and most forcefully in δεῖ) of holiness are enveloped in the notion that God, who gives the Holy Spirit, prompts believers toward sanctification. The indi-catives and imperatives of holiness in the Hebraic tradition are fluid and not artificial; they are two sides of the same coin. In other words,

42. Tomson, *Paul and the Jewish Law*, p. 19.

43. Tomson, *Paul and the Jewish Law*, p. 91 n. 142.

44. Jewett, *The Thessalonian Correspondence*, p. 104. Cf. Spicq, 'Les Thessalo-niciens', pp. 1-13.

45. Cf. Donfried, 'Cults of Thessalonica', p. 338, where he also argues that the problem in 1 Thess. 4.3-8 is the σκεῦος.

46. N. Turner, *A Grammar of New Testament Greek*. III. *Syntax* (by J.H. Moulton; Edinburgh: T. & T. Clark, 1963), p. 263.

47. קדש (Qados) means essentially (1) belonging to Yahweh (in the priestly tradition) as God sets the people apart for his purpose; therefore people, sabbath (Exod. 16.23), assembly (Exod. 12.16), heaven (Ps. 20.6), Mount Zion (Ps. 2.6) are said to be holy; (2) participating in the ethical and moral holiness of God (in the prophetic tradition).

48. Exod. 29.43; 1 Sam. 2.2; Lev. 19.2; Pss. 18.30; 101.2, 6; 1 Pet. 1.15.

sanctification is not the process of human moral perfection by means of the imperatives, but an appropriation through faith of one's union with God and a practical realization of God's purpose through the simultaneous working of the Holy Spirit. Therefore, Paul exhorts the Thessalonians in the opening sentence of this unit to learn: 'how you ought to live and to please God, just as you are doing, you do so more and more' (4.2).

This rhetoric of sanctification as the will of God not only defines for the Thessalonians the purpose of their lifestyle, it also evokes awareness that the Holy Spirit is constantly guiding, enabling and empowering them to be conscious of the presence of God and to live in a way pleasing to God.[49] As such, to live a sanctifying life is to live a life in conscious awareness that every moment of existence presents a chance to encounter God's presence.

The holiness calls to marriage, sexual, and business propriety may be best explained by 'the fact that κλητὴ (called) ἁγία [holiness] is found at Exo 12.16 and Lev 23.2ff. (for מִקְרָא קֹדֶשׁ) [which] may have favoured the combination of κλητός [call] and ἅγιος [holy]…'[50] Again, Paul alludes to the Old Testament motif and freely uses Jewish rhetorical inventions and devices. The past tense ἐκάλεσεν indicates that the initial call of God occurred when the congregations turned to God from idols. A persecuted community cannot drift or give in but must remain true to the calling of God. The power or authenticity of the gospel is seen, not so much in the sectarian holy status claim of the community, but in the transformed lives of the community despite persecution and pressure. The rhetorical intent here is to persuade the audience that God has called them with a purpose. Hope is nurtured as the calling language identifies for them the purpose of their calling.

The fourth appearance of election language is in 1 Thess. 5.9: 'For God did not place/appoint us into wrath but to obtain salvation through our Lord Jesus Christ', which is found in the *probatio* of 4.1–5.11, where the salvation of the apocalyptic hope is discussed. Continuing to encourage the audience to have a sense of purpose, 1 Thess. 5.9 provides motivation both for vigilance by the community and for the hope that they are living with the Lord whether they wake or sleep.

---

49. Burke explains purpose in terms of actualization of good and dependence on God's acts, Burke, *Rhetoric of Religion*, p. 221; and his discussion of purpose in Aristotelian tradition in *A Grammar of Motives* (Berkeley: University of California Press, 1969), pp. 292-300.

50. K.L. Schmidt, 'καλέω κτλ.', *TDNT*, III, pp. 492-96 (496).

The political context of the this verse and its context will help us understand the dynamic rhetoric of Paul. Donfried claims that 1 Thess. 5.3 is 'a frontal attack on the *Pax et Securitas programme* of the early Principate';[51] 4.15 and 5.2 are politically loaded sentences. The word παρουσία ('coming') is taken from the Dominical tradition.[52] παρουσία means the coming, arrival, or presence of a person, emperor, king, or other official in a city.[53] The helmet as the hope of salvation (5.8) may be linked to the helmeted head of Roma.[54] The word 'Lord' (κύριος) clearly denotes a royal figure, politically the emperor[55] and religiously the epiphany of a god.[56] Of course, during Paul's day, emperors were revered as gods. Paul is using the vivid and popular imagery of his day to convey his rhetoric of hope.

The basis for this rhetoric of hope is that 'God has not destined us for wrath, but to obtain salvation through our Lord Jesus Christ' (5.9). Wanamaker wrongly asserts that τιθέναι 'denote[s] God's role in predestining people to wrath or salvation'.[57] The discussion whether 'περιποίησιν with the objective genitive σωτηρίας has the active sense of acquiring or obtaining'[58] has been a protracted but futile one. While Rigaux attempts to make a distinction between the active and the passive subject of περιποίησις ('to obtain'), Volf points out that the syntax within and outside the New Testament does not imply an effort of the subject to act in order to obtain salvation.[59] I.H. Marshall concludes, 'The phrase simply means "to obtain possession" and allows (but does not demand) human cooperation with God in attaining that goal'.[60]

The stronger argument for the passive subject of περιποίησις is the use

---

51. Donfried, 'Cults of Thessalonica', p. 344.

52. As R.H. Gundry argues in 'The Hellenization of Dominical Tradition and Christianization of Jewish Tradition in the Eschatology of 1–2 Thessalonians', *NTS* 33 (1987), pp. 161-78.

53. E. Peterson, ''Απάντησις', *TDNT*, I, pp. 380-81; A. Oepke, 'παρουσία κτλ.', *TDNT*, V, p. 860.

54. Donfried, 'Cults of Thessalonica', p. 341.

55. W. Foerster, 'κύριος', *TDNT*, III, pp. 1054-58, observes that the imagery was used more and more in the first and second centuries.

56. W. Radl, *Ankunft des Herrn* (Frankfurt: Peter Lang, 1981), pp. 173-81.

57. Wanamaker, *Epistles to the Thessalonians*, p. 187.

58. Wanamaker, *Epistles to the Thessalonians*, p. 187.

59. Volf, *Paul and Perseverance*, p. 23. Therefore, περιποίησις is a *nomen actionis* with a passive subject, e.g. receive an inheritance as an heir.

60. Marshall, *1 and 2 Thessalonians*, p. 209.

of the prepositional phrase 'salvation is through Christ alone' (διὰ τοῦ κυρίου ἡμῶν Ἰησοῦ Χριστοῦ).[61] In other words, the Christological formulation[62] of assurance of the Thessalonians' salvation indicates that Christ has accomplished it and will bring the benefactions to completion. Therefore, 'be sober, and put on the breastplate of faith and love, and for a helmet the hope of salvation' (5.8). The end is not yet here, but it will surely come. There is hope, for the salvation that their benefactor will bring.

What is the purpose of the election language here? The words τιθέναι εἰς (to be translated as 'appoint' rather than 'destined') express God's purpose. The reference to wrath is not a reminder to the audience of the ultimate fate of the evil ones, because God does not 'appoint' wrath.[63] What is 'ordained' or 'appointed' is the salvation, rather than determined destinies for the sheep and goats.

The election language pertains to the salvation of believers as well. In 1 Thess. 1.10, Paul has written that 'Jesus...saves us from the *coming* wrath'. The notion of salvation is understood as future and not present reality, as the words 'hope of salvation' (ἐλπὶς σωτηρίας) in 5.8 show. The creation motif of this word 'appointment' (τιθέναι) is common in Old Testament literature.[64] This creation of God is viewed in a continuum of past, present, and future. Therefore, this motif implies that God's creation is still in process. The 'appointment' of Christians is declared clearly in both positive and negative qualifications: 'not...in the wrath but to obtain salvation'. This appointment is the goal, couched with the connotation of purpose. It is formulated as τιθέναι εἰς, which denotes 'divine

61. So Marshall, *1 and 2 Thessalonians*, p. 140; Morris, *1 and 2 Thessalonians*, p. 161; Volf, *Paul and Perseverance*, p. 25.

62. B. Riguax says v. 9 is a Hebraism because of the double accusative ('Tradition et Rédaction dans I Th. V. 1-10', *NTS* 21 [1974–75], pp. 318-40 [333]). Cf. Gen. 17.5; Isa. 28.16; and Rom. 4.17 and 9.33. Plevnik, however, thinks Paul is modifying a pre-Pauline formula (J. Plevnik, 'Parousia as Implication of Christ's Resurrection: An Exegesis of 1 Thess. 4.13-18', in J. Plevnik [ed.], *Word and Spirit: Essays in Honor of David Martin Stanley* [Willowdale, Ontario: Regis, 1975], pp. 195-97). Note that the participial clause τοῦ ἀποθανόντος ὑπὲρ ἡμῶν ('who died for us') speaks of the suffering Christ.

63. For the eschatological understanding of this term, see Best, *1 and 2 Thessalonians*, p. 216.

64. Cf. Gen. 1.17; 17.5; Pss. 32.7; 103.9; Job 38.10; Jer 1.5; 1 Kgs 9.3; Isa. 26.1; etc. See D.W. Maurer, 'τίθημι', *TDNT*, VIII, pp. 154-60 (154).

determination unto something'.[65] It is usually but improperly translated as 'predestine' or 'elect'.[66]

But Paul's rhetoric assures the Thessalonians that their appointment means that their lives are pregnant with divine purpose. Such eschatological hope allows them to live in the difficult present situation in the strength and hope of the future. Thus, the rhetoric here functions as a movement of hope, evoking that hope as the believer is made aware of God's purpose for one's life in a unifying reality of past, present, and future.[67]

Paul's injunction 'in the name of the Lord Jesus' was to ask working Christians 'to keep away from brothers who are *ataktoi*'; this may be a way of detaching oneself from the patron–client relationship. The reference to 'those not working but being the busy bodies' suggests the problem may be caused by the *ataktoi*. The problem may be a social strife for the patron in the city. Paul would not want such a problem to hinder the mission of the church in Thessalonica. More probably, the political problem of causing 'bad witness' for the church and 'false realized eschatology' to the outsiders is too great a risk to take.[68] So Paul admonishes them to live a quiet life. Quiet does not mean passive, inactive; quiet means not causing social and political problems in such a way that the mission of the church is in jeopardy. Given the commitment of a social ethic, Paul wants Christians in Thessalonica not to burden other Christians, but continue to do good for the welfare system of the city.

The fact that Paul sees it necessary for himself to work and not to burden anyone at Thessalonica may indicate that the majority poor are not to be burdened. Paul's message of autobiography is an imitation rhetoric that exhorts the *ataktoi* poor not to burden others. The *ataktoi* are most probably the poor because if they were the rich, their refusal to work would not be a burden to anyone. If they would work, they would be able to support themselves and the poorer brethren in Jerusalem (2 Cor. 8.4).

65. As Volf (*Paul and Perseverance*, p. 21) argues; the usages in Acts 13.47, Isa. 49.6 (LXX), 1 Pet. 2.8 support this interpretation.

66. So Maurer, 'τίθημι', p. 157; E. von Dobschütz, *Die Thessalonicher-Briefe* (ed. F. Hahn; Göttingen: Vandenhoeck & Ruprecht, 1974), p. 212; Morris, *1 and 2 Thessalonians*, p. 160; Volf, *Paul and Perseverance*, p. 21.

67. On rhetoric as a movement of hope in a unifying whole, see W. Ong, *Rhetoric, Romance, and Technology* (London: Cornell University Press, 1971), pp. 12-13.

68. Jewett mentions the 'disenfranchised laborers who were known to be restive under Roman rule' (*The Thessalonian Correspondence*, p. 125).

Eschatology and ethics are inseparable in Pauline thinking.[69] Living is a matter of ethical living in Jesus Christ. The ethical question pertains to the wholeness of life. 'Ethics must be concrete, but not devoid of hope.'[70] Pauline ethics in the Thessalonian correspondence finds its base in eschatology. Paul responded to the question of 'times and seasons' with the ethical advice of 'not sleeping' (negatively expressed), being watchful (positively expressed)[71]—being ever ready for the parousia. Paul does not give them a time table—an eschatological answer. Paul asked them to be sober—an ethical answer.

4. *Rhetoric of Hope in the Context of Cognitive Dissonance*

The last appearance of the calling language is in 1 Thess. 5.24: 'The one who calls you is faithful, and he will do', which possesses rhetoric of hope. 1 Thessalonians 5.23 is a homiletic benediction in the epistolary closing (5.23-28) which recapitulates the previous arguments of the *probatio* (4.1–5.11).[72] Together with the wish-prayer of 3.13 and 5.23 it encapsulates the main arguments of the whole letter. The use of δέ ('and' in 5.23) has its connective function here. In short, this benediction is not written out of formality but is part and parcel of the whole rhetoric. The benediction has also the customary usage of *affectus* (emotional language) with the *recapitulatio* of the proof in the *peroratio*.[73] The *propositio* of 1.9-10 is recapitulated in 3.11-13 and 5.23-24. The benediction summarizes the argument of ethics, holiness, and apocalyptic expectation. Verse 24 colors the benediction with the tone of assurance from the recipient of the prayer, that is, the Faithful One. The subject prayed to is 'the One who calls' (πιστὸς ὁ καλῶν).

The act of salvation is linked to the faithfulness of God, as the reference or title of God in 5.24 indicates. The God who calls them is faithful; therefore, God will do it. He is not the God who called them once and left them

---

69. R. Evans, 'Eschatology and Ethics: A Study of Thessalonica and Paul's Letters to the Thessalonians' (PhD Dissertation, University of Basel, 1967).

70. Evans, 'Eschatology and Ethics', p. 172.

71. While the synoptic traditions do not use negative expression of 'do not sleep', the positive expression of 'being watchful' is found in Mk 13.34, 35; Mt. 24.43; Lk. 12.37, 39.

72. R. Jewett ('Form and Function of the Homiletic Benediction', *ATR* 51 [1969], pp. 19-34) says that benedictions or wish-prayers serve to summarize the preceding section.

73. Cf. Aristotle, *Rhet.* 3.19.1.

there. Whereas in 1 Thess. 4.7 God's calling is stated in the past tense, in 1 Thess. 5.24 the present tense is used to indicate that God is still calling the faithful. The omitted object of what God 'does' (ποιήσει) is best supplied from the preceding verse: God will sanctify them.

The wholeness of God's sanctifying action is emphasized. God will sanctify them to be complete (ἁγιάσαι ὑμᾶς ὁλοτελεῖς) and keep them blameless (ἀμέμπτω...τηρηθείη), spirit, soul, and body (ὁλόκληρον ὑμῶν τὸ πνεῦμα καὶ ἡ ψυχὴ καὶ τὸ σῶμα) till the end-time. The word 'complete' (ὁλοτελεῖς) indicates the completeness of God's sanctifying work. The wholeness concept is further emphasized by the three anthropological terms which seem to indicate a polemic usage of a disfragmented anthropological view on the part of some of the audience. Jewett is correct in observing that the wording of 'spirit and soul and body' reflects the audience's tripartite view of human nature.[74] Since trichotomous language is atypical for Paul, and since we observe the dualistic understanding of the sexual ethics of the 'rebels' (ἄτακτοι) in 1 Thess. 4.7 above, we may conclude that Paul's emphasis on 'wholeness' (ὁλοτελής) is a correction of the audience's misconception. In other words, Paul's theology affirms body, spirit, and soul, while the audience may view the body as degenerative, and the spirit of humans as divine.[75] Paul's understanding of anthropology, holiness, and the God of Shalom is distinctively Jewish.

This wholeness of salvation corresponds to the title of God (in 5.23): the God of Shalom (ὁ θεὸς τῆς εἰρήνης). The word εἰρήνης ('peace' or 'shalom') is an 'all-encompassing term for salvation'[76] or 'the sum total of gospel blessings'.[77] He is the *God of Shalom,* not in the sense of orderliness but in the comprehensiveness of his salvation.[78] Furthermore, the aorist optative of ἁγιάσαι is perhaps intended by Paul to 'embrac[e] the whole process'[79] of salvation as well.

Paul reassures his audience that God's salvation is not yet completed at this juncture in history. In 1 Thess. 1.10, Jesus is the subject of salvation;

74. Jewett infers this from the Gnostic-like anthropology, cf. *The Thessalonian Correspondence*, pp. 107-108.

75. This does not necessarily imply the origin of Gnosticism in Thessalonica, because such dualistic belief was prevalent throughout the Greco-Roman world. Cf. E. Schweizer, 'πνεῦμα, πνεματικός', *TDNT*, VI, pp. 390-91.

76. Marshall, *1 and 2 Thessalonians*, p. 161.

77. Bruce, *1 and 2 Thessalonians*, p. 129.

78. G. von Rad and W. Foerster, 'εἰρήνη κτλ.', *TDNT*, II, pp. 402-408.

79. Wanamaker, *Epistles to the Thessalonians*, p. 206.

in 1 Thess. 5.9, Jesus Christ is the agent of God. Then, in 5.10, Christ is described as the one who 'died for us so that we…might live with him'. The implied subject of 'we live' (ζήσωμεν), that is, the 'we', is inclusive of both the readers who are 'watching' and those who are 'sleeping'. Therefore, ζήσωμεν ('we live') refers to the possibility of living with Christ in the eschatological salvation of the future:[80] 5.23-24 then serves as affirmation of the divine benefactor's commitment (he who calls is faithful) and his resolution to realization (will do).

From what we have observed in this pericope, we note that, because the function of this benediction serves to summarize the arguments of the whole letter, and because the calling language is used within that benedictory recapitulation, therefore, the calling language used here does explicate and unify the rhetoric of hope, assurance, and purpose. The subject of hope, assurance and purpose is the God of Shalom himself. The purpose is God's calling of the congregation into sanctification (comprehensive salvation) and wholeness (complete salvation). The assurance is that God is faithful and God is the call*ing* One. The hope is the 'yet-to-be' end of history—the coming of our Lord Jesus Christ.

The consolation and correction styles point to the greatest need of the audience in 1 Thessalonians—eschatological hope. The triadic formulation, 'faith, love, hope', appears in 1.3 and 5.8. Timothy reports to Paul the good news of their 'faith and love' (3.6), presumably without hope so that Paul is going to 'supply what is lacking' (τὰ ὑστερήματα) in their faith (3.10). The hope motif continually reappears in 1.10, 2.19, and 3.13, with particular regard to the parousia (παρουσία) in 2.19, 3.13, 4.15, and 5.23. Paul uses an epideictic genre to furnish hope to the Thessalonians in their context of affliction. We may conclude that Paul in 1 Thessalonians is addressing the problems not by critical reproof but through reinforcement and reconfirmation. The epideictic genre of the first letter serves to correct the problem of hopelessness by means of praise through exhortation or paraenesis.

1 Thessalonians is an epideictic letter that serves to praise and reaffirm the congregation in the midst of crisis and dissonance. The epideictic genre (παραμυθούμενοι in 1 Thess. 2.12 and 5.14) of performative acts are: act of God to call, act of Thessalonians to trust. God's will for the

---

80. Marshall, *1 and 2 Thessalonians*, p. 141; Volf, *Paul and Perseverance*, p. 22. Jewett likewise claims that 'Paul cited in a clarified apocalyptic context in 1 Thess. 5.23, insisting that humans are to be kept intact until the parousia' (*The Thessalonian Correspondence*, p. 175).

believers is that they rejoice, pray, give thanks (5.18), abstain from unchastity (4.3), and lead a life worthy of God (2.12). The responses of the Thessalonians to God are: faith in him (1.8), turning to him (1.9), having courage in him (2.2), and having their being in him (1.1). Paul gives thanks (1.2; 2.13; 3.9), lives a life worthy of God as he has been taught by God (4.9), prays for the Thessalonians without ceasing (1.2-3). In the face of great opposition (1 Thess. 2.2; also 'in all our distress and affliction' in 1 Thess. 3.7) and Paul's absence, the praise rhetoric strategizes to build up an affective relationship between Paul and the congregation, as well as to sustain them to go through tribulation, and to supply the hope that is missing in their faith and love. The need for the rhetoric of hope is doubly compounded by the absence of Paul (agent of benefactor) and Christ (benefactor) in the suffering context of the Thessalonians. The coming of Paul to the Thessalonians will be the full presence of hope for the Thessalonians to cope with their problems. Thus, to a certain extent the apostolic parousia parallels Christ's parousia.

In fact, the rhetoric of hope is necessary because the presence of the living God is elusive (3.9; 4.8, 17). Yet, it is possible because the living God is nevertheless ineffably present. J.G. van der Watt speaks of God as 'consciously present':

> The way in which God is 'consciously present' is a godly way, a true way. His actions resulting from this 'presence' will reflect the quality and nature expected of the true God! Being God, this life is, for one thing, absolute. God is (present participle) the living God; he does not derive his life from elsewhere. As the living God, he can also give life, as was evidenced, for instance, in his raising of Christ.[81]

Indeed, God is the Father who chooses (1.4), calls (2.12), gives the Spirit (4.8), wills the believer's sanctification (4.3), and makes each believer perfectly holy (5.23). Such is the loving-parent God who is active in their lives; such is the living and true God they are going to serve.[82] Being the divine agent of the loving parent, the Lord Jesus Christ has died and been raised for the sake of the Thessalonian congregation (1.10; 4.14; 5.10); he is destined to be the salvific and sanctifying instrument (5.9, 18), the deliverer of divine wrath and giver of peace for believers (1.10; 5.28);

---

81. J.G. van der Watt, 'The Use of ZAW in 1 Thessalonians: A Comparison with ZAW/ZWH in the Gospel of John', in Collins (ed.), *The Thessalonian Correspondence*, p. 359.

82. See van der Watt, 'The Use of ZAW in 1 Thessalonians', pp. 356-69.

and he is the source of their hope as they wait for his return (1.3, 10; 4.15; 5.23).

A rhetoric of hope often portrays the rightness of the favored people and the damnation of the enemies in 1 Thessalonians. 1 Thessalonians falls within the epideictic genre, in which praise and blame are prominent subjects.[83] For instance, the rhetorical structure of the letter from the beginning to the end contains the argument of hope. The letter begins with the epistolary prescript (1.1) which draws the readers' attention to the writer. The *exordium* (1.2-10) begins with the thanksgiving (1.2-5) that confirms the virtues of the people as signs of God's grace upon the people. Then the *exordium* (1.6-10) reviews the past actions of the community as evidence of hope. Clarification of apostolic example (2.1-12) in the *narratio* (2.1–3.13) posits the 'rightness' of the apostle and the 'wrong-ness' of the hinderers. The case of the Judean example serves to reinforce the ground of hope by indicting the sins of the oppositors. Paul's repeated and determined effort to revisit the Thessalonians (2.17-20) reinforces the conviction of confidence: hope, joy, crown, boast, glory. Timothy's visit (3.1-5) to represent Paul and the result of Timothy's visit (3.6-10) shows the righteousness of the Thessalonians. Transitus in benedictory style (3.11-13) of the narratio gives conviction of hope. Then, Paul deliberates on traditional teaching in the *probatio* (4.1–5.11): hope in the traditional maintenance of marriage, business (4.1-8), and communal ethics (4.9-12); hope for the dead (4.13-18); hope in watchfulness for the imminent parousia (5.1-11). The *peroratio* (5.12-22) ends the letter with hope and peacefulness in congregational life (5.12-22). The epistolary closing (5.23-28) concludes the rhetoric of hope with praise to God and blessings from God to the people of covenanted love. The rhetoric of hope clarifies and accepts the normality of suffering and of cognitive dissonance.

5. *Conclusions*

The calling and election language of Paul has its goal in motivating the audience to live a life honorable to God. Paul is encouraging (παρα–καλέω), comforting (παραμυθέομαι), and urging (μαρτύρομαι) them to lead lives worthy of God (1 Thess. 2.12). The rhetorical intent of 1 Thessalonians is exhortational in reconfirmation and correction. He had the same intent when he sent Timothy to strengthen (στηρίζω) and

83. Jewett, *The Thessalonian Correspondence*, p. 71.

encourage (παρακαλέω) them (1 Thess. 3.2). And he has the same intent for the Thessalonians themselves: therefore encourage (παρακαλέω) one another and build each other up (οἰκοδομέω), just as in fact you are doing (1 Thess. 5.11). They are to be benefactors to each other for the purpose of catalyzing the benefactions of God throughout Macedonia.

The election/calling language in 1 Thessalonians is encouraging and assuring language. In addition to that, the language of calling/election in 1 Thessalonians is quite prominent, and it offers hope, purpose, and encouragement. The rhetoric of hope is germane in the apocalyptic theology of Paul, which is a rhetoric of recapitulating the End (who is Jesus Christ).[84] That rhetoric of hope encourages the Thessalonians by declaring the working presence of God, Christ, and the Holy Spirit in their midst, confirming his own 'nursely' and fatherly example and concern, and nurturing the community by an exhortation of faith, love, and hope in the midst of a hostile environment. Paul at times also recasts the elitist election language of the audience and intertestamental traditions christologically so that his rhetoric sustains the audience in the tension of God's faithfulness and the apocalyptic hope and joy.

The three words—'appoint', 'choose', and 'call' (ἐκλεγή, αἵρεομαι and καλέω)—have a common denominator in God's purpose and not in human manipulation or predetermination. The subject of these words is always God, who initiates an event with a purpose. The purpose may be holiness, enduring affliction, obtaining glory, sharing salvation, or rendering good resolve and good work. And there does not seem to be any orthodox Calvinist versus Arminian controversy in the Pauline usage of calling language in Thessalonians.

Calling or election is therefore God's work of creating, sustaining, saving, and sanctifying his creation out of love and grace. It is the divine purpose to call his creation into relationship with him. The divine yearning is expressed in the shalom benediction of 1 Thessalonians 5. Calling language therefore affirms the possibility of experiencing the shalom (wholeness and harmony) of God in the destructive perils of life.

---

84. See my article, 'Revelation 5 in the Light of Pannenberg's Christology: Christ the End of History and the Hope of the Suffering', *AJT* [*Asia Journal of Theology*] 8 (October 1994), pp. 308-34, for adapting Pannenberg's view and arguing that the cultural-religious world-view of apocalyptic generates hope when one knows Jesus Christ as the end of history.

INDEXES

INDEX OF REFERENCES

OLD TESTAMENT

POSTBIBLICAL JEWISH LITERATURE

INDEX OF AUTHORS

JOURNAL FOR THE STUDY OF THE NEW TESTAMENT
SUPPLEMENT SERIES